For the Students at
Murray State University, Murray, KY

General Psychology

Taken from:

Psychology: Core Concepts, Fifth Edition
By Philip G. Zimbardo, Robert L. Johnson, and Ann L. Weber

PEARSON
Custom
Publishing

PEARSON
and

Taken from:

Pyshcology: Core Concepts, Fifth Edition
By Philip G. Zimbardo, Robert L. Johnson, and Ann L. Weber
Copyright © 2006, 2003, 2000 by Philip G. Zimbardo
Published by Allyn and Bacon
A Pearson Education Company
Boston, Massachusetts 02116

This special edition published in cooperation with Pearson Custom Publishing.

Printed in the United States of America

10 9 8 7 6 5 4 3 2 1

ISBN 0-536-97047-5

2005500042

AK

Please visit our web site at *www.pearsoncustom.com*

PEARSON CUSTOM PUBLISHING
75 Arlington Street, Suite 300, Boston, MA 02116
A Pearson Education Company

Brief Contents

Contents

Chapter 2

Biopsychology and the Foundations of Neuroscience 40

Chapter 3

States of Consciousness   88

Chapter 4

Psychological Development   126

Sensation and Perception   178

Chapter 5

Learning   224

Chapter 6

Chapter 7

Stress, Health, and Well-Being   392

Chapter 10

Chapter 11

Personality   442

Chapter 12

Psychological Disorders   482

Chapter 14

Social Psychology   564

Appendix

Making Sense of the Data: Descriptive and Inferential Statistics   A-1

To the Student . . .

There is one simple formula for academic success, and the following demonstration will show you what it is. Study this array of letters for a few seconds:

IBMUFOFBICIA

Now, without peeking, write down as many of the letters as you can (in the correct order).

Most people remember about five to seven letters correctly. A few people get them all. How do these exceptional few do it? They find a pattern. (You may have noticed some familiar initials in the array above: IBM, UFO, FBI, CIA.) Finding the pattern greatly eases the task because you can draw on material that is already stored in memory. In this case, all that needs to be remembered are four "chunks" of information instead of 12 unrelated letters.

The same principle applies to material you study for your psychology class. If you try to remember each piece of information as a separate item, you will have a difficult time. But if instead you look for patterns, you will find your task greatly simplified—and much more enjoyable. So, how can you identify the patterns? With a little help from your friendly authors, who have developed several learning features that will make meaningful patterns what you are reading in this text stand out clearly:

▪ *Core Concepts:* We have organized each major section of every chapter around a single, clear idea called a Core Concept. For example, one of the four Core Concepts in the "Memory" chapter says:

Human memory is an information processing system that works constructively to encode, store, and retrieve information.

The Core Concept, then, becomes the central idea around which about 10 pages of material—including several new terms—are organized. As you read the chapter, then, keeping the Core Concept in mind will help you encode the new terms and ideas related to that concept, store them in your memory, and later retrieve them when you are being tested.

Key Questions: Each Core Concept is introduced by a Key Question that also serves as a main heading in the chapter. Here, for example, is a Key Question from the Memory chapter:

WHY DOES MEMORY SOMETIMES FAIL US?

Key Questions such as this will help you anticipate the most important point, or the Core Concept, in the section. In fact, the Core Concept always provides a brief answer to the Key Question. Think of the Key Question as the high beams on your car, helping you focus on what lies ahead. Our key questions should also serve as guides for you to be posing questions of your own about what your are reading.

Psychology in Your Life: Psychology has many connections with events in the news and in everyday life, and we have explored one of these connections at the end of each major section in every chapter. What make psychology so fascinating to us and to our students are all the ways in which things learned in this course directly apply to events and experiences in the real worls. To illustrate, here are some examples from the "Memory" chapter:

- Would You Want a "Photographic" Memory?
- "Flashbulb" Memories: Where Were You When . . . ?
- On the Tip of Your Tongue
- Improving Your Memory with Mnemonics

Such connections—practical, down to earth, and interesting—link your reading about psychology with your real-life experiences. They also help you critically evaluate many of the psychological ideas you encounter in the popular press. Also begin to notice how often you read stories about "research shows that . . ." By the end of this course, you will become a much wiser consumer of such information—some of which is often false or misleading.

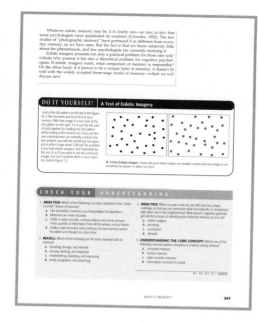

- ***Do It Yourself!*** We have scattered active-learning demonstrations (such as the one at the beginning of this student preface) throughout the book. Besides being fun, these activities have the serious purpose of illustrating principles discussed in the text. In the "Memory" chapter, for example, one Do It Yourself! box helps you find the capacity of your short-term memory; another lets you test your "photographic memory" ability.

- ***Check Your Understanding and Review Tests:*** Whether you're learning psychology, soccer, or the saxophone, you need feedback on your progress, and that's exactly what you will get from the Check Your Understanding quizzes and the Review Tests. These exercises will let you determine how well you have mastered the material.

- ***Using Psychology to Learn Psychology:*** In a section near the end of every chapter, we explain how you can apply your new knowledge of psychology to make your studying more effective. For example, in Chapter 2, "Biopsychology," we tell you how to put your understanding of the brain to work for more efficient learning. Similarly, at the end of the chapter on "Emotion and Motivation," we explain how to use a new psychological concept of "flow" to boost your own academic motivation. Thus, Using Psychology to Learn Psychology not only reinforces points that you have studied, it brings the material home with immediate and practical applications to your life in college.

CONNECTION: CHAPTER 12

Retrograde amnesia involves loss of memory for information acquired in the past.

- ***Connection Arrows:*** Important topics in other chapters are often cross-referenced with an arrow in the margin, as you can see in the sample here. The accompanying reference gives you either a preview or reminder of concepts covered in other chapters. This feature helps you see the interrelatedness of ideas in psychology.

- ***Chapter Summaries:*** We have made our summaries rather brief—intended to provide you with an overview of main points in each chapter. They remind you of the patterns instead of loading you with the details. One caution: They are not a substitute for reading the chapters! One helpful hint: Read the summary before you read the rest of the chapter to get a flavor of what's ahead, then reread the summary after you finish the chapter. Reading the summary before will help you organize the material so that it can be more easily encoded and stored in your memory. And, naturally, reviewing the summary after reading the chapter will reinforce what you have just learned so that you can retrieve more of it in the future.

■ *Our Recommended Books and Videos:* Your authors hope that your interest in psychology will give you new lenses with which to look at the world beyond this book. When you do, you will discover something related to behavior and mental processes nearly everywhere. To pique this interest, every chapter offers a list of relevant, stimulating books and videos that will extend the scope of your learning.

We have built into this text many other learning features, such as the marginal glossary, and the extensive references list (which can be a good resource for term papers). You will learn more about these as you use the book; but if you want a bit more information on our purposes for including these features, please read the Instructor's Preface.

We have one final suggestion to help you succeed in psychology: While this book is filled with examples to illustrate the most important ideas, you will remember these ideas longer if you generate your own examples as you study. This habit will make the information yours, as well as ours. And so, we wish you a memorable journey through the field we love.

Phil Zimbardo
Bob Johnson
Ann Weber

SUPPLEMENTS FOR STUDENTS

■ *Grade Aid Study Guide:* This robust study guide, written by Diane Finley of Prince George's Community College, is filled with guided activities and in-depth exercises to promote student learning. Each chapter includes "Before You Read," presenting a brief chapter summary and learning objectives; "As You Read," offering a collection of demonstrations, activities, and exercises; "After You Read," containing three short practice quizzes and one comprehensive chapter exam; "When You Have Finished," presenting web links for further information and a crossword puzzle using key terms from the text. An appendix includes answers to all practice tests and crossword puzzles.

■ *Companion Website:* Connecting the textbook to the internet, this unique tool includes learning objectives, annotated web links, flashcard glossary terms, and online practice tests organized by chapter. Visit this site at www.ablongman.com/zimbardo5e.

■ *MyPsychLab:* This interactive and instructive multimedia resource can be used to supplement a traditional lecture course or to administer a course entirely online. It is an all-inclusive tool, a text-specific e-book plus multimedia tutorials, audio, video, simulations, animations, and controlled assessments to completely engage students and reinforce learning. Fully customizable and easy to use, MyPsychLab meets the individual teaching and learning needs of every instructor and every student. Visit the site at www.mypsychlab.com.

▐ *Mind Matters II CD-ROM:* A unique tool that combines major concepts with interactivity, this CD-ROM offers a wide range of learning opportunities, including activities with immediate feedback, video clips of historic experiments and current research, animations, simulations, and an interactive glossary of key terms. To see sample modules, visit www.ablongman .com/mindmatters.

▐ *Evaluating Psychological Information:* This workbook, *Sharpening Your Critical Thinking Skills,* 4th edition, developed by James Bell, focuses on helping students evaluate psychological research systematically and improving critical thinking skills.

▐ *How to Write Psychology Papers,* 2nd edition: Les Parrott provides a brief overview for writing APA-style psychology papers, including information on overcoming paper panic, using the Internet, preparing a working reference list, avoiding plagiarism, and using inclusive language.

▐ *Discovering Psychology Telecourse Study Guide:* In this *Telecourse Study Guide,* each chapter corresponds to one program, expands on the material covered in the program, specifies appropriate reading assignments, and reviews material covered in the text. In addition, the study guide includes learning objectives; reading assignments; key people and terms; video program summaries and test questions with answer key; textbook test questions with answer key; essay questions; student activities; additional book, article, and film resources; and annotated websites. All vocabulary and review questions are keyed to *Psychology: Core Concepts.*

▐ *Study Card for Introduction to Psychology, © 2005:* Colorful, affordable, and packed with useful information, Allyn & Bacon/Longman's Study Cards make studying easier, more efficient, and more enjoyable. Course information is distilled down to the basics, helping students quickly master the fundamentals, review a subject for understanding, or prepare for an exam.

To the Instructor . . .

We teachers of psychology have a little secret that we usually don't talk about, even among ourselves: Every introductory text contains more material than a student can possibly learn while taking the first course in psychology. Yet most texts try to cram ever more material into each new edition because the knowledge base in our field continues to grow at an exponential pace.

There is much that we want our students to know. Since the 4th edition of this text, neuroscience has revealed many more brain mechanisms underlying development, thinking, learning, perception, and every other subfield of psychology. At the same time, gender and culture issues have grown in prominence. Likewise, genetic variables have competed for the spotlight, as fallout from the human genome project has forced psychologists to consider anew the old questions about nature and nurture.

Cognitive psychologists, too, have been busy expanding the frontiers of knowledge about implicit memory, concept learning, and cognitive development. But they have been pressured by their colleagues working on "hot" cognition research to recognize the role of emotion in memory and thinking. Meanwhile, on the clinical front, psychologists have been accumulating evidence for psychological therapies of demonstrable effectiveness—some of which challenge the hegemony of Prozac and Valium.

And, of course, the terrorist attacks of September 11, 2001, have refocused our attention on the origins of aggression and violence. As we write this, the revelations of the horrendous abuses of Iraqi prisoners by American Army reservist MPs raise the fundamental questions of situational versus dispositional explanations for such pathological behavior. Are there just a few bad apples, or was that behavior the product of a systematic corruption of good soldiers in the bad barrel of a war prison?

Obviously, we, as writers of an introductory psychology text, must wrestle with several problems. How can we include the exciting new developments in the field and still acquaint students with all the classic studies, historical trends, and multiple perspectives in the field? How can we add what is new and clearly valuable to understanding the human condition without cutting out a lot of what has been traditional—and, at the same time, keep the book within manageable proportions? How can we make psychology meaningful to students without overwhelming them with information?

For this 5th edition of *Psychology: Core Concepts*, your authors have again had to make difficult choices, and we hope you will agree with most of them. The fact that each instructor has the opportunity to introduce additional materials in class eases the pressure somewhat. Accordingly, we hope you will feel free to let this book give students a broad overview of the field, while you emphasize your favorite topics and concepts. In fact, one of the things you, as a teacher, can do far better than any text is to model how a psychologist thinks and solves problems.[1]

But, as psychologists, we realize that the problem for students is not just one of sheer volume and information overload; it is also a problem of meaningfulness. With this in mind, we have again found inspiration in a classic study of chess players. As you may recall, Adrian de Groot (1965) and his colleagues (Chase & Simon, 1973) showed that experts did no better than novices at remembering the locations of pieces on a chess board when the pieces were placed at random. Only when the patterns made sense—because they represented positions that would be found in real games—did the experts show a big advantage of their experience. Clearly, meaningful patterns are easier to remember than random arrangements.

In applying this finding to *Psychology: Core Concepts*, 5th edition, our goal has been to help students take the first steps toward becoming more expert psychologists by revealing to them meaningful patterns that occur throughout the field of psychology. We have developed a number of special pedagogical features in our text that help us achieve this goal:

■ *Core Concepts:* We have organized the major sections of every chapter around a single, clear idea that we call a Core Concept. Here is an example from the chapter on "Sensation and Perception":

> The brain senses the world indirectly because the sense organs convert stimulation into the language of the nervous system: neural impulses.

To borrow an old saying, the Core Concepts become the "forest," while the details of the chapter become the "trees."

■ *Key Questions:* The main headings in each chapter appear in question form, as in this example, which introduces the Core Concept shown above:

HOW DOES STIMULATION BECOME SENSATION?

Fundamental questions such as these help students anticipate and focus on the most important idea, the Core Concept, which serves as a brief answer to the Key Question. Both the Key Questions and the Core Concepts later reappear as organizing features of the Chapter Summary.

---

[1]In this vein, we commend to you a new book, *What the Best College Teachers Do* (Bain, 2004). It lays out the results of a 15-year study of college teachers who were nominated as "the best" by their students and colleagues. One of the factors that all of the best had in common was helping students learn how to think and solve problems like experts in their disciplines.

■ **Psychology in Your Life:** One reason that psychology continues to fascinate and involve so many students stems from its obvious relevance to the events in their lives. We explore one of these links between psychology and life at the end of each main division of every chapter. Here are some examples:

■ Emotional Differences between Men and Women Depend on Culture

■ The Origins of Sexual Orientation

■ A Critical Look at "Learning Styles"

■ How Psychoactive Drugs Affect the Nervous System

■ Explaining Unusual People and Unusual Behavior

Such real-life explorations not only make psychology come alive, but they also promote critical thinking by helping students evaluate some of the pop psychology they encounter in the media. We believe that learning how psychologists think about real-life issues can help your students become wiser consumers of information in the public media pertaining to mind, brain, and behavior.

■ **Do It Yourself!** These active-learning boxes offer simple and effective demonstrations of principles discussed in the text. Many are borrowed from demonstrations we have used successfully in our own classrooms. They include, among other topics, locating one's blind spot, demonstrating the concept of mental set, finding the capacity of working memory, checking one's locus of control, wrestling with IQ test items, and second-guessing a surprising social psychology experiment.

■ **Using Psychology to Learn Psychology:** In a special section at the end of every chapter, we consider how some aspect of the chapter applies to studying and learning. For example, in the context of biopsychology, we show students how to put their knowledge of the brain to work for more efficient learning. Similarly, in the discussion of thinking, students learn how the psychology of expertise (as in de Groot's studies of chess masters) applies to their mastery of the concepts in psychology. Thus, "Using Psychology to Learn Psychology" not only reinforces points that students have learned, it brings the material home with immediate and practical applications to their college lives.

▎ *Connection Arrows:* Uniquely in this book, important topics in other chapters are often cross-referenced with an arrow in the margin, as you saw in the previous paragraph. These icons are used in place of the phrase, "as we will see in Chapter X." A brief explanatory note accompanies these arrows, giving students a headline preview of the discussion to be found in the referenced chapter. We intend this feature to convey the sense of psychology as a web of interconnecting ideas.

▎ *Our Recommended Books and Videos:* At the end of each chapter in the 5th edition, you'll find a short section in which we list our top picks of worthwhile books and rentable videos, both classics and more contemporary works. Each has been selected by our media guru, Ann Weber, as illustrative of some concept in the chapter.

▎ *Multiple Perspectives on Terrorism:* Finally, this edition of *Psychology: Core Concepts* again addresses the problem of terrorism. In the social psychology chapter we bring together the concepts developed in our discussions of aggression, violence, and conflict, applying them to build an understanding of terrorism. Doing this requires what may be psychology's greatest strength: the use of multiple perspectives, including biopsychology, social learning, and cognitive psychology, as well as perspectives drawn from sociology, history, political science, and other disciplines.

Along with these unique features, this new edition of *Psychology: Core Concepts* offers the breadth and depth of content plus the tried-and-true pedagogical devices that are standard for any modern introductory psychology text:

▎ *Marginal glossaries:* In this 5th edition of *Psychology: Core Concepts,* the most important terms again appear in **boldface,** with their glossary definitions readily accessible in the margin. Then, at the end of the book, a comprehensive Glossary section gathers together all the terms and definitions from each chapter.

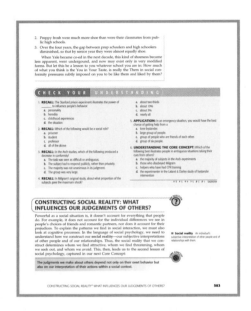

▎ *Check Your Understanding and Chapter Review Tests:* Reviewers have told us that they want a book that promotes active reader involvement. The 5th edition of *Psychology: Core Concepts* does this in many ways. One of the most important for student learning is the Check Your Understanding feature, which offers a brief quiz at the end of each main chapter section. This is a quick checkup for the student to determine if she or he has gotten the main points from what was just read. We have written these quizzes so that they reinforce specific information from the chapters as well as some of the more abstract concepts. Accordingly, some questions call for simple recall, while others call for deeper analysis or application of material. In addition, at least one question in each Check Your Understanding quiz is aimed squarely at the Core Concept of the section. Similarly, the Review Test at the end of each chapter helps students assess their overall retention and understanding of the material in that chapter before going on to start the next one.

▎ *Chapter Summaries:* The goal of each Chapter Summary is to provide students with a brief overview of the main points in that chapter, organized around the Key Questions and Core Concepts. We hope that you will advise your students to review these chapter summaries *before* reading the chapter, to get a preview of the chapter content and organization, and then again *after* having read the chapter, to reinforce their learning.

■ *Culture and gender:* Nearly every chapter brings in a culture- or gender-related concept. We have not trivialized this material by setting it aside in special boxes. Rather, culture and gender have been fully integrated with whatever psychological topic is being presented in the running text.

What is new to this edition? We think you and your students will like the following additions and modifications.

■ *The Seven Modern Perspectives: Updated:* The Big Seven major modern perspectives have been updated to include trait psychology and the developmental viewpoint—both of which had long been ignored in the "perspectives" section of this and other texts. The modern perspectives we list in this edition are: *biological, developmental, cognitive, clinical, behavioral, trait,* and *social-cultural.* As you can surmise, evolution and neuroscience now fall under the biological perspective, while the clinical perspective includes both humanistic and psychodynamic psychologies.

■ *State of the Art:* Each chapter ends in a "State of the Art" section, which briefly characterizes and reviews what's known and also points to the unknowns that are ripe for research. One of the things we're trying to do here is to get budding young researchers thinking about what the unsolved problems and big mysteries are in psychology.

■ *Making the abstract concrete:* You will find a new emphasis on providing concrete examples of abstract concepts, along with an increased use of metaphors and similes, where appropriate—all designed to help students assimilate unfamiliar and abstract ideas. We think your students will find this especially helpful in mastering difficult concepts in biopsychology.

■ *Fewer boldfaced terms:* In response to reviewers' requests, we have been more selective about the terms we deem important enough to put in boldface and include in the marginal glossary. Again the goal is to avoid information overload, while calling students' attention to the most important terms.

■ *More judicious use of connection arrows in the margins:* While we have retained these icons as a tactic for conveying the vital connections of ideas and principles within our field, reviewers have advised us that less would be more—that fewer would be more useful to readers and, at the same time, provide a cleaner, less-cluttered look for the text.

This edition has also undergone a major developmental revision for content coverage and accuracy. While no book can be altogether free of slipups, we think you'll agree that this edition does an extraordinarily good job of getting psychology right.

We think you will like the introduction to psychology presented in this book—both the content and the pedagogical features. After all, it's a text that relies consistently on well-grounded principles of psychology to teach psychology.

INSTRUCTOR SUPPLEMENTS

The following supplements will also enhance teaching and learning for you and your students:

■ *Instructor's Manual:* This helpful teaching companion features at-a-glance grids, handouts, lecture enhancements, detailed chapter outlines, activities for the classroom, and other valuable course organization material for new and experienced instructors.

▮ *Test Bank:* Paul Wellman of Texas A&M University has provided an updated test bank containing over 2000 questions, including multiple choice, true/false, short answer, and essay (each with an answer justification). All questions are labeled with a page reference, difficulty ranking, and a type designation. This product is also available in TestGen computerized version for use in creating tests in the classroom.

▮ *PowerPoint Presentation:* David Lundberg-Kenrick has created a Power-Point package with detailed outlines of key points for each chapter supported by charts, graphs, diagrams, and other visuals from the textbook. The presentation also contains links to the companion website for corresponding activities.

▮ *The Allyn & Bacon Introduction to Psychology Transparency Set:* This set of approximately 200 full-color transparencies is available upon adoption of the text from your local Allyn & Bacon sales representative.

▮ *Allyn & Bacon Digital Media Archive for Psychology, 4.0:* This comprehensive CD-ROM includes charts, graphs, maps, tables, and figures, with audio clips and video clips and links to relevant web sites.

▮ *Insights into Psychology, Volumes I–IV:* A new set of video resources prepared to accompany Allyn & Bacon's texts in introductory psychology, each video consists of 15 to 16 topics, each supported by 2 to 3 video clips. Critical thinking questions accompany each clip. In addition, the video guide provides further critical thinking questions and Internet resources for more information.

▮ *Blockbuster Guide for Introduction to Psychology:* NEW! The *Blockbuster Guide* is a unique print resource for instructors who enjoy enhancing their classroom presentations with film. With heavy coverage of general, abnormal, social, and developmental psychology, this guide suggests a wide range of films to use in class and provides activities, questions for reflection, and other pedagogical tools to make the use of film more effective in the classroom.

▮ *MyPsychLab:* This interactive and instructive multimedia resource can be used to supplement a traditional lecture course or to administer a course entirely online. It is an all-inclusive tool, a text-specific e-book plus multimedia tutorials, audio, video, simulations, animations, and controlled assessments to completely engage students and reinforce learning. Fully customizable and easy to use, *MyPsychLab* meets the individual teaching and learning needs of every instructor and every student. Visit the site at www.mypsychlab.com.

▮ *CourseCompass:* Powered by Blackboard, this course management system uses a powerful suite of tools that allows instructors to create an online presence for any course.

▮ *Discovering Psychology Telecourse Videos:* Written, designed, and hosted by Phil Zimbardo, this set of 26 half-hour videos is available for class use from the Annenberg/CPB collection. The collection includes two completely new programs and more than 15 new sequences that bring students up-to-date in some of the latest developments in the field. A perfect complement to *Psychology: Core Concepts,* this course supplement is a landmark educational resource that reveals psychology's contribution not only to understanding the puzzles of behavior but also to identifying solutions and treatments to ease the problems of mental disorders. It has won numerous prizes and is widely used in the United States and internationally.

■ **Discovering Psychology Telecourse Faculty Guide:** The *Telecourse Faculty Guide* provides guidelines for using *Discovering Psychology* as a resource within your course. Keyed directly to *Psychology: Core Concepts,* the faculty guide includes the complete Telecourse Study Guide plus suggested activities; suggested essays; cited studies; instructional resources, including books, articles, films, and websites; video program test questions with answer key; and a key term glossary.

A NOTE OF THANKS

Nobody ever realizes the magnitude of the task when taking on a textbook-writing project. Susan Hartman and Kelly May, our Acquisitions Editors, deftly guided (and prodded) us through this process. The vision of the 5th edition confronted reality under the guidance of Pamela Barter, our tenacious Developmental Editor, who made us work harder that we had believed possible. We suspect that Pam may be able to leap tall buildings in a single bound, but we know with certainty that she has the X-ray eyes of an editor. Time and again she spotted glitches and potentially troublesome wording that had slipped passed the six less-penetrating eyes of your authors.

The job of making the manuscript into a book fell to Joe Sweeney, Production Supervisor, and Margaret Pinette, our puckish copyeditor, in whom we met a stickler for style with a great sense of humor. We think they did an outstanding job—as did our tireless photo researcher, the tenacious Sarah Evertson, who had the class and brass to get photos from even the most reluctant of sources.

We are sure that none of the above would be offended if we reserve our deepest thanks for our spouses and closest colleagues. Phil thanks his wonderful wife, Christina Maslach, for her endless inspiration and for modeling what is best in academic psychology.

Ann thanks her long-suffering spouse, John Quigley, for always and readily encouraging her efforts and assuring her that she's "the best." It will surprise no one who knows her that Ann also thanks her six cats and one perfect dog for their abiding, accepting love and for providing perspective and acceptance, no matter what. She also would like to thank her students and colleagues in the Department of Psychology, UNC at Asheville, for providing feedback, input, and inspiration of the teaching profession as well as the minutia of composing a book—lessons, examples, gimmicks, and especially ideas and images that don't work and so have to be deleted before the manuscript ever sees the light of publication!

Bob is grateful to his spouse and friend, Michelle, who put up with long conversations on topics psychological, Bob's undone household chores, and much gratification delayed—mostly without complaint. She has been a wellspring of understanding and loving support. His thanks, too, go to Rebecca, their daughter, who has taught him the practical side of developmental psychology—and now, much to her own astonishment, possesses a graduate degree in psychology. In addition, he thanks his friends and colleagues Mike Vasey, Suzy Horton, and Kandis Mutter, who read and commented on the previous edition and on portions of the new manuscript. It would be impossible to thank them enough.

Many experts and teachers of introductory psychology also shared their constructive criticism with us on every chapter and feature of the 5th edition of this text:

Michele Breault, Truman State University

Jay Brown, Southwest Missouri State University

Wanda Clark, South Plains College

John Conklin, Camosun College (Canada)

Michelle L. Pilati Corselli, Rio Hondo College

Sara DeHart-Young, Mississippi State University

Janet DiPietro, John Hopkins University

Diane Finley, Prince George's Community College

Krista Forrest, University of Nebraska at Kearney

Rick Froman, John Brown University

Jack Hartnett, Virginia Commonwealth University

Michael Hillard, Albuquerque TVI Community College

Brian Kelley, Bridgewater College

Sheila Kennison, Oklahoma State University

Dawn Lewis, Prince George's Community College

Deborah Long, East Carolina University

Cindy Nordstrom, Southern Illinois University

Jeff Pedroza, Santa Ana College

Laura Phelan, St. John Fisher College

Skip Pollock, Mesa Community College

Lynne Schmelter-Davis, Brookdale, County College of Monmouth

Patricia Stephenson, Miami Dade College

Stacy Walker, Kingwood College

We also thank the reviewers of the 4th edition of *Psychology: Core Concepts* and hope that they will recognize their valued input in all that is good in this text:

Lynn Haller, Morehead State University

Carol Hayes, Delta State

Richard Mascolo, El Camino College

Nancy Mellucci, Los Angeles Community College District

Ginger Osborne, Santa Ana State

Vernon Padgett, Rio Hondo College

Mark Shellhammer, Fairmont State College

We would lastly like to thank reviewers of our past editions for their input and insight:

Gordon Allen, Miami University

Beth Barton, Coastal Carolina Community College

Linda Bastone, Purchase College, SUNY

Michael Bloch, University of San Francisco

Susan Beck, Wallace State College

John H. Brennecke, Mount San Antonio College

T. L. Brink, Crafton Hills College

Sally S. Carr, Lakeland Community College

Saundra Ciccarelli, Gulf Coast Community College

Authur Gonchar, University of LaVerne

Peter Gram, Pensacola Junior College

Mary Elizabeth Hannah, University of Detroit

Carol Hayes, Delta State University

Peter Hornby, SUNY Plattsburgh

Laurel Krautwurst, Blue Ridge Community College

Judith Levine, SUNY Farmingdale

Margaret Lynch, San Francisco State University

Marc Martin, Palm Beach Community College

Steven Meier, University of Idaho

Yozan Dirk Mosig, University of Nebraska

Melinda Myers-Johnson, Humbolt State University

Michael Nikolakis, Faulkner State College

Faye Plascak-Craig, Marian College

Chris Robin, Madisonville Community College

Christina Sinisi, Charleston Southern University

Mario Sussman, Indiana University of Pennsylvania

John Teske, Elizabethtown College

Robert Wellman, Fitchburg State University

If you have any recommendations of your own that we should not overlook for the next edition, please write to us! Address your comments to:

Dr. Ann Weber

Department of Psychology, CPO #1960

UNC at Asheville

Asheville, NC 28804-8508

or send e-mail to:

weber@unca.edu

Thanks to all of our colleagues whose feedback has improved our text. Thanks also to all instructors of this most-difficult-to-teach course for taking on the pedagogical challenge and conveying to students their passion about the joys and relevance of psychological science and practice.

ABOUT THE AUTHORS

Phil Zimbardo

Philip Zimbardo, Ph.D., Stanford University professor, has been teaching the Introductory Psychology course for nearly 50 years and has been writing the basic text for this course, as well as the Faculty Guides and Student Workbooks, for the past 35 years. In addition, he has helped to develop and update the PBS-TV series, *Discovering Psychology,* that is used in many high school and university courses both nationally and internationally. He has been called the "Face and Voice of Psychology" because of this popular series and his other media presentations. Zimbardo also loves to conduct and publish research on a wide variety of subjects, as well as teaching and engaging in public and social service activities. He has published more than 300 professional and popular articles and chapters and 50 books of all kinds. He is currently engaged in writing a trade book on the psychology of evil that relates his classic Stanford Prison Experiment to the abuses at Iraq's Abu Ghraib Prison. Please see these websites for more information: www.zimbardo.com, www.prisonexperiment.org, www.psychologyMatters.org.

Robert Johnson

Robert Johnson, Ph.D, taught introductory psychology for 28 years at Umpqua Community College. He is especially interested in applying psychological principles to the teaching of psychology and in encouraging linkages between psychology and other disciplines. In keeping with those interests, Bob founded the Pacific Northwest Great Teachers Seminar, of which he was the director for 20 years. He was also one of the founders of PT@CC (Psychology Teachers at Community Colleges), serving as its executive committee chair during 2004. That same year he also received the Two-Year College Teaching Award given by the Society for the Teaching of Psychology. Bob has long been active in APA, APS, the Western Psychological Association, and the Council of Teachers of Undergraduate Psychology.

Bob loves to write about psychology almost as much as he loves to teach. Aside from his contributions as a coauthor of *Psychology: Core Concepts,* he is particularly proud of his articles in *Teaching of Psychology.* Recently he began a term as the editor of *The General Psychologist,* the newsletter of the Society for General Psychology (Division 1 of APA). And, he is working on a book that brings to light what Shakespeare had to say about psychology.

Bob and his wife live on the North Umpqua River in southern Oregon, where they can go kayaking in their front yard or bicycling in the valleys of the Cascade Mountains. In his spare time he likes making pottery and Thai curries.

Ann L. Weber

Ann L. Weber, Ph.D., is professor of psychology at the University of North Carolina at Asheville, where for almost three decades she has taught General Psychology, Social Psychology, and the Psychology of Close Relationships, among other courses. She came to UNCA after completing her undergraduate work at The Catholic University of America and graduate work at The Johns Hopkins University. *Psychology: Core Concepts* is one of her many student-oriented texts and study guides, in addition to scores of books and other writings on close relationships, loss, and grief. As a consultant, she conducts workshops on subjects from managing stress and surviving breakups to learning humor and perspective from relationships with pets. Her many recognitions for teaching include UNCA's Distinguished Teacher Award and the Outstanding Teacher Award from the International Association for Relationship Research. Currently she is writing and developing courses on psychology in film and the relationships between people and animals. She and her husband live in the mountains of western North Carolina with five cats, two dogs, and a steady stream of fostered companion animals.

USING PSYCHOLOGY TO LEARN PSYCHOLOGY:
Studying with Key Questions and Core Concepts

Mind, Behavior, and Psychological Science

PEOPLE REFERRED TO HIM as Clever Hans because, to all appearances, he was exceptionally smart. But another characteristic made his case truly remarkable: Hans was a horse. His celebrity grew from public demonstrations in which he apparently solved math problems. "What is 12 plus 7?" a bystander might ask, and Hans would tap 19 times with his hoof. He wasn't *always* right, mind you, but most of the time Hans gave correct answers to problems involving simple addition, subtraction, multiplication, and division— even square roots. Nor were his presumed talents limited to math: When presented with questions written on large cards, Hans would spell out answers by tapping the ground to indicate letters on an alphabet board.

As Hans's fame spread throughout Europe and America, he became the world's most famous animal. But the scientific community, as you might expect, had its skeptics. Could a horse think and reason? Surely not. But then, how could they explain Hans's apparent talents?

One fall day in 1904, a committee of scientists, assembled by Carl Stumpf, Director of the Berlin Psychological Institute, paid a visit to Hans's owner, Wilhelm von Osten to investigate the matter. The group brought a variety of backgrounds to the task, including psychology, zoology, and veterinary medicine. For good measure, Stumpf also brought along a circus animal trainer and a prominent politician. For his part, Mr. Von Osten obligingly put Hans through his intellectual paces, while the committee

● Clever Hans

observed. Their initial skepticism soon gave way to fascination at the horse's performance. More important for the committee's mission, they found no hint that von Osten was cheating.

Nevertheless, one of the committee members, psychologist Oskar Pfungst, remained suspicious. He wondered whether the horse might be responding to cues unconsciously given by von Osten. Dr. Pfungst, therefore, proposed a more controlled test of Hans's abilities. Could the horse correctly answer questions when its owner Osten did not know the answer or was out of sight? Sure enough, when von Osten was not allowed to see the written questions, Hans failed the test. Likewise, when von Osten could see the questions but was required to stand behind a curtain or otherwise outside the horse's field of vision, Hans could not answer.

Von Osten was deeply disappointed with the results. But, to his credit, he cooperated with Pfungst to find out exactly what sorts of cues the horse had been sensing. A slight lean forward served as the signal for Hans to start tapping. The "stop" sign could be a subtle straightening of von Osten's posture, a rise of his eyebrows, or even a flaring of his nostrils. Hans, it turned out, was a clever horse, indeed—clever at reading almost imperceptible physical cues. When it came to verbal and math skills, however, his abilities were just average . . . for a horse.

KEY QUESTION

WHAT IS PSYCHOLOGY—AND WHAT IS IT *NOT*?

In a generic sense, everyone is a psychologist. We all study people, analyze their behavior, try to understand what they are thinking and feeling, and attempt to predict what they will do next. But there is a real difference between the commonsense psychology your Uncle Felix or Aunt Ethyl uses in everyday life and the psychology you will learn about in the following pages. We have already glimpsed the latter in Dr. Pfungst's skeptical "show-me-the-evidence" approach. More specifically, the working definition of psychology that we will use throughout this book is a part of our Core Concept for this section of the chapter:

CORE CONCEPT

Psychology is a broad field, with many specialties, but fundamentally psychology is the science of behavior and mental processes.

We can find the original meaning of **psychology** in the Greek roots of the word. *Psyche* means "mind"—which the ancient Greeks believed to be separate and distinct from the physical body—and the suffix *-ology* means "a field of study." Therefore, "psychology" literally means "the study of the mind." Psychologists today, however, use the broader definition that we included in our Core Concept: Psychology includes not only *mental processes* but also *behaviors*. That is to say, psychology's domain extends across both directly observable behaviors (talking, smiling, and crying, for example) and the internal mental processes that can be only indirectly observed (such as thinking, feeling, and desiring). As you will see later in the chapter, psychologists have not always agreed on these boundaries for their field—particularly on whether subjective mental processes could be explored by a discipline that claims to be a science.

The other important part of our definition, then, involves this scientific aspect of psychology. In brief, the *science* of psychology is based on objective,

■ **Psychology** The science of behavior and mental processes.

verifiable evidence obtained with the same care used by Pfungst in his study of Clever Hans. Giving you a more complete explanation of what we mean by the science of psychology will occupy much of the rest of the chapter.

For the moment, we want to focus on a point that is only implied in our definition of psychology: the notion that psychology is *not* mere speculation about human nature, nor is it a body of folk wisdom about people that "everybody knows" to be true. Throughout this book you will find many examples of such "commonsense" ideas that psychological science has shown to be false. Could some of your own beliefs be among them? We challenge you to find out by taking the quiz in the box, "Do It Yourself! Is it Psychological Science or Psychobabble?"

DO IT YOURSELF! | Is It Psychological Science or Psychobabble?

"Show me the evidence!" is the rallying cry of critical thinking. This rule has not penetrated our popular culture, where books tell us that men are from Mars and women are from Venus and that some people think with the "left brain" and others with the "right brain." In fact, much that is called "psychology" by the popular press and on TV is not based on science at all. Likewise, it is a good bet that you will find many volumes in the "Psychology and Self-Help" section of your local bookstore that are based on nothing more than speculation, exaggeration, or misunderstanding—what we call *pseudopsychology* and psychologist Carol Tavris (2000) more scathingly labels *psychobabble*. Whichever term you prefer, your authors hope that this book will help you spot bogus psychology for what it is.

Now, let's put a sampling of your psychological beliefs to the test. Some of the following statements are true, and some are false. Don't worry if you get a few—or all—of the items wrong: You will have lots of company. The point is that what so-called common sense teaches us about psychological processes may not withstand the scrutiny of a scientific test. Mark each of the following statements as "true" or "false." (The answers are given at the end.)

_____ 1. It is a myth that most people use only about 10% of their brains.

_____ 2. During your most vivid dreams, your body may be paralyzed.

_____ 3. Psychological stress can cause physical illness.

_____ 4. The color red exists only as a sensation in the brain. There is no "red" in the world outside the brain.

_____ 5. Bipolar (manic–depressive) disorder is caused by a conflict in the unconscious mind.

_____ 6. The newborn child's mind is essentially a "blank slate" on which

everything he or she will know is "written" (learned) by experience.

_____ 7. Everything that happens to us leaves a permanent record in memory.

_____ 8. You were born with all the brain cells that you will ever have.

_____ 9. Intelligence is a nearly pure genetic trait that is fixed at the same level throughout a person's life.

_____ 10. Polygraph ("lie detector") devices are remarkably accurate in detecting physical responses that, in the eye of a trained examiner, reliably indicate when a suspect is lying.

Answers: The first four items are true; the rest are false. Below you will find some brief explanations for each item; you will find more detail in the chapters indicated in parentheses.

1. *True:* This *is* a myth. We use all parts of our brains every day. (See Chapter 2, "Biopsychology and the Foundations of Neuroscience.")

2. *True:* During our most vivid dreams, which occur during rapid eye movement sleep (REM), the voluntary muscles in our body are paralyzed, with the exception of those controlling our eyes. (See Chapter 3, "States of Consciousness.")

3. *True:* The link between mind and body can make you sick when you are under chronic stress. (See Chapter 10, "Stress, Health, and Well-Being.")

4. *True:* Strange as it may seem, all sensations of color are created in the brain itself. Light waves do have different frequencies, but they have no color. The brain interprets the various frequencies of light as different colors. (See Chapter 5, "Sensation and Perception.")

5. *False:* There is no evidence at all that unconscious conflicts play a role in bipolar disorder. Instead, the evidence suggests a strong biochemical component. The disorder usually responds well to certain drugs, hinting that it involves faulty brain chemistry. Research also suggests that this faulty chemistry may have a genetic basis. (See Chapter 12, "Mental Disorders," and Chapter 13, "Therapies for Mental Disorders.")

6. *False:* Far from being a "blank slate," the newborn child has a large repertoire of built-in abilities and protective reflexes. The "blank slate" myth also ignores the child's genetic potential. (See Chapter 4, "Psychological Development.")

7. *False:* Although many details of our lives are remembered, there is no evidence that memory records all the details of our lives. In fact, we have good reason to believe that most of the information around us never reaches memory and that what does reach memory often becomes distorted. (See Chapter 7, "Memory.")

8. *False:* Contrary to what scientists thought just a few years ago, some parts of the brain continue to create new cells throughout life. (See Chapter 2, "Biopsychology and the Foundations of Neuroscience.")

9. *False:* Intelligence is the result of both heredity and environment. Because it depends, in part, on environment, your level of intelligence (as measured by an IQ test) can change throughout your life. (See Chapter 8, "Thinking and Intelligence.")

10. *False:* Even the most expert polygrapher can incorrectly classify a truth-teller as a liar or fail to identify someone who is lying. Objective evidence supporting the accuracy of lie detectors is meager. (See Chapter 9, "Emotion and Motivation.")

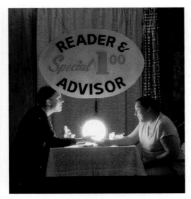

● Fortune tellers, astrologers, and other practitioners of pseudopsychology don't bother to verify their claims with the same care that Pfungst used to test Clever Hans.

Psychology and Critical Thinking

The Clever Hans incident occurred one hundred years ago. Yet, people today seem as eager as ever to embrace fantastic claims—especially those of mysterious powers of the mind and supernatural influences on our personalities. For evidence, we have to look no further than the horoscope in the daily newspaper. Never mind that astrology has been thoroughly debunked (Schick & Vaughn, 2001)[1]. And the same goes for graphology (the bogus science of handwriting analysis), fortune telling, and the purported power of subliminal messages in the movies or on TV to persuade us to buy certain products or vote for certain politicians. All fall under the heading of **pseudopsychology:** phony, unscientific psychology masquerading as the real thing.

One of the goals your authors have for this book is to help you differentiate between psychology and pseudopsychology—that is, to *think critically* about claims made under the name of psychology. Most people, of course, think of themselves as good thinkers—just using common sense—but, as we will see over and over again in this book, what masquerades as psychological common sense has often turned out to be wrong. "Common sense," after all, has led many people to accept uncritically the polygraph (the so-called lie detector), the superiority of certain racial groups, demonic possession as a cause of mental illness, the brutal brain operation sometimes called the "lobotomy," and the notion that horrific deeds (such as the recent torture of prisoners in Iraq) are perpetrated by just a few "bad apples."

Harmful Effects of Pseudopsychology So, what's the big deal if people want to believe such things? We—your authors, Drs. Phil, Bob, and Ann—suggest that there are two sets of problems.

First, those who uncritically accept the claims of pseudoscientific psychology risk depriving themselves of some *real* psychological insights that are even more interesting and useful. To give one example, few people realize that we humans are highly susceptible to **confirmation bias.** That is, we pay attention to events that confirm our beliefs and ignore evidence that contradicts them (Halpern, 2002). Knowledge of the confirmation bias helps us understand why, for example, astrology fans usually remember those days when the horoscope seems accurate and forget the days when it misses the mark.

The second set of problems with pseudopsychology involves the potential for more serious harm. For example, unfounded psychological beliefs (*pseudopsychology*) can waste time, money, and talent—even lives—as you will see when we discuss false "recovered memories" of sexual abuse (in Chapter 7) or when the presumption of female intellectual inferiority keeps women out of "men's jobs." Some people still don't know that psychological science long ago demonstrated that memory is not always accurate and that neither sex is intellectually inferior to the other (Neisser et al., 1996).

Pseudopsychology can also provide a fertile field for fraud. This happens when people are bilked by fortune-tellers, handwriting analysts (graphologists), or astrologers, who claim to have special knowledge of personality. Still another form of harm (of special concern to psychologists) involves diminished public support for legitimate psychological science.

■ **Pseudopsychology** Erroneous assertions or practices set forth as being scientific psychology.
■ **Confirmation bias** The tendency to attend to evidence that complements and confirms our beliefs or expectations, while ignoring evidence that does not.

---

[1]Throughout this book you will find that we use brief citations in parentheses calling your attention to a complete bibliographic reference found in the "References" section, beginning on p. R-1, near the end of this book. These brief in-text citations give the authors' last names and the publication date. With the complete reference in hand, your library can help you find the original source.

Merely raising questions about accepted pseudoscientific beliefs can sometimes be dangerous. For example, in some parts of the United States only a few decades ago, those who dared to question the presumed mental and moral inferiority of African Americans were sometimes beaten, jailed, or lynched. Even today, in many regions of the world, posing critical questions about the status of women or particular racial groups still carries dire consequences.

Dangerous Therapies: The Facilitated Communication Fiasco   Yet another potential harmful consequence of pseudoscientific psychology lurks in unvalidated therapies for psychological disorders. Let's consider an example involving *facilitated communication,* a widely acclaimed treatment for *autism* (a developmental disorder that can severely impair attention, language, and social functioning) that was popular in the 1990s. The treatment (which we will explain in a moment) is based on the erroneous belief that autism sufferers can have impressive verbal abilities that lie hidden by their disorder.

● When skeptical psychologists tested the claims for facilitated communication, they found that it wasn't the autistic children who were responsible for the messages.

In brief, facilitated communication is a method by which a helper (or *facilitator*) attempts to communicate with an autistic person by asking questions and then assisting the person to respond by typing or pointing to letters on a letter board. (You can see how this is done in the accompanying photo.) You may have already identified the problem with this method: making sure that it is the autistic person who is really responding, rather than the facilitator.

Initially, the reports on facilitated communication were promising—even enthusiastic. But some psychologists were skeptical. They pointed out that the glowing reports were simply anecdotes, lacking in strict scientific controls. They also expressed concern that the helper might be consciously or unconsciously guiding the child's hand to produce the messages. (You have probably noticed the parallels with the case of Clever Hans.)

Sure enough, when studies of facilitated communication were done under controlled conditions, the results showed the skeptics' concerns to be well founded (Cabay, 1994; Wheeler et al., 1993). When the facilitator knew the questions being asked, the autistic child would seem to give sensible answers. But when "blinders" were applied—by hiding the questions from the facilitator—the answers were inaccurate or nonsensical. In fact, the experiments that demonstrated the flaws in facilitated communication employed essentially the same design that Dr. Pfungst used almost a century before to test Clever Hans.

Sadly, even though facilitated communication had extended hope to beleaguered parents and teachers, psychological research dashed those hopes. Moreover, the consequences of an uncritical belief in facilitated communication proved worse than false hopes. Not only did the use of facilitated communication mean that more effective treatments were delayed, but many parents blamed themselves when their children did not respond as expected to the treatment (Levine et al., 1994). Worst of all may have been the false accusations of sexual abuse derived from facilitated messages thought to have come from the autistic children (Bicklen, 1990; Heckler, 1994). The controlled studies left little doubt that the messages describing abuse originated wholly in the minds of the facilitators. In the wake of these findings, the American Psychological Association (2003b) denounced facilitated communication as a failure and relegated it to the junk pile of ineffective therapies.

The Skeptical Psychologist   So, what lesson can you, as a student of psychology, draw from the facilitated communication fiasco and from the case of Clever Hans? After all, you won't be able to run your own scientific test on every fantastic-sounding claim that comes along. We hope that you will develop a skeptical, critical attitude about reports of amazing new treatments, dramatic psychological "breakthroughs," and products that claim to help you develop "untapped potential." And, we hope you will always pause to ask: Is there a simpler explanation? Has someone done a controlled test? Could the claims be merely the result of people's *expectations*—that is, could *confirmation bias* be at work? By doing so, you will have adopted the skeptical, show-me-the-evidence attitude of a good psychologist. This is exactly the approach that we will take on the journey through psychology that we begin in this chapter.

What Do Psychologists Do?

In the next few pages you will discover that psychology is a more diverse field than most people realize. Many students enroll in their first psychology course expecting that it will deal mainly with mental disorders and psychological therapies. But they soon find that psychology is also about learning, memory, perception, intelligence, personality, social interaction, thinking, emotion, and many more concepts that we will explore throughout this book. In the remainder of this section, we will first confront a stereotype about psychologists, and then we will show you three main ways to be a psychologist. After that, you will learn about some of the field's principal areas of specialization and, finally, about the difference between psychologists and psychiatrists.

Not All Psychologists Are Therapists   Contrary to the popular stereotype, psychologists are not all therapists. You will find them at work almost everywhere: in education, industry, sports, prisons, government, churches and temples, private practice, and in the psychology departments of colleges and universities (see Figure 1.1). Psychologists also work for athletic teams, engineering firms, consulting firms, and the courts (both the judicial and the NBA variety). In these diverse settings, they perform a wide range of tasks, including teaching, research, assessment, equipment design—and psychotherapy. Psychology's specialties are too numerous to cover them all here, but we can give you the flavor of the field by first dividing psychology into three broad categories.

Three Ways Of Doing Psychology   Broadly speaking, we can divide psychology into three main branches or categories: *experimental psychology, teaching of psychology,* and *applied psychology.* **Experimental psychologists** are the workhorses who do the basic research in psychology. Most are faculty members at a college or university. This group, also called *research psychologists,* is the smallest of the three major branches of psychology (Frincke & Pate, 2004).

The second category, **teachers of psychology,** overlaps with the experimentalists, because most researchers also teach classes at the colleges or uni-

■ **Experimental psychologists**
Psychologists who do research on basic psychological processes—as contrasted with applied psychologists; also called *research psychologists.*

■ **Teachers of psychology**
Psychologists whose primary job is teaching, typically in high schools, colleges, and universities.

● **FIGURE 1.1**   Work Settings of Psychologists

(Updated information from *Employed Doctoral Scientists and Engineers, by Sector of Employment, Broad Field of Doctorate and Sex: 2001,* National Science Foundation.)

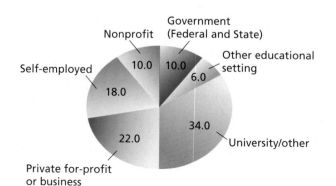

versities where they do their experimental work. Increasingly, however, large numbers of psychologists are hired by high schools, colleges, and universities primarily to teach. Community colleges alone employ some 9000 psychologists in teaching positions across the United States (Johnson & Rudmann, 2004).

Applied psychologists use the knowledge developed by experimental psychologists to tackle human problems, such as training, equipment design, and psychological treatment. Applied psychologists work in a wide variety of places such as schools, clinics, factories, social service agencies, airports, hospitals, and casinos. All told, some 64% of the doctoral-level psychologists in the United States work primarily as applied psychologists, and that percentage has been steadily increasing since the 1950s (Kohout & Wicherski, 2000; Rosenzweig, 1992; Stapp et al., 1985).

Applied Psychological Specialties   What, exactly, do applied psychologists do? Here are profiles of some of the most popular applied specialties:

- *Industrial and organizational psychologists* (often called *I/O psychologists*) specialize in modifying the work environment to maximize productivity and morale. Some I/O psychologists develop interview and testing procedures to help organizations select new employees; some develop programs to train and retain employees; and others specialize in market research.

- *Sports psychologists,* as you might expect, work with athletes to help them maximize their performance. They deal with enhancing motivation, controlling emotions under pressure, and planning practice sessions. Many major sports franchises have sports psychologists on staff.

- *Engineering psychologists* work at the interface between people and equipment. Some design devices, such as control panels or airplane instrument displays, for easy and reliable human use. Some do psychological detective work to discover what went wrong in accidents attributed to "human error." Engineering psychologists are usually employed by private industry or the government and often work on a team with other scientists.

- *School psychologists* have expertise in the problems of teaching and learning. Typically, they work for a school district, where they diagnose learning and behavior problems and consult with teachers, students, and parents. School psychologists may spend a good deal of time administering, scoring, and interpreting psychological tests.

- *Rehabilitation psychologists* serve with physicians, nurses, counselors, and social workers on teams that may treat patients with both physical and mental disorders, such as stroke, spinal cord injury, alcoholism, drug abuse, or amputation. Some work in a hospital setting. Others work for social service agencies and for sheltered workshops that provide job training for people with disabilities.

- *Clinical psychologists* and *counseling psychologists* work with people who have problems with social and emotional adjustment or those who face difficult choices in relationships, careers, or education. About half of all doctoral-level psychologists list clinical or counseling psychology as their specialty (American Psychological Association, 2003c). The clinician is more likely to have a private practice involving psychological testing and long-term therapy, while the counselor is more likely to work for an agency or school and to spend fewer sessions with each client.

More information on the career possibilities in psychology can be found in *Careers in Psychology for the Twenty-First Century,* published by the American Psychological Association (2003a).

■ **Applied psychologists**
Psychologists who use the knowledge developed by experimental psychologists to solve human problems.

PSYCHOLOGY IN YOUR LIFE: KNOWING THE DIFFERENCE BETWEEN A PSYCHOLOGIST AND A PSYCHIATRIST

Students sometimes worry that their psychology professors are going to "psychoanalyze" them. Apparently, they believe that psychologists stand ever vigilant—just waiting for signs of mental disorder to appear. To put your mind at rest, this is only a stereotype: People commonly think that all psychologists are *clinical* psychologists—but you have already learned that isn't true. In fact, many psychologists have no training at all in the diagnosis and treatment of mental disorders.

One other point of confusion blurs the public image of psychology: the distinction between *psychology* and *psychiatry*. **Psychiatry** is a medical specialty, not a part of psychology. Psychiatrists hold MD (Doctor of Medicine) degrees and have also had specialized training in the treatment of mental and behavioral problems. Therefore, psychiatrists are licensed to prescribe medicines and to perform other medical procedures. Consequently, psychiatrists tend to view patients from a *medical* perspective. In the public mind, however, psychiatry often gets confused with clinical psychology because both professions treat people suffering mental disorders. Psychologists like to point out that, while psychiatric training emphasizes mental illness, it gives short shrift to basic *psychological* topics, such as perception, learning, psychological testing, and developmental issues.

By contrast with psychiatry, psychology is a much broader field, encompassing many different specialties. Each specialty—such as experimental, engineering, teaching, and I/O psychology—has its own focus. As we have seen, most have nothing to do with the diagnosis and treatment of mental disorders. Moreover, while psychologists typically hold doctoral degrees, their training is not in medicine. (Only a few psychologists have taken the necessary medical coursework that qualifies them to prescribe drugs for psychological problems.) Instead, graduate training in psychology focuses on training in research methods, along with advanced study in a particular psychological specialty.

So, now you can sound smarter than most people when you talk about psychology and psychiatry. But, what about the difference between a psychologist and a *psychoanalyst*? We'll look into that in the next section.

■ **Psychiatry**   A medical specialty dealing with the diagnosis and treatment of mental disorders.

CHECK YOUR UNDERSTANDING

1. **RECALL:** Experiments showing facilitated communication to be ineffective were similar to the experiment that exposed Clever Hans. Specifically, what did both experimental procedures have in common?
   a. Neither the horse nor the autistic children could see the questions.
   b. Neither Von Osten nor the facilitators could see the questions.
   c. Both Hans and the autistic children were given incentives for producing correct answers.
   d. In both situations, correct answers were given about half the time.

2. **APPLICATION:** The *confirmation bias* refers to a mental process that explains, among other things, why people
   a. engage in risky behavior.
   b. seek help from psychiatrists.
   c. believe in astrology.
   d. become autistic.

3. **RECALL:** Which one would be considered an applied psychologist?
   a. an I/O psychologist
   b. a psychologist doing basic research
   c. a professor of psychology at the university
   d. a psychiatrist

4. **APPLICATION:** Which one of the following would be most likely to do research on learning or memory?
   a. an applied psychologist
   b. an I/O psychologist
   c. a psychiatrist
   d. an experimental psychologist

5. **UNDERSTANDING THE CORE CONCEPT:** Psychology is different from other disciplines, such as psychiatry, that deal with people because
   a. psychology focuses on mental disorder.
   b. psychology is a broader field, covering all aspects of behavior and mental processes.
   c. psychologists must have doctoral degrees.
   d. psychologists do research.

WHAT ARE PSYCHOLOGY'S HISTORICAL ROOTS?

KEY QUESTION

People have probably always speculated about <u>human behavior and mental processes</u>. Written records, dating back some 25 centuries to the Greek philosophers Socrates, Plato, and Aristotle, include ideas about consciousness and madness. They observed that emotions can distort thinking and that our perceptions are merely interpretations of the external world. Most people today would probably agree with many of these ancient ideas—and so would modern psychology.

On the other hand, the Greeks also came up with some psychological notions that now seem quaint or amusing. They believed, for example, that emotions flow from the heart, the liver, and the spleen and that mental disorder could be caused by excessive bile. Following their lead, we still use the metaphor of "heartfelt" emotions, and we may "vent the spleen" when we are angry.

● The ancient Greeks believed that anger, such as we see in this enraged driver, comes from the spleen, but it never occurred to them to put their theories to a controlled test.

But we can give the Greeks only partial credit for laying the historical foundations for psychology. At roughly the same time, Asian and African societies were developing their own psychological ideas. In Asia, Yoga and Buddhism were exploring consciousness, which they attempted to control with meditation. Meanwhile, in Africa, other explanations for personality and mental disorder were emerging from traditional spiritual beliefs (Berry et al., 1992). Based on these *folk psychologies*, shamans (healers) developed therapies rivaling in effectiveness the treatments used in Western psychology and psychiatry today (Lambo, 1978). It was, however, the Greek tradition and, later, the Roman Catholic Church that most influenced the tortuous development of Western psychology as a science.

Oddly—and significantly—it never occurred to any of the ancient thinkers to put their speculations to a test, in the same way that Pfungst tested his suspicions about Clever Hans. In the Greek mind, truth came from casual observation, logic, and the authority of experts. Then, a few hundred years later, when the medieval Church gained control of Europe, clerics sought to minimize inquiry into human nature because they had little interest in the "world of the flesh." In fact, the Church taught that the mind and soul operate completely outside the natural laws that govern worldly objects and events. For medieval Christians, the human mind—like the mind of God—presented an unsolvable mystery.

This view prevailed until the 17th century, when French philosopher René Descartes (*Day-CART*) dared to assert that human sensations and behaviors are based on activity in the nervous system. His idea fit well with exciting new discoveries about the biology of nerve circuits in animals. For example, science had just shown how the sense organs convert stimulation into the nerve impulses and muscular responses. This discovery allowed scientists, for the first time, to see that there were biological processes (rather than mysterious spiritual forces) behind sensation and simple reflexive behaviors. Yet, despite these major advances, psychology itself would not become a distinct scientific discipline for another two centuries after Descartes. As we will see, it took two revolutionary ideas to make a science of psychology possible.

Before we get to that, however, let's take a moment to state our Core Concept for this section, which emphasizes five of the competing viewpoints that emerged in the early days of psychology, as the field struggled to become a science:

> Modern psychology developed from several conflicting traditions, including structuralism, functionalism, Gestalt psychology, behaviorism, and psychoanalysis.

After you have studied this section, you should be able to explain the basic assumptions of each tradition and the issues on which they were in conflict.

Structuralism: Focus on Structure—and the Founding of Scientific Psychology

One of the two revolutionary ideas to shape the early development of psychology emerged in the mid-1800s. In his book *On the Origin of Species* (1859), Charles Darwin suggested a biological kinship between humans and animals. For psychologists this would mean that discoveries about animal biology and behavior could be applied (with caution, of course) to people. So, for example, Helmholtz's pioneering research on nerve impulses in frogs helped psychologists understand human reflexes. Likewise, Darwin's insight meant that Pavlov's later work on learning in dogs could also throw light on human learning—as we shall see in Chapter 6.

The second big idea that shaped the early science of psychology arose in chemistry, where scientists had noticed patterns in properties of the chemical elements that led them to develop the *periodic table*. At one stroke, the periodic table made the processes underlying chemical reactions clear. This achievement particularly intrigued one Wilhelm Wundt, a German scientist (who, incidentally, became the first person to call himself a "psychologist"). Wundt wondered: Could a similar approach simplify our understanding of the mind? Could he discover "the elements of conscious experience"? Wundt's quest for the elements of consciousness became known as **structuralism,** because it focused on revealing the most basic "structures" or components of the mind (Fancher, 1979).

To pursue his dream of establishing a science of consciousness, in 1879 Wundt established an institute for psychological research at the University of Leipzig. There, in a new laboratory, Wundt and his students began to conduct studies on what they supposed to be the "elements" of consciousness: sensation and perception, memory, attention, emotion, cognition, learning, and language. All our mental activity, they asserted, was combinations of such basic processes. In their experiments, they presented trained volunteers with a variety of simple stimuli and asked them to respond with the press of a lever or a description of their sensations—a technique called **introspection.**

■ **Structuralism** A historical school of psychology devoted to uncovering the basic structures that make up mind and thought. Structuralists sought the "elements" of conscious experience.

■ **Introspection** The process of reporting on one's own conscious mental experiences.

From the outset, structuralism was a magnet for critics, who attacked and ridiculed Wundt from all sides. In particular, many objected to his introspective method as being too subjective. After all, they said, how can we judge the accuracy of people's description of their thoughts and feelings?

But, Wundt has had the last laugh—even though structuralism no longer exists as a recognized "school" of psychology. Psychologists still rely on his introspective method for obtaining dream reports and evidence of perceptual changes, such as those you will experience in the Necker cube demonstration in the upcoming "Psychology in Your Life" section. And, for one more reason, Wundt, if he were alive today, would still be laughing: The topics that he and his students first identified and explored can be found as chapter headings in every introductory psychology text, including this one.

● In 1879, Wilhelm Wundt (1832–1920) founded the first formal laboratory devoted to experimental psychology. He's shown here (center) in his laboratory in Leipzig in 1912.

Functionalism: Focus on Function

One of the most vocal of Wundt's critics, the American psychologist William James, argued that structuralism's approach was far too narrow. (He also said that it was boring—which didn't help his already strained relationship with Wundt [Fancher, 1979].) James argued that psychology should include the *function* of consciousness, not just its *structure*. In a famous metaphor, he pictured a "stream of consciousness" as a mental process that had no static structure but was continually flowing, changing, and interacting with the environment. Appropriately, James's brand of psychology became known as **functionalism.**

James found Charles Darwin's ideas much more interesting than Wundt's. In particular, he liked Darwin's emphasis on organisms *adapting* to their environments. James therefore proposed that psychology should explain how people adapt—or fail to adapt—to the everyday world outside the laboratory. Recurring bouts of depression probably added to his concern with problems of everyday living (Ross, 1991).

Where did this approach lead the functionalists? Much of their work had a practical bent: They were the first *applied* psychologists. James wrote extensively on the development of learned "habits," emotions, the psychology of religion, and teaching. Appropriately, one of his followers, John Dewey, founded the "progressive education" movement, which emphasized learning by *doing*, rather than by merely listening to lectures and memorizing facts.

Gestalt Psychology: Focus on the Whole instead of the Parts

Another challenge to Wundt's structuralism came from a rebellious group in his native Germany. In some respects, their approach, known as **Gestalt psychology,** was exactly the opposite of the structuralism: The Gestalt psychologists were interested in how we construct "perceptual wholes" (or *Gestalts*, in German), such as our perception of a face, rather than just a conglomeration of lines, colors, and textures. (The structuralists, you will remember, focused on the parts, or elements of consciousness, not on the whole.) But, for Gestalt psychology, understanding perception was merely the means to the even more

■ **Functionalism** A historical school of psychology that believed mental processes could best be understood in terms of their adaptive purpose and function.
■ **Gestalt psychology** A historical school of psychology that sought to understand how the brain works by studying perception and perceptual learning. Gestalt psychologists believed that percepts consist of meaningful wholes (in German, *Gestalts*).

important end of understanding how the brain works. Like both the structuralists and functionalists, psychologists of the Gestalt "school" (or philosophical approach) relied on introspection.

Prominent Gestalt psychologists include Max Wertheimer, who studied visual illusions and ambiguous figures, such as the Necker cube, which you will see in a moment (page 000). Another psychologist, Wolfgang Köhler, extended the reach of Gestalt psychology to *insight learning,* an overlooked form of learning marked by sudden "Aha!" experiences. We will see much more of the Gestaltists in our study of perception (Chapter 5).

Behaviorism: Eliminate the Mind and Focus on Behavior

A particularly feisty group, known as the *behaviorists,* disagreed with nearly everyone. Most notably, they proposed the novel idea that consciousness should not be a part of psychology at all! John B. Watson, the leader of the behavioral movement, argued that a true and objective science of psychology should deal solely with observable events: *stimuli* from the environment and the organism's *responses.* **Behaviorism,** said Watson, should be the science of *behavior*—not the mind.

In general, behaviorism rejected any psychology of subjective mental processes. But, in particular, behaviorists objected to *introspection,* the practice of asking people to report on their mental experiences—a technique that the structuralists, functionalists, and Gestalt psychologists all used. Watson and his behaviorist followers cared nothing about what people were *thinking.* Instead, they wanted to know how people would *act* (for example, whether a child would respond with fear to a rabbit which, on an earlier presentation, had been accompanied by a sudden loud noise).

We will encounter behaviorism again in the next section of the chapter because it is one of the ancestral lines of psychology that continues to live on in the present day.

Psychoanalysis: Focus on the Unconscious Mind

Yet another objection to Wundt's approach to psychology came from medicine—specifically from the Viennese physician Sigmund Freud and his disciples, who were pioneering the *psychoanalytic method* of treating mental disor-

CONNECTION: CHAPTER 6

John Watson and his colleague Rosalie Rayner performed a notorious study in which they taught a young boy, Albert, to fear furry objects.

■ **Behaviorism** A historical school (as well as a modern perspective) that has sought to make psychology an objective science that focused only on behavior—to the exclusion of mental processes.

● Sigmund Freud (1856–1939), shown here in the office of his Vienna home, developed the psychodynamic approach to behavior.

ders. Their conceptual approach, called **psychoanalysis,** asserted that mental disorders arise from conflicts in the *un*conscious mind. Accordingly, they maintained that the definition of psychology should be expanded to include the unconscious.

Because psychoanalytic theory remains a force in modern psychology, we will talk more about Freud and his ideas later in the chapter. But, for now, you should know that psychoanalysis and behaviorism outlasted structuralism, functionalism, and Gestalt psychology. Today, few would call themselves structuralists, functionalists, or Gestaltists. Yet—and this is the important point—the legacies of these early approaches, along with those of behaviorism and psychoanalytic theory, can be found woven through the fabric of modern psychology. We will return for a big-picture overview of modern psychology, a field still marked by multiple viewpoints, right after we show you how a famous image makes two profound points.

■ **Psychoanalysis**   An approach to psychology based on Sigmund Freud's assertions, which emphasize unconscious processes. The term is used to refer broadly both to Freud's psychoanalytic theory and to his psychoanalytic treatment method.

PSYCHOLOGY IN YOUR LIFE: AN INTROSPECTIVE LOOK AT THE NECKER CUBE

The cube in Figure 1.2A will trick your eye—or, more accurately, it will trick your brain. If you look at it for a few moments, it will suddenly seem to change perspectives. For a time you may see it as if from the upper right (Figure 1.2B), and then it will abruptly shift and appear as though you were seeing it from the lower left (Figure 1.2C).

It may take a few moments to see the shift. But, once you see it change, you won't be able to prevent it from alternating back and forth, seemingly at random. Try showing the cube to a few friends and asking them what they see.

We feel compelled to confess that the alternating-cube phenomenon was not discovered by a psychologist. Rather, it was first noticed by Swiss geologist Louis Necker in 1832, while he was looking at cube-shaped crystals under a microscope. Since that time, it has been known in his honor as the Necker cube. For our purposes, Necker's amazing cube illustrates two important points.

First, it illustrates the much-maligned process of *introspection,* pioneered by Wundt and his students. Please note that the only way we can demonstrate that the Necker cube changes perspectives in our minds is by having people look at it and report what they see. And why is this important to psychology? Only the hardest of the hard-core behaviorists would deny that something happens mentally within a person looking at the cube. Moreover, whatever it is involves more than simply seeing lines on a page. In fact, the Necker cube demonstrates that we add *meaning* to our sensations—a process called *perception,* which will be a main focus of a later chapter. *The take away message is that we don't simply sense the world as it "really" is, but we perceive it by adding our own interpretations.*

The second important point is this: The Necker cube can serve as a metaphor for the multiple perspectives in psychology. Just as there is no single right way to see the cube, there is no single perspective in psychology that gives us one right understanding of behavior and mental processes. Put another way, to understand psychology fully, we must alternately shift our view points among multiple perspectives. And what are those perspectives? We will explore seven of the most important ones in the next section.

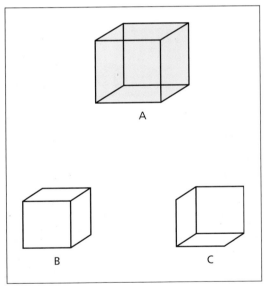

● **FIGURE 1.2**   The Necker Cube Perspective

1. **RECALL:** The ancient Greeks' approach to psychology was not scientific because they
   a. failed to check their opinions against controlled observations.
   b. were more interested in art and music than in truth.
   c. believed that all truth was revealed in sacred texts given by their gods.
   d. lived in an age before precise measuring instruments had been developed.

2. **RECALL:** René Descartes made a science of psychology possible when he suggested that
   a. science should be based entirely on common sense rather than on religion.
   b. sensations and perceptions are the result of activity in the nervous system.
   c. the elements of conscious experience could be arranged into a periodic table.
   d. psychology should be a branch of philosophy.

3. **RECALL:** One of the roots of cognitive psychology sought to identify the "elements of conscious experience." Adherents to this viewpoint were called

   a. structuralists.
   b. functionalists.
   c. Gestalt psychologists.
   d. behaviorists.

4. **APPLICATION:** Which of the following is a method you would use to tell whether a friend had experienced a perceptual shift while viewing the Necker cube?
   a. behaviorism
   b. introspection
   c. structuralism
   d. sensation

5. **UNDERSTANDING THE CORE CONCEPT:** Modern psychology has strong roots in all of the following traditions except
   a. Greek philosophy.
   b. biology.
   c. astrology.
   d. functionalism.
   e. structuralism.

WHAT ARE THE PERSPECTIVES PSYCHOLOGISTS USE TODAY?

During the past century, the picture of psychology was both enriched and complicated by ideas borrowed from many sources. The result is a field that resembles a slightly dysfunctional family, with a few common interests and lots of family squabbles. In our Core Concept we simplify this family portrait by focusing on seven especially important viewpoints:

Seven main perspectives characterize modern psychology: the biological, developmental, cognitive, clinical, behavioral, trait, and sociocultural views.

The champions of each view see behavior and mental processes in a slightly different way—much like seven painters portraying the same scene from different vantage points. You are likely to find experimental psychologists and teachers of psychology holding any of these viewpoints. Among applied psychologists who do counseling, therapy, and personnel selection work, however, the trait and clinical views predominate. As you read the following pages, you should focus on the important ideas that distinguish each view from the others.

The Biological View

The **biological view** emphasizes how your physical makeup and the operation of your brain influence your personality, preferences, behavior patterns, and abilities. More specifically, psychologists taking the biological approach search

■ **Biological view** The psychological perspective that searches for the causes of behavior in the functioning of genes, the brain and nervous system, and the endocrine (hormone) system.

for the causes of behavior in heredity, in the nervous system and the endocrine (hormone) system, and in the effects of environmental insults such as disease (*not* insults of the other kind). As you might imagine, the biological view has strong roots in medicine and biological science. Often, the enterprise of biological psychology, along with biology, neurology, and other disciplines interested in brain processes, is referred to as **neuroscience.**

Neuroscience is a "hot" area at the moment. Thanks to spectacular advances in computers and brain-imaging techniques, neuroscientists have made amazing strides in understanding the brain during the past decade. Among their achievements, they have begun to unravel the mystery of how our eyes and brain convert light waves into vision. They have also learned how damage to certain parts of the brain can destroy specific abilities, such as speech, social skills, or memory. And they have discovered brain wave patterns associated with the hidden world of sleep and dreams.

One important variation on the biological view again draws on the ideas originally proposed by the famous British scholar and naturalist Charles Darwin. **Evolutionary psychology** suggests that many human traits arise from hereditary characteristics established in our remote ancestral past. In this view, our genetic makeup—including our most deeply ingrained behaviors—were shaped by the conditions faced by our ancestors thousands of years ago.

All through the history of the species, environmental forces have pruned the human family tree, favoring the survival and reproduction of those individuals with the most adaptive mental and physical characteristics. Charles Darwin called this *natural selection.* Through this process, the physical characteristics of a species evolve (change) in the direction of characteristics that give the fittest organisms a competitive advantage.

Proponents of evolutionary psychology say that virtually all human behavior—even the most destructive behavior, such as warfare, homicide, and racial discrimination—has grown out of genetic tendencies that once may have helped humans adapt and survive. This approach has also suggested some highly controversial explanations for certain gender differences—why, for instance, men typically have more sexual partners than do women.

● The biological view led to the discovery that certain patterns of brain waves are associated with the hidden world of dreams.

The Developmental View

Change may be the only constant in our lives. In the **developmental view,** psychological change results from an interaction between the *heredity* programmed in our genes and the experiences presented by our *environment.* A big question, however, involves the relative contributions made by our genes and by our surroundings in shaping who we become: Which counts most heavily, heredity or environment, *nature* or *nurture?*

Developmental psychologists also study how we change as we grow older and how we change by developing social skills, learning language, and assimilating the expectations of our culture. Much of their research has focused on *child* development. Increasingly, however, developmental psychologists have begun to look at how development unfolds in teens and adults. In the developmental chapter of this book, we will explore the sweeping patterns of psychological change seen across the lifespan, from before birth to old age.

The Cognitive View

The next of psychology's multiple modern perspectives suggests that our thoughts and actions arise from the way we *interpret* our experiences. From this viewpoint, understanding ourselves requires that we look in our minds, as well as our biology.

■ **Neuroscience** The field devoted to understanding how the brain creates thoughts, feelings, motives, consciousness, memories, and other mental processes.
■ **Evolutionary psychology**
A relatively new specialty in psychology that sees behavior and mental processes in terms of their genetic adaptations for survival and reproduction.
■ **Developmental view**
The psychological perspective emphasizing changes that occur across the lifespan.

● Humanistic psychologists are interested in discovering how self-actualizing individuals, such as Martin Luther King, Jr., are able to unleash their potential for leadership and creativity.

CONNECTION: CHAPTER 11

Freud's *theory of personality* emphasized the unconscious causes of everyday behavior, as well as mental disorder.

■ **Cognitive view** The psychological perspective emphasizing mental processes, such as learning, memory, perception, and thinking, as forms of information processing.

■ **Cognitions** Mental processes, such as thinking, memory, sensation, and perception.

■ **Cognitive neuroscience** A hybrid field emphasizing brain activity as information processing.

■ **Clinical view** The psychological perspective emphasizing mental health and mental illness. Psychodynamic and humanistic psychology are variations on the clinical view.

■ **Psychodynamic psychology** A clinical viewpoint emphasizing the understanding of mental disorders in terms of unconscious needs, desires, memories, and conflicts.

■ **Humanistic psychology** A clinical viewpoint emphasizing human ability, growth, potential, and free will.

In the **cognitive view,** our actions are profoundly influenced by the way we process information streaming in from our environment. Cognitive psychologists study all sorts of mental processes, or **cognitions**—thoughts, expectations, perceptions, and memories, as well as states of consciousness. You might think of them as the heirs to the best of the structuralist, functionalist, and Gestalt traditions.

Modern cognitive psychologists` have also borrowed from linguistics the idea that our most basic language abilities are wired into our brains at birth (Pinker, 2002). From computer science they have borrowed the metaphor of the brain as a biological computer—designed as a processor of information (Gardner, 1985; Gazzaniga, 1998a; Sperry, 1988). And from medicine they have borrowed the technology that now allows visualizing the activity of the brain and connecting it to mental processes. Cognitive psychologists who are especially interested in the connections among mind, brain, and behavior have pioneered a hybrid field called **cognitive neuroscience.**

The Clinical View

A special interest in mental health and mental disorder characterizes the **clinical view.** Most commonly, you will find its adherents practicing counseling or psychotherapy. But the two main groups that comprise this perspective— *psychodynamic psychology* and *humanistic psychology*—have taken this interest in different directions.

Psychodynamic Psychology The term *psychodynamic* comes from the belief that the mind (psyche) is a reservoir of energy (dynamics). Accordingly, **psychodynamic psychology** says that we are motivated primarily by the energy of irrational desires generated in our unconscious minds (Murray et al., 2000). This approach has been especially attractive to practitioners who specialize in psychotherapy. As a result, the psychodynamic perspective has emphasized the treatment of mental disorders over scientific research.

The best-known representative of the psychodynamic approach was Sigmund Freud, who founded *psychoanalysis* (and whom we met earlier in our tour of psychology's historical "schools"). Originally a medical technique devised to treat mental disorders, psychoanalysis portrays the mind as a sort of mental boiler that holds the rising pressure of unconscious sexual and destructive desires, along with memories of traumatic events. Even today, most psychoanalysts are medical doctors with a specialty in psychiatry and advanced training in Freudian methods. (And now you know the difference between a *psychologist* and a *psychoanalyst*.)

Humanistic Psychology The other main variation on the clinical view is called **humanistic psychology.** According to this perspective, your actions are hugely influenced by your self-concept and by your need for personal growth and fulfillment. Far more than the psychoanalysts, humanistic therapists emphasize the positive side of our nature: human ability, growth, and potential.

Led by the likes of Abraham Maslow (1968, 1970, 1971) and Carl Rogers (1951, 1961, 1977), humanistic psychologists have also rejected what they saw as the cold, mechanical approach of scientific psychology. In its place, they have offered a model of human nature emphasizing the free will people have to make choices affecting their lives. They have also pressed psychology to take a greater interest in feelings and the self-concept (Cushman, 1990). As you might have suspected, humanistic psychologists have not produced a great deal of scientific research, although their voluminous writings have had a major impact on the practice of counseling and psychotherapy.

The Behavioral View

A wholly different approach harks back to John Watson and the early days of psychology. *Behaviorism* says we should look for the causes of behavior in our environment rather than in our biology or our minds (Murray et al., 2000). This **behavioral view**, then, calls attention to the ways rewards and punishments shape how we act.

As we saw a few pages ago, in our discussion of psychology's historical roots, behaviorism first emerged as a revolution against the subjective methods used by Wundt, James, and others in the structuralist and functionalist traditions. In brief, the behaviorists totally reject a science of inner experience. Instead, they choose to study the person entirely from the outside, focusing only on what they can observe directly: the effects of people, objects, and events on behavior. And this is still the approach taken by hard-core behaviorists (although we will see in Chapter 6 that some renegades, calling themselves *cognitive behaviorists,* have opened behaviorism's door to mental processes). The behaviorists have made their greatest contribution by giving us a detailed understanding of how the environment affects learning—especially through rewards and punishments.

B. F. Skinner, the most influential American behaviorist, argued that the concept of "mind" has led psychology in circles, chasing something so subjective that it cannot even be proved to exist (Skinner, 1987, 1989, 1990). (Think about it: Can you prove that you have a mind?) As Skinner noted wryly, "The crucial age-old mistake is the belief that . . . what we feel as we behave is the cause of our behaving" (Skinner, 1989, p. 17).

The Trait View

The Greeks, who seem to have had their hands in almost everything, proclaimed that our personalities are ruled by four body *humors* (fluids): blood, phlegm, melancholer, and yellow bile. Depending on which fluid is most abundant, your personality might be sanguine (dominated by blood), slow and deliberate (phlegm), melancholy (melancholer), or angry and aggressive (yellow bile).

We no longer buy into the ancient Greek typology, of course, but their idea of personality traits lives on in modern psychology, especially among psychologists interested in personality and personality testing. *Traits*, to a psychologist, mean long-lasting personality characteristics, such as introversion or extraversion—as contrasted with temporary mood states. This **trait view** is common among psychologists who do mental testing, including clinical, counseling, and I/O psychologists.

Among experimentalists and teachers of psychology, you will find the trait view especially among those who are interested in the field of personality. We will see later in the book that proponents of this trait perspective have identified five major personality dimensions, cleverly named the *Big Five*. Significantly, these dimensions have proved to be valid for classifying people living in virtually any culture around the world.

The Sociocultural View

Who could deny that people exert powerful influences on each other? The **sociocultural view** makes this idea of *social influence* the focus of psychology. Social psychologists have used this perspective to probe the mysteries of liking, loving, prejudice, aggression, obedience, and conformity.

And, speaking of culture (as we were a moment ago), even social psychologists overlooked the effects of the larger social context called **culture** until

CONNECTION: CHAPTER 11

People's personalities differ on five major trait dimensions, cleverly called the *Big Five*.

■ **Behavioral view** A psychological perspective that finds the source of our actions in environmental stimuli, rather than in inner mental processes.
■ **Trait view** A psychological perspective that views behavior and personality as the products of enduring psychological characteristics.
■ **Sociocultural view** A psychological perspective emphasizing the importance of social interaction, social learning, and a cultural perspective.
■ **Culture** A complex blend of language, beliefs, customs, values, and traditions developed by a group of people and shared with others in the same environment.

● Cross-cultural psychologists, such as this researcher in Kenya, furnish important data for checking the validity of psychological knowledge.

recently. As a complex blend of human language, beliefs, customs, values, and traditions, culture exerts profound influences on all of us—as we can readily see by comparing people in, say, the California-Mexican culture of San Diego with the Scandinavian-based culture of Minnesota. Psychology's blindness to culture was due, in part, to the beginnings of scientific psychology in Europe and North America, where most psychologists lived and worked under similar cultural conditions (Lonner & Malpass, 1994; Segall et al., 1998).

Now the perspective has begun to broaden. Although nearly half of the world's half-million psychologists still live and work in the United States, it is encouraging to note that interest in psychology is also growing in countries outside of Europe and North America (Pawlik & d'Ydewalle, 1996; Rosenzweig, 1992, 1999). Even so, most of our psychological knowledge still has a North American/European flavor (Cushman, 1990). Recognizing this bias, cross-cultural psychologists have begun the long task of reexamining the "laws" of psychology across cultural and ethnic boundaries (Fowers & Richardson, 1996; Gergen et al., 1996; Segall et al., 1998; Triandis, 1994, 1995).

To summarize the perspectives we have just covered, please have a look at Table 1.1. There you will find an overview of the main viewpoints that make up the spectrum of modern psychology. A few moments taken to fix these perspectives in your mind will pay big dividends in your understanding of the chapters that follow, where we will refer to them often.

The Changing Face of Psychology

Modern psychology is a field in flux. Over the last several decades, the biological, cognitive, and developmental perspectives have become dominant. And, among psychologists espousing a sociocultural perspective, those who put the emphasis on culture are gaining ascendancy. Meanwhile, the behavioral camp seems to be losing ground, as are the Freudian folk, among those holding the clinical perspective. We also call your attention to an especially noteworthy trend among psychologists who are women and members of minority groups.

Ethnic minorities—especially Asians, African Americans, and Latinos—are becoming psychologists in increasing numbers (Kohout, 2001). Even more striking is the new majority status of women in psychology. In 1906, only 12% of American psychologists listed were women, according to a listing in *Amer-*

TABLE 1.1	Seven Major Perspectives in Modern Psychology		
Perspective	Overview	What Determines Behavior?	Problems and Questions for Study
Biological	We are essentially complex biological systems that respond to both hereditary and environmental influences. This view includes *evolutionary psychology*.	Behavior is determined by brain structure and chemicals and by inborn responses to external cues for survival and reproduction.	How do the nervous system, endocrine system produce behavior and mental processes? Evolutionary psychologists seek to learn how behaviors may be linked to evolutionary changes that conferred a survival or reproductive advantage on our ancestors.
Developmental	People undergo predictable patterns of change throughout their lives.	Behavior determined by the interaction of nature and nurture (heredity and environment).	What are the patterns that characterize developmental change? What are the genetic and environmental influences underlying these patterns?
Cognitive	People are information-processing systems.	Behavior is the result of our mental interpretations of our experience.	What factors influence our mental processes, including sensation, perception, learning, memory, and language?
Clinical	The clinical approach includes two main variants: ▮ *Psychodynamic psychology* emphasizes dark forces in the unconscious. ▮ *Humanistic psychology* emphasizes human growth and potential.	Psychodynamic theory sees behavior arising from unconscious needs, conflicts, repressed memories, and childhood experiences. Humanistic theory focuses on the influence of self-concept, perceptions, interpersonal relationships, and need for personal growth.	Psychodynamic focus: How can our understanding of the unconscious mind help us understand and treat mental disorders? Humanistic focus: What factors encourage high self-esteem and mental health, and how can this knowledge be used in counseling and therapy?
Behavioral	Our behavior is primarily shaped by learning.	In accordance with the laws of behavioral learning, we respond to stimulus cues and to our history of rewards and punishments.	What are the "laws" that associate our responses with stimulus conditions? And how can they be applied to improve the human condition?
Trait	Individual differences result from differences in our underlying patterns of stable characteristics (traits).	Behavior results from each person's unique combination of traits.	How many fundamental traits are there? How can we use trait patterns to predict behavior?
Sociocultural	People are social animals, so human behavior must be interpreted in its social context.	Behavior is heavily influenced by culture, social norms and expectations, and social learning.	Under what conditions is the social and cultural situation predictive of behavior? How are social influences different across cultures?

ican Men of Science (named with no irony intended). By 1921 the proportion had risen above 20%. And now, women receive approximately two-thirds of the new doctorates awarded in psychology each year (Kohout, 2001).

Although psychology has always included a higher proportion of women than any of the other sciences, women have too often found gender-related biases in their psychological career paths (Furumoto & Scarborough, 1986). For example, G. Stanley Hall, one of the pioneers of American psychology, maintained that academic work would ruin a woman's health and cause deterioration of her reproductive organs. Nevertheless, as early as 1905 the American Psychological Association elected its first female president, Mary Whiton Calkins (Furumoto, 1991). Calkins had earlier been denied a doctorate by Harvard University because of her gender even though she had completed all the requirements. In these early days of psychology, as in all fields of science, women were pressured to choose between marriage and career. Amazingly, even those who managed a career were usually limited to teaching at women's colleges, positions with less prestige. Still, they made important contributions to their developing field, as you can see in a sampling presented in Table 1.2.

TABLE 1.2	Early Contributions Made by Women in Psychology	
	Research Area	Institutional Affiliation
Christine Ladd Franklin	logic and color vision	Johns Hopkins University
Kate Gordon	memory and attention	Mt. Holyoke, Carnegie Tech.
Julia Gulliver	dreams and the subconscious self	Rockford University
Alice Hinman	attention and distraction	University of Nebraska
Lillien Martin	psychophysics	Wellesley College
Anna McKeag	pain	Bardwell School
Naomi Norsworthy	abilities of the child	Columbia Teachers College
Millicent Shinn	child development	unaffiliated
Helen Thompson	mental traits	Mt. Holyoke College
Margaret Washburn	perception	Vassar College
Mabel Williams	visual illusions	unaffiliated

Source: The 1906 edition of *American Men of Science.*

 PSYCHOLOGY IN YOUR LIFE: PSYCHOLOGY AS A MAJOR

Becoming a fully fledged psychologist requires substantial training beyond the bachelor's degree. The psychology graduate student takes advanced classes in one or more specialized areas and develops skills as a scholar, researcher, and perhaps as a practitioner. Upon completion of the program, the student receives a master's or doctor's degree, typically a PhD (Doctor of Philosophy), an EdD (Doctor of Education), or a PsyD (Doctor of Psychology).

Satisfying careers are available, however, at various levels of education in psychology. In most states, a license to practice psychology requires a graduate degree, usually a doctorate, and a supervised internship. Most college and university teaching or research jobs in psychology also require a doctorate.

A master's degree, typically requiring two years of study beyond the bachelor's level, may qualify you for employment as a psychology instructor at the high school level or as an applied psychologist in certain specialties, such as counseling. Master's-level psychologists are common in human service agencies, as well as in private practice (although many states do not allow them to advertise themselves as "psychologists"). In addition, many practitioners with master's degrees in the related field of social work offer therapy for emotional problems.

Holders of associate degrees and bachelor's degrees in psychology or related human services fields may find jobs as psychological aides and technicians in agencies, hospitals, nursing homes, and rehabilitation centers. If this is your goal, however, you should know that salaries at this level are relatively low (Kohout, 2000). A bachelor's degree in psychology, coupled with training in business or education, can also lead to interesting careers in personnel management or education.

If you would like further information about job prospects and salary levels for psychologists, the U.S. Department of Labor's *Occupational Outlook Handbook* is a good place to look. Your college's career or counseling center probably has a copy.

1. **APPLICATION:** Which of the following approaches to psychology would say that the differences between the behavior of males and females are the result of different survival and reproduction issues faced by the two sexes?
   a. psychoanalytic theory
   b. evolutionary psychology
   c. the trait view
   d. the sociocultural perspective

2. **RECALL:** Mental processes such as perception, thinking, and remembering are sometimes called
   a. cognition.
   b. affective events.
   c. neural nets.
   d. dependent variables.

3. **APPLICATION:** If you were a teacher trying to understand how students learn, which of the following viewpoints would be most helpful?

   a. the cognitive view
   b. psychoanalytic theory
   c. evolutionary psychology
   d. the trait view

4. **UNDERSTANDING THE CORE CONCEPT:** Which of the following sets of factors is *all* associated with the perspective indicated?
   a. memory, personality, environment: the behavioral perspective
   b. changes through the lifespan, changes as the result of mental disorders, changes a result of social pressure: the developmental perspective
   c. mental health, mental disorder, mental imagery: the trait perspective
   d. neuroscience, evolutionary psychology, genetics: the biological perspective

ANSWERS: 1.b 2.a 3.a 4.d

HOW DO PSYCHOLOGISTS DEVELOP NEW KNOWLEDGE?

As early as 1880, psychologists were challenging the claims of spiritualists and psychics (Coon, 1992). But even today, psychology continues to dispute the unfounded claims of *pseudoscience,* which seem to blossom faster than they can be nipped in the bud. Modern sources of questionable psychology include practitioners of astrology, palmistry, graphology, biorhythm analysis, and any number of psychics, seers, and prophets who claim to have special insights into people's personalities and to be able to predict their futures.

So, what makes psychology different from the pseudoscientific approaches to understanding people? Answer: None of the pseudosciences has survived trial by the *scientific method,* which is a way of rigorously testing ideas against objective observations. Instead, pseudoscience is based on mere speculation and anecdote—and on human gullibility.

You might think this a snobbish view for psychologists to take. Why can't we make room for many different approaches to the understanding of people? In fact, we do. Psychologists have no problem with sociology, anthropology, and psychiatry, for example, as partners in the enterprise of understanding people. Psychologists reject only those approaches that claim to have "evidence" but offer only anecdotes and testimonials.

So, what makes psychology a real science? Again, it's the *method.* As our Core Concept for this section says:

■ **Scientific method** A five-step process for empirical investigation of a hypothesis under conditions designed to control biases and subjective judgments.
■ **Empirical investigation** An approach to research that relies on sensory experience and observation as research data.

Psychologists, like researchers in all other sciences, use the scientific method to test their ideas empirically.

What is this marvelous method? Simply put, the **scientific method** is a process for putting ideas to an objective pass–fail test. At the heart of this testing procedure is **empirical investigation,** the collecting of objective information

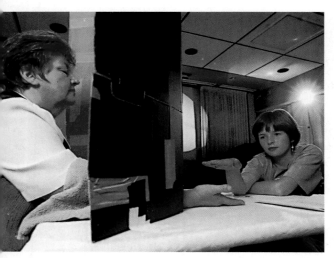

● Emily Rosa's experiment

firsthand by making careful measurements based on direct experience. Literally, *empirical* means "experience based"— as contrasted with speculation based solely on faith, hope, authority, or common sense. To investigate a question empirically is to collect evidence yourself, rather than relying solely on a logical argument or appealing to the opinion of "experts." Ultimately, a main goal of psychological science is to develop explanations for behavior and mental processes—explanations based on solid empirical studies. We call these explanations *theories.*

In brief, a **theory** is a testable explanation for a set of facts or observations (Kerlinger, 1985; Kukla, 1989). Please note that this definition may be quite different from the way you customarily use the term. In everyday language, "theory" can mean "wild speculation" or a mere "hunch"—an idea that has no evidence to support it. "It's only a theory," people may say. But *theory* means something quite different to a scientist. The essence of a scientific theory is its power to explain the facts and its ability to be tested objectively. Some theories have a great deal of evidence to support them, while others are highly speculative. Examples of well-supported theories include Einstein's theory of relativity, the germ theory of disease, Darwin's theory of natural selection, and, in psychology, social learning theory (which we will discuss in Chapter 6).

To illustrate the scientific method in action, we would remind you how Dr. Pfungst put Clever Hans to the test. But to take a more recent example, let's look at a simple and elegant psychological experiment published in the *Journal of the American Medical Association* by . . . a fourth grader (Rosa et al., 1998)! Meet Emily Rosa of Loveland, Colorado. Emily's school science project, it turned out, challenged a widely held belief in the power of *therapeutic touch* (TT).

In the early 1990s, TT was touted as a medical therapy, and Emily's mother, a nurse, had explained to her how TT practitioners attempted to promote healing by moving their hands over the patient's body without directly touching it. In doing so, they believed that they were detecting and manipulating an energy field radiating from the body. These practitioners claimed they could use TT to treat a wide range of medical and psychological problems—from colic to cancer and arthritis to depression (Gorman, 1999). So effective was it believed to be that the technique was being taught in more than 100 colleges and universities in 75 countries and used by nurses in at least 80 U.S. hospitals.

But did it really work, or was it just another example of flawed common sense? Emily Rosa suspected that TT practitioners were really detecting their own beliefs and expectations, rather than a "human energy field." So, she put their claims to a simple experimental test, the details of which we will use to illustrate the scientific method.

The Five Steps of the Scientific Method

Testing any scientific assertion requires five steps. (See Figure 1.3.) These steps are essentially the same whether the study involves psychology, biology, chemistry, astronomy, or any other scientific discipline. Thus, it is the *method* that makes these fields scientific, not their subject matter. Ideally, a researcher (such as Emily Rosa) who follows the scientific method will proceed as follows.

Developing a Hypothesis   The first step calls for coming up with a testable idea, or prediction. Scientists call this prediction a **hypothesis.** The term literally means "little theory" because it often represents only one piece of a larger

■ **Theory**   A testable explanation for a set of facts or observations. In science, a theory is *not* just speculation or a guess.

■ **Hypothesis**   A statement predicting the outcome of a scientific study; a statement describing the relationship among variables in a study.

1. Developing a hypothesis

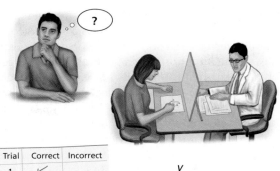

2. Performing a controlled test

3. Gathering objective data

Trial	Correct	Incorrect
1	✔	
2		✔
3	✔	✔
4		

4. Analyzing the results

Report #1   2   3

5. Publishing, criticizing, and
   replicating the results

theoretical puzzle. For example, a hypothesis stating that introverted people are attracted to extraverted people might be part of a larger, more complex theory tying together all the factors that affect romantic attraction. Sometimes, however, a hypothesis can be just an interesting idea that piques the scientist's curiosity—as was the case in Emily Rosa's experiment. Her hypothesis came simply from questioning the value of a treatment (therapeutic touch) that everyone "knew" to be effective.

Like any good scientist, Emily stated her hypothesis in such a way that it could be tested and *falsified* (shown to be either correct or incorrect). To make her suspicion testable, Rosa had to follow an ironclad requirement of all scientific research: She had to give **operational definitions** for all the terms in her hypothesis. That is, she had to specify the exact procedures (operations) she would use in setting up the experimental conditions and measuring the results.

Emily wondered: Could TT practitioners accurately sense the presence of her hand when it was placed above one of their hands but out of sight? She hypothesized that they could not. In our earlier example, the study of Clever Hans, Dr. Pfungst also operationalized his hypothesis by stating that the horse could not give the right number of taps with its hoof when it couldn't see its owner or when the owner couldn't see the written questions. Here again, the hypothesis was stated *operationally*—in terms of the procedures that would be used to test it.

So far, so good. But, of course, a scientific study must not stop with a hypothesis. The great failing of pseudosciences like astrology is that they never take the other steps necessary to verify or reject their assertions. Among scientists, however, a hypothesis will be taken seriously only after it has been subjected to rigorous testing.

Performing a Controlled Test   A hypothesis must undergo an "ordeal of proof"—a test that it will either pass or fail. Here's how Emily Rosa conducted her test: She invited each of 21 TT practitioners (varying in experience from 1 to 27 years) to determine which of their two hands (thrust, palms up, through

■ **Operational definitions**   Specific descriptions of concepts involving the conditions of a scientific study. Operational definitions are stated in terms of how the concepts are to be measured or what operations are being employed to produce them.

holes in a screen) was closest to one of her own hands (held palm down, a few inches from either of the practitioner's hands).

In order to control the conditions of her experiment, Rosa varied only one part of the situation on each trial: whether her hand was above the subject's left or right hand. We call this variable condition the **independent variable.** Think of the independent variable as a condition that the experimenter changes *independently* of all the other carefully controlled experimental conditions. The independent variable always involves a systematic variation on the conditions that the experimenter is evaluating in a study. In Pfungst's study of Clever Hans, the independent variable involved systematically changing the conditions so that (a) Hans could not see his owner or (b) the owner could not see the questions being asked.

In Rosa's experiment on therapeutic touch, control over the experimental conditions would have been laughable if she had simply held her hand alternately above the volunteers' left and right hands or followed some other predictable pattern. That is, had the volunteers been able to guess which response was correct, the results of the experiment would have meant nothing. The solution was *random presentation* of the stimulus, which meant that chance alone determined the order in which the stimulus was presented. **Random presentation** is one tool in the experimenter's bag of tricks for controlling expectations that can skew the results of a study. In Rosa's experiment, randomization was achieved by a coin flip, which determined whether she presented her hand above the practitioner's left or right hand. And in Pfungst's study, randomization meant that there was no predictable pattern (such as 2, 4, 6, 8 . . .) in the correct answers to the problems presented to Hans and his trainer.

Gathering Objective Data   In the third step of the scientific method, the scientist collects objective **data**: information gathered by direct observation. Such data depend only on the manipulations of the experimental conditions (the independent variable). The data must *not* depend on the experimenter's hopes, expectations, or personal impressions. In Emily Rosa's experiment, the data consisted of the number of correct and incorrect responses during the test—whether the practitioners responded correctly to the placement of her hand. Such responses are referred to as the **dependent variable.** The term comes from the assumption that the responses of participants in an experiment *depend* directly on the conditions to which they have been exposed. As a result, the data will depend on how the independent variable has been manipulated. (You might think of the independent variable as the *stimuli* you are studying and the dependent variable as the *responses* made by the participants in your experiment.)

In designing an experiment, the dependent variable must also be given an operational definition. That is, the researcher must specify the procedures (operations) that were used in measuring the responses being observed. This is exactly what Emily Rosa did when she described how she required her participants to respond with guesses of "left" or "right." The dependent variable in Pfungst's study consisted of the horse's hoof-tapping response to each question presented.

Analyzing the Results and Accepting or Rejecting the Hypothesis   In the fourth step of the scientific method, the researcher examines the results (the data) to see whether the hypothesis survived the test. Based on that analysis, the hypothesis is accepted or rejected. This usually requires some special mathematical tools, particularly if the data require a close call. Statistical analysis can tell the researcher whether the observed results rise to the level of *significance*—that is, whether the results are likely due to the independent variable or merely due to chance.

■ **Independent variable** A stimulus condition so named because the experimenter changes it independently of all the other carefully controlled experimental conditions.
■ **Random presentation** A process by which chance alone determines the order in which the stimulus is presented.
■ **Data** Pieces of information, especially information gathered by a researcher to be used in testing a hypothesis. (Singular: *datum.*)
■ **Dependent variable** The measured outcome of a study; the responses of the subjects in a study.

from "The Cartoon Guide to Statistics" by Larry Gonick & Wollcott Smith

A detailed explanation of statistics is beyond the scope of this book. In fact, it's a subject for a whole course in itself. But to give you a glimpse of this world, your authors have provided a brief introduction to statistics in the Appendix near the end of the book. There you will find a summary of key points and examples of how psychological concepts are *quantified* (measured and expressed as numbers) and how those quantities can provide meaning and understanding.

In Rosa's experiment, the statistical analysis was remarkably simple. The chances of getting a correct answer merely by guessing were 50%. That is, half the time the TT practitioners could be expected to give the right answer, even if they had no ability to sense the "human energy field." So, Rosa set this standard: Her subjects would have to perform significantly above the chance level to support the claim that they can detect a "human energy field." They did not, so she concluded that practitioners of therapeutic touch were not sensing human energy fields.

Much the same analysis applied to Pfungst's study, where the chance level of correct responses would be near zero, and any consistent level of correct responses would have supported the hypothesis that Clever Hans could read and calculate. That hypothesis, however, was rejected, because Hans' responses were incorrect when cues from his owner were controlled.

Publishing, Criticizing, and Replicating the Results   In the fifth step of the scientific method, researchers must find out whether their work can withstand the scrutiny and criticism of the scientific community. To do so, they might communicate their results to colleagues by publishing them in a professional journal, presenting a paper at a professional meeting, or writing a book. (You may recall that Emily Rosa published her results in *The Journal of the American Medical Association*.) Then they wait for the critics to respond.

If colleagues find the study interesting and important—and especially if it challenges a widely held theory—they may look for flaws in the research design: Did the experimenter choose the participants properly? Were the statistical analyses done correctly? Could other factors account for the results?

Some critics complained that Rosa's experiment was not an accurate representation of the conditions under which therapeutic touch is done: They claimed that TT depends on the transfer of emotional energy during a medical crisis, and because Emily was not sick she didn't have disturbances in her energy field that could be detected by TT practitioners.

Critics could have checked Rosa's work by *replicating* it. To **replicate** her experiment they would redo it, perhaps under slightly different control conditions, to see whether they would get the same results. But, as far as we know, Rosa's experiment was never replicated. (Nor was Pfungst's.) At this point then, we can say that Rosa's experimental results have withstood the scientific test. We should also note that Emily's research earned her a check for $1000 from the Skeptics Society. She also received a plaque from the *Guinness Book of Records* for being the youngest researcher to have a paper published in a major medical journal.

Criticism and replication of research is a part of a thorough, and sometimes intimidating, screening process that goes on behind the scientific scenes to filter out poorly conceived and executed research. As a result, fewer than 2% of the papers submitted to psychological journals get into print without major revisions. In fact, the majority never see print at all (Eichorn & VandenBos, 1985). Journal editors and book publishers (including the publishers of this book) routinely seek the opinion of several expert reviewers for each submission before agreeing to publish it. Different reviewers often focus their criticism on different facets of the study (Fiske & Fogg, 1990). As a result, the author usually receives helpful, if sometimes painful, suggestions for revision. Only when a hypothesis has survived all these tests will editors put it in print and scholars tentatively accept it as scientific "truth." We should emphasize, however, that scientific findings are always tentative, forever in jeopardy from a new study that might require a new interpretation and relegate previous work to the scientific scrap heap. Granted, it is an imperfect system, but it is the best method ever developed for testing ideas about the natural world.

Five Types of Psychological Research

We're not out of the scientific woods yet—even though we have covered the basic steps of science's experimental method. We still need to discuss the various forms that psychological research may take. In addition to *experiments*, like Emily Rosa's research, these include *correlational studies, surveys, naturalistic observations,* and *case studies*. Each, we will see, has its advantages and limitations.

In brief, an experiment is the tool scientists use to investigate *cause and effect* under tightly controlled conditions—as when a psychologist wants to find out whether a certain type of therapy can alleviate depression. In contrast, correlational studies are used to study *relationships* found in events that have occurred naturally in the real world, where the researcher has much less control over the research conditions. A correlational study would be used to investigate a possible relationship between parenting styles and delinquency. Unlike a true experiment, a correlational study can never prove a cause-and-effect relationship. Finally, we will look at three kinds of *descriptive* research: case studies, naturalistic observations, and surveys. In these, the goal is simply to describe the characteristics of individuals or groups. Political pollsters, for example, do descriptive research.

Experiments   Emily Rosa's study is an example of an **experiment,** a form of research in which the researcher controls all the conditions and directly manipulates the independent variable. Not only did Rosa and her colleagues design

■ **Replicate**   In research this refers to doing a study over to see whether the same results are obtained. As a control for bias, replication is often done by someone other than the researcher who performed the original study.

■ **Experiment**   A kind of research in which the researcher controls all the conditions and directly manipulates the conditions, including the independent variable.

the apparatus used in their study, but they established the conditions under which subjects were tested. Virtually everything about the experiment was under their control.

Every experiment, including Rosa's, is designed to answer this question: Does the manipulation of the independent variable *cause* the predicted change in the dependent variable? To determine this, the experimenter designs two or more ways of treating the participants whose responses are being studied. Thus, in the therapeutic touch study, Rosa created two possible treatment conditions by varying which of the participants' hands she placed her own hand near. To give another example, in an experiment designed to study a new drug, the two treatments might involve two different groups of volunteers. One would get the experimental drug, while others receive a **placebo** (*pla-SEE-bo*), a "drug" with no medical value, such as a sugar pill).

© The New Yorker Collection 1993. Ronald Reilly from Cartoonbank.com. All Rights Reserved

When two groups are used, those exposed to the special treatment (e.g., the new drug) are said to be in the *experimental condition* of the study. These individuals make up the **experimental group.** Meanwhile, those in the other group, the **control group,** are placed in the *control condition,* where they may receive a placebo or no treatment at all. Thus, the control group is used as a standard against which to compare the subjects in the experimental condition. (See Figure 1.4.)

When an experimenter uses two or more groups of volunteer subjects, it is important to avoid any systematic bias in the way individuals are assigned to the groups. In a drug study, for example, it wouldn't do for one group to have sicker people than the other or for all the women to be assigned to the experimental group and all the men placed in the control group. A good solution involves **random assignment,** where people are assigned to each group by chance alone. One way to do this would be to list volunteers alphabetically and assign alternating names to the experimental and control groups. In this way, chance minimizes any potential differences between the two groups.

CONNECTION: CHAPTER 5

For many people who are in pain, the brain responds to *placebos* in much the same way that it responds to pain-relieving drugs.

■ **Placebo** Substances that appear to be drugs but are not. Placebos are often referred to as "sugar pills" because they might contain only sugar, rather than a real drug. Placebos cause a *placebo effect* in many people who take them.
■ **Experimental group** Participants in an experiment who are exposed to the treatment of interest.
■ **Control group** Participants who are used as a comparison for the experimental group. The control group is not given the special treatment of interest.
■ **Random assignment** A process used to assign individuals to various experimental conditions by chance alone.

● **FIGURE 1.4** Experimental Groups and Control Groups in a Drug Study.
Well-designed experiments often compare the responses of an experimental group and a control group, as in this design for evaluating a new drug.

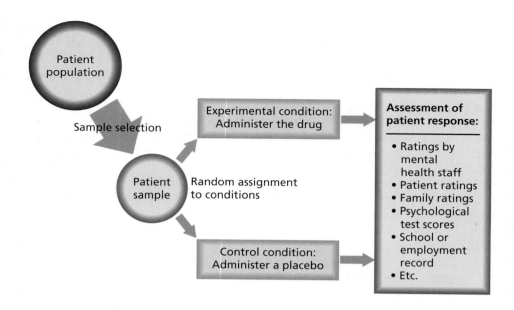

Correlational Studies Sometimes, for practical or ethical reasons, the researcher cannot control the situation well enough for a careful experiment. Here's an example: Suppose that you wanted to test the hypothesis that children who ingest lead-based paint (common in older homes, especially in low-income urban housing) have a higher incidence of learning disabilities. You couldn't do an experiment to verify this hypothesis. Why? In an experiment you would manipulate the independent variable by deliberately giving toxic lead-based paint to an experimental group of children. Obviously, this would be hazardous and unethical.

Fortunately, we can find a way around the problem—but at the expense of some control over the research conditions. The solution is a **correlational study.** In correlational research you, in effect, look for an "experiment" that has already occurred by chance, not by design, in the world outside the controlled conditions of the laboratory. So, in a correlational study on the effects of ingesting lead-based paint, you might look for a group of children who had already been exposed to leaded paint and compare them to another group who had not been exposed. As a further control, you should try to match the groups so that they are comparable in every conceivable respect (such as age, family income, and gender), except for their exposure to leaded paint.

The drawback to a correlational study is that you can never be sure that the groups are really similar in every way. Because you can't randomly assign subjects or manipulate the independent variable, you cannot say with certainty that the condition of interest was the *cause* of the effects you observed. So, even if you observe more learning disabilities among children who were exposed to lead-based paint, you cannot conclude that exposure to the paint *caused* the disabilities. The most you can say is that lead-based paint is *correlated* or associated with learning disabilities. As scientists often put it: *Correlation does not necessarily mean causation.*

Scientists usually express the degree of correlation as a number. So, the next step requires calculating a statistic known as the *correlation coefficient,* often symbolized in formulas by the letter *r.* The correlation coefficient summarizes the relationship between the two variables. It can range from a negative number (as low as –1.0) to a positive number (as high as +1.0).

We won't go into the details of calculating the correlation coefficient here. (Any introductory statistics book will tell you how to do it.) The important

■ **Correlational study** A form of research in which the relationship between variables is studied, but without the experimental manipulation of an independent variable. Correlational studies cannot determine cause-and-effect relationships.

idea is to develop a feeling for what *positive correlation, negative correlation,* and *zero correlation* mean. If the variables have no relationship at all, their correlation is 0. You would expect a zero correlation between shoe size and GPA, for example. If, however, the two variables show a relationship in which they vary in the same direction (as one variable's scores increase, so do the other's) then we say they have a **positive correlation.** An example of a positive correlation is the moderate relationship between SAT scores and college grades (which is approximately +0.4).

In contrast, when one variable decreases as the other increases, they have a **negative correlation,** and their correlation coefficient would have a negative sign. You would probably find a negative correlation between the amount of alcohol consumed by college students and their grade-point averages. In our earlier example, we predicted that lead levels in the blood would be negatively correlated with IQ scores.

It is important to understand that *a correlation can show a strong relationship even when it is negative.* (Note: Professors often ask test questions about this.) Let us suppose that a measure of anxiety (such as a checklist of anxiety-related symptoms) shows a negative correlation of –0.7 between anxiety and time spent studying. In other words, more study is associated with less anxiety. Even though this is a negative correlation, it shows a *stronger* relationship than, for example, the positive correlation between SAT scores and grades (+0.4).

● Jane Goodall used the method of naturalistic observation to study chimpanzee behavior.

Surveys   If you want to know about people's attitudes, preferences, or other characteristics, you don't need to do an experiment or a correlational study. You can simply ask them for the information, using a **survey.** This is the method used by political pollsters and marketing consultants, as well as by many researchers in psychology and sociology. Surveys typically ask people for their responses to a prepared set of questions. The survey method offers the advantage of generating large numbers of respondents with relative ease. But the value of a survey is only as good as the clarity of its questions and the accuracy and honesty of the respondents' reports (Schwarz, 1999).

Naturalistic Observations   When the researchers want to know how individuals act in their natural surroundings (as opposed to the artificial conditions of a laboratory), they may use the method of **naturalistic observation.** Naturalistic observation might be a good choice for studying child-rearing practices, people's shopping habits, or public courting behaviors. The method is also used extensively to study animal behavior in the wild. It was, in fact, the approach used by Jane Goodall in her classic studies of chimpanzee culture. Thus, the setting for a naturalistic observation could be as varied as a shopping mall, a classroom, a home, or a remote wilderness. But, because the researcher merely observes, rather than controlling the conditions or manipulating the independent variable, naturalistic observations are made under far less controlled conditions than are experiments.

Case Studies   Yet another kind of research, the **case study,** focuses on only a few individuals—sometimes just one. The method is usually reserved for the in-depth study of unusual people with rare problems or unusual talents. For example, in his book *Creating Minds,* Howard Gardner (1993) used the case study method to explore the thought processes of seven highly creative individuals, including Einstein, Picasso, and Freud. Psychoanalysts have also used this approach, calling it the *clinical method,* to develop theories about mental

■ **Positive correlation**   A correlation coefficient indicating that the variables change simultaneously in the same direction: as one grows larger or smaller, the other grows or shrinks in a parallel way.
■ **Negative correlation**   A correlation coefficient indicating that the variables change simultaneously in opposite directions: as one becomes larger, the other gets smaller.
■ **Survey**   A technique used in descriptive research, typically involving seeking people's responses to a prepared set of verbal items.
■ **Naturalistic observation**   A form of descriptive research involving behavioral assessment of people or animals in their home surroundings.
■ **Case study**   Research involving a single individual (or, at most, a few individuals).

disorder based on material gathered from their patients. The disadvantages of the case study method, of course, lie in its subjectivity and its small sample size. These limitations restrict the researcher's ability to draw conclusions that can be applied with confidence to other individuals. Nevertheless, the case study can sometimes give us valuable insights that could be obtained in no other way.

Sources of Bias in Research (or Anywhere Else)

Think of an issue on which you have strong feelings and opinions—perhaps abortion, euthanasia, or capital punishment. On such topics, our emotions make it difficult to reason objectively. Likewise, emotionally loaded topics can bring out biases that affect the ways an experimenter designs a study, collects the data, or interprets the results. Fortunately, the scientific method, with its public procedures and openness to replication, provides a powerful means to check on an experimenter's bias. Still, scientists would rather save themselves embarrassment by identifying and controlling their biases before they hit print. Here are some forms of bias to which they must be alert.

Personal bias involves an individual's beliefs, preferences, assumptions, or prejudices. Often these are not obvious to the individual holding such biases. For example, in his book *Even the Rat Was White*, psychologist Robert Guthrie (1998) points out the personal bias in the long tradition of using mainly white subjects in psychological research. Whatever form it takes, personal bias can cause scientists to notice only the evidence confirming their hypotheses and to ignore contrary data.

Expectancy bias also affects observations when observers expect—and look for—certain outcomes. (Expectancy bias is closely related to *confirmation bias*, which we discussed earlier in this chapter.) We can see expectancy bias at work in a classic study in which psychology students timed groups of rats running through a maze (Rosenthal & Jacobson, 1968a). The experimenters told some students that their rats were especially bright; other students heard that their rats were slow learners. (In fact, the experimenters had randomly selected both groups of rats from the same litters.) Amazingly, the students' data showed that rats believed to be bright outperformed their supposedly duller littermates.

These sources of bias can not only lead to erroneous conclusions, but they can also be expensive. Imagine that you are a psychologist working for a pharmaceutical company that wants you to design a test for a new drug. With millions of dollars riding on the outcome, you will want to do it right. But what about the doctors who are going to be prescribing the drug to patients in your study? Surely those doctors will have high hopes for the drug, as will their patients. And so the stage is set for bias to creep into your study along with people's expectations.

We have seen that a common strategy for controlling expectancy bias in a drug study is to keep participants in the research experimentally "blind," or uninformed, about whether they are getting the real drug or a placebo. An even better strategy is to keep *both* the participants and the experimenter clueless about which group receives what treatment. In a drug study, this would mean that neither the researchers nor the participants would know (until the end of the study) which individuals were getting the new drug and which were getting the placebo. Such a research strategy is called a **double-blind study.** This strategy assures that the experimenters will not inadvertently treat the experimental group differently from the control group, so that neither group will get any clue about the expected response to the pills they are taking.

Aside from these forms of observer bias, researchers must also try to identify other possible influences on the behavior being studied—influences other

■ **Personal bias** The researcher allowing personal beliefs to affect the outcome of a study.

■ **Expectancy bias** The researcher allowing his or her expectations to affect the outcome of a study.

■ **Double-blind study** An experimental procedure in which both researchers and participants are uninformed about the nature of the independent variable being administered.

than the independent variable. Such *confounding variables* are factors that could be confused with the independent variable and thus distort the results. Consider, for example, a study of a stimulant drug (such as Ritalin) used to control hyperactive behavior among schoolchildren. What might be some confounding variables? The drug's effect might differ because of different body weights, eating schedules, and time, method, or setting of administration. Unless arrangements are made to control all such possible confounding variables—that is, to expose all the subjects to identical conditions—the researcher has no way of knowing which factors really produced the results.

CONNECTION: CHAPTERS 3 AND 13

Paradoxically, stimulants seem to calm hyperactive behavior in children with *ADHD.*

Ethical Issues in Psychological Research

A final issue we will consider involves the ethics of research. In psychology, ethical issues surround the possibility that individuals might be hurt or unduly distressed by participating in a poorly conceived psychological study. No researcher would want this to happen, yet the issues are not always clear. Is it ethical, for example, to subject people to severe frustration in an experiment involving a problem that is impossible to solve? Or, in an experiment on aggression, what about deliberately provoking people by insulting them? What degree of unease is too high a price to pay for the knowledge gained from the experiment? These are difficult, but important, questions, and not all psychologists would answer them in exactly the same way.

To provide some guidelines for researchers, the American Psychological Association has published "Ethical Principles of Psychologists and Code of Conduct" (2002), a statement advising researchers of their ethical obligation to shield subjects from potentially harmful procedures. Further, the statement admonishes researchers that information acquired about people during a study must be held confidential and must not be published in such a way that individual rights to privacy are compromised. Nevertheless, gray areas still appear, making ethical problems of research a continuing issue (Ilgen & Bell, 2001; Kimmel, 1991; Knapp & VandeCreek, 2003; Pomerantz, 1994; Rosenthal, 1994).

Deception   The use of *deception* poses an especially knotty problem. Under most circumstances, the "Ethical Principles" states that participation in research should be voluntary and informed. That is, we should advise volunteers of what challenges they will face and give them a real opportunity to drop out of the study. But what if you are interested in the "good Samaritan" problem, the conditions under which people will help a stranger in distress? If you tell people that you have contrived a phony emergency situation and ask them if they are willing to help, you will spoil the very effect that you are trying to study. Consequently, the guidelines do allow for deception under some conditions, provided that no substantial risks are likely to accrue to the participants.

But who, you might ask, is to judge the risks? Most places where research is done now have watchdog committees, called *institutional review boards (IRBs)* that make these judgments by examining all studies proposed to be carried out within an institution, such as a college, university, or clinic. When deception is used, the APA guidelines require that participants be informed of the deception as soon as is possible without compromising the study's research goals. Individuals used in deceptive research must also be *debriefed* after the study to make sure that they suffer no lasting ill effects. Despite these precautions, some psychologists stand opposed to the use of deception in any form of psychological research (Baumrind, 1985; Bower, 1998d).

Animal Studies   Another long-standing ethical issue surrounds the use of laboratory animals, such as rats, pigeons, and monkeys. As far back as the mid-1800s, scientists used animals in their research for a variety of reasons. These included the relative simplicity of animals' nervous systems and the relative ease with which a large number of individuals could be maintained under controlled conditions. Animals have also served as alternatives to human subjects when a procedure was deemed risky or outright harmful. Concerned about the issue as long ago as 1925, the American Psychological Association established a Committee on Precautions in Animal Experimentation, which adopted guidelines for animal research (Dewsbury, 1990). The American Psychological Association's "Ethical Principles of Psychologists" (2002) also directs researchers to provide decent living conditions for animal subjects and to weigh any discomfort caused them against the value of the information sought in the research. A 1985 federal law also imposes legal restrictions on animal research (Novak & Suomi, 1988).

Recent years have seen a renewal of concern, both inside and outside of psychology, about the use of animals as subjects, particularly when the research involves painful or damaging procedures, such as brain surgery, electrode implants, and pain studies. Some people feel that the limitations should be more stringent on studies using humanlike animals, such as chimpanzees. Others believe that limitations or outright bans should apply to all animal research, including studies of simple animals such as sea slugs (which are often used in neurological studies). Many psychologists, however, support animal research under the APA guidelines (Blum, 1994). At present, the issue remains a hot one.

Questions Science Cannot Answer

It is important to understand that science is not the best approach for finding answers to every important question in our lives. Even scientists don't take a scientific approach to everything. The scientific method is merely the best way to find answers to testable questions about the natural world—the world of atoms and animals, of stones and stars, and of behavior and mental processes. On the other hand, science is *not* appropriate for answering questions that cannot be empirically tested—such as questions of ethics, morality, religious beliefs, or preferences. To see what we mean, please look at Table 1.3, which shows some of the questions that science can never answer.

TABLE 1.3	What Questions Can the Scientific Method *Not* Answer?

The scientific method is not appropriate for answering questions that cannot be put to an objective, empirical test. Here are some examples of such issues:

Topic	Question
Ethics	Should scientists do research with animals?
Values	Which culture has the best attitude toward work and leisure?
Morality	Is abortion morally right or wrong?
Preferences	Is rap music better than blues?
Aesthetics	Was Picasso more creative than Van Gogh?
Existential issues	What is the meaning of life?
Religion	Does God exist?
Law	What should be the speed limit on interstate highways?

Although science can help us understand such issues, the answers ultimately must be settled by logic, faith, legislation, consensus, or other means that lie beyond the scope of the scientific method.

PSYCHOLOGY IN YOUR LIFE: GETTING IN DEEPER

Whatever your intended major field of study, you will want to learn more about the professional role your chosen field will expect of you. You can do this in several ways: by attending events sponsored by your major department, by getting to know your professors personally, and by taking out student memberships in professional organizations. You should also develop a habit of scanning the field's main magazines, journals, and newsletters. For those readers who are considering a major in psychology, we suggest that you investigate the following resources.

Professional Organizations in Psychology The largest and oldest professional association for psychologists, the American Psychological Association (APA), has well over 150,000 members and affiliates (American Psychological Association, 2004). The American Psychological Society (APS) was formed just a few years ago to give a stronger voice to academic and research psychologists. Although the APS is a much smaller organization, it has won wide respect; many psychologists belong both to the APA and to the APS.

These groups have student memberships that include nearly all privileges at a fraction of full membership costs. If you are thinking of majoring in psychology, ask your instructor for information about student membership in a professional psychology association. Also consider attending a state, regional, or national convention to get a better view of what psychologists are really like. These conventions also offer an opportunity for students to present their own research. You could do so, too.

Consider, also, joining a student psychology group, if your school has one. If none is available, you may be able to organize a psychology club or a chapter of a national honorary society, such as Psi Beta (at a two-year college) or Psi Chi (at a four-year college or university).

Psychology-Related Journals and Magazines Professional groups sponsor newsletters or journals that help keep their members abreast of new developments in the field. Psychology majors should begin looking over a few of the main ones every month. Some publish general-interest articles, while others contain highly technical reports tailored for those with specialized

● Dr. Phil Zimbardo, one of your authors, served as president of the American Psychological Association in 2002.

advanced training. We suggest taking your first plunge into the psychological literature with one or more of these:

- *Monitor on Psychology*—the monthly news magazine of the APA
- *Current Directions in Psychological Science*—a semimonthly APS journal that provides short reviews on trends and controversies in all areas of psychology
- *American Psychologist*—the flagship journal of the APA
- *Psychological Science*—the premiere journal of the APS

In addition, there are several popular magazines in which you may find psychological articles of interest:

- *Discover*—a science magazine written for the general public
- *Scientific American*—another general-interest science magazine
- *Science News*—a weekly magazine consisting of brief blurbs on breaking news in all areas of science, including psychology
- *The Skeptical Inquirer*—a take-no-prisoners, pseudoscience-bashing magazine published by CSICOP, the Committee for the Scientific Investigation of Claims of the Paranormal

Don't feel that you must keep up on the entire psychological literature. Nobody can. Read what interests you in these publications.

Electronic Resources in Psychology The printed psychological literature is vast and growing quickly. As a result, anyone wanting to find out what is known on a special topic must know how to access the information on the Internet and in an electronic database. There are several general databases available, such as Expanded Academic Index and Ebsco Academic Search Elite. The best electronic resource specifically for psychology is PsychInfo, an online computer database offered by the American Psychological Association. Most such resources require a paid subscription, although they may be available through your campus library.

In addition, a huge amount of free information about psychology is available on the Internet. A good place to start looking would be the American Psychological Association's home page on the World Wide Web at http://www.apa.org or the American Psychological Society's home page at http://www.psychologicalscience.org. Remember that web addresses often change. Remember, also, that anyone can put anything on the Internet, so be skeptical!

CHECK YOUR UNDERSTANDING

1. **RECALL:** A theory is
   a. an unsupported opinion.
   b. a testable explanation for the data.
   c. the opposite of a fact.
   d. a statement that has not yet been supported with facts.

2. **RECALL:** A scientific study should begin with
   a. a controlled test.
   b. a hypothesis.
   c. data collection.
   d. risk/gain assessment.

3. **APPLICATION:** Which of the following could be an operational definition of "fear"?
   a. an intense feeling of terror and dread when thinking about some threatening situation
   b. panic
   c. a desire to avoid something
   d. moving away from a stimulus

4. **ANALYSIS:** The conditions involving the independent variable could also be thought of as

a. stimuli.
b. responses.
c. cognitions.
d. experimenter biases.

5. **RECALL:** Which is the only form of research that can determine cause and effect?
   a. a case study
   b. a correlational study
   c. a naturalistic observation
   d. an experimental study

6. **ANALYSIS:** Random assignment of subjects to different experimental conditions is a method for controlling differences between
   a. the dependent variable and the independent variable.
   b. the experimental group and the control group.
   c. empirical data and subjective data.
   d. heredity and environment.

7. **RECALL:** In which kind of research does the scientist have the most control over variables that might affect the outcome of the study?
   a. a case study
   b. a correlational study
   c. an experimental study
   d. a naturalistic observation

8. **ANALYSIS:** Which one of the following correlations shows the strongest relationship between two variables?
   a. +0.4
   b. +0.38
   c. −0.7
   d. 0.05

9. **ANALYSIS:** Which one of the following is a good method for controlling expectancy bias?
   a. performing a case study
   b. joining a professional organization
   c. consulting the "Ethical Principles of Psychologists and Code of Conduct"
   d. doing a double-blind study

10. **UNDERSTANDING THE CORE CONCEPT:** Religion, art, the humanities, and the pseudosciences don't require controlled research, but the sciences (such as psychology) require that theories be tested against
    a. controlled observations.
    b. expert opinion.
    c. common sense.
    d. intuition and "gut" reactions.

USING PSYCHOLOGY TO LEARN PSYCHOLOGY

Studying with Key Questions and Core Concepts

In this book, your authors have attempted to help you find meaningful patterns that will aid you in making a mental map (sometimes called a *cognitive map*) of every chapter. To do so, we have built in many learning devices. Among the most important are the Key Questions and the Core Concepts. Let us show you how using these features can make your study of psychology easier.

The Key Questions, which take the place of the familiar section headings in each chapter, give you a "heads up" by signaling what to watch for as you read. For example, one of the Key Questions from this chapter asked, "What are the perspectives psychologists use today?" It alerted you to the idea that psychologists have some special ways of looking at mind and behavior that are different from those used in the past. You are much more likely to remember these new concepts if you approach them with an appropriate question in mind (Bransford et al., 1986; Brown & Campione, 1986; Glaser, 1984). You can also use the

Key Question as a review-check of your understanding of each section before the next test. If you have a study partner, try asking each other to give detailed answers to the key questions.

You can think of Core Concepts as brief responses to the Key Questions. They also highlight the central idea in each chapter section—as previews of coming attractions. It is important to realize that a Core Concept is not a complete answer but a capsule summary of ideas to be fleshed out. As you come to understand the meaning of a Core Concept, you will see that the details of the section—the terms, names, and important research—will fall easily into place. And to reinforce your understanding, it is a good idea to revisit the Core Concept after you have finished reading the section. In fact, this is precisely what the brief end-of-section quizzes (Check Your Understanding) are designed to do.

Another good way to use the Core Concepts is to see if you can explain how the terms in boldface link to the Core Concepts. Let's take the second Core Concept in this chapter, which says:

Modern psychology developed from several conflicting traditions, including structuralism, functionalism, Gestalt psychology, behaviorism, and psychoanalysis.

Can you explain, for example, how the term *introspection* relates to this Core Concept? (Sample answer:

Only the behaviorists, among the historical schools in psychology, refused to use introspection because it was subjective.)

Together, then, the Key Questions and Core Concepts are designed to pose important questions that lead you to the big ideas in the chapter. They will help you step back from the details to see meaningful patterns.

CHAPTER SUMMARY

● WHAT IS PSYCHOLOGY—AND WHAT IS IT *NOT*?

All psychologists are concerned with some aspect of behavior and mental processes. Unlike the pseudosciences, scientific psychology demands solid evidence to back up its claims. Within psychology there are many specialties that fall within three broad areas. Experimental psychologists primarily do research, but they often teach, as well. Those who are primarily teachers of psychology work in a variety of settings, including colleges, universities, and high schools. Applied psychologists practice many specialties, such as engineering, school, rehabilitation psychology, clinical psychology, and counseling. In contrast with psychology, psychiatry is a medical specialty that deals with mental disorder.

● Psychology is a broad field, with many specialties, but fundamentally psychology is the science of behavior and mental processes.

● WHAT ARE PSYCHOLOGY'S HISTORICAL ROOTS?

Psychology has its roots in several often-conflicting traditions stretching back to the ancient Greeks. René Descartes helped the study of the mind to become scientific, based on his insight that sensations and behaviors are linked to activity in the nervous system. The formal beginning of psychology as a science is traced to the establishment by Wundt of the first psychological laboratory in 1879. Wundt's structuralism advocated understanding mental processes such as consciousness by investigating their contents and structure. Another early school of psychology, known as functionalism, argued that mental processes are best understood in terms of their adaptive purposes and functions. Also in opposition to structuralism, Gestalt psychology focused on perceptual "wholes," rather than parts of consciousness. Psychoanalysis differed from the other schools of psychology by emphasizing the unconscious, while behaviorism staked its uniqueness on a rejection of introspection.

● Modern psychology developed from several conflicting traditions, including structuralism, functionalism, Gestalt psychology, behaviorism, and psychoanalysis.

● WHAT ARE THE PERSPECTIVES PSYCHOLOGISTS USE TODAY?

Modern psychology has seven main viewpoints. The biological view looks for the causes of behavior in physical processes such as brain function and genetics. Using cutting-edge technology, neuroscientists using this perspective have made many discoveries about brain function. Many biological psychologists take an evolutionary approach, assuming that human behavior and mental processes are based on genetic adaptations for survival and reproductive advantage. This approach has developed influential theories that explain gender differences and aggressive behavior. The developmental view calls attention to mental and behavioral changes that occur throughout the lifespan. Such changes result from the interaction of heredity and environment. The cognitive view emphasizes information processing; it has made many discoveries about learning, memory, sensation, perception, language, and thinking. Cognitive neuroscientists are especially interested in the link between the brain and mental processes. The clinical view focuses on mental health and mental disorder. One clinical variation, known as psychodynamic psychology, pioneered by Sigmund Freud, proposes that behavior and thought are influenced by inner, often unconscious, psychological forces and conflicts. Its impact has been greatest in therapy. A competing clinical approach, called humanistic psychology, characterizes human functioning as motivated by a desire to grow, be productive, and fulfill human potential. Both have influenced our understanding of personality and the practice of psychotherapy. The behavioral view rejects mentalistic explanations and explains behavior in terms of observable stimuli and responses. It has given us powerful insights into the nature of learning. The trait view emphasizes enduring personality characteristics, and it is popular among applied psychologists involved in mental testing and clinical work. The sociocultural view recognizes the power of society and cultural context on individual thought, feeling, and action, notably through social learning. Cross-cultural psychologists, who take a sociocultural perspective, are working to incorporate information about other cultures into a field that has historically been dominated by psychologists from Europe and the United States.

● **Seven main perspectives characterize modern psychology: the biological, developmental, cognitive, clinical, behavioral, trait, and sociocultural views.**

● HOW DO PSYCHOLOGISTS DEVELOP NEW KNOWLEDGE?

Psychology differs from the pseudosciences, such as astrology, in that it employs the scientific method to check its ideas empirically—based on direct observations. The scientific method consists of five steps: (1) developing a hypothesis, (2) performing a controlled test, (3) gathering objective data, (4) analyzing the results and accepting or rejecting the hypothesis, and (5) pub-

lishing, criticizing, and replicating the results. Variations on this scientific method include experiments, correlational studies, and several kinds of descriptive research, such as surveys, naturalistic observations, and case studies. Each differs in the amount of control the researcher has over the conditions being investigated. Everyone, including the scientist, has biases. Researchers can fall prey to personal bias and expectancy bias, as well as confounding variables. One way that scientists control for bias in their studies involves the double-blind control method.

Psychologists must conduct their work by following a code of ethics, established by the American Psychological Association, for the humane treatment of subjects. Still, some areas of disagreement remain. These especially involve the use of deception and the use of animals as experimental subjects. And, despite the power of science to help us learn about the natural world, there are many important nonscientific questions that science simply cannot answer.

● **Psychologists, like researchers in all other sciences, use the scientific method to test their ideas empirically.**

REVIEW TEST

For each of the following items, choose the single best answer. The answer key appears at the end.

1. Psychology's scientific origins are usually traced to the late 19th century, when _____ established the first psychological laboratory.
   a. William James
   b. Wilhelm Wundt
   c. Sigmund Freud
   d. John B. Watson

2. "To understand consciousness or behavior, you must focus on the probable purpose of an action or process." This statement reflects the arguments of
   a. humanism.
   b. functionalism.
   c. structuralism.
   d. behaviorism.

3. According to the _____ approach, which is a variation of the _____ view, a person's behavior and personality develop as a result of unconscious inner tensions and conflicts.
   a. evolutionary/biological
   b. introspective/cognitive
   c. psychodynamic/clinical
   d. structuralist/behavioral

4. Which of psychology's seven perspectives says that psychology should *not* study mental processes, such as sensation, perception, memory, thinking, motivation, and emotion?

   a. biological
   b. cognitive
   c. clinical
   d. behavioral

5. According to the evolutionary approach in modern psychology, human behavior is the result of the natural selection of behaviors that promote
   a. cultural conformity.
   b. ability to process information.
   c. survival and reproduction.
   d. conflict between individual goals and societal limits.

6. All of the following areas are applied psychology specialties, except
   a. cognitive psychology.
   b. counseling psychology.
   c. clinical psychology.
   d. school psychology.

7. Scientific psychology employs empirical investigation methods. This means that the data collected must be based on
   a. firsthand sensory evidence.
   b. logic.
   c. the observer's subjective interpretation of events.
   d. established traditions of philosophical inquiry.

8. To study the effects of childhood abuse on adult adjustment patterns, you would do
   a. an experimental study.
   b. a correlational study.
   c. a double-blind study.
   d. an evolutionary study.

9. In psychological research, a _____ is a relationship between the events or variables being studied.
   a. model
   b. dependent variable
   c. hypothesis
   d. correlation

10. A researcher wonders how to stimulate young schoolchildren to be more creative. She randomly divides a class of first graders in half, reading stories to one group and having members of the other group take turns making up stories to go with the same set of titles. After two weeks, those who made up stories are producing more work in their reading, writing, and art classes than those who merely listened as she read stories to them. Which one of the following statements is *not* true about this study?
   a. The experimental group was the group that made up their own stories.
   b. The dependent variable involves the amount of work produced by the two groups of children.
   c. There are two levels or conditions in the independent variable.
   d. This is an example of a case study.

ANSWERS: 1.b 2.b 3.c 4.d 5.c 6.a 7.a 8.b 9.d 10.d

KEY TERMS

Psychology (p. 2)
Pseudopsychology (p. 4)
Confirmation bias (p. 4)
Experimental psychologists (p. 6)
Teachers of psychology (p. 6)
Applied psychologists (p. 7)
Psychiatry (p. 8)
Structuralism (p. 10)
Introspection (p. 10)
Functionalism (p. 11)
Gestalt psychology (p. 11)
Behaviorism (p. 12)
Psychoanalysis (p. 13)

Biological view (p. 14)
Neuroscience (p. 15)
Evolutionary psychology (p. 15)
Developmental view (p. 15)
Cognitive view (p. 16)
Cognitions (p. 16)
Cognitive neuroscience (p. 16)
Clinical view (p. 16)
Psychodynamic psychology (p. 16)
Humanistic psychology (p. 16)
Behavioral view (p. 17)
Trait view (p. 17)

Sociocultural view (p. 17)
Culture (p. 17)
Scientific method (p. 21)
Empirical investigation (p. 21)
Theory (p. 22)
Hypothesis (p. 22)
Operational definitions (p. 23)
Independent variable (p. 24)
Random presentation (p. 24)
Data (p. 24)
Dependent variable (p. 24)
Replicate (p. 26)
Experiment (p. 26)

Placebo (p. 27)
Experimental group (p. 27)
Control group (p. 27)
Random assignment (p. 27)
Correlational study (p. 28)
Positive correlation (p. 29)
Negative correlation (p. 29)
Survey (p. 29)
Naturalistic observation (p. 29)
Case study (p. 29)
Personal bias (p. 30)
Expectancy bias (p. 30)
Double-blind study (p. 30)

ARTICLE

Morgeson, F. P., Seligman, M. E. P., Sternberg, R. J., Taylor, S. E., & Manning, C. M. (1999). Lessons learned from a life in psychological science: Implications for young scientists. *American Psychologist, 54,* 106–115. Interested in becoming a psychologist? Read this article by a panel of well-known psychologists discussing their early careers and what they know now that they wish they had known then.

BOOKS

Burr, C. (2004). *The emperor of scent: A true story of perfume and obsession.* New York: Random House. We know least about our most ancient sense. Yet, in this true story, when a likable scientist claims he has discovered the true inner workings of the sense of smell, he is dismissed by peers, must struggle to publish his findings in *Nature,* and next meets with resistance from the fragrance industry. This book is an exposé of scientific publication as well as an exploration of the olfactory sense.

Hunt, M. (1993). *The story of psychology.* New York: Doubleday. These fascinating anecdotes, summaries, and documentation cover the lives and times of what Morton Hunt calls "the Magellans of the mind," from ancient philosophy to modern research.

Pinker, S. (2003). *The blank slate: The modern denial of human nature.* New York: Viking. Steven Pinker, MIT psychology professor and author of *How the Mind Works* and *The Language Instinct,* uses wit, poetry, and comedy to argue against the notion that the human infant's brain is a "blank slate" at birth, insisting rather than evolution provides strong, inherited, survival-oriented skills—with ample room for shaping by culture and experience.

Salsburg, D. (2001). *The lady tasting tea: How statistics revolutionized science in the twentieth century.* San Francisco: W. H. Freeman & Co. With intriguing stories, this author shows how the mathematics of probability made it possibly not only to discover but to test scientific findings.

Schick, T., Jr., & Vaughn, L. (1999). *How to think about weird things,* 2nd ed. Mountain View, CA: Mayfield. Become a "critical consumer" of science by distinguishing good research from bad and keeping an open mind while maintaining high standards in explaining baffling behavior and phenomena such as astrology, ESP, creationism, channeling, and near-death experiences.

VIDEO

Fast, cheap, and out of control. (1997, color, 82 min). Directed by Errol Morris; starring Dave Hoover, George Mendonca, Ray Mendez, and Rodney Books. This documentary has interviews with four eccentric "geniuses"—a lion tamer, a topiary gardener, an expert on the African naked mole rat, and an MIT robotics scientist—mixed with B-movie footage and running commentary on life and human nature.

Key Question Chapter Outline

CORE CONCEPTS

Psychology in Your Life

Evolution has fundamentally shaped psychological processes because it favors genetic variations that produce adaptive behavior.

Choosing Your Children's Genes

Within your lifetime, parents may be able to select genetic traits for their children. What price will we pay for these choices?

The brain coordinates the body's two communications systems, the nervous system and the endocrine system, which use similar chemical processes to communicate with targets throughout the body.

How Psychoactive Drugs Affect the Nervous System

Chemicals used to alter thoughts and feelings usually affect the actions of hormones or neurotransmitters. In so doing, they may also stimulate unintended targets, where they produce unwanted side effects.

The brain is composed of many specialized modules that work together to create mind and behavior.

Brain Damage and Behavior

Everyone knows somebody who has suffered brain damage from an accident, a tumor, or a stroke. The symptoms suggest which part of the brain was damaged.

USING PSYCHOLOGY TO LEARN PSYCHOLOGY
Putting Your Knowledge of the Brain to Work

Biopsychology and the Foundations of Neuroscience

I HADN'T NOTICED DAD dragging the toe of his right foot ever so slightly as he walked. But my mother noticed it on their nightly tour of the neighborhood, when he wasn't keeping up with her brisk pace. I just figured that he was slowing down a bit in his later years.

Dad, too, casually dismissed his symptom, but Mom was persistent. She scheduled an appointment with the doctor. In turn, the doctor scheduled a brain scan that showed a remarkably large mass—a tumor—on the left side of Dad's brain. You can see what the neurologist saw in Figure 2.1—an image taken ear-to-ear through the head.

When I saw the pictures, I knew immediately what was happening. The tumor was located in an area that would interfere with tracking the position of the foot. As I remembered learning in my introductory psychology class, each side of the brain communicates with the opposite side of the body—so it made sense that the tumor showing so clearly on the left side of Dad's brain (right side of the image) was affecting communications with his right foot.

The neurologist also told us that the diseased tissue was not in the brain itself. Rather, it was in the saclike layers surrounding the brain and spinal cord. That was good news, in an otherwise bleak report. Still, the mass was growing and putting pressure on the brain. The recommendation was surgery—which occurred after an anxious wait of a few weeks.

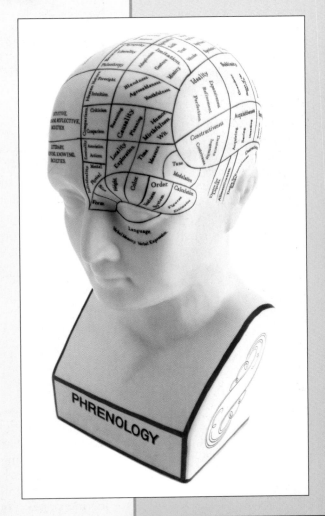

This image, showing a side-to-side section toward the back of the head, reveals a large mass on the left side of the brain, in a region involved with tracking the position of the right foot. Visible at the bottom is a cross section of the cerebellum. Also visible are the folds in the cerebral cortex covering the brain. Near the center, you can see two of the brain's ventricles (hollow spaces filled with cerebrospinal fluid), which are often enlarged, as they are here, in Alzheimer's disease. The scan is of the father of one of your authors.

During this difficult time, I remember feeling grateful for my professional training. As a psychologist, I knew something about the brain, its disorders, and treatments. This allowed me to shift perspectives—from son to psychologist and back again. It helped me deal with the emotions that rose to the surface when I thought about the struggle for the organ of my father's mind.

Sadly, the operation did not produce the miraculous cure for which we had hoped. Although brain surgery is performed safely on thousands of patients each year—many of whom receive immense benefits in the quality and lengths of their lives—one has to remember that it is a procedure that is usually done on very sick people. In fact, the operation did give Dad some time with us that he may otherwise not have had.

—RJ

You, too, probably know someone—a relative or a friend—who has suffered a brain injury. It might have involved a tumor, an auto accident, a combat wound, encephalitis (inflammation of the brain), a stroke, or some other trauma, including a difficult birth. This chapter is a tribute to the scores of thousands who have incurred such injuries and allowed themselves to be studied by scientists trying to understand how the brain works. In the following pages, you will learn about the resulting discoveries, as we explore the physical basis of mind and behavior.

So, what do we know about the brain? In the simplest terms, it is about the size of a grapefruit, it weighs about 3 pounds, and it has a pinkish-gray and wrinkled surface. But such bland facts give us no hint of the brain's amazing structure and capabilities. The home of some 100 billion nerve cells, each making connections with up to 10 thousand other nerve cells, the human brain is the most complex structure known. Its intricate circuitry makes our largest computers seem primitive by comparison. Indeed, its cells outnumber all the stars in the galaxy.

At birth, the brain has an extra supply of nerve cells, and many surplus ones die in the first few years of our lives. By adolescence the number stabilizes. Although our brains generate some new nerve cells throughout our lives, the total remains essentially constant once we reach adulthood (Barinaga, 2003a; Gage, 2003; Kempermann & Gage, 1999). This neural stability may be essential for the continuity of learning and memory over a long lifetime (Rakic, 1985). Even so, the nerve cells in our brains do continue to expire at a low rate: A mere 200,000 will die every day of your adult life (Dowling, 1992). Fortunately, because we start out with so many and generate some new ones along the way, we end up with more than 98% of our supply after 70 years.

As for its capabilities, the brain uses its vast nerve circuitry to regulate all our body functions, control our behavior, generate our emotions and desires, and process the experiences of a lifetime. In addition—and unlike any ordinary computer—the brain has circuits capable of producing emotions, motives, and insights. This dazzling array of abilities may seem to involve something far more than a mere knot of nervous tissue lying inside our heads—and it does! Yet, when disease, drugs, or accidents destroy brain cells, the biological basis of the human mind becomes apparent. We are then forced to recognize that biology underlies all human sensation and perception, learning and memory, passion and pain, reason—and even madness.

Most remarkable of all, the human brain has the ability to think about itself. This is one of the fascinations for researchers in **biopsychology,** a rapidly growing specialty that lies at the intersection of biology, behavior, and mental processes. Increasingly, biopsychologists are collaborating with cognitive psychologists, biologists, computer scientists, chemists, neurologists, linguists and others interested in the connection between brain and mind— how the circuitry of the brain produces mental processes and behavior. The result is a vibrant interdisciplinary field known as **neuroscience** (Kandel & Squire, 2000).

In this chapter, you will see that biopsychologists and other neuroscientists have made many discoveries that have practical applications in everyday life. For example, we now know that sleep patterns are controlled by specific parts of the brain—with the result that we now have effective treatments for a variety of sleep disorders. Likewise, the attraction of certain psychoactive drugs, such as cocaine, heroin, and methamphetamine, makes sense only when we understand how these drugs interact with chemicals made in the brain. And, as we pointed out earlier, a little knowledge of biopsychology will be helpful when someone you know sustains brain damage as the result of an accident, stroke, or Alzheimer's disease.

We will begin our exploration of biopsychology and neuroscience at the most basic level—by considering the twin domains of *genetics* and *evolution,* both of which have shaped our bodies and minds. Then, we will examine the *endocrine system* and the *nervous system,* the two communication channels carrying messages throughout the body. Finally, we will focus on the brain itself. As we follow this path, please keep in mind that we are not asking you to undertake a mere academic exercise: You will be learning how biological processes shape your every thought, feeling, and action.

CONNECTION: CHAPTER 3

Neuroscientists have discovered the causes and treatments for many *sleep disorders.*

■ **Biopsychology** The specialty in psychology that studies the interaction of biology, behavior, and mental processes.
■ **Neuroscience** A relatively new interdisciplinary field that focuses on the brain and its role in psychological processes.

HOW ARE GENES AND BEHAVIOR LINKED?

Just as fish have an inborn knack for swimming and most birds are built for flight, we humans also have *innate* (inborn) abilities. At birth, the human brain is already "programmed" for language, social interaction, self-preservation, and many other functions, as we can see in the interaction between babies and their caregivers. Babies "know," for example, how to search for the breast and how to communicate through coos and cries. We'll look more closely at the menu of innate human behaviors in our discussion of human development (Chapter 4), but for now, this is the question: How did such potential come to be woven into the brain's fabric?

The scientific answer rests on the concept of **evolution,** the process by which succeeding generations of organisms change as they adapt to changing environments. We can observe evolution in action on a microscopic level, when an antibiotic doesn't work because a strain of bacteria has evolved a resistance. Over much longer time spans, generations of larger and more complex organisms also change, as they adapt to changing climates, competitors, diseases, and food supplies. In our species, for example, change has favored large brains suited to language, complex problem-solving, and social interaction.

Our Core Concept for this section makes this evolutionary process the link between genetics and behavior.

> Evolution has fundamentally shaped psychological processes because it favors genetic variations that produce adaptive behavior.

The idea of evolution is both simple and powerful. In this section we begin our explanation of evolution with the story of Charles Darwin, who gave the idea of evolutionary change to the world. Then, we will consider an idea Darwin never knew: how *genetics* produces the molecular machinery that makes evolution work—and ultimately influences all our psychological processes.

Evolution and Natural Selection

Although he had trained both for medicine and the ministry, Charles Darwin decided that biology was his calling. So, in 1831, he signed on as a naturalist aboard HMS *Beagle,* a British research vessel commissioned to survey the coastline of South America. Returning five years later with numerous specimens and detailed records of the many unusual life-forms and fossils he had found, Darwin also brought home the radical idea of a relationship among species. Struck by the similarities among the various animals and plants he studied, Darwin concluded that all creatures, including humans, share a common ancestry.

He knew this notion flew in the face of accepted scholarship, as well as the religious doctrine of creationism. So, in his famous book, *On the Origin of Species* (1859), Darwin carefully made the case for the evolution of life. And controversial it was. The essential features of his argument, however, withstood withering attacks, and eventually the theory of evolution created a fundamental change in the way people saw their relationship to other living things (Keynes, 2002; Mayr, 2000).

What was the evidence that led Darwin to his radical conclusion about the evolution of organisms? Again and again on the voyage, he had observed organisms that were exquisitely adapted to their environments: flowers that attracted certain insects, birds with beaks perfectly suited to cracking certain seeds. He had also observed *variation* among individuals within a species:

■ **Evolution** The gradual process of biological change that occurs in a species as it adapts to its environment.

Some finches, for example, had bigger, stronger beaks than others, just as some humans are taller than others or have better eyesight (Weiner, 1994). Such variations gave some individuals an advantage over others in the struggle for survival and reproduction. This, then, suggested a mechanism for evolution: a "weeding out" process that he called **natural selection.** By means of natural selection, those individuals best adapted to the environment are more likely to flourish and reproduce; those that are poorly adapted will tend to leave fewer progeny, and their line may die out. (You may have heard this described as "survival of the fittest," a term Darwin disliked.) For the fortunate individuals whose ancestors had accumulated new traits that allowed them to adapt and survive, the result "would be the formation of a new species," claimed Darwin (1859).

Applied to psychology, evolution makes sense of many things that would otherwise seem arbitrary. For example, evolutionary psychologists have pointed out that human *phobias* (extreme and incapacitating fears) almost always involve stimulation that signaled danger to our ancestors (snakes, lightning, blood), rather than dangerous conditions of more recent origin (radiation, electricity, automobiles). In the same way, the fact that we spend about a third of our lives asleep makes much more sense in an evolutionary context (sleep kept our ancestors out of trouble in the dark) than it does as an adaptive behavior in a modern world with artificial lights. Evolution also explains certain innate preferences and distastes, such as the attractiveness of sweets and fatty foods (good sources of valuable calories for our ancestors) and a dislike for bitter-tasting substances (often a sign of poisons).

"Evolution" is, of course, an emotionally loaded term, and many people misunderstand its real meaning. For example, some believe that Darwin's theory says humans "come from monkeys." But neither Darwin nor any other evolutionary scientist has ever said that. Rather, they say we had a common ancestor millions of years ago—a big difference. Another evolutionary misconception holds that behavior can alter hereditary traits. But giraffes didn't get long necks from stretching to reach leaves high in the trees. Instead, the doctrine of natural selection says that the ancestors of modern giraffes were variants that had a survival advantage over their shorter-necked cousins. Over

■ **Natural selection** The driving force behind evolution, by which the environment "selects" the fittest organisms.

● More than 98% of our genetic material is also found in chimpanzees (Gibbons, 1998). This supports Darwin's idea that humans and apes had a common ancestor.

time, then, the longer-necked trait came to dominate the population. In the same way, evolving human traits, such as a big brain adapted for language, gave our ancestors an advantage in the competitive struggle for survival and reproduction (Buss et al., 1998).

We should be clear that the basic principles of evolution, while still controversial in some quarters, have been accepted by virtually all scientists for more than a century. That said, we should note that evolutionary theory is a controversial newcomer to psychology. It is not that psychologists dispute Darwin—most do not. Rather, the controversy centers on whether an evolutionary approach places too much emphasis on *nature*, the biological basis of psychology, and not enough emphasis on *nurture*, the role of learning. This *nature–nurture controversy* is a long-standing issue in psychology that we will meet again and again throughout this book. Sometimes it is also called the *heredity vs. environment* issue.

CONNECTION: CHAPTERS 4 AND 8

The *nature–nurture controversy* is a prominent issue in developmental psychology and in intelligence testing.

In later chapters we will discuss specific evolutionary explanations that have been advanced to explain aggression, jealousy, sexual orientation, physical attraction and mate selection, parenting, cooperation, temperament, morality, and (always a psychological hot potato) gender differences. But for now, let us turn our attention to the biological underpinnings of evolutionary change.

Genetics and Inheritance

Remarkably, Darwin knew nothing of genetics. Although he correctly described how natural selection works, he lived long before scientists understood the biology behind evolutionary change. From our perspective, some 150 years after Darwin, we know that the individual variations that caught his attention arise from random genetic differences among individuals.

In principle, the genetic code is quite simple. Much as the microscopic pits in a CD encode information that can become pictures or music, your *genes* encode information that can become your inherited traits. Consider your own unique combination of traits. Your height, weight, facial features, and hair color, for example, all originate in the encoded genetic "blueprint" inherited from your parents and inscribed in every cell nucleus in your body. Psychologists have shown that many of our psychological characteristics, too, are influenced by genetics, including basic temperament, tendency to fears, and certain behavior patterns (Pinker, 2002).

Yet, despite your genetic heritage, you are a unique individual—different from either of your parents. One source of difference lies in your experience, in the environment in which you grew up—distinct in time and, perhaps, in place from that of your parents. The other main source of difference between you and your parents comes from heredity—the random combination of traits that each parent passed on to you from past generations in their own family lines. These include the color of your hair, eyes, and skin, as well as aspects of your personality. This hybrid inheritance produced your unique **genotype,** the genetic pattern that makes you different from anyone else on earth.

If the genotype is the "blueprint," then the resulting physical structure is the **phenotype.** All your physical characteristics make up your phenotype, including not only your visible traits but also the chemistry and "wiring" of your brain. We should hasten to point out that, while the phenotype is based in biology, it is not completely determined by heredity. Heredity never acts alone but always in partnership with the environment, which includes such biological influences as nutrition, disease, and stress. For example, poor medical care that results in a birth defect counts as an environmental influence on the phenotype.

■ **Genotype** An organism's genetic makeup.
■ **Phenotype** An organism's observable physical characteristics.

Now, with these ideas about heredity, environment, genotypes, and phenotypes fresh in mind, let's turn to the details of heredity and individual variation that Darwin never knew.

Chromosomes, Genes, and DNA   In the film *Jurassic Park*, scientists recovered the genetic code for dinosaurs and created an island full of reptilian problems. The story, of course, was science fiction, yet the film rested on an important scientific fact: Every cell nucleus in the body carries a complete set of biological instructions for building the organism. For humans, these instructions are contained in 23 pairs of chromosomes, which, under a high-powered microscope, look like tiny twisted threads. Zooming in for a close look, we find that each chromosome consists of a long and tightly coiled chain of **DNA** (deoxyribonucleic acid), a molecule that just happens to be especially well-suited to storing this biological information.

Genes are the "words" that make up the organism's instruction manual. Encoded in discrete segments of DNA, each gene contributes to the operation of the organism by specifying a single protein. Thousands of such proteins, in turn, serve as the building blocks for the organism's physical characteristics (the phenotype) and the regulation of the body's internal operations. Genes, because they are not precisely the same in each individual, are also the biological source of the variation that caught Darwin's attention.

The genes occur in sequence on the **chromosomes,** like a string of words in a coded sentence. But the chromosomes are much more than mere genetic paragraphs. They also contain "punctuation" that indicates where each gene begins and ends, along with instructions specifying how and when the genes are to be expressed (Gibbs, 2003). Although these instructions are not yet well understood, genetic scientists have shown that the instructions for gene expression are crucial to the proper functioning of every cell in our bodies. Errors in gene expression can lead to physical and developmental problems, including mental retardation. At the extreme, flawed gene expression can produce fatal diseases.

On a still smaller scale (now we're getting beyond the power of microscopes to resolve), genes are composed of even smaller molecular units called *nucleotides* that serve as individual "letters" in the genetic "words." But instead of a 26-letter alphabet, the genetic code uses just four nucleotides, even though a particular gene may require hundreds of nucleotides to specify a particular protein.

Physically, the nucleotides fit together in pairs, rather like the opposing teeth in a zipper. Then, when a protein is needed, the nucleotides in the appropriate segment of DNA "unzip," forming a jagged pattern, or template, from which the protein is built. (See Figure 2.2.)

So, how many genes does it take to make a human? According to current estimates, the complete package of human DNA contains approximately 30,000 genes—surprisingly few, in view of the human organism's complexity (Netting & Wang, 2001; Pennisi, 2003). Together with their supplemental instructions, your genes reside on 46 chromosomes, arranged in 23 pairs. One in each pair came from your mother, with the remaining 23 being your father's genetic contribution. As if that weren't complicated enough, duplicate copies of all this genetic information are crammed inside the billions of cell nuclei throughout your body. It's much the same as a large corporation that relies on many individual computers, each of which requires its own copy of the operating system software.

Two of the 46 chromosomes warrant special mention: the **sex chromosomes.** Named X and Y for their shape, these chromosomes carry genes encoding for a male or a female phenotype. We all inherit one X chromosome from

■ **DNA**   A long, complex molecule that encodes genetic characteristics. DNA is an abbreviation for *deoxyribonucleic acid.*

■ **Gene**   Segment of a chromosome that encodes the directions for the inherited physical and mental characteristics of an organism. Genes are the functional units of a chromosome.

■ **Chromosome**   Tightly coiled threadlike structure along which the genes are organized, like beads on a necklace. Chromosomes consist primarily of DNA.

■ **Sex chromosomes**   The X and Y chromosomes that determine our physical sex characteristics.

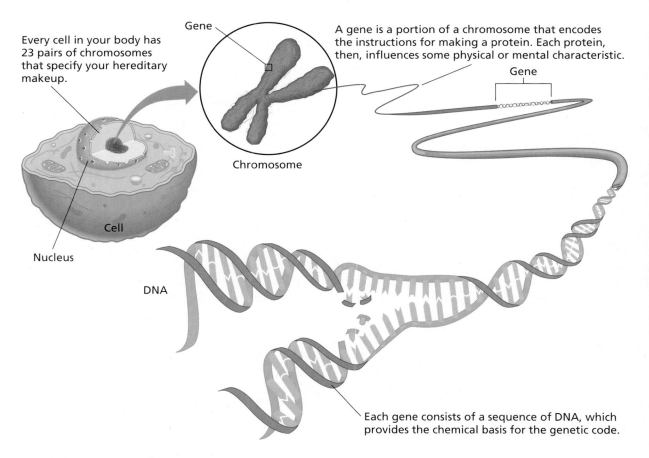

Every cell in your body has 23 pairs of chromosomes that specify your hereditary makeup.

Gene

A gene is a portion of a chromosome that encodes the instructions for making a protein. Each protein, then, influences some physical or mental characteristic.

Gene

Chromosome

Cell

Nucleus

DNA

Each gene consists of a sequence of DNA, which provides the chemical basis for the genetic code.

● **FIGURE 2.2** DNA, Genes, and Chromosomes

A chromosome is composed mainly of a tightly coiled strand of DNA, an incredibly long molecule. Each chromosome contains thousands of genes, along with instructions for the "when" and "how" of gene expression. Genes themselves are segments of DNA. Each gene contains instructions, coded in the four-nucleotide alphabet, for making a protein. The Human Genome Project recently identified the sequence of nucleotides in all 23 pairs of our chromosomes.

our biological mothers. In addition, we receive either an X (for females) or a much smaller Y (for males) from our biological fathers. When they pair up, two X chromosomes (XX) contain the code for femaleness, while an XY pair codes for maleness. In this sense, then, the chromosomes we get from our fathers determine our biological sex.

It is important to note that you do not inherit copies of *all* your father's and mother's genes. Rather you get half of each, randomly shuffled—which explains why siblings all have slightly different genotypes (unless they are identical twins). This random shuffling and recombining of parental genes produces the variation that Darwin viewed as the raw material for evolution.

Genetic Explanations for Psychological Processes   Most of the foregoing discussion of heredity and genetics could apply equally to fruit flies and butterflies, hollyhocks and humans. All organisms follow the same basic laws of heredity. The differences among different species arise, then, from different genetic "words" spelled with the same four letters of life's universal four-letter alphabet.

And what does all this have to do with psychology? Simply put, genes influence our psychological characteristics as well as our physical traits. In later chapters we will explore the extent to which genes affect such diverse human attributes as intelligence, personality, mental disorders, reading and language disabilities, and (perhaps) sexual orientation. (See Bouchard, 1994; Caspi et al., 2002; DeAngelis, 1997; Gelernter, 1994; Hamer, 1997; Lai et al., 2001; Plomin, Owen, & McGuffin, 1994; Plomin & Rende, 1991; Saudino, 1997). Even our fears can have some genetic basis (Hariri et al., 2002). But, because genetic psychology is still a field in its infancy, we don't yet know how or to what extent genes are involved in most psychological processes (Hamer, 2002; Plomin, 2003).

In only a few cases can we hold a single gene responsible for a psychological disorder. For example, just one abnormal gene has been linked to a rare pattern of impulsive violence found in several members of a Dutch family (Brunner et al., 1993). Most other genetically influenced disorders appear to involve multiple genes, often on more than one chromosome (Boomsma, Anokhin, & de Geus, 1997; Plomin, 2000). Experts think it likely that multiple genes contribute, for example, to schizophrenia, a severe mental disorder, and to Alzheimer's disease, a form of dementia. (See Morrison-Bogorad & Phelps, 1997; Plomin, Owen, & McGuffin, 1994; Skoog et al., 1993; St. George-Hyslop, 2000).

CONNECTION: CHAPTER 12

Schizophrenia is a psychotic disorder that affects about one out of 100 persons.

So, does this mean that heredity determines our psychological destiny? Will you grow up to be like your Uncle Henry? Not to worry. To reiterate: Heredity never acts alone. *Both* heredity and environment always work together to influence our behavior and mental processes (Pinker, 2002). Even identical twins, who share the same genotype, display individual differences in appearance and personality that result from their distinct experiences, such as exposure to different people, places, chemicals, and diseases. Moreover, studies show that, when one identical twin acquires a psychological disorder known to have a genetic basis (schizophrenia, for example), the other twin does not necessarily develop the same disorder. This is the takeaway message: *Never attribute psychological characteristic to genetics alone* (Ehrlich, 2000a, b; Mauron, 2001).

An example of the interaction between heredity and environment—and one of the rays of hope that have come from biopsychology—can be seen in a condition called *Down syndrome.* Associated with an extra chromosome 21, this disorder includes markedly impaired physical development, as well as mental retardation. Only a few years ago, people with Down syndrome faced bleak and unproductive lives, shut away in institutions, where they depended almost wholly on others to fulfill their basic needs. Now, a better understanding of the disorder, along with a deeper appreciation for the interaction between genetics and environment, has changed that outlook. Although no cure has been found, today we know that people with Down syndrome are capable of considerable learning, despite their genetic impairment. With special programs that teach life skills, those with Down syndrome now learn to care for themselves, work, and establish some personal independence.

 PSYCHOLOGY IN YOUR LIFE: CHOOSING YOUR CHILDREN'S GENES

Scientists already have the ability to control and alter the genetics of animals, like Dolly, the late and famous fatherless sheep that was cloned from one of her mother's cells. But what are the prospects for genetic manipulation in people? Scientists working on the Human Genome Project have recently completed a "first draft" of the human genetic code (Pennisi, 2001). The rest of the 21st century will see us mining this data for insight into the genetic basis for many physical and mental disorders. High on the list will be disorders that affect millions: cancer, heart disease, schizophrenia, and Alzheimer's disease. But not all the promise of human genetics lies in the future. We can already sample fetal cells and search for certain genetic disorders, such as Down syndrome. Data drawn from the Human Genome Project will greatly expand this ability. Psychologists also expect it to teach us something about the genetic basis for human differences in abilities, emotions, and resistance to stress (Kosslyn et al., 2002).

Right now, with a little clinical help, parents can select the sex of a child with a fair degree of certainty. And, within your lifetime, parents may be able to select specific genes for their children, much as you select the components of a deli sandwich. It is likely that we will learn to alter the DNA in a developing fetus in order to add or delete certain physical and mental traits (Henig, 1998). This might be done by infecting the fetus with a harmless virus containing desirable genes that will alter or replace the genetic blueprint in every cell of the body. Another approach might involve injecting *stem cells* ("generic" cells that have not fully committed themselves to becoming a particular type of tissue) that have desirable genetic characteristics (Doetsch, 2002). But what will be the price of this technology?

This developing genetic knowledge will surely create some new problems, as well as promises. Take *cloning,* for example. While most people do not favor the cloning of entire humans, the possibility exists of cloning specific organs or tissues—again from stem cells, a procedure currently under severe restrictions by the U.S. government. Proponents point out that cloned organs could potentially cure heart, liver, and kidney failure, as well as diabetes and arthritis (Pool, 1998). But one difficulty arises from the source of cells for such research. Because donor embryos most often come from extras produced during *in vitro* fertilization procedures, many people oppose this work (Wheeler, 1999). Eventually, perhaps, we will learn to build a new organ out of the recipient's own cells.

There will be psychological issues, as well. Undoubtedly, parents in this brave new genetic world will want their children to be smart and good looking—but, we might wonder, by what standards will intelligence and looks be judged? And what will be the costs? Will everyone be able to place an order for their children's genes—or only the very wealthy? You can be certain that the problems we face will be simultaneously biological, psychological, political, and ethical (Fackelmann, 1998; Patenaude, Guttmacher, & Collins, 2002).

In general, the more we learn about behavior genetics, the more clearly we can see the powerful biological forces that shape human potential and life experience. We can also glimpse the problems to be faced when we learn to manipulate these genetic forces. Already, psychologists are called on to provide guidance about how genetic knowledge can best be applied (Bronheim, 2000; Plomin, 1997; Plomin & McClearn, 1993), particularly in helping people assess genetic risks in connection with family planning. We invite you to grapple with these issues by answering the following questions:

▌ If you could select three genetic traits for your children, which ones would you select?

▌ How would you feel about raising children you have adopted or fostered but to whom you are not genetically related?

▌ If a biological child of yours might be born disabled or fatally ill because of your genetic heritage, would you have children anyway? What circumstances or conditions would affect your decision?

▌ If you knew you might carry a gene responsible for a serious medical or behavioral disorder, would you want to be tested before having children? And would it be fair for a prospective spouse to require you to be tested before conceiving children? Or would it be fair for the state to make such a requirement?

These questions, of course, have no "right" answers; but the answers you give will help you define your stand on some of the most important issues we will face in the 21st century.

HOW DOES THE BODY COMMUNICATE INTERNALLY?

You are driving on a winding mountain road, and suddenly a car is coming directly at you. At the last instant, you and the other driver swerve in opposite directions. Your heart pounds—and it keeps pounding for several minutes after the danger has passed. Externally, you have avoided a potentially fatal accident. Internally, your body has responded to two kinds of messages from its two communication systems.

One of these is the fast-acting *nervous system*, with its extensive network of nerve cells that carries messages in pulses of electrical and chemical energy throughout the body. It is this network that first comes to your rescue in an emergency, carrying the orders that accelerate your heart and tense your muscles for action. The other communication network, the slower-acting *endocrine system*, sends follow-up messages that support and sustain the emergency response initiated by the nervous system. To do this, the endocrine glands, including the pituitary, thyroid, adrenals, and gonads, use the chemical messengers we call *hormones.* Coincidentally, communication between nerve cells also relies on chemicals that are suspiciously similar to hormones, as we shall see.

It is important to understand that the two internal message systems cooperate to arouse us not only in stressful situations, such as the narrowly avoided auto accident, but in happier emotional circumstances, such as when you receive an unexpected "A" on a test or fall in love. They also work together when we are in states of low arousal, to keep the vital body functions operating smoothly. This cooperation between the endocrine system and the nervous system is coordinated by the nervous system's chief executive, the brain—which brings us to our Core Concept:

> The brain coordinates the body's two communications systems, the nervous system and the endocrine system, which use similar chemical processes to communicate with targets throughout the body.

Why is this notion important for your understanding of psychology? For one thing, these two communication systems are the biological bedrock for all our thoughts, emotions, and behaviors. For another, when the biology goes awry, the result can be a variety of unfortunate effects on the brain and mental functions, such as stroke, Alzheimer's disease, and schizophrenia. Still another reason for studying the biology behind the body's internal communications is that it helps us understand how drugs, such as caffeine, alcohol, and Prozac, can change the chemistry of the mind.

We will begin our tour of these vital communication systems with a close look at the building block of the nervous system: the *neuron*. Next, we will see how networks of neurons, each having similar functions, work together as components of the *nervous system*. Then, we will consider the *endocrine system*, a network of glands that operates in parallel with the nervous system to send information throughout the body. Finally, in the last section of the chapter, we will probe the mysteries of that "great raveled knot" of neurons: the *brain* itself.

The Neuron: Building Block of the Nervous System

On the most basic level, every part of the nervous system is made of the same components, called *nerve cells* or neurons. In simplest terms, a **neuron** is merely a cell specialized to receive, process, and transmit information to other cells. And neurons do that very efficiently. A typical neuron may receive information from a thousand other neurons and, within a fraction of a second, "decide" to pass it along at speeds up to 100 meters per second to a thousand more neurons—sometimes as many as 10,000 (Pinel, 2003).

Types of Neurons While neurons vary in shape and size, they all have essentially the same structure, and they all send messages in essentially the same way. Still, biopsychologists distinguish three major classes of neurons according to their location and function: *sensory neurons, motor neurons,* or *interneurons.* (See Figure 2.3.) **Sensory neurons,** or *afferent neurons,* act like one-way streets that carry traffic from the sense organs *toward* the brain. Accordingly, afferent neurons treat the brain to all your sensory experience, including vision, hearing, taste, touch, smell, pain, and balance. For example, when you test the water temperature in the shower with your hand, afferent neurons carry the message toward the brain. By contrast, **motor neurons,** or *efferent neurons,* form the one-way routes that transport messages *away* from the brain to the muscles, organs, and glands. So, in our shower example, the motor neurons deliver the message from the brain that tells your hand just how much to move the shower control knob.

■ **Neuron** Cell specialized to receive and transmit information to other cells in the body—also called a *nerve cell.* Bundles of many neurons are called *nerves.*

■ **Sensory neuron** Nerve cell that carries messages from sense receptors toward the central nervous system. Also called an *afferent neuron.*

■ **Motor neuron** Nerve cell that carries messages away from the central nervous system toward the muscles and glands. Also called an *efferent neuron.*

● **FIGURE 2.3** Sensory Neurons, Motor Neurons, and Interneurons

Information about the water temperature in the shower is carried by thousands of *sensory neurons* (afferent neurons) from the sense organs to the central nervous system. In this case, the message enters the spinal cord and is relayed, by *interneurons,* to the brain. There, the information is assessed and a response is initiated (turn the water temperature down!). These instructions are sent to the muscles by means of *motor neurons* (efferent neurons). Large bundles of the message-carrying fibers from these neurons are called *nerves.*

Skin receptors

Muscle

Sensory neuron

Motor neuron

Interneuron

Spinal cord

Pain message to brain

Anterior cingulate cortex (midline)

Sensory cortex

Sensory and motor neurons rarely communicate directly with each other, except in the simplest of reflexive circuits. Instead, they usually rely on the go-between **interneurons** (also shown in Figure 2.3), which make up most of the billions of cells in the brain and spinal cord. Interneurons relay messages from sensory neurons to other interneurons or to motor neurons, sometimes in complex pathways. In fact, the brain itself is mostly a network of billions of intricately connected interneurons.

How Neurons Work   A look at Figure 2.4 will help you visualize the parts of a neuron. The "receiver" parts, which accept most of the incoming messages, consist of finely branched fibers called **dendrites.** These dendritic fibers extend outward from the cell body, where they act like a net, collecting messages received by direct stimulation (such as pressure, light, and sound) or from the activity of neighboring neurons.

Significantly, neuroscientists have discovered that dendrites can undergo subtle modifications when we learn (Barinaga, 2000; Kennedy, 2000; Matus, 2000). This discovery has launched a search for drugs that might encourage the changes in dendrites associated with learning. While students will probably never be able to take a pill instead of a psychology class, they may one day be able to ingest harmless chemicals that will help them remember what they have read or heard in class. For the moment, the best we have to offer is coffee—which actually acts as a mild, but temporary, stimulus to the dendrites (Julien, 2001). (The evidence that caffeine promotes learning is controversial.)

Dendrites complete their job by passing incoming messages to the central part of the neuron, the *cell body* or **soma.** Not only does the soma contain the

■ **Interneuron**   A nerve cell that relays messages between nerve cells, especially in the brain and spinal cord.
■ **Dendrite**   A branched fiber that extends outward from the main cell body and carries information into the neuron.
■ **Soma**   The part of a cell (such as a neuron) containing the nucleus, which includes the chromosomes. Also called the *cell body.*

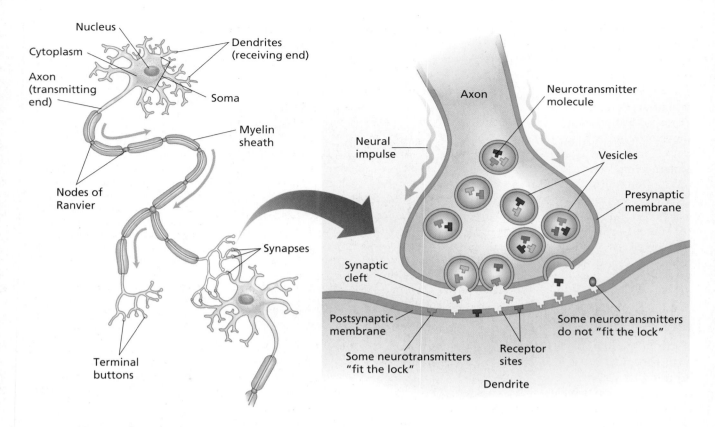

● **FIGURE 2.4** Structure and Function of the Neuron

A typical neuron receives thousands of messages at a time through its *dendrites* and *soma* (cell body). When the soma becomes sufficiently aroused, its own message is then passed to the *axon,* which transmits it by means of an *action potential* to the cell's *terminal buttons.* There tiny *vesicles* containing *neurotransmitters* rupture and release their contents into the *synapse* (synaptic cleft). Appropriately shaped transmitter molecules arriving at the postsynaptic membrane can dock at *receptors,* where they stimulate the receiving cell. Excessive transmitter is taken back into the "sending" neuron by means of *reuptake.*

cell's nucleus and life-support machinery, it also has the executive job of assessing all the messages the cell receives from the dendrites (and also directly from other neurons). In this process, the input from a single synapse carries little weight, because a typical neuron may receive messages from hundreds or even thousands of other neurons. And, to make the situation more complex, some of these messages can be *excitatory* (saying, in effect, "Fire!") or *inhibitory* ("Don't fire!"). Just how aroused the cell body becomes depends on the sum total of all the incoming messages.

When excitation triumphs over inhibition, the aroused neuron may generate a message of its own, sent through a single "transmitter" fiber, the **axon,** which can extend over considerable distances. In a college basketball player, the axons connecting the spinal cord with the toes can be more than a meter in length. At the other end of the scale, the axons of interneurons in the brain may span only a tiny fraction of an inch.

The Action Potential Nerve cells employ both electrical and chemical signals to process and transmit information. As we have seen, an impulse in a single neuron begins when a stimulus, such as a sound, a pinprick, or messages from other nerve cells, make the soma excited. When the arousal reaches a critical level, an electrical impulse occurs in the axon, like the electronic flash of a camera. When this happens, the cell is said to "fire."

■ **Axon** In a nerve cell, an extended fiber that conducts information from the *soma* to the *terminal buttons.* Information travels along the axon in the form of an electric charge, called the *action potential.*

Much like the battery in that camera, the axon gets its electrical energy from charged chemicals, called *ions*. In its normal, resting state, the ions within the cell give the axon a small negative charge, appropriately called the **resting potential.** But this positive/negative imbalance is easily upset. When the cell body becomes excited, it triggers a cascade of events, known as the **action potential,** that temporarily reverses the charge and causes an electrical signal to race along the axon. This happens when tiny pores open in a small area of the axon's membrane adjacent to the soma, allowing a rapid influx of positive ions. This rapidly changes (we're talking 1/1000 of a second here) the internal charge in that part of the axon from negative to positive. Then, like a row of falling dominoes, these changes progress down the axon, causing an electrical signal to race from the soma toward the axon ending. There's no halfway about this action potential: Either the axon "fires" or it doesn't. Neuroscientists call this the **all-or-none principle.**

Almost immediately, the cell's "ion pump" flushes out the positively charged ions and restores the neuron to its resting potential, ready to fire again. Incredibly, the whole complex cycle may take place in less than a hundredth of a second. It is a mind-boggling performance—but this is not the end of the matter. The information carried by the action potential still must traverse a tiny gap before reaching another cell.

Synaptic Transmission   The gap between nerve cells, called the **synapse,** acts as an electrical insulator, preventing the charge speeding down the axon from jumping to the next cell (see Figure 2.4). To pass the message across the *synaptic gap* (or *synaptic cleft*), a neuron must initiate a process in tiny bulblike structures called **terminal buttons,** found at the ends of the axon. There, in a remarkable sequence of events known as **synaptic transmission,** the electrical message morphs into a chemical message that easily flows across the synaptic cleft between neurons. This occurs in the following way.

■ **Resting potential**   The electrical charge of the axon in its inactive state, when the neuron is ready to "fire."

■ **Action potential**   The nerve impulse caused by a change in the electrical charge across the cell membrane of the axon. When the neuron "fires," this charge travels down the axon and causes neurotransmitters to be released by the terminal buttons.

■ **All-or-none principle**   Refers to the fact that the action potential in the axon occurs either full-blown or not at all.

■ **Synapse**   The microscopic gap that serves as a communications link between neurons. Synapses also occur between neurons and the muscles or glands they serve.

■ **Terminal buttons**   Tiny bulblike structures at the end of the axon, which contain neurotransmitters that carry the neuron's message into the synapse.

■ **Synaptic transmission**   The relaying of information across the synapse by means of chemical neurotransmitters.

DO IT YOURSELF! | Neural Messages and Reaction Time

For only a dollar you can find out how long it takes for the brain to process information and initiate a response.

Hold a crisp dollar bill by the middle of the short side, so that it dangles downward. Have a friend put his or her thumb and index fingers on opposite sides and about an inch away from the center of the bill, as shown in the illustration. Instruct your friend to pinch the thumb and fingers together and attempt to catch the bill when you drop it.

If you drop the bill without warning (being careful not to signal your intentions), your friend's brain will not be able to process the information rapidly enough to get a response to the hand before the dollar bill has dropped safely away.

What does this demonstrate? The time it takes to respond reflects the time it takes

for the sensory nervous system to take in the information, for the brain to process it, and for the motor system to produce a response. All

this involves millions of neurons; and, even though they respond quickly, their responses do take time.

1 in. gap between fingers and bill

● Michael J. Fox suffers from Parkinson disease, caused by a deficiency of dopamine in his brain.

Neurotransmitters   At the terminal buttons, the electrical impulse causes a rupture in the small bubble-shaped *vesicles* (sacs) containing **neurotransmitters,** which are chemicals used in neural communication. (Again, see Figure 2.4.) The vesicles quickly spill their contents—about 5000 transmitter molecules each—into the synaptic cleft (Kandel & Squire, 2000). There, the transmitter molecules diffuse across the gap. If they have the right shape (that is, a shape that complements that of special *receptors* in the membrane of the target cell), the neurotransmitters fit into the receptors, like a key fitting into a lock. This lock-and-key process stimulates the receiving neuron and carries the message forward.

After the transmitter molecules have done their work, they are broken down by other chemicals and recycled back to the terminal buttons, where they are reassembled and reused. In addition, many of the transmitter molecules get recycled before docking at a receptor site. Through a process called *reuptake*, these transmitters are intercepted as they are floating within the synapse and drawn back intact into vesicles. Reuptake, then, has the effect of "turning the volume down" on the message being transmitted between neurons. When we later discuss drug therapy for mental disorders (in Chapter 13), reuptake will be an important term because some important drugs—such as the well-known Prozac—interfere with the reuptake process.

Neuroscientists have identified dozens of different neurotransmitters. Table 2.1 distinguishes several that have proved especially important in psychological functioning. Imbalances in these neurotransmitters are also thought to underlie certain disorders, such as schizophrenia and Alzheimer's disease, as well as poisoning by black widow spider venom and botulism toxin. It shouldn't surprise us, then, that many drugs used to treat mental disorders employ chemicals that act like neurotransmitters or otherwise affect the action of neurotransmitters on nerve cells. Likewise, drugs of abuse (heroin, cocaine, methamphetamine, for example) either mimic, enhance, or inhibit our brains' natural neurotransmitters. We will talk more about neurotransmitters and their relation to drug action in the "Psychology in Your Life" section, coming up.

Plasticity   Neurons have the ability to send messages that produce simple reflexes, as when you automatically withdraw your hand from a painfully hot plate. But neurons also have the ability to *change*—to make new connections or to strengthen old ones. This is a hugely important process known as **plasticity.** It means that the nervous system, and especially the brain, has the ability to adapt or modify itself as the result of experience (M. Holloway, 2003; Kandel & Squire, 2000). Earlier we discussed one form of plasticity that involves the changes within dendrites that are associated with learning. Another form involves making new connections among neurons—as when neurons sprout new dendrites, for example. This process is also believed to be associated with learning. Plasticity may also account for the brain's ability to compensate for injury, as in a stroke or head trauma—a controversial concept (Pinel, 2003). In all these ways, then, plasticity is a property that allows the brain to be restructured and "reprogrammed" by experience.

Here is a more subtle point: Because of its neural plasticity, the physical structure of the brain can be changed by its interactions with the outside world (Barinaga, 1996; LeDoux, 2002; Singer, 1995). For example, as a violin player gains expertise, the motor area linked to the fingers of the left hand becomes larger (Juliano, 1998). Increased brain area also develops for the index finger used by a blind reader who learns to use Braille (Elbert et al., 1995; LeDoux, 1996). Usually these changes are beneficial. Occasionally, however, intensely traumatic experiences can also alter the brain's emotional responsiveness in detrimental ways (Arnsten, 1998; Caldwell, 1995; Mukerjee, 1995). Thus, the

■ **Neurotransmitters** Chemical messengers that relay neural messages across the synapse. Many neurotransmitters are also hormones.
■ **Plasticity** The nervous system's ability to adapt or change as the result of experience. Plasticity may also help the nervous system adapt to physical damage.

TABLE 2.1	Seven Important Neurotransmitters		
Neurotransmitter	Normal function	Problems associated with imbalance	Substances that affect the action of this neurotransmitter
Dopamine	Produces sensations of pleasure and reward Used by CNS neurons involved in voluntary movement	Schizophrenia Parkinson's disease	Cocaine Amphetamine Methylphenidate (Ritalin) Alcohol
Serotonin	Regulates sleep and dreaming, mood, pain, aggression, appetite, and sexual behavior	Depression Certain anxiety disorders Obsessive–compulsive disorder	Fluoxetine (Prozac) Hallucinogenics (e.g., LSD)
Norepinephrine	Used by neurons in autonomic nervous system and by neurons in almost every region of the brain Controls heart rate, sleep, stress, sexual responsiveness, vigilance, and appetite	High blood pressure Depression	Tricyclic antidepressants Beta-blockers
Acetylcholine	The primary neurotransmitter used by efferent neurons carrying messages from the CNS Also involved in some kinds of learning and memory	Certain muscular disorders Alzheimer's disease	Nicotine Black widow spider venom Botulism toxin Curare Atropine
GABA	The most prevalent inhibitory neurotransmitter in neurons of the CNS	Anxiety Epilepsy	Barbiturates "Minor" tranquilizers (e.g., Valium, Librium) Alcohol
Glutamate	The primary excitatory neurotransmitter in the CNS Involved in learning and memory	Release of excessive glutamate apparently causes brain damage after stroke	PCP ("angel dust")
Endorphins	Pleasurable sensations and control of pain	Lowered levels resulting from opiate addiction	Opiates: opium, heroin, morphine, methadone

brain cells of soldiers who experience combat or people who have been sexually assaulted may undergo physical changes that can produce a permanent hair-trigger responsiveness. This can cause them overreact to mild stressors and even to merely unexpected surprises. Taken together, such findings indicate that neural plasticity can produce changes both in the brain's function and in its physical structure in response to experience (Sapolsky, 1990).

Glial Cells: A Support Group for Neurons   Interwoven among the brain's vast network of neurons is an even greater number of *glial cells* that were once thought to "glue" the neurons together. (The name comes from the Greek word for "glue.") In fact, glial cells do provide structural support for neurons, as well as help in forming new synapses (Gallo & Chittajallu, 2001). New evidence suggests that they may also be a crucial part of the process we call *learning* (Fields, 2004). In addition, the multitalented **glial cells** form a *myelin sheath*, a fatty insulation around many axons in the brain and spinal cord. Like the covering on an electrical cable, the myelin sheath insulates and protects the cell and helps speed the conduction of impulses along the axon (see Figure 2.4). Unfortunately, certain diseases, such as multiple sclerosis (MS), attack the myelin sheath, especially in the motor pathways. The result is poor conduction of nerve impulses, which accounts for the increasing difficulty MS patients have in controlling movement.

CONNECTION: CHAPTER 10

Extremely threatening experiences can cause posttraumatic stress disorder, which can produce physical changes in the brain.

■ **Glial cells**   Cells that bind the neurons together. Glial cells also provide an insulating covering (the myelin sheath) of the axon for some neurons, which facilitates the electrical impulse.

So there you have the two main building blocks of the nervous system: neurons, with their amazing plasticity, and their supportive glial cells, which protect the neurons and help to propagate neural messages. But, wondrous as these individual components are, we should point out that, in the big picture of behavior and mental processes, a single cell doesn't do very much. It takes thousands upon millions of neurons flashing their electrochemical signals in synchronized waves back and forth through the incredibly complex neural networks in your brain to produce thoughts, sensations, and feelings. Similarly, all your actions arise from waves of nerve impulses delivered to your muscles, glands, and organs through the nervous system. Yet, as we will see in the next "Psychology in Your Life" section, the effects of psychoactive drugs, such as tranquilizers, antidepressants, and painkillers, rely on altering the chemistry underlying these waves at the level of individual cells and their synapses (Deadwyler & Hampson, 1995; Ferster & Spruston, 1995). For the moment, however, let's turn our attention to the neural networks themselves—networks which, together, make up the *nervous system.*

Divisions of the Nervous System

If you could observe a neural message as it moves from stimulus to response, you would see the signal make a seamless transition from one part of the nervous system to another. It might begin, for example, as a signal in the eyes, then travel to the brain for extensive processing, and finally reemerge from the brain as a message instructing the muscles to respond. In fact, the **nervous system,** made up of all the nerve cells in the body, functions as a single, complex, and interconnected unit. Nevertheless, we find it convenient to distinguish among divisions of the nervous system, based on their location and on the type of processing they do. The most basic distinction recognizes two major divisions: the *central nervous system* and the *peripheral nervous system.* (See Figure 2.5.)

■ **Nervous system** The entire network of neurons in the body, including the central nervous system, the peripheral nervous system, and their subdivisions.

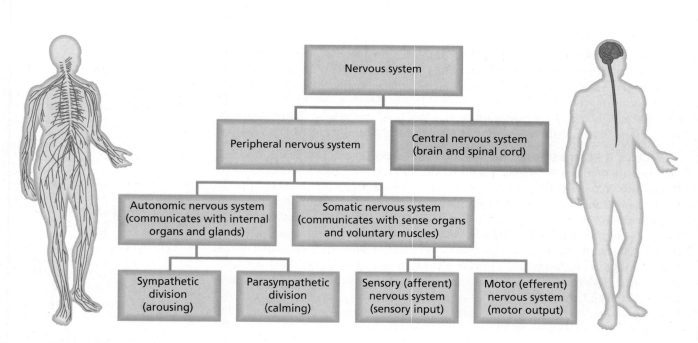

● **FIGURE 2.5** Organization of the Nervous System

This figure shows the major divisions of the nervous system. (Note: It does *not* show the flow of information in the nervous system!)

The Central Nervous System Comprised of the *brain* and *spinal cord,* the **central nervous system** (CNS) serves as the body's "command central." The brain, filling roughly a third of the skull, makes complex decisions, coordinates our body functions, and initiates our behaviors. The spinal cord, playing a supportive role, serves as a sort of neural cable, connecting the brain with parts of the peripheral nervous system extending into the trunk and limbs. (The nerve pathways connecting the brain with the eyes, ears, nose, tongue, skin and muscles of the head, and internal organs do not pass through the spinal cord.)

The spinal cord has another job, too. It takes charge of simple, swift **reflexes** that do not require brain power, such as the knee-jerk reflex your physician elicits with a tap on the knee. We know that the brain does not get involved in these simple reflexes, because a person whose spinal cord has been severed may still be able to withdraw a limb reflexively from a painful stimulus—even though the brain doesn't sense the pain. The brain is required, however, for *voluntary* movements. That's why damage to the nerves of the spinal cord can produce paralysis of the limbs or trunk. As you might expect, the extent of paralysis depends on the location of the damage. In general, the higher the site of damage, the greater the extent of the paralysis. This fact helps explain why an injury high in the spinal cord paralyzed the late actor Christopher Reeve from his neck down.

The Peripheral Nervous System The **peripheral nervous system** (PNS) also plays a supportive role, connecting the central nervous system with the rest of the body through bundles of sensory and motor axons, called *nerves.* Its many branches carry messages between the brain and the sense organs, the internal organs, and the muscles. In this role, the peripheral nervous system carries the incoming messages that tell your brain about the sights, sounds, tastes, smells, and textures of the world. Likewise, it carries the outgoing signals that tell your body's muscles and glands how to respond.

You might think of the PNS, therefore, as operating a pick-up-and-delivery service for the central nervous system. If, for example, an aggressive dog approaches you, your PNS picks up the auditory information (barking, growling, snarling) and visual information (bared teeth, hair standing up on the neck) and delivers it to the brain. Quickly, brain circuits assess the situation (Danger!) and communicate with other circuits that give orders for a hasty retreat. The PNS then delivers those orders to mobilize your heart, lungs, legs, and other body parts needed in response to the emergency. It does this through its two major divisions: the *somatic nervous system* and the *autonomic nervous system.* One deals with our external world, the other with our internal responses. (A few moments spent studying Figure 2.5 will help you understand these divisions and subdivisions.)

The Somatic Division of the PNS Think of the **somatic nervous system** as the brain's communications link with the outside world. Its sensory component connects the sense organs to the brain, and its motor component links the CNS with the body's skeletal muscles, the muscles that control voluntary movements. (We met these two divisions earlier in our discussion of sensory and motor neurons.) So, for example, when you see a slice of pizza, the visual image is carried by the somatic division's *afferent* system. Then, if all goes well, the *efferent* system sends instructions to muscles that propel the slice of pizza in just the right direction, into your open mouth.

The Autonomic Division of the PNS The other major division of the PNS takes charge of the pizza once it heads down your throat. It is now in the province of the **autonomic nervous system** (*autonomic* means self-regulating or independent). This network carries signals that control our internal organs to perform

■ **Central nervous system** The brain and the spinal cord.
■ **Reflex** A simple, unlearned response triggered by stimuli—such as the knee-jerk reflex set off by tapping the tendon just below your kneecap.
■ **Peripheral nervous system** All parts of the nervous system lying outside the central nervous system. The peripheral nervous system includes the autonomic and somatic nervous systems.
■ **Somatic nervous system** A division of the peripheral nervous system that carries sensory information to the central nervous system and also sends voluntary messages to the body's skeletal muscles.
■ **Autonomic nervous system** The portion of the peripheral nervous system that sends communications between the central nervous system and the internal organs and glands.

such jobs as regulating digestion, respiration, heart rate, and arousal. Amazingly, it does so without our having to think about it—all unconsciously. The autonomic system also works when you are asleep. Even during anesthesia, it can sustain the most basic vital functions.

And—wouldn't you know?—biopsychologists further divide the autonomic nervous system into two major parts: the *sympathetic* and *parasympathetic divisions* (as shown in Figure 2.6). The **sympathetic division** arouses the heart, lungs, and other organs in stressful or emergency situations, when our responses must be quick and powerfully energized. Often called the "fight-or-flight" system, the sympathetic division carries messages that help us respond quickly to a threat either by attacking or fleeing. The sympathetic system also creates the tension and arousal you feel during an exciting movie, a first date, or an oral presentation. Perhaps you can bring to mind what the sympathetic division of your autonomic nervous system was doing during your last public-speaking effort. Was it hard to breathe? Were your palms sweaty? Did your stomach feel queasy?

In contrast, the **parasympathetic division** applies the neural brakes, returning our internal responses to a calm and collected state. But even though it has an opposing action, the parasympathetic division works cooperatively with the sympathetic system, like two children on a teeter-totter. Figure 2.6 shows the most important connections made by these two autonomic divisions.

■ **Sympathetic division**   The part of the autonomic nervous system that sends messages to internal organs and glands that help us respond to stressful and emergency situations.

■ **Parasympathetic division**
The part of the autonomic nervous system that monitors the routine operations of the internal organs and returns the body to calmer functioning after arousal by the sympathetic division.

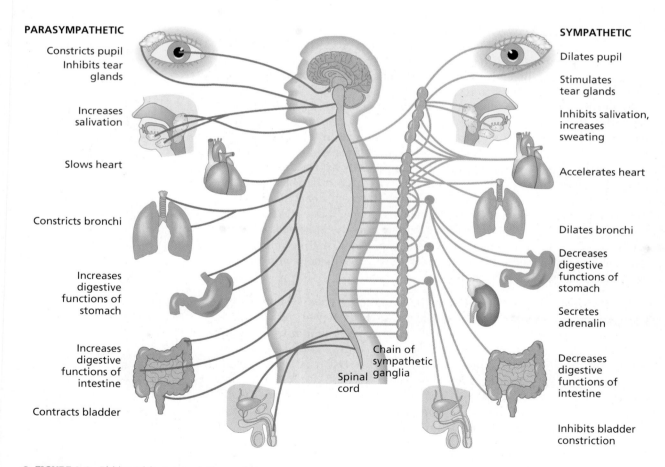

PARASYMPATHETIC

Constricts pupil
Inhibits tear glands

Increases salivation

Slows heart

Constricts bronchi

Increases digestive functions of stomach

Increases digestive functions of intestine

Contracts bladder

SYMPATHETIC

Dilates pupil

Stimulates tear glands

Inhibits salivation, increases sweating

Accelerates heart

Dilates bronchi

Decreases digestive functions of stomach

Secretes adrenalin

Decreases digestive functions of intestine

Inhibits bladder constriction

Chain of sympathetic ganglia
Spinal cord

● **FIGURE 2.6**   Divisions of the Autonomic Nervous System

The *parasympathetic nervous system* (at left) regulates day-to-day internal processes and behavior. The *sympathetic nervous system* (at right) regulates internal processes and behavior in stressful situations. On their way to and from the spinal cord, sympathetic nerve fibers make connections with specialized neural clusters called *ganglia*.

Now, having completed our whirlwind tour of the nervous system, we return our attention briefly to its partner in internal communication, the *endocrine system*. Again, we will remind you that this system makes use of many of the same chemicals employed in neural communication. In the nervous system we called them *neurotransmitters,* but when we find these chemicals at work in the endocrine system, we call them *hormones.*

The Endocrine System

Consider this little-known fact: Your bloodstream carries *information,* along with oxygen and nutrients. It does so by serving as the communication pathway for the **endocrine system,** shown in Figure 2.7. The glands comprising the endocrine system (which takes its name from the Greek *endo* for "within" and *krinein* for "secrete") transmit information by releasing **hormones** into the bloodstream. Much like neurotransmitters in the nervous system, hormones are chemical messengers that influence not only body functions but behaviors and emotions (Damasio, 2003; LeDoux, 2002). For example, hormones from the pituitary stimulate body growth. Hormones from the ovaries and testes influence sexual development and sexual responses. Hormones from the adrenals produce the arousal accompanying fear. And hormones from the thyroid control metabolism (the body's rate of energy use). Once secreted into the blood,

■ **Endocrine system** The hormone system—the body's chemical messenger system, including the endocrine glands: pituitary, thyroid, parathyroid, adrenals, pancreas, ovaries, and testes.

■ **Hormone** A chemical messenger used by the endocrine system. Many hormones also serve as neurotransmitters.

Thyroids and parathyroids

Adrenals

Pancreas

Ovaries

Testes

Pituitary

● **FIGURE 2.7** Endocrine Glands in Females and Males

The pituitary gland (shown at right) is the "master gland," regulating the endocrine glands, whose locations are illustrated at left. The pituitary gland is under the control of the hypothalamus, an important structure in the limbic system.

TABLE 2.2	Hormonal Functions of Major Endocrine Glands
These Endocrine Glands . . .	Produce Hormones That Regulate . . .
Anterior pituitary	Ovaries and testes Breast milk production Metabolism Reactions to stress
Posterior pituitary	Conservation of water in the body Breast milk secretion Uterus contractions
Thyroid	Metabolism Physical growth and development
Parathyroid	Calcium levels in the body
Pancreas	Glucose (sugar) metabolism
Adrenal glands	Fight-or-flight response Metabolism Sexual desire (especially in women)
Ovaries	Development of female sexual characteristics Production of ova (eggs)
Testes	Development of male sexual characteristics Sperm production Sexual desire (in men)

hormones circulate throughout the body until delivered to their target muscles, glands, and organs. Table 2.2 outlines the major endocrine glands and the body systems they regulate.

Under normal (unaroused) conditions, the endocrine system works in parallel with the parasympathetic nervous system to sustain our basic body processes. But in a crisis, the endocrine system shifts into a new mode, supporting the actions of the sympathetic nervous system. So, when you encounter a stressor or an emergency (such as the speeding car headed at you), the hormone *epinephrine* (sometimes called *adrenalin*) is released into the bloodstream, sustaining the body's defensive reaction that we called "fight or flight." In this way, the endocrine system finishes what your sympathetic nervous system started, by keeping your heart pounding and your muscles tense, ready for action.

Later in the book we will see what happens when this stress state persists too long. For example, people who have stressful jobs or unhappy relationships may develop a chronically elevated level of stress hormones in their blood, keeping them in a state of perpetual arousal. But the price of continued arousal is dear. The body may not withstand such long-term stress without suffering some physical consequences.

CONNECTION: CHAPTER 10

Prolonged stress messages can produce physical and mental disorders by means of the *general adaptation syndrome*.

At the base of your brain, a "master gland," called the **pituitary gland,** attempts to keep all these endocrine responses under tight control. (See Figure 2.7.) It does so by sending out hormone signals of its own through the blood. But the pituitary itself is really only a midlevel manager. It takes orders, in turn, from the brain—in particular from a small neural nucleus to which it is physically appended: the *hypothalamus*. We will have more to say about this important brain structure in a moment.

For now, we want to emphasize the idea that the peripheral nervous system and the endocrine system provide parallel means of communication, coordinated by their link in the brain. Ultimately, the brain decides which messages will be sent through both networks. We will turn our attention to this

■ **Pituitary gland** The "master gland" that produces hormones influencing the secretions of all other endocrine glands, as well as a hormone that influences growth. The pituitary is attached to the brain's hypothalamus, from which it takes its orders.

master "nerve center"—the brain—right after exploring, in "Psychology in Your Life," how the concepts you have just learned about can explain the effects of psychoactive drugs.

 ## PSYCHOLOGY IN YOUR LIFE: HOW PSYCHOACTIVE DRUGS AFFECT THE NERVOUS SYSTEM

The mind-altering effects of marijuana, LSD, cocaine, narcotics, tranquilizers, and sedatives entice millions of users. Millions more jolt their brains awake with the caffeine of their morning coffee, tea, or cola and the nicotine in an accompanying cigarette. Then at night they may reverse the cycle with alcohol and sleeping pills. But how do these substances achieve their effects? The answer to that question involves the ability of *psychoactive drugs* to enhance or inhibit natural chemical processes in our neural circuits.

The ecstasy and the agony of these drugs come mainly from their effects on brain synapses. Some drugs impersonate neurotransmitters by mimicking their effects in the brain. Others act less directly by enhancing or dampening the effects of neurotransmitters. We call those that enhance or mimic neurotransmitters **agonists.** Nicotine, for example, is an agonist because it acts like the neurotransmitter acetylcholine. This has the effect of "turning up the volume" in the acetylcholine pathways (the acetylcholine-using bundles innervating the muscles and connecting certain parts of the brain). By contrast, we call chemicals that dampen or inhibit the effects of neurotransmitters **antagonists.** Curare and botulism toxin are antagonists because they interfere with the neurotransmitter acetylcholine—effectively "turning the volume down." In general, agonists facilitate and antagonists inhibit messages in parts of the nervous system using that transmitter.

The well-known antidepressant Prozac (fluoxetine) does its work as an agonist in the brain's serotonin pathways, where it makes more serotonin available (see Figure 2.8). But, because serotonin's effects are complex, fluoxetine can cause not only changes in mood but, occasionally, undesirable changes in sleep patterns, appetite, and thinking (*Physician's Desk Reference*, 2004).

■ **Agonist** Drug or other chemical that enhances or mimics the effects of neurotransmitters.

■ **Antagonist** Drug or other chemical that inhibits the effects of neurotransmitters.

● **FIGURE 2.8** Serotonin Pathways in the Brain

Each neurotransmitter is associated with certain neural pathways in the brain. In this cross section of the brain you see the main pathways for serotonin. Drugs that stimulate or inhibit serotonin will selectively affect the brain regions shown in this diagram.

■ Neural pathway Bundle of nerve cells that follow generally the same route and employ the same neurotransmitter.

Why the unwanted side effects? The answer to that question involves an important principle about the brain's design. Within the brain are many bundles of neurons—**neural pathways**—that connect different components of the brain. Moreover, each pathway employs only certain neurotransmitters. This fact allows a drug affecting a particular transmitter to target specific parts of the brain. Unfortunately for the drug-takers, different pathways may employ the same neurotransmitter for widely different functions. Thus, serotonin pathways, for example, affect not only mood but sleep, appetite, and cognition. So, taking Prozac (or one of its chemical cousins with other brand names) may treat depression but, at the same time, have side effects on other psychological processes—which explains why the drug ads must list the major possible side effects.

In fact, no psychoactive drug exists that acts like a "magic bullet" that can strike only one precise target in the brain, to work its wonders without causing collateral effects.

CHECK YOUR UNDERSTANDING

1. **RECALL:** Of the body's two main communication systems, the _____ is faster, while the _____ sends longer-lasting messages.

2. **RECALL:** The _____ division of the autonomic nervous system increases the heart rate during an emergency, while the _____ division slows the heart rate after an emergency is over.

3. **RECALL:** Which of the following might carry a neural impulse across the synapse?
   a. an electrical charge
   b. dopamine
   c. the blood
   d. the cerebrospinal fluid

4. **RECALL:** Which part of the brain communicates directly with the "master gland" of the endocrine system?
   a. the cortex
   b. the brain stem
   c. the cerebellum
   d. the hypothalamus

5. **RECALL:** Make a sketch of two connecting neurons. Describe the location and function of the dendrites, soma, axon, myelin sheath, terminal buttons, synapse.

6. **APPLICATION:** Some people seem to have high blood pressure because they have an anxiety response while having their blood pressure taken at the doctor's office. Which part of the nervous system produces this anxiety response?
   a. the somatic nervous system
   b. the sympathetic nervous system
   c. the parasympathetic nervous system
   d. the spinal cord

7. **UNDERSTANDING THE CORE CONCEPT:** The chemical messengers in the brain are called _____, while in the endocrine system they are called _____.

ANSWERS: 1. nervous system/endocrine system 2. sympathetic/parasympathetic 3. b 4. d 5. See Figure 2.4 6. b 7. neurotransmitters/hormones

HOW DOES THE BRAIN PRODUCE BEHAVIOR AND MENTAL PROCESSES?

KEY QUESTION

In September 1848, a 25-year-old American railroad worker named Phineas Gage sustained a horrible head injury when a charge of blasting powder drove an iron rod into his face, up through the front of his brain, and out through the top of his head. (See accompanying photo.) Amazingly, he recovered from this injury and lived another 12 years—but as a psychologically changed man (Fleischman, 2002; Macmillan, 2000). Those who knew him remarked that Gage, once a dependable and likeable crew boss, had become an irresponsible and rowdy ruffian. In essence, he was no longer himself. "Gage was no longer Gage" (Damasio, 1994, p. 8). We cannot help but wonder: Had the site of Gage's injury—the front of his brain—been the home of his "old self"?

Phineas Gage's accident also raises another question: What is the connection between mind and body? Humans have, of course, long recognized the existence of such a link—although they didn't always know the brain to be the organ of the mind. Even today we might speak, as they did in Shakespeare's time, of "giving one's heart" to another or of "not having the stomach" for something when describing disgust. Today we know that love doesn't flow from the heart, nor courage from the digestive system. We now know that emotions, desires, and thoughts originate in the brain. (The news hasn't reached songwriters, who have yet to pen a lyric proclaiming, "I love you with all my brain.") At last, neuroscientists are unraveling the mysteries of this complex organ, revealing it—perhaps a little less romantically than the songwriters do—as a collection of distinct modules that work together like the components of a computer. This new understanding of the brain becomes the Core Concept for this final section of the chapter:

● Author Phil Zimbardo (left) with the skull of Phineas Gage.

The brain is composed of many specialized modules that work together to create mind and behavior.

As you study the brain in the following pages, you will find that the brain's modular components have specialized functions (Cohen & Tong, 2001). Some take responsibility for sensations, such as vision and hearing. Some have a part in regulating our emotional lives. Some contribute to memory. Some generate speech and other behaviors. This is the point: The specialized parts of the brain, like an efficient committee, usually manage to work together. Fortunately, from the perspective of a brain owner, many of these brain modules do so automatically and without conscious direction, as when an infant "knows" to look at a person's eyes. But, when something goes wrong with one or more of the brain's components, as in a stroke or Alzheimer's disease—or as happened to Phineas Gage—the biological basis of thought or behavior captures our attention.

Let's begin the story of the brain by seeing how neuroscientists go about opening their windows on its inner workings. As you will see, much of what we know about the brain's inner workings comes from observations of people with brain disease and head injuries—people like Gage.

Windows on the Brain

The brain can never actually touch velvet, taste chocolate, have sex, or see the blue of the sky. It only knows the outside world secondhand, through changing patterns of electrochemical activity in the peripheral nervous system, the neural network that shuttles messages in and out. The brain, the undisputed master of the body and seat of our personality, has no power to act on its own. To do its bidding, the brain must rely on the neural and endocrine communications networks that carry its messages to the muscles, organs, and glands throughout the body.

And what would you see if you could peer beneath the bony skull and behold the brain? The wrinkled appearance of its surface, rather like a giant walnut, offers no hint of the brain's internal structure or function. For that, we need the *EEG, CT scans,* and *MRIs.*

Sensing Brain Waves with the EEG   Neuroscientists have learned a great deal about the brain by studying its electrical activity. Using a sensitive device called the **electroencephalograph** (or **EEG**), they can—without opening the skull—record the extremely weak voltage patterns called *brain waves*, sensed by electrodes pasted on the scalp. Much as the lights can tell you which parts of a city are most "alive" at night, the EEG senses which parts of the brain are most active. It can identify, for example, electrical patterns involved in moving the hand or processing a visual image. The EEG can also reveal abnormal waves caused by brain malfunctions, such as occurs in *epilepsy* (a seizure disorder that arises from an electrical "storm" in the brain).

That said, however, the EEG is not a very precise instrument. Within the limits of its sensitivity, it indiscriminately records the brain's electrical activity in the region of the electrode. And because there may be fewer than a dozen electrodes used, the electrical picture of the brain is not detailed. Moreover, the EEG electrodes sample not only the "flash" discharges of the action potential, they also sense other, more subtle electrical charges, such as those in the soma. The result is a coarse, moment-to-moment summary of the electrical activity in millions and millions of neurons lying near the surface of the brain—making it all the more amazing that we can sometimes read the traces of mental processes in the EEG signature, as we will see in more detail in the next chapter.

Mapping the Brain with Electric Probes   Half a century ago, the great Canadian neurologist Wilder Penfield opened another window on the brain by "mapping" its pinkish-gray surface with a pen-shaped electric probe. During brain surgery, Penfield stimulated patients' exposed brains with an electrode (a thin wire that conducts a mild electric current, on the order of a flashlight battery) and recorded their responses. (His patients were kept awake, but under local anesthesia, so they felt no pain.)

This was not just an experiment. As a surgeon, Penfield needed to identify the exact boundaries of the diseased brain areas, to avoid removing healthy tissue. But, as he did so, Penfield was able to demonstrate that the brain's surface is divided into distinct regions, each with different functions. Stimulating a certain spot might cause the left hand to move; another site might produce a sensation, such as a flash of light. Stimulating still other sites might provoke a memory from childhood (Penfield, 1959; Penfield & Baldwin, 1952). Later, other scientists followed Penfield's lead and probed structures deeper in the brain. There they found that electrical stimulation could set off elaborate sequences of behavior and emotions. The overall conclusion from such work is unmistakable: Each region of the brain has its own specific functions.

Computerized Brain Scans   Advances in brain science during the last couple of decades have opened new windows on the brain by employing sophisticated procedures collectively known as *brain scans*. Some make images with X rays, others use radioactive tracers, and still others use magnetic fields (Pinel, 2003). Thanks to such scanning methods, scientists can now make vivid pictures of brain tissue without opening the skull and physically invading the brain. Medically, these methods also help neurosurgeons locate brain abnormalities such as tumors or stroke-related damage. Psychologically, the images they obtain from brain scans can show where our thoughts and feelings are processed because specific regions of the brain seem to "light up" when a person reads, speaks, solves problems, or feels certain emotions (Raichle, 1994).

The most common brain-scanning methods currently used are CT scanning, PET scanning, and MRI (Barinaga, 1997a; Mogilner et al., 1993):

■ **Electroencephalograph** or **EEG**
A device for recording brain waves, typically by electrodes placed on the scalp. The record produced is known as an electroencephalogram (also called an EEG).

- **CT scanning,** or **computerized tomography,** creates a computerized image of the brain from X rays passed through the brain at various angles. Tomography (from the Greek *tomos,* "section") detects the soft-tissue structures of the brain that X rays normally do not reveal (see Figure 2.9). CT scanning creates a static image of brain structure.

- **PET scanning,** or **positron emission tomography,** produces an image showing brain activity (rather than brain structure). One common PET technique does so by sensing the concentration of low-level radioactive glucose (sugar), which concentrates in the most active brain circuits. Areas of high concentration show up as brightly colored on the image.

- **MRI,** or **magnetic resonance imaging,** makes highly detailed pictures from tissue responses to powerful pulses of magnetic energy. (Another example of an MRI image can be seen in Figure 2.1, at the beginning of the chapter.) While standard MRI images show brain structure, a newer technique called *functional magnetic resonance imaging (fMRI)* can distinguish more active brain cells from less active ones (Alper, 1993; Collins, 2001). Thus, fMRI allows neuroscientists to determine which parts of the brain are most active during various mental activities. The fMRI technique also produces more detailed images than does PET, as you can see in Figure 2.9.

Each scanning method has its particular strengths and weaknesses. For example, PET is good at tracking the brain's activity, but not as good as MRI for distinguishing the fine details of brain structure. But neither PET nor MRI work well in studying processes that occur at rates faster than a few seconds, such as a startle response. To capture such short-lived "conversations" among brain cells requires the EEG—which, unfortunately, is limited in its detail (Raichle, 1994). Currently, no single scanning technique gives biopsychologists a perfectly clear "window" on the brain.

Three Layers of the Brain

What is seen through these windows on the brain depends, of course, on what brain one is examining. Birds and reptiles manage to make a living with a brain that consists of little more than a stalk that regulates the most basic life processes. Creatures with more complex brains—we humans, for example—have essentially the same stalk, the **brain stem.** From an evolutionary perspective, then, this is the part of the brain with the longest ancestry. On top of that stalk, we and our mammalian cousins have evolved two more layers, known as the *limbic system* and the *cerebrum.* (See Figure 2.10)

So, where in the brain do we really live? Is there a module that houses the "self," the real *you*? That question has no easy answer. There are certain parts of the brain stem that you couldn't do without—modules that govern your most vital functions, such as heart rate, breathing, and blood pressure. If something goes radically wrong here, the *you* could vanish. Yet, these are brain-stem functions that are essentially the same as those of any other person, or even a rat or a lizard. For the most part, they operate outside consciousness. Surely, the *you* resides somewhere else.

Perhaps we can find *you* in the brain's middle layer, especially in the limbic system's circuits that generate emotions, memories, and desires. And, although these certainly sound more like the characteristics that make us human, we also should think back to the lesson of Phineas Gage. The iron rod that blasted through his skull and made him a different person didn't touch his brain stem or limbic region. Rather it tore through the parts of the brain's topmost layer, destroying circuits that help us "put it all together"—circuits that combine and integrate our emotions, memories, and desires with thoughts,

● **FIGURE 2.9** Windows on the Mind
Images from brain-scanning devices. From top: PET, MRI, EEG. Each scanning and recording device has its strengths and weaknesses.

■ **CT scanning** or **computerized tomography** A computerized imaging technique that uses X rays passed through the brain at various angles and then combined into an image.
■ **PET scanning** or **positron emission tomography** An imaging technique that relies on the detection of radioactive sugar consumed by active brain cells.
■ **MRI** or **magnetic resonance imaging** An imaging technique that relies on cells' responses in a high-intensity magnetic field.
■ **Brain stem** The most primitive of the brain's three major layers. It includes the medulla, pons, and the reticular formation.

Cerebrum

Cerebral cortex:
(outer layer of cerebrum)
involved in complex
mental processes

Thalamus:
relays sensory
information

Hypothalamus:
manages the body's
internal state

Limbic system:
regulates emotions
and motivated behavior

Hippocampus:
involved in memory

Reticular formation:
controls alertness

Pons:
involved in regulation
of sleep

Cerebellum:
regulates coordinated
movement

Spinal cord:
pathway for neural fibers
traveling to and from brain

Optic tract:
vision

Amygdala:
involved in emotion
and memory

Pituitary gland:
regulates glands
all over body

Brain stem:
sets brain's general alertness
level and warning system

● **FIGURE 2.10**   Major Structures of the Brain
From an evolutionary perspective, the brain stem and cerebellum represent the oldest part of the brain; the limbic system evolved next; and the cerebral cortex is the most recent achievement in brain evolution.

sensations, and perceptions. Is that where you really live? Again, the answer is not simple, but we will pursue it by examining each of these three layers in more detail.

The Brain Stem and Its Neighbors   If you have ever fought to stay awake in class, you have struggled with your brain stem. Most of the time, however, it does its many jobs less obtrusively and less obnoxiously. We can infer one of its jobs from the brain stem's location, linking the spinal cord with the rest of the brain. In this position, the brain stem serves as a conduit for nerve pathways that carry messages traveling up and down the spinal pathway between body and brain. Significantly, these pathways cross as they traverse this region. Therefore, *the crossover of the sensory and motor pathways means that each side of the brain connects to the opposite side of the body.* The left side of the brain controls the right side of the body, and the left side of the body sends sensory signals to the right side of the brain. This is an important idea to remember later, when we try to understand the symptoms seen in brain-injured patients.

Components of the Brain Stem   More than just a go-between, the brain stem also connects several important information-processing regions, four of which we will mention here: the *medulla,* the *pons,* the *reticular formation,* and the *thalamus.* (See Figure 2.11.) From an evolutionary standpoint, they are all ancient structures, which can be found in the brains of creatures as diverse as penguins, pigs, pandas, pythons, porcupines, and people.

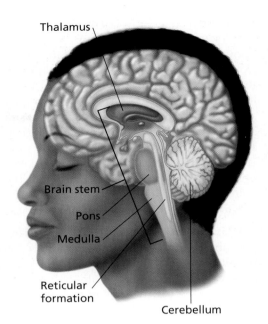

Thalamus

Brain stem

Pons

Medulla

Reticular
formation

Cerebellum

● **FIGURE 2.11** The Brain Stem and
Cerebellum

These structures in the central core of the brain
are primarily involved with basic life processes:
breathing, pulse, arousal, movement, balance,
and early processing of sensory information.

The **medulla,** appearing as a bulge low in the brain stem, regulates basic body functions, including breathing, blood pressure, and heart rate. It operates on "automatic pilot"—without our conscious awareness—to keep our internal organs operating without our having to think about them. An even bigger bulge called the **pons** (the Latin word for *bridge*) appears just above the medulla, where it houses nerve circuits that regulate the sleep and dreaming cycle. True to its name, the pons also acts as a "bridge" that connects the brain stem to the *cerebellum.*

Running through the center of everything, the **reticular formation** consists of a pencil-shaped bundle of nerve cells that forms the brain stem's core. One of the reticular formation's jobs is keeping the brain awake and alert. Others include monitoring the incoming stream of sensory information and directing attention to novel or important messages. It was the reticular formation against which you were struggling when you became drowsy in class.

From the reticular formation, nerve fibers run, like phone lines, in many directions, but especially down to the spinal cord and up to a small pair of football-shaped structures called the **thalamus.** Perched atop the brain stem, the thalamus lies near the geographic center of the brain. It is also central to the brain in another way: Like the central processing chip in a computer, the thalamus directs nearly all the brain's incoming and outgoing sensory and motor traffic. Accordingly, it receives information from all the senses (except smell) and distributes it to appropriate processing circuits throughout the brain. Incoming visual information, for example, enters the thalamus by way of the optic nerve and is then relayed on to the "gray matter" areas at the back of the brain that specialize in visual perception. Likewise, motor functions use routes between the brain's movement-control areas and the thalamus, which distributes instructions to the neural pathways serving muscles in all parts of the body. And, if that were not enough, the thalamus also seems to have a role in focusing attention—which seems appropriate enough for a structure with its connections to almost everything.

The Cerebellum Lying at the back of the brain stem, the **cerebellum** looks very much like a miniature add-on brain (its name literally means "little brain"), as you can see in Figure 2.11. Although seemingly separate—not actually a part

■ **Medulla** A brain-stem structure that controls breathing and heart rate. The sensory and motor pathways connecting the brain to the body cross in the medulla.
■ **Pons** A brain-stem structure that regulates brain activity during sleep and dreaming. The name *pons* derives from the Latin word for "bridge."
■ **Reticular formation** A pencil-shaped structure forming the core of the brain stem. The reticular formation arouses the cortex to keep the brain alert and attentive to new stimulation.
■ **Thalamus** The brain's central "relay station," situated just atop the brain stem. Nearly all the messages going into or out of the brain go through the thalamus.
■ **Cerebellum** The "little brain" attached to the brain stem. The cerebellum is responsible for coordinated movements.

of the brain stem—it works cooperatively with the brain stem and higher brain centers to control those complex movements that we perform without consciously thinking about the details—such as walking, dancing, or drinking from a cup (Spencer et al., 2003; Wickelgren, 1998b). Research also implicates the cerebellum in helping us keep a series of events in order—as we do when listening to the sequence of notes in a melody (Bower & Parsons, 2003). It also gets involved in producing habitual responses on cue—as when you learn to salivate at the sound of the lunch bell (Hazeltine & Ivry, 2002; Raymond et al., 1996; Seidler et al., 2002).

Taken together, the brain stem and cerebellum control the most basic functions of movement and of life itself. Note, again, that much of their work is automatic, functioning largely outside our awareness. The next two layers, however, assert themselves more obviously in consciousness.

The Limbic System: Emotions, Memories, and More   We're sorry about your pet canary or goldfish. Only mammals come equipped with a fully developed **limbic system,** a diverse collection of structures that wrap around the thalamus, vaguely in the shape of a pair of ram's horns. (See Figures 2.10 and 2.12.) Together, these structures give mammals greatly enhanced capacity for emotions and memory. These characteristics, it turns out, offer the huge advantage of mental flexibility—so the organism doesn't have to rely solely on the instincts and reflexes that dominate the behavior of simpler creatures.

This layer not only houses modules that process memories and regulate complex motives and emotions, but it is involved in feelings of pleasure and pain. It is also the limbic system that produces fear, rage, and ecstasy. In general, the limbic system elaborates on the simpler urges arising lower in the brain to make mammalian behavior more complex than the behavior of organisms, like fish or birds, with less complex brains.

Two important limbic structures take their names from their shapes. One, the **hippocampus,** is shaped (vaguely) like a sea horse. Hence, its name—again from Greek. (Actually, there is one hippocampus on each side of the brain, making two *hippocampi.* See Figure 2.12.) The hippocampus's job is to connect your present with your past and to help you remember locations of things in space (Bilkey, 2004; Fyhn et al., 204; Leutgeb et al., 2004). We can best see how this pair of brain structures works by pondering the regrettable case of H. M., a man who lost his hippocampi.

In 1953, when H. M. was in his early 20s, he underwent a radical and experimental brain operation, intended to reduce the frequency of the seizures that threatened his life (Hilts, 1995). The surgery, which removed most of the hippocampus on both sides of H. M.'s brain, was successful in reducing the frequency of his seizures and may have saved his life. But in another sense, it was a total failure: Ever since the operation, new experiences disappear from his memory almost as soon as they happen. Like the legendary Rip Van Winkle, H. M. draws a blank for the intervening years. He continues to believe he is living in 1953. Later in the book, we will see that H. M. has much to teach us about the structure of memory. Suffice it for now to note that his case illustrates that the hippocampus is a vital part of the brain's memory system. (We hope you will remember H. M., when we revisit him a few chapters hence.)

Another limbic structure, the **amygdala,** also takes its name from its shape: *amygdala* (again in Greek) means "almond." (See Figure 2.12.) Its function was first revealed by Heinrich Klüver and Paul Bucy (1939), who suspected that the amygdala had a role in emotion. To test this idea, they surgically snipped the connections to the amygdala on both sides of the brain in rhesus monkeys. After surgery, these normally foul-tempered beasts became docile and easy to handle, a change so dramatic that it surprised even Klüver and Bucy. Many

■ **Limbic system**   The middle layer of the brain, involved in emotion and memory. The limbic system includes the hippocampus, amygdala, hypothalamus, and other structures.
■ **Hippocampus**   A component of the limbic system, involved in establishing long-term memories.
■ **Amygdala**   A limbic system structure involved in memory and emotion, particularly fear and aggression. Pronounced *a-MIG-da-la.*

Fear and apprehension:
Amygdala

Hunger and eating:
Hypothalamus

Learning and memory:
Hippocampus

● **FIGURE 2.12** The Limbic System

The structures of the limbic system are involved with motivation, emotion, and certain memory processes.

studies since then have shown conclusively that the amygdala is involved not only in aggression but in fear—and probably in other emotional responses (Damasio, 2003; LeDoux, 1996; Whalen, 1998). With this in mind, you shouldn't be surprised to hear that the amygdala also seems to have a role in helping us remember emotionally charged events, such as the September 11 attacks or the explosions of the space shuttles *Columbia* and *Challenger*.

The limbic system also contains several "pleasure centers" that give us the good feelings accompanying eating, sex, and other rewarding activities (Olds & Fobes, 1981; Pinel, 2003). On the street, drugs like cocaine, methamphetamine, and heroin generate wild rushes of pleasure and stimulate limbic "pleasure centers," which all seem to involve the neurotransmitter dopamine. But you don't have to take drugs or undergo brain surgery to stimulate the limbic system. The stimulation of food, drink, or sex will indirectly activate limbic pathways, too (Carlson, 2004), as will exciting activities, such as riding a roller-coaster. Studies also show that the rewarding effects from a dose of rich chocolate stimulate the same brain circuits (Small, 2001).

In the laboratory, studies have shown that rats seem to like mild stimulation in these regions. They like it very much, indeed. In fact, if left on their own to press a lever that delivers a mild electric current to one of these sites, they may stimulate themselves up to 10,000 time an hour! Rats will also pay a high price to get this pleasurable stimulation, including crossing a grid that gives painful shocks to their feet, to reach a lever that can send the obviously pleasurable stimulation to their brains. In a few cases, humans too have been given stimulation in the "pleasure centers" (for medical reasons during brain surgery). And what do they say it feels like? The feeling depends on which "pleasure center" is being stimulated, but the sensation at some locations has been likened to an orgasm. Happily, people who have had this experience do not become so obsessed by it as do rats (Valenstein, 1973).

We have already met another limbic structure, the **hypothalamus,** that has many tasks to perform. Rich with blood vessels, as well as with neurons, it primarily serves as your brain's blood-analysis laboratory. By constantly monitoring the blood, it detects small changes in body temperature, fluid levels, and nutrients. When it detects an imbalance (too much or too little water, for example), the hypothalamus immediately responds with orders that regulate appetite, thirst, and body temperature control, among other responses. Because of these functions, the hypothalamus has a major role in motivation.

The hypothalamus makes its influence felt in other ways, as well. It sends neural messages to "higher" processing areas in the brain—making us aware of the needs it senses (hunger, for example). It also exerts its control through the pituitary gland, the body's master gland, which lies attached to the underside of the hypothalamus. As we saw earlier, the hypothalamus links the nervous system with the endocrine system. Thus, messages from the hypothalamus may tell the pituitary gland (the C.E.O. of the endocrine system) to release certain hormones, which then flow through the bloodstream to regulate such responses as heart rate, blushing, sweating, and goose pimples.

Does the hypothalamus have any role in our emotions? It hosts some of the brain's reward circuits, or "pleasure centers," which generate the feeling-good emotions associated with gratifying the hunger, thirst, and sex drives. A second link with emotion involves the hypothalamus's job of regulating the body's responses during emotional arousal. It does so by sending messages to the internal organs via the autonomic nervous system and, as we have noted, to the pituitary gland. In turn, the pituitary regulates the endocrine (hormone) response to emotional arousal and stress.

The Cerebral Cortex: The Brain's Thinking Cap
When you look at a whole human brain, you mostly see the bulging *cerebral hemispheres*—a little bigger than your two fists held together. The nearly symmetrical hemispheres form a thick cap that hides most of the limbic system and the brain's central core. Its thin outer layer forms the **cerebral cortex** (cortex comes from Latin for "bark" or "shell"), with its distinctive wrinkled appearance. The seat of our most awesome mental powers, the cortex and its supporting structures account for two-thirds of the brain's total mass. Flattened out, the cortical surface would cover an area roughly the size of a newspaper page, but the wrinkling and folding enable its billions of cells to squeeze into the tight quarters inside your skull. As a result, only about a third of the cortex is visible on the brain's surface.

Although we humans take pride in our large brains, it turns out that ours are not the largest. All large animals have large brains—a fact more closely related to body size than to intelligence (Pinel, 2003). Nor is the wrinkled cortex a distinctively human trait. Again all large animals have highly convoluted cortexes. We do have more massive cortexes for our body weight than do other big-brained creatures (Carlson, 2004). Yet, human uniqueness lies more in the

CONNECTION: CHAPTER 9

The hypothalamus contains important control circuits for the basic *motives* and *drives*.

● The cerebral hemispheres of the human brain.

■ **Hypothalamus**   A limbic structure that serves as the brain's blood-testing laboratory, constantly monitoring the blood to determine the condition of the body.

■ **Cerebral cortex**   The thin gray-matter covering of the cerebral hemispheres, consisting of a ¼-inch layer dense with cell bodies of neurons. The cerebral cortex carries on the major portion of our "higher" mental processing, including thinking and perceiving.

function of our brains, rather than their size. Although no one is sure exactly how or why our species evolved such a large cortex (Buss, 2004), we know that it hosts an amazing array of abilities.

Lobes of the Cerebral Cortex

In the late 1700s, the famous Austrian physician Franz Joseph Gall threw his considerable scientific weight behind the idea that specific regions of the brain control specific mental faculties, such as hearing, speech, movement, vision, and memory. Unfortunately, he carried this otherwise sensible idea to muddle-headed extremes. In his theory of *phrenology*, Gall claimed that the brain had specific regions devoted to such traits as spirituality, hope, benevolence, friendship, destructiveness, and cautiousness. Moreover, he asserted that these traits could be detected as bumps on the skull.

These ideas captured the public's attention and became enormously popular, even though Gall was mostly wrong about the details of his theory. But he was absolutely right on one small but important point—which is the reason we mention phrenology in this book: his doctrine of *localization of function*, which stated that *different regions of the brain perform different tasks.* Gall merely got the tasks and the locations wrong. We can forgive him, perhaps, because no one in those days had discovered a scientific method for determining exactly which functions were performed by which parts of the brain.

The technology Gall needed was invented about a century later by two German surgeons. In 1870, on a battlefield of the Franco-Prussian War, Gustav Fritsch and Eduard Hitzig seized an unusual opportunity to study living human brains. Their technique (which seems extreme by modern standards) involved a jolt of electricity to the exposed cortex of unfortunate soldiers who had had parts of their skulls blown away in battle. Not surprisingly, most of the cortical regions they tested gave no response: These were the so-called silent areas. But sometimes the stimulation would cause an arm or leg or some other body part to move, notably when a certain strip of tissue in the *frontal lobes* received the electric current (see Figure 2.13). Thus, Fritsch and Hitzig discovered a region, now called the *motor cortex,* that controls a specific function: voluntary movement of body parts. Later research, of course, has expanded on this work by finding functions for the silent areas all over the cortex. In fact, investigations have extended Gall's doctrine of localization of function to deeper regions beneath the cortex. As a result, the entire brain has now been mapped. Let's see what this map looks like.

The Frontal Lobes   Your choice of major, your plans for the summer, and your ability to answer test questions all depend on the cortical regions at the front of your brain, aptly named the **frontal lobes.** Here we find modules working together to perform our higher mental functions, such as planning, deciding, and perceiving (Helmuth, 2003a; Koechlin et al., 2003; Shimamura, 1996). The biological substrates of personality and temperament have important components here, too. We know this from accidents that damage the frontal lobes and produce devastating effects, such as we saw earlier in the case of Phineas Gage.

At the back of the frontal lobe lies a special strip of cortex capable of taking action on our thoughts. Known as the **motor cortex,** this area takes its name from its function: controlling the body's motor movement by sending messages via the motor nerves to the voluntary muscles. As you can see in Figure 2.14, the motor cortex contains an upside-down map of the body. We have represented its functions by the *homunculus* (the cartoonish "little man" in the figure). A look at the motor homunculus reveals that certain parts of the body

● A phrenology bust showing the supposed locations of mental faculties, such as intuition, morality, friendship, and dignity. Although phrenologists correctly proposed that the brain is organized in modules, the specifics of their theory turned out to be completely wrong.

■ **Frontal lobes**   Cortical regions at the front of the brain that are especially involved in movement and in thinking.
■ **Motor cortex**   A narrow vertical strip of cortex in the frontal lobes, lying just in front of the central fissure; controls voluntary movement.

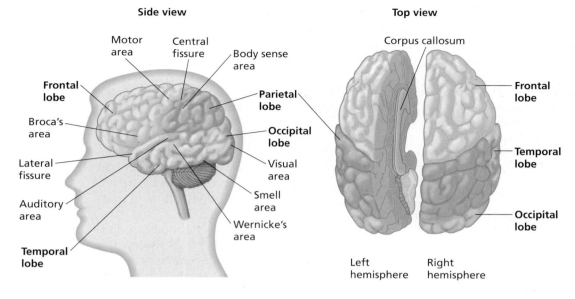

Side view

Motor area
Central fissure
Body sense area
Frontal lobe
Broca's area
Lateral fissure
Auditory area
Temporal lobe
Parietal lobe
Occipital lobe
Visual area
Smell area
Wernicke's area

Top view

Corpus callosum
Frontal lobe
Temporal lobe
Occipital lobe
Left hemisphere
Right hemisphere

● **FIGURE 2.13** The Cerebral Cortex

Each of the two hemispheres of the cerebral cortex has four lobes. Different sensory and motor functions have been associated with specific parts of each lobe. The two hemispheres are connected by a thick bundle of fibers called the corpus callosum.

● **FIGURE 2.14** The Motor Cortex and the Somatosensory Cortex

Actions of the body's voluntary muscles are controlled by the motor cortex in the frontal lobe. The somatosensory cortex in the parietal lobe processes information about temperature, touch, body position, and pain. The diagram below shows the proportion of tissue devoted to various activities or sensitivities in each cortex.

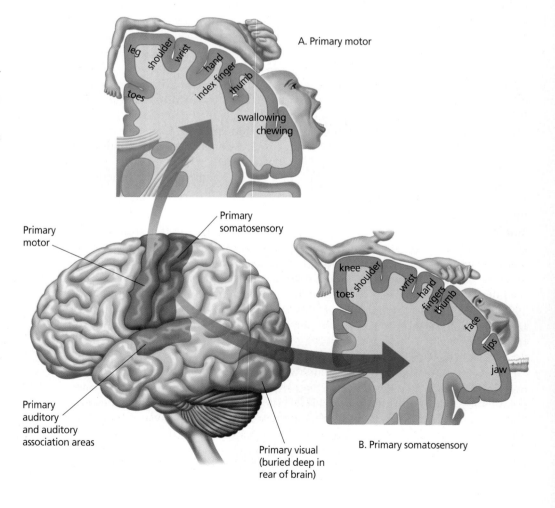

A. Primary motor

leg
shoulder
wrist
hand
index finger
thumb
toes
swallowing
chewing

Primary motor
Primary somatosensory

Primary auditory and auditory association areas

Primary visual (buried deep in rear of brain)

B. Primary somatosensory

knee
shoulder
toes
wrist
hand
fingers
thumb
face
lips
jaw

are disproportionately represented, with the lips, tongue, and hands being particularly exaggerated. One of its largest areas is devoted to the fingers (especially the thumb), reflecting the importance of manipulating objects. (Could this also reflect our human fondness for using "rules of thumb"? Perhaps not.) Another major area sends messages exclusively to the muscles of the face, used in expressions of emotion. Please remember, however, that commands from the motor cortex on one side of the brain control muscles on the opposite side of the body, as we saw in our opening vignette.

The Parietal Lobes   Behind each frontal lobe and running along the top of the brain lie two large patches of cortex that specialize in sensation (see Figure 2.13). These **parietal lobes** allow us to sense the warmth of a hot bath, the smoothness of silk, the pressure and movement of a rude elbow, and the gentleness of a caress. A special parietal strip, known as the **somatosensory cortex,** mirrors the adjacent strip of motor cortex that we found in the frontal lobe. This somatosensory cortex has two main functions. First, it serves as the primary processing area for the sensations of touch, temperature, pain and pressure from all over your body (Graziano et al., 2000; Helmuth, 2000). Second, it relates this information to a mental map of the body to help you locate the source of these sensations.

Other maps in the parietal lobes keep track of the position of body parts, so they prevent you from biting your tongue or stepping on your own toes. And, when your leg "goes to sleep" and you can't feel anything but a tingling sensation, your body position has temporarily disabled the nerve cells that carry sensory information to body maps in the parietal lobe. (It was such a parietal body map that was affected by the tumor described in our opening vignette.)

Besides processing sensation and keeping track of body parts, the parietal lobes—especially the one in the right hemisphere—allow us to locate, in three-dimensional space, the positions of external objects detected by our senses. Meanwhile, the left hemisphere's parietal lobe has its own special talents. It specializes in locating the source of speech sounds, as when someone calls your name. It also works with the temporal lobe to extract meaning from speech and writing.

The Occipital Lobes   During the Apollo 11 mission to the moon, lunar module pilot Edwin Aldrin reported back to Earth that he was experiencing mysterious flashes of light. This celestial display apparently resulted from cosmic rays stimulating his **occipital lobes,** at the back of the brain (see Figure 2.13). Similarly—if less pleasantly—you, too, will "see stars" when a sharp blow to your head bounces your brain around and stimulates its occipital lobes. Under more normal circumstances, the occipital lobes receive stimulation relayed from the eyes to the **visual cortex,** which constructs our moving picture of the outside world.

To create this picture, the brain divides up the incoming visual input and sends it to separate cortical areas for the processing of color, movement, shape, and shading—as we will see in more detail in Chapter 5. There is even a distinct patch of cortex dedicated to the recognition of human faces and another for perception of the human body (Downing et al., 2001; Holden, 1997; Turk et al., 2002). But the occipital lobes do not do all this work alone. As we have noted, they rely on adjacent association areas in the parietal lobes to locate objects in space. They also work with temporal regions to produce visual memories (Ishai & Sagi, 1995; Miyashita, 1995).

The Temporal Lobes   When the phone rings or a horn honks, the sound registers in your **temporal lobes,** on the lower side of each cerebral hemisphere

■ **Parietal lobes**   Cortical areas lying toward the back and top of the brain; involved in touch sensation and in perceiving spatial relationships (the relationships of objects in space).
■ **Somatosensory cortex**   A strip of the parietal lobe lying just behind the central fissure. The somatosensory cortex is involved with sensations of touch.
■ **Occipital lobes**   The cortical regions at the back of the brain, housing the visual cortex.
■ **Visual cortex**   The visual processing areas of cortex in the occipital and temporal lobes.
■ **Temporal lobes**   Cortical lobes that process sounds, including speech. The temporal lobes are probably involved in storing long-term memories.

(see Figure 2.13). There lies the *auditory cortex,* which helps you make sense of the sounds. In most people, a specialized section of auditory cortex on the brain's left side is dedicated to processing speech sounds. Other parts of the temporal lobes assume the task of storing long-term memories. This is not surprising, because the hippocampus lies directly beneath the temporal lobe—and, if you remember H. M., you will remember that the hippocampus is involved in forming memories.

The first detailed description of temporal lobe function was written at neurosurgeon Wilder Penfield's operating table over 50 years ago. As his electrical probe touched the temporal lobe's auditory cortex of patients under local anesthesia, they often reported hearing sounds, such as buzzing noises. More surprising, when the probe strayed into nearby temporal regions, it occasionally touched a memory. One patient abruptly exclaimed, "I can see Seven-Up Bottling Company—Harrison Bakery," two of Montreal's large illuminated advertisements. Another patient reported, "There was a piano over there and someone playing. I could hear the song, you know." Still another cried out, "Now I hear people laughing—my friends in South Africa." He was surprised because he seemed to be laughing with his cousins on a South African farm, although he knew he was in surgery in Montreal (Penfield, 1975; Penfield & Jasper, 1954; Penfield & Rasmussen, 1950; Penfield & Roberts, 1959). Such reports leave little doubt that the temporal lobes are involved in both hearing and memory.

The Cooperative Brain

Like a championship team, no individual part of the brain takes sole responsibility for emotion, memory, personality, or any other complex psychological characteristic—contrary to the beliefs of Gall and his phrenologists. There are no single "brain centers" for any of the major functions of the mind—attention, consciousness, learning, memory, thinking, language, emotion, or motivation. Rather, every mental and behavioral process involves the coordination and cooperation of many brain networks (Damasio, 2003; LeDoux, 2002). For example, when you do something as simple as answering a ringing telephone, you hear it in your temporal lobes, interpret its meaning with the help of the frontal lobes, visually locate it with your occipital lobes, initiate grasping the phone on the orders of your frontal and parietal lobes, and engage in thoughtful conversation, again using frontal-lobe circuitry. Nor are we talking just about the cortex. Even the cortex cannot do its work without communicating with circuits lying deep beneath the surface: the limbic system, thalamus, brain stem, cerebellum, and other structures.

With the brain's democratic division of labor in mind, it shouldn't surprise you to learn that the largest proportion of the human cortex is devoted to integrating and interpreting information gathered from the sensory parts of the

TABLE 2.3	Major Functions of the Cortical Lobes
Lobe	Functions
Frontal	Movement, speech, abstract thought
Parietal	Sensations of touch, body position, hearing
Temporal	Hearing, smell, vision
Occipital	Vision

brain. Collectively, these regions are known as the **association cortex.** Diverse parts of the association cortex, then, interpret sensations, lay plans, make decisions, and prepare us for action—precisely the mental powers in which we humans excel and which distinguish us from other animals. We have these capabilities because we have more cortical area committed to making associations than does any nonhuman species.

And now that we have seen how the four lobes in each hemisphere have specialized functions and that we depend on the cooperation of each of the parts, let's turn to some evidence that the two cerebral hemispheres are also specialists at different tasks. These differences fall under the heading of *cerebral dominance*—a commonly misunderstood concept.

Cerebral Dominance

In the mid 1800s, at about the same time that Phineas Gage was recovering from his accident, a French neurologist named Paul Broca was studying patients who had speech impairments that resulted from brain injuries. An especially important case involved a man known in the medical books as "Tan"—a name derived from the only word he was able to speak. After Tan's death, an autopsy revealed severe damage in the left front portion of his brain. This clue prompted Broca to study other patients who had developed *aphasia*—the loss of speech caused by brain damage. Again and again, Broca found damage to the same spot, later named *Broca's area*, that had been damaged in Tan's brain. (See Figure 2.13.) This pattern was one of the early suggestions that the two sides of the brain specialize in different tasks. Subsequent work has confirmed and extended Broca's findings:

▮ Brain-damaged patients suffering paralysis on the right side of their bodies often develop speech disturbances, suggesting that speech production involves the frontal lobe, usually in the left hemisphere. (Again, please recall that the left hemisphere controls the right side of the body.)

▮ Damage to other areas in the left parietal and left temporal lobes commonly produces problems in understanding language.

People with right-sided brain injuries less often have speech problems, but they are more likely to have difficulties with *spatial orientation* (locating themselves or external objects in three-dimensional space). They may, for example, feel lost in a previously familiar place or be unable to assemble a simple jigsaw puzzle. Musical ability is also associated with the right hemisphere, particularly with Broca's area (Holden, 2001; Janata et al., 2002; Zatorre & Krumhansl, 2002).

While the two hemispheres appear to be near mirror images of each other, they assume different functions. This tendency for the hemispheres to take charge of different tasks is called **cerebral dominance.** But what many people don't understand about cerebral dominance is this: While some processes are more under the control of the left hemisphere, and others are predominantly right-hemisphere tasks, *both hemispheres work together to produce our thoughts, feelings, and behaviors.*

That's the broad-brush picture of cerebral dominance. Now, let's look at some details, beginning with some new research showing that the dominance pattern is not always the same from one person to another. This work uses a technique called *transcranial magnetic stimulation* (TMS), involving powerful magnetic pulses that can disable parts of the brain temporarily and without causing damage. When TMS is applied to the language areas of the brain, the results show that some people—about 1 in 10 individuals, and mostly left-handers—process language primarily on the *right* side of the brain. Another 1 in

▮ **Association cortex** Cortical regions throughout the brain that combine information from various other parts of the brain.
▮ **Cerebral dominance** The tendency of each brain hemisphere to exert control over different functions, such as language or perception of spatial relationships.

10—again, mostly left-handers—have language functions distributed equally on both sides of the brain (Knecht et al., 2002).

Other studies have shown that, while one hemisphere usually dominates language functions, both sides of the brain get involved. The left side is usually more dominant in processing the "what," or *content,* of speech. The right hemisphere, by contrast, assumes the role of processing the *emotional tone* of speech (Vingerhoets, 2003). In fact, the right hemisphere is usually more involved than the left in interpreting the emotional responses of others. The control of one's own negative emotions, such as fear and anger, stems from the right frontal lobe, while the left frontal lobe regulates the positive emotions, such as joy. (For more information, see Beeman & Chiarello, 1998; Davidson, 1992a, b; Heller et al., 1998; McIntosh & Lobaugh, 2003; Posner & Raichle, 1994; Springer & Deutsch, 1993).

Different though they may be, the two hemispheres don't compete with each other (except under the most unusual conditions, which we will describe in a moment). Rather, they make different contributions to the same task. In the lingo of neuroscience, they have different *processing styles.* For example, on matching tasks performed in the psychology lab, the left hemisphere matches objects analytically and verbally—by similarity in function, as in matching eating utensils (*knife* with *spoon*). By contrast, the right hemisphere matches things that look alike or fit together to form a visual pattern—such as matching *coin* to *clock,* which are both round objects (Gazzaniga, 1970; Sperry, 1968, 1982). In general, we can describe the left hemisphere's processing style as more *analytic* and *sequential,* while the right hemisphere interprets experience more *holistically* and *spatially* (Reuter-Lorenz & Miller, 1998).

The differences between the two sides of the brain have captured the public's interest in recent years. Knowing a fad when they see it, smarmy pseudoscientists have proclaimed that people can be typed as "right-brained" or "left-brained." But we want to emphasize that this distinction is simplistic and misleading. The evidence by no means warrants categorizing people in this way. In reality, the differences between the two hemispheres do not outweigh their similarities (Banich, 1998; Trope et al., 1992). Further, as we have seen, the two hemispheres normally don't work either in isolation from each other or at cross-purposes. Rather, they cooperate, each by making its own complementary contribution to our mental lives (see Figure 2.15).

There are, however, some exceptions that have actually proved the rule. In a few rare cases, the cerebral hemispheres cannot work together—because they have been disconnected. We are referring to individuals whose brains have

● **FIGURE 2.15** Specialization Commonly Found in the Cerebral Hemispheres

Left hemisphere

- Regulation of positive emotions

- Control of muscles used in speech

- Control of sequence of movements

- Spontaneous speaking and writing

- Memory for words and numbers

- Understanding speech and writing

Right hemisphere

- Regulation of negative emotions

- Responses to simple commands

- Memory for shapes and music

- Interpreting spatial relationships and visual images

- Recognition of faces

been surgically "split." Their story has much to teach us about cerebral dominance in the normal human brain.

The Split Brain: "I've Half a Mind to . . ."

Imagine what your world might be like if the halves of your brain could not communicate. Would you be, literally, "of two minds"? (Or feel "beside yourself"?) A rare surgical procedure, used to treat severe epilepsy, has given us some answers to such question. The procedure requires that surgeons cut the **corpus callosum,** the bundle of nerve fibers responsible for transferring information between the two hemispheres (Figure 2.16).

The purpose of the surgery is to prevent abnormal electrical rhythms from "echoing" back and forth between the hemispheres and developing into a full-blown seizure (Trope et al., 1992; Wilson et al., 1977). Indeed, after the operation, most patients' seizures diminish in severity. More remarkably (to psychologists), these *split-brain patients* appear mentally and behaviorally unaffected under all but the most unusual conditions. But what really grabbed psychologists' attention were certain odd responses that these individuals made on cleverly contrived tests conducted by Nobel Prize winner Roger Sperry (1968) and his colleague Michael Gazzaniga (1970).

For example, split-brain patients could not identify an unseen object, such as a ball, when it was placed in the left hand—although they had no trouble naming the object when it was shifted to the right hand. Or, in another test, most split-brain patients said they saw nothing when an image of a spoon was flashed briefly on the left side of the visual field. Yet, at the same time, the patient's right hand could reach under a visual barrier and pick the spoon out of an array of other objects.

To understand these strange results, you will need some insider information about the pathways used to get visual information from the eyes to the occipital cortex. This is the tricky part: Visual information coming *from each eye* divides into two streams that flow to the opposite sides of the brain. (Figure 2.17 can help you visualize the sensory pathways involved.) For people with intact brains, this fork in the visual road poses no problem. Thanks to the connecting pathways through the corpus callosum, information from both sides of the visual field is accessible to both hemispheres.

In split-brain patients, however, information sharing across the corpus callosum can't happen. Yet, under everyday conditions outside the laboratory, they get along surprisingly well. They simply scan a scene with their eyes, which sends essentially the same visual information to both sides of the brain.

■ **Corpus callosum** The band of nerve cells that connects the two cerebral hemispheres.

● **FIGURE 2.16** The Corpus Callosum
Only the corpus callosum is severed when the brain is "split." This medical procedure prevents communication between the cerebral hemispheres. Strangely, split-brain patients act like people with normal brains under most conditions. Special laboratory tests, however, reveal a duality of consciousness in the split brain.

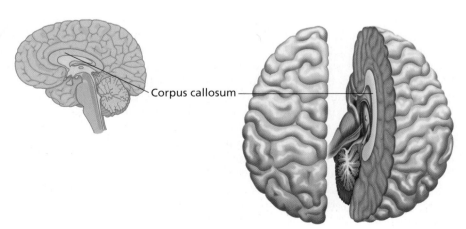

Corpus callosum

There are two things to notice in this illustration, in which the person is looking at the
center of the pizza. First, the information from
the left side of the retina in each eye corresponds to the right side of the pizza. Con-
versely, the right visual field senses the left side
of the pizza. (This happens because the lens of
the eye reverses the image.) Second, please
notice that the left sides of both retinas in the
eyes send images to the brain's left visual
cortex, while the right sides of the retinas send
images to the right visual cortex. As a result,
when the eyes are fixated in the center, each
side of the brain "sees" the opposite side of
the pizza.

Only when the two hemispheres of split-brain patients get entirely different
messages does the bizarre psychological reality of the split brain show itself—
as it did in the Sperry and Gazzaniga experiments.

Now, put yourself in an experimenter's shoes, and see if you can explain
why the split-brain patient responds as shown in Figure 2.18. Why is he able
to match, using the left hand, the image seen on the left side of the screen?
And, why does he fail the same test when he uses the right hand? (Remember, from our discussion of the brain stem, that each hemisphere communicates with the *opposite* side of the body.)

The patient in the figure has been asked to identify an object that had been
visualized only by the brain's right hemisphere (because the image had been
flashed only on the left side of the screen). The identification task was easily
performed by the left hand, which is connected to the right hemisphere, but
impossible for the right hand, which communicates with the left hemisphere.
So, before reading the caption for Figure 2.18, would you predict that the
patient could, or could not, name the object seen on the screen?

Some altogether unexpected effects of having a split brain also showed up
in patient reports of their everyday experiences. For example, one patient told
how his left hand would unzip his pants or unbutton his shirt at inappropriate times, especially when he was under stress. In fact, it was usually the left
hand that would play such tricks. But why? The researchers theorize that the
right hemisphere—which has little language ability, but which controls the left
hand—was merely trying to find a way to communicate (Sperry, 1964). It's
almost as if the right hemisphere were saying, "Look at me!"

Match   Mismatch

● **FIGURE 2.18** Testing a Split-Brain
Patient
When a split-brain patient uses the left hand to
find a match to a hidden object flashed briefly
in the left visual field, eye–hand coordination
is normal, because both are registered in the
right hemisphere. (The patient, however, cannot name the object because speech is mainly
a left-hemisphere function.) Alternatively, when
asked to use the right hand to match an object
seen in the left visual field, the patient cannot
perform the task and mismatches a pear with
some other object, such as a glass–although
the patient can now name the object in his
hand!

Such cerebral antics point up the most interesting finding in Sperry and
Gazzaniga's work: the *duality of consciousness* observed in split-brain patients.
It was as if each patient were two separate individuals. When different stimuli were presented to opposite sides of the brain (as in Figure 2.18), the two
hemispheres could respond independently. For example, the right hemisphere
might direct the left hand to select a pear, and the left hemisphere might tell
the right hand to select a glass. In other tests, they found that right-hemisphere
responses tended to respond more emotionally, while the left hemisphere was
more analytic. As expected, the left hemisphere typically had much more language fluency than did the right.

We must be cautious about generalizing such findings from split-brain
patients to individuals with normal brains, says Gazzaniga (1998a, b). He suggests that we think of the human mind as neither a single nor a dual entity
but rather as a *confederation of minds,* each specialized to process a specific kind
of information. If so, the input from these many separate "miniminds" must
be synthesized and coordinated for action by still other (poorly understood)
executive processors in the brain. The corpus callosum, then, is a connecting
pathway that helps our confederation of minds share information. And so, we
come full circle to a Core Concept that we encountered at the beginning of this
section: The brain is composed of many specialized modules that work
together to create mind and behavior (Baynes et al., 1998; Strauss, 1998).

PSYCHOLOGY IN YOUR LIFE: BRAIN DAMAGE AND BEHAVIOR

Nearly everybody knows someone who has suffered brain damage from an
accident, a stroke, or a tumor—such as we described in the chapter-opening
vignette. Your new knowledge of the brain and behavior will help you understand the problems such people must face. And if you know what abilities
have been lost or altered, you can usually make a good guess as to which
part of the brain sustained the damage—especially if you bear in mind two
simple principles:

1. Each side of the brain communicates with the opposite side of the body.
   Thus, if symptoms appear on one side of the body, it is likely that the other
   side of the brain was damaged. (See Figure 2.19.)

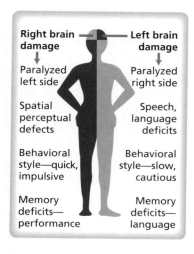

FIGURE 2.19 Effects of Damage to the Cerebral Hemispheres

2. For most people, speech is mainly a left-hemisphere function.

Now we invite you to use your knowledge of the brain to guess where the damage probably occurred in the brains of the following individuals:

■ Edna had a *stroke* (an interruption of blood supply to a part of the brain) and lost her ability to speak, although she could still understand speech. Where did the stroke most likely affect her brain?

■ Theo was in an auto accident, which left him with jerky, uncoordinated movements. Brain scans revealed no damage to his cerebral cortex. So, where did the accident have its effect in the brain?

■ Just prior to her seizures, Lydia has a strange sensation (an "aura") that feels like pinpricks on her left leg. What part of her brain generates this sensation?

Edna's case could have a happy ending. Depending on her age, physical condition, the extent of the stroke, and how quickly she received medical attention, she may get some or all of her speech back. Even if Broca's area in her left frontal lobe has been permanently damaged, other parts of Edna's brain may be able to take over some of the lost function. As we have noted, neuroscientists call this the *plasticity* of the brain. Long-term therapy for Edna will emphasize speech therapy.

Theo may also regain some or all his abilities, especially if the affected neural cells in his cerebellum were merely bruised but not destroyed in the accident. Long-term treatment for him will involve physical therapy. Both Edna and Theo may also need psychological therapy to help them cope with any permanent loss of function.

Lydia has epilepsy, originating in her right somatosensory cortex. Like most people with epilepsy, she will probably receive significant help from antiseizure medications. The chances are good that she will be completely symptom-free when the drugs are properly adjusted.

A lesson from all these cases is that people who suffer from brain damage can often receive significant help. Note, too, that help may come in many forms, both physical and mental. Perhaps the most important long-term therapy, however, is social support—a good thing to remember if you know someone who has suffered brain damage. (For more information on social support under stress, see Chapter 10, "Stress, Health, and Well-Being.")

CHECK YOUR UNDERSTANDING

1. **RECALL:** Which technique for studying the brain relies on the brain's electrical activity?
   a. EEG
   b. MRI
   c. PET
   d. CT

2. **RECALL:** Name the three main layers of the human brain discussed in the text: _____, _____, and _____.

3. **APPLICATION:** A brain tumor in the limbic system is most likely to produce changes in a person's
   a. coordination.
   b. vision.
   c. sleep patterns.
   d. emotions.

4. **RECALL:** Make a sketch showing the four lobes of the cerebral cortex. Indicate the main functions of each lobe. Which hemisphere of the brain controls language in most people? Which hemisphere of your brain controls your left hand?

5. **RECALL:** In the split-brain operation, what part of the brain is severed?
   a. the left hemisphere
   b. the right hemisphere
   c. the corpus callosum
   d. the occipital lobe

6. **ANALYSIS:** The split-brain patient in Figure 2.18 has trouble using the _____ hand to select the object flashed on the left side of the screen.
    a. right
    b. left
    (*Hints:* Which hemisphere controls each hand? Which hemisphere processes information from the left side of the visual field?)

7. **UNDERSTANDING THE CORE CONCEPT:** The brain is composed of many specialized and interconnected modules that work together to create mind and behavior. Can you name at least two specialized parts of the brain that are known to work together? What is the result of the collaboration of the structures you have named?

BIOPSYCHOLOGY: THE STATE OF THE ART

Now that we have had a look at the biology behind psychology, you must be wondering how to put together all the details we have covered. For example, how do all the separate modules in the brain cooperate in processing information, making decisions, and initiating action? The frank answer: No one knows precisely how the components of the brain manage to work together (Horgan, 1993). Do we need a more detailed map of the brain's interconnections? Perhaps. But even if we knew every connection for every nerve cell in the brain, we still wouldn't understand how it senses, thinks, and feels. We would be long on detail and short on insight. What we really need is a good *model,* or theory, of the brain that tells us how the parts work in synchrony. The lack of such a theory represents one of the two biggest mysteries in biopsychology.

The other mystery involves genes and psychological processes. During the last decade, scientists have made great strides in deciphering the human genome, but we still have only the sketchiest understanding of how genes regulate our thoughts, feelings, desires, and actions. How, for example, does a genetic tendency for depression become activated? Does it require some sort of "trigger" from the environment? And, how do the genes communicate with the brain?

So, at the beginning of the 21st century, these are the two burning issues that lie at the cutting edge of theory and research in biopsychology. Students just now entering the field will have the opportunity to find the answers.

USING PSYCHOLOGY TO LEARN PSYCHOLOGY

Putting Your Knowledge of the Brain to Work

The old idea that we use only 10% of our brains is bunk. We hope this chapter has shown you that every part of the brain has a known function, and it gets used every day—but not necessarily for intellectual purposes. We now know that much of the brain merely controls basic biological functions. This tells us that simply engaging more of our brains is not the royal road to increased brain power.

So, have neuroscientists found anything that you can use to improve your memory, especially for the concepts you are learning in your classes? Among their most important discoveries is the revelation that many different regions of the cerebral cortex are involved in learning and memory (Kandel & Squire, 2000). Accordingly, if you can bring more of this cerebral circuitry to bear on your studies (about biopsychology, for example), your brain will lay down a wider web of memories.

To be more specific, reading the material in this book will help you form verbal (language) memories, parts of which involve circuits in the temporal cortex. Taking notes brings the motor cortex of the frontal lobes into play, adding a "motor memory" component to your study. Scanning the accompanying photos, charts, and drawings adds visual and spatial memory components in the occipital and parietal lobes. Listening actively to your professor's lectures and discussing the material with a study partner will engage the auditory regions of the temporal cortex and lay down still other memory traces. Finally, study time spent anticipating what questions will appear on the exam will involve regions of the frontal lobes in your learning process.

In general, the more ways that you can deal with the material—the more sensory and motor channels you can employ—the more memory components you will build in your brain's circuitry. As a result, when you need to remember the material, you will have more possible ways of accessing what you have learned. So, put your knowledge of your brain to work in your studying!

CHAPTER SUMMARY

● HOW ARE GENES AND BEHAVIOR LINKED?

Charles Darwin's theory of evolution explains behavior as the result of natural selection. Variation among individuals and competition for resources lead to survival of the most adaptive behavior, as well as the fittest features. This principle underlies human behavior, as well as that of other animals. Research in genetics has clarified the biological basis for natural selection and inheritance. Our chromosomes contain thousands of genes, carrying traits inherited from our parents. Each gene consists of a DNA segment than encodes for a protein. Proteins, in turn, serve as the building blocks for the organism's structure and function, including the functioning of the brain. While a draft of the human genome was recently completed, we do not yet know precisely how specific genes influence behavior and mental processes.

● Evolution has fundamentally shaped psychological processes because it favors genetic variations that produce adaptive behavior.

● HOW DOES THE BODY COMMUNICATE INTERNALLY?

The body's two communication systems are the nervous system and the endocrine system. The neuron, the basic unit of the nervous system, is specialized for processing information. It receives messages by means of stimulation on the dendrites and soma and, when sufficiently aroused, generates an action potential along the axon. Neurotransmitter chemicals relay the message to receptors on cells across the synapse.

The nervous system, composed of billions of interconnected neurons, has two main divisions: the central nervous system (the brain and the spinal cord) and the peripheral nervous system. The peripheral nervous system, in turn, can be divided into the somatic nervous system (further divided into sensory and motor pathways) and the autonomic nervous system, which communicates with internal organs and glands. The somatic division of the autonomic NS is most active under stress, while the parasympathetic division attempts to maintain the body in a more calm state.

The glands of the slower endocrine system also communicate with cells around the body by secreting hormones into the bloodstream. Its activity is controlled by the pituitary gland, attached to the base of the brain, where it receives orders from the hypothalamus.

Psychoactive drugs affect the nervous system by influencing the effects of neurotransmitters. Moreover, they may act as agonists or antagonists. Unfortunately for drug users, many neural pathways in the brain may employ the same neurotransmitter, causing unwanted side effects.

● The brain coordinates the body's two communications systems, the nervous system and the endocrine system, which use similar chemical messengers to communicate with targets throughout the body.

● HOW DOES THE BRAIN PRODUCE BEHAVIOR AND MENTAL PROCESSES?

Early medicine learned about the brain from the study of brain-injured persons, such as Phineas Gage. In modern times, researchers have opened windows on the brain, using the EEG to sense the brain's electrical activity, along with electric probes sometimes used to stimulate the brain during surgery. In recent years, computer technology has led to brain-scanning techniques, such as CT, PET, MRI, and fMRI—each having its advantages and disadvantages.

We can conceive of the brain as being organized in three integrated layers. The brain stem and associated structures (including the medulla, reticular formation, pons, thalamus, and cerebellum) control many vital body functions, along with influencing alertness and motor movement. The limbic system (including the hippocampus, amygdala, and hypothalamus) plays vital roles in motivation, emotion, and memory. The cerebral cortex contains highly specialized modules—each with distinct functions. Its frontal lobes involve both motor functions and higher mental functions. The parietal lobes specialize in sensation, especially the senses of touch and body position. The occipital lobes deal exclusively with vision, while the temporal lobes have multiple roles involved in vision, hearing, and smell. Even though the functions of the brain are highly localized within specific modules, they normally work seamlessly together.

The two cerebral hemispheres are also differently specialized. Language, analytical thinking, and positive emotions are regulated by specific parts of the left hemisphere, while circuits in the right hemisphere control spatial interpretation, visual and musical memory, and negative emotions. If the hemispheres are surgically severed, as when the corpus callosum is cut in split-brain patients, a duality of consciousness emerges. In such cases, each hemisphere functions independently and has no direct awareness of stimulation or cognitive activities affecting the other. In people with intact brains, however, the two hemispheres communicate and cooperate with each other.

● **The brain is composed of many specialized modules that work together to create mind and behavior.**

REVIEW TEST

For each of the following items, choose the single best answer. The correct answers appear at the end.

1. According to Darwin's theory of natural selection,
   a. the environment chooses organisms that are more complex and more advanced.
   b. the members of a species that are best adapted to their environment are more likely to survive and produce more offspring.
   c. giraffes evolved longer necks because they were constantly reaching for the tender, higher leaves in the tall trees in their environment.
   d. evolution is a process whereby experience modifies an organism's genes.

2. Although Darwin never knew it, evolution takes advantage of genetic _____ that aid survival and reproduction of the individual.
   a. variations
   b. environments
   c. thoughts
   d. diseases

3. During a neural impulse, a neuron "fires" when
   a. it is physically contacted by another cell that is transmitting the signal.
   b. an electric charge travels down the axon.
   c. it contracts and releases powerful chemicals directly into the bloodstream.
   d. signals entering at the axon travel the length of the cell and exit through the dendrites.

4. Neurotransmitters are released by the terminal buttons into the _____, and hormones are released by the endocrine system into the _____.
   a. sympathetic nervous system/parasympathetic nervous system
   b. cortex/brain stem
   c. left hemisphere/right hemisphere
   d. synaptic cleft/bloodstream

5. Which one of the following is an example of behavior controlled primarily by the autonomic nervous system?

a. typing a sentence accurately on a keyboard
b. solving a mathematical problem
c. breathing and swallowing while asleep
d. feeling hungry

6. Which form of brain scanning employs radioactive tracers to reveal the most active regions of the brain?
   a. EEG
   b. CT
   c. PET
   d. MRI

7. Which of the following statements identifying the locations of important brain structures is true?
   a. The hypothalamus is part of the brain stem.
   b. The medulla is part of the limbic system.
   c. The occipital lobe is part of the cerebral cortex.
   d. all of the above

8. Which of the three brain layers is often thought of as the "emotional brain"?
   a. the brain stem and cerebellum
   b. the limbic system
   c. the autonomic nervous system
   d. the cerebrum

9. What part of the cerebral cortex is most involved with initiating and controlling body movements?
   a. the frontal lobes
   b. the hippocampus
   c. the temporal lobes
   d. the occipital lobes

10. The left hemisphere of the cerebral cortex is usually more involved than the right hemisphere in activities such as
   a. recognizing and appreciating visual stimuli.
   b. enjoying and appreciating music.
   c. using spoken and written language.
   d. understanding spatial relationships.

ANSWERS: 1.b 2.a 3.b 4.d 5.c 6.c 7.c 8.b 9.a 10.c

KEY TERMS

Biopsychology (p. 43)

Neuroscience (p. 43)

Evolution (p. 44)

Natural selection (p. 45)

Genotype (p. 46)

Phenotype (p. 46)

DNA (p. 47)

Gene (p. 47)

Chromosome (p. 47)

Sex chromosomes (p. 47)

Neuron (p. 52)

Sensory neuron (p. 52)

Motor neuron (p. 52)

Interneuron (p. 53)

Dendrite (p. 53)

Soma (p. 53)

Axon (p. 54)

Resting potential (p. 55)

Action potential (p. 55)

All-or-none principle (p. 55)

Synapse (p. 55)

Terminal buttons (p. 55)

Synaptic transmission (p. 55)

Neurotransmitters (p. 56)

Plasticity (p. 56)

Glial cells (p. 57)

Nervous system (p. 58)

Central nervous system (p. 59)

Reflex (p. 59)

Peripheral nervous system (p. 59)

Somatic nervous system (p. 59)

Autonomic nervous system (p. 59)

Sympathetic division (p. 60)

Parasympathetic division (p. 60)

Endocrine system (p. 61)

Hormone (p. 61)

Pituitary gland (p. 62)

Agonist (p. 63)

Antagonist (p. 63)

Neural pathway (p. 64)

Electroencephalograph or EEG (p. 66)

CT scanning or computerized tomography (p. 67)

PET scanning or positron emission tomography (p. 67)

MRI or magnetic resonance imaging (p. 67)

Brain stem (p. 67)

Medulla (p. 69)

Pons (p. 69)

Reticular formation (p. 69)

Thalamus (p. 69)

Cerebellum (p. 69)

Limbic system (p. 70)

Hippocampus (p. 70)

Amygdala (p. 70)

Hypothalamus (p. 72)

Cerebral cortex (p. 72)

Frontal lobes (p. 73)

Motor cortex (p. 73)

Parietal lobes (p. 75)

Somatosensory cortex (p. 75)

Occipital lobes (p. 75)

Visual cortex (p. 75)

Temporal lobes (p. 75)

Association cortex (p. 77)

Cerebral dominance (p. 77)

Corpus callosum (p. 79)

OUR RECOMMENDED BOOKS AND VIDEOS

ARTICLE

Nash, M. R. (2001, July). The truth and the hype of hypnosis. *Scientific American, 285,* 46–49, 52–55. Everyone has ideas and images of hypnosis: glittering watches, drowsy subjects commanded to feel "verrry sleepy . . ." Modern cognitive science now illuminates how and why hypnosis works in pain relief, memory retrieval, and other applications.

BOOKS

Ackerman, D. (2004). *An alchemy of mind: The marvel and mystery of the brain.* New York: Scribner. Poet and naturalist Diane Ackerman investigates the "crowded chemistry lab" of the human nervous system, discovering how identity emerges within the "three-pound blob" that is the brain.

Finger, S. (1999). *Minds behind the brain.* New York: Oxford University Press. Historian Stanley Finger uses biographical sketches to study the development of brain science from ancient times to the present.

Johnson, S. (2004). *Mind wide open: Your brain and the neuroscience of everyday life.* Writer Steven Johnson describes his own experience undergoing brain scans, empathy tests, and neurofeedback, presenting the results and discussing the processes revealed. If you want to know what such tests feel like and mean, here are clear explanations and inviting glimpses into brain science.

Keynes, R. (2002). *Darwin, his daughter, and human evolution.* New York: Penguin Putnam. Randal Keynes, great-great-grandson of the author of *Origin of Species,* explores how Charles Darwin's affection for his family, and grief at the loss of his children, influenced his quest to understand the origins of emotions and social bonds.

LeDoux, J. (2003). *The synaptic self: How our brains become who we are.* New York: Penguin Books. Descartes asserted that "I think, therefore I am." Neuroscientist Joseph LeDoux once spotted a T-shirt that countered, "I don't know—so maybe I'm not." For LeDoux, getting the joke shows that the brain's hardwired pathways interact with one's unique experiences, producing not only conscious experience, but the unique self. His book is as absorbing as a mystery, with instructive humor.

MacMillan, M. (2002). *An odd kind of fame: Stories of Phineas Gage.* Cambridge, MA: MIT Press. In the mid-19th century, a railway worker in Vermont suffered and survived a horrendous brain injury after an accidental explosion. One hundred and fifty years later, Phineas Gage remains famous in neuropsychology because the injury, mainly to his frontal lobe, altered his personality more than any bodily function—thus pinpointing the brain site of individuality. This is a well-researched, poignant history.

Reeve, C. (1999). *Still me.* New York: Ballantine Books. Actor Christopher Reeve, a movie star rendered quadriplegic by a horseback riding accident, recounted what was changed, remained the same, and even became better after his injury.

VIDEOS

Awakenings. (1990, color, 121 min.). Directed by Penny Marshall; starring Robin Williams, Robert DeNiro, Julie Kavner. Based on Oliver Sacks's collection of the same title, this is the true story of "sleeping sickness" patients who, after decades in a vegetative state, were briefly "awakened" by one doctor's synthetic dopamine therapy. Does medicine have the right to treat patients if the experimental "cure" might offer only temporary hope?

Inherit the Wind. (1960, B&W, 127 min.). Directed by Stanley Kramer; starring Spencer Tracy, Fredric March, Gene Kelly, Dick York. This wonderful adaptation of the stage play is based on the 1925 "monkey trial" of John Scopes, a Tennessee man prosecuted for teaching evolution in his public school class. Watch the movie—then research the facts about the real people behind the characters.

Minority Report. (2002, color, 144 min.). Directed by Steven Spielberg; starring Tom Cruise, Colin Farrell, Samantha Morton. Adapted from Philip K. Dick's futuristic sci-fi short story (a saga that has inspired several movies). In a future society, elite police units predict and prevent crimes before they occur by telepathically interpreting the visions of prophetic brains. Is individual brainpower a common social resource? And is crime detection its best application?

Unbreakable. (2000, color, 107 min.). Directed by M. Night Shyamalan. Starring Bruce Willis, Samuel L. Jackson, Robin Wright Penn. An unhappy man in a troubled marriage realizes he is invulnerable to illness or injury—and acutely sensitive to evil—after meeting an eccentric invalid who is vulnerable to everything. How powerfully does the body shape one's personality and purpose in life?

CORE CONCEPTS

Consciousness can take many forms, while other mental processes occur simultaneously outside our awareness.

Consciousness changes in cycles that correspond to our biological rhythms and to the patterns of stimulation in our environment.

▼

An altered state of consciousness occurs when some aspect of normal consciousness is modified by mental, behavioral, or chemical means.

Psychology in Your Life

The Unconscious—Reconsidered

An empirical approach suggests a simpler unconscious than the one portrayed by Sigmund Freud.

Sleep Disorders

Insomnia, sleep apnea, narcolepsy, and daytime sleepiness can be hazardous to your health—and perhaps even to your life.

Dependence and Addiction

Psychoactive drugs alter brain chemistry, and they can produce physical or psychological addiction. But is addiction a disease or a character flaw?

USING PSYCHOLOGY TO LEARN PSYCHOLOGY:
Connecting Consciousness with Memory

States of Consciousness

ONE RAINY SWISS SUMMER day in the early 19th century, a housebound trio of writers eagerly challenged each other to craft ghost stories. Yet, after several days of uninspired effort, Mary Wollstonecraft Shelley feared she would come up empty handed. Then one night, with the problem turning over in her mind, she went to bed and soon fell asleep, only to awaken some time later with horrific dream images in her head. She later recalled them clearly:

> My imagination, unbidden, possessed and guided me ... I saw the pale student of unhallowed arts kneeling beside the thing he had put together. I saw the hideous phantasm of a man stretched out, and then ... show signs of life, and stir with an uneasy, half vital motion ... [The creator] would rush away from his odious handiwork, horror-stricken.

Early the next day she penned the words: "It was on a dreary night of November ..." (Shelley, 1831, p. x). Thus began her "ghost story," *Frankenstein, or The Modern Prometheus.*

Mary Shelley was far from the first to have been inspired by a dream. From ancient times, dreams have been regarded as sources of insight, creativity, and prophecy. We can see this, for example, in the Old Testament story of the Israelite Joseph, who interpreted Pharaoh's dreams of fat and lean cattle as predicting first the years of plenty and then the years of famine that lay in store for the Egyptian kingdom (Genesis, 41:i–vii).

● Spanish painter Salvador Dali found inspiration for his work in his dreams.
© 2004 Gala-Salvador Dali Foundation, Figueres, Spain, © Salvador Dali Museum, Inc. St. Petersburg, Florida, USA/ Bridgeman Art Library

In more modern times, the English poet Samuel Taylor Coleridge attributed the imagery of his poem "Kubla Khan" to a dream (possibly drug-induced) that he experienced after reading a biography of the famed Mongol warrior. Likewise, painters such as surrealist Salvador Dali have found their dreams to be vivid sources of imagery. Composers as varied as Mozart, Beethoven, the Beatles, and Sting have all credited their dreams with inspiring certain works. And in the scientific world, chemist August Kekule's discovery of the structure of the benzene molecule was sparked by his dream of a snake rolled into a loop, grasping its own tail tucked in its mouth. Even the famous horror writer Stephen King claims to have harvested story ideas from his own childhood nightmares.

Dreaming represents just one of many states of consciousness that are possible for the human mind. Others include, of course, our familiar state of wakefulness and the less-familiar states of dreamless sleep, hypnosis, and meditation, as well as the chemically altered states produced by alcohol and other drugs. But that's not all. Behind these conscious states, the brain has other levels of processing that occur outside consciousness (Wallace & Fisher, 1999). These range from information readily available in memory (What is seven times nine?) to the operations occurring in the deep, primitive regions of the brain, which control basic biological functions, such as blood pressure and body temperature. Somewhere between these extremes are parts of the mind that somehow deal with our once-conscious memories and gut-level responses, as varied as this morning's breakfast and your most embarrassing moment. As we will see, this netherworld of nonconscious ideas, feelings, desires, and images has been a magnet for controversy ever since Freud suggested that dreams may reflect our unrecognized fears and desires. In this chapter we will evaluate this claim and others that have been made for consciousness and the "deeper" levels of processing in the mind.

HOW IS CONSCIOUSNESS RELATED TO OTHER MENTAL PROCESSES?

In simplest terms, we can define **consciousness** as the process underlying the mental model we create of the world of which we are aware. It is also a part of the mind into which we can potentially retrieve a fact, an idea, an emotion, or a memory of an experience and recombine them in the processes we call "thinking." It's the part of the mind that helps us combine both reality and fantasy—the "movie" in your head. For example, if you see a doughnut when you are hungry, consciousness forms an image of the doughnut (based on external stimulation) and consults memory, which associates the image with food and also allows you to imagine eating the doughnut. Most likely, under these circumstances your consciousness will quickly fill with doughnutty imagery. But exactly *how* the brain does this is perhaps psychology's greatest mystery. How do the patterns in the firing of billions of neurons become the conscious image of a doughnut—or of the words and ideas on this page?

Folk wisdom merely attributes consciousness to an *anima,* a spirit or inner life force, an explanation that takes us no closer to understanding how consciousness works. A Biblical variation on this theme connects consciousness to the soul—although the Bible also suggests that evil spirits or devils sometimes take over consciousness and cause bizarre behavior. (See Mark 5, for example.)

■ **Consciousness** The process by which the brain creates a model of internal and external experience.

For psychologists, the big difficulty presented by consciousness is that it is so subjective and illusive—like searching for the end of the rainbow (Damasio, 1999, 2000). That lesson was driven home when the structuralists attempted to dissect conscious experience more than a century ago. As you will recall, the structuralists used a simple technique called introspection: People were asked to report on their own conscious experience. The slippery, subjective nature of consciousness quickly became obvious to nearly everyone, and psychologists began to despair that science would never find a way to study objectively something so private as conscious experience. (Think about it: How could you prove that you have consciousness?)

◄ **CONNECTION:** CHAPTER 1

Wundt and the structuralists pioneered the use of introspection in their search for "the elements of conscious experience."

The problem seemed so intractable that, early in the 20th century, the notorious and influential behaviorist John Watson declared that the mind was out of bounds for the young science of psychology. Mental processes were little more than by-products of our actions, he said. (You don't cry because you are sad, you are sad because some event makes you cry.) Under Watson's direction, psychology became simply the science of behavior. And so, psychology not only lost its consciousness but also lost its mind!

● Francis Crick says that our consciousness is "no more than the behavior of a vast assembly of nerve cells and their associated molecules."

The psychology of consciousness remained in limbo until the 1960s, when a coalition of cognitive psychologists, neuroscientists, and computer scientists brought it back to life (Gardner, 1985). They did so for two reasons. First, many psychological issues had come to light that needed a better explanation than behaviorism could deliver: quirks of memory, perceptual illusions, drug-induced states (which were very popular in the 1960s). The second reason for the reemergence of consciousness came from technology. Scientists were acquiring new tools—especially computers, which allowed them to scan the brain and also gave them a model that could be used to explain how the brain processes information.

■ **Cognitive neuroscience**   An interdisciplinary field involving cognitive psychology, neurology, biology, computer science, linguistics, and specialists from other fields who are interested in the connection between mental processes and the brain.

The combination of new tools and pressing problems, then, led to a multidisciplinary effort that became known as **cognitive neuroscience.** It includes scientists from a variety of fields, including cognitive psychology, neurology, biology, computer science, and linguistics—all interested in how the brain processes information and creates conscious experience. From the perspective of cognitive neuroscience, the brain acts like a biological computing device with vast resources—among them being 100 billion transistor-like neurons, each with thousands of interconnections—capable of creating the complex universe of imagination and experience we think of as consciousness (Chalmers, 1995; Churchland, 1995; Crick, 1994).

In this chapter we will see how neuroscientists have renewed the quest to understand the multiple conscious states of which we are capable, including sleep, dreaming, hypnosis, and drug-altered consciousness. We will also introduce you briefly to the mental processes that occur outside of consciousness, laying the groundwork for more in-depth exploration of that world in later chapters on emotion, motivation, perception, and memory. As we travel this path, please keep the following Core Concept readily available to your consciousness:

CORE CONCEPT

Consciousness can take many forms, while other mental processes occur simultaneously outside our awareness.

The big picture that emerges is one of a conscious mind that can take on a variety of roles, as we will see, but one that must focus sequentially, first on one thing and then another, like a moving spotlight (see Tononi & Edelman,

1998). Consciousness is not good at multitasking: So, if you try to drive while talking on your cell phone, you must shift your attention back and forth between tasks (Rubenstein et al., 2001; Strayer et al., 2003). Meanwhile, **nonconscious processes** have no such restriction and can work on many jobs at once—which is why you can walk, chew gum, and breathe simultaneously. In more technical terms, consciousness must process information serially, while nonconscious brain circuits can processes many streams of information in parallel. We will begin our exploration of these multifarious mental states and levels with a look at some of the tools and techniques that have opened up this line of research.

Tools for Studying Consciousness

As you will recall from the previous chapter, high-tech tools, such as the MRI, PET, and EEG, have opened new windows through which researchers can look into the brain to see which regions are active during various mental tasks—showing us the "what" of consciousness. These imaging devices, of course, do not show the actual contents of conscious experience, but they quite clearly reveal distinct groups of brain structures that "light up," for example, when we read or speak (See Figure 3.1.) The resulting images have left no doubt that conscious processing involves simultaneous activity in many brain circuits, especially in the cortex and in the pathways connecting the thalamus to the cortex. But, to glimpse the underlying mental processes—the "how" of consciousness—psychologists have devised other, even more ingenious, techniques. We will see many of these techniques throughout this chapter—in fact, throughout this book. For the moment, though, we will give you just two examples, as previews of coming attractions.

Mental Rotation   A classic experiment by Roger Shepard and Jacqueline Metzler (1971) showed that it's not merely a metaphor when people speak of "turning things over" in their conscious minds. Using images like those in Figure 3.2, Shepard and Metzler asked volunteers to decide whether the two images in each pair show the same object in different positions. They reasoned that, if the mind actually rotates these images when comparing them, people would take longer to respond when the difference between the angles of the images

■ **Nonconscious processes**   Any brain process that does not involve conscious processing, including both preconscious memories and unconscious processes.

● **FIGURE 3.1**   PET Scans of the Brain at Work

These PET scans show how different regions of the brain become active during different conscious tasks.

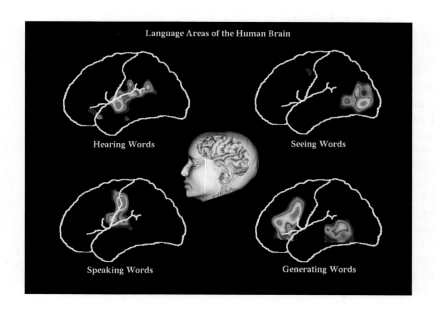

Language Areas of the Human Brain

Hearing Words

Seeing Words

Speaking Words

Generating Words

These figures are similar to those used in Shepard and Metzler's mental rotation experiment. Results showed that people took longer to decide whether the images were the same or different, as the angles through which the images in each pair were rotated. You might try your own test to verify their findings.

A

B

C

in each pair is increased. And that is exactly what they found. If you try this experiment on your friends, it is likely that they, too, will respond more quickly to pair A—where the images have been rotated through a smaller angle—than to pairs B and C.

Zooming in with the Mind   Another clever approach to the "how" of consciousness takes a different twist: Stephen Kosslyn found that we can use our conscious minds to "zoom in," camera-like, on the details of our mental images. To demonstrate this, Kosslyn (1976) first asked people to think of objects, such as an elephant or a cat or a chair. Then he asked questions about details of the imagined object (for example, "Is it a black cat?" or "Does it have a long tail?"), recording how long it took for his subjects to answer. He discovered that the smaller the detail he asked for, the longer subjects needed for a response. Subjects required extra time, Kosslyn proposed, to make a closer examination of their mental images. Both the Shepard and Metzler and the Kosslyn experiments suggest that we consciously manipulate our visual images in much the same way that we might manipulate physical objects in the outside world (Kosslyn, 1983). You can try this yourself with the demonstration in the accompanying box, "Do It Yourself! Zooming in on Mental Images."

Ask a friend to close his or her eyes and imagine a house. Then, ask your friend to describe the color of the roof, the front door, and doorbell button. Using a watch or clock that displays seconds, record the amount of time it takes to get each answer. Based on Kosslyn's research, which item would you predict would require the longest response time? The shortest?

You will probably find that the smaller the detail you ask for, the longer it takes your friend to respond. Kosslyn interpreted this to mean that people need the extra time to "zoom in" on a mental image to resolve smaller features. In other words, we examine our mental images in the same way that we examine physical objects in the external world in order to perceive the "big picture" or the details.

● **FIGURE 3.3**

As we progress through the chapter, you will learn about other techniques used by neuroscientists to study consciousness and its allied mental processes. Now, let's see what picture has emerged from this work.

The Conscious and Nonconscious Minds

William James likened ordinary waking consciousness to a flowing stream that carries ever-changing sensations, perceptions, thoughts, memories, feelings, motives, and desires. This "stream of consciousness" can include awareness both of ourselves and of stimulation from our environment. And, as we have seen, it can also include physical sensations from within, such as hunger, thirst, pain, and pleasure.

Freud used another metaphor, comparing consciousness to the tip of an iceberg, which belies a much larger presence beneath the surface. A large body of evidence now confirms Freud's insight that much of the mind lurks and works out of sight, beneath the level of awareness—although probably not in exactly the way Freud believed, as we will see later. Most of the time our nonconscious machinery quietly operates in parallel with the conscious mind, but occasionally a nonconscious motive or emotion becomes so strong that it emerges into consciousness—as when a peculiar fragrance associated with an emotional memory suddenly brings that emotion to consciousness or when a growing hunger drive spills into awareness as a "Mac attack." To get a better perspective on these processes, we will first consider the major functions of consciousness. Then we will review what research and theory can tell us about the architecture that organizes the layers of mind below its surface.

What Consciousness Does for Us   At this very moment, your consciousness is focused on these words, written in black letters on a white page. But the words don't stand alone. They have meaning, which also flows through consciousness as you read. You can, of course, shift the spotlight of your attention to something else—music in the background, perhaps—and as you do so, the words on the page slip into the fringes of awareness. You may be moving your eyes across the page, but the meaning does not really register. (Every student has had this experience.)

Now, if we can have your attention again, we'd like to remind you that consciousness has many functions. But three especially important ones were illustrated by the scenario in the previous paragraph (Solso, 2001; Tononi & Edelman, 1998):

▌ Consciousness restricts our attention. Because consciousness processes information serially, it limits what you notice and think about. In this way, consciousness keeps your brain from being overwhelmed by stimulation. It is also the property that will not let you concentrate on what you are reading when you shift your attention to music playing in the background.

▌ Consciousness provides a mental "meeting place," where sensation can combine with memory, emotions, motives, and a host of other psychological processes. Thus, consciousness is the canvas on which we create a meaningful picture from the stimulation offered by our internal and external worlds. This is the aspect of consciousness that links meaning to words on a page or connects the emotion of joy to the sight of an old friend's face.

▌ Consciousness allows us to create a mental model of the world that we can manipulate. Unlike simpler organisms, we are not prisoners of the moment: We don't just react reflexively to stimulation. Instead, we can use a conscious model of our world that draws on memory, bringing both the past and the future into awareness. With this model in mind, we can think and plan by manipulating our mental world to evaluate alternative responses and imagine how effective they will be. It is this feature of consciousness that helps you generate your own examples for concepts in this text—or keeps you from being too brutally honest with a friend wearing clothes you don't like.

These three features—restriction, combination, and manipulation—apply in varying degrees to all states of consciousness, whether dreaming, hypnosis, meditation, a drug state, or our "normal" waking state. On the other hand, nonconscious processes operate in a much different way, as we have said. To show you how this region of the mind works, let's begin by distinguishing two levels of nonconscious processing.

Levels of the Nonconscious Mind   Sigmund Freud originally proposed that processing outside awareness could influence our conscious thoughts, feelings, dreams, fantasies, and actions. And, while many cognitive psychologists would reject most details of Freud's theory as little more than fantasies, they would retain the notion that the nonconscious mind has two main divisions, often called the *preconscious* and the *unconscious*.

The Preconscious   Psychologists define memories of events (a date last weekend, for example) and facts (Salem is the capital of Oregon) that have once been the focus of attention as **preconscious memories.** They can return to consciousness with relative ease when something cues their recall. Otherwise, they lie in the background of the mind, just beyond the boundary of consciousness until needed. Preconsciousness doesn't operate under the serial, one-thing-at-a-time limitation of consciousness. On the other hand, it doesn't have the ability consciousness has for actively manipulating information.

The Unconscious A dictionary might define the term *unconscious* as the absence of all consciousness, as in one who has fainted, become comatose, or is under anesthesia. But there is another meaning for unconscious that refers to cognition occurring without awareness. In this sense, the **unconscious** refers to many levels of processing that occur without awareness, ranging from brain systems that run on "automatic pilot" to those that can have subtle influences on consciousness and behavior (Kihlstrom, 1987). You can get some idea of how these unconscious processes affect us if you think about how you often follow a familiar route to work or school without apparent thought. Let us show you another way that psychologists have demonstrated the existence of this sort of unconscious processing in the laboratory.

A Demonstration of Unconscious Processing Try filling in the blanks to make a word from the following stem:

D E F __ __ __

Using a technique called priming, psychologists can have some influence on the answers people give to such problems without their being conscious that they were influenced. In the example just given, there are a number of possible ways to complete the word stem, including *defend, defeat, defect, defile, deform, defray, defuse,* and *define.* We don't know for sure what your answer was, but we have carefully set you up to increase the probability that you would pick the word *define.* To do so, we deliberately "primed" your response by twice using the word *define* in the two paragraphs preceding our test. With priming methods such as this, psychologists have a powerful tool for probing the interaction of conscious and unconscious processes.

PSYCHOLOGY IN YOUR LIFE: THE UNCONSCIOUS— RECONSIDERED

As we have seen, the term *unconscious* can have many meanings. In Freud's psychoanalytic theory, for example, powerful unconscious forces actively work to block (or repress) sexual desires and traumatic memories (Freud, 1925). If allowed to break through into consciousness, these would cause extreme anxiety, Freud taught. In this view, the unconscious mind, then, serves as a mental dungeon where terrible urges and threatening memories can be kept "locked up" outside of awareness.

Ever since Freud, the art and literature of the Western world have been captivated by the idea of an unconscious mind filled with dark and sinister motives and memories. For example, Joseph Conrad's novel *Heart of Darkness* tells the story of a person's internal and unconscious struggle with the most evil of desires for power, destruction, and death. Unconscious desires can be sexual, as well. What else could account for the dubious success of the titillating stories splashed so obviously across the pages of the tabloids and the screens of the "soaps"?

■ **Preconscious memories** Information that is not currently in consciousness but can be recalled to consciousness voluntarily or after something calls attention to them.

■ **Unconscious** In classic Freudian theory, a part of the mind that houses memories, desires, and feelings that would be threatening if brought to consciousness. Many modern cognitive psychologists view the unconscious in less sinister terms, merely as a collection of mental processes that operate outside of awareness—but not typically suppressing information or working at odds with consciousness.

CONNECTION: CHAPTER 10

In Freud's *psychoanalytic theory,* the unconscious makes up the major part of the mind. In this view, it serves as the source of sexual and aggressive desires.

Freud also taught that we "forget" anniversaries because we have unconscious reservations about the relationship. He said that we choose mates who are, on an unconscious level, just substitutes for our fathers and mothers. And he gave us the concept of the "Freudian slip," which one wag defined as, "saying one thing when you really mean your mother."

In essence, Freud's view is just a variation on the anima hypothesis mentioned earlier: He placed the ego—the rational decision-maker part of the mind—at the center of consciousness. There, said Freud, it assumes the responsibility of keeping the sexual and aggressive forces of the unconscious in check. But was he right? While most psychologists today would say that Freud's views were better as metaphors than as objective science, his ideas are still widely accepted by the general public.

Advances in research methods (such as priming) have made it possible to analyze unconscious thought processes in ways never dreamed of by Freud (Kihlstrom, 1990; Kihlstrom et al., 1992; Rozin, 1976). As a result, the mind beneath consciousness does not appear to be so dramatic or sinister as Freud portrayed it. Rather, a cognitive view suggests a much simpler structure than the complicated censoring and repressing system that Freud proposed (Greenwald, 1992).

For the most part, the nonconscious mind seems to devote its resources to simple background tasks such as screening the incoming stream of sights, sounds, smells, and textures, rather than to repressing memories of traumatic experiences. This ability also provides a quick appraisal of events for their attractiveness or harmfulness (LeDoux, 1996). These unconscious pathways can even save your life, as when you react "without thinking" to a swerving car or a deadly snake on the path in front of you. In this fashion, the less-than-conscious mind works with consciousness, rather than against it. Ironically, the cognitive view of an unconscious that monitors, sorts, discards, and stores the flood of data we encounter may give the unconscious a larger role than Freud originally conceived.

CHECK YOUR UNDERSTANDING

1. **RECALL:** Who objected most strenuously to defining psychology as the science of consciousness?
   a. the cognitive psychologists
   b. the behaviorists
   c. the humanists
   d. the neurologists

2. **RECALL:** According to cognitive neuroscience,
   a. consciousness does not exist.
   b. creativity arises from altered states of consciousness.
   c. consciousness is a product of the brain.
   d. the conscious mind has little access to the larger world of mental activity in the unconscious.

3. **APPLICATION:** Suppose you wanted to sample the contents of preconsciousness in a group of volunteers. Which technique would be most appropriate?

   a. Give them MRI scans.
   b. Ask them to recall specific memories to consciousness.
   c. Do a priming experiment.
   d. Have them undergo psychoanalysis.

4. **UNDERSTANDING THE CORE CONCEPT:** Which of the following is a description of consciousness suggested by the Core Concept for this section?
   a. Consciousness processes information serially.
   b. Consciousness allows us to respond reflexively, without thinking.
   c. Consciousness controls the autonomic nervous system.
   d. Consciousness makes us more alert.

WHAT CYCLES OCCUR IN EVERYDAY CONSCIOUSNESS?

If you are a "morning person," you are probably at your peak of alertness soon after you awaken. But this mental state doesn't last all day. Like most other people, you probably experience a period of mental lethargy in the afternoon. At this low point in the cycle of wakefulness, you may join much of the Latin world, which wisely takes a siesta. Later, your alertness increases for a time, only to fade again during the evening hours. Punctuating this cycle may be periods of heightened focus and attention (as when you are called on in class) and periods of reverie, known as daydreams. Finally, whether you are a "morning" or "night" person, you eventually drift into that third of your life spent asleep, where conscious contact with the outside world nearly ceases.

Psychologists have traced these cyclic changes in consciousness, looking for reliable patterns. Our Core Concept for this section of the chapter summarizes what they have found:

> Consciousness changes in cycles that correspond to our biological rhythms and to the patterns of stimulation in our environment.

In this section we will devote most of our attention to the cyclic changes in consciousness involved in sleep and nocturnal dreaming. We begin, however, with another sort of "dreaming" that occurs while we are awake.

Daydreaming

In the mildly altered state of consciousness that we call **daydreaming,** attention turns inward to memories, expectations, and desires—often with vivid mental imagery (Roche & McConkey, 1990). Daydreaming occurs most often when people are alone, relaxed, engaged in a boring or routine task, or just about to fall asleep (Singer, 1966, 1975). But is daydreaming normal? You may be relieved to know that most people daydream every day. (In fact, it is abnormal if you do not!) Research shows, however, that young adults report the most frequent daydreams, with the amount of daydreaming declining significantly with increasing age (Singer & McCraven, 1961).

Daydreams can serve valuable, healthy functions (Klinger, 1987). They often dwell on practical and current concerns in people's lives, such as classes, goals (trivial or significant), and interpersonal relationships. As we ruminate on these concerns, daydreaming can help us make plans and solve problems.

On the other hand, daydreams can feature persistent and unwelcome wishes, worries, or fantasies. What can you do if that happens? Suppose that you decide to stop entertaining a particular thought—fantasies of an old flame, a persistent tune running through your head, or worries about a grade. Studies suggest that deliberate efforts to suppress unwanted thoughts are likely to backfire. In the "white bear" experiment (Wegner et al., 1987), students were asked to speak into a tape recorder about anything that came to mind. They were instructed, however, not to think about "a white bear." The results: Despite the instructions, the students mentioned a white bear about once per minute! Obviously, trying to suppress a thought or put something out of your mind can result in an obsession with the very thought you seek to escape. Yet, when you don't try to censor your thoughts but, instead, allow your mind to roam freely, as daydreaming and fantasy naturally do, unwanted or upsetting thoughts usually become less intrusive and finally cease (Wegner, 1989).

● Daydreaming, common among people of all ages, may be a source of creativity.

■ **Daydreaming** A common (and quite normal) variation of consciousness in which attention shifts to memories, expectations, desires, or fantasies and away from the immediate situation.

And how do daydreams compare with dreams of the night? No matter how realistic our fantasies may be, daydreams are rarely as vivid as our most colorful night dreams. Neither are they as mysterious—because they are more under our control. Nor do they occur, like night dreams, under the influence of biological cycles and the strange world that we call sleep. It is to this world that we now turn our attention.

Sleep: The Mysterious Third of Our Lives

If you live to be 90, you will have slept for nearly 30 years. Even though this means we "lose" a third of our lives, most of us take this lengthy alteration of daily consciousness for granted. In fact, we often anticipate sleep with pleasure. But what is this mysterious mental state? Once the province of psychoanalysts, prophets, poets, painters, and psychics, the world of sleep has now become a vibrant field of study for scientific researchers, who have shown that sleep must be understood as one of our natural biological cycles (Beardsley, 1996). We begin our exploration of this realm of altered consciousness with an examination of these cycles.

Circadian Rhythms   All creatures fall under the influence of nature's cyclic changes, especially the daily pattern of light and darkness. Among the most important for we humans are those known as **circadian rhythms,** bodily patterns that repeat approximately every 24 hours. (*Circadian* comes from the Latin *circa* for "about" + *dies* for "a day.") Internal control of these recurring rhythms resides in a "biological clock" that sets the cadence of such functions as metabolism, heart rate, body temperature, and hormonal activity. Although we don't know precisely how this clock works, we know its locus is the hypothalamus—the suprachiasmatic nucleus, to be exact (Pinel, 2003). This group of cells receives input from the eyes, and so is especially sensitive to the light–dark cycles of day and night (Barinaga, 2002). From a biological perspective, then, the cycle of sleep and wakefulness is just another circadian rhythm.

For most individuals, the normal sleep–wakefulness pattern is naturally a bit longer than a day in length. When placed for long periods in an environment in which there are no time cues, most people settle into a circadian cycle of about 25 hours. But under more normal circumstances, the pattern undergoes daily readjustment by our exposure to light and by our habitual routines (Dement & Vaughan, 1999).

Anything that throws off your biological clock affects how you feel and behave. Work schedules that shift from day to night are notorious for such effects (Dement & Vaughan, 1999; Moore-Ede, 1993). Staying up all night studying for an exam will have similar consequences. Likewise, flying across several time zones results in jet lag because the internal circadian cycle is disrupted by your new temporal environment. If it is 1:00 A.M. to your body but only 10:00 P.M. to the people around you, you must use energy and resources to adapt to your surroundings. The resulting symptoms of jet lag include fatigue, irresistible sleepiness, and temporary cognitive deficits. Air travelers should note that our biological clocks can adjust more readily to longer days than to shorter ones. Therefore, traveling eastbound (losing hours in your day) creates greater jet lag than traveling westbound (gaining hours). Apparently, it is easier to stay awake a bit longer than it is to fall asleep sooner than usual.

The Main Events of Sleep   Sleep has been a mystery for most of human history—until late one night in 1952. It was then that graduate student Eugene Aserinsky decided to make recordings of his sleeping son's brain waves and muscle movements of the eyes (Brown, 2003). The session proceeded uneventfully for about an hour and a half, with nothing but the slow rhythms of sleep

■ **Circadian rhythms**   Physiological patterns that repeat approximately every 24 hours—such as the sleep–wakefulness cycle.

appearing as tracks on the EEG. Then suddenly, a flurry of eye movements appeared. The recording showed the boy's eyeballs darting back and forth, as though he were watching a fast-changing scene. At the same time, the brain wave patterns told Aserinsky that the boy was alert. Expecting to find that his son had awakened and was looking around, Aserinsky entered the bedroom and was surprised to see him lying quietly, with his eyes closed and fast asleep. What was going on? Wisely, the researcher ran more volunteers through the same procedure, and he found that essentially the same pattern occurred periodically throughout the night in all of them.

About every 90 minutes during sleep, we enter a stage called **REM sleep,** marked by rapid eye movements (REM) beneath closed eyelids. These take place for several minutes and then abruptly cease (Aserinsky & Kleitman, 1953). The interim periods, without rapid eye movements, are known as **non-REM (NREM) sleep.** And what happens in the mind and brain during these two different phases of sleep?

To find out, researchers awakened sleepers during either REM sleep or NREM sleep and asked them to describe their mental activity (Dement & Kleitman, 1957). The NREM reports typically contained either brief descriptions of ordinary daily events or no mental activity at all. By contrast, REM reports were usually filled with vivid cognitions, featuring fanciful, bizarre scenes. In other words, rapid eye movements were a sign of dreaming. Strangely, while the eyes dance during REM sleep, the voluntary muscles in the rest of the body are immobile—paralyzed—a condition now known as **sleep paralysis.** From an evolutionary perspective, we can see that this probably kept our ancestors from wandering out of their caves and into trouble while acting out their dreams. (In case you're wondering: Sleepwalking and sleep talking don't occur during REM sleep but in the deepest stage of NREM sleep.) We'll have much more to say about dreaming in a moment. For now, let's see how REM sleep fits with the other phases of sleep.

The Sleep Cycle Imagine that you are a volunteer subject in a laboratory specializing in sleep research. Already connected to EEG recording equipment, you soon become comfortable with the wires linking your body to the machinery, and you are settling in for a night's sleep. While you are still awake and alert, the EEG shows your brain waves pulsing at a rate of about 14 cycles per second (cps). As you begin to relax and become drowsy, they slow to about 8 to 12 cps. When you fall asleep, the EEG shows further changes. Then, over the course of the night, your brain waves begin a cycle of activity much like the pattern you see in Figure 3.4—a cycle that repeats itself over and over through the night. A closer look at the recording of this cycle the next morning will show several distinct stages, each with a characteristic EEG signature (see Figure 3.5):

- In Stage 1 sleep, the EEG displays some slower (theta) activity, along with fast brain (beta) waves similar to those seen in the waking state.

- During the next phase, Stage 2, the generally slower EEG is punctuated by sleep spindles—short bursts of fast electrical activity that reliably signals the end of Stage 1.

- In the following two stages (3 and 4), the sleeper enters a progressively deeper state of relaxed sleep. The heart rate and breathing rate slow down. Brain waves also slow dramatically, with delta waves appearing for the first time. The deepest point in the sleep cycle occurs, in Stage 4, about a half hour after sleep onset.

- As Stage 4 ends, the electrical activity of the brain increases, and the sleeper climbs back up through the stages in reverse order.

■ **REM sleep** A stage of sleep that occurs approximately every 90 minutes, marked by bursts of rapid eye movements occurring under closed eyelids. REM sleep periods are associated with dreaming.
■ **Non-REM (NREM) sleep** The recurring periods, mainly associated with the deeper stages of sleep, when a sleeper is not showing rapid eye movements.
■ **Sleep paralysis** A condition in which a sleeper is unable to move any of the voluntary muscles, except those controlling the eyes. Sleep paralysis normally occurs during REM sleep.

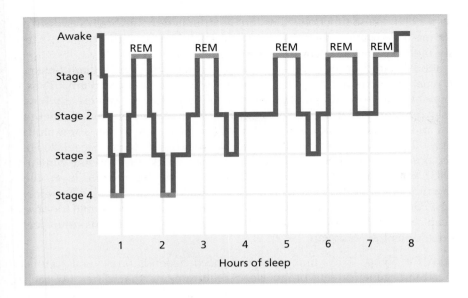

● **FIGURE 3.4** Stages Of Sleep

In a typical night, the deepest sleep (Stages 3 and 4) occurs mainly in the first few hours. As the night progresses, the sleeper spends more and more time in the stages of light sleep and in REM sleep.

● **FIGURE 3.5** EEG Patterns in Stages of Sleep

As the sleeper reaches Stage 1 again, fast beta waves recorded by the EEG reappear. In addition, the sleeper now enters REM sleep for the first time. Then, after a few minutes of REMing, the entire cycle begins to repeat itself.

Over the course of an average night's sleep, most people make the circuit up and down through the stages of sleep four to six times. In each successive cycle, the amount of time spent in deep sleep (Stages 3 and 4) decreases, and the amount of time spent in REM sleep increases. During the first cycle, the REM period may last only 10 minutes, while in the last cycle, we may spend as much as an hour REMing. A look at Figure 3.3 will show you how this pattern plays out through a typical night's sleep. Studying this pattern will not only help you understand your normal night's sleep but will also provide the framework for understanding the abnormal patterns found in most sleep disorders, which we will consider a little later. Again, please note the three most important features of normal sleep: (a) the 90-minute cycles, (b) the occurrence of deepest sleep near the beginning of the night, and (c) the increase in REM duration as sleep progresses.

What do you suppose would happen if a person were deprived of a substantial amount of REM sleep for a whole night? Laboratory studies show that REM-deprived subjects feel tired and irritable the next day. Then, during the following night, they spend much more time in REM sleep than usual, a condition known as **REM rebound.** This observation suggests that one of the functions of sleep is to satisfy a basic biological need for REM. Sleep-deprived college students take note: Because we get most of our REM sleep during the last few cycles of the night, we inevitably suffer some REM deprivation and REM rebound if we cut our night's sleep short.

The Function of Sleep   Sleep is so common among animals that it surely must have some essential function, but sleep scientists disagree on what that function is (Maquet, 2001; Pinel, 2003; Rechtschaffen, 1998). There are several possibilities. Evolutionary psychology suggests that sleep may have evolved because it enabled animals to conserve energy and stay out of harm's way at times when there was no need to forage for food or search for mates (Dement &

■ **REM rebound** A condition of increased REM sleep caused by REM-sleep deprivation.

Vaughan, 1999). These functions, then, are coordinated by the brain's circadian clock. Some experiments also suggest that sleep aids mental functioning, particularly memory and problem-solving (Wagner et al., 2004).

Yet another function of sleep was poetically described by William Shakespeare, when he spoke of "sleep that knits up the ravelled sleave of care." Thus, sleep may have a restorative function for the body and mind. But exactly how might sleep restore us? It may be a time when the body replenishes its energy supplies and purges itself of toxins built up during the day. In fact, some studies suggest that damaged brain cells do get repaired during sleep (Siegel, 2003). Another possibility has been proposed by Francis Crick and Graeme Mitchison (1983), who believe that sleep and dreams help the brain to flush out the day's accumulation of unwanted and useless information—much like reformatting a computer disk. Truth be told, however, no one has been able to show how sleep actually restores us—although there's no doubt that it makes us feel restored (Dement & Vaughan, 1999).

The Need for Sleep How much sleep we need depends on several factors. For one thing, genetics sets broad sleep requirements that differ for each species. And although sleep duration is influenced by circadian rhythms, there is some individual variation (Barinaga, 1997b; Haimov & Lavie, 1996). Part of that variation is genetic, but the amount of sleep we require is linked to our personal characteristics and habits. For example, those who sleep longer than average tend to be more nervous, worrisome, artistic, creative, and nonconforming. Short sleepers tend to be more energetic and extroverted (Hartmann, 1973). And, it is no surprise that the amount of exercise a person gets influences the need for sleep. Oddly, however, strenuous physical activity during the day increases the amount of slow-wave sleep in Stage 4, but it has no effect on REM time (Horne, 1988).

From a developmental perspective, we see that sleep duration and the shape of the sleep cycle change over one's lifetime. As Figure 3.6 shows, newborns sleep about 16 hours per day, with half that time devoted to REM. During childhood, those numbers gradually decline. Young adults typically sleep seven to eight hours (although they may need more), with about 20% REM. By old age, we sleep even less, with only 15% of sleep spent in REM. You can find out whether you are getting enough sleep by answering the questions in the accompanying "Do It Yourself!" box.

● **FIGURE 3.6** Patterns of Human Sleep Over a Lifetime

The graph shows changes with age in the total amounts of REM and NREM sleep and in the percentage of time spent in REM sleep. Note that, over the years, the amount of REM sleep decreases considerably, while NREM diminishes less sharply.

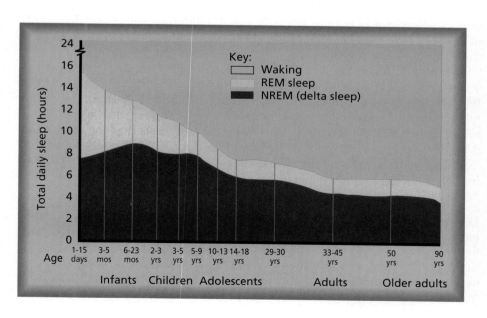

Many college students operate in a chronic state of sleep deprivation. Because their schedules are crowded with study, work, and social events, students may convince themselves that they need only a few hours sleep each night. And, in fact, the average college student sleeps only about 6.8 hours a night (Hicks, 1990). Does too little sleep really make a difference in how well you perform in your classes? Psychologist Cheryl Spinweber (1990) has found that sleep-deprived undergraduates get lower grades than their counterparts who get enough sleep.

How can you tell if you need more sleep? Answer the following questions honestly:

1. Do you often get sleepy in your classes?
2. Do you sleep late on weekends?
3. Do you usually get sleepy when you get bored?
4. Do you often fall asleep while reading or watching TV?
5. Do you usually fall asleep within five minutes of going to bed?
6. Do you awake in the morning feeling that you are not rested?
7. Would you oversleep if you did not use an alarm clock to drive you out of bed?

If you answered "Yes" to any of these questions, chances are that you are shorting yourself on sleep. You may also be paying the price in the quality of your learning and in your grades.

Sleep Debt versus the Circadian Clock So, how much sleep do we humans need—and what happens if we don't get enough? Your mother was right: Most adults need to sleep about eight hours, or a bit more, to feel good and function efficiently. But that's only an average. For different individuals, the amount of sleep needed ranges from about six to nine hours (although most people need more sleep than they think they do). In the sleep laboratory, when volunteers are placed in a dark room and allowed to sleep without interruption and without reference to clocks, the average adult settles into a pattern that produces about eight and one-half hours of sleep each night. Yet, in their daily lives most Americans get significantly less—night after night (Maas, 1999). This creates a sleep shortage that researcher William Dement calls a **sleep debt** (Dement & Vaughan, 1999).

People who pile up a chronic sleep debt usually don't realize it (Dement, 2000; Dement & Vaughan, 1999). They may be groggy and sleepy when the alarm clock rouses them in the morning. But they don't see this as a sign of a sleep debt because their circadian clocks make them "wake up" and begin to feel alert over the next few hours. Afternoon drowsiness may be attributed to a big lunch—which, in truth, does not cause sleepiness. (It's the clock, again.) They may also rationalize away their struggle to stay awake in a meeting or class by telling themselves that sleepiness is a normal response to boredom (Van Dongen et al., 2003). In fact, the normal response to boredom is restlessness—not sleepiness—unless one is sleep deprived.

What is actually happening is that the sleep-deprived individual gets caught in a daily tug-of-war between the pulls of a sleep debt and our relentless circadian rhythms. But our internal clocks can fool us, too. Even when we have not had enough sleep, the clock in the brain can make us feel relatively alert at certain times of the day—usually late morning and late afternoon. But this alertness can also be illusory. With a chronic sleep debt, you are never as alert and mentally efficient as you could be if the sleep debt were paid with a few good nights of sleep (Van Dongen et al., 2003). Unfortunately, the sleep debt is sometimes "paid" with a tragedy—as happened dramatically a few years ago, when *Exxon Valdez*, a giant tanker, ran aground, spilling oil across a pristine bay in the Alaskan wilderness. The ensuing investigation revealed that a crew member who was steering the ship at the time had had only six hours of sleep in the previous two days.

Of special interest to students is this fact: Sleep deprivation can have a devastating effect on cognitive and motor functioning (Pilcher & Walters, 1997). In plainer language, William Dement says that a big sleep debt "makes you stupid" (Dement & Vaughan, 1999, p. 231). Evidence of this is found in a study

■ **Sleep debt** A sleep deficiency caused by not getting the amount of sleep that one requires for optimal functioning.

that deprived one group of volunteers of sleep and gave another group enough alcohol to make them legally drunk (their blood alcohol content reached .1 percent). After 24 hours of sleep loss—like staying up all night studying for a test—the sleepy volunteers were performing just like the intoxicated group on tests of thinking and coordination (Fletcher et al., 2003).

Unfortunately, sleep-deprived people usually don't realize how impaired they actually are. Further, the pressures and opportunities of modern life commonly make us underestimate the amount of sleep we need. We may also believe that we can combat sleepiness and successfully reduce our need for sleep by dint of will power and caffeine. But such measures never give us the clarity of mind that a good night's sleep does. As a result, we may struggle much of our lives with a chronic sleep deficit, never realizing why we must wage a daily battle with drowsiness.

Dreaming: The Pageants of the Night

Every night of your life, you experience a spectacular series of events staged only in your dreams. What produces these fantastic cognitive spectacles? And, what—if anything—do they mean? As we saw earlier, sleep scientists now know that dreams occur regularly throughout the night, most often in REM sleep. They have also identified the parts of the brain that control dreaming—including, especially, parts of the brain stem. What remains most mysterious about this stage of sleep is why we dream.

The ancient Israelites interpreted dreams as messages from God. Their Egyptian contemporaries attempted to influence dreams by sleeping in temples dedicated to the god of dreaming, Serapis. And in India, the sacred Vedas described the religious significance of dreams. Meanwhile, in China dreaming held an element of risk. During a dream, the ancient Chinese believed, the soul wandered about outside the body. For that reason they were reluctant to awaken a sleeper hastily, lest the soul not find its way back to the body (Dement, 1980).

From the perspective of many African and Native American cultures, dreams were an extension of waking reality. Consequently, when traditional Cherokee Indians dreamed of snakebite, they received appropriate emergency treatment upon awakening. Likewise, when an African tribal chieftain dreamed of England, he ordered a set of European clothes; and, when he appeared in the new togs, his friends congratulated him on making the trip (Dement, 1980).

In contrast with such folk theories, sleep scientists have approached dreaming with this question: What function do dreams have? On a biological level, dreams may be necessary for healthy brain functioning, although the evidence for that is not certain (Siegel, 2003). From a cognitive perspective, some experts see dreams as meaningful mental events, serving pressing cognitive needs or reflecting important events or fantasies in the dreamer's mental world. Others argue that dreams are merely the brain's random activity during sleep—and, therefore, their content may have no special meaning. Let's look at both sides of this debate on the meaningfulness of dreams.

Dreams as Meaningful Events   At the beginning of the 20th century, Sigmund Freud laid out the most complex and comprehensive theory of dreams and their meanings ever developed—a theory that has since enjoyed enormous influence, despite a lack of scientific evidence to support it (Squier & Domhoff, 1998). In this view, dreams represent "the royal road to the unconscious," lined with clues to an individual's hidden mental life. For this reason, Freud made the analysis of dreams the cornerstone of psychoanalysis, as set out in his classic book *The Interpretation of Dreams* (1900).

● Death-related images appear more often in dreams of Mexican American college students than in those of Anglo-American college students. This probably occurs because death is more prominently a part of Mexican culture, as can be seen in this figure, used in the Day of the Dead celebration.

Freud's Theory of Dreams   In psychoanalytic theory, dreams have two main functions: to *guard* sleep (by disguising disruptive thoughts with symbols) and to serve as sources of wish fulfillment. Freud believed that dreams play their guardian role by relieving psychic tensions created during the day. They serve their wish-fulfillment function by allowing the dreamer to work harmlessly through unconscious desires.

In his explanation of the meaning of dreams, Freud distinguished between the **manifest content**—the dream's story line—and the **latent content**—the (supposed) symbolic meaning of the dream. Psychoanalytic therapists, therefore, scrutinize the manifest content of their patients' dreams for clues that relate to latent motives and conflicts that may lurk in the unconscious. For example, clues relating to sexual conflicts might take the form of long rigid objects or containers which, in Freudian theory, symbolize the male and female genitals.

Must you be a trained psychoanalyst to understand dreams? Not necessarily. The manifest content in many of our dreams has a fairly obvious connection to our waking lives. You have probably noticed that frightening dreams often relate to life stressors that have found their way into your sleeping thoughts. Research has lent support to such observations. For example, one study found that individuals depressed about divorce often had dreams that were fixed on past relationships (Cartwright, 1984). By analyzing the patterns and content of your own dreams, you may find it is not difficult to assign meaning to many of the images and actions you recall (Hall, 1953/1966; Van de Castle, 1994). We must emphasize, however, that there is no solid scientific support for Freudian interpretations of latent dream content.

Dreams Vary by Culture, Gender, and Age   Freudian dream analysis has also been challenged on the grounds that Freud was not always scrupulous in his research. For example, he asserted that boys frequently dream of strife with their fathers—but he did no careful studies to verify his theoretical suspicions. Rather, on the basis of a few cases, he jumped to the conclusion that such dreams were signs of unconscious sexual jealousy. Many other explanations are possible, however, as anthropologists have shown by studying dreams of the Trobriand Islanders. Boys in that culture don't dream of their fathers so much as their uncles, who act as the disciplinarians in that society (Malinowski, 1927; Segall et al., 1990). Freud's theory, then, may be an example of the confirmation bias.

Modern sleep scientists have taken a more objective approach to dreams than Freud did (see Domhoff, 1996). They now know that the content of dreams varies by age, gender, and culture. Children are more likely to dream about animals than adults are, and the animals in their dreams are more likely to be large, threatening, and wild. In contrast, college students dream more usually of small animals, pets, and tame creatures. This may mean that children feel less in control of their world than adults do and so may find that world depicted in scarier imagery while they sleep (Van de Castle, 1983, 1994).

Women everywhere more commonly dream of children, while men more often dream of aggression, weapons, and tools (Murray, 1995). In a sample of over 1800 dreams collected by dream researcher Calvin Hall, American women dreamed about both men and women, while men dreamed about men twice as often as about women. In another sample of over 1300 dreams, Hall found that hostile interactions between characters outnumbered friendly exchanges and that 64% of dreamed emotions had a negative complexion, such as anger and sadness (Hall, 1951, 1984).

The highly specific effects of culture can be seen in reports from the West African nation of Ghana, where dreams often feature attacks by cows (Barnouw,

◀ **CONNECTION: CHAPTER 1**

The *confirmation bias* leads us to notice evidence that agrees with our views and ignore evidence that does not.

■ **Manifest content**   The story line of a dream, taken at face value without interpretation.
■ **Latent content**   The symbolic meaning of objects and events in a dream. Latent content is usually an interpretation based on Freud's psychoanalytic theory or one of its variants. The latent content of a dream involving clocks might involve fear of the menstrual cycle and, hence, of one's sexuality.

1963). Likewise, Americans frequently find themselves embarrassed by public nakedness in their dreams, although such reports rarely occur in cultures where people customarily wear few clothes. Images of death appear more often in the dreams of Mexican American college students than in the dreams of Anglo American students, probably because concerns about death are more a part of life in Latin American cultures (Roll et al., 1974). In general, the cross-cultural research lends support to Rosalind Cartwright's hypothesis (1977) that dreams merely reflect life events that are important to the dreamer.

Dreams and Recent Experience   Sleep research has also found—as we might expect—that dream content frequently connects with recent experience. If you're struggling with your taxes all day, you're likely to dream about your taxes at night, especially during your first REM period. Typically, the first dream of the night connects with events of the previous day. Then, dreaming in the second REM period (90 minutes later) may build on a theme that emerged during the first REM period. And so it goes through the night, like a rumor passed from one person to another: The final dream that emerges may have a connection—but only a remote one—to events of the previous day. But because the final dream of the night is the one most likely to be remembered, we may not recognize the link with the previous day's events (Cartwright, 1977; Kiester, 1980).

Dreams and Cognition   The relationship between dreams and recent experience may belie yet another possible function of dreams. Comparisons of individuals who were selectively deprived of REM sleep with those deprived of NREM sleep suggest that REM sleep helps us remember—although we must add that this conclusion is still controversial (Kinoshita, 1992; Maquet, 2001; Siegel, 2001; Stickgold et al., 2001; Winson, 1990). It may be that REM sleep is a normal part of weaving new experiences into the fabric of old memories (Barinaga, 1994; Cartwright, 1978; Dement, 1980; Karni et al., 1994).

Dreams as Random Activity of the Brain   Not everyone believes that dream content has any special meaning of consequence—certainly not any latent content that warrants psychoanalytic interpretation. In particular, the **activation-synthesis theory** says that dreams result when the sleeping brain tries to make sense of its own spontaneous bursts of activity (Leonard, 1998; Squier & Domhoff, 1998). In this view, dreams have their origin in periodic neural discharges emitted by the sleeping brain stem. As this energy sweeps over the cerebral cortex, the sleeper experiences impressions of sensation, memory, motivation, emotion, and movement. Although the cortical activation is random, and the images it generates may not be logically connected, the brain tries to make sense of the stimulation it receives. To do so, the brain synthesizes or pulls together the "messages" in these random electrical bursts by creating a coherent story. A dream, then, could merely be the brain's way of making sense out of nonsense.

The proponents of this theory, J. Allan Hobson and Robert McCarley (1977), argued that REM sleep furnishes the brain with an internal source of needed stimulation. This internal activation promotes the growth and development of the brain at the time when the sleeping brain has blocked out external stimulation. Dream content, therefore, results from brain activation, not unconscious wishes or other meaningful mental processes. While Hobson (1988, 2002) claims that the story line in our dreams is added as a "brainstorm afterthought," he does acknowledge that dream content may nevertheless have some psychological meaning in that the dream story is influenced by culture, gender, personality factors, and recent events. Thus, when brain activations are synthesized, dreams seem familiar and meaningful.

■ **Activation-synthesis theory**
The theory that dreams begin with random electrical *activation* coming from the brain stem. Dreams, then, are the brain's attempt to make sense of—to *synthesize*—this random activity.

Dreams as a Source of Creative Insights Even if Hobson and McCarley are right—that dreams have no special meaning other than an attempt by the brain to make sense out of nonsense—they could still be a source of creative ideas. In fact, it would be astonishing if we did not turn to such wild and sometimes wonderful scenes in the night for inspiration. As we have seen, writers, composers, and scientists have done just that.

"Dream explorer" Robert Moss (1996) cites 19th-century physiologist Herman von Helmholtz, who insisted that creative dreaming would result from doing three things: (1) first, saturating yourself in a problem or issue that interests you; (2) next, letting your creative ideas incubate by not pushing yourself for a solution but by shifting attention to something that is relaxing; and (3) finally, allowing yourself time to experience illumination, a sudden flash of insight into the answer you seek.

● Sleep and dreaming have inspired much art, as we see here in Rousseau's *Sleeping Gypsy*.

Moss himself recommends the following technique to find creative guidance in your dreams: First, bring to mind an expert whom you admire in your field of endeavor. Before you go to sleep, imagine you are asking this person for help in solving your problem; then tell yourself to dream the answer. If you wake from a dream, quickly write or sketch all you can recall—no matter what the dream was about. Later, when you review your notes, you may find that your approach to the problem has been "given a distinct tilt" (Moss, 1996, p. 318). Your later interpretation of your dream thoughts might surprise you with insights you didn't even know you could achieve. Perhaps, if you take creative control of your dreams, you can create your own "monster," just as Mary Shelley did.

PSYCHOLOGY IN YOUR LIFE:
SLEEP DISORDERS

You may be among the more than 100 million Americans who get insufficient sleep or poor-quality sleep (Dement & Vaughan, 1999). Some of these sleep problems are job related. Among people who work night shifts, for example, more than half nod off at least once a week on the job. And it may be no coincidence that some of the world's most serious accidents—the disastrous radiation emissions at the Three Mile Island and Chernobyl nuclear plants and the massive toxic chemical discharge at Bhopal—have occurred during late evening hours when people are likely to be programmed for sleep. Sleep experts speculate that many accidents occur because key personnel fail to function optimally as a result of insufficient sleep—as we noted earlier in the case of the *Exxon Valdez* oil spill (Dement, 1980; Dement & Vaughan, 1999).

Along with these job-related sleep problems, there are several clinical sleep disorders that sleep researchers have studied in their laboratories. Some are common, while others are both rare and bizarre. Some are relatively benign, and some are potentially life threatening. The single element that ties them together is a disruption in one or more parts of the normal sleep cycle.

Insomnia is usually the diagnosis when people feel dissatisfied with the amount of sleep they get. Its symptoms include chronic inability to fall asleep quickly, frequent arousals during sleep, or early-morning awakening. Insomnia sufferers number about one-third of all adults, making this the most common of sleep disorders (Dement & Vaughan, 1999).

■ **Insomnia** The most common of sleep disorders—involving insufficient sleep, the inability to fall asleep quickly, frequent arousals, or early awakenings.

CONNECTION: CHAPTER 13

Cognitive behavioral therapy combines cognitive and behavioral techniques in treating psychological disorders.

● Insomnia is a complex disorder caused by a variety of psychological, environmental, and biological factors. This college student anxiously contemplates her inability to get enough rest for the next day's classes.

■ **Sleep apnea** A respiratory disorder in which the person intermittently stops breathing many times while asleep.

■ **Night terrors** Deep sleep episodes that seem to produce terror, although any terrifying mental experience (such as a dream) is usually forgotten upon awakening. Night terrors occur mainly in children.

An occasional bout of sleeplessness is normal, especially when you have exciting or worrisome events on your mind. These incidents pose no special danger in themselves, unless attempts are made to treat the problem with barbiturates or over-the-counter "sleeping pills." These drugs disrupt the normal sleep cycle by cutting short REM sleep periods (Dement, 1980). As a result, they can actually aggravate insomnia by making the user feel less rested and more sleepy. Much more effective is psychological treatment employing cognitive behavioral therapy, which has had remarkable success (Smith, 2001).

Sleep apnea, another common disorder, may be apparent only in a person's complaints of daytime sleepiness and a sleep partner's complaints about snoring. Behind the curtain of the night, the cause can be found in an abnormal breathing pattern. The apnea sufferer actually stops breathing for up to a minute, as often as several hundred times each night! (In case you're concerned, the brief cessation of breathing a few times each hour during the night is normal.) Most commonly, this results from collapse of the airway when the sleeper's muscle tone relaxes. The result is another major symptom of sleep apnea: frequent loud snoring, occurring each time the patient runs short of oxygen and tries mightily to get air through the collapsed airway (Seligson, 1994). As breathing stops and the sleeper's blood oxygen level plummets, the body's emergency system kicks into gear, causing distress hormones to course through the body. In the process, the sleeper awakens briefly, begins breathing again, and then falls back to sleep. Because most of this happens in deep sleep, there is usually no memory of the episode.

Failure to recognize the nature of the problem can cause sufferers—and their families and coworkers—to interpret unusual daytime behavior as laziness or neglect. While this may be disruptive to relationships, sleep apnea can also have harmful biological effects that include elevated blood pressure, and can put dangerous levels of stress on the blood vessels and heart (Anch et al., 1988; Stavish, 1994a).

Occasional episodes of sleep apnea are likely to occur in premature infants, who may need physical stimulation to start breathing again. Further, any tendency toward sleep apnea can be aggravated by putting a young child to bed on its stomach. (Sleep scientists strongly recommend "back to sleep.") Obviously, the problem can be lethal, and it is one possible cause of sudden infant death syndrome (SIDS). Until their underdeveloped respiratory systems mature, these infants must remain connected to breathing monitors. For adults with sleep apnea, permanent breathing failure is not a strong concern. In adults, treatment focuses on the hundreds of nightly apnea episodes, which can be alleviated by use of a device that pumps extra air into the lungs and keeps the airway open during sleep.

Night terrors, which occur primarily in children, pose no health threat. Typically, a night terror attack presents itself as the screaming of a terrified-looking child who is actually in Stage 4 sleep and very difficult to awaken. When finally alert, the child may still feel fearful but have no specific memory of what mental events might have caused the night terror. In fact, the whole experience is likely to be more memorable to the beleaguered family members than it is to the child.

Unlike garden-variety nightmares, sleep-terror episodes occur in deep sleep, rather than in REM sleep. In this respect they are like sleepwalking and sleep talking, which also occur in Stage 4. All three of these conditions seem to have a genetic component. In themselves, they are not dangerous, although sleepwalkers can inadvertently climb out of upper-story windows or walk into a busy street—so it pays to take some precautions. In most cases, sleepwalking and night terrors will diminish or disappear in adulthood, but if they pose persistent and chronic problems, the individual should be evaluated by a sleep specialist.

Narcolepsy, one of the most unusual of sleep disorders, produces sudden daytime sleep attacks, often without warning. But these are no ordinary waves of drowsiness. So suddenly do these sleep attacks develop that narcolepsy sufferers have reported falling asleep while driving a car, climbing a ladder, or scuba diving under 20 feet of water. Narcoleptic sleep attacks may also be preceded by a sudden loss of muscle control, a condition known as *cataplexy*.

Strangely, anything exciting can trigger a narcoleptic episode. For example, these patients commonly report that they fall asleep while laughing at a joke or even while having sex. Obviously, narcolepsy can be dangerous—and not so good for intimate relationships, either.

Assembling the pieces of this puzzle of symptoms, we find that narcolepsy is fundamentally a disorder of REM sleep. Specifically, a sleep recording will show that the narcolepsy victim has an abnormal sleep-onset REM period. That is, instead of waiting the usual 90 minutes to begin REMing, the narcoleptic person enters REM as sleep begins. You may have already guessed that the accompanying cataplexy is simply REM sleep paralysis.

Studies of narcoleptic animals show that the disorder is a genetic problem affecting the sleep-control circuitry in the brain stem (Harder, 2004). It has no known cure, but we have drugs that diminish the frequency of both the sleep attacks and the cataplexy. And now that we know that the cause is biological, narcoleptic patients are no longer sent to psychotherapy aimed at searching for the unconscious conflicts that were once assumed to underlie the disorder.

So, what should you do if you suspect that you have a serious sleep disorder, such as chronic insomnia, sleep apnea, or narcolepsy? An evaluation by a sleep expert is the place to start. Many hospitals have sleep disorder clinics to which your physician or clinical psychologist can refer you.

● The discovery of narcolepsy in dogs showed that the disorder has a biological basis.

■ **Narcolepsy** A disorder of REM sleep, involving sleep-onset REM periods and sudden daytime REM-sleep attacks usually accompanied by cataplexy.

CHECK YOUR UNDERSTANDING

1. **RECALL:** Which statement is true about daydreaming?
    a. Most people can easily suppress unwanted thoughts.
    b. Most people daydream every day.
    c. Daydreams usually serve as an escape from the concerns of real life.
    d. Daydreams are usually more vivid than night dreams.

2. **RECALL:** All of the following are related to our circadian rhythms, except
    a. sleep.
    b. dreaming.
    c. jet lag.
    d. daydreaming.

3. **RECALL:** Suppose that you are working in a sleep laboratory, where you are monitoring a subject's sleep recording during the night. As the night progresses, you would expect to see that
    a. the four-stage cycle gradually lengthens.
    b. REM periods become longer.
    c. Stage 3 and 4 sleep periods lengthen.
    d. dreaming becomes less frequent.

4. **RECALL:** According to the activation-synthesis theory, dreams are
    a. replays of events during the previous day.

b. an attempt by the brain to make sense of random activity in the brain stem.
    c. a storylike episode that provides clues about problems in the unconscious mind.
    d. wish fulfillments.

5. **APPLICATION:** Which of the following symptoms suggests the presence of a sleep disorder?
    a. a brief cessation of breathing once or twice a night
    b. a REM period at the beginning of sleep
    c. needing nine hours of sleep each night in order to feel rested
    d. not remembering your dreams

6. **UNDERSTANDING THE CORE CONCEPT:** Our Core Concept states that consciousness changes in cycles that normally correspond to our biological rhythms and to the patterns of our environment. Which of the following illustrates this concept?
    a. priming
    b. consciousness, preconsciousness, and the unconscious
    c. REM rebound
    d. sleep and dreaming

ANSWERS: 1.b 2.d 3.b 4.b 5.b 6.d

WHAT OTHER FORMS CAN CONSCIOUSNESS TAKE?

Children stand on their heads or spin around to make themselves dizzy. You may seek similar sensations on hair-raising theme-park rides or by sky diving. But why do people do these strange things to themselves? One view says that "human beings are born with a drive to experience modes of awareness other than the normal waking one; from very young ages, children experiment with techniques to change consciousness" (Weil, 1977, p. 37). So, sleep, dreams, fantasies, and thrilling experiences offer compelling alternatives to everyday conscious experience.

In this section of the chapter, we will see how certain psychological techniques, such as hypnosis and meditation, can alter consciousness, too. But, for some people, these conventional alternatives may not provide the states of consciousness they seek. Instead, they may turn to drugs that alter ordinary awareness. We will also examine this approach to changing consciousness. Our discussion of drugs will include both legal substances, such as alcohol, tobacco, and caffeine, and illegal drugs, such heroin, PCP, cannabis, and amphetamines. So, what is the theme that ties these altered states of consciousness together? The Core Concept of this section says:

An altered state of consciousness occurs when some aspect of normal consciousness is modified by mental, behavioral, or chemical means.

While this may, at first, sound simplistic, it carries the important implication that altered states do not involve any mysterious or paranormal phenomena that defy rational explanation. Rather, altered states are modifications of ordinary consciousness that we can study with the tools of science. Let's begin with what is known about hypnosis.

Hypnosis

The cartoon images have it wrong. Neither the hypnotist's eyes nor fingertips emit strange, mesmerizing rays that send subjects into a compliant stupor—nor does a dangling shiny bauble have the power to control people's minds.

● A roller coaster ride is one way to alter your consciousness.

● Hypnosis can help to control pain in many individuals. Here, a woman is learning hypnotic techniques that she will use in natural childbirth.

A more accurate (but much less dramatic) picture would show the hypnotist making suggestions to promote concentration and relaxation (Barber, 1976, 1986). Soon the subject appears to be asleep, although he or she can obviously hear suggestions and carry out requests. In some cases, the individual under hypnosis also seems to have amazing powers to ignore pain, remember long-forgotten details, and create hallucinations. But what mental processes make these things happen? To find out, we will explore several viewpoints on the nature of hypnosis. Then, we will consider some of its valid and practical uses by psychologists.

The term *hypnosis* derives from *Hypnos,* the name of the Greek god of sleep. Yet, the EEG record tells us that ordinary sleep plays no role in hypnosis, even though hypnotized individuals may appear to be in a relaxed, sleeplike state. (There is no unique EEG signature for hypnosis.) Most authorities would say **hypnosis** involves a state of awareness characterized by deep relaxation, heightened suggestibility, and focused attention.

When deeply hypnotized, some people have the special ability to respond to suggestion with dramatic changes in perception, memory, motivation, and sense of self-control (Orne, 1980). And, yes, stage hypnotists can make carefully selected volunteers quack like a duck or seem to like the taste of a bitter lemon. After the experience is over, people often report that they experienced heightened responsiveness to the hypnotist's suggestions and felt that their behavior was performed without intention or any conscious effort.

Hypnotizability Dramatic stage performances of hypnosis give the impression that hypnotic power lies with the hypnotist. However, the real star is the person who is hypnotized. The hypnotist is more like an experienced guide showing the way. Some individuals can even practice self-hypnosis, or autohypnosis, by inducing the hypnotic state through self-administered suggestions.

The single most important factor in achieving a hypnotic state is a participant's susceptibility. Experts call this hypnotizability, and they measure it by a person's responsiveness to standardized suggestions. Individuals differ in this susceptibility, varying from complete unresponsiveness to any suggestion, at one extreme, to total responsiveness to virtually every suggestion, at the other. A highly hypnotizable person may respond to suggestions to move their arms, walk about, experience hallucinations, have amnesia for important memories, and become insensitive to painful stimuli. And, we should add, because hypnosis involves heightened suggestibility, any "recovered memories" obtained by this means are highly suspect.

Figure 3.7 shows the percentage of college-age people who achieved various levels of hypnotizability the first time they were given a hypnotic induction test. For example, a hypnotist may test a new subject's acceptance of suggestion by saying, "Your right hand is lighter than air," and observing whether the subject allows his or her arm to float upward. High scorers are more likely than low scorers to experience pain relief, or hypnotic analgesia, and to respond to hypnotic suggestions for experiencing perceptual distortions.

Hypnosis as an Altered State The experts disagree about the psychological mechanisms involved in hypnosis (Fromm & Shor, 1979; Kihlstrom, 1998; Kirsch & Lynn, 1995, 1998; Woody & Sadler, 1998). Some believe that hypnosis is a distinct state of consciousness, quite separate from sleep or our normal waking state (Fromm & Shor, 1979). Other experts propose that hypnosis is simply heightened motivation (Barber, 1979; Kirsch & Braffman, 2001). In this view, hypnotic subjects are not entranced but merely motivated to focus their attention and to channel more energy into suggested activities. They are hypnotized because they want or expect to be, so they focus on expressing and achieving the responses the hypnotist tries to evoke. Still other experts think

● **FIGURE 3.7** Level of Hypnosis Reached at First Induction

This graph shows the results achieved by 533 subjects hypnotized for the first time. (Hypnotizability was measured by the 12-item Stanford Hypnotic Susceptibility Scale.)

■ **Hypnosis** An induced state of awareness, usually characterized by heightened suggestibility, deep relaxation, and highly focused attention.

CONNECTION: CHAPTER 12

Extreme forms of dissociation are associated with clinical disorders, known as *dissociated states*. These include *dissociative identity disorder* (formerly called "multiple personality disorder").

that hypnosis is usually a social process, involving role playing, often to please the hypnotist (Sarbin & Coe, 1972).

A widely held view, originally proposed by researcher Ernest Hilgard (1992), portrays hypnosis as a dissociated state, involving a "hidden observer" in the person's mind, operating in parallel with normal consciousness. Hilgard has shown that hypnotized individuals who say they feel no pain when their hand is placed in ice water will nevertheless respond affirmatively to the instruction, "If some part of you does feel pain, please raise your right index finger." Hilgard believed that attention to the painful sensation was shifted to the hidden observer, leaving normal consciousness blissfully unaware.

Recent theories have attempted to find common ground among these perspectives. And perhaps all have a bit of the truth. It may be that hypnosis, like the normal waking state, can cover a whole range of dissociated states, intensified motives, heightened expectations, and social interactions (Kirsch & Lynn, 1995; Woody & Sadler, 1998).

Practical Uses of Hypnosis   Stage tricks aside, what is hypnosis good for? Because it can exert a powerful influence on psychological and body functions in some people, hypnosis can be a useful tool for researchers (Bowers, 1983; Hilgard, 1968, 1973; Miller & Bowers, 1993; Nash, 2001). By using normal volunteers under hypnosis, an experimenter can induce temporary mental conditions, such as anxiety, depression, or hallucinations, instead of having to find individuals who already have these problems. For example, in one study of the psychological issues associated with hearing loss, college students given the hypnotic suggestion to become deaf on cue reported feeling paranoid and excluded because they could not hear what other subjects were saying and assumed they were being deliberately whispered about and excluded (Zimbardo et al., 1981).

Hypnosis has uses in psychological treatment, too. For instance, it can be an effective tool in desensitizing phobic patients who are afraid of heights or spiders. It can also be a part of a relaxation training program designed to combat stress. In addition, therapists find it useful for eliminating unwanted behaviors, such as smoking. A frequently used technique calls for planting posthypnotic suggestions that can diminish a patient's cravings (Barnier & McConkey, 1998; Kihlstrom, 1985). By means of posthypnotic suggestion, a therapist can also induce the patient to forget events that occurred during or before the hypnotic session, an effect called *posthypnotic amnesia*.

Finally, hypnosis has a place in medical and dental treatment, especially for managing pain during procedures in which the patient wants to avoid the risks of anesthesia (Nash, 2001). For example, the Lamaze method of natural childbirth uses a hypnosis-like procedure as a primary means of pain control. However, it is important to note that not everyone can be hypnotized deeply enough for effective analgesia (Callahan, 1997; Miller & Bowers, 1993; Orne, 1980). Still, in some cases, hypnosis alone will allow patients to undergo treatments that would otherwise cause excruciating pain (Finer, 1980). And for some highly suggestible individuals, hypnosis may actually be superior to conventional anesthesia for controlling pain. Moreover, for certain individuals, hypnosis works better to mask pain than does acupuncture, aspirin, Valium, or even morphine (Stern et al., 1977).

How does hypnosis produce pain relief? Hilgard's hidden-observer explanation is one possibility, although other scientists have taken a more biological approach to the problem. Currently there is no universally accepted explanation, although we can rule out one contender. Experiments have demonstrated that endorphins, which account for the pain-relieving property of placebos, are *not* responsible for hypnotic analgesia (Grevert & Goldstein, 1985; Mayer,

CONNECTION: CHAPTER 2

Endorphins are the body's own opiate-like substances.

1979; Watkins & Mayer, 1982). We will consider another possibility, called the *gate-control theory,* in our discussion of pain, coming up in Chapter 5. For now, we will accept hypnosis as a valuable tool about which much remains to be learned concerning the ways in which it alters consciousness.

Meditation

Many religions and traditional psychologies of the Asian and Pacific cultures use forms of **meditation** to direct consciousness away from worldly concerns and temptations. Although the purpose of meditation varies among practitioners, many use it to seek some form of spiritual enlightenment and to increase self-knowledge and well-being. Although meditators may use a variety of techniques, they commonly begin by concentrating on a repetitive behavior (such as breathing), assuming certain body positions (yogic postures), and minimizing external stimulation. (You can see the similarities with hypnosis.)

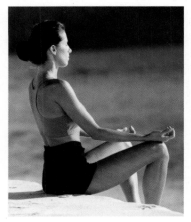

● Meditation produces relaxation and, perhaps, new insights.

To view meditation as an altered state of consciousness may reflect a particularly Western worldview, because Asian beliefs about the mind are typically different from those of Western cultures (Austin, 1998, Rosch, 1999). Buddhism, for example, teaches that the visible universe is an illusion of the senses. To become enlightened, a Buddhist tries to control bodily yearnings, to stop the ordinary experiences of the senses and mind, and to discover how to see things in their truest light. Thus, in the Buddhist view, meditation more accurately captures reality. In contrast, Western cognitive scientists often view meditation as an altered form of consciousness, and they aspire to understand it and to harness it for therapeutic purposes (Barinaga, 2003b).

What exactly are the mental and physical effects of meditation? Experienced meditators show changes in their brain-wave patterns (Kasamatsu & Hirai, 1966). Along the same lines, a recent study by Richard Davidson and his colleagues showed that meditation produces frontal lobe changes that are also associated with positive emotions (Davidson et al., 2003). Other studies have linked meditation with beneficial changes in blood pressure and stress hormones (Seeman et al., 2003). And, as still other studies have shown, meditation produces relaxation and reduces anxiety, especially in people who function in stress-filled environments (Benson, 1975; Bjork, 1991; Shapiro, 1985; van Dam, 1996). In many ways, then, meditating is like resting, because it has been found to reduce various signs of bodily arousal (Dillbeck & Orme-Johnson, 1987; Holmes, 1984; Morrell, 1986). As for some of the more subjective benefits attributed to meditation, such as its power to bring new understandings and meaning to one's life, such issues lie beyond the limits in which science can operate objectively.

Psychoactive Drug States

For millennia, humans have used alcohol, opium, cannabis, mescaline, coca, caffeine, and other drugs to alter their everyday perceptions of reality. Especially under stress, people throughout the world take drugs for pleasure, for relaxation, or just to avoid the unpleasantness of their lives. Some drugs such as LSD are taken by those seeking the hallucinations they produce. Other drugs (alcohol is an example) can act as "social lubricants," to help people feel comfortable with each other. Still other drugs are used by individuals seeking a euphoric "rush," a "buzz," a state of tranquility, or even stupor. What, if anything, do all these drugs have in common?

To some extent, all **psychoactive drugs** impair the brain mechanisms that usually help us make good decisions (Gazzaniga, 1998a). In addition, the most widely abused drugs—cocaine, heroin, and amphetamines—all stimulate the

■ **Meditation** A state of consciousness often induced by focusing on a repetitive behavior, assuming certain body positions, and minimizing external stimulation. Meditation may be intended to enhance self-knowledge, well-being, and spirituality.

■ **Psychoactive drugs** Chemicals that affect mental processes and behavior by their effects on the brain.

brain's "reward circuits." From an evolutionary perspective, we know that our brains are built to find pleasure in many substances (such as the taste of sweet or fatty foods) that helped our ancestors survive and reproduce. Cocaine, heroin, and amphetamines trick the brain by exploiting these same mechanisms with strong, direct, and pleasurable signals that make our bodies "think" that these substances are good for us (Nesse & Berridge, 1997).

Cultural trends influence drug-taking behavior, too. The United States saw this vividly during the 1960s and 1970s, when the country entered a period of casual experimentation with recreational drugs and other mind-altering techniques. By 1989, nearly 55% of American high school seniors had reported using one or more illegal drugs in their senior year (Johnston et al., 1989). Data from several sources, including emergency room visits, drug arrests, and surveys, indicate that overall illicit drug use has declined since the early 1990s. There has been, however, a rise in drug use among young teenagers (Martin, 1999). Credit for the overall decline in illicit drug use is often claimed by proponents of antidrug education programs, although the evidence does not show most of these programs to be especially effective (Murray, 1997).

Let us now have a closer look at the most commonly used and abused psychoactive drugs. We do so by grouping them in categories: *hallucinogens, opiates, depressants,* and *stimulants* (see Table 3.1). In general, we will find that all the drugs in each category will have similar effects on the mind and brain.

Hallucinogens Drugs known as **hallucinogens** produce changes in consciousness by altering perceptions, creating hallucinations, and blurring the boundary between self and the external world. For example, an individual experiencing hallucinogenic effects might listen to music and suddenly feel that he or she is producing the music or that the music is coming from within. Most hallucinogenic drugs act in the brain at specific receptor sites for the neurotransmitter serotonin (Jacobs, 1987).

Commonly used hallucinogens include mescaline (made from a type of cactus), psilocybin (from a mushroom), LSD or "acid," and PCP (also called phencyclidine). Both LSD and PCP are synthetic drugs made in chemical laboratories. PCP, or "angel dust," was a favorite of young people who used hallucinogens until the word got around that the intensity and duration of its effects were quite unpredictable. The drug produces a strange dissociative reaction, in which the user feels disembodied or removed from parts of his or her personality. Users may become confused, insensitive to pain, and feel separated (dissociated) from their surroundings.

Cannabis, derived from the hemp plant (used, therefore, to make rope, as well as dope), also acts as a hallucinogen. Its active ingredient is THC (tetrahy-

◀ **CONNECTION: CHAPTER 2**

Serotonin is a neurotransmitter involved with reward, sleep, memory, and depression.

■ **Hallucinogens** Drugs that create hallucinations or alter perceptions of the external environment and inner awareness.

● When psychologists talk about drugs, they include legal substances such as tobacco and caffeine, two extremely popular stimulants in most cultures.

TABLE 3.1	Psychoactive Drugs: Medical Uses, Effects, Likelihoods of Dependence		
		Dependence	
Category	Medical Uses	Psychological	Physical
Opiates			
Morphine	Painkiller, cough suppressant	High	High
Heroin	Under investigation	High	High
Codeine	Painkiller, cough suppressant	Moderate	Moderate
Methadone	Treatment of heroin addiction	Low	High
Hallucinogens			
Mescaline	None	None	Unknown
Psilocybin	None	Unknown	Unknown
LSD	None	None	None
PCP	Veterinary anesthetic	Unknown	High
Cannabis	Reduces nausea from chemotherapy	Low	Low
Depressants			
Barbiturates	Sedative, sleep, anticonvulsant, anesthetic	Moderate–high	Moderate–high
Benzodiazepines	Antianxiety, sleep, anticonvulsant, sedative	Low–moderate	Low–moderate
Alcohol	Antiseptic	Moderate	Moderate
Rohypnol	None in U.S. (elsewhere for sedation, anesthesia, and treatment of insomnia)	Low–moderate	Low–moderate
Stimulants			
Amphetamines	Weight control, counteract anesthesia	High	High
Methamphetamine	ADHD, weight control (rarely)	High	High
MDMA (ecstasy)	None (originally developed as an appetite suppressant)	Moderate	Moderate
Cocaine	Local anesthetic	High	High
Nicotine	Gum, patch for cessation of smoking	Low–high	Low–high
Caffeine	Weight control, stimulant in acute respiratory failure, analgesia	Low	Low

drocannabinol), found in both the plant's dried leaves and flowers (marijuana) and in its solidified resin (hashish). Most commonly it is smoked, although it can also be eaten.

The experience obtained from ingesting THC depends on its dose. Small doses may create mild, pleasurable highs, and larger doses can cause long hallucinogenic reactions. Unlike alcohol, its effects can last for many hours—and long after users feel themselves to be impaired (Julien, 2001). The pleasant effects include altered perception, sedation, pain relief, mild euphoria, and distortions of space and time—similar in some respects to the effects of heroin (Wickelgren, 1997). Alternatively, depending on the social context, and expectations, the effects can be an unpleasant mixture of fear, anxiety, and confusion. Cannabis also produces temporary failures in memory, as well as impairments in motor coordination (Julien, 2001). Those who work or drive under its influence suffer a higher risk of accidents (Moskowitz, 1985)—and those who study under its influence are likely to remember nothing.

Some habitual cannabis users become psychologically addicted to its pleasurable effects. So, they crave the drug so often that it interferes with other pursuits, including school or work. Nevertheless, the potential for physical dependence on this drug is lower than most other psychoactive substances (Grinspoon et al., 1997; Pinel, 2003). On a more positive note, cannabis has some medical uses, especially in the treatment of nausea associated with chemotherapy and in reducing pressure in the eye associated with glaucoma (Julien, 2001). Needless to say, its use, even under prescription, is controversial.

What causes the mind-altering effects of this drug? In the brain, THC causes the release of dopamine, which suggests an effect on the brain's reward system (Carlson, 2004). Neuroscientists have also discovered cannabis receptors in the brain (Wilson & Nicoll, 2002). This suggests that the brain makes its own THC-like chemicals, which it uses to modulate information flow. So, marijuana and hashish produce their mind-altering effects by exploiting the natural chemistry of the brain. It is no wonder, then, that they can interfere with cognition, because these receptors are particularly abundant in pathways involving learning, thinking, and memory.

Opiates Another class of drugs, known as **opiates,** includes morphine, heroin, and codeine—all made from the opium poppy. These are highly addictive drugs that suppress physical sensation and response to stimulation, including painful stimulation. From a medical standpoint, morphine and codeine have particularly good analgesic (pain-relieving) properties that result from their similarity to the body's own pain-relieving chemicals, the endorphins.

Derived from morphine, heroin originally was developed in 19th-century Germany by the Bayer Company (of aspirin fame), but it was abandoned because it is even more highly addictive than morphine. For the intravenous heroin user, however, the drug is attractive because it gives a strong rush of pleasurable sensations. These feelings of euphoria supplant all worries and awareness of bodily needs, although—surprisingly—there are no major changes in cognitive abilities. Under the influence of these drugs, the user is usually able to converse normally and to think clearly. Unfortunately, serious addiction is likely once a person begins to inject heroin. To avoid heightened sensitivity to pain and the intense cravings of withdrawal, the addict must take the drug frequently—at least daily—making it a very expensive habit to maintain. Because addicts often steal to support their habit, the use of heroin underlies much of the property crime in cities around the world.

Methadone, a synthetic opiate, can be taken orally and therefore doesn't require injection. It has essentially the same euphoric, analgesic, and addictive effects as heroin, but when taken orally methadone doesn't produce the same "rush" because the drug level in the brain increases slowly. This feature makes methadone useful as a substitute for heroin in drug treatment programs, in which the patient is switched to methadone and then gradually weaned from opiates altogether.

Paradoxically, patients who take opiates for pain control under medical supervision rarely become highly addicted. The reason for the difference in effects between the use of opiates for pleasure and for pain is unclear. It appears, however, that the presence of pain causes opiates to affect parts of the brain other than the "reward centers" involved in pleasure. The practical point is this: There is little to fear from the legitimate medical use of these drugs for controlling pain (Melzack, 1990).

Depressants Drugs that slow the mental and physical activity of the body by inhibiting activity in the central nervous system are collectively known as **depressants.** (Depressants don't necessarily make people feel clinically depressed, in the sense of "sad.") They include barbiturates (usually prescribed for sedation), benzodiazepines (antianxiety drugs), and alcohol (a social stimulant and nervous system depressant). By inhibiting the transmission of messages in the central nervous system, depressants tend to slow down the men-

■ **Opiates** Highly addictive drugs, derived from opium, that can produce a profound sense of well-being and have strong pain-relieving properties.

■ **Depressants** Drugs that slow down mental and physical activity by inhibiting transmission of nerve impulses in the central nervous system.

tal and physical activity of the body. In appropriate dosages, depressants can relieve symptoms of pain or anxiety, but overuse or abuse of depressants is dangerous because these drugs impair reflexes and judgment. They may also be addictive.

Barbiturates, commonly used in "sleeping pills," can induce sleep. Unfortunately, they have the side effect of reducing REM-sleep time. This leaves the user feeling unrested, despite a full night's sleep. In addition, withdrawal from barbiturates causes severe REM rebound, filling sleep with unpleasant dreams. Worse yet, overdoses of barbiturates may cause loss of consciousness, sometimes to the point of coma and even death. Fatal reactions to barbiturates are made all the more likely because the lethal dose is relatively close to the dose required for inducing sleep or other desired effects. The chance of accidental overdose can be compounded by alcohol or other depressant drugs, which magnify the depressant action of barbiturates (Maisto et al., 1995).

The benzodiazepines (pronounced *BEN-zo-dye-AZ-a-peens*), commonly prescribed to treat anxiety, are safer than barbiturates. Physicians frequently prescribe them to calm patients without causing sleepiness or sedation. For this reason, they are often referred to as "minor tranquilizers"—the best-known and most widely prescribed of which include Valium and Xanax. (The tranquilizing drugs used to treat psychotic disorders work differently and are not classified as depressants.)

While the benzodiazepines are relatively safe, compared to barbiturates, they can also be overused and abused. Addiction occurs and is of special concern because these drugs are so commonly prescribed. Overdoses produce poor muscle coordination, slurred speech, weakness, and irritability, while withdrawal symptoms include increased anxiety, muscle twitching, and sensitivity to sound and light. Significantly, the benzodiazepines are almost never taken by recreational drug users because people who are not suffering from anxiety usually do not like their effects (Wesson et al., 1992).

Alcohol, another drug that acts as a brain depressant, was one of the first psychoactive substances used by humankind. Under its influence, people have a variety of reactions that involve loosening of inhibitions. At first, this may seem like a contradiction: How can a depressant make people less inhibited? What actually happens is that the alcohol depresses activity in the brain circuits that normally control self-monitoring of our thoughts and behavior. The result depends on the context and the personality of the imbiber, who may become more talkative or quiet, friendly or abusive, ebullient—or, sometimes, psychologically depressed. Alcohol's effects also depend on whether other drugs, such as MDMA ("ecstasy") or rohypnol (the "date-rape drug"), are being used simultaneously. Such drugs are believed by users to enhance social interaction and empathy, although their effects can easily spin out of control, especially in combination with alcohol (Gahlinger, 2004).

Physically, alcohol in very small doses can induce relaxation and even slightly improve an adult's reaction time. In slightly larger amounts, it can impair coordination and mental processing—sometimes even when drinkers believe their performance has been improved. Moreover, it is quite easy for alcohol to accumulate in the system because the body may not metabolize it as fast as it is ingested. In general, the body breaks down alcohol at the rate of only one ounce per hour, and greater amounts consumed in short periods stay in the body and depress activity in the central nervous system. When the level of alcohol in the blood reaches a mere 0.1% (1/1000 of the blood), an individual experiences deficits in thinking, memory, and judgment, along with emotional instability and coordination problems. In most parts of the United States, this level of blood alcohol automatically qualifies a driver as being legally drunk.

● Physical dependence, tolerance, and addiction to alcohol often begin with binge drinking, common on many college campuses.

CONNECTION: CHAPTER 13

Benzodiazepines are used to treat anxiety-related problems, such as panic disorder and obsessive–compulsive disorder.

Distillers, brewers, and wine makers spend millions of dollars annually depicting the social and personal benefits of alcoholic beverages. And, to be sure, many adults use alcohol prudently. Nevertheless, an estimated 5 to 10% of American adults who use alcohol drink to the extent that it harms their health, career, or family and social relationships (Julien, 2001). Physical dependence, tolerance, and addiction all develop with prolonged heavy drinking—of the sort that often begins with binge drinking, common on college campuses. When the amount and frequency of drinking alcohol interferes with job or school performance, impairs social and family relationships, and creates serious health problems, the diagnosis of alcoholism is appropriate (see Julien, 2001; Vallee, 1998).

Abuse of alcohol has become a significant problem for about 15 million Americans (Pinel, 2003). The effects of the problem are much more widespread, however. When ingested by pregnant women, alcohol can affect the fetus. In fact, alcohol use by expectant mothers is a leading cause of mental retardation (Committee on Substance Abuse, 2000). Estimates suggest that 40% of Americans see the effects of alcohol abuse in a family member (Vallee, 1998). For many Americans aged 15 to 25, the problem becomes a lethal one: Alcohol-related automobile accidents are the leading cause of death in this age group.

Stimulants   In contrast with depressants, **stimulants** speed up central nervous system activity. The result is a boost in both mental and physical activity level. Surprisingly, stimulants can also increase concentration and reduce the hyperactive behavior seen in attention-deficit/hyperactivity disorder (ADHD). With narcoleptic patients, they also have a use in preventing sleep attacks.

Recreational users of certain stimulants seek still other effects: intense pleasurable sensations, increased self-confidence, greater energy and alertness, and euphoria. Cocaine, in particular, packs what may be the most powerfully rewarding punch of any illegal drug (Landry, 1997). Crack, an especially addictive form of cocaine, produces a swift, pleasurable high that wears off quickly. Amphetamine (often called "speed") and related drugs have effects comparable to cocaine. Among these, a particularly powerful variant known as methamphetamine came into widespread use during the 1990s. Still another stimulant known as MDMA (often called "ecstasy") has grown popular in the "rave" culture, where it has a reputation for creating a feeling of euphoria and for energizing young users to dance for hours, sometimes leading to dehydration, convulsions, and other unpleasant consequences (Gahlinger, 2004; Yacoubian et al., 2004). Ecstasy is also known to impair memory (Verbaten, 2003).

Stimulant drugs hold other dangers, as well. Heavy amphetamine and cocaine users may experience frightening hallucinations and paranoid delu-

CONNECTION: CHAPTER 13

ADHD is a relatively common disorder of attention span and behavior, usually diagnosed in children but sometimes found in adults.

■ **Stimulants**   Drugs that arouse the central nervous system, speeding up mental and physical responses.

● Brain changes during use of drugs can be seen on PET-scan images. Much less activity is seen in the limbic system of the brain under the influence of amphetamines.

BASELINE   AMPHETAMINE

sions—symptoms also associated with severe mental disorder. And these drugs can send users on an emotional roller coaster of euphoric highs and depressive lows. This leads users to increase the frequency and dosage, quickly making the abuse of these drugs spiral out of control. Yet another danger accrues to "secondhand" users: children who were exposed to cocaine in their mother's blood while in the womb. Studies show that such children are at increased risk for developing cognitive problems, emotional difficulties, and behavior-control disorders (Vogel, 1997b).

Two other stimulants that you may not even think of as psychoactive drugs are caffeine and nicotine—yet their effects on the brain are swift and powerful. Within 10 minutes, two cups of strong coffee or tea deliver enough caffeine to have a measurable effect on the heart, blood circulation, and signaling in the brain. Nicotine inhaled in tobacco smoke can have similar effects within just seconds. Both drugs are addictive, and both augment the effects of the natural rewarding chemicals released by the brain. In this way, nicotine and caffeine tease the brain's reward pathways into responding as if using these substances were associated with something beneficial for us. Fortunately, in the case of caffeine, the negative effects are minor for most people. Further, caffeine has a built-in "braking" action that limits its intake because high dosages also produce uncomfortable anxiety-like feelings.

In contrast to caffeine, nicotine is a much more dangerous drug for two reasons: Nicotine is highly addictive, and it has been associated with a variety of health problems, including cancer, emphysema, and heart disease. In fact, the negative impact of smoking on health is greater than that of all other psychoactive drugs combined—including heroin, cocaine, and alcohol. According to the U.S. Public Health Service, smoking is the leading cause of preventable disease, with a human cost of more than 350,000 deaths annually. As a result, the American Medical Association has formally recommended that the U.S. Food and Drug Administration regard nicotine as a drug to be regulated. Currently, however, nicotine is both legal and actively promoted—with a $2.7 billion budget from the tobacco industry. Although antismoking campaigns have been somewhat effective in reducing the overall level of smoking in the United States, some 47 million Americans still smoke. Most worrisome is the fact that more than 3 million teenagers smoke, and their numbers are increasing by about 3000 who start every day (Gardyn & Wellner, 2001; Julien, 2001).

PSYCHOLOGY IN YOUR LIFE: DEPENDENCE AND ADDICTION

We have seen that psychoactive drugs can alter the functioning of neurons in your brain and, as a consequence, temporarily change your consciousness. Once in your brain, they usually act on synapses to block or stimulate neural messages. In this way, drugs profoundly alter the brain's communication system, affecting perception, memory, mood, and behavior.

Significantly, a given dose of many psychoactive drugs comes to have a weaker consciousness-altering effect with continued use. As a result, the user needs larger and larger dosages to achieve the same effect. This reduced effectiveness with repeated use of a drug is called **tolerance.** Hand-in-hand with tolerance goes **physical dependence**—a process in which the body adjusts to and comes to need the substance, in part because the production of neurotransmitters in the brain is affected by the frequent presence of the drug (Wickelgren, 1998d). A person with a physical dependence requires the drug in his or her body and may suffer unpleasant withdrawal symptoms if the drug is not present. Further, a person who develops tolerance to a highly

◀ **CONNECTION:** CHAPTER 2

Most psychoactive drugs mimic neurotransmitters or enhance or dampen their effects at the synapses.

■ **Tolerance** The reduced effectiveness a drug has after repeated use.
■ **Physical dependence** A process by which the body adjusts to, and comes to need, a drug for its everyday functioning.

● The line between substance use and abuse is easy to cross for those who become addicted.

■ **Addiction** A condition in which a person continues to use a drug despite its adverse effects—often despite repeated attempts to discontinue using the drug. Addiction may be based on physical or psychological dependence.

■ **Withdrawal** A pattern of uncomfortable or painful physical symptoms and cravings experienced by the user when the level of drug is decreased or the drug is eliminated.

■ **Psychological dependence** A desire to obtain or use a drug, even though there is no physical dependence.

addicting drug such as heroin becomes less sensitive to all sorts of natural reinforcers, including the pleasures of friendship, food, and everyday entertainment: The drug, in increasing dosages, becomes the only thing capable of providing pleasure (Helmuth, 2001a). **Addiction** is said to occur when the person continues to use a drug in the face of adverse effects on his or her health or life—often despite repeated attempts to stop.

Withdrawal involves uncomfortable physical and mental symptoms that occur when drug use is discontinued. It can include physical trembling, perspiring, nausea, increased sensitivity to pain, and, in the case of extreme alcohol withdrawal, even death. Although heroin and alcohol are the drugs that most commonly come to mind when we think of withdrawal symptoms, nicotine and caffeine, as well as certain sleeping pills and "tranquilizing" drugs, can also cause unpleasant withdrawal symptoms.

Individuals may find themselves craving or hungering for the drug and its effects, even though they are not physically dependent—a condition known as **psychological dependence** or psychological addiction. This usually results from the powerfully rewarding effects that many psychoactive drugs produce. Psychological dependence can occur with many drugs, including caffeine and nicotine, prescription medications, and over-the-counter drugs.

Addiction, whether biological or psychological, ultimately affects the brain (Gazzaniga, 1998a; Koob & Le Moal, 1997; Nestler, 2001). Consequently, in the view of many public health professionals, this makes both forms of addiction brain diseases (Leshner, 1997). On the other hand, the general public has been reluctant to view drug addicts as people who have an illness. Instead, the public often thinks of addicts as weak or bad individuals who should be punished (MacCoun, 1998).

What difference does our characterization of addiction make? When addicts are seen as persons suffering from a disease, they are most logically placed in treatment programs. By contrast, when they are seen as persons with character defects, addicts are sent to prison for punishment—which does little to break the cycle of drug use, crime, and addiction.

Strange as it may seem, some experts argue that viewing addiction as a disease may also interfere with the effective treatment of drug addicts. How could this be? The disease model of addiction, with its emphasis on biological causes and medical treatment, does little to deal with the social and economic context in which addictions develop. This may account for the fact that psychologically based treatment programs that treat alcohol abuse as a behavioral problem may work better than medically based programs (Miller & Brown, 1997).

We can also see the blind spots of the disease model in heroin addiction. Treatment programs have a notoriously poor record with heroin addicts who have picked up their habits on the streets of the United States. On the other hand, they had far greater success with the thousands of veterans who became addicted to the heroin that was readily available to troops in Vietnam. What made the difference? The addicted veterans did not remain in the environment where they had become addicted—which was the wartime culture of Vietnam. Instead, they returned home to an environment that was not usually so supportive of a heroin habit. In contrast, heroin users who become addicted in the United States tend to return, after treatment, to the same environment that originally led to their addiction.

Whether physical or psychological, disease or character flaw, drug addiction poses many personal and social problems. Clearly, this is a field that has much room for new ideas and new research.

1. **RECALL:** Hypnosis is sometimes used by psychological researchers to
   a. study the effects of psychoactive drugs.
   b. induce amnesia for traumatic experiences.
   c. cure patients suffering from severe mental disorders.
   d. create mental states, such as anxiety or euphoria.

2. **RECALL:** Psychoactive drugs usually create their effects by _____ in the brain.
   a. disabling dendrites
   b. stimulating reward circuits
   c. causing delayed stress reactions
   d. altering memories

3. **RECALL:** Which of the following statements is true?
   a. Research has proven conclusively that addiction is a brain disease.
   b. Most public health professionals view addiction as a character weakness.
   c. Some psychologists suggest that treating addiction as a disease ignores the social and economic factors that surround the problem.
   d. The cycle of addiction is most efficiently broken with a combination of punishment for relapses and drugs that counteract the effects of psychoactive drugs.

4. **APPLICATION:** Which of the following groups of drugs have the opposite effects on the brain?
   a. hallucinogens and stimulants
   b. opiates and sedatives
   c. stimulants and depressants
   d. depressants and opiates

5. **UNDERSTANDING THE CORE CONCEPT:** An altered state of consciousness occurs when some aspect of normal consciousness is modified either by mental, behavioral, or chemical means. This suggests that:
   a. some states of consciousness are mystical phenomena that cannot ever be explained.
   b. all states of consciousness are controlled by unconscious needs, desires, and memories.
   c. altered states of consciousness are the primary source of creativity in our minds.
   d. psychologists can study altered states of consciousness with scientific methods.

ANSWERS: 1.d 2.b 3.c 4.c 5.d

CONSCIOUSNESS: THE STATE OF THE ART

We have seen that, aside from our familiar state of wakefulness, consciousness can occur in many forms. More surprising, perhaps, is the discovery that mental processing can also occur outside of consciousness. We have also seen that neuroscientists have developed techniques with which they can study these once private and subjective worlds that occur both in consciousness and in the preconscious and unconscious. Among their achievements with these techniques, scientists have flung open the gates of the sleeping and dreaming mind. They have also learned much about the workings of the mind under the influence of hypnosis, meditation, and drugs.

What remains to be learned? Still hotly debated and poorly understood is the function of dreams: Do they mean anything, or are they merely a by-product of an always-active brain cut off from the outside world? Also remaining to be discovered are better treatments for certain sleep disorders, such as narcolepsy and insomnia, as well as more effective treatments for addictions.

But the biggest and most elusive prize of all is a full understanding of consciousness itself. How can the activity of neurons "lighting up" in our brains produce the ongoing movie-of-the-mind that we call consciousness? At this point, no one really knows.

Connecting Consciousness with Memory

Expand your consciousness? In the strictest sense, it is not really possible, because consciousness has a limited capacity. As we noted at the beginning of the chapter, consciousness can focus on only one thing at a time. What can be expanded, however, is the access your consciousness has to information you have stored in preconscious memory. Learning how to do this can be of tremendous help to students who need to absorb a large amount of information and to prove it on an exam.

You will, of course, have an advantage if you face an exam with your consciousness unimpaired by the massive sleep debt that students sometimes incur in an "all-nighter" study session. No amount of caffeine can bring your sleep-deprived consciousness back to optimum functioning. Just as your teachers have always preached, it is far better to spread your studying over several days or weeks, rather than trying to learn everything at once and losing sleep over it.

It can also help when we reach Chapter 7 to understand that consciousness is fundamentally the same as working memory, a mental "work space" that holds only a few items at once. Because of its severely limited capacity, you cannot possibly hold in consciousness all the information you need to remember for an exam. Most of the material must be stored outside of consciousness in preconscious long-term memory. The trick is to be able to bring it back into consciousness when needed. Here are some strategies that you may find helpful in doing this:

1. *Study for the gist*. Students sometimes think their professors ask "trick questions," although professors almost never do so intentionally. In reality, a good exam question will show whether students understand the meaning of a term—the gist—rather than having merely memorized a definition. A twofold study strategy can help you get the gist of a concept. First, paraphrase the definition given in the text or in class. Second, think of an example from your own experience that illustrates the concept.

2. *Look for connections among concepts*. Even if you have the gist of the concepts you have studied, you will probably need to know how those concepts are related to each other. The professor may ask you to explain, for example, what happens to the *sleep cycle* in people with *narcolepsy*. Therefore a good study strategy is to ask yourself: "How is this new concept related to what I learned previously?"

3. *Anticipate the most likely cues*. Just because you know the material doesn't mean that the exam questions will make the right answer spill from long-term memory back into consciousness. It pays, therefore, to spend some of your study time thinking about the kinds of questions your professor might ask. For example, you may have learned about the effects of various psychoactive drugs, but you could be stumped when the professor asks you to explain why alcohol is more like the barbiturates than the opiates. (Do you know?) You can often anticipate such questions by noting what the professor emphasizes in lecture. It also helps to think of the kinds of questions that your professor is known to favor. (A study partner helps a lot with this.) Some of the most frequently seen test questions begin with terms such as "Explain," "Evaluate," or "Compare and contrast."

In general, the relationship between consciousness and memory suggests that learning the kind of material required in your college classes requires that the material be actively processed while it is in consciousness. To do so effectively, it must be made meaningful. This requires making connections between new information and information that is already in your memory. It also requires organizing the information so that you see how it is interconnected. And, finally, it requires anticipating the cues that will be used to bring it back to consciousness.

CONNECTION: CHAPTER 7

Working memory (also called short-term memory) is a main component of consciousness, but it holds only a small number of items at any time.

● HOW IS CONSCIOUSNESS RELATED TO OTHER MENTAL PROCESSES?

Consciousness represents one of the major mysteries of psychology. Cognitive scientists agree that consciousness involves restricted attention. It also involves the mental model we create of our internal and external world. Consciousness employs mental processes that not only integrate all the mental activity in our awareness, but allow us to manipulate their contents. Moreover, consciousness exists in various states, including the normal waking state, states of sleep and dreaming, hypnosis, meditation, and drug states. Aspects of consciousness can be studied with the techniques of cognitive psychology.

In addition to consciousness, the mind has many nonconscious modes that can operate outside awareness. These include the preconscious and various levels of unconscious processing. While consciousness is limited to serial processing, the mind can process information nonconsciously in parallel channels. New technologies and techniques have opened windows on conscious processes for researchers. Increasingly, cognitive scientists are disputing the Freudian concept of an unconscious that works in opposition with the conscious mind.

● **Consciousness can take many forms, while other mental processes occur simultaneously outside our awareness.**

● WHAT CYCLES OCCUR IN EVERYDAY CONSCIOUSNESS?

Consciousness shifts and changes in everyday life, commonly taking the form of daydreaming, sleep, and nocturnal dreams. Although the function of sleep is not altogether clear, everyone agrees that sleep and wakefulness are part of the circadian cycle. Sleep researchers have revealed the features of the normal sleep cycle, including the four stages of sleep, which undergo 90-minute cycles, including both REM and non-REM periods. Over the course of the night, each ensuing sleep cycle involves

less deep sleep and more REM sleep. The sleep cycle also changes dramatically with age. Most adults need at least eight hours of sleep every night.

The function of dreams is also unclear, but they often occur in REM sleep. While Freud's dream theory has been influential, it has no empirical support. Dreams have, however, always been a source of inspiration and creativity for humankind.

Aberrations in the sleep cycle can produce various sleep disorders. Narcolepsy is a disorder of REM sleep, insomnia involves shortened sleep, and sleep apnea involves abnormalities in deep sleep. Other disorders of a less serious nature include night terrors, sleep talking, and sleepwalking.

● **Consciousness changes in cycles that correspond to our biological rhythms and to the patterns of stimulation in our environment.**

● WHAT OTHER FORMS CAN CONSCIOUSNESS TAKE?

Altered states of consciousness include hypnosis, meditation, and the effects of psychoactive drugs. From a cognitive-neuroscience perspective, these may involve changes in psychological processes rather than entirely new forms of awareness. Hypnosis remains a puzzle, although it is known to block pain and have other uses in therapy and research. Likewise, experts dispute whether meditation is a distinct state of consciousness, even though it has measurable effects on arousal. To understand the effects of psychoactive drugs, it is helpful to group them as hallucinogens, opiates, depressants, and stimulants. Most psychoactive drugs that are abused produce sensations of pleasure and well-being that make the drugs especially attractive and potentially addictive.

● **An altered state of consciousness occurs when some aspect of normal consciousness is modified by mental, behavioral, or chemical means.**

REVIEW TEST

For each of the following items, choose the single correct or best answer. The correct answers appear at the end of the test.

1. What was the objection by Watson and other behaviorists to the study of consciousness?

   a. Conscious processes cannot be directly observed and measured.

   b. Consciousness could not be accessed by introspection.

   c. Consciousness is not affected by rewards and punishments.

   d. Consciousness is the result of an inner life force, which they did not have the tools to study.

2. Imaging techniques, such as MRI and PET scans, allow cognitive scientists to connect mental activity with

   a. cognition.

   b. behavior.

   c. brain activity.

   d. priming.

3. Which of the following is *not* one of the functions of consciousness cited by your text?

   a. restricting attention to what is relevant

   b. combining sensation with memory

   c. manipulating a mental image of the world

   d. relinquishing control to enhance self-awareness

4. Which one of the following did Freud believe to be a function of the unconscious mind?
   a. protecting consciousness from sexual desires and traumatic experiences
   b. regulation of sleep, wakefulness, blood pressure, heart rate, body temperature, and habit patterns
   c. the construction of grammatically correct sentences, without having to think consciously about the grammatical rules
   d. logical thinking

5. Rapid eye movements are reliable behavioral signs that
   a. an individual has reached the deepest level of sleep.
   b. one has achieved a genuine meditative state.
   c. a sleeper is dreaming.
   d. a person is very low in hypnotizability.

6. Which one of the following is a sleep disorder characterized by brief interruptions when the sleeper stops breathing, wakens, resumes breathing, and falls back asleep?
   a. apnea
   b. daytime sleepiness
   c. insomnia
   d. analgesia

7. Which of the following statements about hypnosis is true?
   a. Hypnosis is actually a form of NREM sleep.
   b. Hypnotizability relies on a person's ability to respond to suggestion.

c. Anyone can be hypnotized if the hypnotist knows the most effective techniques to use.
   d. The less intelligent or educated a person is, the more hypnotizable he or she will be.

8. Psychology has verified that meditation can be useful for producing
   a. a deeper understanding of oneself.
   b. enlightenment.
   c. a state of relaxation.
   d. heightened cognitive arousal.

9. Which of the following drugs would be most likely to produce hallucinations (sensory experiences with no basis in reality)?
   a. nicotine
   b. mescaline
   c. alcohol
   d. benzodiazepines

10. Three major effects sought by users of _____ are increased alertness, greater self-confidence, and euphoria.
    a. stimulants
    b. depressants
    c. opiates
    d. hallucinogens

ANSWERS: 1.a 2.c 3.d 4.a 5.c 6.a 7.b 8.c 9.b 10.a

KEY TERMS

Consciousness (p. 90)

Cognitive neuroscience (p. 91)

Nonconscious processes (p. 92)

Preconscious memories (p. 96)

Unconscious (p. 96)

Daydreaming (p. 98)

Circadian rhythms (p. 99)

REM sleep (p. 100)

Non-REM (NREM) sleep (p. 100)

Sleep paralysis (p. 100)

REM rebound (p. 101)

Sleep debt (p. 103)

Manifest content (p. 105)

Latent content (p. 105)

Activation-synthesis theory (p. 106)

Insomnia (p. 107)

Sleep apnea (p. 108)

Night terrors (p. 108)

Narcolepsy (p. 109)

Hypnosis (p. 111)

Meditation (p. 113)

Psychoactive drugs (p. 113)

Hallucinogens (p. 114)

Opiates (p. 116)

Depressants (p. 116)

Stimulants (p. 118)

Tolerance (p. 119)

Physical dependence (p. 119)

Addiction (p. 120)

Withdrawal (p. 120)

Psychological dependence (p. 120)

ARTICLE

Nash, M. R. (2001, July). The truth and hype of hypnosis. *Scientific American, 285,* 46–49, 52–55. Everyone has images of hypnosis: the shiny watch, the command to become "verrry sleepy . . ." Advances in cognitive science have left the fascination and much of the mystery intact, while answering questions about how hypnosis works in alleviating pain, retrieving memories, and other applications.

BOOKS

Alper, M. (2001). *The "God" part of the brain: A scientific interpretation of human spirituality and God.* New York: Rogue Press. Every culture has some forms of religion. Does this mean that the capacity for faith is hardwired into our brains, like any other feature our species shares? Matthew Alper suggests that religion is a brain-based capacity for human adaptation and survival. Does brain-based belief affect the validity of religious experience?

Coren, S. (1996). *Sleep thieves: An eye-opening exploration into the science and mysteries of sleep.* Free Press Paperbacks. Coren gives us the "A to ZZZZs of sleep," including whether dogs and cats dream, determining whether you are getting enough sleep, how to help children sleep better, and the dangers of Daylight Savings Time.

Hobson, A. (2002). *Dreaming: An introduction to the science of sleep.* New York: Oxford University Press. Have you wakened from realistic dreams, confused about what is real? Hobson identifies the qualities that distinguish one's dreaming from waking life and links these to specific brain processes.

Jaynes, J. (2001). *The origin of consciousness in the breakdown of the bicameral mind.* New York: Mariner Books/Houghton Mifflin. Reissued since its original publication in 1976, this continually popular and intriguing work examines how consciousness may have originally evolved when the brain's two hemispheres, connected but separate, "heard" each other—and were experienced by early humans as the voices of spirits, gods—and finally of the self. Don't be disheartened by the mega-title; it's highly readable and provocative.

Mindell, A. (2000). *Dreaming while awake: Techniques for 24-hour lucid dreaming.* Charlottesville, VA: Hampton Roads Publishing Company. Dreams weave together our conscious ideas and concerns, so that while awake we may learn to detect the "seeds of dreaming" and influence their presentation in our dreams, perhaps solving problems and enhancing bodily healing in the process.

Peacock, R., & Gorman, R. (Eds.). (1998). *Sleep: Bedtime reading.* Universe Publishing. Wide awake and trying not to worry about it? Try some bedtime reading by the best authors. Includes short works by authors ranging from Alice Walker to John Updike, along with poetry, pictures, and photographs—all designed to take your mind off what's keeping you awake so you can get some rest.

Samorini, M., Calliope, T., & Montgomery, R. (2002). *Animals and psychedelics: The natural world and the instinct to alter consciousness.* New York: Park Street Press. How natural is it for people to deliberately alter consciousness by ingesting psychoactive substances? From observations of our nonhuman relatives, pretty natural! Like humans, wild animals and insects seek out substances (e.g., caffeine, nectar) that alter perception, possibly expanding their behavioral responses—thus increasing adaptation and survival. How and why do substances stop expanding and begin impairing the mind?

VIDEOS

Leaving Las Vegas. (1995, color, 111 min.). Directed by Mike Figgis; starring Nicolas Cage, Elisabeth Shue. Unable and unwilling to quit, an alcoholic moves to Las Vegas to drink himself to death, falling in love with a prostitute who accepts his death wish. Cage's Oscar-winning performance highlights the moments of lucidity, silliness, pleasure, and repulsiveness of chronic alcoholism.

The Matrix. (1999, color, 136 min.). Directed by Andy Wachowsky & Larry Wachowski; starring Keanu Reeves, Laurence Fishburne, Carrie-Anne Moss. Neo, a computer hacker, is drafted by a group of techno-rebels in a suspenseful, subversive exploration of mind control and illusion. The film considers how artificial intelligence might be employed to produce immersion in artificial reality. (See also sequels *Matrix Reloaded* and finally *The Matrix Revolutions,* both 2003, for Neo's further adventures).

Mesmer. (1994, color, 107 min.). Directed by Roger Spottiswoode; starring Alan Rickman, Amanda Ooms. In 18th-century Vienna and Paris, Franz Anton Mesmer discovers the power of "animal magnetism" to heal the sick. Derided as a charlatan, his methods dubbed "mesmerism," Mesmer brings clinical hypnosis to Paris, where it becomes an entertainment for the bored aristocracy (in the doomed reign of Marie Antoinette). Mesmer's true story is interesting, here romanticized with subplots and piqued with terrific dialogue.

CORE CONCEPTS

Development is a process of growth, change, and consistency brought about by an interaction of heredity and environment.

Newborns have innate abilities for finding nourishment, interacting with others, and avoiding harmful situations, while the developing abilities of infants and children rely more on learning.

Infants and children face especially important developmental tasks in the areas of language acquisition, cognition, and social relationships—tasks that lay a foundation for further growth in adolescence and adulthood.

▼

Adolescence offers new developmental challenges growing out of physical changes, cognitive changes, and socioemotional pressures.

▼

Nature and nurture continue to produce changes throughout life, but in adulthood these changes include both growth and decline.

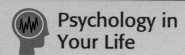

Psychology in Your Life

Psychological Traits in Your Genes

While genes contribute to your thoughts and behaviors, you shouldn't assume that biology is everything.

Does Your Child Measure Up?

The developmental milestones are averages, but children show great variation in their development.

Childhood Influences on Your Personality

Erikson's theory says that your personality is shaped by a series of developmental crises.

The Development of Moral Thinking

Moral dilemmas reveal stages of moral reasoning—but not necessarily moral behavior.

The Last Developmental Challenges You Will Face

The final years of life present a challenge, but a new picture of aging is emerging.

USING PSYCHOLOGY TO LEARN PSYCHOLOGY:
Cognitive Development in College Students

Psychological Development

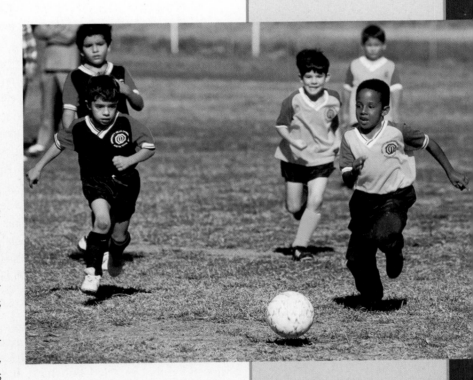

WHAT COULD GRAB MEDIA interest more effectively than a story of twins separated at birth and reunited as adults? Many such tales have come out of the twin-study project at the University of Minnesota. But what really attracts journalists are the reports of uncanny similarities between identical twins who were raised by different parents, taught by different teachers, influenced by different peers and siblings, and sometimes even raised in different cultures.

Take, for example, the "Jim Twins." Separated just a few weeks after they were born, identical twins Jim Springer and Jim Lewis were adopted separately and raised apart. Yet something drove them on parallel paths, even though those paths didn't cross again for 39 years. At their reunion, the "Jim twins" discovered some remarkable correspondences in their habits, preferences, and experiences. Some examples:

▌ They achieved nearly identical scores on tests of personality, intelligence, attitudes, and interests.

▌ Medically, both have mildly high blood pressure and have had spells that they mistakenly thought were heart attacks; both have had vasectomies; both suffer from migraine headaches.

▌ Both chain-smoke Salem cigarettes and drink Miller Lite beer.

- Both had been indifferent students: Jim Lewis had dropped out in the 10th grade, while Jim Springer had managed to graduate from high school.

- Both had been married twice, and both of their first wives were named Linda. Both of their second wives were named Betty. Both men like to leave love notes around the house.

- Lewis had three sons, including one named James Alan. Springer had three daughters, plus a son named James Allan.

- Both had owned dogs named Toy.

- Both drive Chevrolets, chew their fingernails, like stock-car racing, and dislike baseball.

- Both had been sheriff's deputies.

- Both do woodworking as a hobby. Lewis likes to make miniature picnic tables, and Springer makes miniature rocking chairs. Both had built white benches around trees in their yards.

When he first read about the two Jims in a newspaper, psychologist Thomas Bouchard knew their case presented a rare opportunity to study the relative effects of heredity and environment and how they unfold over time in the process we call *development* (Holden, 1980a, b; Jackson, 1980; Lykken et al., 1992). The Jims agreed to participate and so became the first of some 115 pairs of reunited twins (plus four sets of reared-apart triplets) to be studied over the next 20 years at the University of Minnesota.

Another remarkable pair, Oskar Stör and Jack Yufe, were also separated at birth, and from that point on their lives went in almost unbelievably different directions. Stör was raised by his grandmother in Czechoslovakia and attended a Nazi-run school during World War II, while Yufe was taken to Trinidad, where he was raised as a Jew by his biological father. Oskar is now married, a strong union man, and a devoted skier, while Jack is separated, a businessman, and a self-styled workaholic. Still, alongside these huge differences, the researchers again found some striking similarities in seemingly trivial behavior patterns. Both twins wear neatly clipped moustaches; both read magazines from back to front; both have a habit of storing rubber bands on their wrists; both flush the toilet before using it; both like to dunk buttered toast in coffee; and both think it is funny to sneeze loudly in public.

A Critical Look at the Twin Studies   As compelling as these correspondences are, we must interpret them with care (Phelps et al., 1997). Let's begin that interpretation by putting on our critical thinking caps and confronting the same questions that puzzled Bouchard and his colleagues: What might account for the remarkable similarities they were uncovering in the lives of reunited identical twins? How much was genetics? How much was coincidence? Were there any other explanations that could account for their results? As so often happens in psychology, the answers are complex.

To see these two twin pairs in a broader perspective, you need to know that they are "outliers"—extreme among the twins studied at Minnesota, even though they have received a lion's share of media coverage. Although Bouchard and his colleagues found many unexpected developmental similarities between individuals in all the twin pairs they studied, most were not nearly so much alike as Oskar and Jack or the Jims. Bouchard acknowledges that many of the similarities are just coincidences (The Mysteries, 1998). Yet, it is precisely such coincidences that make the news and catch our eye. But, says twin researcher Richard Rose, "If you bring together strangers who were born on the same day in the same country and ask them to find similarities between them, you may find a lot of seemingly astounding coincidences" (Horgan, 1993). While mere coincidence does not offer a very dazzling explanation, the alternatives seem absurd. No one seriously suggests, for example, that the names of Betty and Linda could have been written into the genes of the two Jims or that heredity really specifies storing rubber bands on one's wrists.

The real story, then, is both less dramatic and more important: Identical twins do show remarkable similarities, but mainly in the characteristics you might expect: intelligence, temperament, gestures, posture, and pace of speech—all of which do make sense as traits that could be genetically influenced. And, the fact that fraternal twins and other siblings show fewer similarities also suggests that hereditary forces are at work—in all of us, whether we are twins or not. Bouchard (1994) himself takes a rather extreme position, suggesting that heredity accounts for up to 80% of the similarities observed among identical twins (What We Learn, 1998). Critics aren't so sure.

● Twin studies are one way to study the relative importance of nature and nurture, but they must be interpreted with caution. This photo shows the identical "Bob Twins," who, like the "Jim Twins," grew up not knowing of each other's existence. Both sport mustaches and smoke a pipe; both have engineering degrees; and both married teachers named Brenda. It is unlikely that all the similarities—striking as they may be—are caused by genetics.

Identical Twins Are Not Identical So, what objections do the critics raise concerning the twin studies Bouchard and his colleagues have been conducting? First, they note that, stunning as the similarities between identical twins may seem, the effect of the environment also shows up in each pair of twins. None of the twin pairs displays behavior that is identical across the board. And the fact that twins reared together typically are more alike than those reared apart provides further testimony to the effect of environment. The additional fact that the personalities of most twin pairs become less alike as they age provides still further evidence that the environment, as well as heredity, is at work (McCartney et al., 1990). We should note, too, that many of the twin pairs studied by Bouchard had been reunited for some time before he found them—an environmental condition that could easily accentuate, or even *create,* similarities. This was true, for example, of Oskar Stör and Jack Yufe, the Nazi and Jew twins, who met five months before Bouchard got to them. In fact, says psychologist Leon Kamin, Bouchard's twins face strong incentives to exaggerate their similarities and minimize their differences in order to please the research team and to attract media attention (Horgan, 1993). (Since their story broke in the press, Stör and Yufe have hired agents, made paid appearances on TV, and sold their story to a Hollywood film producer.)

A second sort of criticism points out that because identical twins look alike, people often treat them alike. This is an environmental factor that can easily account for many similarities in behavior. For example, some people's faces look good with moustaches, and, if a pair of twins has such faces, people may encourage them to grow moustaches—whether or not they have been raised together. The resulting similarity, then, can be due as much to environment as it is to heredity.

Finally, the critics also remind us that scientists' hopes and expectations can influence their conclusions in this sort of research. Because Bouchard and other investigators of identical twins expect to find some hereditary influences, their attention will be drawn more to similarities than to differences. In fact, this is what people often do when they meet: Their conversation jumps from topic to topic until they discover common interests, attitudes, experiences, or activities.

◀ **CONNECTION: CHAPTER 1**

The *expectancy bias* can distort perceptions and research findings.

So, is there any point of consensus about the twin studies and about the effects of heredity and environment? Bouchard and his critics all would say that neither heredity nor environment ever acts alone to produce behavior or mental processes. They always *interact*. That is, from a developmental perspective, heredity and environment work together throughout a person's life. In addition, most would agree that the important findings coming out of the Minnesota twin research have nothing to do with unique and amazing similarities between particular twins. Rather, they have to do with the similarities found across all the identical twin pairs they studied: Twins show extraordinary similarities with each other in personality, attitudes, facial expressions, and temperament—almost everything, oddly enough, except their choice of mates: The spouses of identical twins were no more similar to each other than were people who would have been chosen at random (El-Hai, 1999). What the twin studies really did was to remind us that we are products of *both* heredity and environment—nature *and* nurture.

HOW DO PSYCHOLOGISTS EXPLAIN DEVELOPMENT?

Broadly speaking, **developmental psychology** is the psychology of growth, change, and consistency through the lifespan. It asks how thinking, feeling, and behavior change through infancy, childhood, adolescence, and adulthood. It also seeks to understand how the brain changes, how our bodies change, and what effects these changes have on sensation, perception, cognition, motivation, emotion, and personality. And developmental psychology seeks to discover the threads of consistency—the "who we are"—that provide continuity throughout our lives. Beyond describing change and consistency, developmental psychologists also want to understand the fundamental forces that *cause* development. And that's, of course, where the two broad influences of heredity and environment come in. For developmental psychology, the big questions about heredity and environment are (a) How much weight does each wield? and (b) How do they interact?

Psychologists often refer to this as the **nature–nurture issue:** *Nature* refers to the effects of heredity and *nurture* to the influence of environment. Because this issue is so central to developmental psychology, we have highlighted it in the first Core Concept of this chapter:

> Development is a process of growth, change, and consistency brought about by an interaction of heredity and environment.

The most important word here is **interaction:** Heredity and environment are always entwined in an inseparable relationship. The story of development, then, is the story of the *nature–nurture interaction* over the lifespan.

The Nature–Nurture Interaction

It was probably Shakespeare who first brought the terms *nature* and *nurture* together (Gottesman, 1997), when Prospero describes the futility of his efforts to civilize his beastlike servant Caliban:

> A devil, a born devil, on whose nature
> Nurture can never stick; on whom my pains,
> Humanely taken, all, all lost, quite lost . . .
>
> —*The Tempest*, Act 4, Scene 1

■ **Developmental psychology** The psychological specialty that studies how organisms change over time as the result of biological and environmental influences.

■ **Nature–nurture issue** The long-standing discussion over the relative importance of nature (heredity) and nurture (environment) in their influence on behavior and mental processes.

■ **Interaction** A process by which forces work together or influence each other—as in the interaction between the forces of heredity and environment.

More important, Shakespeare seems to have grasped the idea that nature and nurture can work in partnership—the idea of *interaction* that has not always been obvious to others. Those who had missed this important point have long argued over which of these forces—nature *or* nurture—is the more important influence on our thoughts and behaviors. It also reappears in the debate over racial differences and gender differences, as we will see a few chapters hence.

Although people continue to ask, "Is it nature *or* nurture?" psychologists today are more interested in understanding how heredity and environment *work together* to produce our personalities and our mental abilities (Bronfenbrenner & Ceci, 1994; Dannefer & Perlmutter, 1990). We know that virtually every human characteristic (with the trivial exceptions of certain physical traits, such as eye color) is shaped by both an individual's biological inheritance and experience (de Waal, 1999). That is, *nature and nurture interact*. If you are good at, say, math or music, your ability is really the result of a combination of genetic potential and experience. Heredity establishes your potential, but experience determines how your potential will be realized. To put it yet another way: Nature *pro*poses, and nurture *dis*poses.

Still, we may ask: Which of our traits does heredity affect most? And which are most heavily influenced by learning or other environmental factors (such as disease or nutrition)? And it's worth noting that answering such questions can pose some hazards. For example, we know that in the genetic disorder known as Down syndrome, biology has a strong influence. In this condition, the output of abnormal chromosomes leads to mental retardation—and there is no cure. The hazard of knowing about the genetic basis for Down syndrome is that the parents or teachers of children with such disorders may simply conclude that biology determines the child's destiny and give up hope. By focusing on the genetic side of the disorder, they may overlook effective learning-based treatments that can measurably improve the living skills of these individuals.

Mindful of such dangers, psychologists have nevertheless forged ahead in the study of hereditary and environmental contributions to thought and behavior. To do so, they have invented several clever methods for weighing the effects of nature and nurture. These include studies of twins and studies of adopted children. Briefly, we will examine how these two methods work, as well as their strengths and weaknesses.

Twin Studies Twins, as we have seen in Bouchard's studies, can give us some tantalizing clues about the relative contribution of nature and nurture, especially when the twins have been separated since birth. But identical twins separated at birth and later reunited are a scarce resource. For that reason, psychologists have also devised ways to tease out the effects of nature and nurture from studies comparing identical and fraternal twins who were reared together. Because **identical twins** have precisely the same genotype and **fraternal twins** have (on the average) 50% of their genes in common, hereditary effects should show up more strongly in identical twins. (In studies comparing these two twin types, the fraternal twins serve as a sort of *control group*). Such studies have given us valuable information on the genetics of mental and behavioral disorders, including alcoholism, Alzheimer's disease, schizophrenia, depression, and panic disorder (Eley, 1997; Plomin et al., 1994; Pool, 1997).

Adoption Studies If you adopted a baby, would he or she grow up to resemble you more than the biological parents? This is the sort of question asked by psychologists who do adoption studies. By comparing the characteristics of adopted children with those of their biological and adoptive family members, developmental psychologists have yet another method for separating the effects of heredity and environment. Similarities with the biological family point to the effects of nature, while similarities with the adoptive family

■ **Identical twins** A pair who started life as a single fertilized egg, which later split into two distinct individuals. Identical twins have exactly the same genes.
■ **Fraternal twins** A pair who started life as two separate fertilized eggs that happened to share the same womb. Fraternal twins, on the average, have about 50% of their genetic material in common.

◄ **CONNECTION: CHAPTER 1**

The *control group* in a study serves as a standard against which other groups can be compared.

suggest the influence of nurture. This work, in concert with twin studies, has revealed genetic contributions to a variety of psychological characteristics, such as intelligence, sexual orientation, temperament, and impulsive behavior—all of which we will see in more detail elsewhere in this book (Bouchard, 1994; Dabbs, 2000; Hamer, 1997; Saudino, 1997; Wright & Mahurin, 1997).

Gradual versus Abrupt Change

Most of us cringe with embarrassment when our parents tell stories on us, especially about the "cute" things we said or did as children. What makes children's antics so cute, of course, is that they don't think like adults. But how do children *become* adults? Is there a predictable *pattern* they follow as their thought and language and social relationships become more and more adult-like? Such questions raise a second issue related to our Core Concept: whether the developmental changes produced by nature and nurture happen abruptly or gradually—whether we go through clearly defined "stages" or change more gradually and continually throughout our lives.

According to the **continuity view,** change is gradual. Children become more skillful in thinking, talking, or acting in much the same way that they become taller: through a gradual developmental process. We know that skilled behaviors often develop in this fashion, as you can see in the trial-and-error process of a child learning to walk or eat with a spoon. The more interesting question, of course, is whether complex mental processes, such as development of thought and language, follow the same pattern.

Psychologists who take the opposing **discontinuity view** see development as more abrupt—as a succession of changes that produce different behaviors in different age-specific life periods, or *stages,* such as infancy, childhood, and adolescence. In this view, development can occur in bursts. That is, development can be *discontinuous.* You can observe this discontinuous process at work in beginning readers who suddenly discover the connection between letters and sounds. (For a graphical comparison of the continuity and discontinuity views, see Figure 4.1.)

■ **Continuity view** The perspective that development is gradual and continuous—as opposed to the discontinuity (stage) view.

■ **Discontinuity view** The perspective that development proceeds in an uneven (discontinuous) fashion—as opposed to the continuity view.

● In a remarkable series of self-portraits, we see developmental changes in the face of the painter Rembrandt.

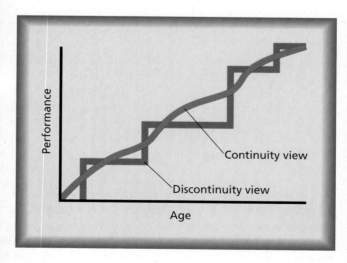

● **FIGURE 4.1** Continuity versus Discontinuity

The continuity view sees development as a process of continual change, while the discontinuity view sees development as a series of steps, or stages.

You may have heard parents dismissing a child's misbehavior or moodiness as "just going through a stage," such as the "terrible twos," when children are becoming more mobile and independent. But for psychologists who subscribe to the discontinuity view, stages are not simply difficult times. These psychologists define **developmental stages** as periods of life initiated by distinct transitions (changes) in physical or psychological functioning. From a stage perspective, specific abilities, such as walking, talking, or abstract reasoning, appear at specific ages or life periods because different developmental processes come into play. In general, developmental psychologists who take the discontinuity view find that people go through the same stages in the same order—but not necessarily at the same rate.

■ **Developmental stages** Periods of life initiated by significant transitions or changes in physical or psychological functioning.

PSYCHOLOGY IN YOUR LIFE: PSYCHOLOGICAL TRAITS IN YOUR GENES

Eye color and the shape of your earlobes are purely genetic traits. Even some food aversions, such as a distaste for broccoli, can be anchored in the genes. But, as far as we know, heredity by itself determines none of our more complex psychological characteristics (Horgan, 1993). Where personality traits, temperament, interests, and abilities are concerned, heredity always acts in combination with environment. Outgoing people, for example, aren't just born that way; they have also been encouraged to let their tendencies to extraversion show. Still, it's fair for developmental psychologists and biopsychologists to ask which psychological characteristics have strong genetic links.

A genetic contribution to general intelligence, for example, is well established—although psychologists disagree over the magnitude of heredity's role (Plomin et al., 1994). There is also a good possibility that genes contribute to your sexual orientation (Hamer et al., 1993). And it just may be that an interest in skydiving, rock climbing, or other risky behavior has a substantial genetic component (Hamer, 1997). The evidence suggests that genes also contribute to your basic temperament and personality, including all of the "Big Five" personality factors (Bouchard, 1994; Plomin, 1997).

Likewise, some clinical disorders are associated with genetic abnormalities (Eley, 1997; Gibbs, 1995; Mann, 1994; Plomin et al., 1994). One of the first to be discovered was Huntington's disease, a rare problem that causes aggressive behavior and mental deterioration beginning in midlife (Cattaneo et al., 2002). Depression, a far more common problem, can also have genetic roots (although this doesn't mean that everyone who gets depressed has a genetic problem). Similarly, twin studies have revealed a strong genetic contributes to schizophrenia, a major mental disorder. Fear, too, can have a hereditary basis, especially in those who suffer from a condition known as panic disorder. So can anxiety, the basis for repetitive "neurotic" rituals, such as compulsively checking and rechecking the alarm-clock setting, seen in obsessive–compulsive disorder. There's also evidence that the violence that may occur in an antisocial personality and the uncontrollable outbursts of Tourette's syndrome stem ultimately from the genes. And, if you are older, you may worry that every instance of forgetting is a sign of Alzheimer's disease, which (in some forms) arises from a genetic flaw that takes first the memory and then the rest of the mind.

Thus, we see that many psychological traits, both desirable and undesirable, have a connection to our genes, as well as in our experience. But, at the risk of playing the same tune too often, we must emphasize: Genetics is not everything. While heredity is involved in nearly all we do, human behaviors also are shaped by environment. And by "environment" we mean not only

CONNECTION: CHAPTER 11

The *Big Five* are fundamental traits that reliably distinguish different personality patterns among people in all cultures.

● The genetic code, written in DNA, contains our complete hereditary blueprint, grouped into genes and chromosomes.

the influence of learning (including the impact of all our experiences) but also physical factors such as nutrition and physical stress (Brown, 1999).

Unfortunately, people sometimes go to extremes by seeing hereditary effects everywhere. A strong hereditarian stance can, for example, lead to unfair labeling of people as having "bad blood," if they come from troubled or abusive families. Just as disturbing, hereditarian expectations can create complacency and self-centeredness in those whose parents have desirable characteristics, such as high intelligence or good looks. Either way, expectations about genetic influences can create a self-fulfilling prophecy, which leads people to live up (or down) to their expectations. If you expect to be smart and successful (or stupid and a failure), chances are you won't be disappointed.

CHECK YOUR UNDERSTANDING

1. **RECALL:** Psychologists have resolved the nature–nurture controversy by saying that we are the products of
   a. heredity.
   b. environment.
   c. both heredity and environment.
   d. neither heredity nor environment.

2. **APPLICATION:** Which of the following statements is most accurate with regard to the "Jim twins"?
   a. We cannot say for certain that their similarities are mainly genetic.
   b. It is reasonably certain that their similarities come from shared early experiences.
   c. It has been proven that their similarities are just chance.
   d. They are similar because they were raised in the same family environment.

3. **RECALL:** Which perspective says that developmental change is a gradual process?
   a. the continuity view
   b. the discontinuity view
   c. the hereditarian view
   d. the environmental view

4. **UNDERSTANDING THE CORE CONCEPT:** Which one of the following best exemplifies a developmental change that results from and interaction of heredity and environment?
   a. the appearance of facial hair in a teenage boy
   b. eye color
   c. a child learning to talk
   d. winning the lottery

ANSWERS: 1.c 2.a 3.a 4.c

WHAT CAPABILITIES DOES THE CHILD POSSESS?

People used to think that babies began life as a "blank slate"—with an empty brain and no abilities. In modern times, however, that picture has changed. We now see newborns as possessing a remarkable set of abilities that they acquired through their genes. They are social creatures, also adept at locating food and avoiding potential harm. These *innate* (inborn) abilities are the focus of the Core Concept for this section:

Newborns have innate abilities for finding nourishment, interacting with others, and avoiding harmful situations, while the developing abilities of infants and children rely more on learning.

To be sure, the newborn's capabilities are limited—but they are effective enough to promote survival. The newborn arrives in the world already "knowing," for example, how to get nourishment by suckling and how to get attention by cooing and crying. Still, it is helpful to think of the newborn's basic abilities as a sort of scaffold to which new and more complex abilities are added as the child grows and develops.

To explain where these abilities come from and how they develop, we will organize our discussion around three important developmental periods: the *prenatal* period, the *neonatal* (newborn) period, and *infancy.* You will notice that, in each phase, development builds on the abilities and structures laid down earlier.

Prenatal Development

The **prenatal period** spans the nine months between conception and birth. As every mother has sensed, it is a time of furious developmental activity that readies the organism for life on its own outside the womb. In this prenatal period, it passes successively through three stages, which we will describe in a bit more detail.

Shortly after conception, the fertilized egg, also known as a **zygote,** begins to grow through cell division. First one cell becomes two; two become four; and when the number reaches about 150, the zygote implants itself in the lining of the uterus—a process that is completed about 10 days after conception. At this point it becomes an **embryo** (along with those cells that will form into the placenta and other supportive structures).

During the embryonic phase, the genetic plan determines how all the organs that will later be found in the newborn infant begin to form. In this stage, the embryo's cells begin to specialize as components of particular organ systems, a process known as *differentiation.* (Before differentiation, certain cells in the embryo, known as *embryonic stem cells,* are capable of forming into any organ of the body.)

At first, the embryo's cells form distinct layers. Those in the outer layer become the nervous system and the skin. Cells in the middle layer become muscles, bones, blood vessels, and certain internal organs. Those in the inner layer differentiate on a path that will eventually make them into the digestive system, lungs, and glands. By the end of the first month the initial single cell of the zygote has developed into an embryo with millions of specialized cells. Eventually this process of cell division and differentiation, which continues throughout the prenatal period, produces all the tissues and organs of the body.

The first rudimentary "behavior"—a heartbeat—appears when the embryo is about three weeks old and one-sixth of an inch long. A few weeks later, when it is not yet an inch in length, the embryo makes reflexive responses to stimulation. These behaviors occur long before the brain has developed to the point where it can think or direct behaviors.

After the eighth week, the developing embryo is called a **fetus.** Spontaneous movements commanded by the somatic nervous system begin at about this time, although the mother doesn't usually feel these movements until the 16th week after conception (Carmichael, 1970; Humphrey, 1970). By this point, the fetus has grown to about 7 inches long (the average length at birth is 20 inches).

Teratogens: Prenatal Toxins Specialists used to think that the womb shielded the developing organism from nearly all environmental assaults, but we now know better. Although the **placenta** (an organ that develops between the embryo/fetus and the mother) screens out some potentially dangerous substances, many can pass through this interface. These toxic substances, called **teratogens,** include viruses (including HIV, the AIDS virus), certain drugs, and other chemicals. Among the most common teratogens are nicotine and alcohol.

The effects of these teratogens vary from slight to devastating, depending on the type, amount of exposure, and stage of prenatal development in which exposure occurs. Fetal alcohol syndrome is one of the more worrisome disorders that can occur in children of mothers who drink heavily during pregnancy. The symptoms can include mental retardation, poor motor coordination, impaired attention, and hyperactivity.

● As the brain grows in the developing embryo, it forms as many as 250,000 new neurons per minute.

■ **Prenatal period** The developmental period before birth.
■ **Zygote** A fertilized egg.
■ **Embryo** In humans, the name for the developing organism during the first eight weeks after conception.
■ **Fetus** In humans, the term for the developing organism between the embryonic stage and birth.
■ **Placenta** The organ interface between the embryo or fetus and the mother. The placenta separates the bloodstreams, but it allows the exchange of nutrients and waste products.
■ **Teratogens** Substances from the environment, including viruses, drugs, and other chemicals, that can damage the developing organism during the prenatal period.

Prenatal Development of the Brain   Prenatally, the brain grows new neurons at the amazing rate of up to 250,000 per minute. By birth it has produced some 100 billion (Dowling, 1992). All originate from a proliferation of cells at the top of the embryo's hollow *neural tube*. (Your own brain and spinal cord have a hollow core that harks back to your embryonic days.) These furiously multiplying cells eventually become the brain; but, to do so, they must embark on a once-in-a-lifetime journey. As new brain cells are produced, they actually migrate out of the neural tube and then extend their axons and dendrites to make connections with other newly formed neurons. Exactly how they manage to make the proper connections to form a functioning brain is still the subject of much research. The basic plan for "wiring" the brain, however, must be contained in the genetic code.

The Neonatal Period: Abilities of the Newborn Child

What is the sensory world like for the newborn? The father of American psychology, William James, guessed that everything must be an overwhelming jumble of stimuli—"One great blooming, buzzing confusion" (James, 1890). We now know that his views grossly underestimated infants' capabilities. Long before babies achieve motor coordination and locomotion, they take in vast amounts of information about their surroundings, filtering and processing stimulation that attracts, interests, or upsets them. They also have an amazing behavioral repertoire that they use to respond to and manipulate their environment.

During the **neonatal period** (newborn period), which covers the time from birth to one month of age, neonates are capable of responding to stimulation from all of their senses. For example, newborn babies will turn their heads toward anything that strokes their cheeks—a nipple or a finger—and begin to suck it. They can also respond to taste: the sweeter the fluid, the more continuously and forcefully an infant will suck (Lipsitt et al., 1976). They smile when they smell banana essence, and they prefer salted to unsalted cereal (Bernstein, 1990; Harris et al., 1990). However, they recoil from the taste of lemon or shrimp or the smell of rotten eggs. And, as early as 12 hours after birth, they show distinct signs of pleasure at the taste of sugar water or vanilla. All these responses are part of the ability the newborn has to seek nourishment—as the Core Concept for this section suggested.

What else can newborns do with their senses? Minutes after birth, their eyes scan their surroundings, although their vision is not, at first, especially sharp. In fact, babies are born rather nearsighted, with an optimal focus of about 12 inches—ideal for looking at faces. Their distance vision, however, is poor, with a visual acuity of about 20/500 (which means that they can discriminate at 20 feet stimuli that most older children can see clearly at 500 feet). Moreover, good vision requires the operation and coordination of a great many receptor cells in the eye's retina, in the visual pathways, and in the occipital cortex of the brain. At birth, relatively few of these connections are laid down. But these immature systems develop very rapidly, and the baby's visual abilities soon become quite effective (Banks & Bennett, 1988).

Early on, infants can perceive large objects that display a great deal of contrast. By the age of one month, a child can detect contours of a head at close distances. At seven weeks, the baby can scan the features of the caregiver's face, and, as the caregiver talks, the baby can contact his or her eyes. Just as heredity biases infants to prefer human voices over other sounds, it programs them to prefer human faces to most other visual patterns (Fantz, 1963). Although newborns can see colors, their ability to differentiate colors, such as red from orange from blue, becomes dramatically better a month or two after

■ **Neonatal period**   In humans, the neonatal (newborn) period extends through the first month after birth.

birth (Teller, 1998). At three months, the baby can perceive depth and is well on the way to enjoying the visual abilities of adults. And it may surprise you to know that infants seem to possess a rudimentary ability to "count" objects they see: They know, for example, the difference between two dolls and three (Wynn, 1992, 1995). Such *core knowledge* serves as the foundation for the later development of more complex skills, such as are required for arithmetic (Spelke, 2000). They also have strong auditory preferences, one being a greater attraction to female voices than to those of men. Neonates also shift their attention to sound patterns they have heard before; and within a few weeks of birth they begin to recognize their mothers' voice (Carpenter, 1973; DeCasper & Fifer, 1980; DeCasper & Spence, 1986; Spelke & Owsley, 1979).

Aside from their sensory abilities, babies are born with a remarkable set of behavioral reflexes that provide a biological platform for later development. Among these reflexes, the *postural reflex* allows babies to sit with support, and the *grasping reflex* enables them to cling to a caregiver. And, in their cooing and crying, babies also have some rudimentary tools for social interaction. These and other innate responses equip newborns with the essential tools for survival and "instinctive" know-how. In addition, babies have built-in safety features that help them avoid or escape from unpleasant stimulation, such as loud noises, bright lights, strong odors, and painful stimuli. All of this, of course, makes much evolutionary sense because these abilities are highly adaptive and promote survival.

Infancy and Childhood: Building on the Neonatal Blueprint

Following the neonatal period, the child enters **infancy,** a period that lasts until approximately 18 months of age—the time when speech has become well developed. (The Latin root *infans* means "incapable of speech.") It is a time of rapid, genetically programmed growth and still-heavy reliance on the repertoire of reflexes and "instinctive" behaviors that we discussed above. All of these abilities arise from a nervous system that continues to develop at a furious pace. At birth and for the first few years of life, many potential brain circuits are not fully connected, a fact that helps to explain why most people have a poor memory for events that occurred before they were about 3½ years of age (Bauer, 2002; Howe & Courage, 1993). In order to complete the process of forming the brain's circuitry, the neonatal brain shifts its emphasis from producing new cells to a different mode of growth. The genetic program now emphasizes the branching of axons and dendrites (Kolb, 1989). As the dendrites and axons grow and connect, the total mass of neural tissue in the brain continues to increase rapidly—by 50% in the first two years. By 4 years of age it has nearly doubled its birth size.

As nerve fibers grow and connections form in the young brain, stimulation is necessary to make them permanent and functional. Those connections that are not used are lost through a process called *synaptic pruning*. This destruction of unused connections does not destroy the neurons themselves. Rather it returns them to an uncommitted state, awaiting a role in future development (Johnson, 1998). In some cases, however, vital neural connections may be broken, as can happen in children born with congenital cataracts of the eyes. If the cataracts are not treated early, neural connections in the visual system are irretrievably lost.

The genetic program (along with the physical limitations imposed by the size of the skull) does not allow the tremendous growth of brain circuitry to continue indefinitely. So, the neural growth rate gradually diminishes. Finally, by about 11 years of age, the brain attains its ultimate mass.

■ **Infancy** In humans, infancy spans the time between the end of the neonatal period and the establishment of language—usually at about 18 months to 2 years.

Learning Assumes a Role in Development Infancy is also a period during which youngsters begin to exploit their abilities for *learning*. Babies start to build up their knowledge of the world by observing relations between important sensory events, as when a certain tone of the mother's voice signals it is time to eat. This involves a fundamental form of learning that psychologists call *classical conditioning* (it's the same sort of learning that makes your mouth water at the sight of a pizza or makes some people faint at the sight of blood). This form of learning in babies was demonstrated by an experiment in which newborns were taught to anticipate pleasurably sweet sensations by first stroking the babies' foreheads and then giving them sugar water. After several trials, the stroking alone would cause the babies to turn their heads in the direction from which the sweet fluid had been delivered—a learned anticipation of more of the same (Blass, 1990).

CONNECTION: CHAPTER 6

Classical conditioning is a form of learning, originally studied by Pavlov, in which one event signals the occurrence of another.

Infants also use their learning ability to expand their social interaction skills. We have seen, for example, that young babies can learn to distinguish their mother's voice. Likewise, they learn to associate their caregiver with certain odors. And, as any parent will tell you, babies quickly learn how to manipulate their parents by cooing, smiling, and crying. Learning and memory also underlie the surprising ability of newborns to imitate simple facial expressions, such as sticking out the tongue or rounding the mouth (Meltzoff, 1998; Meltzoff & Prinz, 2002). In general, as development proceeds through infancy, learning assumes an ever-larger role in producing even more complex behaviors.

Social Abilities As the foregoing discussion suggests, infants are built for social interaction, and they not only respond to, but also interact with, their caregivers from the moment of birth. Film studies of this interaction reveal a remarkable degree of *synchronicity*: close coordination between the gazing, vocalizing, touching, and smiling of mothers and infants (Martin, 1981). And while babies respond and learn, they also send out messages to those willing to listen to and love them. The result of this interaction can be seen in studies showing how the feelings of mothers and infants are coordinated (Fogel, 1991). So, a 3-month-old infant may laugh when his or her mother laughs and frown or cry in response to her display of negative emotion (Tronick et al., 1980).

Attachment Ideally, social development begins with the establishment of a close emotional relationship between a child and a parent figure. Psychologists call this **attachment,** although the popular media often refer to it as "bonding." By either name, this relationship is especially important because it lays the foundation for all other relationships that follow.

CONNECTION: CHAPTER 9

"Instinct" is a common but imprecise term that refers to behaviors that have a strong genetic basis.

Attachment behaviors appear to occur "instinctively" in many species, although they are not necessarily limited to the infant's interactions with the biological parents. One striking example occurs in **imprinting,** the powerful attraction of infants of some species (notably in birds) to the first moving object or individual they see. A baby chick hatched by a mother duck will form an attachment to its surrogate mother—even though it is a chicken, not a duck. The imprinted chick will even follow its duck-mother right up to the water's edge when she and her ducklings go for a swim. (You may also recall *The Ugly Duckling,* the children's tale about imprinting.) Thus, the imprinting tendency is an innate predisposition, although the organism's environment and experience determine what form it will take. While imprinting occurs most clearly in birds, a similar, but more complex, process may account for the attachment between human infants and their caregivers.

Although humans apparently have an inborn need for attachment, there is no guarantee that parents will always respond to this need. What, then, can

■ **Attachment** The enduring social-emotional relationship between a child and a parent or other regular caregiver.
■ **Imprinting** A primitive form of learning in which some young animals follow and form an attachment to the first moving object they see and hear.

babies do to increase the chances of getting the contact they want? Unlike a baby chick, human babies are not mobile enough at birth to use their own locomotion to get closeness or attention from a caregiver. When they want to get close to the attachment figure (e.g., their mother), they cannot simply crawl or move toward her. But they can emit signals—such as smiling, crying, and vocalizing—to promote responsive behavior (Campos et al., 1983). And few can resist a baby's smile! According to John Bowlby (1973), infants will form attachments to any individual who consistently and appropriately responds to their signals.

Some observers have suggested that attachment begins as early as the first few weeks (Ainsworth, 1973; Ainsworth et al., 1978; Bowlby, 1969, 1973). One study found, for example, that when mothers left the room, their 2- to 4-month-old babies' skin temperature dropped, a sign of emotional distress (Mizukami et al., 1990). In these youngsters, skin temperature dropped even more when a stranger replaced the mother. In contrast, skin temperature remained steady if the mother stayed in the room—even if the stranger was present. Apparently, children only a few months old rely on their caretakers as a "safe base," even before they can indicate attachment with crying or locomotion (Bee, 1994).

● Konrad Lorenz (1903–1989), a researcher who pioneered the study of imprinting, dramatically demonstrated what can happen when young birds become imprinted on an object other than their mother.

The Strange Situation   Developmental psychologist Mary Ainsworth spent a career studying the various forms attachment takes. She did this by observing young children in a variety of carefully contrived "strange situations." For example, she separated children from their mothers by a barrier or placed them alone in an unfamiliar room (Ainsworth, 1989; Ainsworth et al., 1978; Ainsworth & Wittig, 1969; Lamb, 1999). Using such methods in a variety of cultures, Ainsworth found that the children's responses fell into two main categories, reflecting either secure attachment or insecure attachment. Securely attached children felt close to their mothers, safe, and more willing to explore or tolerate a novel experience—confident that they could cry out for help or be reunited with the missing parent. Insecurely attached children were more likely to react to the "strange situation" in one of two ways: with anxiety and ambivalence or with avoidance. The anxious-ambivalent children wanted contact but cried with fear and anger when separated and proved difficult to console even when reunited with their mothers. The avoidant children acted as though they were unconcerned about being separated from their mothers, not crying when they left and not seeking contact when they returned. Avoidant children may be showing the effects of repeated rejection, no longer seeking attachment because their efforts have failed in the past (Shaver & Hazan, 1994).

Attachment fascinates researchers because patterns established in infancy may persist in a variety of childhood and even adult behaviors, influencing later-life job satisfaction, relationship choices, and intimacy experiences—although the current research carries mixed messages on this issue. (See Berk, 2004, for a more detailed review.) As children grow up and become adults, they no longer restrict their attachment to their primary caregiver. While they may retain their childhood attachment style, they gradually widen their attachments to include peers, friends, teachers, coworkers, and others in their community. We should emphasize, however, that—powerful as attachment is—individuals who lack healthy attachments in infancy and childhood are not necessarily doomed to failure in life. While attachment problems are good predictors of later problems with social relationships, many people do succeed in overcoming attachment difficulties (Kagan, 1996, 1998). Further, cross-cultural psychologists have cautioned us that attachment patterns may differ somewhat from culture to culture. For example, Japanese mothers make more physical

● Children become attached to their caregivers, and parents likewise become attached to their children. Love and responsibility help offset the daily struggles for survival faced by poor families the world over.

Identify which one of the following three self-descriptions you most agree with (adapted from Shaver & Hazan, 1994):

1. I am somewhat uncomfortable being close to others; I find it difficult to trust them completely, difficult to allow myself to depend on them. I am nervous when anyone gets too close, and love partners often want me to be more intimate than I feel comfortable being.

2. I find that others are reluctant to get as close as I would like. I often worry that my partner doesn't really love me or won't want to stay with me. I want to get very close to my partner, and this sometimes scares people away.

3. I find it relatively easy to get close to others and am comfortable depending on them. I don't often worry about being abandoned or about someone getting too close to me.

WHAT YOUR CHOICE MEANS

We realize that it is probably obvious to you which of the statements above is "best." Nevertheless, just considering the alternatives should help you understand attachment styles—and, perhaps, yourself—a little better. Here's our interpretation: If you selected the first statement, you agreed with the attitude that reflects an avoidant, insecure attachment. This style was chosen by 25% of Shaver and Hazan's respondent sample. The second statement reflects an anxious-ambivalent, insecure attachment style, selected by 20% of the sample. The third statement reflects a secure attachment style, the most common pattern identified, accounting for 55% of respondents (Shaver & Hazan, 1994).

What do these styles signify for later life? Through interviews, observations, and questionnaires, researchers have identified several consequences of attachment style, secure or insecure, in adulthood (see Ainsworth, 1989; Collins & Read, 1990; Hazan & Shaver, 1990; Kirkpatrick & Shaver, 1992; Shaver & Hazan, 1993, 1994; Simpson, 1990):

■ Secure individuals have more positive self-concepts and believe that most other people are good-natured and well-intentioned. They see their personal relationships as trustworthy and satisfying.

■ Secure respondents are satisfied with their job security, coworkers, income, and work activity. They put a higher value on relationships than on work and derive their greatest pleasure from connections to others.

■ Insecure, anxious-ambivalent persons report emotional extremes and jealousy. They feel unappreciated, insecure, and unlikely to win professional advancement. They make less money than those with other attachment styles, working more for approval and recognition than financial gain. They fantasize about succeeding but often slack off after receiving praise.

■ Avoidant people fear intimacy and expect their relationships to fail. They place a higher value on work than on relationships and generally like their work and job security. They follow a workaholic pattern, but (not surprisingly) they are dissatisfied with their coworkers.

■ Secure individuals tend to choose as partners others who are secure. After breakups, avoidant individuals claim to be less bothered by the loss of the relationship, although this may be a defensive claim, with distress showing up in other ways (e.g., physical symptoms).

---

contact with infants, while American mothers make more eye contact (Rothbaum et al., 2000). With such caveats in mind, we now invite you to take the quiz in the "Do It Yourself!" box, "What's Your Attachment Style?"

Contact Comfort Why do infants become attached to caregivers in the first place? An evolutionary explanation says that attachment safeguards an infant's survival by assuring the support and protection it requires. Through natural selection, individuals with genetic tendencies to "attach" will survive, thrive, and pass those tendencies along to their own offspring.

In addition to protection, could attachment also be the child's way of encouraging the parents to provide food—its most basic physical need? This idea has been dubbed the "cupboard theory": Infants become attached to those who provide the "cupboard" containing the food supply. This theory has been a favorite of those who believe that nursing is the basis for healthy relationships. But does the cupboard theory really explain the parent–child bond?

To understand how psychologists have dealt with this issue, we have to imagine the way many people looked at child rearing in the 1940s and 50s, when the cupboard theory prevailed. Freud had convinced most physicians that young infants and children were so mentally undeveloped that the only thing of real importance in their lives was the breast or the bottle. Nothing like adult social relationships entered their little minds—which explains why no one worried about the lack of touching or other displays of affection given premature infants in incubators or older children in orphanages (Blum, 2002; Sapolsky, 2002).

Psychologists Harry and Margaret Harlow guessed that a more fundamental cause of attachment involves physical contact (Harlow, 1965; Harlow &

Harlow, 1966). To see if they were right, they decided to test this idea against the cupboard theory in an animal model, using infant monkeys who had been separated from their mothers at birth. The Harlows placed orphaned baby monkeys in cages where they had access to two artificial *surrogate mothers*. One was a simple wire figure that provided milk through a nipple—a "cupboard," but little else. The other was a cloth-covered figure providing no milk but offering abundant stimulation from its soft terry-cloth cover. Confirming their expectations, the Harlows observed that their baby monkeys spent many hours nestled close to the cloth mother but little time with the wire model, despite the nourishment the latter provided. Moreover, when the baby monkeys were frightened, they sought comfort by clinging to the cloth figure. They also used it as a base of operations when exploring new situations. With these observations, then, the Harlows were able to show that the infant monkeys become attached to and prefer a "mother" figure that provides **contact comfort,** the stimulation and reassurance derived from physical touch.

Human infants need contact comfort, too. The lack of a close, loving relationship in infancy even affects physical growth. We know this from observations of children in emotionally detached or hostile family environments: Such children have slower growth and bone development. They may grow again if removed from the poor environment, but their growth is stunted again if they are returned to it, a phenomenon known as *psychosocial dwarfism*. A related condition, which has no organic basis but results from lack of parental love and nurturing, is known as *failure to thrive,* seen in wasted-looking, withdrawn, and apathetic infants. Accordingly, in some hospitals that recognize the power of contact comfort, premature infants and others born at risk are scheduled to receive regular holding and cuddling by staff members and volunteers. Clearly, a close, interactive relationship with loving adults is a child's first step toward healthy physical growth and normal socialization.

Maturation and Physical Abilities Sitting, crawling, and walking—like the growth of the brain, the growth spurt of puberty, and the onset of menopause—all occur on their own biological time schedules. Psychologists use the term **maturation** for the unfolding of these genetically programmed processes of growth and development over time. When organisms are raised under adequate environmental conditions, their maturation follows a predictable pattern. In humans, maturation generates all of the sequences and patterns of behavior seen in Figure 4.2.

Even when maturation takes the leading role, we must keep in mind the *interaction* of biology and environment. So, in the sequence for motor control shown in Figure 4.2, a child learns to walk without special training following a time-ordered pattern that is typical of all physically capable members of our species. Indeed, in cultures where children are carried in cradle boards, walking occurs on a similar schedule (Dennis & Dennis, 1940). Despite this hereditary pattern, however, we find that environmental influences can sometimes play a part. So, in the West Indies, where infants receive vigorous massage after the daily bath and frequent practice in moving their legs while being held, children sit and walk a little earlier, on the average, than do children in the United States (Hopkins & Westra, 1988). On the other hand, lack of human contact can have the opposite effect, as in children who had spent their lives lying in cribs in Iranian orphanages were observed to be very slow in learning to sit and walk (Dennis, 1960).

Harking back to our discussion of continuity and discontinuity, physical growth in humans has always been viewed as a *continuous* process whose rate changes with age, slowing over time after a rapid start in the early years. This picture of continuous physical growth has been qualified, however, as the

● One of Harlow's monkeys and its artificial terry-cloth mother. Harlow found that the contact comfort mothers provide is essential for normal social development.

■ **Contact comfort** Stimulation and reassurance derived from the physical touch of a caregiver.
■ **Maturation** The process by which the genetic program manifests itself over time.

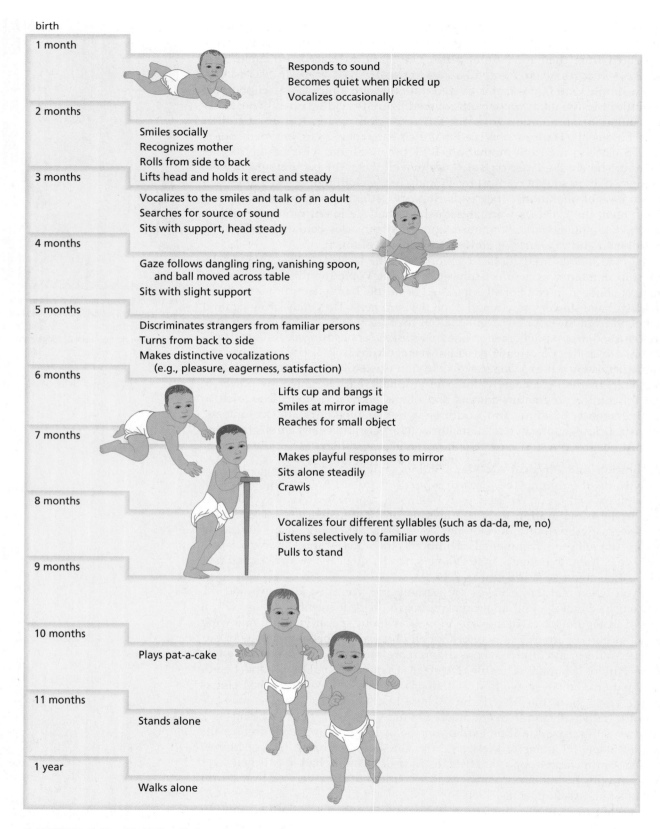

birth

1 month

Responds to sound
Becomes quiet when picked up
Vocalizes occasionally

2 months

Smiles socially
Recognizes mother
Rolls from side to back
Lifts head and holds it erect and steady

3 months

Vocalizes to the smiles and talk of an adult
Searches for source of sound
Sits with support, head steady

4 months

Gaze follows dangling ring, vanishing spoon,
    and ball moved across table
Sits with slight support

5 months

Discriminates strangers from familiar persons
Turns from back to side
Makes distinctive vocalizations
    (e.g., pleasure, eagerness, satisfaction)

6 months

Lifts cup and bangs it
Smiles at mirror image
Reaches for small object

7 months

Makes playful responses to mirror
Sits alone steadily
Crawls

8 months

Vocalizes four different syllables (such as da-da, me, no)
Listens selectively to familiar words
Pulls to stand

9 months

10 months

Plays pat-a-cake

11 months

Stands alone

1 year

Walks alone

● **FIGURE 4.2** Maturational Timetable for Motor Control

This figure shows average ages at which each behavior is performed. There are considerable individual differences in the *rate* of development, so the time at which each response occurs is variable. Most infants, however, follow the *sequence* of development outlined here.

result of reports showing that growth in the length of infants' bodies occurs in discontinuous "bursts." Developmentalists call this *saltation* (from the Latin *saltare*, "to leap"). In fact, all through infancy and childhood physical growth involves an alternation between active and inactive growth phases (Lampl et al., 1992). Typically, infants go for several days showing no growth at all, and then suddenly they enter a growth spurt, in which they can add as much as one-half inch in length in 24 hours!

To summarize, we have seen that neonates come equipped to accomplish three basic tasks of survival: finding sustenance (feeding), maintaining contact with people (for protection and care), and defense against harmful stimuli (withdrawing from pain or threat). Such tasks require a set of innate abilities, and these abilities, in turn, form a foundation on which learning and physical maturation build the perceptual skills, the ability to understand experiences, and basic thinking skills that continue to develop during infancy, childhood, and throughout life (von Hofsten & Lindhagen, 1979).

 PSYCHOLOGY IN YOUR LIFE: DOES YOUR CHILD MEASURE UP?

It is risky to discuss the ages by which a child "should" achieve certain physical and mental skills. Children show great variation in their development. Some children walk by 11 months, about half do so by their first birthdays, and nearly all achieve this milestone by 15 months of age. So if your child, or a child you know, hasn't started walking and talking by age 1, you shouldn't panic. Likewise, you shouldn't be worried if your child isn't talking by the average time suggested in the baby books. Einstein was slow to talk, too.

On the other hand, large differences from the averages should not be ignored. If a child still isn't beginning to walk and talk by age 2, the caregiver should consult a specialist, such as a pediatrician or developmental psychologist, to see whether something is wrong. It is well to remember, also, that a delay in one area, such as the onset of speech, does not mean that the child is "retarded" or will be generally slow in other areas. Not only are there great variations among children, but variations occur normally within an individual child.

What developmental standards would a specialist use? Certainly, a child should be responsive to people almost from the moment of birth. All the major reflexes discussed in the previous section should be present. (These should be checked by the pediatrician.) Then, as the child develops, you will want to watch at the appropriate times for the abilities listed in Figure 4.2. Doing so will not only help you follow the child's progress, but it will make you more knowledgeable about the process of psychological development.

CHECK YOUR UNDERSTANDING

1. **RECALL:** Which of the following does not appear before birth?
   a. the heartbeat
   b. movement of limbs
   c. growth and migration of neurons
   d. vocalizations

2. **RECALL:** After birth, brain development emphasizes the
   a. migration of neurons.
   b. development of connections among neurons.
   c. development of the brain stem.
   d. multiplication of neurons.

3. **APPLICATION:** You are a psychologist working in a pediatric hospital. What would you recommend as one of the most important things that the staff could do for newborn babies to promote their healthy development?
   a. Talk to them.
   b. Touch them.
   c. Make eye contact with them.
   d. Feed them on demand.

4. **APPLICATION:** You would expect your newborn baby to
   a. quickly learn to recognize the sound of his or her name.
   b. react negatively to a taste of lemon.
   c. prefer the father's deeper voice to the mother's higher voice.
   d. smile when eating.

5. **RECALL:** Mary Ainsworth found two main types of attachment,
   a. shy and bold.
   b. introverted and extraverted.
   c. secure and insecure.
   d. strong and weak.

6. **UNDERSTANDING THE CORE CONCEPT:** Which one of the following is an innate ability that promotes survival?
   a. the grasping reflex
   b. recognition of the mother's face
   c. toilet training
   d. sharp vision

ANSWERS: 1.d 2.b 3.b 4.b 5.c 6.a

WHAT ARE THE DEVELOPMENTAL TASKS OF INFANCY AND CHILDHOOD?

Three of the greatest accomplishments of your life include acquiring your native language, developing your ability to think and reason, and forming relationships with the important people in your life. Each of these serve as the basis for further development later in life. And we will see that, as children work through these tasks, they undergo profound psychological changes. Here's how our Core Concept states the main idea of this section:

Infants and children face especially important developmental tasks in the areas of language acquisition, cognition, and social relationships—tasks that lay a foundation for further growth in adolescence and adulthood.

As we will see below, the developmental differences between children and adults are huge, but the differences in language, thought, and socialization are not simply the result of adults' greater experience or store of information. The differences between children and adults also involve the unfolding of crucial maturational processes. Let us first observe these processes at work on the task of language acquisition.

How Children Acquire Language

One of the defining characteristics of humans is the use of complex *language*—our ability to communicate through spoken and written words and gestures. From a developmental perspective, human language acquisition is awe-inspiring: Newborn children know no words at all, yet in only a few years virtually all of them become fluent speakers of any language they hear spoken regularly—or *see,* in the case of gestural languages such as American Sign Language. What makes them such adept language learners? Developmental specialists believe that human infants possess innate (inborn) abilities that help them with this task (Pinker, 1994).

Language Structures in the Brain According to the *innateness theory of language,* children acquire language not merely by imitating but by following an inborn program of steps to acquire the vocabulary and grammar of the language in their environment. Psycholinguist Noam Chomsky (1965, 1975) has proposed that children are born with mental structures—built into the brain—that make it possible to comprehend and produce speech. Many experts agree with Chomsky that innate mental machinery orchestrates children's language learning (Hauser, Chomsky, & Fitch, 2002). Indeed, research based on the Human Genome Project has provided evidence that the foundations of language are, in part, genetic (Liegeois et al., 2001). One such mechanism, we have seen, lies in Broca's area, the motor speech "controller" in the cerebral cortex. Chomsky refers to these speech-enabling structures collectively as a **language acquisition device** or **LAD.**

In Chomsky's theory, the LAD—like a computer chip—contains some very basic rules, common to all human languages. One such rule might be the distinction between nouns (for names of things) and verbs (for actions). These innate rules, Chomsky argues, make it easier for children to discover patterns in languages to which they are exposed.

What other evidence does Chomsky have to suggest that the foundations of language are innate? Children worldwide proceed through very similar stages of learning their native languages. A logical hypothesis for explaining this pattern would be that children possess inborn "programs" for language development that automatically run at certain times in the child's life. Despite the cross-cultural similarities in the sequence, however, language learning is not precisely the same across cultures. Such variations suggest that children's built-in capacity for language is not a rigid device but a set of "listening rules" or guidelines for perceiving language (Bee, 1994; Slobin, 1985a, b). For example, babies pay attention to the sounds and rhythms of the sound strings they hear others speak (or in sign language, see), especially the beginnings, endings, and stressed syllables. Relying on their built-in "listening guides," young children deduce the patterns and rules for producing their own speech.

In general, language researchers have been impressed with the fact that most young children are both ready to acquire language and flexible about its final form and context. This is equally true for children exposed to any of the world's 4000 spoken languages, as well as to gestural communication systems, such as American Sign Language. Such adaptability suggests that the LAD in children is flexible, not rigidly programmed (Goldin-Meadow & Mylander, 1990; Meier, 1991). Recent research also suggests that the effect can also go the other way: The language we learn as children also fine-tunes the structure of the brain, as when English speakers "wire" their brains to distinguish the sounds /r/ and /l/, sounds that cannot be distinguished by many Japanese speakers (Iverson et al., 2003).

Babbling: A Foundation for Language Besides their ability to perceive speech sounds, infants have a natural ability to produce language sounds. Part of this tendency arises from a vocal apparatus that is biologically adapted for speech. As a result, infants babble, producing speechlike sounds and syllables such as "mamama" or "beebee" well before they begin to use true words. Infants at this stage may also follow conversational "rules," such as taking turns with vocalizations (Jaffe et al., 2001). Amazingly, during this *babbling stage*, babies make nearly all sounds heard in all languages. Eventually, however, learning narrows the repertoire down to the sounds of the language that the baby hears (Clark & Clark, 1977; Mowrer, 1960).

Acquiring Vocabulary and Grammar Inborn language abilities don't tell the whole story, for children must *learn* the words and the structure of a particular language. Accordingly, learning the basic grammar and vocabulary in the native language represents an important project for children in their first few years of life—and they are excellent language learners. At age 2, the average

■ **Language acquisition device or LAD** A biologically organized mental structure in the brain that facilitates the learning of language because (according to Chomsky) it is innately programmed with some of the fundamental rules of grammar.

FIGURE 4.3 Growth in Grade-School Children's Vocabulary

The number of words in a child's vocabulary increases rapidly during the grade school years—an even faster rate of increase than during the preschool years. The chart shows total vocabulary, including words that a child can use (production vocabulary) and words that a child can understand (comprehension vocabulary). These data were reported in 1995 by J. M. Anglin of the University of Waterloo, Ontario, Canada.

■ **Grammar** The rules of a language, specifying how to use words, morphemes, and syntax to produce understandable sentences.

■ **Morphemes** The meaningful units of language that make up words. Some whole words are morphemes (example: "word"); other morphemes include grammatical components that alter a word's meaning (examples: "-ed," "-ing," and "un-").

child has a vocabulary of nearly a thousand different words (Huttenlocher et al., 1991). By the age of 6, that number has burgeoned to an astounding 10,000 words (Anglin, 1993, 1995). Assuming that most of these words are learned after the age of 18 months, this works out to about nine new words a day, or almost one word per waking hour (Bower, 1998c; Carey, 1978). Even more surprising, the pace of vocabulary acquisition picks up between about ages 6 and 10, as you can see in Figure 4.3.

What is the pattern by which children develop vocabulary and grammar? Developmental psychologists recognize three initial stages: the *one-word stage,* the *two-word stage,* and *telegraphic speech.* During the *one-word stage,* which begins at about 1 year of age, children utter single concrete nouns or verbs, such as "Mama" or "drink." Later, they learn to put words together to express more complex ideas.

The Naming Explosion At around 18 months of age, children's word learning accelerates rapidly. At this age, children may delight in pointing to objects and naming them. Researchers have called this phase the "naming explosion" because children begin to acquire new words, especially names for objects, at a rapidly increasing rate. Soon they also discern that some words are not names but actions (verbs) that describe how named objects and persons affect each other.

After about six months, the naming explosion subsides and children begin to use one-word utterances in different sequences to convey more complex meanings. When these words come in pairs, they are said to enter the *two-word stage,* and the range of meanings children can convey increases tremendously. Studies of different languages show that, around the world, children's two-word utterances begin to divide their experience into certain categories. For example, children speaking languages as diverse as English, Samoan, Finnish, Hebrew, and Swedish were found to talk mostly about three categories of ideas: movers, movable objects, and locations (Braine, 1976). When young Alexis kicks a ball, for example, the mover is Alexis and the movable object is the ball. Alexis can express this relationship in the two-word sequence, "Alexis ball." It is in the two-word stage, at about 2 years, that children first develop the language rules called *grammar.* This allows them to move past simple naming and combine words into sentences.

The Rules of Grammar: Putting Words Together Even if you have a limited vocabulary, you can combine the same words in different sequences to convey a rich variety of meanings. For example, "I saw him chasing a dog" and "I saw a dog chasing him" both use exactly the same words, but switching the order of the words "him" and "dog" yields completely different meanings. **Grammar** makes this possible: It is a language's set of rules about combining and ordering words to make understandable sentences (Naigles, 1990; Naigles & Kako, 1993). Different languages may use considerably different rules about grammatical combinations. In Japanese, for example, the verb always comes last, while English is much more lax about verb position.

In their early two- and three-word sentences, children's speech is *telegraphic:* short, simple sequences of nouns and verbs without plurals, tenses, or function words like "the" and "of." For example, "Ball hit Evie cry" is *telegraphic speech.* To develop the ability to make full sentences, children must learn to use other forms of speech, such as modifiers (adjectives and adverbs) and articles (the, those), and they must learn how to put words together—grammatically. In English, this means recognizing and producing the familiar subject-verb-object order, as in "The lamb followed Mary."

Finally, children need to acquire grammatical skill in using **morphemes,** the meaningful units that make up words. Morphemes mark verbs to show tense (walk*ed,* walk*ing*) and mark nouns to show possession (Maria*'s,* the people*'s*) and plurality (fox*es,* child*ren*). Often, however, children make mistakes because they do not know the rule or apply an inappropriate one (Marcus, 1996). One common error, known as **overregularization,** applies a rule too widely and creates incorrect forms. For example, after learning to make past tense verb forms by adding *-d* or *-ed,* children may apply this "rule" even to its exceptions, the irregular verbs, creating such nonwords as *hitted* and *breaked.* Learning to add *-s* or *-es* to make plurals, children may apply the rule to irregular nouns, as in *foots* or *mouses.*

Other Language Skills Words and the grammatical rules for combining them are only some of the ingredients of communication. To communicate well, children also need to learn the social rules of conversation. They must learn how to join a discussion, how to take turns talking and listening, and how to make contributions that are relevant. Adult speakers use body language, intonation, and facial expressions to enhance their communication. They also use feedback they get from listeners and are able to take the perspective of the listener. Children must master these skills in order to become successful communicators—to become part of a human language community.

As they grow older, children also begin to express abstract meanings, especially as their thoughts extend beyond the physical world and into their psychological world. For example, after the age of 2, children begin to use words such as *dream, forget, pretend, believe, guess,* and *hope,* as they talk about internal states (Shatz et al., 1983). They also use words such as *happy, sad,* and *angry* to refer to emotional states. Finally, after cognitive advances that occur later in childhood, they understand and use highly abstract words such as *truth, justice,* and *idea.*

What is the major point that stands out amid the complexities of language acquisition? It is part of our Core Concept: Language is a major developmental task of childhood—for which children are exquisitely prepared. And the way they acquire and use language suggests that these early steps on the path to adulthood involve a combination of learning and innate processes that unfold on their own developmental timetables.

Cognitive Development: Piaget's Theory

If you have ever known a toddler going through the naming explosion, you have seen that children have an insatiable appetite for labeling things they know. Behind this labeling is their emerging ability for thinking, perceiving, and remembering. The next few pages will focus on the ways that these mental abilities emerge, a process called *cognitive development.*

Psychologists interested in cognitive development ask such questions as: When do children realize that objects still exist even when they can't see them? Do they know that it is possible to hold ideas that aren't true? Can they understand that people have desires and dreams, but objects do not? Developmental psychologists investigate not only *what* children think but *how* they think.

In this section we will emphasize the pioneering work on cognitive development by the late Swiss psychologist Jean Piaget (although there are other points of view). For nearly 50 years, Piaget observed children's intellectual development and formulated his observations into a comprehensive theory.

Piaget began this quest to understand the child's mind by carefully observing the behavior of his own three children. His methods were simple: He would pose problems to them, observe their responses, slightly alter the situations, and once again observe their responses. Piaget attended especially to the developmental transitions and changes in his children's thinking, reasoning, and

■ **Overregularization** Applying a grammatical rule too widely and creating incorrect forms.

problem solving. This focus led to a *discontinuous stage model* of development, which emphasized Piaget's view that children undergo a revolution in thought at each stage. We will see below that three key ideas distinguish Piaget's approach: (1) *schemas*, (2) the interaction of *assimilation* and *accommodation*, and (3) the *stages of cognitive development*.

Schemas   To illustrate the concept of schemas, think of some four-legged animals. Now think of some that are friendly. Then think of one that barks. You might have started by imagining elephants, tigers, cats, and dogs (all four-legged), then narrowed your choices down to cats and dogs (four-legged and friendly), and finally to just dogs (which bark). You could do this easily only because you have developed mental structures (mental programs) that enable you to interpret concepts and events. Piaget termed such mental structures **schemas.** We have schemas for concepts, such as "dog" and "development." We have schemas for actions, such as eating with chopsticks. We also have schemas for solving problems, such as finding the area of a circle or dealing with a crying baby. In general, schemas are mental structures that guide thinking. According to Piaget, they are also the building blocks of development. Schemas form and change as we develop and organize our knowledge to deal with new experiences and predict future events. As you read this, you are building a schema about schemas!

Assimilation and Accommodation   In Piaget's system, two dynamic processes underlie all cognitive growth: *assimilation* and *accommodation*. **Assimilation** is a mental process that modifies new information to fit with existing schemas—with what is already known. So, a baby who knows how to suck from a nipple will use assimilation to deal with new objects such as a finger or a new toy. Likewise, an older child might assimilate a new word such as "pepperoni" to describe a favorite kind of pizza. You, too, experience assimilation when you read about a favorite actor's new film or gain skill in using a new program on your computer.

By contrast, **accommodation** is a process of *restructuring or modifying schemas* to incorporate new information. For example, a child's simplistic "bird" schema, which includes any flying object, undergoes accommodation when the child learns that a butterfly is not a bird. Adults experience accommodation of their mental schemas, too. For example, the Internet has caused widespread accommodation in the schemas people use to conceptualize shopping and communicating. You, too, may need to modify a schema when the professor in your psychology course says something that surprises you—such as, "Children have innate language abilities," when you had always assumed that language was acquired entirely by learning. As a result, your schema about newborn children may change to accommodate your new knowledge.

For Piaget, cognitive development results from the continual interweaving of assimilation and accommodation. Through these two processes, the individual's behavior and knowledge become less dependent on concrete external reality and more reliant on internal thought. In general, *assimilation* makes new information fit our existing views of the world, and *accommodation* changes our views to fit new information.

Piaget's Stages of Cognitive Development   The way a child thinks about the world progresses through four revolutionary changes. Piaget described these changes in terms of four stages of cognitive growth: the *sensorimotor stage* (infancy), the *preoperational stage* (early childhood), the *concrete operational stage*

● Although an infant will begin to suck a bottle just the way he or she sucked a breast (assimilation), the infant will soon discover that some changes are necessary (accommodation). The child will make an even greater accommodation in the transitions from bottle to cup.

■ **Schemas**   In Piaget's theory, mental structures or programs that guide a developing child's thought.

■ **Assimilation**   A mental process that modifies new information to fit it into existing schemes.

■ **Accommodation**   A mental process that restructures existing schemes so that new information is better understood.

(middle childhood), and the *formal operational stage* (adolescence). At each stage, distinct styles of thinking emerge as the child progresses from sensory reaction to logical thought. It is important to note that all children progress through these stages in the same sequence, although one child may take longer to pass through a given stage than does another child.

The Sensorimotor Stage (Birth to about age 2) We have seen that children enter the world equipped with many innate and reflexive behaviors, such as those for clinging, sucking, and crying. None of these require thought—in the sense of the complex mental activity seen in problem solving later in childhood. Instead, children in the **sensorimotor stage** give mainly reflexive or "instinctive" motor responses to stimulation, with very little "thinking" involved. Piaget called this *sensorimotor intelligence*. Not everything is automatic, however. As we have seen, children at this stage are also capable of simple learning, even though the circuitry in the cortex is not yet well connected. They learn to recognize people they see frequently. And they learn to coordinate their body parts to grasp and explore attractive objects (a rattle, perhaps) or to avoid things that they dislike (such as the taste of a lemon wedge).

A major development of significance for later thinking and learning appears in the second year: the ability to make mental images, or internal mental representations, of objects. With the power of **mental representation,** children can now form mental images of objects and events and begin to use them in thinking and problem solving.

Gradually, the child takes mental representation one step farther by realizing that objects continue to exist even when they are out of sight. This ability, called **object permanence,** liberates the child from the present and from his or her immediate surroundings. (This makes the game of peekaboo interesting to a young child.) The basics are in place by one year of age, but the ability for object permanence continues to develop through the second year (Flavell, 1985). At the same time, language begins to appear, and so words become another way to make mental representations. Together these forms of representational thought become the major accomplishment of the sensorimotor stage.

The Preoperational Stage (from about 2 to 6 or 7 Years of Age) The cognitive advances in the next developmental stage, the **preoperational stage,** grow out of the ability to represent objects mentally. One of these advances involves the emerging sense of self as distinctive from other people and objects in the environment. Another advance involves the ability to solve simple problems using mental representation (such as searching different places for a lost toy). Yet, despite these abilities, the child cannot solve problems requiring logical thought. Other important limiting features of the child's mind in this period are *egocentrism, animistic thinking, centration,* and *irreversibility.*

■ **Egocentrism,** a self-centered focus, causes children to see the world only in terms of themselves and their own position. Further, they assume that others see the world in the same way that they do. So, when you are talking to a preoperational child on the phone, she may say, "Look at my new dollie!" assuming you can see things on her end of the line. As a result of this egocentrism, preoperational children are not yet able to fully empathize with others or take others' points of view. For this reason, children may act in ways that have destructive or hurtful consequences, even though they don't intend to upset or harm others. Egocentrism also makes it difficult for a child at this stage to share toys or food.

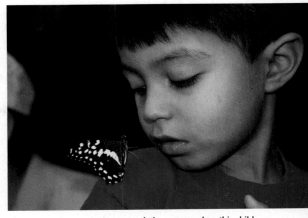

● Accommodation occurs when this child learns that a butterfly does not fit his schema for "bird."

● Object permanence, the perception that objects exist independently of one's own actions or awareness, develops gradually during the first stage of cognitive development and is solidly formed before age one. The baby in these pictures clearly believes that the toy no longer exists once it is obscured by the screen.

■ **Sensorimotor stage** The first stage in Piaget's theory, during which the child relies heavily on innate motor responses to stimuli.
■ **Mental representation** The ability to form internal images of objects and events.
■ **Object permanence** The knowledge that objects exist independently of one's own actions or awareness.
■ **Preoperational stage** The second stage in Piaget's theory, marked by well-developed mental representation and the use of language.
■ **Egocentrism** In Piaget's theory, the self-centered inability to realize that there are other viewpoints beside one's own.

- **Animistic thinking** involves the belief that inanimate objects have life and mental processes, just as people do. For example, if a child slips and bangs her head on the table, she might complain about the "bad table," blaming it for hurting her.

- **Centration** involves the inability to understand an event because the child focuses attention too narrowly, while ignoring other important information. That is, the child can "center" on only one bit of information at a time. So, for example, a thirsty child may insist on drinking a "big glass" of juice, preferring a tall narrow container to a short wide one, mistakenly assuming that the height of the glass ensures that it will hold more juice, while ignoring the other relevant dimension of width. (See the "Do It Yourself!" box below.)

- **Irreversibility** is the inability to think through a series of events or the steps involved in solving of a problem and then to reverse course, returning to the mental starting point. In short, preoperational children lack the ability to do and then undo an act in their minds. To give a concrete example, Sam might see Mary spill a box of raisins on the table and think, "Wow! Mary has lots more raisins than I have in my little box." But preoperational Sam cannot mentally reverse the process and think, "If she put them all back in the box, it would look like the same amount I have in mine." This inability—to do a mental "experiment," then undo it and mentally try another approach—represents the biggest obstacle to logical thinking in the preoperational child.

While we might see these as limitations, keep in mind that they are also the characteristics that make children at this stage most charming and interesting—and different from older children and adults.

The Concrete Operational Stage (from about 7 to about 11 Years of Age)   At the next stage, children break through the barrier of *irreversibility* to understand, for the first time, that many things may stay essentially the same, even when their superficial appearance changes. In this **concrete operational stage,** they can understand that a short, wide glass can hold as much juice as a tall, narrow one or that the spilled raisins must fit back in the box. So, the problems that defeated the preoperational child now yield to a new understanding of the way that volume is *conserved.* Similarly, they now understand that a string of red beads is not longer than an identical string of blue beads, even though the red beads are stretched out in a line while the blue beads lie in a small pile. They realize that the beads *look* different in their grouping, but

- **Animistic thinking**   A preoperational mode of thought in which inanimate objects are imagined to have life and mental processes.
- **Centration**   A preoperational thought pattern involving the inability to take into account more than one factor at a time.
- **Irreversibility**   The inability, in the preoperational child, to think through a series of events or mental operations and then mentally reverse the steps.
- **Concrete operational stage**   The third of Piaget's stages, when a child understands conservation but still is incapable of abstract thought.

DO IT YOURSELF! | Playing with Children–Piagetian Style

If you have access to a child, you can try out some of the problems Piaget posed for his children in order to study their thinking. For example, with a preoperational or concrete operational child, it's always fun to give a conservation problem that involves pouring liquid from a tall, narrow container into a short, wide one. Begin by pouring the same amounts into two identical vessels, such as glass measuring cups. Get the child to agree that you are

starting with the same amount in each. Then pour the liquid from one vessel into a shallow pan. Ask the child, "Does one of these have more than the other, or are they both the same?" Then see if your child's responses fit with Piaget's observations.

Piaget found that the concrete operational child–who understands conservation–will know that the volume of liquid remains the same, regardless of the shape of the container. The

preoperational child will think that the shallow pan has less because the liquid does not come up as far on the container. This shows that the younger child does not know that volume is conserved, regardless of the shape of the container. Piaget claimed that it also showed that the younger child cannot reason about both height and width simultaneously.

this does not mean that they *are* different in number. This new ability, called **conservation,** represents one of the most important cognitive breakthroughs that most 7-year-olds have made.

Along with the new ability to understand conservation, children at this stage acquire the capability for performing **mental operations.** They have overcome the problem of irreversibility, so they now can solve problems by manipulating concepts entirely in their minds. This allows the concrete operational child to think things through before taking action. As a result, they may be less impulsive. They are also less gullible, giving up many "magical" notions, such as the belief in Santa Claus, that they now know to be impossible.

Using their ability for performing mental operations, concrete operational children begin to use simple reasoning to solve problems. The symbols they use in reasoning are, however, still mainly symbols for concrete objects and events, not abstractions. The limitations of their concrete thinking are shown in the familiar game of "20 questions," the goal of which is to determine the identity of an object by asking the fewest possible yes/no questions of the person who thinks up the object. A child of 7 or 8 usually sticks to very specific questions ("Is it a bird?" "Is it a cat?"), but does not ask the higher-level questions that more efficiently narrow down the possibilities for the correct answer ("Does it fly?" "Does it have fur?").

The *formal operational stage,* Piaget's final stage of cognitive development, we will save for our discussion of adolescence, when the individual overcomes the limitations of the previous stages, undergoing yet another cognitive revolution. Suffice it to say for now that this final stage involves the development of abstract thought.

Beyond Piaget: Contemporary Perspectives on Cognitive Development Most psychologists accept the broad picture that Piaget painted of development (Beilin, 1992; Flavell, 1996; Lourenço & Machado, 1996). However, newer research suggests that the transition between one stage and another is less abrupt—more continuous—than Piaget's theory implies. Also, researchers have shown that children are, in some ways, more intellectually sophisticated at each stage than Piaget had found (Munakata et al., 1997). Studies show, for example, that some mental representation occurs as early as three months of age, rather than in the second year, as Piaget had thought (Gulya et al., 1998). Recent research also shows that by one year of age infants develop the complex idea that people have intentions that may differ from their own (Baldwin, 2000; Tomasello, 2000).

Some psychologists believe that what Piaget saw as limitations on preoperational thought may actually be the inability to *express* thoughts (Bauer, 2002). So, preoperational children may actually *understand* some of the same concepts that older children do, but they may still lack the skills to perform accordingly. For example, a 5-year-old child who has watched her father prepare breakfast in the past can watch him and understand what he is cooking but may not be able to describe it to her visiting grandmother or express why she likes her pancakes "the way Daddy fixes them." Researchers have found, in contrast with Piaget's notion of centration, that young children (ages 3 and 4) understand that the "insides" of objects, although they are invisible, are not necessarily identical to their external appearances (Gelman & Wellman, 1991). And, in contrast with Piaget's claims about animistic thinking, 3- to 5-year-old children, when pressed to do so, are consistently able to distinguish between real and purely mental (imaginary) entities (Wellman & Estes, 1986). Finally, studies of emotional development have shown that preoperational children can understand that other people have internal emotional responses that do not always jibe with their outward expressions (Bower, 1997b).

● This 5-year-old girl is aware that the two containers have the same amount of colored liquid. However, when the liquid from one is poured into a taller narrow container, she indicates that there is more liquid in the taller one. She has not yet grasped the concept of conservation, which she will understand by age 6 or 7.

■ **Conservation** The understanding that the physical properties of an object or substance do not change when appearances change but nothing is added or taken away.
■ **Mental operations** Solving problems by manipulating images in one's mind.

Other developmental psychologists counter that Piaget's theory is not as rigid as its critics claim. Rather, it is flexible enough to accommodate new findings. And, say Piaget's supporters, it underwent continual change throughout his long career (Lourenço & Machado, 1996).

What is really needed, says Robert Siegler, is a new metaphor for development (Siegler, 1994). Instead of the abrupt changes implied by stage theories, he proposes that we think of "waves." The wave metaphor, he says, better fits both the scientific data and our everyday experience, which shows the variability of children's behavior. For example, a child may, during a single day, use several different strategies to solve the same linguistic problem: "I ate," "I eated," and "I ated." This is not the pattern we would find if a child were making a sudden leap from one stage to another. Instead, says Siegler, this is a pattern of overlapping developmental waves, where each wave can be thought of as the ebb and flow in the strength of a cognitive strategy (Azar, 1995).

Social and Emotional Development

Our health, happiness, and even our survival depend on forming meaningful, effective relationships, in the family, with peers—and, later in life, on the job. This means that children need to begin the long process of learning the rules their society uses for governing its members' social and political interactions. They must also learn to monitor their own feelings and behavior and understand those of others.

As we have seen, Piaget taught that the preoperational child assumes other people share his or her view of the world. To grow beyond this egocentric perspective, the child must develop a **theory of mind.** This consists of an awareness that others may have beliefs, desires, and emotions different from one's own and that these mental states underlie their behavior (Frith & Frith, 1999). The theory of mind is also a set of expectations about how people will act in certain situations—such as when given a present or when spoken to angrily. This accomplishment is fundamental to successful social interaction, whether it be play, work, or establishing friendships and partnerships.

Smiling is one simple but important way people begin social and emotional interactions. So essential is a smile to human communication that a baby's first smile is probably generated automatically by genetically controlled processes. In fact, smiles occur in babies throughout the world (Gazzaniga, 1998a). The delight parents take in a baby's first smile represents the beginning of lifelong lessons in social behavior. People smile not only as a sign of positive feelings but also because their audience expects such a facial expression (Fridlund, 1990). However, social and emotional development involves much more than a winning smile. On the "nature" side, psychologists have found that an innate disposition or *temperament* influences our responsiveness to others. And, on the "nurture" side, psychologists have found many environmental factors that influence socialization. We will analyze these two important concepts more deeply.

Temperament Psychologists use the term **temperament** for an individual's inherited, "wired-in" pattern of personality and behavior. Harvard researcher Jerome Kagan, who has studied temperament in thousands of children, observed that about 10 to 15% of infants are "born shy" or "born bold" (Kagan, 1994a, b; Kagan et al., 1986; Kagan & Snidman, 1991). In response to physical and social stimulation, shy babies are more easily frightened and less socially responsive than bold babies. Because of a baby's temperament, people are less likely to interact and be playful with the shy baby, accentuating the child's initial disposition.

■ **Theory of mind** An awareness that other people's behavior may be influenced by beliefs, desires, and emotions that differ from one's own.

■ **Temperament** An individual's characteristic manner of behavior or reaction—assumed to have a strong genetic basis.

While basic temperaments can be recognized almost at birth, they are not written in stone (Kagan, 1996). (Remember: Nature always interacts with nurture.) Experience and parenting styles can modify the way temperament expresses itself. For example, a bold child reared by bold parents will certainly experience and respond to the world differently from a bold child reared by timid or fearful parents. Likewise, if a shy baby's parents recognize the child's withdrawal and gently play with her and encourage her to interact, the child may become more outgoing than her temperament would otherwise have predicted. Thus family members and friends can teach every individual a variety of responses to the world, all within his or her temperamental range. Nor is one temperament ideal for all situations. We should "remember that in a complex society like ours, each temperamental type can find its adaptive niche" (Kagan, quoted in Gallagher, 1994, p. 47).

Socialization   To help children find the most adaptive niches for their abilities and temperaments, parents socialize their offspring. *Socialization*, however, doesn't just happen it childhood. It is the lifelong process of shaping an individual's behavior patterns, values, standards, skills, attitudes, and motives to conform to those regarded as desirable in a particular society (Hetherington & Parke, 1975). We first learn about these things, of course, from our parents, so developmental psychologists have looked at the effects of various *parenting styles* on children's personalities and social behaviors. Aside from parents, many individuals and institutions exert pressure on the child to adopt socially approved values. Among these, the school and leisure-time influences, such as television and peers, have heavy influences. And, increasingly, many preschool children are shaped by their experiences in day care. Of these, let's first take a look at parenting styles.

Four Parenting Styles and Their Effects   Most approaches to child rearing fall into one of four distinct parenting styles that developmental psychologists have found in families all over the world (Baumrind, 1967, 1971; Darling & Steinberg, 1993; Russell et al., 2002). (As you read about these, you might try to imagine how you would have turned out differently if your parents had used one of the other approaches.) *Authoritarian parents* often live by the slogan, "Spare the rod and spoil the child." They demand conformity and obedience, and they tolerate little discussion of rules, which they enforce with punishment or threats of punishment. In an alternative approach, *authoritative parents* can be demanding, too. They have high expectations of their children, which they enforce with consequences. But unlike authoritarian parents, they combine high standards with warmth and respect for the child's views: They are quite willing to listen to a child's ideas and feelings and they often encourage a democratic family atmosphere. Authoritative parents usually place a heavy emphasis on reasoning and explaining in order to help their children learn to anticipate the consequences of their behavior. Taking a third approach, *permissive parents* set few rules and allow the children to make their own decisions. Like authoritative parents, they are caring and communicative, but permissive parents give most decision-making responsibility to their children. Permissive parents believe that children can learn better from the consequences of their own actions than they can from following rules set by their parents. *Uninvolved parents* tend to be either indifferent or rejecting, sometimes to the point of neglect or abuse (Maccoby & Martin, 1983). Typically parents in this group lead such stress-filled lives that they have little time or energy for their children. (See Table 4.1.)

You can probably guess the usual outcomes of these different parenting styles. Research shows that children with authoritative parents tend to be confident, self-reliant, and enthusiastic—overall, happier, less troublesome, and

TABLE 4.1	Features of the Four Parenting Styles		
Style	Emotional involvement	Authority	Autonomy
Authoritative	Parent is warm, attentive, and sensitive to child's needs and interests.	Parent makes reasonable demands for the child's maturity level; explains and enforces rules.	Parent permits child to make decisions in accord with developmental readiness; listens to child's viewpoint.
Authoritarian	Parent is cold and rejecting; frequently degrades the child.	Parent is highly demanding; may use coercion by yelling, commanding, criticizing, and reliance on punishment.	Parent makes most decisions for the child; rarely listens to child's viewpoint.
Permissive	Parent is warm, but may spoil the child.	Parent makes few or no demands—often out of misplaced concern for child's self-esteem.	Parent permits child to make decisions before the child is ready.
Uninvolved	Parent is emotionally detached, withdrawn, and inattentive.	Parent makes few or no demands—often lacking in interest or expectations for the child.	Parent is indifferent to child's decisions and point of view.

Source: From DEVELOPMENT THROUGH THE LIFESPAN 3rd ed. by L. E. Berk. Copyright © 2004 by Pearson Education. Published and reprinted by permission of Allyn & Bacon, Boston, MA.

more successful. Those with authoritarian parents tended to be anxious and insecure. Those with permissive or uninvolved parents are typically less mature, more impulsive, more dependent, and more demanding. Thinking back to our earlier discussion of attachment, these findings shouldn't be surprising. Generally speaking, authoritative parents take a more involved, interactive role in their children's lives—forming a stronger social-emotional attachment—than do the other three types of parents. This lays a strong foundation for prosocial behavior in the developing child.

Effects of Day Care As working parents make increasing use of day care for their children, we should ask the following question: How necessary is it to have a full-time caregiver? The question is an urgent one in the United States and Canada, where over half of all mothers with children under age 3 are employed, and more children are cared for by paid providers than by relatives (Scarr, 1997, 1998; Statistics Canada, 2002; U.S. Bureau of the Census, 2002).

The research on this issue sends mixed messages. First the good news: Most children thrive in day care. They do as well—sometimes better—both intellectually and socially as children raised at home by a full-time parent. Now the bad news: Some poor-quality day care experiences influence children to be aggressive, depressed, or otherwise maladjusted. Fortunately, the overwhelming majority of day care centers do a fine job (Bower, 1996; Clarke-Stewart, 1989; NICHD Early Child Care Research Network, 2003).

As important as day care is in our society, it is comforting to note that having alternative caregivers does not in itself cause psychological problems. Rather, difficulties appear most often in poorly staffed centers where large numbers of children get little attention from only a few adults (Howes et al., 1988; NICHD Early Child Care Research Network, 2000). Another source of difficulty results from the unfortunate fact that children who are placed in the poorest-quality day care programs are most often from the poorest, most disorganized, and most highly stressed families. Developmental psychologist Laura Berk (2004) concludes that this volatile combination of inadequate day care and family pressure places some children at high risk for emotional and behavioral problems. Yet, she says, using this evidence to curtail day care services would be mistaken, because forcing a parent on a marginal income to stay home may expose children to an even greater level of risk.

All this means that day care is, in itself, neither good nor bad. It is the quality of care, whether given by a parent or a paid provider, that makes all the difference. Development expert Sandra Scarr (1998) says:

> There is an extraordinary international consensus among child-care researchers and practitioners about what quality child care is: It is warm, supportive interactions with adults in a safe, healthy, and stimulating environment, where early education and trusting relationships combine to support individual children's physical, emotional, social, and intellectual development.... (p. 102)

School and Leisure Influences Children and adolescents in the United States and other industrialized countries have much more free time than do children elsewhere in the world. In nonindustrialized societies, children average some six hours a day working at some sort of chores or labor. By comparison, the typical American child spends less than one-half hour at such tasks. Moreover, the amount of free time available to U.S. children has increased dramatically over the last several generations (Larson, 2001). While long, hard work may teach discipline and responsibility, there is little evidence that it produces positive changes in cognitive development.

On the other hand, American children also spend more time (on the average) doing schoolwork than did children in years past—although not as much as their foreign counterparts in other industrialized countries. Still, there is time left over: How is it spent? Much is taken up watching television, talking on the telephone, or surfing the Internet (the consequences of which are largely unknown at present). The largest amount of discretionary time, however, is spent "hanging out" with friends. Surprisingly, however, many children spend the majority of their "free" time in structured activities, such as clubs and other organizations, art and music lessons, and sports—although this varies greatly from child to child (Larson, 2000).

Is the time of our nation's children well spent? Certainly some of it is unproductive or even counterproductive. For example, spending a great deal of time watching violent TV is predictive of aggressive behavior (Strasburger, 1995). Still, only the most unfeeling person would argue that all a child's time should be accounted for in developmentally productive activities. Clearly, the increase in leisure time, as well as increased access to information and the media, is a trend that is sweeping over industrialized nations. Where it may lead will be a subject for future research.

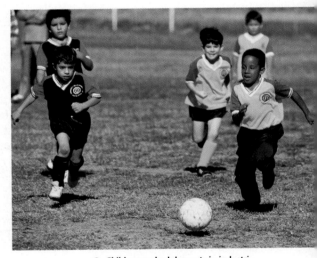

● Children and adolescents in industrialized societies average about six hours a day of discretionary time. Many choose to spend this time in organized activities, such as sports, although the most popular pursuit is "hanging out" with friends.

Gender Differences in Socialization Anyone who has watched young boys and girls playing has noticed gender differences in their social interaction. The sexes usually prefer to segregate themselves—a pattern that holds across cultures (Maccoby, 1998, 2000). In their play, boys are typically more aggressive than girls, although there are certainly exceptions. Girls tend to organize themselves into small, cooperative groups. By contrast, boys often form larger groups that have a hierarchical structure, or "pecking order." In these groups, individual boys continually compete for higher-ranking positions. They frequently resort to aggressive tactics, such as hitting, shoving, and verbal threats. Evolutionary psychologists believe that these gender differences have an innate basis (Buss, 1999), which may be related, in part, to gender differences in testosterone levels (Dabbs, 2000). This does not mean, of course, that environmental factors, such as parenting styles and peer influences, make no difference. Social-cognitive theorists like Kay Bussey and Albert Bandura (1999) attempt to counter this view by reminding us that children also *learn* gender roles and gender-related behaviors, such as aggressiveness, competitiveness, or cooperation.

 ## PSYCHOLOGY IN YOUR LIFE: CHILDHOOD INFLUENCES ON YOUR PERSONALITY

Your personality and your social relationships are a unique blend of your temperament, attachment style, and many other forces that have acted on you through life. But are there common problems that everyone faces at certain points in life—problems that generate predictable personality changes across the lifespan? A theory of personality proposed by psychoanalyst Erik Erikson says yes.

As a middle-aged immigrant to America, Erik Erikson (1963) became aware of conflicts and choices he faced because of his new status. This caused him to reflect on the many such conflicts every individual must face in the continuing process of development. Before reading further, please take a moment to do as Erikson did: Recall some of the conflicts or challenges you have experienced in childhood. These will give you a vantage point from which to understand Erikson's theory—and your own personality.

Erikson's Theory of Psychosocial Development Erikson saw human development as a sequence of **psychosocial stages,** defined by common problems that emerge throughout life, from infancy to old age. As the term implies, all involve our social relationships. When people face these challenges, he said, they make choices that influence the growth of their personalities. Good choices lay the foundation for healthy growth during later stages.

Erikson identified eight such stages. With each succeeding stage, a new challenge comes into focus, as shown in Table 4.2. The problem must be satisfactorily resolved at a given stage if an individual is to cope successfully with the new problems that present themselves in later stages. Here we will review the psychosocial stages of childhood; later in the chapter we will review the issues experienced in adolescence and adulthood.

Trust versus Mistrust In the first stage of psychosocial development, you needed to develop a basic sense of trust in your environment and in those who cared for you. This trust is a natural accompaniment to a strong attachment relationship with a caregiver who provides food, warmth, and the comfort of physical closeness. But if these basic needs were not met, Erikson suggested, you experienced a developmental crisis that he called *trust versus mistrust*. At this stage, inconsistent parenting, lack of physical closeness and warmth, or the frequent absence of a caring adult may produce a lasting sense of mistrust, insecurity, and anxiety. Children facing such conditions will not be prepared for the second stage in their psychological development. The healthy personality requires a foundation of trust from which the individual can become more adventurous.

Autonomy versus Self-Doubt In the second stage, as you acquired skills in walking and talking, you also expanded your ability to interact with objects and people. If you entered this stage with a sense of trust in others, these new abilities should have brought you a comfortable sense of autonomy (independence) and of being a capable and worthy person. Too much restriction or criticism at this stage may have led to self-doubts—hence, the term

■ **Psychosocial stages** In Erikson's theory, the developmental stages refer to eight major challenges that appear successively across the lifespan, which require an individual to rethink his or her goals, as well as relationships with others.

TABLE 4.2	Erikson's Psychosocial Stages		
Age/Period (approximate)	Principal Challenge	Adequate Resolution	Inadequate Resolution
0 to 1½ years	Trust vs. mistrust	Basic sense of safety, security; ability to rely on forces outside oneself	Insecurity, anxiety
1½ to 3 years	Autonomy vs. self-doubt	Perception of self as agent; capable of controlling one's own body and making things happen	Feelings of inadequacy about self-control, control of events
3 to 6 years	Initiative vs. guilt	Confidence in oneself as being able to initiate, create	Feeling of lack of self-worth
6 years to puberty	Competence vs. inferiority	Adequacy in basic social and intellectual skills; acceptance by peers	Lack of self-confidence; feelings of failure
Adolescence	Identity vs. role confusion	Comfortable sense of self as a person, both unique and socially accepted	Sense of self as fragmented, shifting, unclear sense of self
Early adulthood	Intimacy vs. isolation	Capacity for closeness and commitment to another	Feeling of aloneness, loneliness, separation; denial of intimacy needs
Middle adulthood	Generativity vs. stagnation	Focus of concern beyond oneself, to family, society, future generations	Self-indulgent concerns; lack of future orientation
Late adulthood	Ego-integrity vs. despair	Sense of wholeness; basic satisfaction with life	Feelings of futility, disappointment

for this stage: *autonomy versus self-doubt*. Harsh demands made on you beyond your ability—such as attempting toilet training too early—could have discouraged your efforts to persevere in mastering new tasks. Such demands also can lead to stormy scenes of confrontation, disrupting the supportive parent–child relationship. In contrast, the 2-year-old who insists on the right to do something without help, in response to appropriate demands, acts out of a need to affirm his or her autonomy and adequacy.

Initiative versus Guilt   If you developed a basic sense of trust and autonomy during your preschool days, you probably entered the grade school years as a child who could comfortably initiate intellectual and motor tasks. For example, children in this stage want to do things for themselves, such as choose what to wear or what to eat. The danger at this stage comes from overcontrolling adults, who demand an impossible degree of self-control ("Why can't you sit still?"), with the result that the child is overcome by feelings of inadequacy and guilt. The term for this stage reflects these two alternatives: *initiative versus guilt*. Caregivers' responses to self-initiated activities either encourage or discourage the freedom and self-confidence needed for the next stage.

Competence versus Inferiority   If you successfully resolved the crises of the three earlier stages, you were ready to develop your skills and competencies in a more systematic way. During the elementary school years, school activities and sports offer arenas for learning more complex intellectual and motor skills, while peer interaction offers the chance to develop social skills. Successful efforts in these pursuits lead to feelings of competence. Some youngsters, however, become discouraged spectators rather than performers, or they experience failure that leaves them with a sense of inferiority. The term for this stage, therefore, is *competence versus inferiority*.

A Critical Reflection on Erikson's Theory   How much confidence should we place in Erikson? Although widely respected, his developmental theory does have some shortcomings. Based mainly on clinical observation, it lacks a rigorous scientific basis. Moreover, as some critics point out, Erikson's list of developmental issues does not adequately capture the problems faced by girls and women. Nonetheless, your authors suggest that Erikson's work should be seen as a comprehensive pioneering effort that has encouraged us to look at the life cycle as a whole, putting into perspective both the unfolding changes and the continuity of life experience.

CONNECTION: CHAPTER 1

Clinical observation is a form of the *case study* method.

CHECK YOUR UNDERSTANDING

1. **RECALL:** Noam Chomsky has presented evidence supporting his theory that
   a. children learn language by imitating their parents.
   b. children are born with some rules of grammar programmed into their brains.
   c. vocabulary is innate, but grammar is learned.
   d. different languages may have entirely different rules of grammar.

2. **RECALL:** Match the ability/limitation with the Piagetian stage at which it becomes an important characteristic of thinking.
   a. centration
   b. abstract thought
   c. innate schemes
   d. conservation

   i. sensorimotor stage
   ii. preoperational stage
   iii. concrete operational stage
   iv. formal operational stage

3. **RECALL:** A child's acquisition of grammar first becomes apparent at
   a. the babbling stage.
   b. the one-word stage.
   c. the two-word stage.
   d. the concrete operational stage.

4. **APPLICATION:** Imagine that you are a family counselor. Which parenting style would you encourage parents to adopt in order to encourage their children to become confident and self-reliant?
   a. authoritative
   b. authoritarian
   c. permissive
   d. uninvolved

5. **UNDERSTANDING THE CORE CONCEPT:** There are many developmental task that children must face in the areas of language, thought, and social interaction. Can you name one in each of these areas?

ANSWERS: 1. b   2. a. ii, b. iv, c. i, d. iii   3. c   4. a   5. Language: both vocabulary and grammar. Thought processes: for example, young children are not capable of abstract reasoning. (Piaget's theory suggests other differences at each stage.) Social relationships: attachment, development of a theory of mind.

WHAT CHANGES MARK THE TRANSITION OF ADOLESCENCE?

Most early theorists assumed that the major work of development occurred before adolescence. After that, they assumed, the psyche was set for life and would undergo few important changes. Modern research disputes these older views. Modern psychologists agree that we have a remarkable capacity for developmental change throughout our lifespan (Kagan, 1996, 1998). Again in adolescence the big changes lie in three important areas—as our Core Concept says:

Adolescence offers new developmental challenges growing out of physical changes, cognitive changes, and socioemotional pressures.

So, when does *adolescence* begin? Or, to put the question more personally, what event first made you think of yourself as an adolescent? Chances are that it had something to do with your sexual maturation, such as a first menstrual period or a nocturnal ejaculation. Psychologists mark the beginning of **adolescence** as the onset of *puberty,* when sexual maturity, or the ability to reproduce, is attained. However, they cannot so precisely identify the point at which adolescence ends and adulthood begins.

Adolescence and Culture

Variations among cultures compound the difficulty of specifying the span of adolescence. Although the physical changes that take place at this stage are universal, the social and psychological dimensions of adolescence depend on the cultural context. For example, if you enter your teen years in a society that celebrates puberty as the entry to adulthood and rewards you with the power to make responsible choices, you will have a very different experience from someone whose culture condemns teenagers as confused and potentially dangerous troublemakers.

In fact, most nonindustrial societies do not identify an adolescent stage as we know it. Instead, children in these societies move directly into adulthood with **rites of passage.** These rituals usually take place at about the time of puberty and serve as a public acknowledgment of the transition from childhood to adulthood. Rites of passage vary widely among cultures, from extremely painful rituals to periods of instruction in sexual and cultural practices or periods of seclusion involving survival ordeals. For example, in some tribal groups, the young person may be asked to take a meditative journey alone or to submit to symbolic scarring or circumcision surrounded by friends and family. Once individuals have completed the passage, there is no ambiguity about their status: They are adults, and the ties to their childhood have been severed.

Our own society has few transition rituals to help children clearly mark their new adolescent status or for adolescents to know when they have become young adults. One such rite of passage for many middle-class teenagers in America is qualifying for a driver's license. Another is high school graduation. Both provide a young person with an added measure of freedom and independence that is not available to children.

Although many issues are important in adolescence, we will focus on a few of the most important developmental tasks that confront adolescents in the United States and the industrialized Western world: coming to terms with physical maturity, a new level of cognitive development, redefining social roles and emotional issues, dealing with sexual opportunities and pressures, and the development of moral standards. Each of these issues is just one component of the central task of establishing one's identity. We begin with the physical changes that mark the end of childhood and the onset of adolescence.

Physical Maturation in Adolescence

One of the first signs of approaching adolescence is the *pubescent growth spurt.* Two to three years after the onset of the growth spurt, **puberty,** or sexual maturity, is reached. Puberty for males begins with the production of live sperm (usually at about age 14 in the United States), while for girls it begins at *menarche,* the onset of menstruation (usually between ages 11 and 15). These serve as indicators that the **primary sex characteristics**—the sex organs and genitals—are undergoing dramatic change, accompanied by equally dramatic changes in the **secondary sex characteristics,** the enlargement of breasts and

● Body image becomes especially important in the teenage years.

■ **Adolescence** In industrial societies, a developmental period beginning at puberty and ending (less clearly) at adulthood.
■ **Rites of passage** Social rituals that mark the transition between developmental stages, especially between childhood and adulthood.
■ **Puberty** The onset of sexual maturity.
■ **Primary sex characteristics** The sex organs and genitals.
■ **Secondary sex characteristics** Gender-related physical features that develop during puberty, including facial hair and deepening voice in males, widened hips and enlarged breasts in females, and the development of pubic hair in both sexes.

the widening of hips in girls, the deepening of the voice and appearance of facial hair in boys, and the sprouting of pubic hair in both sexes.

Simultaneously, boys and girl generally become more aware of their own appearance, often judging themselves harshly by the standards they think other people may be applying to them. And, unfair as it may be, physical attractiveness does influence the way people think about each other (Hatfield & Rapson, 1993). Thus, one of the most formidable tasks of adolescence involves coming to terms with one's physical self by developing a realistic yet accepting *body image* (one's personal and subjective view of one's own appearance). This image is dependent not only on measurable features, such as height and weight, but also on perceptions of other people's assessments and on cultural standards of physical beauty. During adolescence, dramatic physical changes and heightened emphasis on peer acceptance (especially acceptance by sexually attractive peers) intensifies concern with one's body image.

Approximately 44% of American adolescent girls and 23% of boys claimed that they have "frequently felt ugly and unattractive"; similar data have been found across many cultures (Offer et al., 1981, 1988). Physical appearance is clearly one of the biggest concerns among adolescents (Perkins & Lerner, 1995). Girls' self-concepts are particularly tied to perceptions of their physical attractiveness, while boys seem more concerned with their physical prowess, athletic ability, and effectiveness in achieving goals (Lerner et al., 1976; Wade, 1991). In general, girls and women are more dissatisfied with their weight and shape than are males, and they experience more conflict about food and eating (Rolls et al., 1991). These differences probably mirror a cultural preoccupation with female beauty and male strength—an inevitable source of concern because not all adolescents can embody the cultural ideals of attractiveness. There are also cultural influences on self-concept; some research indicates that the self-esteem of white adolescents of both sexes is more tied to physical attractiveness than is that of black adolescents (Wade, 1991). Over time, adolescents seem to become more accepting of their appearances. Nonetheless, the attainment of acceptable body images can be a difficult task.

Cognitive Development in Adolescence

Adolescence brings with it Piaget's final stage of cognitive growth, involving the ability for abstract and complex thought. In this **formal operational stage,** the individual begins to ponder introspective problems involving ways of becoming better accepted by peers, along with abstract and intangible issues, such as fairness, love, and reasons for existence. With these formal operational reasoning powers, adolescents and adults now approach life's problems in a way that demonstrates their ability to use abstractions and to adopt thinking strategies that are not merely random guesswork. In the "20 questions" game we mentioned earlier, they impose their own structures on the task, starting with broad categories and then formulating and testing hypotheses in light of their knowledge of categories and relationships. Their questioning moves from general categories ("Is it an animal?") to subcategories ("Does it fly?") and then to specific guesses ("Is it a bird?") (Bruner et al., 1966).

Behind these changes in thinking are some profound changes occurring inside the body. Concentrations of the hormones estrogen and testosterone rise to high levels. At the same time, the frontal lobes of the brain, a region involved in social and emotional behaviors, is undergoing a "remodel," involving growth of new circuits, loss of some old ones, and changes in the balance of neurotransmitters (Spear, 2000). All of this probably contributes to increases among adolescents in sensation-seeking and risk-taking behaviors, as well as to increasing preoccupation with body image, sex, and social-emotional issues.

■ **Formal operational stage** The last of Piaget's stages, during which abstract thought appears.

involves the increasing fluidity among roles as worker and family member: Men no longer (at least, not as often) define themselves only as workers and family providers, and women are less likely to define themselves solely as wives and mothers. For most people this provides an expanded source of social support and an increased sense of well-being.

At this writing, same-gender couples are visibly forming family units, getting married, and raising children. And, as every reader of this book will be aware, this has become highly politicized. You can be sure that research on gay and lesbian families is forthcoming from psychologists, but at present we have only a few dozen studies. Remarkably, they almost uniformly suggest that same-sex couples can have healthy, nurturing relationships, and that their children are as well-adjusted as are children from heterosexual couples (APA Online, 2004; see also Redding, 2001, 2002; Rooney, 2002).

Finally, we should note that the population is becoming older, as increasing numbers of people live long enough to become elderly. Moreover, *baby boomers* (those born in the "baby boom" right after World War II) are retiring, and retirement is becoming both an issue and an opportunity for more people. The research says that women (as a group) are less prepared for retirement than are men, although among retirees the majority report being happier than they were during their working years (Kim & Moen, 2001). If our society is to face the problems of an older population, with even more time on their hands than teenagers have, we will need a far more extensive research base dealing with this group.

 ## PSYCHOLOGY IN YOUR LIFE: THE LAST DEVELOPMENTAL CHALLENGES YOU WILL FACE

At the beginning of the 20th century, only 3% of the U.S. population was over 65. One hundred years later that figure is about 13%. When the baby boom generation reaches this age over the next few years, nearly one-fourth of our population will be in this oldest group.

If you are now a 20-year-old college student, you will be in your mid-40s by the year 2030, and you will have witnessed a profound demographic shift (change in population characteristics). By that time, more than 80 million Americans will be over 60 years of age. For the first time in history, the number of people in the 60-plus age group will outnumber those under 20 years of age. This will represent a dramatic reversal of all previous demographics and a potentially significant shift away from today's youth-oriented culture (Pifer & Bronte, 1986). Among the effects: Tattoos and body piercings will become common in nursing homes, and there will also be far fewer people to pay the Social Security and Medicare bills.

With drastic changes in our society's age distribution looming, it is more crucial than ever to understand the nature of aging as well as the abilities and needs of the elderly (Roush, 1996). The problem of dealing with an aging population is even more pressing in Third World countries, where incomes and standards of living are low and where health care resources are minimal (Holden, 1996a). And, on a personal level, it may be helpful to anticipate some of the developmental challenges you will face in the last phase of your life.

Ego-Integrity versus Despair   According to Erikson, an increasing awareness of your own mortality and of the changes in your body, behavior, and social roles will set the stage for late adulthood. Erikson called the crisis he identified at this stage *ego-integrity versus despair*. Ego-integrity, the healthy end of

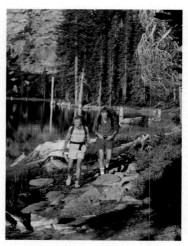

● Older people who pursue high levels of environmental stimulation tend to maintain higher levels of cognitive abilities.

this dimension, involves the ability to look back on life without regrets and to enjoy a sense of wholeness. For those whose previous crises had unhealthy solutions, however, aspirations may remain unfulfilled, and these individuals may experience futility, despair, and self-deprecation. Sadly, they often then fail to resolve the crisis successfully at this final developmental stage.

In general, Erikson characterizes old age as a time of new challenges. What are the tasks of old age, and what resources and limitations must we confront as we look ahead to the autumn of our lives? In a series of interviews with middle-aged and older men and women, Ryff (1989) found that nearly everyone of both sexes defined "well-being" in terms of relationships with others: being a caring, compassionate person and having a good social support network. Respondents also emphasized the value of accepting change, enjoying life, and cultivating a sense of humor.

New Perspectives on Aging   From a biological perspective, aging typically means decline: Energy reserves are reduced, cell machinery functions less efficiently, and muscle tone diminishes. From a cognitive perspective, however, we will see that aging is no longer synonymous with decline (Qualls & Abeles, 2000). In fact, many abilities, including expert skills and some aspects of memory, may improve with age (Azar, 1996; Krampe & Ericsson, 1996). A lifetime's accumulation of experience may finally culminate in wisdom—if the mind remains open and active. Thus, we see that theories of aging are models of balance or trade-offs: In old age, a person may lose energy reserves but gain an ability to control emotional experiences and thereby conserve energy. Thus, we can expect two kinds of changes—gains and losses—as we grow older (Baltes, 1987).

Some of the most obvious changes that occur with age affect people's physical appearances and abilities. As we age, we can expect our skin to wrinkle, our hair to thin and gray, and our height to decrease an inch or two. Our hearts and lungs operate less efficiently, so we can expect decreased physical stamina. We can also expect some of our senses to dull. These changes occur and develop gradually, so we have ample opportunity to gauge them and try to adjust. Successful aging takes into consideration both individual potential and realistic limits (Baltes, 1993). Consider how an individual might make the most of the following resources he or she has, given each of the changes accompanying aging:

▍ *Vision:* As we age, the lenses in our eyes become discolored and less flexible, affecting both color vision and distance vision. Most people over 65 experience some loss of visual acuity, and without corrective lenses half of the elderly would be considered legally blind. Glasses do aid in adjusting to these changes in vision, however, especially for night driving or close work such as reading.

▍ *Hearing:* Diminished hearing is common among those 60 and older, especially the ability to hear high-frequency sounds. Problems can ensue if the loss is undetected or denied (Maher & Ross, 1984; Manschreck, 1989). A person may come to believe that others are deliberately whispering to avoid being heard, leading to a mild form of paranoia (belief that one is being victimized). Those with a hearing loss might explain others' actions inaccurately because they lack information and blame their misinterpretations on evil intentions instead of simple bad hearing (Zimbardo et al., 1981). Fortunately, early hearing-aid therapy can be more effective than later psychotherapy. Hearing aids can compensate for much of one's hearing loss. In addition, those close to someone with a probable hearing loss can help them by speaking in lower-pitched tones, enunciating clearly, and reducing background noise.

- *Thinking, learning, and problem-solving:* A great fear about aging is that it is accompanied by the loss of mental abilities. But is this fear justified? Certain parts of the brain, particularly the frontal lobes, do lose mass as we age, but there is little evidence that this causes a general mental decline in healthy adults. Performance on tasks requiring imagination, such as vivid imagery strategies for memorizing, does seem to decline with age (Baltes & Kliegl, 1992). And, people do acquire information more slowly by the time they are in their 70s and 80s. By that age, many older people—but not all—begin to show some decline in cognitive abilities. The older the group, the more variation we find (Kramer & Willis, 2002). On the other hand, the decline for the average person may not be as severe as folk wisdom had assumed (Helmuth, 2003c). Brain imaging studies suggest that older people's brains compensate by processing information differently, bringing more regions into play (Cabeza, 2002; Helmuth, 2002). In fact, there is new research showing that moderate physical fitness training improves cognitive abilities in older adults and may forestall or even prevent age-related mental decline (Colcombe et al., 2004). Moreover, the evidence suggests that some abilities actually improve with age. Vocabulary, for example, is consistently better in older adults, as are social skills. And, accomplished with regard to skilled performance, musicians have been shown to improve well into their 90s (Krampe & Ericsson, 1996). Psychologists are now exploring age-related gains in wisdom, such as expertise in practical knowledge and life experience (Baltes, 1990).

- *Memory:* A common complaint among older adults is that their ability to remember things is not as good as it used to be. Most of these age-related memory difficulties appear in a part of the memory system that processes and stores new information (Poon, 1985). Aging does *not* seem to diminish access to knowledge or events that occurred long ago. So, an elderly person may have to ask the name of a new acquaintance once or twice before finally remembering it but may have no trouble recalling the names of old friends or celebrities. A more important concern might be that people explain memory loss differently depending on the age of the forgetful person. Using a double standard, younger adults attribute other young adults' memory failures to lack of effort but those of older adults to loss of ability (Parr & Siegert, 1993).

  Particularly worrisome to older people is **Alzheimer's disease,** a degenerative disorder of the brain that produces both diminished thinking abilities and memory problems. Ultimately, it can cause death. Alzheimer's disease is estimated to occur in about 4% of the population over the age of 65, with the incidence increasing with age, to over 50% in people beyond age 85 (National Institute on Aging, 2004). One of the early signs involves memory problems, causing many older persons to become anxious when they are unable to remember a name or an event—a difficulty to which they would have given little thought when younger. It is an especially frightening disorder because it can render people helpless, rob them of their ability to make new memories, and make them forget loved ones.

- *Sexual functioning:* One myth about aging is that elderly people cannot or should not be sexually active. Belief in such a myth can be a greater obstacle than any physical limitations to experiencing satisfying sex in late adulthood. There is no age, for either men or women, at which the capability for arousal or orgasm ceases. (This is particularly true now that drugs, such as the well-advertised Viagra, have enhanced erectile ability for millions of older men.) And while sex loses its reproductive functions in late adulthood, it doesn't lose its capacity for providing pleasure. Regular sexual

■ **Alzheimer's disease**
A degenerative brain disease usually noticed first by its debilitating effects on memory.

practice also enhances healthy aging because it provides arousal, aerobic exercise, fantasy, and social interaction (Ornstein & Sobel, 1989). Experience and creativity clearly compensate for minor physical changes or losses of physical stamina.

▌ *Social interaction:* An unfortunate consequence of living a long life is outliving some friends and family members. In addition, the reduced mobility associated with aging can make people become somewhat less active socially in later adulthood. While older adults reduce the extent of their social contacts, they remain more invested in those ties they choose to keep. Maintaining even a single intimate relationship can markedly improve personal health, as can living with a beloved pet (Siegel, 1990). Research shows that as people age, they tend to engage in **selective social interaction,** maintaining only the most rewarding contacts for the investment of precious physical and emotional energy (Carstensen, 1987, 1991; Lang & Carstensen, 1994).

▌ *Emotions:* While old age is often seen as a time of depression and restriction of emotions, the evidence doesn't support this view in healthy older adults, although age often improves people's ability to *control* their emotions—when they want to (Lawton, 2001). Moreover, older individuals report experiencing more positive emotions and fewer negative emotions than do younger adults (Mroczek, 2001).

What can be done for those who experience trouble or personal difficulty in aging? Many elderly people have discovered particular strategies that help them age successfully. For example, older adults can remain both active and close to people by doing volunteer work in the community, joining clubs and classes, or spending time with grandchildren. In addition, we might learn lessons from other cultures where older citizens are respected and venerated for their wisdom. Before this happens, however, people must overcome stultifying stereotypes of the elderly as incapable and incompetent (Brewer et al., 1981).

What, then, would be a good strategy for dealing with the challenges of aging? Perhaps successful aging consists of making the most of gains while minimizing the impact of losses (Schulz & Heckhausen, 1996). Additionally, it is helpful to realize that losses of specific abilities need not represent threats to one's sense of self. As one's physical and psychological resources change, so do one's goals (Carstensen & Freund, 1994). In this fashion, late adulthood may be a time not of increasing frustration, but of increasing fulfillment.

DEVELOPMENTAL PSYCHOLOGY: THE STATE OF THE ART

Developmental psychology has shown beyond doubt that development—physical, cognitive, social, and emotional—continues throughout the lifespan. And, the older we get, the more diversity we find among our age mates, even though we are facing many of the same issues or "life crises."

The most recent research has shown us that people at all ages have more abilities than had been believed by previous generations of developmental psychologists. We now know, for example, that newborns can imitate facial expressions, that infants can count, and that thinking can be sharp in the elderly.

Much remains to be discovered, however. Highly effective treatments for many disorders connected to development, such as autism and Alzheimer's

■ **Selective social interaction**
Choosing to restrict the number of one's social contacts to those who are the most gratifying.

disease, remain just out of reach. The decoding of the human genome also promises insights into developmental problems—but those problems, too, remain unsolved. And finally (although this developmental "to-do" list is incomplete), the major social changes occurring in our society—including the redefinition of work and family, retirement, increased leisure time, instant access to information, and gender equality—all are having their effects on development in ways that we don't yet fully understand.

CHECK YOUR UNDERSTANDING

1. **RECALL:** According to Erikson, a person who successfully faces the issue of intimacy versus isolation will have
    a. a meaningful career.
    b. children.
    c. a thirst for knowledge.
    d. social support.

2. **RECALL:** According to Erikson, people at midlife most want to
    a. have the freedom and independence to pursue their leisure interests.
    b. hang out with their friends.
    c. make a contribution to their career, society, or future generations.
    d. maintain or improve their physical appearance.

3. **APPLICATION:** A major demographic shift is now in progress. This change involves
    a. a culture that is increasingly focusing on youth.
    b. an increase in the average age of the population.
    c. the roles of worker and parent becoming more rigidly defined.
    d. fewer women assuming professional roles.

4. **UNDERSTANDING THE CORE CONCEPT:** Old age eventually means that the person will experience decline in which of the following?
    a. thinking and problem-solving abilities
    b. social support from family
    c. vision and hearing
    d. emotional well-being

ANSWERS: 1. d   2. c   3. b   4. c

USING PSYCHOLOGY TO LEARN PSYCHOLOGY

Cognitive Development in College Students

Does your arrival at the formal operational stage, in the middle or high school years, signal the end of the cognitive line? Or, will your thinking abilities continue to develop as you go on through college? Or, if you are a "nontraditional" student, will your cognitive development continue apace with your younger counterparts? A study by developmental psychologist William Perry suggests that your perspective on learning will change and mature as your college experience unfolds. This prediction is based on a sample of students that Perry followed through their undergraduate years at Harvard and Radcliffe. Specifically, he found that students' views of psychology and their other social science courses changed radically, as did their view of what they were there to learn (Perry, 1970, 1994).

At first, students in Perry's study had the most difficulty coming to grips with the diverse and conflicting viewpoints they encountered in their courses. For example, many confronted, for the first time, the idea that reasonable people can disagree—even about their most cherished "truths" concerning good and evil, God, nature, and human nature:

> A few seemed to find the notion of multiple frames of reference wholly unintelligible. Others responded with violent shock to their confrontation in dormitory bull sessions, or in their academic work, or both. Others experienced a joyful sense of liberation. (Perry, 1970, p. 4)

In dealing with this academic culture shock, Perry's students passed through a series of distinct intellectual stages that were reminiscent of Piaget's stages. And, although they arrived at college at different levels of cognitive maturity and continued to develop at different rates, all progressed through the same intellectual stages in the same sequence. Here are some of the highlights of this intellectual journey:

▪ Students at first typically see a college or university as a storehouse of information—a place to learn the

Right Answers. Thus, they believe it is the professor's job to help students find these answers.

■ Sooner or later, students discover an unexpected—perhaps shocking—diversity of opinion, even among the experts. At this stage, college students are likely to attribute conflicting opinions to confusion among poorly qualified experts.

■ Eventually, students begin to accept diverse views as legitimate—but only in the fuzzy areas (such as psychology, other social sciences, and humanities) where experts haven't yet found the Right Answers. They decide that, in subjects where the Right Answers haven't been nailed down, professors grade them on "good expression" of their ideas.

■ Next, some students (not all) discover that uncertainty and diversity of opinion are everywhere—not just in the social sciences and humanities. They typically solve this problem in their minds by dividing the academic world into two realms: (a) one in which Right Answers exist (even though they haven't all been discovered) and (b) another in which anyone's opinion is as good as anyone else's. Often, at this stage, they perceive math and the "hard" sciences as the realm of Right Answers, leaving the social sciences and humanities in the realm of opinion.

■ Finally, the most mature students come to see that multiple perspectives exist in all fields of study.

The students who achieve the final stage begin to see "truth" as tentative. They now realize that knowledge is always building and changing—even in the "hard" sciences. And they realize that a college education is not just learning an endless series of facts. Rather, it is learning about the important *questions* and major *concepts* of a field. In this book we have called them "Key Questions" and "Core Concepts."

At what stage do you find yourself?

CHAPTER SUMMARY

● HOW DO PSYCHOLOGISTS EXPLAIN DEVELOPMENT?

Developmental psychologists study change and growth in physical and mental functioning throughout the life span. They have resolved the old nature–nurture issue by pointing out that nature and nurture always interact. Nevertheless, the issue continues to be debated. To weigh the relative contributions of heredity and environment, psychologists employ a variety of methods, including observations of identical twins, fraternal twins, and adopted children. The resulting studies show that many complex behaviors have a genetic component. Another controversy in developmental psychology involves continuity versus discontinuity. Psychologists who speak of developmental stages are taking the discontinuity view.

● Development is a process of growth, change, and consistency brought about by an interaction of heredity and environment.

● WHAT CAPABILITIES DOES THE CHILD POSSESS?

While the newborn mind was once considered a "blank slate," we now know that newborns possess certain innate abilities that help them survive. During the prenatal period, the organism progressively becomes a zygote, an embryo, and a fetus. Teratogens can damage the organism at any of these stages. Development of the brain proceeds at a rapid pace during the prenatal period, laying the foundation for the neonate's abilities to find food, interact with others, and avoid harm. Developmental research shows that infants are born with many sensory capabilities, preferences, and motor reflexes, plus the abilities to learn new responses that develop throughout childhood.

Developmental psychologists have been especially interested in the relationship between child and mother (or other caregiver). Ainsworth found that children may become either securely or insecurely attached. Attachment patterns established in infancy often persist into adulthood. Harlow's research suggests that infants seek contact comfort in the relationship with the mother.

Developmental psychologists have also looked carefully at the sequence of physical maturation and the influence of experience—particularly social interaction and physical contact—on the times at which various physical abilities, such as sitting and walking, develop.

● Newborns have innate abilities for finding nourishment, interacting with others, and avoiding harmful situations, while the developing abilities of infants and children rely more on learning.

● WHAT ARE THE DEVELOPMENTAL TASKS OF INFANCY AND CHILDHOOD?

Young children are biologically equipped to learn language and motivated to communicate. Many experts believe that children have "language acquisition devices" built into their brains. Psychologists find that language development proceeds in a predictable sequence, involving the babbling stage, the one- and two-word stages, and telegraphic speech, as children acquire vocabulary at an almost unbelievable rate. Grammar appears when the child begins to put words together.

Piaget's theory says that assimilation and accommodation are the two basic processes affecting our mental schemes and so underlie cognitive development. Piaget also proposed that children's cognitive development goes through four stages: the sensorimotor, the preoperational, the concrete operational, and the formal operational stages. New abilities, such as mental representation, object permanence, conservation, and mental operations, mark the emergence of successive stages. Newer theory and research have, however, modified many of Piaget's ideas.

Social and emotional development require that the child learn the rules of society and also develop a theory of mind. The basis for socialization is an innate temperament, which can be modified by experience, particularly by the four parenting styles: authoritative, authoritarian, permissive, and uninvolved. Day care is every more frequently used in the United States, and the research shows it can have positive effects on children. Children are also influenced by peers, school, and the media. Gender differences in socialization appear in the types of friendships formed by boys and girls.

Certain developmental disorders are most frequently seen in childhood, including mental retardation, autism, dyslexia, and ADHD. In most cases, existing treatments can help, but they are far from cures for these disorders.

Erikson's theory proposes that personality develops through a series of crises, each focused on resolving an issue about oneself and others. These issues define four stages of psychosocial development in childhood, characterized by these issues: trust versus mistrust, autonomy versus self-doubt, initiative versus guilt, and competence versus inferiority.

● Infants and children face especially important developmental tasks in the areas of language acquisition, cognition, and social relationships—tasks that lay a foundation for further growth in adolescence and adulthood.

● WHAT CHANGES MARK THE TRANSITION OF ADOLESCENCE?

The meaning of adolescence varies from culture to culture, although developmental psychologists define adolescence as a stage that starts at puberty. For Americans, the transitions of adolescence typically focus on rapid physical maturation and the development of a sexual, social, and gender identity, although there are few distinct rites of passage. Cognitive development in adolescence involves emerging abstract thought, which accompanies the formal operational stage. Peers become increasingly influential, and, for most, the family diminishes in influence. Some become delinquent. For the majority, the journey through adolescence is not unduly traumatic, but for some it is marked by loneliness or even suicide.

Sexual issues are especially important in adolescence, whether they be homosexual or heterosexual. For the latter group, the past decade has witnessed a decline in sexual intercourse among adolescents.

Kohlberg's theory of moral reasoning, built on Piaget's foundation, is also a stage theory. In Kohlberg's view, lower stages involve concerns with personal consequences, and higher stages have a broader focus on principles of ethical living. It seems to be applicable across a variety of cultures, although some critics have raised issues of gender bias in the theory.

● Adolescence offers new developmental challenges growing out of physical changes, cognitive changes, and socioemotional pressures.

● WHAT DEVELOPMENTAL CHALLENGES DO ADULTS FACE?

The challenges of adulthood focus on social needs, particularly achieving intimacy and a sense of generativity. In recent years, major social changes in sex roles and the configuration of the family, career paths, and retirement have occurred, all of which affect the course of psychological development. In later adulthood, individuals must maintain a sense of integrity despite some physical changes and losses.

Erikson believed that successful resolution of earlier life crises can enable one to face the end of life with acceptance and even a sense of satisfaction. New perspectives on aging, however, show that this period of life is marked by both gains and losses, notably in vision, hearing, intelligence, memory, sexual functioning, and social interaction. For some aging is very difficult, but for others it is a time of increasing fulfillment.

● Nature and nurture continue to produce changes throughout life, but in adulthood these changes include both growth and decline.

REVIEW TEST

For each of the following items, choose the single correct or best answer. The correct answers appear at the end.

1. "Nature" refers to the effects of _____ and "nurture" refers to the effects of _____.
   a. continuity; discontinuity
   b. parents; peers
   c. assimilation; accommodation
   d. heredity; environment

2. A psychologist taking the discontinuity view might see development as

   a. a gradual process.
   b. a matter of learning.
   c. entirely genetic.
   d. a series of stages.

3. About eight weeks after conception, the developing human organism is known as
   a. a zygote.
   b. an embryo.
   c. a fetus.
   d. a neonate.

4. Which of the following is true of the physical abilities of the newborn infant?
   a. At birth, babies already have preferences for particular tastes and smells and dislikes for others.
   b. Just moments after birth, a neonate may turn in the direction of a voice or reach out an exploring hand.
   c. While babies are born with poor eyesight, they soon learn to detect large objects and high-contrast patterns.
   d. all of the above

5. Which of the following utterances illustrates overregularization in language development?
   a. "Babababa."
   b. "Me gots two foots and two handses."
   c. "Drink milk, all gone."
   d. "Want cookie."

6. "Hey! That's not fair," complains Judi. "Tonio has more ice cream than me." Actually, both Judi and Tonio received a single scoop, but Tonio has stirred his around so it seems to fill the dish, while Judi's scoop is more compact. Judi's complaint indicates that she has not yet acquired the concept of _____ that affects how children think about the physical properties of things.
   a. centration
   b. egocentrism
   c. conservation
   d. object permanence

7. Harry and Margaret Harlow conducted landmark studies of the behaviors of baby monkeys who were separated from their mothers and had access only to mother "dummies" in their cages. This work confirmed that

a. genuine attachment is possible only with the infant's biological mother.
b. contact comfort and physical touch are important for healthy early development.
c. the "cupboard theory of attachment" is true for both humans and nonhumans.
d. nonhuman infants will imprint on and restrict social behavior to the first visually prominent thing they see after birth.

8. For Erikson, the psychosocial crisis of _____ is addressed by skill development and social interaction during the elementary school years, when children must explore their abilities, talents, and peer relationships.
   a. trust versus mistrust
   b. autonomy versus doubt
   c. competence versus inferiority
   d. identity versus role confusion

9. The briefest summary of the concerns and issues of adult development might simply be
   a. success and security.
   b. power and conquest.
   c. youth and beauty.
   d. love and work.

10. In late adulthood, loss of _____ has often been associated with feelings of paranoia and social isolation.
   a. intellectual abilities
   b. sexual functioning
   c. one's spouse
   d. hearing

ANSWERS: 1. d 2. d 3. c 4. d 5. b 6. c 7. b 8. c 9. d 10. d

KEY TERMS

Developmental psychology (p. 130)
Nature–nurture issue (p. 130)
Interaction (p. 130)
Identical twins (p. 131)
Fraternal twins (p. 131)
Continuity view (p. 132)
Discontinuity view (p. 132)
Developmental stages (p. 133)
Prenatal period (p. 135)
Zygote (p. 135)
Embryo (p. 135)
Fetus (p. 135)
Placenta (p. 135)

Teratogens (p. 135)
Neonatal period (p. 136)
Infancy (p. 137)
Attachment (p. 138)
Imprinting (p. 138)
Contact comfort (p. 141)
Maturation (p. 141)
Language acquisition device or LAD (p. 145)
Grammar (p. 146)
Morphemes (p. 146)
Overregularization (p. 147)
Schemas (p. 148)
Assimilation (p. 148)

Accommodation (p. 148)
Sensorimotor stage (p. 149)
Mental representation (p. 149)
Object permanence (p. 149)
Preoperational stage (p. 149)
Egocentrism (p. 149)
Animistic thinking (p. 150)
Centration (p. 150)
Irreversibility (p. 150)
Concrete operational stage (p. 150)
Conservation (p. 151)
Mental operations (p. 151)
Theory of mind (p. 152)

Temperament (p. 152)
Psychosocial stages (p. 156)
Adolescence (p. 159)
Rites of passage (p. 159)
Puberty (p. 159)
Primary sex characteristics (p. 159)
Secondary sex characteristics (p. 159)
Formal operational stage (p. 160)
Generativity (p. 168)
Alzheimer's disease (p. 171)
Selective social interaction (p. 172)

OUR RECOMMENDED BOOKS AND VIDEOS

ARTICLE

Sapolsky, R. (2001, November). The loveless man . . . who invented the science of love. *Scientific American,* 95–96. This is a review of Blum's *Love at Goon Park,* a study of attachment theorist Harry Harlow, the depressed yet disciplined scientist who isolated and studied miserable, lonely monkeys and discovered the importance to them (and to us) of touch, connection, and mother love.

BOOKS

Blum, D. (2002). *Love at Goon Park: Harry Harlow and the science of affection.* Boulder, CO: Perseus Books. Today we take for granted the importance of touch in expressing consolation, closeness, and sexual attraction, but the concept only became commonplace in the 1950s, with psychologist Harry Harlow's work on "contact comfort" among infant monkeys. From Harlow's controversial research and poignant photographs of frightened baby monkeys came research on human attachment as well as applications to romantic love. ("Goon Park" was the nickname for the often mis-read address of Harlow's University of Wisconsin laboratory at "600 N. Park").

Colapinto, J. (2001). *As nature made him: The boy who was raised as a girl.* New York: HarperPerennial. When a newborn boy lost his penis in a botched circumcision, his parents were advised by an "expert" to raise him as a girl, with a girl's name, clothing, and new gender instruction. Originally presented as a successful effort in identity shaping, the treatment became a developmental nightmare for the growing child, who at 14 decided to live life as a male instead. Presenting family with sympathy and doctors with disdain, the narrative becomes a gripping story of an individual in the cross-fire of nature and nurture.

Haddon, M. (2004). *The curious incident of the dog in the night-time.* New York: Vintage. This acclaimed first novel presents the journal of an autistic teenage boy who undertakes the search for the killer of his neighbor's dog. The light mystery is secondary to the intriguing perspective of this unemotional boy, a mathematical genius who remains baffled by others' motives and emotions.

Kagan, J., Snidman, N., Arcus, D., & Reznick, J. S. (1994). *Galen's prophecy.* New York: HarperCollins. This interesting, engaging exploration of temperament, its origins, varieties, and lifelong influence on behavior and personality, is told with examples and case studies.

Kindlon, D. J., & Thompson, M. (1999). *Raising Cain: Protecting the emotional life of boys.* New York: Ballantine Books. Of about 16,000 murders every year in the United States, 95% are com-mitted by young *men.* The authors argue that masculinity is so narrowly defined that boys grow up in a culture of cruelty, tough-ness, and suppressed emotion—all to prove they are becoming men. Here they blend personal stories with theory to explore alternatives that allow boys the emotions essential to healthy life.

Kilbourne, J. (2000). *Can't buy my love: How advertising changes the way we think and feel.* New York: Free Press. The average Ameri-can is exposed to over 3000 advertisements a day, all promising that love, sex, power, or self-esteem can be acquired simply by purchasing clothing, cosmetics, shoes, or cars. Educational psychol-ogist and media expert Jean Kilbourne explores these manipulative messages and the damage they do—especially to young women and girls.

Snowdon, D. (2001). *Aging with grace: What the nun study teaches us about leading longer, healthier, and more meaningful lives.* New York: Bantam Doubleday Dell. In the late 1980s, the author undertook a study of aging and disability in a community of elderly Catholic nuns; but he eventually found he could not maintain a scholarly distance from them and began to care and learn about them individually. Here he presents the lessons he learned from them about the blend of community, commitment, activity, and health.

VIDEOS

Boys Don't Cry. (1999, color, 119 min.). Directed by Kimberly Peirce; starring Hilary Swank, Chloë Sevigny, Peter Sarsgaard. This is based on the true story of a girl in rural Nebraska who successfully passes as a boy—until a discovery has violent consequences. This story may be hard to watch, both because it depicts violence and be-cause you know it's true. What makes gender impersonations alternately acceptable, even entertaining—or tragically infuriating?

Marvin's Room. (1996, color, 98 min.). Directed by Jerry Zaks; starring Meryl Streep, Diane Keaton, Leonardo DiCaprio. Estranged sisters face family crises as one, who is sick, calls on help from the other, who is losing a battle with her teenaged son. This cinematic tangle of family tensions, insights, and oversights still summarizes the messiness of real-life family relationships.

Welcome to the Dollhouse. (1996, color, 87 min.). Directed by Todd Solondz; starring Heather Matarazzo, Brandon Sexton, Jr., Daria Kalinina, Matthew Faber. The pain of puberty is depicted through the eyes of a young woman whose suburban parents are amazingly unsympathetic and favor her baby sister and whose school experi-ence seems to be the Seventh Grade from Hell. The film has good performances and a lot of humor.

CORE CONCEPTS

The brain senses the world indirectly because the sense organs convert stimulation into the language of the nervous system: neural messages.

The senses all operate in much the same way, but each extracts different information and sends it to its own specialized processing region in the brain.

▼
Perception brings *meaning* to sensation, so perception produces an interpretation of the world, not a perfect representation of it.

Psychology in Your Life

A Critical Look at Subliminal Persuasion
Subliminal perception occurs, but individual differences in perceptual thresholds make widespread use of subliminal persuasion unworkable.

The Experience of Pain
Pain is more than just a stimulus; it is an experience that varies from person to person. Pain control methods include drugs, hypnosis, and—for some—placebos.

Seeing and Believing
Magicians and politicians rely on the fact that we don't merely sense the world, we perceive it.

USING PSYCHOLOGY TO LEARN PSYCHOLOGY:
Studying for the Gestalt

Sensation and Perception

CAN YOU IMAGINE WHAT your world would be like if you could no longer see colors—but merely black, white, and gray? Such a bizarre sensory loss actually befell Jonathan I., a 65-year-old New Yorker, following an automobile accident (Sacks, 1995). Apparently the trauma of the crash caused damage to a region in his brain that processes color information. At first, Jonathan also had some amnesia for reading letters of the alphabet, which all seemed like nonsensical markings to him. But, after five days, his inability to read disappeared. His loss of color vision, however, persisted as a permanent condition, known as *cerebral achromatopsia* (pronounced *ay-kroma-TOP-see-a*).

As you might expect, Jonathan became depressed by this turn of events in his life. The problem was aggravated by the fact that he was a painter whose profession was based on representing his visual images of the world in vivid colors. Now this world of colors was all gone, all drab, all "molded in lead." When he looked at his own paintings, which had seemed bursting with special meaning and emotional associations, all he now saw were unfamiliar and meaningless objects on canvas.

Curiously, Jonathan also lost his memory of color and eventually the names for colors. He could no longer even imagine, for instance, what "red" once looked like. What Jonathan's experience dramatically demonstrated to the researchers and clinicians who studied him and tried to help him was the nonobvious neurological truth that colors do not really exist "out there." Rather, the world of color is constructed by the sensory and perceptual processes in the brain.

Jonathan's story has a more or less happy ending, one that reveals much about the resilience of the human spirit. First, Jonathan became a "night person," traveling and working at night and socializing with other night people. (As we will see in this chapter, good color vision depends on bright illumination such as daylight; most people's color vision is not as acute in the dark of night.) He also became aware that what remained of his vision was remarkably good, enabling him to read license plates from four blocks away at night. Jonathan began to reinterpret his "loss" as a "gift" in which he was no longer distracted by color, so that he could now focus his work more intensely on shape, form, and content. Finally, he switched to painting only in black and white, and critics acclaimed his "new phase" as a success. He has also become good at sculpting, which he had never attempted before his accident. So, as Jonathan's world of color died, a new world of "pure forms" was born in his perception of the people, objects, and events in his environment.

● To hunt small flying objects at night, bats rely on the sensory system of echolocation, a kind of sonar. Bats emit high-frequency sounds that bounce off insects, revealing their locations so the bats can find and eat them.

■ **Sensation** The process by which stimulation of a sensory receptor produces neural impulses that the brain interprets as a sound, a visual image, an odor, a taste, a pain, or other sensory image. Sensation represents the first series of steps in processing of incoming information.

What are the lessons we can learn from Jonathan's experience? His unusual sensory loss tells us that our picture of the world around us depends on an elaborate sensory system that processes incoming information. In other words, we don't experience the world directly, but instead through a series of "filters" that we call our *senses*. By examining such cases of sensory loss, psychologists have learned much about how the sensory processing system works. And, on a more personal level, case studies like Jonathan allow us momentarily to slip outside our own experience to see more clearly how resilient humans can be in the face of catastrophic loss.

Although the very private processes that connect us with the outside world extend deep into the brain, we will begin our chapter at the surface—at the sense organs. This is the territory of *sensory psychology*. We will define **sensation** simply as the process by which a stimulated receptor (such as the eyes or ears) creates a pattern of neural messages that represent the stimulus in the brain, giving rise to our initial experience of the stimulus. An important idea to remember is that sensation involves changing stimulation (such as a pinprick, a sound, or a flash of light) into a form the brain can understand (neural signals)—much as a cell phone converts an electronic signal into sound waves you can hear.

In this chapter you will see how all our sense organs, in some fundamental ways, are much alike. They all transform physical stimulation (such as light waves) into the neural impulses that give us sensations (such as light and dark). Along the way, you will learn about the psychological basis for color, odor, sound, texture, and taste. When you have finished the chapter, you will know why tomatoes and limes seem to have different hues, why a pinprick feels different from a caress, and why seeing doesn't always give us an accurate basis for believing.

Happily, under most conditions our sensory experience is highly reliable. So, when you catch sight of a friend, the sensation usually registers clearly, immediately, and accurately. Yet, we humans do have our sensory limitations—just as other creatures do. In fact, we lack the acute senses so remarkable in many other species: the vision of hawks, the hearing of bats, the sense of smell of rodents, or the sensitivity to magnetic fields found in migratory birds. So, is there a human specialty? Our species has evolved the sensory equipment that enables us to process a wider range and variety of sensory input than any other creature.

Beyond that fact, our ultimate destination in this chapter lies, far beyond mere sensation, in the amazing realm of *perception*. There we will uncover the psychological processes that attach meaning and personal significance to the sensory messages entering our brains. *Perceptual psychology* will help you understand how we assemble a series of tones into a familiar melody or a barrage of shapes and shadings into a familiar face. More generally, we will define **perception** as a mental process that elaborates and assigns meaning to the incoming sensory patterns. Thus, *perception creates an interpretation of sensation*. Perception answers questions such as: Is the tomato ripe? Is the sound a church bell or a doorbell? Does the face belong to someone you know?

In this chapter, you will also learn that many complex acts of sensing and perceiving occur behind the scenes, so effortlessly, continuously, and flawlessly that we pay them little conscious mind. Even more fundamentally, you will learn the sobering fact that our minds lack direct access to the outside world. No matter what we do, the information we get about external events must always be filtered through our sense organs and then combined with our unique mix of memories, emotions, motives, and expectations. So, the inner world of sensation and perception is the only world we can ever know.

As you can see, the boundary of sensation blurs into that of perception. Perception is essentially an interpretation and elaboration of sensation. Seen in these terms, sensation refers just to the initial steps in the processing of a stimulus. It is to these first sensory steps that we now turn our attention.

HOW DOES STIMULATION BECOME SENSATION?

A thunderstorm is approaching, and you feel the electric charge in the air make the hair stand up on your neck. Lightning flashes, and a split second later you hear the thunderclap. It was close by, and you smell the ozone left in the wake of the bolt, as it sizzled through the air. Your senses are warning you of danger.

Our senses have other adaptive functions, too. They aid our survival by directing us toward certain stimuli, such as tasty foods, which provide nourishment. Our senses also help us locate mates, seek shelter, and recognize our friends. Incidentally, our senses also give us the opportunity to find pleasure in music, art, athletics, food, and sex.

How do our senses accomplish all this? The complete answer is complex, but it involves one elegantly simple idea that applies across the sensory landscape: Our sensory impressions of the world involve *neural representations* of stimuli—not the actual stimuli themselves. The Core Concept puts it this way:

> **The brain senses the world indirectly because the sense organs convert stimulation into the language of the nervous system: neural messages.**

As we have noted, the brain never receives stimulation directly from the outside world. Its experience of a tomato is not the same as the tomato itself—although we usually assume that the two are identical. Neither can the brain receive light from a sunset, reach out and touch velvet, or inhale the fragrance of a rose. It must always rely on secondhand information from the go-between sensory system, which delivers only a coded neural message, out of which the brain must create its own experience. (See Figure 5.1.) Just as you cannot receive phone messages without a telephone receiver to convert the electronic energy into sound you can hear, your brain also needs its sensory system to

■ **Perception** A process that makes sensory patterns meaningful. It is perception that makes these words meaningful, rather than just a string of visual patterns. To make this happen, perception draws heavily on memory, motivation, emotion, and other psychological processes.

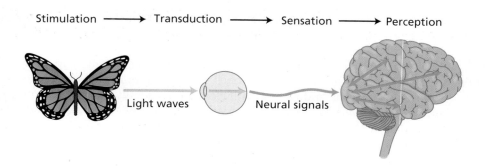

● **FIGURE 5.1** Stimulation Becomes Perception

For visual stimulation to become meaningful perception, it must undergo several transformations. First, physical stimulation (light waves from the butterfly) are transduced by the eye, where information about the wavelength and intensity of the light is coded into neural signals. Second, the neural messages travel to the sensory cortex of the brain, where they become sensations of color, brightness, form, and movement. Finally, the process of perception interprets these sensations by making connections with memories, expectations, emotions, and motives in other parts of the brain. Similar processes operate on information taken in by the other senses.

convert the stimuli from the outside world into neural signals that it can comprehend.

To understand more deeply how the world's stimulation becomes the brain's sensation, we need to think about three attributes common to all the senses: *transduction, sensory adaptation,* and *thresholds.* They determine which stimuli will actually become sensation, what the quality and impact of that sensation will be, and whether it grabs our interest. These attributes determine, for example, whether a tomato actually registers in the sensory system strongly enough to enter our awareness, what its color and form appear to be, and how strongly it bids for our attention.

Transduction: Changing Stimulation to Sensation

The idea that basic sensations, such as the redness and flavor of our tomato, are entirely creations of the sense organs and brain may seem incredible to you. But remember that all sensory communication with the brain flows through neurons in the form of neural signals: Neurons cannot transmit light or sound waves or any other external stimulus. Accordingly, none of the light bouncing off the tomato ever actually reaches the brain. In fact, light only gets as far as the back of the eyes, where the information it contains is converted to neural messages. Likewise, the chemicals that signal taste make their way only as far as the tongue, not all the way to the brain.

In all the sense organs, it is the job of the *sensory receptors* to convert incoming stimulus information into electrochemical signals—neural activity—the only language the brain understands. As Jonathan I.'s case suggests, sensations, such as "red" or "sweet" or "cold," occur only when the neural signal reaches the cerebral cortex. The whole process seems so immediate and direct that it fools us into assuming that the sensation of redness is characteristic of a tomato or the sensation of cold is a characteristic of ice cream. But they are not! (You can demonstrate to yourself how light is not necessary for sensations of light with the demonstration in the "Do It Yourself!" box, "Phosphenes Show That Your Brain Creates Sensations.")

Psychologists use the term **transduction** for the sensory process that converts physical energy, such as light or sound waves, into the form of neural messages. Transduction begins with the detection by a sensory neuron of the physical stimulus (such as the sound wave made by a vibrating guitar string). When the appropriate stimulus reaches a sense organ, it activates specialized neurons, called *receptors,* which respond by converting their excitation into a nerve signal. This happens in much the same way that a bar-code reader (which is, after all, merely an electronic receptor) converts the series of lines on a frozen pizza box into an electronic signal that a computer can match with a price. In our own sensory system, it is the neural impulse that carries a code of the sensory event in a form that can be further processed by the brain. To

■ **Transduction** Transformation of one form of energy into another—especially the transformation of stimulus information into nerve signals by the sense organs. Without transduction, ripe tomatoes would not appear red (or pinkish-gray, in the case of tomatoes purchased in many grocery stores).

get to its destination, this information-carrying signal travels from the receptor cells along a *sensory pathway* by way of the thalamus to specialized sensory processing areas in the brain. From neural impulses arriving from these pathways, the brain then extracts information about the basic qualities of the stimulus, such as its intensity, pitch, and direction. Please keep in mind, however, that the stimulus itself terminates in the receptor: The only thing that continues on into the nervous system is *information* carried by the neural impulse.

Sensory Adaptation

If you have ever jumped into a cool pool on a hot day, you know that sensation is critically influenced by *change*. In fact, a main role of our stimulus detectors is to announce changes in the external world such as a flash of light, a splash of water, a clap of thunder, the prick of a pin, or the burst of flavor from a dollop of salsa. Thus, our sense organs are change detectors. Their receptors specialize in gathering information about new and changing events.

The great quantity of incoming sensation would quickly overwhelm us, if not for the ability of our sensory systems to adapt. **Sensory adaptation** is the diminishing responsiveness of sensory systems to prolonged stimulation, as when you adapted to the feel of swimming in cool water. Unless it is quite intense or painful, stimulation that persists without changing in intensity or some other quality usually shifts into the background of our awareness. To give another example, you probably did not realize, until we called your attention to it, that your sense of touch had adapted to the press of furniture against your body. On the other hand, any change in the stimulation you are receiving (if an air conditioner suddenly becomes louder or higher-pitched, for example)

● A swimmer must undergo sensory adaptation when jumping into cool water.

■ **Sensory adaptation** Loss of responsiveness in receptor cells after stimulation has remained unchanged for a while, as when a swimmer becomes adapted to the temperature of the water.

will draw your attention. Incidentally, sensory adaptation is why the background music often played in stores is so unmemorable: It has been deliberately selected and filtered to remove any large changes in volume or pitch that might distract attention from the merchandise. (Do you see why it's not a good idea to listen to interesting music while you are studying?)

Thresholds

What is the weakest stimulus that an organism can detect? How dim can a light be and still be visible? How soft can music be and still be heard? These questions refer to the **absolute threshold** for different types of stimulation, which is the minimum amount of physical energy needed to produce a sensory experience. In the laboratory, a psychologist would define this operationally as the intensity at which the stimulus is detected accurately half of the time over many trials. Obviously, this threshold will vary from one person to another. So, if you point out a faint star to a friend who says he cannot see it, the star's light is above your absolute threshold (you can see it) but below that of your friend (who cannot).

A faint stimulus does not abruptly become detectable as its intensity increases. Because of the fuzzy boundary between detection and nondetection, a person's absolute threshold is not absolute! In fact, it varies continually with our mental alertness and physical condition. Experiments designed to determine thresholds for various types of stimulation were among the earliest studies done by psychologists—who called this line of inquiry *psychophysics*. Table 5.1 shows some typical absolute threshold levels for several familiar natural stimuli.

We can illustrate another kind of threshold with the following imaginary experiment. Suppose you are relaxing by watching television on the one night you don't need to study, while your roommate busily prepares for an early morning exam. Your roommate asks you to "turn it down a little" to eliminate the distraction. You feel that you should make some effort to comply but really wish to leave the volume as it is. What is the least amount you can lower the volume to prove your good intentions to your roommate while still keeping the volume clearly audible? Your ability to make judgments like this one depends on your **difference threshold,** the smallest physical difference between two stimuli that can still be recognized as a difference.

If you turn the volume knob as little as possible, your roommate might complain, "I don't hear any difference" or "You haven't turned it down enough." By "enough," your roommate probably means his or her difference threshold. Even if you have adjusted the volume downward slightly, the difference might not be large enough to detect. If you hear the difference, it exceeds your own difference threshold; if your roommate can hear the differ-

◄ **CONNECTION: CHAPTER 1**

An *operational definition* describes a concept in terms of the operations required to produce, observe, or measure it.

■ **Absolute threshold**   The amount of stimulation necessary for a stimulus to be detected. In practice, this means that the presence or absence of a stimulus is detected correctly half the time over many trials.

■ **Difference threshold**   The smallest amount by which a stimulus can be changed and the difference be detected half the time.

TABLE 5.1	Approximate Perceptual Thresholds of Five Senses
Sense Modality	**Detection Threshold**
Light	A candle flame at 30 miles on a dark, clear night
Sound	The tick of a mechanical watch under quiet conditions at 20 feet
Taste	One teaspoon of sugar in two gallons of water
Smell	One drop of perfume diffused into the entire volume of a three-bedroom apartment
Touch	The wing of a bee falling on your cheek from a distance of one centimeter

Source: From ENCYCLOPEDIC DICTIONARY OF PSYCHOLOGY 3rd ed. Copyright © 1986 by Dushkin/McGraw-Hill, a division of The McGraw-Hill Companies. Adapted and reprinted by permission of the publisher.

In this simple demonstration, you will see how detection of change depends on the intensity of the background stimulation. Find a three-way lamp equipped with a bulb having equal wattage increments, such as a 50–100–150 watt bulb. (Wattage is closely related to brightness.) Then, in a dark room, switch the light on to 50

watts. This will unmistakably increase brightness. Changing from 50 to 100 watts will also seem like a large increase. But why does the last 50-watt increase (from 100 to 150 watts) appear only slightly brighter? Your sensory system does not give you a sensation of the exact brightness. Rather, it compares the stimu-

lus change to the background stimulation, translating the jump from 100 to 150 watts as a mere 50% increase (50 watts added to 100) compared to the earlier 100% increase (50 watts added to 50). This illustrates how your brain computes sensory relationships, rather than absolutes.

---

ence, it exceeds his or hers. Suppose you start adjusting the volume and ask your roommate to "say when"—to stop you when the adjustment is sufficient to be detected. This minimal amount of change in the signal that is still recognizable is the **just noticeable difference (JND).** The terms *difference threshold, just noticeable difference,* and *JND* are used interchangeably by psychologists.

Investigation of the JND for different senses has yielded some interesting insights into how human stimulus detection works. It turns out that *the JND is always large when the stimulus intensity is high, and small when the stimulus intensity is low.* Psychologists refer to this idea—that the size of the JND is proportional to the intensity of the stimulus—as **Weber's law.** And what does Weber's law tell us about adjusting the TV volume? If you have the volume turned up very high, you will have to turn the volume down a lot to make the difference noticeable. On the other hand, if you already have the volume set to a very low level, so that you can barely hear it if you listen carefully, a small adjustment will probably be noticeable enough for your roommate. The same principle operates across all our senses. Knowing this, you might guess that a weight lifter would notice the difference when small amounts are added to light weights, but it would take a much larger addition to be noticeable with heavy weights.

What does all this mean for our understanding of human sensation? The general principle is this: We are built to detect *changes* in stimulation and *relationships* among stimuli. You can see how this works in the box, "Do It Yourself! An Enlightening Demonstration of Sensory Relationships."

● Signal detection theory says that the background stimulation would make it less likely for you to hear someone calling your name on a busy downtown street than in a quiet park.

Signal Detection Theory

A deeper understanding of absolute and difference thresholds comes from *signal detection theory* (Green & Swets, 1966). Originally developed for engineering electronic sensors, signal detection theory uses the same concepts to explain both the electronic sensing of stimuli by devices, such as your TV set, and by the human senses, such as vision and hearing.

According to **signal detection theory,** sensation depends on the characteristics of the stimulus, the background stimulation, and the detector. You may have noticed, for example, that you get more out of an 8 o'clock class if your nervous system has been aroused by a strong cup of coffee. Similarly, a person's interests and biases can affect the "signals" he or she gets from the evening news.

Signal detection theory also helps us understand why thresholds are variable—why, for example, you might notice a certain sound one time and not the next. The classical theory of thresholds ignored the effects of the perceiver's physical condition, judgments, or biases. Thus, in classical psychophysics (the study of stimulation, thresholds, and sensory experience), if a signal were

■ **Just noticeable difference (JND)** Same as the difference threshold.

■ **Weber's law** This concept says that the size of a JND is proportional to the intensity of the stimulus; the JND is large when the stimulus intensity is high and small when the stimulus intensity is low. (This concept has *no* connection with Ann Weber, one of your authors.)

■ **Signal detection theory** Explains how we detect "signals," consisting of stimulation affecting our eyes, ears, nose, skin, and other sense organs. Signal detection theory says that sensation is a judgment the sensory system makes about incoming stimulation. Often, it occurs outside of consciousness. In contrast to older theories from psychophysics, signal detection theory takes observer characteristics into account.

intense enough to exceed one's absolute threshold, it would be sensed; if below threshold, it would be missed. In the view of modern signal detection theory, sensation is not a simple present/absent, yes/no experience.

So, what does signal detection theory offer psychology that was missing in classical psychophysics? One factor is the variability in human judgment. Signal detection theory recognizes that the observer, whose physical and mental status is always in flux, must compare a sensory experience with ever-changing expectations and biological conditions. For example, when something "goes bump in the night" after you have gone to bed, you must decide whether it is the cat, an intruder, or just your imagination. What you decide depends on the keenness of your hearing and what you expect to hear, as well as other noises in the background. By taking into account the variable conditions that affect detection of a stimulus, signal detection theory provides a more accurate portrayal of sensation than did classical psychophysics.

 ## PSYCHOLOGY IN YOUR LIFE: A CRITICAL LOOK AT SUBLIMINAL PERSUASION

Can extremely weak stimulation—stimulation that you don't even notice—affect your mind or behavior? The alluring promise that signals can be processed in your sensory system without awareness lies at the basis of the industry that sells "subliminal" tapes and CDs touted as remedies for obesity, shoplifting, smoking, and low self-esteem. But before you put your money in the mail, let's look at a bit of history and some fundamentals of sensory psychology.

Some years ago, advertising executive James Vicary dramatically announced to the press that he had discovered an irresistible sales technique now known as "subliminal advertising." Vicary said that his method consisted of projecting very brief messages on the screen of a movie theater, urging the audience to "Drink Coke" and "Buy popcorn." He claimed that the ads presented ideas so fleetingly that the conscious mind could not perceive them—yet, he said, the messages would still lodge in the unconscious mind, where they would work on the viewer's desires unnoticed. Vicary also boasted that sales of Coca Cola and popcorn had soared at a New Jersey theater where he tested the technique.

The public was both fascinated and outraged. Subliminal advertising became the subject of intense debate. People worried that they were being manipulated by powerful psychological forces without their consent. As a result, laws were proposed to quash the practice. But aside from the hysteria, was there any real cause for concern? For answers to that question we must return to the concept of *threshold*, the minimum amount of stimulation necessary to trigger a response. The word *subliminal* means "below the threshold" (*limen* = threshold). In the language of perceptual psychology, *subliminal* more specifically refers to stimuli lying near the absolute threshold. Such stimuli may, in fact, be strong enough to affect the sense organs and to enter the sensory system, without causing conscious awareness of the stimulus. But the real question is this: Can subliminal stimuli in this range influence our thoughts and behavior?

Several studies have found that subliminal words flashed briefly on a screen (for less than 1/100 second) can "prime" a person's later responses (Merikle & Reingold, 1990). For example, can you fill in the following blanks to make a word?

S N _ _ _ E L

If you had been subliminally primed by a brief presentation of the appropriate word, it would be more likely that you would have found the right answer, even though you were not aware of the priming stimulus.

Apparently people do respond to stimuli below the absolute threshold, under some circumstances (Greenwald et al., 1996; Reber, 1993). But here is the problem for would-be subliminal advertisers who would attempt to influence us in the uncontrolled world outside the laboratory: Different people have thresholds at different levels. So, what might be *subliminal* for me could well be *supra*liminal (above the threshold) for you. Consequently, the subliminal advertiser runs the risk that some in the audience will notice—and be angry about—a stimulus aimed slightly below the average person's threshold. In fact, *no controlled research has ever shown that subliminal messages delivered to a mass audience can influence people's buying habits.*

But what about those subliminal recordings that some stores play to prevent shoplifting? Again, no reputable study has ever demonstrated their effectiveness. A more likely explanation for any decrease in shoplifting accruing to these tapes lies in increased vigilance from employees who know that management is worried about shoplifting. The same goes for the tapes that claim to help you quit smoking, lose weight, become wildly creative, or achieve other dozens of elusive dreams. In a comprehensive study of subliminal self-help techniques, the U.S. Army found all to be without foundation (Druckman & Bjork, 1991). The simplest explanation for reports of success lies in the purchasers' expectations and in the need to prove that they did not spend their money foolishly. And finally, to take the rest of the worry out of subliminal persuasion, you should know that James Vicary eventually admitted that his claims for subliminal advertising were a hoax (Druckman & Bjork, 1991).

The answer to the fill-in-the-blanks problem, by the way, is "snorkel."

CHECK YOUR UNDERSTANDING

1. **RECALL:** The sensory pathways carry information
   a. from the brain to the muscles.
   b. from the sense organs to the brain.
   c. from the brain to the sense organs.
   d. from the central nervous system to the autonomic nervous system.

2. **RECALL:** Which one refers to the least amount of stimulation that your perceptual system can detect about half the time?
   a. the stimulus threshold
   b. the difference threshold
   c. the absolute threshold
   d. the action threshold

3. **APPLICATION:** Which one would involve sensory adaptation?
   a. The water in a swimming pool seems warmer after you have been in it for a while than it did when you first jumped in.
   b. The flavor of a spicy salsa on your taco seems hot by comparison with the blandness of the sour cream.
   c. You are unaware of a priming stimulus flashed on the screen at 1/100 of a second.
   d. You prefer the feel of silk to the feel of velvet.

4. **RECALL:** Which of the following is a process that adds meaning to incoming information obtained by the sensory systems?
   a. stimulation
   b. sensation
   c. sensory adaptation
   d. perception

5. **UNDERSTANDING THE CORE CONCEPT:** When you hear the sound of a tree falling in the forest, the brain has received nothing but
   a. sound waves from the air.
   b. neural activity in the sensory pathways.
   c. the vibration of the eardrums.
   d. sound waves traveling through the sensory pathways.

ANSWERS: 1.b 2.c 3.a 4.d 5.b

HOW ARE THE SENSES ALIKE? AND HOW ARE THEY DIFFERENT?

Vision, hearing, smell, taste, touch, pain, body position: In certain ways, all these senses are the same. They all transduce stimulus energy into neural impulses. They are all more sensitive to change than to constant stimulation. And they all provide us information about the world—information that has survival value. But how are they different? With the exception of pain, each sense taps a different form of stimulus energy, and each sends the information it extracts to a different part of the brain. These contrasting ideas lead us to the Core Concept of this section:

> The senses all operate in much the same way, but each extracts different information and sends it to its own specialized processing region in the brain.

Each sense organ has a different design, and each sends neural messages to its own specialized region in the brain. So, in the end, *different sensations occur because different areas of the brain become activated.* Whether you hear a bell or see a bell depends ultimately on which part of the brain receives stimulation. We will explore how this all works by looking at each of the senses in turn. First, we will explore the visual system—the best understood of the senses—to discover how it transduces light waves into visual sensations of color and brightness.

Vision: How the Nervous System Processes Light

Animals with good vision have an enormous biological advantage. This fact has exerted evolutionary pressure to make vision the most complex, best developed, and important sense for humans and most other highly mobile creatures. Good vision helps us detect desired targets, threats, and changes in our physical environment and to adapt our behavior accordingly. So, how does the visual system accomplish this?

The Anatomy of Visual Sensation You might think of the eye as a camera the brain uses to make motion pictures of the world (see Figure 5.2). Like a camera, the eye gathers light, focuses it, converts it to neural signals, and sends these signals on their way for subsequent processing into a visual image. The unique characteristic of the eye—what makes the eye different from other sense organs—lies in its ability to extract the information from light waves, which are simply a form of electromagnetic energy. (Visible light is not fundamentally different from radio waves or X rays, as we shall find.) The eye, then, *transduces* the characteristics of light into neural signals that the brain can process. This transduction happens in the **retina,** the light-sensitive layer of cells at the back of the eye that acts much like the light-sensitive chip in a digital camera.

The real work in the retina is performed by light-sensitive cells known as **photoreceptors,** which operate much like the tiny pixel receptors in a digital camera. These photoreceptors consist of two different types of specialized neurons—the rods and cones that absorb light energy and respond by creating neural impulses (see Figure 5.3). But why two sorts of photoreceptors?

Because we sometimes function in near-darkness and sometimes in bright light, we have evolved two ways of processing, using two distinct receptor cell types, named for their shapes. The 125 million tiny **rods** "see in the dark"—that is, they detect low intensities of light at night, though they cannot make

■ **Retina** The thin light-sensitive layer at the back of the eyeball. The retina contains millions of photoreceptors and other nerve cells.

■ **Photoreceptors** Light-sensitive cells (neurons) in the retina that convert light energy to neural impulses. The photoreceptors are as far as light gets into the visual system.

■ **Rods** Photoreceptors in the retina that are especially sensitive to dim light but not to colors. Strange as it may seem, they are rod-shaped.

● **FIGURE 5.2** Structures of the Human Eye

Cornea
Fluid (aqueous humor)
Pupil
Lens
Iris
Muscle
(for focusing lens)

Muscle (for turning eye)
Fluid (vitreous humor)
Retina
Fovea
Blind spot
Blood vessels
Optic nerve

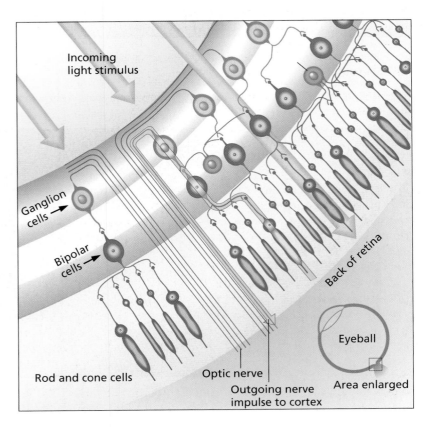

Incoming
light stimulus

Ganglion
cells

Bipolar
cells

Rod and cone cells

Optic nerve

Outgoing nerve
impulse to cortex

Back of retina

Eyeball

Area enlarged

● **FIGURE 5.3** Transduction of Light in the Retina

This simplified diagram shows the pathways that connect three layers of nerve cells in the retina. Incoming light passes through the ganglion cells and bipolar cells first before striking the photoreceptors at the back of the eyeball. Once stimulated, the rods and cones then transmit information to the bipolar cells (note that one bipolar cell combines information from several receptor cells). The bipolar cells then transmit neural impulses to the ganglion cells. Impulses travel from the ganglia to the brain via axons that make up the optic nerve.

the fine distinctions that give rise to our sensations of color. Rod cells enable you to find a seat in a darkened movie theatre.

Making the fine distinctions necessary for color vision is the job of the seven million **cones** that come into play in bright light. Each cone is specialized to detect the light waves we sense either as blue, red, or green. In good light, then, we can use these cones to distinguish ripe tomatoes (sensed as red) from unripe ones (sensed as green). The cones concentrate in the very center of the retina, in a small region called the **fovea,** which gives us our sharpest vision. With movements of our eyeballs, we use the fovea to scan whatever interests us visually—the features of a face or, perhaps, a flower. (You can learn more about the way cones work by trying the "Do It Yourself!" demonstration below.)

There are still other types of cells in the retina, but while they are vital to vision they do not respond directly to light. In particular, the *bipolar cells* have the job of collecting impulses from many photoreceptors (rods and cones) and shuttling them on to the *ganglion cells*, much as an airline "hub" collects passengers from many regional airports and shuttles them on to other destinations. Bundled together, the axons of the ganglion cells make up the **optic nerve,** which transports visual information from the eye to the brain. (See Figures 5.2 and 5.3.) Again, it is important to understand that your visual system carries no light at all beyond the retina—only patterns of nerve impulses conveying *information* derived from the incoming light.

Just as strangely, there is a small area of the retina in each eye where everyone is blind, because that part of the retina has no photoreceptors. This **blind spot** is located at the point where the optic nerve exits each eye, and the result

■ **Cones**   Photoreceptors in the retina that are especially sensitive to colors but not to dim light. You may have guessed that the cones are cone-shaped.

■ **Fovea**   The tiny area of sharpest vision in the retina.

■ **Optic nerve**   The bundle of neurons that carries visual information from the retina to the brain.

■ **Blind spot**   The point where the optic nerve exits the eye and where there are no photoreceptors. Any stimulus that falls on this area cannot be seen.

DO IT YOURSELF! | The Amazing Afterimage

After you stare at a colored object for a while, cells in your retina will become fatigued, causing an interesting visual effect. When you shift your gaze to a blank surface, you can "see" the object in complementary colors—as a visual afterimage. The "phantom flag" demonstration will show you how this works.

Stare at the dot in the center of the green, black, and orange flag for at least 30 seconds. Take care to hold your eyes steady and not to let them scan over the image during this time. Then quickly shift your gaze to the center of a sheet of white paper or to a light-colored blank wall. What do you see? Have your friends try this, too. Do they see the same afterimage? (The effect may not work for people who are color-blind.)

Afterimages may be negative or positive. Positive afterimages are caused by a continuation of the receptor and neural processes following stimulation. They are brief. An example of positive afterimages occurs when you see the trail of a sparkler twirled by a Fourth of July reveler. Negative afterimages are the opposite or

the reverse of the original experience, as in the flag example. They last longer. Negative afterimages operate according to the *opponent-process theory* of color vision, which involves ganglion

cells in the retina and the optic nerve. Apparently, in a negative afterimage, the fatigue in these cells produces sensations of a complementary color when they are exposed to white light.

The "blind spot" occurs at the place on the retina where the neurons from the retina bunch together to exit the eyeball and form the optic nerve. There are no light-sensitive cells at this point on the retina. Consequently, you are "blind" in this small region of your visual field. The following demonstrations will help you determine where this blind spot occurs in your visual field.

DEMONSTRATION 1

Hold the book at arm's length, close your right eye, and fix your left eye on the "bank" figure. Keep your right eye closed and bring the book slowly closer. When it is about 10 to 12 inches away and the dollar sign is in your blind spot, the dollar sign will disappear—but you will not see a "hole" in your visual field. Instead, your visual system "fills in" the missing area with information from the white background. You have "lost" your money!

DEMONSTRATION 2

To convince yourself that the brain fills in the missing part of the visual field with appropriate background, close your right eye again and focus on the cross in the lower part of the figure. Once again, keeping the right eye closed,

bring the book closer to you as you focus your left eye on the cross. This time, the gap in the line will disappear and will be filled in with a continuation of the line on either side. This shows that what you see in your blind spot may not really exist!

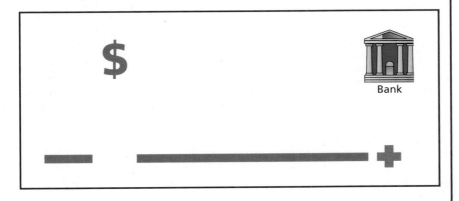

Bank

---

is a gap in the visual field. If your vision is normal, you do not experience blindness there because what one eye misses is registered by the other eye, and the brain "fills in" the spot with information that matches the background. You can find your own blind spot by following the instructions in the "Do It Yourself!" box above.

Processing Visual Sensation in the Brain   We *look* with our eyes but we *see* with the brain. To do so, we use a special processing area in the brain to create visual images from the information imported through the optic nerve (see Figure 5.4). In the *visual cortex*, the brain begins working its magic by transforming the incoming neural impulses into visual sensations of color, form, boundary, and movement. Amazingly, the visual cortex also manages to take the two-dimensional patterns from each eye and assemble them into a three-dimensional world of depth (Barinaga, 1998; Dobbins et al., 1998). With further processing, the cortex ultimately combines these visual sensations with memories, motives, emotions, and sensations of body position and touch to create a representation of the visual world that fits our current concerns and interests (Barinaga, 1999; Batista et al., 1999; de Gelder, 2000; Maunsell, 1995). Now you know why you can be strongly attracted by the visual appeal of appetizing foods if you go grocery shopping when you are hungry.

How the Visual System Creates Brightness   Sensations of **brightness** come from the intensity or *amplitude* of light, determined by how much light reaches the retina (see Table 5.2). Bright light, as from approaching headlights, involves a more intense light wave, which creates much neural activity in the retina, while relatively dim light, from your car's instrument panel, does not. Ultimately, the brain senses brightness by the level of neural activity produced in the retina and passed along through the optic pathways.

CONNECTION: CHAPTER 2

The *visual cortex* lies in the brain's occipital lobe.

■ **Brightness**   A psychological sensation caused by the intensity of light waves.

Light from objects in the visual field projects
images on the retinas of the eyes. Please note
two important things. First, the lens of the eye
reverses the image on the retina—so the image
of the man falls on the right side of the retina
and the image of the woman falls on the left.
Second, the visual system splits the retinal
image coming from each eye, so that part of
the image coming from each eye crosses over
to the opposite side of the brain. (Note how
branches of the optic pathway cross at the
optic chiasma.) As a result, objects appearing
in the *left* part of the visual field *of both eyes*
(the man, in this diagram) are sent to the *right*
hemisphere's visual cortex for processing, while
objects in the *right* side of the visual field *of
both eyes* (the woman, in this diagram) are
sent to the *left* visual cortex. In general, the
right hemisphere "sees" the left visual field,
while the left hemisphere "sees" the right visual
field. (*Source:* From SEEING: Illusion, Brain and
Mind by J. P. Frisby. Copyright © 1979.
Reprinted by permission of J. P. Frisby.)

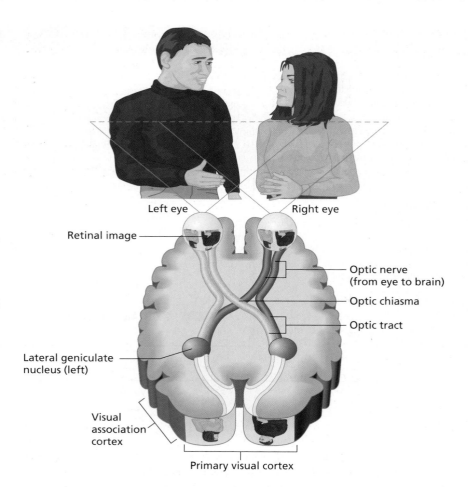

■ **Color** Also called *hue.* Color is *not* a
property of things in the external world. Rather,
it is a *psychological sensation* created in the
brain from information obtained by the eyes
from the wavelengths of visible light.

How the Visual System Creates Color You may have been surprised to learn
that a flower or a ripe tomato, itself, has no **color** or *hue.* Physical objects seen
in bright light seem to have the marvelous property of being awash with color;
but, as we have noted, the red tomatoes, yellow flowers, green trees, blue
oceans, and multihued rainbows are, in themselves, actually quite colorless. Nor
does the light reflected from these objects have color. Despite the way the world
appears to us, color does not exist outside the brain because color is a *sensation*
that the brain creates based on the wavelength of light striking our eyes. Thus,
color exists only in the mind of the viewer—a *psychological* property of our sensory experience. Color is created when the wavelength in a beam of light is
recoded by the photoreceptors in the form of neural impulses and sent to specialized areas of the brain for sensory processing. To understand more fully
how this happens, you must first know something of the nature of light.

TABLE 5.2	Visual Stimulation Becomes Sensation	
Physical Stimulation		**Psychological Sensation**
Wavelength	⟶	color
intensity (amplitude)	⟶	brightness

Color and brightness are the psychological counterparts of the wavelength and intensity of a lightwave. Wavelength and
intensity are physical characteristics of light waves, while color and brightness are psychological characteristics that exist only
in the brain.

The eyes detect the special form of energy that we call *visible light*. Physicists tell us that this light is pure energy—fundamentally the same as radio waves, microwaves, infrared light, ultraviolet light, X rays, and cosmic rays. All are forms of *electromagnetic energy*, consisting of waves that move at light's speed limit of nearly 670 million MPH. These waves differ in their *wavelength*, the distance they travel in making one wave cycle, as they vibrate in space, like ripples on a pond (see Figure 5.5). The light we can see occupies but a tiny segment of the vast **electromagnetic spectrum.** Our only access to this electromagnetic spectrum lies through a small visual "window" called the **visible spectrum.** Because we have no biological receptors sensitive to the other portions of the electromagnetic spectrum, we must employ special detection instruments, such as radios and TVs, to help us convert energy in the range outside our vision into signals we can use.

Within the visible spectrum light waves of different wavelengths give rise to different colors. Longer waves make us see a tomato as red, and medium-length waves give rise to the sensations of yellow and green we see in lemons and limes. The shorter waves from a clear sky stimulate sensations of blue. Thus, it is the wavelength of light from which the eye extracts the information used by the brain to construct colors (see Table 5.2).

Remarkably, our visual experiences of color, form, position, and depth are all based on processing the same stream of sensory information in different parts of the visual cortex. Colors themselves are realized in a specialized area, where humans are capable of discriminating among about five million different hues. Other nearby cortical areas take responsibility for processing information about boundaries, shapes, and movements.

Two Ways of Sensing Colors   Even though color is realized in the cortex, color processing begins in the retina. There, three different types of cones sense different parts of the visible spectrum—to light that we sense as red, green, and blue. This three-receptor explanation for color vision is known as the **trichromatic theory,** and for a time it was considered to account for color vision completely. We now know that the trichromatic theory best explains the initial stages of color vision in the cone cells.

■ **Electromagnetic spectrum**
The entire range of electromagnetic energy, including radio waves, X rays, microwaves, and visible light.

■ **Visible spectrum**   The tiny part of the electromagnetic spectrum to which our eyes are sensitive. The visible spectrum of other creatures may be slightly different from our own.

■ **Trichromatic theory**   The idea that colors are sensed by three different types of cones sensitive to light in the red, blue, and green wavelengths. The trichromatic theory explains the earliest stage of color sensation.

● **FIGURE 5.5**   The Electromagnetic Spectrum

The only difference between visible light and other forms of electromagnetic energy is *wavelength*. (*Source:* Fig. 2.1, p. 27, "The Electromagnetic Spectrum," from PERCEPTION 3rd ed. by Sekuler & Blake. Copyright © 1994. Reprinted by permission of The McGraw-Hill Companies.)

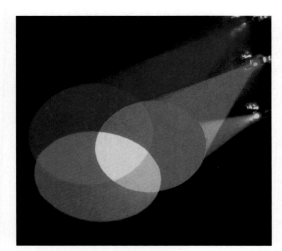

The combination of any two unique hues yields the complement of a third color. The combination of all three wavelengths produces white light, as does the combination of two complementary colors.

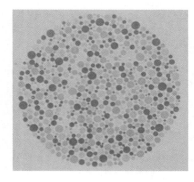

● **FIGURE 5.6** The Ishihani Color Blindness Test

Someone who cannot discriminate between red and green hues will not be able to identify the number hidden in the figure. What do you see? If you see the number 15 in the dot pattern, your color vision is probably normal.

■ **Opponent-process theory** The idea that cells in the visual system process colors in complementary pairs, such as red or green or as yellow or blue. The opponent-process theory explains color sensation from the bipolar cells onward in the visual system.

■ **Afterimages** Sensations that linger after the stimulus is removed. Most visual afterimages are *negative afterimages,* which appear in reversed colors.

■ **Color blindness** Typically a genetic disorder (although sometimes the result of trauma, as in the case of Jonathan) that prevents an individual from discriminating certain colors. The most common form is red–green color blindness.

Another explanation, called the **opponent–process theory,** better explains some cases of color blindness, as well as negative **afterimages** (see the "Do It Yourself!" box on p. 190)—both of which involve *opponent,* or complementary, colors. According to the opponent-process theory, from the bipolar cells onward the visual system processes colors in either-or complementary pairs, such as red or green or as yellow or blue. In all subsequent layers of the visual system, then, the sensation of a certain color, such as red, inhibits the sensation of its complement, green. Taken together, the two theories explain color vision: The trichromatic theory explains color processing in the cones, while the opponent-process theory explains what happens in the bipolar cells and beyond.

Color Blindness Not everyone sees colors in the same way, because some people are born with a color deficiency. At the extreme, complete **color blindness** is the total inability to distinguish colors. More commonly people merely have a color weakness that causes minor problems in distinguishing colors, especially under low-light conditions. People with one form of color weakness can't distinguish pale colors, such as pink or tan. Most color weakness or blindness, however, involves a problem in distinguishing red from green, especially at weak saturations. Those who confuse yellows and blues are rare, about one or two people per thousand. Rarest of all are those who see no color at all and see only variations in brightness. In fact, only about 500 cases of this total color blindness have ever been reported—including Jonathan I., whom we met at the beginning of this chapter. To see whether you have a major color deficiency, look at Figure 5.6 and note what you see. If you see the number 15 in the dot pattern, your color vision is probably normal. If you see something else, you are probably at least partially color blind.

Hearing: If a Tree Falls in the Forest . . .

Imagine how your world would change if your ability to hear were suddenly diminished. You would quickly realize that hearing, like vision, provides you with the ability to locate objects in space, such as the source of a voice calling your name. In fact, hearing may be even more important than vision in orienting us toward distant events. We often hear things, such as footsteps coming up behind us, before we see the source of the sounds. Hearing may also tell us of events that we cannot see, including speech, music, or a car approaching from behind.

But there is more to hearing than its *function.* Accordingly, we will look a little deeper to learn *how* we hear. Specifically, in the next few pages we will review what sensory psychologists have discovered about how sound waves are produced, how they are sensed, and how these sensations of sound are interpreted.

The Physics of Sound: How Sound Waves Are Produced Those Hollywood explosions of spaceships or planets should be absolutely silent! On Earth, the vibrational energy of vibrating objects, such as guitar strings, bells, and vocal cords, transfers to the surrounding medium—usually air—as the vibrating objects push the molecules of the medium back and forth. The resulting changes in pressure spread outward in the form of sound waves that can travel 1100 feet per second in air. In space, however, there is no air or other medium to carry the sound wave, so if you were a witness to a planetary disaster, the experience would be eerily without sound.

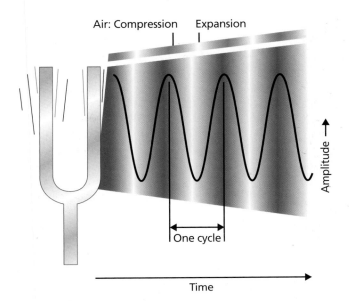

Air: Compression   Expansion

One cycle

Amplitude →

Time

● **FIGURE 5.7** Sound Waves
Sound waves produced by the vibration of a
tuning fork create waves of compressed and
expanded air. The pitch that we hear depends
on the *frequency* of the wave (the number of
cycles per second). High pitches are the result
of high-frequency waves. The *amplitude* or
strength of a sound wave depends on how
strongly the air is affected. In this diagram,
amplitude is represented by the height of
the graph.

Back here on Earth, the purest tones are made by a tuning fork (see Figure 5.7). When struck, a tuning fork produces an extremely simple sound wave that has only two characteristics: *frequency* and *amplitude*. These are the two physical properties of any sound wave that determine how it will be sensed by the brain. **Frequency** refers to the number of vibrations or cycles the wave completes in a given amount of time; it is usually expressed in *cycles per second (cps)* or *hertz (Hz)*. **Amplitude** measures the physical strength of the sound wave (shown in its peak-to-valley height); it is defined in units of sound pressure or energy. When you turn down the volume on your stereo, you are decreasing the amplitude of the sound waves.

Sensing Sounds: How We Hear Sound Waves   Much like vision, the psychological sensation of sound requires that waves be transduced into neural impulses and sent to the brain. This happens in four steps:

1. *Airborne sound waves must be relayed to the inner ear*. In this initial transformation, vibrating waves of air enter the outer ear (also called the *pinna*) and strike the *eardrum,* or **tympanic membrane** (see Figure 5.8). This tightly stretched sheet of tissue transmits the vibrations to three tiny bones: the *hammer, anvil,* and *stirrup,* named for their shapes. These bones immediately pass the vibrations on to the primary organ of hearing, the **cochlea,** located in the inner ear.

2. *The cochlea focuses the vibrations on the basilar membrane*. Here in the cochlea, the formerly airborne sound wave becomes "seaborne," because the coiled tube of the cochlea is filled with fluid. As the bony stirrup vibrates against the oval window at the base of the cochlea, the vibrations set the fluid into wave motion, working on the same principle as a submarine sending a sonar "ping" through the water. In turn, the fluid wave spreads through the cochlea, causing a sympathetic vibration in the **basilar membrane,** a thin strip of tissue running through the cochlea.

3. *The basilar membrane converts the vibrations into neural messages*. The swaying of tiny hair cells on the vibrating basilar membrane (much like the swaying of buildings during an earthquake) stimulates sensory nerve endings connected to the hair cells. The excited neurons, then, transform the mechanical vibrations of the basilar membrane into neural activity.

■ **Frequency**   The number of cycles completed by a wave in a given amount of time, usually a second.
■ **Amplitude**   The physical strength of a wave. This is usually measured from peak (top) to valley (bottom) on a graph of the wave.
■ **Tympanic membrane**   The eardrum.
■ **Cochlea**   The primary organ of hearing; a coiled tube in the inner ear, where sound waves are transduced into nerve messages.
■ **Basilar membrane**   A thin strip of tissue sensitive to vibrations in the cochlea. The basilar membrane contains hair cells connected to neurons. When a sound wave causes the hair cells to vibrate, the associated neurons become excited. As a result, the sound waves are converted (transduced) into nerve activity.

● **FIGURE 5.8** Structures Of The Human Ear

Sound waves are channeled by the outer ear (*pinna*) through the external canal, causing the tympanic membrane to vibrate. The vibration activates the tiny bones in the middle ear (*hammer, anvil,* and *stirrup*). These mechanical vibrations pass from the oval window to the cochlea, where they set internal fluid in motion. The fluid movement stimulates tiny hair cells along the basilar membrane, inside the cochlea, to transmit neural impulses from the ear to the brain along the auditory nerve.

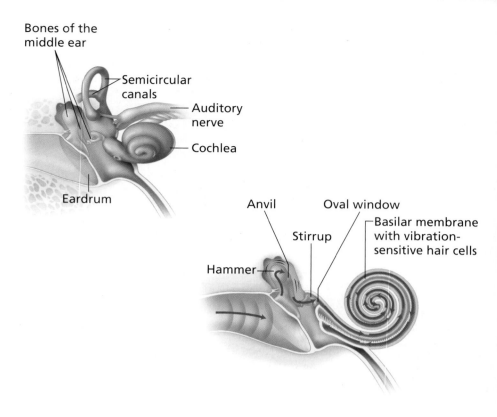

◀ **CONNECTION: CHAPTER 2**

The auditory cortex lies in the brain's *temporal lobes.*

■ **Pitch**   A sensory characteristic of sound produced by the *frequency* of the sound wave.

4. *Finally, the neural messages travel to the auditory cortex in the brain.* Neural signals leave the cochlea in a bundle of neurons called the *auditory nerve.* The neurons from the two ears meet in the brain stem, which passes the auditory information to both sides of the brain. Ultimately, the signals arrive in the *auditory cortex* for higher-order processing.

If the auditory system seems complicated, you might think of it as a sensory "relay team." Sound waves are first funneled in by the outer ear, then handed off from the tissue of the eardrum to bones in the middle ear. Mechanical vibrations of these bones are then passed to the cochlea and basilar membrane, where they finally become neural signals, which are, in turn, passed along to the brain. This series of steps transforms commonplace vibrations into experiences as exquisite and varied as music, doorbells, whispers, shouts, and psychology lectures.

Psychological Qualities of Sound: How We Distinguish One Sound from Another   No matter where they come from, sounds have only three sensory qualities: *pitch, loudness,* and *timbre.* In the following discussion, we will show you how the two *physical* characteristics of a sound wave (frequency and amplitude) manage to produce these three *psychological sensations.*

Sensations of Pitch   A sound wave's *frequency* determines the highness or lowness of a sound—a quality known as **pitch.** High frequencies produce high pitch, and low frequencies produce low pitch, as you see in Table 5.3. As with light, our sensitivity to sound spans only a limited range of the sound waves that occur in nature. The range of human auditory sensitivity extends from

	TABLE 5.3	Auditory Stimulation Becomes Sensation	

Physical stimulation	Waveform	Psychological sensation
Amplitude (intensity)	Loud ——————— Soft	Loudness
Frequency (wavelength)	Low ——————— High	Pitch
Complexity	Pure ——————— Rich	Timbre

Pitch and loudness are the psychological counterparts of the frequency and amplitude (intensity) of a sound wave. Frequency and amplitude are characteristics of the physical sound wave, while sensations of pitch and loudness exist only in the brain. In addition, sound waves can be complex combinations of simpler waves. Psychologically, we experience this complexity as *timbre*. Compare this table with Table 5.2 for vision.

frequencies as low as 20 cps (the lowest range of a subwoofer in a good sound system) to frequencies as high as 20,000 cps (produced by the high-frequency tweeter in your sound system). Other creatures can hear sounds both higher (in dogs, for example) and lower (in elephants) than we can.

How does the auditory apparatus produce sensations of pitch? Two distinct auditory processes share the task, affording us much greater sensory precision than either could provide alone. Here's what happens:

- When sound waves pass through the inner ear, the basilar membrane vibrates (see Figure 5.8). Different frequencies activate different locations on the membrane. Thus, the pitch one hears depends, in part, on which region of the basilar membrane receives the greatest stimulation. This explanation of pitch perception, known as the *place theory*, says that different *places* on the basilar membrane send neural codes for different pitches to the auditory cortex of the brain—much as keys on different places on a piano keyboard can produce different notes. It turns out that the place theory accounts for our ability to hear high tones—above about 1000 Hz (cycles per second).

- Neurons on the basilar membrane respond with different firing rates for different sound wave frequencies, much as guitar strings vibrating at different frequencies produce different notes. And so, the rate of firing provides another code for pitch perception in the brain. This *frequency theory* explains how the basilar membrane deals with frequencies below about 5000 Hz. (Between 1000 and 5000 Hz, hearing is based on both place and frequency.)

Why is there overlap in the processes described by these two theories—specifically for sounds within the range of 1000 to 5000 Hz? Simple. This is the range of human speech, and our hearing has evolved two different ways of making sure that we are especially sensitive to sounds in this range. And,

● **FIGURE 5.9** Intensities of Familiar Sounds

Figure scale (decibel levels):

180 — Rocket launch (from 150 ft)
140 — Jet plane take off (from 80 ft)
130 — Threshold of pain
120 — Loud thunder; rock band
— Twin-engine airplane take off
100 — Inside subway train
— Hearing loss with prolonged exposure
80 — Inside noisy car
— Inside quiet car
60 — Normal conversation
— Normal office
40 — Quiet office
— Quiet room
20 — Soft whisper (5 ft)
0 — Absolute hearing threshold (for 1000-Hz tone)
dB Decibel level

■ **Loudness** A sensory characteristic of sound produced by the *amplitude* (intensity) of the sound wave.
■ **Timbre** The quality of a sound wave that derives from the wave's complexity (combination of pure tones). *Timbre* comes from the Greek word for "drum," as does the term *tympanic membrane*, or eardrum.
■ **Vestibular sense** The sense of body orientation with respect to gravity. The vestibular sense is closely associated with the inner ear and, in fact, is carried to the brain on a branch of the auditory nerve.
■ **Kinesthetic sense** The sense of body position and movement of body parts relative to each other (also called *kinesthesis*).

just to make sure, the auditory canal is shaped to amplify sounds within this speech range.

Sensations of Loudness The **loudness** of a sound is determined by its physical strength or *amplitude* (much as brightness is determined by the intensity of light). More intense sound waves (a shout) produce louder sounds (see Table 5.3), while we experience sound waves with small amplitudes (a whisper) as soft. Amplitude, then, refers to the physical sound wave, and loudness is a psychological sensation.

Because we can hear sound waves across a great range of intensity, the loudness of a sound is usually expressed as a ratio rather than an absolute amount. Specifically, sound intensity is measured in units called decibels (dB). Figure 5.9 shows the levels of some representative natural sounds in decibel units.

Sensations of Timbre The bark of a dog, a train whistle, the wail of an oboe, the clink of a spoon in a cup—all sound distinctively different, not just because they have different pitches or loudness but because they are peculiar mixtures of tones. In fact, most natural sound waves are mixtures rather than pure tones (see Figure 5.10). This complex quality of a sound wave is known as **timbre** (pronounced *TAM-b'r*). Timbre is the property that enables you to recognize a friend's voice on the phone or distinguish between the same song sung by different artists.

Now, with all this information about sound in mind, we are in a position to answer an ancient puzzle: If a tree falls in the forest and there is no ear there to hear it, is there a sound? Based on our knowledge of sensory psychology, we can emphatically say, "No." Even though a falling tree makes strong vibrations in the air, we now know that it produces no physical sound because *sound is not a physical phenomenon*. Rather, sound is a purely *psychological sensation* that requires an ear (and the rest of the auditory system) to produce it.

How Are Auditory and Visual Sensations Alike? Earlier we discussed how visual information is carried to the brain by the optic nerve in the form of neural impulses. Now, we find that, in a similar fashion, auditory information is also conveyed to the brain as neural signals—but by a different pathway. So, why do we "see" visual information and "hear" auditory information? As our Core Concept suggested, the answer lies in the region of the cortex receiving the neural message—not on some unique quality of the message itself. In brief, different regions of the brain, when activated, produce different sensations.

How the Other Senses Are Like Vision and Hearing

Of all our senses, vision and hearing have been studied the most. However, our survival and well-being depend on other senses, too. So, to conclude this discussion of sensation, we will briefly review the processes involved in our sense of body position and movement, smell, taste, the skin senses, and pain. (See Table 5.4.) You will note that each gives us information about a different aspect of our internal or external environment. Yet each operates on similar principles. Each transduces physical stimuli into neural activity, and each is more sensitive to change than to constant stimulation. And, as was the case with vision and hearing, each of these senses is distinguished by the type of information it extracts and by the specialized regions of the brain devoted to it. Finally, you will see two patterns emerging in the way the senses process information. First, as was the case with vision and hearing, the other senses also make use of only a fraction of the available stimulation. Second, you will find that the senses are built to be especially sensitive to *changes* in stimulation.

Position and Movement To act purposefully and gracefully, we need constant information about where our limbs and other body parts are in relation to each other and to objects in the environment. Without this knowledge, even our simplest actions would be hopelessly uncoordinated. (You have probably had just this experience when you tried to walk on a leg that had "gone to sleep.") The physical mechanisms that keep track of body position, movement, and balance actually consist of two different systems.

The **vestibular sense** is the body position sense that orients us with respect to gravity. It tells us how our bodies—especially our heads—are postured, whether straight, leaning, reclining, or upside down. The vestibular sense also tells us when we are moving or how our motion is changing. The receptors for this information are tiny hairs (much like those we found in the basilar membrane) in the *semicircular canals* of the inner ear (refer back to Figure 5.8). These hairs respond to our movements by detecting corresponding movements in the fluid of the semicircular canals. Disorders of this sense can cause extreme dizziness and disorientation.

The **kinesthetic sense,** the other sense of body position and movement, keeps track of body parts relative to each other. Your kinesthetic sense makes you aware of crossing your legs, for example, and tells you which hand is closer to the telephone when it rings. Kinesthesis provides constant sensory feedback about what the muscles in your body are doing during motor activities, such as whether to continue reaching for your cup of coffee or to stop before you knock it over (Turvey, 1996).

Receptors for kinesthesis reside in the joints, muscles, and tendons. These receptors, as well as those for the vestibular sense, connect to processing regions in the brain's parietal lobes—which help us make a sensory "map" of the spatial relationship among objects and events. This processing usually happens automatically and effortlessly, outside of conscious awareness, except when we are deliberately learning the movements for a new physical skill, such as swinging a golf club or playing an instrument.

Smell The sense of smell, or **olfaction,** involves a chain of biochemical events. First, odors (in the form of airborne chemical molecules) interact with receptor

● **FIGURE 5.10** Waveforms of Familiar Sounds

Each sound is a distinctive combination of several pure tones. (*Source:* From THE SCIENCE OF MUSICAL SOUNDS by D. C. Miller. Reprinted by permission of Case Western Reserve University.)

■ **Olfaction** The sense of smell.

TABLE 5.4	Fundamental Features of the Human Senses			
Sense	**Stimulus**	**Sense organ**	**Receptor**	**Sensation**
Vision	Light waves	Eye	Rods and cones of retina	Colors, brightness, patterns, motion, textures
Hearing	Sound waves	Ear	Hair cells of the basilar membrane	Pitch, loudness, timbre
Skin senses	External contact	Skin	Nerve endings in skin	Touch, warmth, cold
Smell	Volatile substances	Nose	Hair cells of olfactory epithelium	Odors (musky, flowery, burnt, minty, etc.)
Taste	Soluble substances	Tongue	Taste buds of tongue	Flavors (sweet, sour, salty, bitter)
Pain	Many intense or extreme stimuli: temperature, chemicals, mechanical stimuli, etc.	Net of pain fibers all over the body	Specialized pain receptors, overactive or abnormal neurons	Acute pain, chronic pain
Kinesthetic and vestibular senses	Body position, movement, and balance	Semicircular canals, skeletal muscles, joints, tendons	Hair cells in semicircular canals; neurons connected to skeletal muscles, joints, and tendons	Position of body parts in space

Frontal lobe of cerebrum	Olfactory bulb
Olfactory tract	Olfactory (I) nerves
Olfactory bulb	Connective tissue
Olfactory nerves	Axon
	Olfactory receptor cell
Olfactory epithelium	Dendrite
	Olfactory hair (cilium)
	Mucus layer
	Substance being smelled

A. View of skull   B. Enlarged aspect of olfactory receptors

● **FIGURE 5.11**   Receptors for Smell

(*Source:* From PSYCHOLOGY AND LIFE 15th ed. by P. G. Zimbardo and R. J. Gerrig. Copyright © 1999 by Pearson Education. Reprinted by permission of Allyn & Bacon, Boston, MA.)

proteins associated with specialized hairs in the nose (Axel, 1995; Buck & Axel, 1991; Mombaerts, 1999). The stimulated nerve cells associated with these hairs (much like the sensitive hairs we found in the inner ear) convey information about the stimulus to the brain's *olfactory bulbs*, where sensations of smell are realized. These olfactory bulbs can be found on the underside of the brain just below the frontal lobes (Mori et al., 1999). (See Figure 5.11.) Unlike all the other senses, smell signals are not relayed through the thalamus, suggesting that smell evolved earlier than the other senses.

In humans, olfaction has an intimate connection with memory: Certain smells, such as a favorite perfume, can evoke emotion-laden memories (Azar, 1998a; Holloway, 1999). Originally, however, smell was probably a system in primitive organisms for detecting and locating food (Moncrieff, 1951). Even today, smell remains a major factor in survival because it helps us detect and avoid potential sources of danger, such as decaying food.

In many animals, the sense of smell is used for communication. For example, insects such as ants and termites and vertebrates such as dogs and cats communicate with each other by secreting and detecting odorous signals called **pheromones**—especially to signal sexual receptivity, danger, territorial boundaries, and food sources. We humans seem to use the sense of smell primarily in conjunction with taste to seek and sample food, but some evidence exists to suggest that people may also use sexual pheromones as well as pheromones that help us identify family members by smell (Azar, 1998b; Filsinger & Fabes, 1985; Holden, 1996b).

Taste   Like smell, taste is a sense based on chemistry. But the similarity doesn't end there: The senses of taste and smell have a cooperative working relationship. Many of the subtle distinctions you may think of as flavors really come from odors. (Much of the "taste" of an onion is odor, not flavor.) You will also notice this when you have a cold, which makes food seem tasteless because your nasal passages are blocked and you can't smell the food.

■ **Pheromones**   Chemical signals released by organisms to communicate with other members of their species. Pheromones are often used by animals as sexual attractants. It is unclear whether or not humans employ pheromones.

Isolated in the laboratory, the sense of taste, or **gustation,** has long been known to have four main qualities: sweet, sour, bitter, and salty. Recently, however, researchers have identified a fifth taste quality called *umami* (Chaudhari et al., 2000). Umami is the flavor associated with monosodium glutamate (MSG), often used in Asian cuisine. It also occurs naturally in protein-rich foods, such as meat, seafood, and cheese.

The taste receptor cells are gathered in *taste buds,* located on the top and side of the tongue, where they can easily sample the molecules in our food and drink. These receptors cluster in small mucous-membrane projections called *papillae,* shown in Figure 5.12. Individuals vary in their sensitivity to taste sensations, a function of the density of these papillae on the tongue (Bartoshuk et al., 1994). Those with more taste buds for bitter flavors are "supertasters," who are more sensitive than regular tasters or extreme "nontasters," which accounts for supertasters' distaste for certain foods, such as broccoli or "diet" drinks. Supertasters also have a survival advantage, because most poisons are bitter (Bartoshuk, 1993).

A specialized nerve "hotline" carries nothing but taste messages to the brain. There taste is realized in a specialized region of the parietal lobe's somatosensory cortex. Conveniently for the brain, this area lies next to the patch of cortex that receives touch stimulation from the face (Gadsby, 2000).

Infants have heightened taste sensitivity, which is why you have probably never met a baby who wouldn't cringe at the bitter taste of lemon. This supersensitivity, however, decreases with age. As a result, many elderly people complain that food has lost its taste—which really means that they have lost much of their sensory ability to detect differences in the taste and smell of food. Compounding this effect, taste receptors can be easily damaged by alcohol, smoke, acids, or hot foods. Fortunately, gustatory receptors are frequently replaced (as are the smell receptors). Because of this constant renewal, the taste system is the most resistant to permanent damage of all your senses, and a total loss of taste is extremely rare (Bartoshuk, 1990).

■ **Gustation** The sense of taste—from the same word root as "gusto"—also called the *gustatory sense.*

A. Top view of tongue

Papilla

B. Enlarged side view of papilla

Taste bud

C. Enlarged view of taste bud

Gustatory cell

● **FIGURE 5.12** Receptors for Taste

(A) Distribution of the papillae on the upper side of the tongue; (B) an enlarged view with individual papillae and taste buds visible; (C) one of the taste buds enlarged.

The Skin Senses Consider the skin's remarkable versatility: It protects us against surface injury, holds in body fluids, and helps regulate body temperature. The skin also contains nerve endings that, when stimulated by contact with external objects, produce sensations of touch, warmth, and cold. Like several other senses, these **skin senses** are connected to the somatosensory cortex located in the brain's parietal lobes.

The skin's sensitivity to stimulation varies tremendously over the body, depending in part on the number of receptors in each area. For example, we are ten times more accurate in sensing stimulation on our fingertips than stimulation on our backs. In general, our sensitivity is greatest where we need it most—on our faces, tongues, and hands. Precise sensory feedback from these parts of the body permits effective eating, speaking, and grasping.

One aspect of skin sensitivity—touch—plays a central role in human relationships. Through touch we communicate our desire to give or receive comfort, support, love, and passion (Fisher, 1992; Harlow, 1965; Masters & Johnson, 1966). Touch also serves as a primary stimulus for sexual arousal in humans. And it is essential for healthy mental and physical development; the lack of touch stimulation can stunt mental and motor development (Anand & Scalzo, 2000; Field & Schanberg, 1990; Spitz, 1946).

 PSYCHOLOGY IN YOUR LIFE: THE EXPERIENCE OF PAIN

If you are in severe pain, nothing else matters. A wound or a toothache can dominate all other sensations. And if you are among the one-third of Americans who suffer from persistent or recurring pain, the experience can be debilitating and can sometimes even lead to suicide (Wallis, 1984). Yet pain is also part of your body's adaptive mechanism that makes you respond to conditions that threaten damage to your body.

Unlike other sensations, pain can arise from intense stimulation of various kinds, such as a very loud sound, heavy pressure, a pinprick, or an extremely bright light. But pain is not merely the result of stimulation. Many people who were born without a limb or have had a limb amputated feel painful sensations that seem to come from the missing part, often called a *phantom limb* (Ramachandran & Blakeslee, 1998). Neurological studies show that the painful phantom sensations do not originate in damaged nerves in the sensory pathways. Rather, the sensations arise in the brain itself. To understand pain, then, we must understand not only painful sensations but mechanisms in the brain that both process and inhibit pain.

The Gate Control Theory No one has yet developed a theory that explains everything about pain, but Melzack and Wall's **gate-control theory** (1965, 1983) explains a lot. In particular it explains why pain can sometimes be blocked by analgesic drugs, competing stimuli, as in acupuncture, and even by the mere expectation of treatment effects. Their proposal asserts that pain depends on the relative amount of traffic in two different sensory pathways which carry information from the sense organs to the brain.

One route, consisting of neurons with a fatty myelin covering on their axons, handles messages quickly; these *fast fibers* deliver most sensory information to the brain. The smaller *slow fibers*, without the fatty sheaths on their axons, send messages more slowly. Very intense stimuli, such as that caused by tissue injury, send strong signals on the slow fibers.

Melzack and Wall hypothesize that competing messages from the fast fibers can block pain messages in the slow fibers. That is, the fast fibers can

■ **Skin senses** Sensory systems for processing touch, warmth, cold, texture, and pain.

■ **Gate-control theory** An explanation for pain control that proposes we have a neural "gate" that can, under some circumstances, block incoming pain signals.

close a sort of "spinal gate," preventing the slow fibers' messages from reaching the brain. Consequently, the level of pain you experience from a wound results from the combination of information coming through these two pathways. When you hit your finger with a hammer, you automatically try to close the "gate" by vigorously shaking your hand to generate fast-fiber signals that block the pain.

The "gate," itself, probably operates in a brain stem region called the *periaqueductal gray (PAG)*. The exact mechanism is unclear, but we do know that pain-blocking opiates and endorphins act on the PAG. There they cause inhibitory neurons to nullify pain messages ascending in the spinal cord (Basbaum et al., 1976; Basbaum & Fields, 1984; Pinel, 2003). Ultimately, pain signals that pass through the gate are routed to the *anterior cingulate cortex*, located along the fissure separating the frontal lobes, where we believe pain to be sensed (Craig & Reiman, 1996; Vogel, 1996).

The spinal gate can be operated top-down by psychological factors, as well. As noted above, we have long known that people's interpretations of events affect whether or not stimuli are perceived as painful (Turk, 1994). For example, soldiers and athletes often suffer severe injuries that cause little pain until the excitement of the battle or contest is over. As we will see in a moment, this mind–body effect on pain is also evident in the action of *placebos* or other sham treatments.

Dealing with Pain Wouldn't it be nice to banish the experience of pain altogether? In reality, such a condition can be deadly. People with congenital insensitivity to pain do not feel what is hurting them, and their bodies often become scarred and their limbs deformed from injuries they could have avoided if their brains were able to warn them of danger. Because of their failure to notice and respond to tissue-damaging stimuli, these people tend to die young (Manfredi et al., 1981). In general, pain serves as an essential defense signal: It warns us of potential harm, and it helps us to survive in hostile environments and to get treatment for sickness and injury.

What can you do if you are in pain? Analgesic drugs, ranging from over-the-counter remedies, such as aspirin and ibuprofen, to prescription narcotics, such as morphine, are widely used and effective. These act in a variety of ways. We have seen that morphine, for example, mimics your body's own pain control substances, the endorphins.

All such drugs—especially the narcotics—can have unwanted side effects. These include addiction or damage to the digestive tract. But, to dispel an old concern, studies have shown that if you must use narcotics to control severe pain, the possibility of your becoming addicted is far less than it would be if you were using narcotics recreationally (Melzack, 1990).

Many people can also learn to control pain by psychological techniques, such as hypnosis, deep relaxation, and thought-distraction procedures (Brown, 1998). You also may be among those for whom pain can also be modified by *placebos*, mock drugs made to appear as real drugs. For example, a placebo may be an injection of mild saline solution (salt water) or a pill made of sugar. Such fake drugs are routinely given to a control group in tests of new pain drugs. Their effectiveness, of course, involves the people's *belief* that they are getting real medicine. It is important to note, however, that the brain's response to a placebo seems to be essentially the same as that of pain-relieving drugs. Because this **placebo effect** is common, any drug deemed effective must prove itself stronger than a placebo.

But how do placebos produce their effects? Apparently the expectation of pain relief is enough to cause the brain to release painkilling endorphins. We believe this is so because brain scans show essentially the same

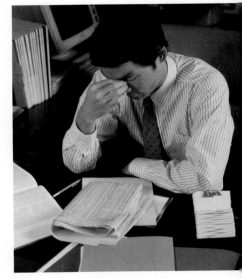

● Pain is affected by experience and circumstance. A person who is unhappy may find the pain of a headache unbearable while another individual, in a more satisfactory job, considers a headache merely annoying.

■ **Placebo effect** A response to a placebo (a fake drug), caused by subjects' belief that they are taking real drugs.

pain-suppression areas "light up" when patients take placebos or analgesic drugs (Petrovic et al., 2002). Further, we find that individuals who respond to placebos report that their pain increases when they take the endorphin-blocking drug, *naltrexone* (Fields, 1978; Fields & Levine, 1984). It is likely that endorphins are responsible for the pain-relieving effects of acupuncture (Price et al., 1984; Watkins & Mayer, 1982).

Pain Tolerance   The threshold of pain varies enormously from person to person. One study, for example, found that electric shocks had to be eight times more powerful to produce painful sensations in their least-sensitive subjects as compared with their most-sensitive subjects (Rollman & Harris, 1987). Another experiment found that brain scans of people who are highly sensitive to pain show greater activation of the thalamus and the anterior cingulate cortex than in scans of those with greater pain tolerance (Coghill et al., 2003). These findings may explain why some people always demand Novocain at the dentist, while others may prefer dental work without the added hassle of an injection.

CHECK YOUR UNDERSTANDING

1. **RECALL:** The eyes have two distinct types of photoreceptors: the *rods,* which detect _____, and the *cones,* which detect _____.
   a. low-intensity light/wavelengths corresponding to colors
   b. motion/shape
   c. bright light/dim light
   d. stimuli in consciousness/stimuli outside of consciousness

2. **RECALL:** The *wavelength* of light causes sensations of _____, while the intensity of light causes sensations of _____.
   a. motion/shape
   b. color/brightness
   c. primary colors/secondary colors
   d. depth/color

3. **RECALL:** The *frequency theory* best explains _____ sounds, while the place theory best explains _____ sounds.
   a. low-pitched/high-pitched
   b. loud/soft
   c. pitch/timbre
   d. simple/complex

4. **RECALL:** Which sense makes use of electromagnetic energy?
   a. hearing   c. pain
   b. taste   d. vision

5. **SYNTHESIS:** What do all of these forms of sensation have in common: vision, hearing, taste, smell, hearing, pain, equilibrium, and body position?
   a. They all arise from stimulation that comes only from outside the body.
   b. They all involve location of stimulation in three-dimensional space.
   c. They all are conveyed to the brain in the form of nerve signals.
   d. They all involve waves having frequency and amplitude.

6. **UNDERSTANDING THE CORE CONCEPT:** Different senses give us different sensations mainly because
   a. they involve different stimuli.
   b. they activate different sensory regions of the brain.
   c. they have different intensities.
   d. we have different memories associated with them.

ANSWERS: 1.a 2.b 3.a 4.d 5.c 6.b

WHAT IS THE RELATIONSHIP BETWEEN SENSATION AND PERCEPTION?

So, we have described how sensory signals have been transduced and transmitted to specific regions of your brain for further processing as visual images, pain, odors, and other sensations. Then what? To understand what that sensory information means, you must enlist your brain's perceptual machinery.

Does a bitter taste mean poison? Does a red flag mean danger? Does a smile signify a friendly overture? The Core Concept of this section emphasizes this perceptual elaboration of sensory information:

Perception brings *meaning* to sensation, so perception produces an interpretation of the world, not a perfect representation of it.

In brief, we might say that the task of perception is to extract sensory input from the environment and organize it into stable, meaningful *percepts*. A **percept,** then, is what we perceive: It is not just a sensation but the associated meaning, as well. Not a simple task, perception must identify features of the world that are invariant (fixed and unchanging) by sorting through a continual flood of information. For example, as you move about the room, the sights in the environment create a rapidly changing, blurred sequence of images—yet you remain sure that it is you who are moving, while the objects around you remain stationary. As we study this complex process, we will first discuss how our perceptual apparatus usually manages to give us an accurate image of the world. Then we will look at some illusions and other instances in which perception apparently fails. Finally, we will examine some theories that attempt to identify the most fundamental principles at work behind the scenes in our perceptual processes.

● **FIGURE 5.13** Who Is This?

Perceptual processes help us recognize Tom Cruise by matching the stimulus to images in memory.

Perceptual Processing: Finding Meaning in Sensation

How does the sensory image of a person (such as the individual pictured in Figure 5.13) become the meaningful percept of someone you recognize? That is, how does mere sensation become an elaborate perception? In the following paragraphs, we will explore some of the physical and mental processes involved in forming perceptions. Let's begin with *feature detectors*—brain cells that operate on the front lines of perceptual processing.

Feature Detectors   To help us make perceptual judgments, our brains have specialized groups of cells dedicated to the detection of specific stimulus features, such as length, slant, color, and boundary (Heeger, 1994; Hubel & Wiesel, 1979; Kandel & Squire, 2000; Lettvin et al., 1959; Maunsell, 1995; Zeki, 1992). There is even a part of the occipital lobe containing cells that are especially sensitive to features of the human face (Carpenter, 1999). Perceptual psychologists call such cells **feature detectors.**

Despite our extensive knowledge of feature detectors, we still don't know exactly how the brain manages to combine (or "bind") the multiple features it detects into a single percept of, say, a face. Psychologists call this puzzle the **binding problem,** and it may be the deepest mystery of perceptual psychology (Kandel & Squire, 2000). Yet, a few pieces of this perceptual puzzle may already be in hand: In order to assemble (bind) these pieces into a meaningful percept, the brain apparently synchronizes the firing patterns in different groups of neurons that have each detected different features of an object—much as an orchestra conductor determines the tempo at which all members of the ensemble will play a musical piece (Barinaga, 1998b; Bower, 1998a; Schechter, 1996).

Bottom-Up and Top-Down Processing   Perception always involves taking sensory data into the system through receptors and sending it "upward" to the cortex, where a basic analysis, involving the feature detectors, is first performed to determine the characteristics of the stimulus: Is it moving? What color is it? Is it loud, sweet, painful, pleasant smelling, wet, hot . . . ? Often it is these characteristics that determine how we finally perceive an object or event, as when deciding which salsa we want at a Mexican restaurant.

■ **Percept**   The meaningful product of perception—often an image that has been associated with concepts, memories of events, emotions, and motives.
■ **Feature detectors**   Cells in the cortex that specialize in extracting certain features of a stimulus.
■ **Binding problem**   Refers to the process used by the brain to combine (or "bind") the results of many sensory operations into a single percept. This occurs, for example, when sensations of color, shape, boundary, and texture are combined to produce the percept of a person's face. No one knows exactly how the brain does this. Thus, the binding problem is one of the major unsolved mysteries in psychology.

Psychologists refer to this as **bottom-up processing.** It is also known as *stimulus-driven processing* because the resulting percept is determined, or "driven," by stimulus features. Other examples include following the motion of a ball, identifying the colors of a flag, and recognizing the sound of a bell. But bottom-up processing is not the only process at work.

A complementary process occurs simultaneously at the "top"—at the highest levels of the cerebral cortex. **Top-down processing** invokes a perceiver's goals, past experience, knowledge, expectations, memory, motivations, or cultural background in the interpretation of an object or event (see Nelson, 1993). You are doing top-down processing when you form a percept based on questions such as these: Will it satisfy my hunger? Is she liberal or conservative? Will that help me get my degree? Because this sort of thinking relies heavily on concepts in the perceiver's own mind, it is also known as *conceptually driven processing.* One more example may clarify what we mean: If you go grocery shopping when you are hungry, top-down processing will probably make you notice ready-to-eat snack foods much more than you would if you had just eaten.

Perceptual Constancies   We can illustrate another aspect of perception with yet another example of top-down processing. Suppose that you are looking at a door, such as the one pictured in Figure 5.14A. You "know" that the door is rectangular, even though your sensory image of it is distorted when you are not looking at it straight-on. Your brain automatically corrects the sensory distortion, so that you perceive the door as being rectangular, as in Figure 5.14B.

This ability to see an object as being the same shape from different angles or distances is just one example of a **perceptual constancy.** In fact, there are many kinds of perceptual constancies. These include *color constancy,* which allows us to see a flower as being the same color in the reddish light of sunset as in the white glare of midday. *Size constancy* allows us to perceive a person as the same size at different distances and also serves as a strong cue for depth perception. *Shape constancy* is responsible for our ability to see the door in Figure 5.14 as remaining rectangular from different angles. Together these constancies help us identify and track objects in a changing world.

■ **Bottom-up processing**   Perceptual analysis that emphasizes characteristics of the stimulus, rather than our concepts and expectations. "Bottom" refers to the stimulus, which occurs at step one of perceptual processing.

■ **Top-down processing**   Perceptual analysis that emphasizes the perceiver's expectations, concept memories, and other cognitive factors, rather than being driven by the characteristics of the stimulus. "Top" refers to a mental set in the brain—which stands at the "top" of the perceptual processing system.

■ **Perceptual constancy**   The ability to recognize the same object as remaining "constant" under different conditions, such as changes in illumination, distance, or location.

● **FIGURE 5.14**   A Door by Any Other Shape Is Still a Door

(A) A door seen from an angle presents the eye with a distorted rectangle image. (B) The brain perceives the door as rectangular.

   (A)   (B)

Perceptual Ambiguity and Distortion

A primary goal of perception is to get an accurate "fix" on the world—to recognize friends, foes, opportunities, and dangers. Survival sometimes depends on accurately perceiving the environment, but the environment is not always easy to "read." We can illustrate this difficulty with the photo of black and white splotches in Figure 5.15. What is it? When you eventually extract the stimulus figure from the background, you will see it as a Dalmatian dog walking to the left with its head down. The dog is hard to find because it blends so easily with the background. The same problem occurs when you try to single out a voice against the background of a noisy party.

But it is not just the inability to find an image that causes perceptual problems. Sometimes our perceptions can be wildly inaccurate because we misinterpret an image. This is a common response to stimulus patterns known as *illusions.*

What Illusions Tell Us about Sensation and Perception When your mind deceives you by interpreting a stimulus pattern in a manner that is demonstrably incorrect, you are experiencing an **illusion.** Typically, illusions become more likely when the stimulus is unclear, when information is missing, when elements are combined in unusual ways, or when familiar patterns are not apparent. Such illusions can help us understand some fundamental properties of sensation and perception—particularly the discrepancy between our percepts and external reality (Cohen & Girgus, 1978).

Let's first examine a remarkable illusion that works at the level of sensation: the black-and-white Hermann grid (Figure 5.16). As you stare at the center of the grid, note how dark, fuzzy spots appear at the intersections of the white bars. But when you focus on an intersection, the spot vanishes. Why? The answer lies in the way receptor cells in your visual pathways interact with each other. The firing of certain cells that are sensitive to light–dark boundaries inhibits the activity of adjacent cells that would otherwise detect the white grid lines. This inhibiting process makes you sense darker regions—the grayish areas—at the white intersections just outside your focus. Even though you know the squares in the Hermann grid are black and the lines are white, this knowledge cannot overcome the illusion, which operates at a more basic, sensory level.

To study illusions at the level of perception, psychologists may employ **ambiguous figures**—stimulus patterns that can be interpreted (top-down) in

■ **Illusion** You have experienced an illusion when you have a demonstrably incorrect perception of a stimulus pattern, especially one which also fools others who are observing the same stimulus. (If no one else sees it the way you do, you could be having a *delusion* or a *hallucination.* We'll take those terms up in a later chapter on mental disorder.)
■ **Ambiguous figures** Images that are capable of more than one interpretation. There is no "right" way to see an ambiguous figure.

● **FIGURE 5.15** An Ambiguous Picture
What is depicted here? The difficulty in seeing the figure lies in its similarity to the background.

● FIGURE 5.16 The Hermann Grid

Why do faint gray dots appear at the intersections of the grid? The illusion, which operates at the sensory level, is explained in the text. (*Source:* "The Hermann Grid" from FUNDAMENTALS OF SENSATON & PERCEPTION by M. W. Levine & J. Shefner. Reprinted by permission of Michael W. Levine.)

A.

Vase or faces?

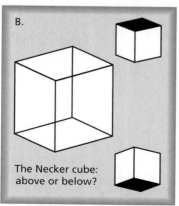

B.

The Necker cube: above or below?

● FIGURE 5.17 Perceptual Illusions

These *ambiguous figures* are illusions of perceptual interpretation.

two or more distinct ways, as in Figures 5.17A and B. Both the vase/faces figure and the Necker cube are designed to confound your interpretations, not just your sensations. Each suggests two conflicting meanings: Once you have seen both, your perception will cycle back and forth between them as you look at the figure. Studies suggest that these alternating interpretations involve the shifting of perceptual control between the left and right hemispheres of the brain (Gibbs, 2001).

Figure 5.18 shows several other illusions thought to operate primarily at the level of perception. All are compelling, and all are controversial—particularly the Müller–Lyer illusion, which has intrigued psychologists for more than 100 years. Disregarding the arrowheads, which of the two horizontal lines in this figure appears longer? If you measure them, you will see that the horizontal lines are exactly the same length. What is the explanation? Answers to that question have been offered in well over a thousand published studies, and psychologists still don't know for sure.

One popular theory, combining both top-down and bottom-up factors, has gathered some support. It suggests that we unconsciously interpret the Müller–Lyer figures as three-dimensional objects. So, instead of arrow heads, we see the ends as angles that project toward or away from us like the inside and outside corners of a building or a room, as in Figure 5.19. The inside corner seems to recede in the distance, while the outside corner appears to extend toward us. Therefore, we judge the outside corner to be closer—and shorter. Why? When two objects make the same size image on the retina and we judge one to be farther away than the other, then we assume that the more distant one is larger.

But what if you had grown up in a culture with no square-cornered buildings? Would you still see one line as longer than the other? In other words, do you have to *learn* to see the Müller–Lyer illusion, or is it "hard-wired" into your brain? The only way to answer such questions is through cross-cultural research. With this in mind, Richard Gregory (1977) went to South Africa to

A. Use a ruler to answer each question.

Which is larger: the brim or the top of the hat?

Top hat illusion

Is the diagonal line broken?

Poggendorf illusion

B. Which of the boxes are the same size as the standard box? Which are definitely smaller or larger? Measure them to discover a powerful illusory effect.

1.

2.

Which central circle is bigger?

Ebbinghaus illusion

Standard

Which horizontal line is longer?

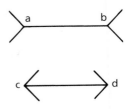

Müller–Lyer illusion

Are the vertical lines parallel?

Zöllner illusion

3.

4.

● **FIGURE 5.18** Five Illusions to Tease Your Brain

Each of these illusions involves a bad "bet" made by your brain. What explanations can you give for the distortion of reality that each of these illusions produces? Are they caused by nature or nurture?

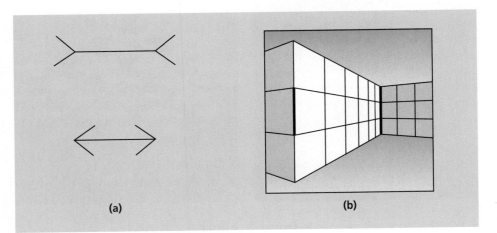

(a)　　　　　　　　　　(b)

● **FIGURE 5.19** The Müller–Lyer Illusion

One explanation for the Müller–Lyer illusion says that your brain thinks it is seeing the inside and outside corners of a building in perspective.

study a group of Zulus who live in what he called a "circular culture." Aesthetically, these people prefer curves to lines and square corners: Their round huts have round doors and windows; they till their fields along curved lines, using curved plows; the children's toys lack straight lines. And, when confronted with the Müller–Lyer, the Zulus saw the lines as nearly the same length. This suggests that the Müller–Lyer illusion is learned. A number of other studies support the conclusion that people who live in "carpentered" environments—where buildings are built with straight sides and 90-degree angles—are more susceptible to the illusion than those who (like the Zulus) live in "noncarpentered" worlds (Segall et al., 1966; Segall et al., 1990; Stewart, 1973).

Applying the Lessons of Illusions Several prominent modern artists, fascinated with the visual experiences created by ambiguity, have used perceptual illusion as a central artistic feature of their work. Consider the two examples of art shown here. *Gestalt Bleue* by Victor Vasarely (Figure 5.20) produces depth reversals like those in the Necker cube, with corners that alternately project and recede. In *Sky and Water* by M. C. Escher (Figure 5.21), you can see birds and fishes only through the process of figure–ground reversal, much like the vase/faces illusion we encountered earlier (in Figure 5.17). The effect of these paintings on us underscores the function of human perception to make sense of the world and to fix on the best interpretation we can make.

To make sense of such illusions, we draw on our personal experiences, learning, and motivation. Knowing this, those who understand the principles of perception often can control illusions to achieve desired effects far beyond the world of painting. Architects and interior designers, for example, create illusions that make spaces seem larger or smaller than they really are. They may, for example, make a small apartment appear more spacious when it is painted in light colors and sparsely furnished. Similarly, set and lighting designers in movies and theatrical productions purposely create visual illusions on film and on stage. So, too, do many of us make everyday use of illusion in our choices of cosmetics and clothing (Dackman, 1986). For example, light-colored clothing and horizontal stripes can make our bodies seem larger, while dark-colored clothing and vertical stripes can make our bodies seem slimmer. In these ways, we use illusions to distort "reality" and make our lives more pleasant.

● **FIGURE 5.20** Victor Vasarely's *Gestalt Bleue*

● **FIGURE 5.21** M. C. Escher's *Sky and Water*

Theoretical Explanations for Perception

The fact that perception is an interpretation and the fact that most people perceive illusions in essentially the same ways suggest that some fundamental psychological principles must be involved. Psychologists looking for these fundamental principles have formulated theories that explain how perception works. Below we will examine two of the classic explanations: the *Gestalt theory* of perception and *learning-based inference*. Although these two approaches may seem contradictory at first, they really emphasize complementary influences on perception. The Gestalt theory emphasizes how we organize incoming stimulation into meaningful perceptual patterns—because of the way our brains are innately structured. On the other hand, learning-based inference emphasizes learned influences on perception, including the power of expectations, context, and culture. In other words, Gestalt theory emphasizes nature, and learning-based inference emphasizes nurture. As you will see, we need both perspectives to understand the complexities of perception. Let's begin with Gestalt theory's view of the *nature* of perception.

CONNECTION: CHAPTER 4

The *nature–nurture* issue centers on the relative importance of heredity and environment.

Perceptual Organization: The Gestalt Theory You may have noticed that a series of blinking lights, perhaps on a theater marquee, can create the illusion of motion, where there really is no motion. Similarly, there appears to be a white triangle in the "Do It Yourself!" box below—but there *is* no white triangle. And, as we have seen, the Necker cube seems to flip back and forth between two alternative perspectives—but, of course, the flipping is all in your mind.

About 100 years ago, such perceptual tricks captured the interest of a group of German psychologists, who argued that the brain is innately wired to perceive not just stimuli by *patterns* in stimulation (Sharps & Wertheimer, 2000). They called such a pattern a *Gestalt*, the German word for "perceptual pattern" or "configuration." Thus, from the raw material of stimulation, the brain forms a perceptual whole that is more than the mere sum of its sensory

DO IT YOURSELF! | Figure Obscures Ground

The tendency to perceive a figure as being in front of a ground is strong. It is so strong, in fact, that you can even get this effect when the perceived figure doesn't actually exist! You can demonstrate this with an examination of the accompanying figure. You probably perceive a fir-tree shape against a ground of red circles on a white surface. But, of course, there is no fir-tree figure printed on the page; the figure consists only of three solid red shapes and a black-line base. You perceive the illusory white triangle in front because the wedge-shaped cuts in the red circles seem to be the corners of a solid white triangle. To see an illusory six-pointed star, look at part B. Here, the nonexistent "top" triangle appears to blot out parts of red circles and a black-lined triangle, when in fact none of these is depicted as such complete figures. Again, this demonstrates that we prefer to see the figure as an object that obscures the ground behind it. (That's why we often call the ground a "*back*ground.")

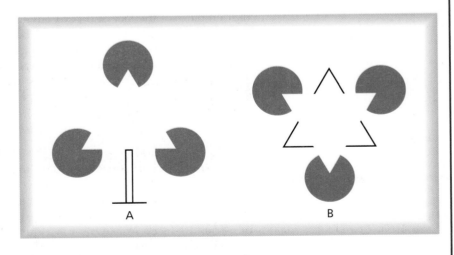

● Subjective Contours

(A) A subjective fir tree; (B) a subjective 6-pointed star.

CONNECTION: CHAPTER 1

Gestalt psychology was one of the historical schools that competed with behaviorism and structuralism.

parts (Prinzmetal, 1995; Rock & Palmer, 1990). This perspective became known as **Gestalt psychology.**

The Gestaltists pointed out that we perceive a square as a single figure, rather than merely four individual lines. Similarly, when you hear a familiar song, you do not focus on the individual notes. Rather, your brain extracts the melody, which is your perception of the overall *pattern* of notes. Such examples, the Gestalt psychologists argued, show that we always organize sensory information into meaningful patterns, the most basic of which are already present in our brains at birth. Because this approach has been so influential, we will examine some of the Gestalt discoveries in more detail.

● In *Weeping Woman,* Picasso challenges our perceptual assumptions by portraying a figure simultaneously from multiple perspectives.

Figure and Ground   One of the most basic of perceptual processes identified by Gestalt psychology divides our perceptual experience into *figure* and *ground*. A **figure** is simply a pattern, or Gestalt, that grabs our attention. Everything else becomes **ground,** the backdrop against which we perceive the figure. A melody becomes a figure heard against a background of complex harmonies, and a spicy pepperoni slice becomes a figure against the ground of cheese, sauce, and bread that make up a pizza. Visually, a figure could be a bright flashing sign or a word on the background of a page. And in the ambiguous faces/vase seen in Figure 5.17A, figure and ground reverse when the faces and vase alternately "pop out" as figure.

Closure: Filling in the Blanks   Our minds seem built to abhor a gap, as you saw in the "Do It Yourself!" box on page 211. Note especially the illusory white triangle—superimposed on red circles and black lines. Moreover, you will note that you have mentally divided the white area into two regions: the triangle and the background. Where this division occurs you perceive *subjective contours:* boundaries that exist not in the stimulus but only in the subjective experience of your mind.

Your perception of these illusory triangles demonstrates a second powerful organizing process identified by the Gestalt psychologists. **Closure** makes you see incomplete figures as wholes by supplying the missing segments, filling in gaps, and making inferences about potentially hidden objects. So, when you see a face peeking around a corner, your mind automatically fills in the hidden parts of the face and body. In general, humans have a natural tendency to perceive stimuli as complete and balanced even when pieces are missing. (Does this ring a _____ with you?) Closure is also responsible for filling in your "blind spot," as you saw on page 191 (Ramachandran, 1992).

In the foregoing demonstrations we have seen how the perception of subjective contours and closure derives from the brain's ability to create percepts out of incomplete stimulation. Now let us turn to the Gestalt laws that explain how we group the stimulus elements that are actually present into Gestalts.

■ **Gestalt psychology**   From a German word (pronounced *gush-TAWLT*) that means "whole" or "form" or "configuration." (A Gestalt is also a *percept.*) The Gestalt psychologists believed that much of perception is shaped by innate factors built into the brain.

■ **Figure**   The part of a pattern that commands attention. The figure stands out against the ground.

■ **Ground**   The part of a pattern that does not command attention; the background.

■ **Closure**   The Gestalt principle that identifies the tendency to fill in gaps in figures and to see incomplete figures as complete.

The Gestalt Laws of Perceptual Grouping   It's easy to see a school of fish as a single unit—as a Gestalt. But, how do we mentally combine hundreds of notes together and perceive them as a single melody? How do we combine the elements of color, shadow, form, texture, and boundary into the percept of a friend's face? And, why have thousands of people reported seeing "flying saucers" or the face of Jesus in the scorch marks on a tortilla? That is, how do we pull together in our minds the separate stimulus elements that seem to "belong" together? This is one of the most fundamental problems that the Gestalt psychologists addressed. As we will see, the Gestaltists made great strides in this area, but the basic processes by which perceptual organization works are still debated today (Palmer, 2002). (This problem is closely related to the *binding problem* that we discussed earlier.)

In the heyday of Gestalt psychology, of course, neuroscience was in its infancy, and there were no MRIs or PET scans. Hence, Gestalt psychologists, like Max Wertheimer (1923) had to focus on the problem of perceptual organization in a different way—with arrays of simple figures, such as you see in Figure 5.22. By varying a single factor and observing how it affected the way people perceived the structure of the array, he was able to formulate a set of **laws of perceptual grouping,** which he inferred were built into the neural fabric of the brain.

According to the **law of similarity,** we group things together that have a similar look (or sound, or feel, and so on). So, when you watch a football game, you use the colors of the uniforms to group the players into two teams because of their similarity, even when they are mixed together during a play. Likewise, in Figure 5.22A you see that the Xs and Os form distinct columns, rather than rows, because of similarity. Any such tendency to perceive things as belonging together because they share common features reflects the law of similarity. You can also hear the law of similarity echoed in the old proverb, "Birds of a feather flock together," which is a commentary not only on human and avian behavior but also on the assumptions we make about perceptual grouping.

Now, suppose that, on one drowsy morning, you mistakenly put on two different-colored socks because they were together in the drawer and you assumed that they were a pair. Your mistake was merely Wertheimer's **law of proximity** (nearness) at work. The proximity principle says that we group things together that are near each other, as you can see in the pairings of the Xs with the Os in Figure 5.22B. On the level of person perception, your parents were invoking the law of proximity when they cautioned you, "You're known by the company you keep."

The Gestalt **law of continuity** can be seen in Figure 5.22C, where the straight line is seen as a single, continuous line, even though it is cut repeatedly by the curved line. In general, the law of continuity says that we prefer smoothly connected and continuous figures to disjointed ones. Continuity also operates in the realm of person perception, where we commonly make the assumption of continuity in the personality of an individual whom we haven't seen for some

■ **Laws of perceptual grouping**
The Gestalt principles of similarity, proximity, continuity, and common fate. These "laws" suggest how our brains prefer to group stimulus elements together to form a percept (Gestalt).
■ **Law of similarity**   The Gestalt principle that we tend to group similar objects together in our perceptions.
■ **Law of proximity**   The Gestalt principle that we tend to group objects together when they are near each other. *Proximity* means *nearness.*
■ **Law of continuity**   The Gestalt principle that we prefer perceptions of connected and continuous figures to disconnected and disjointed ones.

● **FIGURE 5.22**   Gestalt Laws of Perceptual Grouping
(A) Similarity, (B) proximity (nearness), and (C) continuity. In (A) you most easily see the Xs grouped together, while Os form a separate Gestalt. So columns group together more easily than rows. The rows, made up of dissimilar elements, do not form patterns so easily. In (B) dissimilar elements easily group together when they are near each other. In (C), even though the lines cut each other into many discontinuous segments, it is easier to see just two lines—each of which appears to be continuous as a single line cutting through the figure.

FIGURE 5.23 A Bird in the . . .
We usually see what we expect to see—not what is really there. Look again.

time. So, despite interruptions in our contact with that person, we will expect to find him or her to be essentially the same person we knew earlier.

There is yet another form of perceptual grouping that we cannot easily illustrate in the pages of a book because it involves motion. But you can easily conjure up your own image that exemplifies the **law of common fate:** Imagine a school of fish, a gaggle of geese, a clowder of cats, or a simply a marching band. When visual elements (the individual fish, geese, cats, or band members) are moving together, you perceive them as a single Gestalt.

According to the Gestalt perspective, each of these examples of perceptual grouping illustrates the profound idea that our perceptions are influenced by innate patterns in the brain. These inborn mental processes, in a top-down fashion, determine the organization of the individual parts of the percept, just as mountains and valleys determine the course of a river. Moreover, the Gestalt psychologists suggested, the laws of perceptual grouping exemplify a more general principle known as the **law of Prägnanz** ("meaningfulness"). This principle states that we perceive the simplest pattern possible—the percept requiring the least mental effort. The most general of all the Gestalt principles, Prägnanz (pronounced *PRAYG-nonce*) has also been called the *minimum principle of perception.* The law of Prägnanz is what makes proofreading so hard to do, as you will find when you examine Figure 5.23. On the other hand, computers are not very good a perceiving patterns, a fact that is exploited by e-mail advertisers to get terms like *C*A*S*H* or *v.i.a.g.r.a* through your computer's "spam" filter undetected.

Apprehension about the "visual cliff" develops at about the same time an infant is learning to crawl.

The Nature of Depth Perception Are we born with the ability to perceive depth, or must we learn it? As we saw in our discussion of development in the previous chapter, depth perception appears early, although the idea of being cautious when there is danger of falling seems to develop later in infancy. In a famous demonstration, psychologists Eleanor Gibson and Richard Walk placed infants on a Plexiglas-topped table that appeared to drop off sharply on one end. (See the accompanying photo.) Reactions to the *visual cliff* occurred mainly in infants older than 6 months—old enough to crawl. Most readily crawled across the "shallow" side of the table, but they were reluctant to go over the "edge" of the visual cliff—indicating not only that they could perceive depth but that they associated the drop-off with danger (Gibson & Walk, 1960). Developmental psychologists believe that crawling and depth perception are linked in that crawling helps infants develop their understanding of the three-dimensional world.

Using another technique, Bower (1971) found evidence of depth perception in infants only 2 weeks old. By fitting his subjects with 3-D goggles Bower produced powerful "virtual reality" images of a ball moving about in space. When the ball image suddenly appeared to move directly toward the infant's face, the reaction was increased heart rate and obvious anxiety. This suggests that some ability for depth perception is probably inborn or heavily influenced by genetic programming that unfolds in the course of early development. Other depth cues must be learned, as we will see. The result is that everyday depth perception in older children and adults involves a combination of cues. Some of these are *binocular cues,* while others are *monocular cues.*

Binocular Cues Certain depth cues, the **binocular cues,** depend on the use of two eyes. You can demonstrate this to yourself: Hold one finger about 6 inches from your eyes and look at it. Now move it about a foot farther away. Do you

■ **Law of common fate** The Gestalt principle that we tend to group similar objects together that share a common motion or destination.

■ **Law of Prägnanz** The most general Gestalt principle, which states that the simplest organization, requiring the least cognitive effort, will emerge as the figure. *Prägnanz* shares a common root with *pregnant,* and so it carries the idea of a "fully developed figure." That is, our perceptual system prefers to see a fully developed Gestalt, such as a complete circle—as opposed to a broken circle.

■ **Binocular cues** Information taken in by both eyes that aids in depth perception, including binocular convergence and retinal disparity.

feel the change in your eye muscles as you focus at different distances? This feeling serves as one of the main cues for depth perception when looking at objects that are relatively close. The term for this, *binocular convergence,* suggests how the lines of vision from each eye converge at different angles on objects at different distances.

Another binocular depth cue, *retinal disparity,* arises from the difference in perspectives of the two eyes. To see how this works, hold a finger about 12 inches from your face and look at it alternately with one eye and then with the other. Notice how you see a different view of your finger with each eye. Because we see greater disparity when looking at nearby objects than we do when viewing distant objects, these image differences coming from each eye provide us with depth information.

Monocular Cues for Depth Perception Not all cues for depth perception require both eyes. A one-eyed pilot we know, who manages to perceive depth well enough to maneuver the airplane safely during takeoffs and landings, lives as proof that one-eye cues convey a great deal of depth information. Here are some of the **monocular cues** that a one-eyed pilot (or a two-eyed pilot, for that matter) could learn to use while flying:

- If two objects that are assumed to be the same size cast different-sized images on the retina, observers usually judge them to lie at different distances. So, a pilot flying low can learn to use the *relative size* of familiar objects on the ground as a cue for depth and distance. Because of this cue, automakers who install wide-angle rear-view mirrors always inscribe the warning on them, "Objects in the mirror are closer than they appear."

- Lighter-colored objects seem closer to us, and darker objects seem farther away. Thus, *light and shadow* work together as a distance cue. You will notice this the next time you drive your car at night, with the headlights on: Objects that reflect the most light appear to be nearer than more dimly lit objects in the distance.

- We assume that closer objects will cut off our vision of more distant objects behind them, a distance cue known as *interposition.* So, we know that partially hidden objects are more distant than the objects that hide them. You can see this effect right in front of you now, as your book partially obscures the background, which you judge to be farther away.

- As you move, objects at different distances appear to move through your field of vision at a different rate or with a different *relative motion.* Look for this one from your car window. Notice how the power poles or fence posts along the roadside appear to move by at great speed, while more distant objects stay in your field of view longer, appearing to move by more slowly. With this cue, pilots learn to set up a perfect glide path to landing by adjusting their descent so that the end of the runway appears to stay at a fixed spot on the windshield: More distant points appear to move upward, and everything nearer seems to move downward.

- Haze or fog makes objects in the distance look fuzzy, less distinct, or invisible, creating another learned distance cue called *atmospheric perspective.* In the accompanying photo you can see that more distant buildings lack clarity through the Los Angeles smog. At familiar airports most pilots have identified a landmark three miles away. If they cannot see the landmark, they know that they must fly on instruments.

● Air pollution has one useful feature: It provides atmospheric perspective, which helps dwellers in cities such as Los Angeles to judge distance. If you can see it clearly, it must be close!

■ **Monocular cues** Information about depth that relies on the input of just one eye—includes relative size, light and shadow, interposition, relative motion, and atmospheric perspective.

● Quickly scan this photo. Then look away and describe as much as you recall. Turn to page 219 to learn what you, or other perceivers, might not have seen.

Learning-Based Inference: The *Nurture* of Perception In 1866, Hermann von Helmholtz pointed out the important role of learning (or nurture) in perception. His theory of **learning-based inference** emphasized how people use prior learning to interpret new sensory information. Based on this learning, the observer makes *inferences*—guesses or predictions—about what the sensations mean. This theory explains, for example, why you infer a birthday party when you see lighted candles on a cake.

Ordinarily, such perceptual inferences are fairly accurate. On the other hand, we have seen that confusing sensations and ambiguous arrangements can create perceptual illusions and erroneous conclusions. Our perceptual interpretations are, in effect, hypotheses about our sensations. For example, babies learn to expect faces to have certain features in fixed arrangements (pair of eyes above nose, mouth below nose) and that expressions are most easily perceived in the right-side-up arrangement. In fact, we so thoroughly learn about faces in their usual orientation that we fail to "see" facial patterns that violate our expectations. When you look at the two inverted portraits of Britney Spears (Figure 5.24), do you detect any important differences between them? Turn the book upside down for a surprise.

What determines how successful we will be in forming an accurate percept? The most important factors include the *context*, our *expectations*, and our *perceptual set*. We will see that each of these involves a way of narrowing our search of the vast store of concepts in long-term memory.

Context and Expectations Once you identify a context, you form expectations about what persons, objects, and events you are likely to experience (Biederman, 1989). For example, you have probably had difficulty recognizing people you know in situations where you didn't expect to see them, such as in a different city or a new social group. This

● **FIGURE 5.24** Two Perspectives on Britney Spears

Although one of these photos clearly has been altered, they look similar when viewed this way. However, turn the book upside down and look again.

experience undoubtedly made you realize that it is much harder to recognize people outside their usual setting. The problem, of course, is not that they looked different but that the context was unusual: You didn't expect them to be there. Thus, perceptual identification depends on context and expectations as well as on an object's physical properties. To give a more immediate illustration of our expectations being influenced by the context, take a look at the following:

THE CAT

It says THE CAT, right? Now look again at the middle letter of each word. Physically, these two letters are exactly the same, yet you perceived the first as an H and the second as an A. Why? Clearly, your perception was affected by what you know about words in English. The context provided by T__E makes an H highly likely and an A unlikely, whereas the reverse is true of the context of C__T (Selfridge, 1955).

Although context can fool you into misperceiving some stimuli, as in this demonstration, context is an enormously useful cue to identify ambiguous stimuli, such as in recognizing objects in a dimly lit room or deciphering hard-to-read handwriting. So, if you receive a scenic postcard from a friend whose scrawled note describes "having a wonderful time on v____," you rely on context cues to guess that the V-word is probably vacation, and probably not any of the alternatives such as *video, Valium,* or *Venus!*

Perceptual Set Another way learning serves as a platform from which context and expectation exert an influence on perception involves **perceptual set.** Under the influence of perceptual set we have a readiness to notice and respond to certain stimulus cues—like a sprinter anticipating the starter's pistol. In general, perceptual set involves a focused alertness for a particular stimulus in a given context. For example, a new mother is set to hear the cries of her child. Likewise, if you drive a sporty red car, you probably know how the highway patrol has a perceptual set to notice speeding sporty red cars.

Often, a perceptual set leads you to transform an ambiguous stimulus into the one you were expecting. To experience this yourself, read quickly through the series of words that follow in both rows:

FOX; OWL; SNAKE; TURKEY; SWAN; D?CK

BOB; RAY; DAVE; BILL; TOM; D?CK

Notice how the words in the two rows lead you to read D?CK differently in each row. The meanings of the words read prior to the ambiguous stimulus create a perceptual set. Words that refer to animals create a perceptual set that influences you to read D?CK as "DUCK." Names create a perceptual set leading you to see D?CK as DICK. Yet another illustration of perceptual set appears in the "Do It Yourself!" box "You See What You're Set to See."

Cultural Influences on Perception Cross-cultural psychologists have pointed to other ways that learning influences perception (Deregowski, 1980; Kitayama et al., 2003; Segall, 1994; Segall et al., 1966). Consider, for example, the famous Ponzo illusion, shown in Figure 5.25. In your opinion, which bar is longer: the one on top (marked A) or the one on the bottom (marked B)?

■ **Learning-based inference** The view that perception is primarily shaped by learning (or experience), rather than by innate factors.

■ **Perceptual set** Readiness to detect a particular stimulus in a given context—as when a person who is afraid interprets an unfamiliar sound in the night as a threat.

Labels create a context that can impose a perceptual set for an ambiguous figure. Have a friend look carefully at the picture of the "young woman" in part A of the accompanying figure, and have another friend examine the "old woman" in part B. (Cover the other pictures while they do this.) Then, have them look together at part C. What do they see? Each will probably see something different, even though it's the same stimulus pattern. Prior exposure to the picture with a specific label will usually affect a person's perception of the ambiguous figure.

(A) Young woman

(B) Old woman

(C) Now what do you see?

● **FIGURE 5.25** The Ponzo Illusion

The two white bars superimposed on the railroad track are actually identical in length. Because A appears farther away than B, we perceive it as longer.

In actuality, both bars are the same length. (If you've developed a skeptical scientific attitude, you'll measure them!) Research shows, however, that responses to these figures depend strongly on culture-related experiences. Most readers of this book will report that the top bar is longer than the bottom bar, yet people from some cultural backgrounds are not so easily fooled. Why the difference?

The world you have grown up in probably included many structures featuring parallel lines that seemed to converge in the distance: long buildings, airport runways, and tunnels. You may even have stood on a straight railroad track and mused how the rails seem to meet at a faraway point. Psychologists call this *linear perspective* (which is yet another distance cue). Such experiences leave you vulnerable to images, such as the Ponzo illusion (Figure 5.25), in which cues for size and distance are unreliable.

But what about people from cultures where individuals have had far less experience with this cue for distance? Research on this issue has been carried out on the Pacific island of Guam, where there are no Ponzolike railroad tracks (Brislin, 1974, 1993). There, too, the roads are so winding that people have few opportunities to see roadsides "converge" in the distance. People who have spent their entire lives on Guam, then, presumably have fewer opportunities to learn the strong perceptual cue that converging lines indicate distance.

And, sure enough—just as researchers had predicted—people who had lived all their lives on the island of Guam were less influenced by the Ponzo illusion than were respondents from the mainland United States. That is, they were less likely to report that the top line in the figure was longer. These results strongly support the argument that people's experiences affect their perceptions—as Helmholz had theorized.

So, which of the two theories about perception that we have been discussing—Helmholtz's learning theory or the Gestaltists' innate theory—is correct? Both of them are. That is, our perceptual processes show the influence of both nature and nurture. While both theories emphasize top-down processes, Gestalt theory proposes that the brain is innately disposed to influence perception in specific ways. But we can also say with confidence that perception is influenced by experience and learning, as Helmholtz concluded.

PSYCHOLOGY IN YOUR LIFE: SEEING AND BELIEVING

If you assume, as most people do, that your senses give you an accurate and undistorted picture of the outside world, you are mistaken (Segall et al., 1990). Magicians, who base their careers on the difference between appearance and reality, count on fooling people for whom "seeing is believing." And you may have noticed that politicians and marketing experts rely on influencing people's interpretations of events, as well. So we hope that this chapter has shaken your faith in your senses and perceptions . . . just a bit.

Unlike magicians, politicians, and advertisers, perceptual psychologists are happy to reveal how sensation and perception play tricks on all of us (Hyman, 1989). They have developed a number of demonstrations that show how your vivid impressions of the world are really highly processed and interpreted images. We have already seen this in many visual illusions presented in the chapter. But, to drive the point home, consider this statement (which, unfortunately, was printed backwards):

.rat eht saw tac ehT

Please turn it around in your mind: What does it say? At first most people see a sensible sentence that says, "The cat saw the rat." But take another look. The difficulty lies in the power of expectations to shape your interpretation of stimulation.

This demonstration illustrates once again that we don't merely *sense* the world as it is, we *perceive* it. The goal of the process by which stimulation becomes sensation and, finally, perception is to find meaning in our experience. But it is well to remember that we impose our own meanings on sensory experience.

Differences in the ways we interpret our experiences explain why two people can look at the same sunset, the same presidential candidates, or the same religions and perceive them so differently. Perceptual differences make us unique individuals. An old Spanish proverb makes the point elegantly:

En este mundo traidor
No hay verdad ni mentira;
Todo es según el color
Del cristál con que se mira.

In this treacherous world
There is neither truth nor lie;
All is according to the color
Of the lens through which we spy.

Magicians count on the difference between appearance and reality.

● Did you see a woman committing suicide in the photo entitled "The Moment before Death" on page 216? Most people have difficulty identifying the falling woman in the center of the photo because of the confusing background and because they have no perceptual schema that makes them expect to see a person positioned horizontally in midair.

1. **RECALL:** Which of the following is an example of the kind of information that top-down processing contributes to perception?
   a. looking for a friend's face in a crowd
   b. having to wait for your eyes to adjust to the dark in a theater
   c. hearing a painfully loud noise
   d. feeling a pinprick

2. **RECALL:** The illusion in the Hermann grid (Figure 5.16) operates at the level of
   a. stimulation.
   b. sensation.
   c. figure and ground.
   d. perception.

3. **RECALL:** The Gestalt theory proposes that many of our perceptions are determined by
   a. bottom-up factors.
   b. illusions.
   c. ambiguity.
   d. innate factors.

4. **RECALL:** The faces/vase image (in Figure 5.17A) illustrates
   a. similarity.
   b. closure.
   c. figure and ground.
   d. attention as a gateway to consciousness.

5. **APPLICATION:** When two close friends are talking, other people may not be able to follow their conversation because it has many gaps, which the friends can mentally fill in from their shared experience. Which Gestalt principle is illustrated by the friends' ability to fill in these conversational gaps?
   a. similarity
   b. proximity
   c. closure
   d. common fate

6. **UNDERSTANDING THE CORE CONCEPT:** Which of the following best illustrates the idea that perception is not an exact internal copy of the world?
   a. the sound of a familiar tune
   b. the Ponzo illusion
   c. a bright light
   d. jumping in response to a pinprick

ANSWERS: 1.a 2.b 3.d 4.c 5.c 6.b

SENSATION AND PERCEPTION: THE STATE OF THE ART

After more than a century of study, the details of sensation are pretty well known. Perception, on the other hand, has its murky spots. The one great, indisputable finding of perceptual psychology is this: Perception is not a duplicate of reality. And its corollary is the fact that most people still believe that their senses and perceptions don't deceive them. In addition, we know many specifics about the psychology of perception, as identified by Helmholtz, the Gestalt psychologist, and others following in their traditions. It's in the basic neuroscience of perception where the great gaps in our knowledge occur. In particular, the binding problem—the puzzle of how stimulus features, memories, and emotions are combined into a single percept—remains one of psychology's deepest mysteries.

USING PSYCHOLOGY TO LEARN PSYCHOLOGY

Studying for the Gestalt

One of the most mistaken notions about studying and learning is that students should set aside a certain amount of time for study every day. This is not to suggest that you shouldn't study regularly. Rather, it is to say that you shouldn't focus on just putting in your time. So where should you place your emphasis? (And, what does this have to do with perceptual psychology?)

Recall the concept of *Gestalt,* the idea of the meaningful pattern, encountered in this chapter. The Gestalt psychologists taught that we have an innate tendency to understand our world in terms of meaningful patterns. Applied to your studying, this means that your emphasis should be on finding meaningful patterns—Gestalts—in your course work.

In this chapter, for example, you will find that your authors have helped you by dividing the material into three major sections. You can think of each section as a conceptual Gestalt, built around a Core Concept that ties it together and gives it meaning.

The psychological message is this: Organize your study around meaningful units of material. That is, identify a major concept or section of your book, and study that until it makes sense.

And forget about the clock.

CHAPTER SUMMARY

● HOW DOES STIMULATION BECOME SENSATION?

The most fundamental step in sensation involves the transduction by the sense organs of physical stimuli into neural messages, which are sent onward in the sensory pathways to the appropriate part of the brain for further processing. Sensory adaptation occurs when the senses discontinue processing unchanging stimuli.

Not all stimuli become sensations, because some fall below the absolute threshold. Further, changes in stimulation are noticed only if they exceed the difference threshold, making a just-noticeable difference (JND). Classical psychophysics focused on identifying thresholds for sensations and for just-noticeable differences, but a newer approach, called signal detection theory, explains sensation as a process involving context, physical sensitivity, and judgment. And while subliminal perception of stimuli near the absolute threshold is possible under certain conditions, there is no evidence that it has been—or could be—used successfully in the mass media.

● **The brain senses the world indirectly because the sense organs convert stimulation into the language of the nervous system: neural messages.**

● HOW ARE THE SENSES ALIKE? AND HOW ARE THEY DIFFERENT?

All the senses involve transduction of physical stimuli into nerve impulses. In vision, photoreceptors in the retina transduce light waves into neural codes, which retain frequency and amplitude information. This visual information is then transmitted by the optic nerve to the brain's occipital lobes, which converts the neural signals into sensations of color and brightness. Both the trichromatic theory and the opponent process theory are required to explain how visual sensations are extracted. Vision makes use of only a tiny "window" in the electromagnetic spectrum.

In the ear, sound waves in the air are transduced into neural energy in the cochlea and then sent on to the brain's temporal lobes, where frequency and amplitude information are converted to sensations of pitch, loudness, and timbre. Neither our sensations of light or sound are properties of the original stimulus but are creations of the brain.

Other senses include position and movement (the vestibular and kinesthetic senses), smell, taste, the skin senses (touch, pressure, and temperature), and pain. Like vision and hearing, these other senses are especially attuned to detect changes in stimulation. Further, all sensation is carried to the brain by neural impulses, but we experience different sensations because the impulses are processed by different sensory regions of the brain.

The experience of pain can be the result of intense stimulation in any of several sensory pathways. While we don't completely understand pain, the gate-control theory explains how pain can be suppressed by competing sensations or other mental processes. Similarly, the ideal analgesic—one without unwanted side effects—has not been discovered, although placebos work exceptionally well for some people.

● **The senses all operate in much the same way, but each extracts different information and sends it to its own specialized sensory processing region in the brain.**

● WHAT IS THE RELATIONSHIP BETWEEN SENSATION AND PERCEPTION?

There is no exact dividing line between sensation and perception, but psychologists define perception as the stage at which meaning is attached to sensation. We derive meaning from "bottom-up" stimulus cues picked up by feature detectors and from "top-down" processes, especially those involving expectations. What remains unclear is how the brain manages to combine the output of many sensory circuits into a single percept: This is called the binding problem.

By studying illusions and constancies, researchers can learn about the factors that influence and distort the construction of perceptions. Illusions demonstrate that perception does not necessarily form an accurate representation of the outside world.

Perception has been explained by theories that differ in their emphasis on the role of innate brain processes versus learning—nature versus nurture. The Gestalt theory emphasizes innate factors that help us organize stimulation into sensation. In particular, the Gestaltists have described the processes that help us distinguish figure from ground, to identify contours and apply closure, and to group stimuli according to similarity, proximity, continuity, and common fate. Some aspects of depth perception, such as retinal disparity and convergence, may be innate as well. The theory of learning-based inference also correctly points out that perception is influenced by experience, such as context, perceptual set, and culture. Many aspects of depth perception, such as relative motion and atmospheric perspective, seem to be learned.

Despite all we know about sensation and perception, many people uncritically accept the evidence of their senses (and perceptions) at face value. This allows magicians, politicians, and marketers an opening through which they can manipulate our perceptions and, ultimately, our behavior.

● Perception brings *meaning* to sensation, so perception produces an interpretation of the world, not a perfect representation of it.

REVIEW TEST

For each of the following items, choose the single correct or best answer. The correct answers appear at the end.

1. What is the process that converts physical energy, such as sound waves, into neural signals?
   a. sensory adaptation
   b. psychophysics
   c. kinesthesis
   d. transduction

2. Luisa agrees to look after her friends' new baby while they run an errand. Luisa tries to read with the stereo on but keeps listening for signs that the baby might be crying in the bedroom. Several times, Luisa thinks she can hear whimpering—but when she checks the baby, she usually finds her sound asleep. Which of the following best explains why Luisa's sensations are not always accurate?
   a. classical absolute threshold theory
   b. signal detection theory
   c. the law of Prägnanz
   d. Weber's law

3. Which of these sensory structures does not belong with the others?
   a. retina
   b. ganglion cells
   c. basilar membrane
   d. visual cortex

4. Place theory and frequency theory are explanations for processes involved in the sensation of
   a. the hue created by a light's wavelength.
   b. the timbre of sound.
   c. different olfactory stimuli.
   d. the pitch of sound.

5. Which one of the following is the only sense that does not relay information through the thalamus?
   a. olfaction
   b. kinesthesis
   c. the vestibular sense
   d. vision

6. At a crime scene, a detective finds a slip of paper with three symbols printed on it in ink. She cannot identify the source of the figures or which orientation is up. Thus she cannot determine if the figures are the numbers 771 or the letters

ILL. Because she has to guess at the meaning of the figures, her perception of them is
   a. data-driven.
   b. stimulus-driven.
   c. bottom-up.
   d. top-down.

7. Which one of the following is most commonly experienced when a stimulus is ambiguous, information is missing, elements are combined in unusual ways, or familiar patterns are not apparent?
   a. an illusion
   b. common fate
   c. a false alarm
   d. a correct rejection

8. According to Gestalt explanations of how perceptual processes work, when a person encounters an unfamiliar collection of stimuli, he or she will try to
   a. judge whether each stimulus matches a familiar signal.
   b. assemble the parts into a meaningful whole or pattern that makes sense.
   c. analyze each stimulus component separately to ascertain its meaning.
   d. make guesses about its symbolism until finding a matching concept.

9. Research has shown that cultural factors can influence people's perception of
   a. distance.
   b. timbre.
   c. sensory adaptation.
   d. subliminal stimulation.

10. Although the markings in the ceiling tiles are of all different shapes and sizes, you notice that larger, darker spots seem to stand out against a background made up of smaller, lighter ones. Which principle of perceptual grouping explains this distinction?
    a. the law of similarity
    b. the law of proximity
    c. the law of common fate
    d. the principle of closure

ANSWERS: 1.d 2.b 3.c 4.d 5.a 6.d 7.a 8.b 9.a 10.a

Sensation (p. 180)
Perception (p. 181)
Transduction (p. 182)
Sensory adaptation (p. 183)
Absolute threshold (p. 184)
Difference threshold (p. 184)
Just noticeable difference (JND) (p. 185)
Weber's law (p. 185)
Signal detection theory (p. 185)
Retina (p. 188)
Photoreceptors (p. 188)
Rods (p. 188)
Cones (p. 190)
Fovea (p. 190)
Optic nerve (p. 190)
Blind spot (p. 190)

Brightness (p. 191)
Color (p. 192)
Electromagnetic spectrum (p. 193)
Visible spectrum (p. 193)
Trichromatic theory (p. 193)
Opponent-process theory (p. 194)
Afterimages (p. 194)
Color blindness (p. 194)
Frequency (p. 195)
Amplitude (p. 195)
Tympanic membrane (p. 195)
Cochlea (p. 195)
Basilar membrane (p. 195)
Pitch (p. 196)
Loudness (p. 198)

Timbre (p. 198)
Vestibular sense (p. 199)
Kinesthetic sense (p. 199)
Olfaction (p. 199)
Pheromones (p. 200)
Gustation (p. 201)
Skin senses (p. 202)
Gate-control theory (p. 202)
Placebo effect (p. 203)
Percept (p. 205)
Feature detectors (p. 205)
Binding problem (p. 205)
Bottom-up processing (p. 206)
Top-down processing (p. 206)
Perceptual constancy (p. 206)
Illusion (p. 207)

Ambiguous figures (p. 207)
Gestalt psychology (p. 212)
Figure (p. 212)
Ground (p. 212)
Closure (p. 212)
Laws of perceptual grouping (p. 213)
Law of similarity (p. 213)
Law of proximity (p. 213)
Law of continuity (p. 213)
Law of common fate (p. 214)
Law of Prägnanz (p. 214)
Binocular cues (p. 214)
Monocular cues (p. 215)
Learning-based inference (p. 216)
Perceptual set (p. 217)

OUR RECOMMENDED BOOKS AND VIDEOS

BOOKS

Ackerman, D. (1990). *A natural history of the senses.* New York: Vintage. Poet Diane Ackerman's collection of essays discuss smell, touch, taste, hearing, vision, and synesthesia (experiencing a sensation in the "wrong" sense, such as feeling a color or seeing a sound). The book is vivid and inspiring as well as informative.

Cytowic, R. L. (1998). *The man who tasted shapes.* Cambridge, MA: MIT Press. One in 100,000 people experience *synesthesia,* a condition of blended sensory perceptions: Different tastes have distinctive shapes, musical notes have color and form. Better understood than ever before, synesthesia demonstrates the active exploration of the brain and the literally memorable experiences of synesthetes themselves.

Glaser, G. (2002). *The nose: A profile of sex, beauty, and survival.* New York: Pocket Books. Are there fragrances that take you back to your childhood, that remind you of romance, or warn you off novel foods? Most people have "smell stories," but little is known about this most primitive sense. Gabrielle Glaser's absorbing book examines the science, art, history, health, sex, and mythology of our sense of scent.

Jourdain, R. (1998). *Music, the brain, and ecstasy: How music captures our imagination.* New York: Avon Books. The author, a composer himself, examines the nature of sound, music, the experience of making and listening to music, and its links with emotional appeal, satisfaction, mood, and happiness.

Sacks, O. (1998). *The island of the colorblind.* New York: Vintage Books. The latest by the author of *The Man Who Mistook His Wife for a Hat* and *An Anthropologist on Mars,* this fascinating, touching, and funny book describes Sacks's journey to a small island in Micronesia, where all the residents are colorblind, yet experience and describe their world with richness, vividness, and acceptance.

Sheldrake, R. (2003). *The sense of being stared at: And other aspects of the extended mind.* New York: Crown Publishing. In a previous work, Rupert Sheldrake explored whether some dogs know when their owners are coming home. Here he extends his interest in supersensory awareness, examining people's claims of "knowing" when others are about to call them; parents' sensitivity to absent children's experiences; or, as the title suggests, our awareness of being watched and studied.

VIDEOS

Chocolat. (2000, color, 105 min., French). Directed by Lasse Hallström; starring Juliette Binoche, Alfred Molina, Judi Dench, Johnny Depp. The award-winning film is a feast not only for "chocaholics," but for anyone interested in how sensory pleasures are often feared and suppressed by controlling institutions and doctrines. A woman's dessert confections amaze and inspire her customers, while their sensory effects seem to threaten the local authorities.

Immortal Beloved. (1994, color, 125 min.). Directed by Bernard Rose; starring Gary Oldman, Jeroen Krabbe, Isabella Rossellini, Johanna Ter Steege. Ludwig van Beethoven's late-life deafness is explained in this musically rich biography, focusing on the question of the identity of the composer's great love. A few scenes are stunning both to watch and hear, a nice change from films with forgettable scores and soundtracks.

Rashomon. (1950, black-and-white, 88 min.; Japanese). Directed by Akira Kurosawa; starring Toshiro Mifune. A classic film by a master director, *Rashomon* tells the tale of a rape and murder from the perspectives of four very different witnesses, illustrating the intertwining of perception with motivation and emotion. What you see and remember is what you expect, based on your perception of the world—and of yourself.

Key Question / Chapter Outline

CORE CONCEPTS

Psychology in Your Life

What Sort of Learning Does Classical Conditioning Explain?

The Essentials of Classical Conditioning
Applications of Classical Conditioning

▼

Classical conditioning is a basic form of learning in which a stimulus that produces an innate reflex becomes associated with a previously neutral stimulus, which then acquires the power to elicit essentially the same response.

Taste Aversions and Chemotherapy

Your friend risks developing a food aversion when the medicine makes her feel sick.

How Do We Learn New Behaviors by Operant Conditioning?

Skinner's Radical Behaviorism
The Power of Reinforcement
The Problem of Punishment
Operant and Classical Conditioning Compared

▼

In operant conditioning, the consequences of behavior, such as rewards and punishments, influence the chance that the behavior will occur again.

A Checklist for Modifying Operant Behavior

For changing your own behavior or someone else's, a combination of reinforcement and extinction is usually the best bet.

How Does Cognitive Psychology Explain Learning?

Insight Learning: Köhler in the Canaries with the Chimps
Cognitive Maps: Tolman Finds Out What's on a Rat's Mind
Observational Learning: Bandura's Challenge to Behaviorism
Rethinking Behavioral Learning in Cognitive Terms
Brain Mechanisms and Learning
"Higher" Cognitive Learning

▼

According to cognitive psychology, some forms of learning must be explained as changes in mental processes, rather than as changes in behavior alone.

A Critical Look at "Learning Styles"

Many claims are made for different learning styles, but the evidence supporting them is weak.

Learning: The State of the Art

USING PSYCHOLOGY TO LEARN PSYCHOLOGY:
Operant Conditioning Can Help You Study More—and Enjoy It

Learning

SABRA HAD JUST GRADUATED from college, with a degree in graphic arts, and landed a good job at an advertising firm in San Francisco. The work was interesting and challenging, and Sabra enjoyed her new colleagues. The only negative was that her supervisor had asked her to attend an upcoming conference in Hawaii—and take an extra few days of vacation there at the company's expense. The problem was Sabra's fear of flying.

She hadn't had to deal with her fear previously because there was always an alternative. All her life, Sabra had lived close enough to family members that she could easily drive to visit them. And when she went away to college, it was only a 300-mile journey, so she could drive or take the train. But there was no other way to get to Hawaii (except by boat—which would be much too slow for commuting to a business conference). What was she to do?

A friend mentioned having seen an article in the newspaper about a program initiated by one of the airlines to help people overcome their fear of flying. Fortunately, Sabra had a few weeks before the conference started, so she contacted the airline and signed up for three weekend treatment sessions to be held at a local airport.

Sabra arrived at the appointed time, full of expectations and apprehensions—most of which turned out to be wrong. Would she have to see a therapist who would probe her childhood experiences and fantasies? Would they prescribe tranquilizers? Or would they give her some sort of terror-inducing treatment, such as flying upside-down in a small airplane?

In fact, the sessions were organized by a behavioral psychologist who gathered the nine participants in a small conference room. The therapist began by saying that such fears are learned—much as you might learn to cringe when you hear a dentist's drill or the scraping of fingernails on a blackboard. She said that it was not important how such fears got started. This fear-of-flying program would focus on the present, not on the past. Sabra began to feel more relaxed.

After a brief description of the learning-based therapy to be used, the group took a tour of the airport, including the cabin of a passenger jet parked on the Tarmac. Then they went back to "class" to learn the basics of how airplanes work and the physical forces that keep them in the air. The group also watched some videos involving routine flights in a commercial airplane. All in all, this first session went smoothly, and everyone seemed much more at ease than when they started.

The second weekend began with more classroom discussion. Then, the class went back into the airliner, where they took seats and went through a series of relaxation exercises led by the therapist. This training included deep breathing and progressive relaxation of specific muscle groups all over the body. When everyone in the group reported feeling relaxed, they again watched videos of flight on the plane's TV monitors. This was followed by more relaxation exercises. The final activity for the second weekend involved starting the engines and going through the preflight routine—all the way up to takeoff . . . and more relaxation exercises.

The final weekend session was almost identical to the previous one. The only difference was that the "graduation" exercise was an actual flight—a 20-minute trip out over the local countryside and back to the airport. It was, of course, voluntary, but only one of the nine people in the class chose not to go. Sabra went, but not without some anxiety. The therapist, however, encouraged the group to focus on the relaxation exercises they had learned, rather than on their feelings of fear. To the amazement of all who participated, these learning-based techniques helped them through the flight exercise without losing control of their emotional responses. Although no one's fear had vanished completely, everyone was able to bring it under control.

The happiest result was that Sabra was able to go to her meeting in Hawaii—where, by the way, she had a productive conference and a wonderful time. For our purposes we should also note that Sabra has flown several times since then, and she reports that each trip gets just a little easier—just as the psychology of learning would predict.

A Definition of Learning   The program that saved Sabra's job came out of research in *learning*—but not the sort of hit-the-books learning that usually comes to the minds of college students. Psychologists define **learning** broadly, as a process through which experience produces a lasting change in behavior or mental processes. According to this definition, then, Sabra's "flight training" was learning—just as much as taking golf lessons or reading this book are learning experiences.

To avoid confusion, two parts of our definition need some elaboration. First, we should underscore the idea that learning leads to a *lasting change* in behavior. Suppose that you go to your doctor's office and get a particularly unpleasant injection, during which the sight of the needle becomes associated with pain. As a result, the next time you need a shot, you wince when you first see the needle. This persistent change in responding involves learning. But, by the same standard, a simple, reflexive reaction, such as jumping when you hear an unexpected loud noise, does *not* qualify as learning because it produces no

■ **Learning** A lasting change in behavior or mental processes that results from experience.

lasting change—nothing more than a fleeting reaction, even though it does entail a change in behavior.

Second, we should elaborate on the part of the definition that says learning affects *behavior* or *mental processes*. In the doctor's office example above, it is easy to see how learning affects behavior. But mental processes are more difficult to observe. How could you tell, for example, whether a laboratory rat had simply learned the behaviors required to negotiate a maze (turn right, then left, then right . . .) or whether it was following some sort of mental image of the maze, much as you would follow a road map? (And why should we care what, if anything, was on a rat's mind?)

Behavioral Learning versus Cognitive Learning The problem of observing mental events, whether in rats or in people, underlies a long-running controversy between the behaviorists and the cognitive psychologists that threads through this chapter. For over 100 years, the behaviorists have maintained that psychology could be a true science only if it disregarded mental processes and focused exclusively on objective, observable stimuli and responses. On the other side of the issue, cognitive psychologists have contended that the behavioral view is far too limiting and that understanding learning requires that we make inferences about hidden mental processes. In the following pages, we will see that both sides in this dispute have made important contributions to our knowledge.

Learning versus Instincts So, what does learning—either behavioral or cognitive learning—do for us? Nearly every human activity, from working to playing to interacting with family and friends, involves some form of learning. Without learning, we would have no human language. We wouldn't know who our family or friends were. We would have no memory of our past or goals for our future. And without learning, we would be forced to rely on simple reflexes and a limited repertoire of innate behaviors, sometimes known as "instincts."

In contrast with learned responses, instinctive behavior (more properly known as *species-typical behavior*) is heavily influenced by genetic programming. It occurs in essentially the same way across different individuals in a species. We see instincts at work in bird migrations, animal courtship rituals, and a few human behavior patterns, such as nursing in newborns. All these examples involve responses that are influenced relatively little by experience, as compared to learned behaviors such as operating a computer, playing tennis, or wincing at the sight of a needle. In general, human behavior is much more influenced by learning and much less influenced by instincts than that of other animals. For us, learning confers the flexibility to adapt quickly to changing situations and new environments. In this sense, then, learning represents an evolutionary advance over instincts.

Simple and Complex Forms of Learning Some forms of learning can be quite simple. For example, if you live near a busy street, you may learn to ignore the sound of the traffic. This sort of learning, known as **habituation,** involves learning *not to respond* to stimulation. It occurs in all animals that have nervous systems, including insects and worms. Another relatively simple form of learning is seen most obviously in humans: a preference for stimuli to which we have been previously exposed—whether or not the stimulus was associated with something pleasurable or even whether we were aware of the stimulus. This **mere exposure effect** probably accounts for the effectiveness of much advertising (Terry, 2000; Zajonc, 1968, 2001).

Other kinds of learning can be more complex. One involves learning a connection between two stimuli—as when a school child associates the 12 o'clock

● Aversive conditioning has occurred when the mere sight of an object, such as a hypodermic needle, causes an avoidance reaction.

CONNECTION: CHAPTER 9

Instinct refers to motivated behaviors that have a strong innate basis.

■ **Habituation** Learning not to respond to the repeated presentation of a stimulus.
■ **Mere exposure effect** A learned preference for stimuli to which we have been previously exposed.

bell with lunch. And another occurs when we associate our actions with rewarding and punishing consequences, such as praise or a reprimand from the boss or an A or a D from a professor. The first two sections of the chapter will deal with these two types of **behavioral learning,** which we will call *classical conditioning* and *operant conditioning.*

In the third section of the chapter, the focus shifts from external behavior to internal mental processes. Our look at *cognitive learning* will consider how sudden "flashes" of insight and the imitative behavior require theories that go beyond behavioral learning—to explain how we solve puzzles or why children copy behavior they see on TV. We will also discuss the most complex type of learning, which involves the acquisition of concepts, the sort of learning you do in your college classes. Finally, the chapter will close on a practical note, by considering how to use the psychology of learning to help you study more effectively—and enjoy it. We begin, however, with a form of behavioral learning that accounts for many of your likes and dislikes—and, for one of your authors, an extreme dislike of olives.

WHAT SORT OF LEARNING DOES CLASSICAL CONDITIONING EXPLAIN?

CONNECTION: CHAPTER 1

Structuralism and *functionalism* were two of the earliest schools of psychology.

Ivan Pavlov (1849–1936) would have been insulted if you had called him a psychologist. In fact, he had only contempt for the structuralist and functionalist psychology of his time, which he saw as being hopelessly mired in speculation about subjective mental life (Todes, 1997). Pavlov and the hundreds of student researchers who passed through Pavlov's Russian research "factory" were famous for their work on the digestive system, for which Pavlov eventually snared a Nobel prize (Fancher, 1979; Kimble, 1991).

Unexpectedly, however, the experiments on salivation (the first step in digestion) went awry, sending Pavlov and his crew on a detour into the psychology of learning—a detour that occupied Pavlov for the rest of his life. The problem was that the experimental animals began salivating even *before* food was put in their mouths (Dewsbury, 1997). In fact, saliva would start flowing when they saw the food or even when they heard the footsteps of the lab assistant bringing the food.

This response was a puzzle. What, after all, was the biological function of salivating in anticipation of food? When Pavlov and his associates turned their attention to understanding these "psychic secretions" they made a series

■ **Behavioral learning** Forms of learning, such as classical conditioning and operant conditioning, that can be described in terms of stimuli and responses.

● To study classical conditioning, Pavlov placed his dogs in a restraining apparatus. The dogs were then presented with a neutral stimulus, such as a tone. Through its association with food, the neutral stimulus became a conditioned stimulus eliciting salivation.

of discoveries that would change the course of psychology (Pavlov, 1928; Todes, 1997). Quite by accident, they had stumbled upon an objective model of *learning*—one that could be manipulated in the laboratory to tease out the learned connections among stimuli and responses. This discovery, now known as **classical conditioning,** forms the Core Concept of this section:

> Classical conditioning is a basic form of learning in which a stimulus that produces an innate reflex becomes associated with a previously neutral stimulus, which then acquires the power to elicit essentially the same response.

In the following pages we will see that classical conditioning accounts for some important behavior patterns found not only in animals but in people. By means of classical conditioning, organisms learn about cues that help them avoid danger, as well as cues alerting them to food, sexual opportunity, and other conditions that promote survival. First, however, let's examine some of the fundamental features that Pavlov identified in classical conditioning.

The Essentials of Classical Conditioning

It is important to note that Pavlov's work on learning focused on simple, automatic responses known as *reflexes* (Windholz, 1997). Salivation and eye blinks are examples of such reflexes: They are normally triggered by stimuli that have biological significance. The blinking reflex, for example, protects the eyes; the salivation reflex aids digestion.

Pavlov's great discovery was that these reflexive responses could be associated with new stimuli—neutral stimuli that had previously produced no response. Thus, the connection between a reflex and a new stimulus could be *learned*. For example, Pavlov found he could teach his dogs to salivate upon hearing a certain sound, such as the tone produced by a tuning fork or a bell. You have experienced the same sort of learning if your mouth waters when you see a chocolate brownie.

To understand how these "conditioned reflexes" worked, Pavlov's team employed a simple experimental strategy. They first placed an untrained dog in a harness and set up a vial to capture the animal's saliva. Then, at intervals, a tone was sounded, after which the dog was given a bit of food. Gradually, over a number of trials, the dog began to salivate in response to the tone alone. In general, Pavlov and his students found that a **neutral stimulus** (one without any reflex-provoking power, such as a tone or a light), when paired with a natural reflex-producing stimulus (food), will by itself begin to elicit a learned response (salivation) that is similar to the original reflex. It's essentially the same conditioning process behind the association of romance with flowers or chocolate.

The main features of Pavlov's classical conditioning procedure are illustrated in Figure 6.1. At first glance, the terms may seem a bit overwhelming. Nevertheless, you will find it immensely helpful to study them carefully now so that they will come to mind easily later, when we analyze complicated, real-life learning situations, such as the acquisition and treatment of fears, phobias, and food aversions. Here we go . . .

Acquisition Classical conditioning always involves an **unconditioned stimulus (UCS),** a stimulus that automatically—that is, without conditioning—provokes a reflexive response. In Pavlov's experiments, food was used as the UCS because it produced a salivation reflex. In the language of classical conditioning, then, this response is called an *unconditioned reflex* or, more commonly, an **unconditioned response (UCR).** It is important to realize that the UCS–UCR connection involves no learning.

■ **Classical conditioning** A form of behavioral learning in which a previously neutral stimulus acquires the power to elicit the same innate reflex produced by another stimulus.
■ **Neutral stimulus** Any stimulus that produces no conditioned response prior to learning. When it is brought into a conditioning experiment, the researcher will call it a conditioned stimulus (CS). The assumption is that some conditioning occurs after even one pairing of the CS and UCS.
■ **Unconditioned stimulus (UCS)** In classical conditioning, the stimulus that elicits an unconditioned response.
■ **Unconditioned response (UCR)** In classical conditioning, the response elicited by an unconditioned stimulus without prior learning.

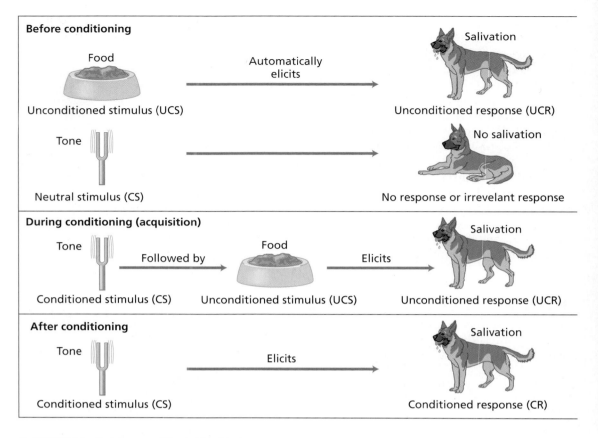

Before conditioning

Food
Unconditioned stimulus (UCS) — Automatically elicits → Salivation
Unconditioned response (UCR)

Tone
Neutral stimulus (CS) — → No salivation
No response or irrelevant response

During conditioning (acquisition)

Tone
Conditioned stimulus (CS) — Followed by → Food
Unconditioned stimulus (UCS) — Elicits → Salivation
Unconditioned response (UCR)

After conditioning

Tone
Conditioned stimulus (CS) — Elicits → Salivation
Conditioned response (CR)

● **FIGURE 6.1** Basic Features of Classical Conditioning

Before conditioning, the food (UCS) naturally elicits salivation (UCR). A tone from a tuning fork is a neutral stimulus and has no effect. During conditioning (the acquisition phase), the tone is paired with the food, which continues to elicit the salivation response. Through its association with the food, the previously neutral tone becomes a conditioned stimulus (CS), gradually producing a stronger and stronger salivation response. (*Source:* From PSYCHOLOGY AND LIFE 15th ed. by P. G. Zimbardo and R. J. Gerrig. Copyright © 1999 by Pearson Education. Published and reprinted by permission of Allyn & Bacon, Boston, MA.)

■ **Acquisition** The initial learning stage in classical conditioning, during which the conditioned response comes to be elicited by the conditioned stimulus.

■ **Conditioned stimulus (CS)** In classical conditioning, a previously neutral stimulus that comes to elicit the conditioned response. Customarily, in a conditioning experiment, the neutral stimulus is called a conditioned stimulus when it is first paired with an unconditioned stimulus (UCS).

■ **Conditioned response (CR)** In classical conditioning, a response elicited by a previously neutral stimulus that has become associated with the unconditioned stimulus.

During the **acquisition** or initial learning stage of classical conditioning, a neutral stimulus (a tone, for example) is paired with the unconditioned stimulus. Typically, after several trials the neutral stimulus will gradually come to elicit essentially the same response as does the UCS. So, in Pavlov's experiment, in which the tone produced salivation, we say that this formerly neutral stimulus has become a **conditioned stimulus (CS).** Although the response to the conditioned stimulus is essentially the same as the response originally produced by the unconditioned stimulus, we now refer to it as the **conditioned response (CR).**

With those terms firmly in mind, look at the graph of acquisition in a typical classical conditioning experiment, which appears in the first panel of Figure 6.2, where gradual acquisition of the conditioned response is reflected in the upward sweep of the line. Note that, at first, only weak responses are elicited by the conditioned stimulus. With continued CS–UCS pairings, however, the conditioned response increases in strength.

In conditioning, as in telling a joke, timing is critical. In most cases, the CS and UCS must be presented *contiguously* (close together in time) so that the organism can make the appropriate connection. The range of time intervals between the CS and UCS that will produce the best conditioning depends on the response being conditioned. For motor responses, such as eye blinks, a short interval of a second or less is best. For visceral responses, such as heart rate and salivation, longer intervals of 5 to 15 seconds work best. Conditioned

● **FIGURE 6.2** Acquisition, Extinction, and Spontaneous Recovery
During acquisition (CS + UCS), the strength of the CR increases rapidly. During extinction, when the UCS no longer follows the CS, the strength of the CR drops to zero. The CR may reappear after a brief rest period, even when the UCS is still not presented; only the CS alone appears. The reappearance of the CR is called "spontaneous recovery." (*Source:* From PSYCHOLOGY AND LIFE 15th ed. by P. G. Zimbardo and R. J. Gerrig. Copyright © 1999 by Pearson Education. Published and reprinted by permission of Allyn & Bacon, Boston, MA.)

fear optimally requires longer intervals of many seconds or even minutes to develop. Taste aversions, we will see, can develop after even longer delays.

These, then, are the building blocks of classical conditioning: the CS, UCS, CR, UCR, and the timing that connects them. So, why did it take Pavlov three decades and 532 experiments to study such a simple phenomenon? There was more to classical conditioning than first met Pavlov's eyes. Along with acquisition, he also discovered the processes of *extinction, spontaneous recovery, generalization,* and *discrimination*—which we will now explore.

Extinction and Spontaneous Recovery   Suppose that, as a result of classical conditioning, your mouth waters at the sound of a bell on the ice cream wagon that cruises your neighborhood. But, does such a conditioned response remain permanently in your behavioral repertoire? The good news, based on experiments by Pavlov's group, suggests that it does not. Conditioned salivation responses in Pavlov's dogs were easily eliminated by withholding the UCS (food) over several trials in which the CS (the tone) was presented alone. In the language of classical conditioning this is called **extinction.** It occurs when a conditioned response is eliminated by repeated presentations of the CS without the UCS. Figure 6.2 shows how the conditioned response (salivation) becomes weaker and weaker during extinction trials.

Now for the bad news: Let's imagine that your mouth-watering conditioned response has been extinguished. (The wagon repeatedly runs out of ice cream just before it gets to your house.) But, after a time (the driver has been on a week's vacation), when you again hear the bell on the ice-cream wagon, the conditioned response may reappear *spontaneously.* The same thing happened in Pavlov's dogs, which began salivating again when they again heard a bell, some time after undergoing extinction training. Pavlov termed this **spontaneous recovery.** Happily, when spontaneous recovery occurs, the conditioned response nearly always reappears at a lower intensity, as you can see in Figure 6.2. In practice, then, the CR can be brought under control, although sometimes this may require several extinction sessions.

The occurrence of spontaneous recovery is of considerable importance in behavior modification therapy for fears. But spontaneous recovery has theoretical importance, too. It tells us that extinction does not involve a complete elimination of the response from the organism's behavioral repertoire. Rather, extinction merely suppresses the conditioned response. What actually seems to be happening during extinction is the learning of a competing response *not to respond* to the conditioned stimulus.

■ **Extinction (in classical conditioning)**   The weakening of a conditioned response in the absence of an unconditioned stimulus.
■ **Spontaneous recovery**
The reappearance of an extinguished conditioned response after a time delay.

CONNECTION: CHAPTER 13

Behavior modification therapies are based on classical conditioning and operant conditioning.

Generalization If you fear spiders, you will probably respond the same way to spiders of all sizes and markings. This is called **stimulus generalization,** a process that involves giving a conditioned response to stimuli that are similar to the CS. Pavlov demonstrated stimulus generalization in his laboratory by showing that a well-trained dog would salivate in response to a bell that made a slightly different sound from the one he had used during conditioning. As you would expect, the closer the sound of the new bell was to the original, the stronger the response.

In everyday life, stimulus generalization is common in people who have acquired fears as a result of traumatic events. Accordingly, a person who has been bitten by a dog may develop a fear of dogs in general, rather than a fear only of the dog responsible for the attack. Likewise, stimulus generalization accounts for an allergy sufferer's sneeze upon seeing a paper flower. In short, by means of stimulus generalization we learn to apply old reflexes in new situations.

Discrimination Learning Although you may have learned to salivate at the sound of the bell on the ice cream wagon, you probably don't drool when the doorbell rings—thanks to *stimulus discrimination.* Much the opposite of stimulus generalization, **stimulus discrimination** occurs when an organism learns to respond to one stimulus but not to stimuli that are similar. Pavlov and his students demonstrated this experimentally when they taught dogs to distinguish between two tones of different frequencies. Once again, their procedure was simple: One tone was followed by food, while another was not. Over a series of trials, the dogs gradually learned the discrimination, evidenced in salivation elicited by one tone and not the other. Beyond the laboratory, discrimination learning can be found in our preferences for one commercial brand over another. Most obviously, perhaps, discrimination is involved in the continuing advertising battle between Pepsi and Coke.

Conditioning an Experimental Neurosis If you have ever had a class in which you couldn't guess what the teacher wanted, you have faced a vexing problem in discrimination learning. To study this problem in the laboratory, Pavlov confronted dogs with the seemingly simple task of distinguishing between a circle and an ellipse. One stimulus was always paired with food and the other was always paired with a painful electric shock. The task became more difficult, however, over a series of trials, when Pavlov gradually changed the ellipse to become more and more circular. And how did the dogs respond? As the discrimination became increasingly difficult, their responses grew more erratic. Finally, as the animals became more confused between the circle and the ellipse, they would snarl and snap at the handlers. Because such agitated responses resemble behavior of "neurotic" people who become irritable and defensive when they have difficult choices to make, this behavior pattern was dubbed **experimental neurosis.** Even today, this pattern stands as a model for the deterioration of behavior seen in both people and animals under stress.

Applications of Classical Conditioning

The beauty of classical conditioning is that it offers a simple explanation for many behaviors, from cravings to aversions. But it offers more than an explanation: It also gives us the tools for eliminating unwanted human behaviors—although Pavlov never attempted any therapeutic applications. It fell to the American behaviorist, John Watson, to first apply classical conditioning techniques to people.

The Notorious Case of Little Albert Conditioned fear in humans was first demonstrated experimentally by John Watson and Rosalie Rayner over 80

■ **Stimulus generalization**
The extension of a learned response to stimuli that are similar to the conditioned stimulus.
■ **Stimulus discrimination** A change in responses to one stimulus but not to stimuli that are similar.
■ **Experimental neurosis** A pattern of erratic behavior resulting from a demanding discrimination learning task, typically one that involves aversive stimuli.

years ago (Brewer, 1991; Fancher, 1979). In an experiment that would be considered unethical today, Watson and Rayner (1920/2000) conditioned an infant named Albert to react fearfully to a white laboratory rat. They created the fear by repeatedly presenting the rat paired with an aversive UCS—the loud sound of a steel bar struck with a mallet. It took only seven trials for "Little Albert" to react with fear at the appearance of the rat (CS) alone. After Albert's response to the rat had become well established, Watson and Rayner showed that his fear readily generalized from the rat to other furry objects, such as a Santa Claus mask and a fur coat worn by Watson (Harris, 1979).

Most likely, the experiment caused Albert only temporary distress, because his fear extinguished rapidly. In fact, Watson and Rayner found it necessary to strengthen the child's response periodically. This need to recondition Albert threatened the whole experiment when, after five days, Watson and Rayner were attempting to show that the child's fear could be generalized to a dog, a rabbit, and a sealskin coat. Watson decided to "freshen the reaction to the rat" by again striking the steel bar. The noise startled the dog, which began to bark at Albert, frightening not only Little Albert but both experimenters (Harris, 1979).

Unlike Little Albert's short-lived aversion to furry objects, some fears learned under extreme conditions can persist for years (LeDoux, 1996). Many sailors were exposed to such conditions during World War II, when the signal used to call them to battle stations was a gong sounding at the rate of 100 rings a minute. For combat personnel aboard ship, this sound was strongly associated with danger—a CS for emotional arousal. The persistent effect of this learning was shown in a study conducted 15 years after the war, when Navy veterans who had experienced combat still gave a strong autonomic reaction to the old "call to battle stations" (Edwards & Acker, 1962).

Like those veterans, any of us can retain a learned readiness to respond to old emotional cues. Fortunately, however, classical conditioning provides some tools for dealing with conditioned fears (Wolpe & Plaud, 1997). A good therapeutic strategy combines extinction of the conditioned fear response with learning a relaxation response to the CS. This *counterconditioning* therapy, then, teaches patients to respond in a relaxed manner to the conditioned stimulus. The technique has been particularly effective in dealing with phobias. It was also part of the treatment used to help Sabra conquer her fear of flying.

Conditioned Food Aversions   As young children, all three of your authors had bad experiences with specific foods. Phil got sick after eating pork and beans in the grade school lunchroom. Ann developed nausea after eating apple fritters. And it was Bob who became ill after overdosing on olives. In all three cases, we associated our distress with the distinctive sight, smell, and taste of the food—but not to anything else in our environment. Even today, the taste, smell, or appearance of the specific food is enough to cause a feeling of nausea.

Unpleasant as it can be, learning to avoid a food associated with illness has survival value. That's why humans and many other animals readily form an association between illness and food—much more readily than between illness and a nonfood stimulus, such as a light or a tone. And, while most forms of classical conditioning require only a short delay between the CS and the UCS, food aversions can develop when a distinctive taste has been separated by hours from the onset of illness. "Must have been something I ate!" we say.

John Garcia and Robert Koelling first recognized this selective CS–UCS connection when they noticed that rats avoided drinking from the water bottles in the chambers where they had previously been made nauseous by radiation. Garcia and Koelling wondered: Could it be the taste of the water in those bottles that the rats were associating with being sick? Subsequent experiments confirmed their suspicions and led to yet another important discovery.

● John Watson and Rosalie Rayner conditioned Little Albert to fear furry objects like this Santa Claus mask (*Discovering Psychology,* 1990).

◀ **CONNECTION: CHAPTER 2**

The *autonomic nervous system* regulates the internal organs.

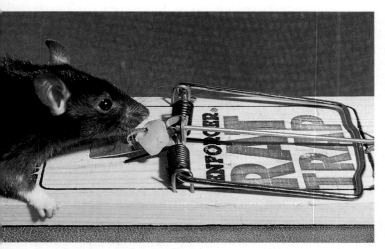

● Bait shyness has survival value.

■ **Taste-aversion learning** A biological tendency in which an organism learns, after a single experience, to avoid a food with a certain taste, if eating it is followed by illness.

● A conditioned taste aversion can make a coyote stop killing sheep.

Garcia and Koelling (1966) found that rats readily learned an association between flavored water and illness, yet the rats could *not* be conditioned to associate flavored water with an electric shock delivered through a grid on the floor of the test chamber. This makes good "sense" from an evolutionary perspective, because illness can easily result from drinking (or eating) poisonous substances but rarely occurs following a sharp pain to the feet. On the other hand, the experiments found that rats easily learned to respond fearfully when bright lights and noise signaled an electric shock—but could *not* learn to connect those light/sound cues and subsequent illness.

A Challenge to Pavlov The problem that conditioned **taste-aversion learning** poses for classical conditioning is that it is not entirely learned. In fact, the tendency to develop taste aversions appears to be a part of our biological nature. And it is this biological basis for taste aversions that has caused psychologists to question some aspects of Pavlov's original theory of classical conditioning.

Unlike conditioning dogs to respond to a tone or a light, food aversions seem to require an innate (and therefore *unlearned*) disposition to associate sickness with food. We know this because people who develop food aversions don't normally make the same association to nonfood items that accompanied the food. For example, when Bob developed an aversion to olives, he did not also learn to avoid other objects in the room at the time, such as a light or a book on the table. It was solely the olives that became an effective conditioned stimulus. Taken together, such observations suggest that organisms have an inborn preparedness to associate certain stimuli with certain consequences, while other CS–UCS combinations are highly resistant to learning.

Moreover, food aversions can develop even when the time interval between eating and illness extends over several hours—as compared with just a few seconds in Pavlov's experiments. Again, this suggests that in food aversions we are not dealing with a simple classically conditioned response as Pavlov understood it but, instead, with a response that is based as much in nature (biology) as it is in nurture (learning).

Conditioning Coyotes: An Application The principles behind conditioned food aversion have been applied to practical problems in the world outside the laboratory. For example, John Garcia and his colleagues demonstrated how aversive conditioning can dissuade wild coyotes from attacking sheep. The researchers did so by wrapping toxic lamb burgers in sheepskins and stashing them on sheep ranches. When roaming coyotes found and ate these morsels, they became sick and—as predicted—developed a distaste for lamb meat. The result was a 30 to 50% reduction in sheep attacks. So powerful was this aversion for conditioned coyotes that, when captured and placed in a cage with a sheep, the coyotes would not get close to it. Some even vomited at the sight of a sheep (Garcia, 1990). Perhaps the most amazing result was this: Despite their success with coyotes, the scientists have been unable to modify the behavior of sheep ranchers to get them to apply the research. Apparently, sheep ranchers have a strong aversion to feeding lamb to coyotes!

So, what is the big lesson of taste aversions for our understanding of classical conditioning? Conditioning involves both nature and nurture. That is, conditioning depends not only on the learned relationship among stimuli and responses but also on the way an organism is genetically attuned to certain stimuli in its environment (Barker et al., 1978; Dickinson, 2001; Pinel, 2003). What any organism can—and cannot—learn in a given setting is to some extent a product of its evolutionary history (Garcia, 1993). This is a concept that Pavlov never understood.

PSYCHOLOGY IN YOUR LIFE: TASTE AVERSIONS AND CHEMOTHERAPY

Imagine that your friend Jena is about to undergo her first round of chemotherapy, just to make sure that any stray cells from the tumor found in her breast will be destroyed. To her surprise, the nurse enters the lab, not with the expected syringe, but with a dish of licorice-flavored ice cream. "Is this a new kind of therapy?" she asks. The nurse replies that it is, indeed. She explains that most patients who undergo chemotherapy experience nausea, which can make them "go off their feed" and quit eating, just when their body needs nourishment to fight the disease. "But," says the nurse, "We have found a way around the problem. If we give patients some unusual food before their chemotherapy, they will usually develop an aversion only to that food." She continued, "Did you ever hear of Pavlov's dogs?"

Cancer patients like Jena often develop aversions to normal foods in their diets to such an extent that they become anorectic and malnourished. The aversions are conditioned responses in which food (the CS) becomes associated with nausea. The problem is aggravated when chemotherapy treatments, which produce the nausea, are administered right after meals. Therapists trained to understand classical conditioning use their knowledge to prevent the development of aversions to nutritive foods by arranging for meals not to be given just before the chemotherapy. And, as in Jena's case, they also present a "scapegoat" stimulus. Thus, patients are given candies or ice cream with unusual flavors before the treatments so that the taste aversion becomes conditioned only to those special flavors. For some patients, this practical solution to problems with chemotherapy may make the difference between life and death (Bernstein, 1988, 1991).

● If this child gets sick tonight, she may develop a taste aversion to this unusual flavor of ice cream.

CHECK YOUR UNDERSTANDING

1. **RECALL:** Classical conditioning is especially useful for understanding which one of the following examples of learning?
   a. a dog that has learned to "sit up" for a food reward
   b. a psychology student who is learning how memory works
   c. a child who, after a painful dental visit, has learned to fear the dentist
   d. an executive who is afraid that she will lose her job

2. **RECALL:** The responses in classical conditioning were originally
   a. innate reflexes.
   b. new behaviors.
   c. premeditated behaviors.
   d. random acts.

3. **APPLICATION:** If you learned to fear electrical outlets after getting a painful shock, what would be the CS?
   a. the electrical outlet
   b. the painful shock
   c. the fear
   d. the time period between seeing the outlet and getting the shock

4. **UNDERSTANDING THE CORE CONCEPT:** Which of the following would be most likely to be an unconditioned stimulus (UCS) involved in classical conditioning?
   a. food
   b. a flashing light
   c. music
   d. money

ANSWERS: 1.c 2.a 3.a 4.a

HOW DO WE LEARN NEW BEHAVIORS BY OPERANT CONDITIONING?

With classical conditioning, you can teach a dog to salivate, but you can't teach it to sit up or roll over. Why? Salivation is a passive, involuntary reflex, while sitting up and rolling over are much more complex responses that we usually think of as voluntary. To a behavioral psychologist, however, such "voluntary" behaviors are really controlled by *rewards* and *punishments*—which have no role in classical conditioning. When rewards or punishments are involved, another important form of learning is at work. Psychologists call it *operant conditioning*. An **operant,** incidentally, is an observable behavior that an organism uses to "operate" in, or have an effect on, the environment. Thus, if you are reading this book to get a good grade on the next test, reading is an operant behavior.

You might also think of **operant conditioning** as a form of learning in which behavior change is brought about by the *consequences* of behavior. The Core Concept of this section puts the idea this way:

> In operant conditioning, the consequences of behavior, such as rewards and punishments, influence the chance that the behavior will occur again.

Common rewarding consequences include money, praise, food, or high grades—all of which can encourage the behaviors they follow. By contrast, punishments such as pain, loss of privileges, or low grades can discourage the behaviors with which they are associated.

As you will see, the theory of operant conditioning is an important one for at least two reasons. First, operant conditioning accounts for a much wider spectrum of behavior than does classical conditioning. And second, it explains new behaviors—not just reflexive behaviors.

Skinner's Radical Behaviorism

The founding father of operant conditioning, American psychologist B. F. Skinner (1904–1990), based his whole career on the idea that the most powerful influences on behavior are its *consequences*. Actually, it wasn't Skinner's idea, originally. He borrowed the concept of behavior being controlled by rewards and punishments from another American psychologist, Edward Thorndike, who had demonstrated how hungry animals would work diligently to solve a problem by trial and error to obtain a food reward. Gradually, on succeeding trials, erroneous responses were eliminated and effective responses were "stamped in." Thorndike called this the **law of effect.** (See Figure 6.3.)

The first thing Skinner did with Thorndike's psychology, however, was to rid it of subjective and unscientific speculation about the organism's feelings, intentions, or goals. What an animal "wanted" or the "pleasure" it felt was not important for an objective understanding of the animal's behavior. As a radical behaviorist, Skinner refused to consider what happens in an organism's mind, because such speculation cannot be verified by observation. For example, eating can be observed, but we can't observe the inner experiences of hunger, the desire for food, or pleasure at eating.

The Power of Reinforcement

While we often speak of "reward" in casual conversation, Skinner preferred the more objective term **reinforcer.** By this he meant any condition that follows and strengthens a response. Food, money, and sex serve this function for

● Taking aspirin for pain usually results in negative reinforcement, because the pain diminishes.

■ **Operant** An observable, voluntary behavior that an organism emits to "operate" on, or have an effect on, the environment.

■ **Operant conditioning** A form of behavioral learning in which the probability of a response is changed by its consequences—that is, by the stimuli that follow the response.

■ **Law of effect** The idea that responses that produced desirable results would be learned, or "stamped" into the organism.

■ **Reinforcer** A condition (involving either the presentation or removal of a stimulus) that occurs after a response and strengthens that response.

● **FIGURE 6.3** A Thorndike Puzzle Box
Unlike Pavlov's dogs, Thorndike's cats faced a problem: how to open the door in the puzzle box to get a food reward lying just outside. To solve this problem, the animals used *trial-and-error learning*, rather than simple reflexive responses. At first, their responses seemed random, but gradually they eliminated ineffective behaviors. And when the effects of their behavior were desirable (that is, when the door finally opened and the animals got the food), they used this strategy on subsequent trials. This change in behavior based on outcome of previous trials is called the *law of effect*. Much the same trial-and-error learning occurs when you learn a skill, such as shooting a basketball.

most people. So do attention, praise, or a smile. All are examples of **positive reinforcement,** which strengthens a response by occurring after the response and making the behavior more likely to occur again.

Most people know about positive reinforcement, of course, but few people understand the other main way to strengthen operant responses. It involves the reinforcement of behavior by the *removal* of an unpleasant or aversive stimulus. Psychologists call this **negative reinforcement.** (The word "negative" here is used in the mathematical sense of *subtract* or *remove,* while "positive" means *add* or *apply.*) So, using an umbrella to avoid getting wet during a downpour is a behavior learned and maintained by negative reinforcement. That is, you use the umbrella to avoid or remove an unpleasant stimulus (getting wet). Likewise, when a driver buckles the seat belt, negative reinforcement occurs as the annoying sound of the seat-belt buzzer stops. Remember, it is the "subtraction" of the unpleasant stimulus that provides negative reinforcement.

Reinforcing Technology: The "Skinner Box" One of B. F. Skinner's (1956) most important innovations was a simple device for studying the effects of reinforcers on laboratory animals: a box with a lever that an animal could press to obtain food, which he called an **operant chamber.** Nearly everyone else called it a "Skinner box," a term he detested. Over the intervening years, the apparatus has been used by thousands of psychologists to study operant conditioning.

The importance of the operant chamber was that it could be set to control the timing and the frequency of reinforcement. These factors, it turned out, are of huge importance in controlling behavior, as you will see in our discussion of *contingencies of reinforcement.* Moreover, the Skinner box could be programmed to conduct experiments at any time—even when the researcher was home in bed.

And speaking of beds, just to set the record straight, we'd like to mention a bit of trivia about the "baby tender" crib Skinner devised for his daughter, Deborah (Benjamin & Nielsen-Gammon, 1999). It consisted of an enclosed, temperature-controlled box—which unfortunately bore a superficial resemblance to the operant chambers used in his experiments. The public learned about the "baby tender" from an article by Skinner in the magazine *Ladies' Home Journal.* Many readers (and also those who did *not* read the article) jumped to wild

● B. F. Skinner is shown reinforcing the animal's behavior in an operant chamber, or "Skinner box." The apparatus allows the experimenter to control all the stimuli in the animal's environment.

■ **Positive reinforcement**   A stimulus presented after a response and increasing the probability of that response happening again.
■ **Negative reinforcement**   The removal of an unpleasant or aversive stimulus, contingent upon a particular behavior. Compare with *punishment.*
■ **Operant chamber**   A boxlike apparatus that can be programmed to deliver reinforcers and punishers contingent on an animal's behavior. The operant chamber is often called a "Skinner box."

● Chimpanzees will work for conditioned reinforcers. Here a chimp has earned plastic tokens, which it is depositing in a "chimp-o-mat" to obtain raisins, a primary reinforcer.

● Parents can use reinforcement contingencies to affect children's behavior.

■ **Reinforcement contingencies**
Relationships between a response and the changes in stimulation that follow the response.
■ **Continuous reinforcement**
A type of reinforcement schedule by which all correct responses are reinforced.
■ **Shaping** An operant learning technique in which a new behavior is produced by reinforcing responses that are similar to the desired response.
■ **Intermittent reinforcement**
A type of reinforcement schedule by which some, but not all, correct responses are reinforced; also called *partial reinforcement*.
■ **Extinction (in operant conditioning)** A process by which a response that has been learned is weakened by the absence or removal of reinforcement. (Compare with *extinction in classical conditioning*.)

conclusions involving child neglect and heartless experimentation. The story of the "baby tender" took on a life of its own, and, years later, stories arose about Deborah Skinner's supposed psychotic breakdown, lawsuits against her father, and eventual suicide—none of which were true. In this case, the truth was not nearly as titillating as the fiction. In fact, Deborah grew up to be a well-adjusted individual who loved her parents.

Contingencies of Reinforcement   College and university students are reinforced for their studying with grade reports two or three times a year. Because that's too long between reinforcers for most students to maintain their academic behavior, professors schedule exams and award grades periodically throughout their courses. They want to encourage continual studying, rather than one big push at the end of the semester.

In any operant learning situation, the timing and frequency of rewards are crucial. How often will reinforcement be given? How much work is needed to earn a reinforcer? Will every response be reinforced—or will reinforcement occur only after a certain number of responses? These are the important questions we will pose in our discussion of **reinforcement contingencies,** which will deal with the many possible ways of associating responses and reinforcers. As you will see, the answers to these questions determine the behavior patterns of organisms, from laboratory rats to students (and their professors).

Continuous versus Intermittent Reinforcement   Suppose you want to teach your dog a trick—say, sitting up on command. It would be a good idea to begin the training program with a reward for every correct response. Psychologists call this **continuous reinforcement.** It's a useful tactic early in the learning process, because rewarding every correct response gives feedback on how well each response was performed. In addition, continuous reinforcement is useful for **shaping** complex new behaviors, such as playing a musical instrument, because the teacher can continually "raise the bar," or increase the standard required for earning a reward, which tells the learner when performance has improved. In general, then, we can say that *continuous reinforcement is the best strategy for teaching and learning new behaviors.*

Continuous reinforcement does have some drawbacks, however. For one thing, an accidental failure to reward a correct response on one trial could easily be misinterpreted as a signal that the response was not correct. For another, continuous reinforcement typically loses its reinforcing quality as the organism becomes satiated, as you can imagine if someone were training you to shoot free throws by rewarding you with chocolate cake. Your first slice of chocolate cake may be highly rewarding, but by the time you have had 10 or 12 slices, the reward value is gone.

Happily, once the desired behavior is well established (for example, when your dog has learned to sit up), the demands of the situation change. The learner no longer needs rewards to discriminate a correct response from an incorrect one. Now is the time to shift to **intermittent reinforcement** (also called *partial reinforcement*), the rewarding of some, but not all, correct responses. A less frequent schedule of reward—perhaps, after every third correct response—can still serve as an incentive for your dog to sit up on command. In general, whether we're dealing with people or animals, *intermittent reinforcement is the most efficient way to maintain behaviors that have already been learned* (Robbins, 1971; Terry, 2000).

A big advantage of intermittent reinforcement comes from the resistance to *extinction* that it produces. Much like the extinction we saw in Pavlovian conditioning, **extinction** also occurs in operant conditioning. The operant version of extinction occurs when reinforcement is withheld, as when a gambler quits playing a slot machine that never pays off. So, why do responses strengthened by partial reinforcement resist extinction much more strongly than do responses that have been rewarded continuously? Imagine two gamblers and two slot machines. One machine inexplicably pays off on every trial, and another, a more typical machine, pays on an unpredictable, intermittent schedule. Now, suppose that both devices suddenly stop paying. Which gambler will catch on first? The one who has been rewarded for each pull of the lever (continuous reinforcement) will quickly notice the change, while the gambler who has won only occasionally (on partial reinforcement) may continue playing unrewarded for a long while.

● Continuous reinforcement is useful for *training* animals, but intermittent reinforcement is better for *maintaining* their learned behaviors.

Schedules of Reinforcement   Now that you are convinced of the power of intermittent reinforcement, you should know that it occurs in two main forms or **schedules of reinforcement.** One, the **ratio schedule,** rewards a subject after a certain *number of responses*. The other, known as an **interval schedule,** provides a reward after a certain *time interval*. Let's look at the advantages and disadvantages of each.

Ratio Schedules   If you pay your employees based on the amount of work they perform, you are using a ratio schedule of reinforcement. Ratio schedules occur any time rewards are *based on the number of responses* (see Figure 6.4). Psychologists make a further distinction between two subtypes of ratio schedules: *fixed ratio* and *variable ratio* schedules.

   Fixed ratio (FR) schedules are found in jobs, where workers are paid on a piecework basis. Suppose that you own a tire factory, and you pay each worker a dollar for every 10 tires produced; you are using a fixed ratio schedule. Under this scheme the amount of work (the number of responses) needed for a reward remains constant. Managers like FR schedules because the rate of responding is usually high (Terry, 2000; Whyte, 1972).

   Variable ratio (VR) schedules are less predictable. Telemarketers—people who make sales pitches by telephone—work on a VR schedule: They never know how many phone calls they must make before they get the next sale. Slot machine players also respond on a variable ratio schedule. In both cases the variable ratio schedule keeps responses coming at a high rate—so high, in fact, that the VR schedule usually produces more responding than any other schedule of reinforcement. In the laboratory, Skinner demonstrated that a variable ratio schedule could entice a hungry pigeon to peck a disk 12,000 times an hour for rewards given, on the average, for every 110 pecks.

Interval Schedules   Time is of the essence on an interval schedule. Accordingly, reinforcement is based on responses made within a certain *time period* (instead of on the number of responses given). (See Figure 6.4.) Psychologists distinguish two kinds of interval schedules: *fixed interval* and *variable interval* schedules.

   Fixed interval (FI) schedules are common in the work world, where they may appear as a monthly paycheck. A student who studies for a weekly quiz is also on a fixed interval

■ **Schedules of reinforcement** Programs specifying the frequency and timing of reinforcements.
■ **Ratio schedule**   A program by which reinforcement depends on the number of correct responses.
■ **Interval schedule**   A program by which reinforcement depends on the time interval elapsed since the last reinforcement.
■ **Fixed ratio (FR) schedules** Programs by which reinforcement is contingent upon a certain, unvarying number of responses.
■ **Variable ratio (VR) schedules** Reinforcement programs by which the number of responses required for a reinforcement varies from trial to trial.
■ **Fixed interval (FI) schedules** Programs by which reinforcement is contingent upon a certain, fixed time period.

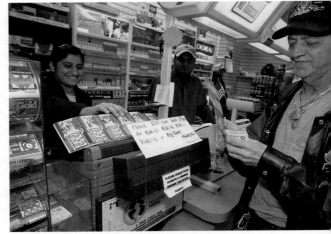

● What schedule of reinforcement encourages this man to buy lottery tickets?

● **FIGURE 6.4** Reinforcement Schedules
These graphs show typical patterns of responding produced by four different schedules of reinforcement. (The hash marks indicate when reinforcement is delivered.) Notice that the steeper angle of the top two graphs shows how the ratio schedules usually produce more responses over a given period of time than do the interval schedules.

■ **Variable interval (VI) schedules** Programs by which the time period between reinforcements varies from trial to trial.
■ **Primary reinforcers** Reinforcers, such as food and sex, that have an innate basis because of their biological value to an organism.
■ **Conditioned reinforcers or secondary reinforcers** Stimuli, such as money or tokens, that acquire their reinforcing power by a learned association with primary reinforcers.
■ **Token economy** A therapeutic method, based on operant conditioning, by which individuals are rewarded with tokens, which act as secondary reinforcers. The tokens can be redeemed for a variety of rewards and privileges.

schedule. Because the interval is invariant, the time period between rewards remains constant. You may have already guessed that fixed interval reinforcement usually results in a low response rate. Ironically, this is the schedule most widely adopted by business. Even a rat in a Skinner box programmed for a fixed interval schedule soon learns that it must produce only a limited amount of work during the interval in order to get its reward. Lever presses beyond the required minimum are just wasted energy. Thus, both rats and humans on fixed interval schedules may display only modest productivity until near the end of the interval, when the response rate increases rapidly. (Think of college students facing a term paper deadline.) Graphically, in Figure 6.4 you can see the "scalloped" pattern of behavior that results from this flurry of activity near the end of each interval.

Variable interval (VI) schedules are, perhaps, the most unpredictable of all. On a VI schedule, the time interval between rewards varies. The resulting rate of responding can be low or high, although not usually as high as for the VR schedule. For a pigeon or a rat in a Skinner box, the variable interval schedule may be a 30-second interval now, 3 minutes next, and a 1-minute wait later. On the job, random visits by the boss occur on a variable interval schedule. Fishing represents still another example: You never know how long it will be before the fish start biting again, but the occasional, unpredictable fish delivers reward enough to encourage fishing behavior over long intervals. And, while waiting for an elevator, it is fun to note which of your companions presses the button as if it controlled the arrival of the elevator on a VI schedule.

Primary and Secondary Reinforcers   It is easy to see why stimuli that fulfill basic biological needs or desires will provide reinforcement: Food reinforces a hungry animal, and water reinforces a thirsty one. Similarly, the opportunity for sex becomes a reinforcer for a sexually aroused organism. Psychologists call such stimuli **primary reinforcers.**

But you can't eat money or drink it. So why does money act as a powerful reinforcer for most people? Neutral stimuli that are associated with primary reinforcers may also acquire a reinforcing effect and become **conditioned reinforcers** or **secondary reinforcers** for operant responses. And that's where money enters the picture; the system works similarly with grades, praise, smiles of approval, gold stars, and various kinds of status symbols. In fact, virtually any stimulus can become a secondary or conditioned reinforcer by being associated with a primary reinforcer. With strong conditioning, secondary reinforcers such as money, status, or awards can even come to be ends in themselves.

The power of conditioned reinforcers has been tapped by mental institutions that have set up so-called *token economies* to encourage desirable and healthy patient behaviors. Under a **token economy,** grooming or taking medication, for example, may be reinforced by plastic tokens awarded by the staff when patients perform these desired behaviors. The tokens can later be exchanged by patients for a wide array of rewards and privileges (Ayllon & Azrin, 1965; Holden, 1978). As an adjunct to other forms of therapy, token economies can help mental patients learn useful strategies for acting effectively in the world (Kazdin, 1994).

Preferred Activities as Reinforcers: The Premack Principle   The opportunity to perform desirable activities can reinforce behavior just as effectively as food or drink or other primary reinforcers. For example, people who work out regularly might use a daily run or fitness class as a reward for getting other tasks done. Likewise, teachers have found that young children will learn to sit still if that behavior is reinforced with the opportunity to run around and make noise (Homme et al., 1963).

The principle at work here says that a preferred activity (running around and making noise) can be used to reinforce a less preferred one (sitting still and listing to the teacher). Psychologists call this the **Premack principle,** after its discoverer, David Premack (1965). He first demonstrated this in thirsty rats, which increased their running in an exercise wheel when they learned that the running would be followed by an opportunity to drink. And, just as Premack had anticipated, another group of rats that were exercise deprived, but not thirsty, increased the amount they drank when drinking was followed by a chance to run in the wheel. In exactly the same way, then, parents can use the Premack principle to get children to engage in otherwise unlikely behavior. For example, the opportunity to play with friends (a preferred activity) could be used to reinforce the less-preferred activity of making the bed or doing the dishes.

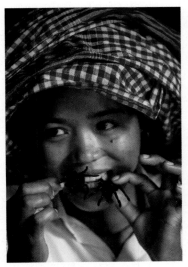

● Foods that many people around the world enjoy may not be a source of reinforcement for the typical North American.

Reinforcement across Cultures   The laws of operant learning apply to all animals with a brain. The biological mechanism underlying reinforcement is, apparently, much the same across species. On the other hand, exactly what serves as a reinforcer varies wildly. Experience suggests that food for a hungry organism and water for a thirsty one will act as reinforcers because they satisfy basic needs related to survival. But what any particular individual will choose to satisfy those needs may depend as much on learning as on survival instincts—especially in humans, where secondary reinforcement is so important. For us, culture plays an especially powerful role in determining what will act as reinforcers. So, while some people would find eating a cricket reinforcing, most people of Euro-American ancestry would not. Similarly, disposing of a noisy cricket might seem both sensible and rewarding to a Baptist and aversive to a Buddhist. And, just to prove our point, we note that watching a game of cricket would most likely be rewarding to a British cricket fan— although punishingly dull to most Americans.

So, culture shapes preferences in reinforcement, but reinforcement also shapes culture. When you first walk down a street in a foreign city, all the differences that catch your eye are merely different ways that people have found to seek reinforcement or avoid punishment. A temple houses cultural attempts to seek rewards from the deity. Clothing may reflect attempts to seek a reinforcing mate or to feel comfortable in the climate. And a culture's cuisine evolves from learning to survive on the native plants and animals. It is in this sense, then, that we can see culture broadly as a set of behaviors originally *learned* by operant conditioning and shared by a group of people.

The Problem of Punishment

Punishment as a means of influencing behavior poses several difficulties, as schoolteachers and prison wardens will attest. In some respects, punishment acts as the opposite of reinforcement. Thus, punishment is an *aversive* consequence used to *weaken* the behavior it follows. But, like reinforcement, punishment comes in two main forms. One, called **positive punishment,** requires the *application of an aversive stimulus*—as, when you touch a hot plate, the painful consequence reduces the likelihood of your repeating that behavior. The other main form of punishment, known as **negative punishment,** results from the *removal of a reinforcer*—as when parents take away a misbehaving teen's car keys.

■ **Premack principle**   The concept, developed by David Premack, that a more-preferred activity can be used to reinforce a less-preferred activity.
■ **Punishment**   An aversive stimulus which, occurring after a response, diminishes the strength of that response. (Compare with *negative reinforcement.*)
■ **Positive punishment**   The application of an aversive stimulus after a response.
■ **Negative punishment**   The removal of an attractive stimulus after a response.

● As Calvin realizes, the probability of someone repeating a response can be decreased if the first response is followed by an aversive consequence, such as a loud noise or angry complaint.

Calvin & Hobbes by Bill Watterson/Universal Press Syndicate.

Unlike reinforcement, however, punishment must be administered consistently. Intermittent punishment is far less effective than punishment delivered after every undesired response. In fact, *not punishing* an occurrence of unwanted behavior can have the effect of rewarding it—as when a supervisor overlooks the late arrival of an employee.

Punishment versus Negative Reinforcement   You have probably noted that punishment and negative reinforcement both involve unpleasant stimuli. So, to avoid confusion, let's see how punishment and negative reinforcement differ, using the following examples (Figure 6.5). Suppose that an animal in a Skinner box can turn off a loud noise by pressing a lever: This action provides negative reinforcement. Now compare that with the other animal in Figure 6.5 for which the loud noise serves as a punishment for pressing the lever.

Please note that punishment and negative reinforcement are used to produce opposite effects on behavior (Baum, 1994). Punishment is used to *decrease* a behavior or reduces its probability of recurring. In contrast, negative reinforcement—like positive reinforcement—always *increases* a response's probability of occurring again.

And remember that the descriptors "positive" and "negative" mean "add" and "remove." Thus, both positive reinforcement and positive punishment involve administering or "adding" a stimulus. On the other hand, negative reinforcement and negative punishment always involve withholding or removing a stimulus. For a concise summary of the distinctions between positive and negative reinforcement and punishment, please see Table 6.1.

● **FIGURE 6.5** Negative Reinforcement and Punishment Compared

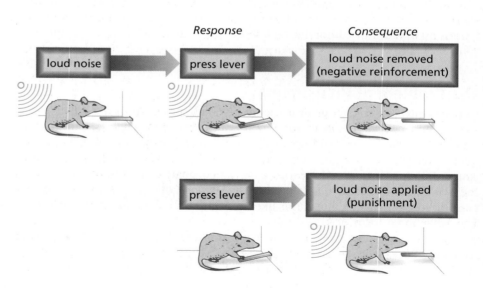

TABLE 6.1	Four Kinds of Consequences		
		Apply (add) stimulus (positive)	Remove (subtract) stimulus (negative)
What is the effect of the stimulus (consequence) on behavior?	The probability of the behavior increases:	**Positive reinforcement** *Example:* An employee gets a bonus for good word—and continues to work hard.	**Negative reinforcement** *Example:* You take aspirin for your headache, and the headache vanishes—so you take aspirin the next time you have a headache.
	The probability of the behavior decreases:	**Positive punishment** *Example:* A speeder gets a traffic ticket—and drives away more slowly.	**Negative punishment** *Example:* A child who has stayed out late misses dinner—and comes homes early next time.

Three important points to keep in mind as you study this table:

1. "Positive" and "negative" mean that a stimulus (consequence) has been added (presented) or subtracted (removed). These terms have nothing to do with "good" or "bad."
2. We can often predict what effect a particular consequence will have, but the only way to know for sure whether it will be a reinforcer or a punisher is to observe its effect on behavior. For example, although we might guess that a spanking would punish a child, it might actually serve as a reinforcer to strengthen the unwanted behavior.
3. From a cognitive viewpoint, we can see that reinforcement consists of the presentation of a pleasant stimulus or the removal of an unpleasant one. Similarly, punishment entails the presentation of an unpleasant stimulus or the removal of a pleasant one.

The Uses and Abuses of Punishment Our society relies heavily on punishment and the threat of punishment to keep people "in line." We put people in jail, fine them, spank them, and give them bad grades, parking tickets, and disapproving looks. And what is the result? Punishment often produces an immediate change in behavior—which, ironically, is reinforcing to the punisher and a major reason why the use of punishment is so widespread. Several other factors also encourage a punishment habit. For one, punishers may feel good while delivering the punishment, sensing that they are "settling a score" or "getting even" or making the other person "pay." This is why we speak of revenge as being "sweet."

But, punishment usually doesn't work as well in the long run as punishers would like (Terry, 2000). Punished children may continue to misbehave, reprimanded employees may still arrive late for work, and, in the United States, many people still commit crimes, despite the fact that we imprison criminals in numbers that far exceed those of any other Western society. So, why is punishment so difficult to use effectively? There are several reasons.

First, *the power of punishment to suppress behavior usually disappears when the threat of punishment is removed* (Skinner, 1953). Drivers will observe the speed limit when they know the highway patrol is watching. Johnny will refrain from hitting his little brother when his parents are within earshot. And you will probably give up your wallet to a mugger who points a gun at you. That is, most people will comply with a demand accompanied by the threat of strong and certain punishment. But they may act quite differently when they know punishment is unlikely. This explains why motorists rarely slow down for "construction speed" signs on the highways: They know that the police rarely enforce these zones. In general, you can be certain of controlling someone's behavior through punishment or threat of punishment only if you can control the environment all of the time. Such total control is usually not possible, even in a prison.

Second, *punishment triggers escape or aggression.* When punished, organisms usually try to flee from or otherwise avoid further punishment. But if escape is blocked, they are likely to become aggressive. Corner a wounded animal,

● Prison riots and other aggressive behavior may result from highly punitive conditions.

and it may savagely attack you. Put two rats in a Skinner box with an electrified floor grid, and the rats will attack each other (Ulrich & Azrin, 1962). Put humans in a harsh prison environment, and they may riot—or, if they are prison guards, they may abuse the prisoners (Zimbardo, 2004c).

Further, in a punitive environment, whether it be a prison, a school, or a home, people learn that punishment and aggression are legitimate means of influencing others, which may explain the smiling faces of the guards seen in the prisoner-abuse photos from Iraq. The punishment–aggression link also explains why abusing parents so often come from abusive families and why aggressive delinquents so often come from homes where aggressive behavior toward the children is commonplace (Golden, 2000). Unfortunately, the well-documented fact that punishment so often leads to aggression remains widely unknown to the general public.

Here's the third reason why punishment is so often ineffective: *Punishment makes the learner apprehensive, which inhibits learning new and better responses.* Unable to escape punishment, an organism may give up its attempts at flight or fight and surrender to an overwhelming feeling of hopelessness. This passive acceptance of a punitive fate produces a behavior pattern called *learned helplessness* (Overmier & Seligman, 1967). In people, this reaction can produce the mental disorder known as depression (Terry, 2000).

CONNECTION: CHAPTER 12

Depression is one of the most common mental disorders.

From the standpoint of a punisher seeking to produce a constructive change in attitudes and behavior, learned helplessness and depression are undesirable outcomes. Whether it produces escape, aggression, or learned helplessness, punishment focuses learners' attention on their own misery—which interferes with new learning. It also fails to help learners see what to do because it focuses attention on what not to do. By contrast, individuals who have not been punished feel much freer to experiment with new behaviors.

And the fourth reason why punitive measures may fail: *Punishment is often applied unequally,* even though that violates our standards of fair and equal treatment. For example, boys are punished more often than girls. Then, too, children (especially grade school children) receive more physical punishment than do adults. And, to give one more example, our schools—and probably our society at large—more often use punishment to control members of racial minority groups than they do to control members of the Caucasian majority (Hyman, 1996; Hyman et al., 1977).

Does Punishment Ever Work?   In limited circumstances, punishment can work remarkably well (Terry, 2000). For example, punishment can halt the self-destructive behavior of autistic children who may injure themselves severely by banging their heads or chewing the flesh off their fingers. In these cases, a mild electric shock or a splash of cold water in the face can quickly put a stop to the unwanted behavior, although the effects may be temporary (Holmes, 2001; Linsheid et al., 1990; Lovaas, 1977; Lovaas et al., 1974).

Before you decide on punishment, we suggest you consider extinction and the rewarding of desirable alternative responses. But, if punishment seems to be the only option, it should at least meet the following conditions (Walters & Grusec, 1977):

- *Punishment should be swift*—that is, immediate. Any delay will decrease its effectiveness, so "You'll get spanked when your father gets home" is a poor punishment strategy.

- *Punishment should be certain*—that is, consistently administered every time the unwanted response occurs. When "bad" behavior goes unpunished, the unintended effect can actually be rewarding.

- *Punishment should be limited in duration and intensity*—just enough to stop the behavior but appropriate enough to "make the punishment fit the crime."

- *Punishment should clearly target the behavior,* not the character of the person.
- *Punishment should be limited to the situation in which the response occurred.*
- *Punishment should not give mixed messages* to the punished person (such as, "You are not permitted to hit others, but I am allowed to hit you").
- *The most effective punishment is usually negative punishment,* such as loss of privileges, rather than the application of unpleasant stimuli, such as pain.

Operant and Classical Conditioning Compared

Now that we have looked at the main features of operant and classical conditioning, let's compare them side by side. As you can see in Table 6.2 and the diagrams in Figure 6.6 it is, most obviously, the *consequences* of behavior—especially, rewards and punishments—that make operant conditioning different from classical conditioning. One note of caution: You can see in the diagram of operant learning that food rewards the dog for sitting up. But you will also see food being presented to the dog as an unconditioned stimulus, in the classical conditioning portion of Figure 6.6. The important thing to observe, however, is that in classical conditioning the food comes *before* the response—and therefore it cannot serve as a reward.

Classical conditioning and operant conditioning also differ in the sequence of stimulus and response. Classically conditioned behavior is largely a response to *past stimulation,* while operant behavior is directed at attaining some *future* reinforcement or avoiding a punishment. To say it another way, operant conditioning requires a stimulus that follows the response, whereas classical conditioning ends with the response. (See Figure 6.7.)

The rewards given in operant conditioning can be especially effective in encouraging *new behaviors*—whether they be pulling slot machine levers, making beds, brushing teeth, going to work, or studying for an exam. Classical conditioning, on the other hand, emphasizes eliciting the *same responses to new stimuli*—such as salivating at the sound of a bell or flinching at the sound of a dentist's drill.

You will also note that extinction works in slightly different ways in the two forms of learning. In classical conditioning, it requires withholding the unconditioned stimulus, while in operant

● Animals can learn to do surprising things with a little help from operant conditioning techniques, such as shaping.

TABLE 6.2	Classical and Operant Conditioning Compared
Classical conditioning	**Operant conditioning**
Behavior is controlled by stimuli that *precede* the response (by the CS and UCS).	Behavior is controlled by consequences (rewards, punishments, etc.) that *follow* the response.
No reward or punishment is involved (although pleasant and aversive stimuli may be used).	Often involves reward (reinforcement) or punishment.
Through conditioning, a new stimulus (the CS) comes to produce "old" (reflexive) behavior.	Through conditioning, a new stimulus (a reinforcer) produces new behavior.
Extinction is produced by withholding the UCS.	Extinction is produced by withholding reinforcement.
Learner is passive (responds reflexively): Responses are involuntary. That is, behavior is *elicited* by stimulation.	Learner is active (operant behavior): Responses are voluntary. That is, behavior is *emitted* by the organism.

● **FIGURE 6.6** The Same Stimulus Plays Different Roles in Classical Conditioning and Operant Conditioning

The same stimulus (food) can play vastly different roles, depending on which type of conditioning is involved. In classical conditioning, it can be the UCS, while in operant conditioning it can serve as a reinforcer for operant behavior. Note also, that classical conditioning involves the association of two stimuli that occur *before* the response. Operant conditioning involves a reinforcing (rewarding) or punishing stimulus that occurs *after* the response.

Classical Conditioning

Operant Conditioning

conditioning the reinforcer must be withheld. In both cases, however, the result is a gradual fading of the response.

Operant conditioning and classical conditioning differ in several other important ways that you see in Table 6.2. For one, operant behavior is not based on an automatic reflex action, as was the dog's salivation or Little Albert's crying. Accordingly, operant behavior seems more "voluntary"—more under the

● **FIGURE 6.7** Classical and Operant Conditioning Can Work Together

A response originally learned through classical conditioning can be maintained and strengthened by operant reinforcement.

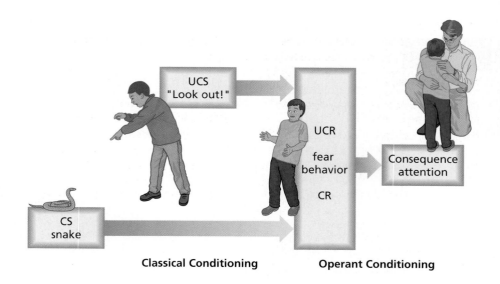

Classical Conditioning   **Operant Conditioning**

control of the responder. To paraphrase a proverb: You can stimulate a dog to salivation (a reflex), but you can't make it eat (an operant behavior).

But don't make the mistake of thinking that classical and operant conditioning are competing explanations for learning. They can be complementary. In fact, responses that were originally learned by classical conditioning will often be maintained later by operant conditioning. How might this happen? Consider a snake phobia. Suppose that the fear of snakes was originally learned by classical conditioning when a snake (CS) was paired with a frightening UCS (someone yelling, "Look out!"). Once the phobic response is established, it could be maintained and strengthened by operant conditioning, as when bystanders give attention to the fearful person (Figure 6.7). Similarly, the attention Bob, one of your authors, gets from refusing to eat olives encourages the aversion that he originally learned by classical conditioning.

 PSYCHOLOGY IN YOUR LIFE: A CHECKLIST FOR MODIFYING OPERANT BEHAVIOR

Think of someone whose behavior you would like to change. For the sake of illustration, let's focus on your nephew Johnny's temper tantrums, which always seem to occur when you take him out in public. Operant conditioning offers a variety of tools that can help, provided you have some control over stimuli that are important to Johnny. Let's consider a checklist of these operant tools: positive reinforcement, punishment, negative reinforcement, and extinction.

▍ *Positive reinforcement* is a good bet, especially if you can find some desirable behavior to reinforce before the unwanted behavior occurs. And don't overlook the Premack principle, by which Johnny gets to do something he likes if he refrains from temper outbursts. Remember, too, that attention can be a powerful reinforcer for unwanted behavior.

▍ *Punishment* may be tempting, but it is always chancy. In addition, it usually has a bad effect on the relationship between punisher and the person being punished. It is also difficult to employ because, unlike positive reinforcement, punishment must be done with unfailing consistency. So, if you do decide to punish Johnny for his tantrums, make sure you do so swiftly, certainly, and without undue harshness. As we said earlier, restriction or loss of privileges (negative punishment) is usually more effective than the application of some aversive consequence (positive punishment).

▍ *Negative reinforcement* has many of the same drawbacks as punishment because it involves unpleasant stimulation. Parents may try—most often unsuccessfully—to use negative reinforcement as a means of encouraging unlikely behavior, such as doing homework, taking out the garbage, or feeding the dog. In its most common form, the parents attempt to use nagging (an aversive stimulus) until the desired behavior occurs, whereupon the nagging presumably stops (negative reinforcement). This tactic rarely works to anyone's satisfaction. (Ironically, Johnny's screaming fit is his own intuitive attempt to manipulate people with negative reinforcement.) The only time negative reinforcement predictably works well is when the aversive conditions were imposed naturally and impersonally—as when you have headache and take aspirin, which produces negative reinforcement when your headache goes away.

▍ *Extinction* is a guaranteed solution, but only if you control all the reinforcers. In Johnny's case, extinction simply means not giving in to the temper tantrum and not letting him have what he wants (attention or candy, for

● The sort of learning displayed by Köhler's chimps defied explanation by the behaviorists—in terms of classical conditioning and operant conditioning. Here you see Sultan, Köhler's smartest animal, solving the problem of getting the bananas suspended out of the reach by stacking the boxes and climbing on top of them. Köhler claimed that Sultan's behavior demonstrated *insight learning*.

example). Instead, you simply allow the tantrum to burn itself out. This may be embarrassing because children often pick the most public places for such displays—a good sign that they are doing so for attention. One big problem with extinction, however, is that it may take a while, so extinction is not a good option if the subject is engaging in dangerous behavior, such as playing in a busy street. Another problem, only recently recognized, is that extinction can unleash a flurry of new trial-and-error behaviors aimed at getting the expected reinforcement (Carpenter, 2001b).

The best approach—often recommended by child psychologists—is to use a combination of tactics. In Johnny's case, they would probably recommend both reinforcing his desirable behaviors and extinguishing his undesirable ones.

We recommend memorizing the four items on this checklist: positive reinforcement, punishment, negative reinforcement, and extinction. Then, whenever you are dealing with someone whose behavior is undesirable, go through the list and see whether one or more of these operant tactics might do the trick. And remember: The behavior you may want to change could be your own!

CHECK YOUR UNDERSTANDING

1. **RECALL:** Thorndike's *law of effect* said that an organism will learn to perform responses that are
   a. rewarded.
   b. reflexive.
   c. prompted.
   d. preceded by a neutral stimulus.

2. **APPLICATION:** Which one of the following is an example of negative reinforcement?
   a. going to the dentist and having a toothache relieved
   b. spanking a child for swearing
   c. taking away a child's favorite toy when the child misbehaves
   d. making a child watch while another child is punished

3. **APPLICATION:** Suppose that you have taught your dog to roll over for the reward of a dog biscuit. Then, one day you run out of dog biscuits. Which schedule of reinforcement would keep your dog responding longer without a biscuit?

   a. continuous reinforcement
   b. intermittent reinforcement
   c. negative reinforcement
   d. noncontingent reinforcement

4. **RECALL:** Which one of the following is a conditioned reinforcer for most people?
   a. money   c. sex
   b. food   d. a sharp pain in the back

5. **UNDERSTANDING THE CORE CONCEPT:** Operant conditioning, in contrast with classical conditioning, emphasizes events (such as rewards and punishments) that occur
   a. before the behavior.
   b. after the behavior.
   c. during the behavior.
   d. at the same time as another stimulus.

ANSWERS: 1.a 2.a 3.b 4.a 5.b

HOW DOES COGNITIVE PSYCHOLOGY EXPLAIN LEARNING?

According to J. D. Watson's (1968) account in *The Double Helix*, the genetic code was cracked one day in a flash of insight following months of trial and error. You may have had a similar, if less famous, experience when solving a problem of your own. Such insightful events present difficulties for behavioral learning because they are hard to explain in terms of Pavlovian reflexes or Skinnerian shaping.

Many psychologists believe that an entirely different process, called *cognitive* learning, is responsible for such "flashes of insight." From this perspective, learning does not always show itself immediately in behavior. Instead, learning may be reflected in mental activity alone. And, to the chagrin of behaviorists, the cognitive view maintains that such mental processes can be examined objectively—as the Core Concept for this section says:

> According to cognitive psychology, some forms of learning must be explained as changes in mental processes, rather than as changes in behavior alone.

Let's see how psychologists have approached this task of examining the covert mental processes behind learning. To do so, we first take you on a trip to the Canary Islands, off the coast of northern Africa.

Insight Learning: Köhler in the Canaries with the Chimps

Isolated on Tenerife in the Canary Islands during World War I, Gestalt psychologist Wolfgang Köhler (*KER-ler*) had time to think long and hard about learning. He was disenchanted with the behaviorists' explanation for learning, which he found too limiting, and so he sought to develop his own theories. To Köhler's way of thinking, mental processes had to be an essential component of learning, even though they had been spurned as unscientific speculation by the behaviorists. To press his point, Köhler took advantage of a primate research facility on Tenerife to study chimpanzee behavior in situations that he contrived to make cognitive learning reveal itself (Sharps & Wertheimer, 2000; Sherrill, 1991).

In one famous study, Köhler showed that his chimps could solve complex problems by combining simpler behaviors they had previously learned separately. This was illustrated by Sultan, the brightest chimp, who had learned to pile up boxes and scramble on top of them to reach fruit suspended high in his cage and to use sticks to obtain fruit that was just out of reach. So, when Köhler presented Sultan with a novel situation, fruit suspended even higher in the air, the chimp first attacked it unsuccessfully with sticks, in trial-and-error fashion. In apparent frustration, Sultan eventually threw the sticks away, kicked the wall, and sat down. According to Köhler's report, the animal then scratched his head and began to stare at some boxes nearby. Suddenly, he jumped up and dragged a box and a stick underneath the fruit, climbed on the box, and knocked down his prize with the stick. Remarkably, Sultan had never before seen or used this combination of responses. This suggested to Köhler that the animals were not mindlessly using conditioned behaviors but were learning by reorganizing their *perceptions* of problems. He ventured that such behavior shows how apes, like humans, learn to solve problems by suddenly perceiving familiar objects in new forms or relationships—a decidedly mental process, rather than a behavioral one. He called this **insight learning** (Köhler, 1925).

Remarkably, behaviorism had no convincing stimulus–response explanation for Köhler's demonstration, except to criticize it as poorly controlled. No stretch of the imagination could plausibly explain Sultan's behavior in stimulus–response terms, as a product merely of classical or operant conditioning. The feats of Köhler's chimps demanded the cognitive explanation of perceptual reorganization. In a similar fashion, rats in Edward Tolman's lab began behaving in ways that also flew in the face of accepted behavioral doctrine. Let's see what they were up to—next.

Cognitive Maps: Tolman Finds out What's on a Rat's Mind

If you have ever given directions to someone or walked through your house in the dark, you have some idea of the *cognitive map* that Edward Tolman (1886–1959) proposed. Technically, a **cognitive map** is a mental image that an

CONNECTION: CHAPTER 5
Gestalt psychology is best known for its work on perception.

■ **Insight learning** A form of cognitive learning, originally described by the Gestalt psychologists, in which problem solving occurs by means of a sudden reorganization of perceptions.
■ **Cognitive map** A mental representation of physical space.

"Well, you don't look like an experimental psychologist to me."

organism uses to navigate through a familiar environment. But could such a simple-minded creature as a rat have such complex mental imagery? And, if so, how could the existence of these cognitive maps be demonstrated?

Mental Images—Not Behaviors A cognitive map, Tolman argued, was the only way to account for a rat quickly selecting an alternative route in a maze when the preferred path to the goal is blocked. In fact, rats will often select the shortest detour around a barrier, even though taking that particular route was never previously reinforced. Rather than blindly exploring different parts of the maze through trial and error (as would be predicted by behavioral theory), Tolman's rats behaved as if they had a mental representation of the maze. (Figure 6.8 shows the arrangement of a maze such as Tolman used.)

● **FIGURE 6.8**   Using Cognitive Maps in Maze Learning

Subjects preferred the direct path (Path 1) when it was open. When it was blocked at A, they preferred Path 2. When Path 2 was blocked at B, rats usually chose Path 3. Their behavior indicated that they had a cognitive map of the best route to the food box. (*Source:* From "Degrees of Hunger, Reward and Nonreward, and Maze Learning in Rats" by E. C. Tolman and C. H. Honzik, *University of California Publication of Psychology,* Vol. 4, No. 16, December 1930.)

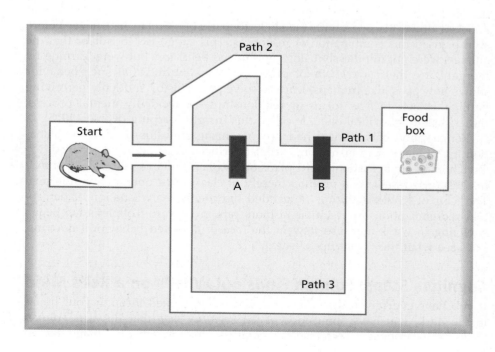

In further support of his claim that learning was mental, not behavioral, Tolman offered another experiment. After rats had learned to run a maze, he flooded it with water and showed that the rats were quite capable of swimming though the maze. Again, this demonstrated that what the animals had learned were not behaviors. Instead of learning merely a sequence of right and left turns, Tolman argued, they had acquired a more abstract mental representation of the maze's spatial layout (Tolman & Honzik, 1930; Tolman et al., 1946).

Learning Without Reinforcement   In yet another simple study that attacked the very foundations of behaviorism, Tolman (1948) allowed his rats to wander freely about a maze for several hours, during which they received no reinforcement at all. Yet, despite the lack of reinforcement (which behaviorists supposed to be essential for maze learning), the rats later were able to negotiate the maze for a food reward more quickly than did rats that had never seen the maze before. Tolman called this *latent learning.*

The Significance of Tolman's Work   What made Tolman's work both significant and provocative was its challenge to the prevailing behavioral views of Pavlov, Watson, and (later) Skinner. While Tolman accepted the idea that psychologists must study observable behavior, he showed that simple associations between stimuli and responses could not explain the behavior observed in his experiments. Tolman's cognitive explanations, therefore, presented a daring challenge to behaviorism (Gleitman, 1991; Kesner & Olton, 1990; Olton, 1992; Tolman, 1932). We should note, in passing, that Jean Piaget's work in developmental psychology (which we described in Chapter 4) was simultaneously challenging behaviorism on another cognitive front.

Subsequent experiments on cognitive maps in rats, chimpanzees, and humans have broadly supported Tolman's work (Menzel, 1978; Moar, 1980; Olton, 1979). More recently, brain imaging has pointed to the hippocampus as a structure involved in "drawing" the cognitive map in the brain (Jacobs & Schenk, 2003). So, it seems clear that Tolman was right: Organisms learn the spatial layout of their environments by exploration, and they do so even if they are not reinforced for exploring. From an evolutionary perspective, this ability to make cognitive maps is highly adaptive in animals that must forage for food (Kamil et al., 1987). And, more generally, Tolman seems to have been right about the cognitive underpinnings of behavioral learning.

In the following section we shall see that Albert Bandura has followed in Tolman's footsteps by challenging a pillar of behaviorism. Bandura proposed that rewards can be effective even if we merely see someone else get them. (After all, this is what makes people buy lottery tickets!) Bandura's work, then, suggests that reinforcement can operate indirectly, through *observation.* Let's see how he demonstrated this idea.

Observational Learning: Bandura's Challenge to Behaviorism

Does observing violent behavior make viewers more likely to become violent? A classic study by Albert Bandura suggests that it does—at least in the children he invited to his lab for a simple experiment. After observing adults seeming to enjoy punching, hitting, and kicking an inflated plastic clown (a BoBo doll), the children later showed similar aggressive behavior toward the doll. Significantly, these children were more aggressive than those in a control condition who had not observed the aggressive models (Bandura et al., 1963). Subsequent studies showed that children will also imitate aggressive behaviors they have seen on film, even when the models were merely cartoon characters.

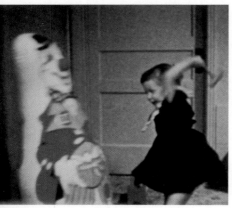

● In the BoBo doll experiment, a boy and girl imitate the aggressive behavior that they have seen from an adult.

■ **Observational learning** A form of cognitive learning in which new responses are acquired after watching others' behavior and the consequences of their behavior.

Learning by Observation and Imitation An important implication of Bandura's BoBo doll study is that imitation can serve us in situations where we have not had a chance to gather personal experience. Thus, we learn by imitation or observation, by watching the behavior of another person, or model. If the model's actions appear successful—that is, if the model seems to find it reinforcing—we may seek to behave in the same way. You can think of learning by observation and imitation as an extension of operant conditioning, in which we observe someone else getting rewarded but act as though we had also received a reward.

Psychologists simply call this **observational learning** or *social lerning*. It accounts for children learning aggressive behavior by imitating aggressive role models who are perceived as successful or admirable or who seem to be enjoying themselves. And it accounts for changes in clothing fashions and the rapid spread of slang expressions, as well as many other learned behaviors. Observational learning is also seen in nonhuman species, as when a mother cat teaches her kittens how to hunt. One study demonstrated that even a creature as simple-brained as the octopus can learn by example from watching the behavior of other octopi (Fiorito & Scotto, 1992). And, not to be outdone, a clever bowerbird in an Australian national park has achieved some notoriety through observational learning by fooling tourists with its imitation of a cell phone ringing (Winters, 2002).

Effects of Media Violence As you might have guessed, much of the research on observational learning has focused on the impact of violence in film and video (Bushman & Anderson, 2001; Huesmann et al., 2003; Johnson et al., 2001). Predictably, the issue is a controversial one (Anderson & Bushman, 2002; Bloom, 2002; Ferguson, 2002; Freedman, 1984, 1996). What we have is *correlational* evidence from more than 50 studies shows that observing violence is associated with violent behavior and more than 100 *experimental* studies pointing to a causal relationship (Huesmann & Moise, 1996; Primavera & Heron, 1996). In addition, we have experimental evidence that viewers of media violence show a reduction in emotional arousal and distress, when they subsequently observe violent acts—a condition known as *psychic numbing* (Murray & Kippax, 1979). Finally, notes social psychologist Elliot Aronson, extensive media violence is undoubtedly one factor contributing to violent tragedies, such as the Columbine High School shootings (Aronson, 2000).

Not all imitation is harmful, of course. By imitation we also learn about charitable behavior, comforting others in distress, and driving on the correct side of the road. In general, we can say that people learn much—both prosocial (helping) and antisocial (hurting) behaviors—through observation of others. This capacity to learn from watching enables us to acquire behaviors efficiently, without going through tedious trial and error. So, while observational learning seems to be a factor in violent behavior, it also enables us to learn socially useful behaviors by profiting from the mistakes and successes of others.

Rethinking Behavioral Learning in Cognitive Terms

In the last few decades of the 20th century, cognitive psychologists ventured deep into the territory of classical and operant conditioning, giving those theories a cognitive tweak (Leslie, 2001). One of the big issues they raised concerns the adaptive value of classical conditioning for an animal (Hollis, 1997). Specifically, Robert Rescorla has shown that the crucial feature of the conditioned stimulus is its *informativeness*—its value in predicting the onset of the unconditioned stimulus (Rescorla, 1972, 1988; Rescorla & Wagner, 1972). We saw this, for example, in food aversions, where a certain taste can serve as a warning of illness.

Research by Leon Kamin extends Rescorla's idea. Kamin (1969) has shown that a learner will form a CS–CR connection only if the CS seems to provide unique information about the UCS. In his laboratory, an aversive unconditioned stimulus, such as a shock, was preceded by multiple warning cues, such as lights, tones, and tastes. Yet, his animal subjects paid attention only to the stimuli that provided the best information about the UCS.

In the wild, the unique wing markings of monarch butterflies serve as conditioned stimuli for butterfly-eating birds that have a learned aversion for monarch butterflies. (They taste awful.) To give a more personal example, you may see smoke as well as smell the acrid odor of something burning before you actually see the flames of a fire. But you may have learned from experience that smoke is not always visible during a fire, while the smell of something burning is a telltale sign of fire. The smell then provides better information about whether there is a fire, so you learned to pay closer attention to the smell than to the sight of smoke.

Following the lead of Bandura, Kamin, and Rescorla, attempts are also being made by cognitive psychologists to broaden the scope of operant conditioning to include mental processes (Church, 2001; DeGrandpre, 2000; Ohlsson, 1996). From this perspective, reinforcement changes not only behavior but the individual's *expectations* for future rewards or punishments in similar situations. An example will probably help: If you are rewarded with a better grade for attending your psychology class, this reward changes your future behavior by changing your expectation that attending future classes will also be rewarding. We will see more of this work in Chapter 14, where we will look at *social cognition*. (See Table 6.3.)

Brain Mechanisms and Learning

On a neural level, learning apparently involves physical changes that strengthen the synapses in groups of nerve cells—a process called **long-term potentiation** (Antonova et al., 2001; Carlson, 2004; Kandel, 2000). In operant conditioning, the brain's reward circuitry also comes into play, especially parts of the limbic system and associated brain structures. These circuits are rich in dopamine receptors, leading many experts to believe that this transmitter is crucial to the brain's sensing of reward (Fiorillo et al., 2003; Shizgal & Avanitogiannis, 2003). In support of this view, we remind you that the highly reinforcing sensations produced by cocaine and amphetamines are due to their action as dopamine agonists.

■ **Long-term potentiation**

A biological process, involving physical changes that strengthen the synapses in groups of nerve cells, which is believed to be the neural basis of learning.

◀ **CONNECTION: CHAPTER 2**

An *agonist* is a chemical that mimics or enhances the effects of a neurotransmitter.

TABLE 6.3	Behavioral Learning and Cognitive Learning Compared
Behavioral Learning	**Cognitive Learning**
Focus on observable events (stimuli and responses) only	Makes inferences about mental processes that are not directly observable
Learning as associations among stimuli and responses	Learning as information processing: The learner seeks useful information from stimuli
Main forms of learning are habituation, classical conditioning, and operant (instrumental) conditioning	Learning also involves insight, observational learning, cognitive maps, and other more complex forms of learning
Developed as a rebellion against the subjective methods of structuralism and functionalism: Behaviorism became the dominant perspective for much of the 20th century.	Developed as a rebellion against the narrow perspective of behaviorism: Cognitive psychology became the dominant perspective at the end of the 20th century.
Big names: Pavlov, Thorndike, Watson, Skinner	Big names: Köhler, Tolman, Bandura, Rescorla

Neuroscientists Eric Kandel and Robert Hawkins (1992) have made a proposal that may connect behavioral learning and cognitive learning at the level of brain pathways. Their theory rests on the discovery that animals with relatively simple nervous systems have a single type of nerve circuit that enables them to learn simple behavioral responses. In the more complex brains of mammals, however, neuroscientists have found a second type of learning circuitry that apparently facilitates higher forms of learning, such as memory for events.

What is the significance of these findings? Kandel and Hawkins speculated that the two types of learning circuits may divide the task of learning along the same line that has long separated behavioral psychologists and cognitive psychologists. Some other psychologists now tentatively agree (Clark & Squire, 1998; Jog et al., 1999). The simpler circuit seems to be responsible for the sort of "mindless" learning that occurs when a dog drools at the sound of a bell or when a person acquires a motor skill, such as riding a bike or swinging a golf club. This kind of learning occurs slowly and improves with repetition over many trials. Significantly, classical conditioning and much of operant learning fit this description. By contrast, the second type of learning circuit seems to be responsible for more complex forms of learning that require conscious processing—the sort of learning that interests cognitive psychologists: concept formation, insight learning, observational learning, and memory for specific events. If further research verifies that this division reflects a fundamental distinction in the nervous system, we will be able to say that those on the behavioral and cognitive extremes were both (partly) right. They were talking about fundamentally different forms of learning.

"Higher" Cognitive Learning

Whatever the neuroscientists finally decide, it seems clear that the learning required in college classes, where you must learn abstract ideas, is different from the stimulus–response learning that Pavlov, Watson, and Skinner studied. Acquiring knowledge about the field of psychology, for example, involves building ing mental images, assimilating concepts, and pondering ways they can be related, compared, and contrasted. By the same token, Sabra's classes taught her *concepts* about flight and about emotional responses. It's not that behavioral conditioning isn't involved in human learning—after all, students *do* work for grades and salivate when they see a pizza—but the principles of behavioral learning don't tell the whole story of "higher" cognitive learning.

The next two chapters will take us deeper into this realm of cognition, where we will discuss memory, thinking, concept formation, problem-solving, and intelligence. There you will find out more about the mental structures that underlie cognitive learning. The problem we will face there is exactly the one that the behaviorists were hoping to avoid: In studying cognition, we must make inferences about processes that we cannot measure directly. Cognitive learning is always about processes that are one step removed from observable behavior. We will find, however, that cognitive psychologists have developed some very clever methods for obtaining objective data on which to base their inferences. The newest of these—coming fully on line in the last decade or so—is brain imaging, which, as we will see, has brought psychologists very close to an objective glimpse at private mental processes.

● Learning is not efficient when the learner is "multitasking"—trying to perform several tasks that demand attention at the same time.

But, before we move on to these topics in the next chapter, let's pause for a critical look at a learning fad that has swept through college classrooms in recent years.

PSYCHOLOGY IN YOUR LIFE: A CRITICAL LOOK AT "LEARNING STYLES"

There is no doubt that people differ in the ways that they approach learning. You can see by looking at your classmates that everyone brings a different set of interests, abilities, temperamental factors, developmental levels, social and cultural experiences, and emotions to bear on learning tasks. But, can we say that these constitute distinct "learning styles"?

Some educators have made claims about learning styles that go far beyond any supporting evidence (Terry, 2000). For example, much has been made of a supposed difference between "left-brained" and "right-brained" learners. But, as we saw in Chapter 2, this dichotomy is based on a fundamental misinterpretation of split-brain research. (In a person with an intact corpus callosum, both hemispheres work cooperatively.) What the proponents of left-brain/right-brain learning styles usually mean is that some people *prefer* learning verbally, while others *prefer* materials that are more visual–spatial. And, like all typologies, this one assumes that people fall neatly into distinct groups, even though it would be more accurate to see people as gradually shading from one end of the spectrum to the other. This questionable assumption may be one reason why little solid evidence exists to show that people who are described as having different learning styles actually do learn differently.

Many other learning style schemes have been proposed, and with them paper-and-pencil tests have appeared on the market for assessing students' learning styles. Unfortunately, most of these schemes have little supporting data to show that people with different scores learn in different ways. An exception may be an ambitious program developed by Sternberg and Grigorenko to assess students on their abilities for logical, creative, and practical thinking—arguably, three distinct forms of "intelligence" (Sternberg, 1994; Sternberg & Grigorenko, 1997). Students in an introductory psychology course were divided into groups that received instruction emphasizing the form of intelligence on which they had scored highest. (A control group of students was deliberately mismatched.) Tests at the end of the course indicated that students did best when the teaching emphasis matched their intellectual style. As a practical matter, however, such a fine-tuned approach is probably not feasible for implementation on a large scale.

On a more positive note, interest in learning styles has alerted teachers and professors to the fact that their material can usually be taught in a variety of ways. Further, the available research suggests everyone learns better when the material can be approached in more than one way—both visual and verbal, as well as through hands-on active learning (see, for example, McKeachie, 1990, 1997, 1999). In recent years, this has led to the development of a variety of teaching methods to augment the lecture-only method that had previously been used almost exclusively in college classrooms.

The practical lesson here is to be skeptical of tests that purport to identify your learning style. Beware also of people who might tell you that you are a visual learner, a reflective learner, or some such other type. This sort of thinking erroneously suggests that each person learns in only one way. It also erroneously suggests that the way we learn is fixed and unchanging. In fact, your college experience presents a wonderful opportunity to learn to think and learn in new and unaccustomed ways.

1. **RECALL:** When their goal path was blocked, Tolman's rats would take the shortest detour around the barrier. This, said Tolman, showed that they had developed
   a. trial-and-error learning.
   b. operant behavior.
   c. cognitive maps.
   d. observational learning.

2. **RECALL:** Cognitive psychologist Robert Rescorla has reinterpreted the process of classical conditioning. In his view, the conditioned stimulus (CS) serves as a
   a. cue that signals the onset of the UCS.
   b. stimulus that follows the UCS.
   c. negative reinforcement.
   d. cognitive map.

3. **APPLICATION:** If you were going to use Bandura's findings in developing a program to prevent violence among middle school children, you might

   a. have children watch videos of aggressive children who are not being reinforced for their aggressive behavior.
   b. have children role-play nonaggressive solutions to interpersonal problems.
   c. have children punch a BoBo doll, to "get the aggression out of their system."
   d. punish children for aggressive acts performed at school.

4. **UNDERSTANDING THE CORE CONCEPT:** Which of the following proved to be difficult to explain in purely behavioral terms?
   a. a trained seal doing a trick for a fish
   b. a dog salivating at the sound of a bell
   c. a chimpanzee using a pile of boxes and a stick to obtain food hung high in its cage
   d. a pigeon learning to press a lever in a Skinner box for a food reward

ANSWERS: 1. c 2. a 3. a 4. c

LEARNING: THE STATE OF THE ART

Psychologists now understand the essential features of behavioral learning: habituation, classical conditioning, and operant conditioning. Arguably, they know more about such learning than about any other facet of psychology. So, is there anything left to learn about learning? Here are three important frontiers that need much more exploration:

▌ We know only a little about the neuroscience behind learning: the nerve circuits, the neurotransmitters, and how they represent our experience (Kandel, 2000). At the most basic level, what *is* learning?

▌ We need more work that bridges the gap between behavioral and cognitive learning. The tools of neuroscience have removed many of the old (and, at the time, valid) objections the behaviorists voiced about the objective study of mental processes. But is cognitive learning just an elaboration of classical conditioning, operant conditioning, and habituation—or is it something fundamentally different?

▌ Third, we have just scratched the surface in our understanding of how we learn about concepts, ideas, and images. This is not only a theoretical issue but a question of urgent practical importance: How can we facilitate such learning in our schools and colleges?

Plenty of work on learning remains to be done by a new generation of researchers who can ask the right questions and look beyond the old controversies.

CHAPTER SUMMARY

Learning produces lasting changes in behavior or mental processes, giving us an advantage over organisms that rely more heavily on reflexes and instincts. Some forms of learning, such as habituation, are quite simple, while others, such as classical conditioning, operant conditioning, and cognitive learning, are more complex.

● WHAT SORT OF LEARNING DOES CLASSICAL CONDITIONING EXPLAIN?

The earliest learning research focused on classical conditioning, beginning with Ivan Pavlov's discovery that conditioned stimuli (after being paired with unconditioned stimuli) could elicit reflexive responses. His experiments on dogs showed how conditioned responses could be acquired, extinguished, and undergo spontaneous recovery in laboratory animals. He also demonstrated stimulus generalization and discrimination learning. John Watson extended Pavlov's work to people, notably in his famous experiment on the conditioning of fear in Little Albert. More recent work, particularly studies of taste aversions, suggest, however, that classical conditioning is not a simple stimulus–response learning process but also has a biological component. In general, classical conditioning affects basic, survival-oriented responses. Therapeutic applications of Pavlovian learning include the prevention of harmful food aversions in chemotherapy patients.

● Classical conditioning is a basic form of learning in which a stimulus that produces an innate reflex becomes associated with a previously neutral stimulus, which then acquires the power to elicit essentially the same response.

● HOW DO WE LEARN NEW BEHAVIORS BY OPERANT CONDITIONING?

A more active form of learning, called instrumental conditioning, was first explored by Edward Thorndike, who established the law of effect, based on his study of trial-and-error learning. B. F. Skinner, expanded Thorndike's work, now called operant conditioning, to explain how responses are influenced by their environmental consequences. His work identified and assessed various consequences, including positive and negative reinforcement, punishment, and an operant form of extinction. The power of operant conditioning involves producing new responses. To do so, Skinner and others examined continuous reinforcement, as well as several kinds of intermittent reinforcement contingencies, including FR, VR, FI, and VI schedules. As for punishment, research has shown that it is more difficult to use than reward because it has several undesirable side effects. There are, however, alternatives, including operant extinction and rewarding of alternative responses, application of the Premack principle, and prompting and shaping new behaviors.

● In operant conditioning, the consequences of behavior, such as rewards and punishments, influence the chance that the behavior will occur again.

● HOW DOES COGNITIVE PSYCHOLOGY EXPLAIN LEARNING?

Much research now suggests that learning is not just a process that links stimuli and responses: Learning is also cognitive. This was shown in Köhler's work on insight learning in chimpanzees, in Tolman's studies of cognitive maps in rats, and in Bandura's research on observational learning and imitation in humans—particularly the effect of observing aggressive models, which spawned many studies on media violence. All of this cognitive research demonstrated that learning did not necessarily involve changes in behavior nor did it require reinforcement. In the past three decades, cognitive scientists have worked on reinterpreting behavioral learning, especially operant and classical conditioning, in cognitive terms, as well as searching for the neural basis of learning. Some educators have, however, taken new developments in learning far beyond the evidence: Specifically, there is little empirical support for most of the claims in the "learning style" literature.

● **According to cognitive psychology, some forms of learning must be explained as changes in mental processes, rather than as changes in behavior alone.**

REVIEW TEST

For each of the following items, choose the single correct or best answer. The correct answers appear at the end.

1. Which one of the following taught that psychology should involve only the analysis of observable stimuli and responses?
   a. Albert Bandura
   b. B. F. Skinner
   c. Sigmund Freud
   d. John Garcia

2. According to Thorndike, rewarded responses are gradually "stamped in," while unrewarded or punished responses are eliminated. He called this
   a. the law of effect.
   b. observational learning.
   c. classical conditioning.
   d. extinction.

3. Which one of the following illustrates a reinforcement contingency?
   a. I always work harder in the morning than I do in the afternoon.
   b. If I don't show up for work, I will be fired.
   c. I get $500 for a week's work.
   d. Money is reinforcing because it buys me things I need and want, such as food, clothes, and entertainment.

4. "The best part of going to the beach," your friend exclaims as you start your vacation, "is getting away from all the stress of work and school." If this is true, then your friend's vacation-taking behavior has been influenced by
   a. positive reinforcement.
   b. negative reinforcement.
   c. extinction.
   d. punishment.

5. Which of the following is *not* a good way to make punishment effective?
   a. Make it swift and brief.
   b. Make it intense.
   c. Deliver it immediately.
   d. Focus it on the undesirable behavior.

6. According to the Premack principle, a reinforcer can be
   a. changes in behavior from its past norms.
   b. anything that rewards rather than penalizes behavior.
   c. a stimulus that becomes associated with an unconditioned stimulus.
   d. the opportunity to engage in any behavior frequently performed by the organism.

7. In his research with rats running mazes, Edward C. Tolman concluded that his animals had
   a. made a CS–UCS connection.
   b. used conditioned reinforcers.
   c. developed a cognitive map.
   d. displayed spontaneous recovery.

8. In Bandura's experiment with the BoBo doll, aggressive behavior resulted from
   a. painful stimulation.
   b. insults.
   c. observational learning.
   d. negative reinforcement.

9. During classical conditioning, for an organism to learn a conditioned association between two stimuli, the UCS must seem to
   a. predict the CS.
   b. be predicted by the CS.
   c. be independent of the CS.
   d. follow the UCR.

10. The biggest problem with the concept of "learning styles" is that
    a. the ways people learn don't fall neatly into distinct learning-style categories.
    b. most people are visual learners—hardly anyone is an auditory learner.
    c. people who think with the right brain don't fit into any known learning style.
    d. most educators don't believe in learning styles.

ANSWERS: 1.b 2.a 3.c 4.b 5.b 6.d 7.c 8.c 9.b 10.a

Learning (p. 226)

Habituation (p. 227)

Mere exposure effect (p. 227)

Behavioral learning (p. 228)

Classical conditioning (p. 229)

Neutral stimulus (p. 229)

Unconditioned stimulus (UCS) (p. 229)

Unconditioned response (UCR) (p. 229)

Acquisition (p. 230)

Conditioned stimulus (CS) (p. 230)

Conditioned response (CR) (p. 230)

Extinction (in classical conditioning) (p. 231)

Spontaneous recovery (p. 231)

Stimulus generalization (p. 232)

Stimulus discrimination (p. 232)

Experimental neurosis (p. 232)

Taste-aversion learning (p. 234)

Operant (p. 236)

Operant conditioning (p. 236)

Law of effect (p. 236)

Reinforcer (p. 236)

Positive reinforcement (p. 237)

Negative reinforcement (p. 238)

Operant chamber (p. 237)

Reinforcement contingencies (p. 238)

Continuous reinforcement (p. 238)

Shaping (p. 238)

Intermittent reinforcement (p. 238)

Extinction (in operant conditioning) (p. 238)

Schedules of reinforcement (p. 239)

Ratio schedule (p. 239)

Interval schedule (p. 239)

Fixed ratio (FR) schedules (p. 239)

Variable ratio (VR) schedules (p. 239)

Fixed interval (FI) schedules (p. 239)

Variable interval (VI) schedules (p. 240)

Primary reinforcers (p. 240)

Conditioned reinforcers or secondary reinforcers (p. 240)

Token economy (p. 240)

Premack principle (p. 241)

Punishment (p. 241)

Positive punishment (p. 241)

Negative punishment (p. 241)

Insight learning (p. 249)

Cognitive map (p. 249)

Observational learning (p. 252)

Long-term potentiation (p. 253)

OUR RECOMMENDED BOOKS AND VIDEOS

BOOKS

Artiss, K. L. (1996). *Mistake making.* Lanham, MD: University Press of America. Why doesn't everyone learn from experience? Some experiences may not be memorable—but certain types of people may also have difficulty making the adjustments necessary for each lesson; and, failing to learn, they end up suffering relentless punishment by repeating their errors and failures. Here's why it may happen—and what to do about it.

Greven, P. (1992). *Spare the child: The religious roots of punishment and the psychological impact of child abuse.* New York: Vintage Books. Imagine a world in which hitting a child is not only politically incorrect, it is also against the law of both man and God. Greven documents the great weight of evidence against any rationale for corporal punishment of children and asserts that we have a moral obligation to develop humane alternatives to beating our kids.

Martel, Yann. (2003). *Life of Pi.* Orlando, FL: Harcourt. No, this is not a math book. It's a fantastic (in both senses) novel about religion . . . and animal learning and behavior. Pi is a young boy from India, where his parents own a zoo and where he becomes a Hindu, a Christian, and a Moslem. When the zoo is sold, the family heads to Canada on a steamer, along with many of their animals. A storm sends the ship to the bottom, and the only survivors are Pi, a wounded zebra, a seasick orangutan, a hyena, and Richard Parker, a Bengal tiger—all in the same lifeboat. That's where Pi's deep understanding of animals comes in handy.

Nierenberg, G. I. (1996). *Doing it right the first time: A short guide to learning from your most memorable errors, mistakes, and blunders.* New York: Wiley. Mainly aimed at managers, this book also offers valuable advice to students (and professors) about how to first become aware of and then detect patterns in our own repeated errors. Some strategies involve focusing attention, learning from others' mistakes, and building accuracy.

Wright, J. (2003). *There must be more than this: Finding more life, love, and meaning by overcoming your soft addictions.* New York: Broadway Books. Educator Judith Wright finds that most people indulge—too much—in "soft addictions" such as watching TV, surfing the Net, gossiping, or shopping. Time spent in these tempting but ultimately unfulfilling activities leaves us needier than before. The key to change is in understanding why these time-wasters feel rewarding and how to find positive reinforcement instead in truly meaningful activity such as interacting with friends or completing valued work.

VIDEOS

A Clockwork Orange. (1971, color, 137 min.). Directed by Stanley Kubrick; starring Malcolm McDowell, Patrick Magee, Adrienne Corri. A classic and still powerful rendition of Anthony Burgess's novel, about a futuristic society's efforts to reform a psychopathic criminal by applying aversive conditioning—with unexpected results.

CORE CONCEPTS

▼

Human memory is an
information processing system
that works constructively to
encode, store, and retrieve
information.

▼

Each of the three memory
stages encodes and stores
memories in a different way,
but they work together to
transform sensory experience
into a lasting record that has
a pattern or meaning.

▼

Whether memories are implicit
or explicit, successful retrieval
depends on how they were
encoded and how they
are cued.

▼

Most of our memory problems
arise from memory's "seven
sins"—which are really
by-products of otherwise
adaptive features of
human memory.

Psychology in Your Life

Would You Want a "Photographic" Memory?
This ability is rare, and those who
have it say that the images can
sometimes interfere with their
thinking.

"Flashbulb" Memories: Where Were You When . . . ?
These especially vivid memories
usually involve emotionally charged
events. Surprisingly, they aren't
always accurate.

On the Tip of Your Tongue
It is maddening when you know the
word, but you just can't quite say it.
But you're not alone. Most people
experience this about once a week.

Improving Your Memory With Mnemonics
There are lots of tricks for learning
lists, but another technique works
better for mastering the concepts
you'll meet in college.

USING PSYCHOLOGY TO LEARN PSYCHOLOGY:
How to Avoid Memory Failure on Exams

Memory

SOME 20 YEARS AGO, 12-year-old Donna Smith began to suffer from severe migraine headaches, which left her sleepless and depressed. Her parents, Judee and Dan, agreed to get her psychiatric help. During an evaluation recommended by her therapist, Donna disclosed—for the first time—that she had been sexually molested at the age of 3 by a neighbor. It was concluded that memories of the assault, buried in her mind for so long, were probably responsible for some of Donna's current problems, so she continued with therapy.

As a teenager, Donna began work with a new therapist, a private social worker specializing in child abuse. In their first session, the therapist asked Donna if she had been sexually abused by her father. Donna denied this but did mention the neighbor's assault. The therapist, however, believed there might be more behind Donna's problems. For many months, she repeatedly asked Donna whether her father had abused her. Finally, Donna told her a lie, claiming her father had once "touched" her, hoping this false claim would enable her therapy to move on. The therapist immediately reported Donna's father to the local sheriff and to the Maryland Department of Social Services (ABC News, 1995).

When Donna realized the drastic consequences of her false claim, she tried to set the record straight, but the therapist dismissed the confession, saying that all abuse victims recant their accusations once they learn their therapists are required to report such claims. The therapist was persuasive, and eventually Donna began to entertain the idea that her conscious memory was a self-delusion—a trick of her mind trying to protect itself from the "real" truth. Reluctantly, she concluded that it must have been her father, not the neighbor, who had assaulted her as a toddler. When the therapist convinced her to tell the story to county authorities, Donna was removed from her home and placed in foster care.

To her parents, these sudden accusations were "like a bomb"—and it got worse. Still in therapy, Donna became convinced her father had been a chronic abuser, and she began to hate him "wholeheartedly." Committed to a psychiatric hospital, she was diagnosed as having several different personalities, one of which claimed that her parents practiced ritual satanic abuse of Donna's younger brothers. The courts forbade Donna's parents to have contact with her. Judee Smith lost her license to run a day care center. Dan Smith, a retired naval officer, was arrested at his home and handcuffed in front of their two young sons. Financially ruined, he was tried on charges of abuse, based solely on his daughter's testimony. His two-week trial ended in a hung jury, and Dan Smith went free.

Shortly after the trial, Donna moved to Michigan with her foster family. In these new surroundings, far away from the system that had supported her fabricated story, she gradually regained perspective and found the courage to tell the truth. She admitted the charges had all been fabrications, and her doctor recommended she be sent back to her family. The Smiths had a tearful reunion and began the slow process of rebuilding lost relationships and trust. "She's been a victim of this system, as much as we've been a victim," says Dan Smith. "You know, there's a lot of healing to be done."

According to Johns Hopkins psychiatrist Paul McHugh, erroneous recovered memories are fabricated from suggestions therapists offer in order to blame psychological problems on long-hidden trauma (ABC News, 1995). Memory expert Elizabeth Loftus agrees, noting that some clinicians are all too ready to accept their clients' memories, even fantastic tales of ritualistic abuse (Loftus, 2003a, b). In the book *Making Monsters,* social psychologist Richard Ofshe argues that clients can unknowingly tailor their recollections to fit their therapists' expectations. He adds that "therapists often encourage patients to redefine their life histories based on the new pseudomemories and, by doing so, redefine their most basic understanding of their families and themselves" (Ofshe & Watters, 1994, p. 6).

Today Donna and her family are "in wonderful shape, back together." Still, the memories of the Smith family's ordeal will remain painful shadows in the background of their lives forever. Fortunately, the same flexibility in human learning and remembering that created these problems can also provide the key to forgiving and healing.

We should emphasize that sexual abuse of children does occur, and it is a serious problem. While estimates vary considerably, it appears that from 4% to 20% of children in the United States experience at least one incident of sexual abuse (McAnulty & Burnette, 2004; Rathus et al., 2000). The issue raised by Donna's case, however, involves false claims of sexual abuse based on faulty "recovered memories." And, while such problems are relatively rare, they have surfaced often enough to alarm psychologists about the widespread misunderstanding people have about memory. Psychologists know that memory does not always make an accurate record of events—even when people are very confident about their recollections.

In fact, Donna's memory works very much like your own. As you will learn in this chapter, everyone has a memory capable of distortion. You will also learn about memory's inner workings and some extraordinary memory abilities. Finally, we will end this chapter on a practical note by considering some steps you can take to improve your memory.

WHAT IS MEMORY?

The best defense against the tricks that memory can play comes from an understanding of how memory works. So, let's begin building that defense with a definition: Cognitive psychologists view **memory** as a system that encodes, stores, and retrieves information—a definition, by the way, that applies equally to an organism or a computer. Unlike a computer's memory, however, human memory is a *cognitive* system, in the sense of the term's Latin root, *cognoscere*, which means "knowing" or "understanding." That is, human memory works closely with the perceptual system, which takes information from the senses and selectively converts it into meaningful patterns that can be stored and accessed later when needed. These memory patterns, then, form the raw material for thought and behavior—allowing you to recognize a friend's face, ride a bicycle, recollect a trip to Disneyland, and (if all goes well) recall the concepts you need during a test. More generally, our Core Concept characterizes the memory system this way:

CORE CONCEPT

> Human memory is an information processing system that works constructively to encode, store, and retrieve information.

And how is memory related to *learning*? You might think of human memory as the cognitive system that processes, encodes, and stores information as we learn and then allows us to retrieve that learned information later. Accordingly, this chapter is an extension of our discussion of cognitive learning in Chapter 6. The focus here, however, will be on more complex *human* learning and memory, as contrasted with the simpler forms of animal learning and conditioning that we studied earlier.

Metaphors for Memory

Human memory has been compared to a library or a storehouse (Haberlandt, 1999). There metaphors capture the ability of memory to hold large amounts of information. Some metaphors for memory, however, can be misleading. That's certainly the case with the "video recorder" metaphor for memory, which leads people to believe that human memory makes a complete and accurate record of everything we experience.

Cognitive psychologists have shown that this "video recorder" metaphor is wrong. In Donna Smith's case, it was dangerously wrong. Instead, cognitive psychologists see human memory as an *interpretive* system that takes in information and, much like an artist, discards details and organizes the rest in meaningful patterns.

Later, when remembering, what actually happens is that you retrieve fragments of memory—like pieces of a jigsaw puzzle. Then, using these fragments, you *reconstruct* the incident (or idea, emotion, or image) by filling in the blanks *as you think it was*, rather than the way it actually was. Most of the time this

● Both people and computers have memory.

■ **Memory** Any system—human, animal, or machine—that encodes, stores, and retrieves information.

● **FIGURE 7.1** The Penny Test

(*Source:* From "Long-Term Memory for a Common Object," by Nickerson and Adams in *Cognitive Psychology,* Vol. 11, Issue #1, 1979, pp. 287–307. Copyright © 1979. Reprinted by permission of Elsevier.)

● Memory encodes the best records for information on which we have focused attention.

■ **Information-processing model**
A cognitive understanding of memory, emphasizing how information is changed when it is encoded, stored, and retrieved.

works well enough that you don't realize just how much of remembrance is really reconstruction.

A look at Figure 7.1 will make you aware of this reconstructive process. Which image in the figure is the most accurate portrayal of a penny? Although pennies are common in our everyday experience, you will probably find that identifying the real penny image is not easy. Unless we are coin collectors, most of us pay little attention to the details of these familiar objects. The result is a vague memory image that serves well enough in everyday life but is sparse on details. So, when retrieving the image of a penny, we automatically fill in the gaps and missing details—without realizing how much of the memory we are actually creating. (The right answer, by the way, is A.)

In general, psychologists have found that we make the most complete and accurate memory records for:

❚ Information on which we have *focused our attention,* such as a friend's words against the background noise of a restaurant

❚ Information in which we are *interested,* such as the courses in your major field

❚ Information that *arouses us emotionally,* such as an especially enjoyable or painful experience

❚ Information that *connects with previous experience,* such as a news item about the star of a movie you saw last week

❚ Information that we *rehearse,* such as memory for material reviewed the night before an exam

The rest of the chapter will unfold this way of thinking about memory, which cognitive psychologists call the **information-processing model.** This view emphasizes how information undergoes systematic changes on its way to becoming a memory—quite different from the naïve perspective of the video-recorder model. It also emphasizes that memory is *functional*—that is, it performs some useful tasks for us. The most basic of these, we will see below, are *encoding, storage,* and *retrieval* of information.

Memory's Three Basic Tasks

In simplest terms, human memory takes essentially meaningless sensory information (such as the sound of your professor's voice) and changes it into meaningful patterns (words, sentences, and concepts) that you can store and use later. To do so, memory must first *encode* the incoming sensory information in a useful format. **Encoding** requires that you *select* some stimulus event from among the vast array of inputs assaulting your senses. Is it a sound, a visual image, or an odor? Then you *identify* the distinctive features of that input. If it's a sound, is it loud, soft, or harsh? Does it fit some pattern, such as a car horn, a melody, a voice? Is it a sound you have heard before? Finally, you mentally tag, or *label*, an experience to make it meaningful. ("It's Dr. Weber. She's my psychology professor!")

For most of our everyday experiences, encoding can be so automatic and rapid that we have no awareness of the process. For example, you can probably recall what you had for breakfast this morning, even though you didn't deliberately try to make the experience "stick" in your mind. Emotionally charged experiences, such as an angry exchange with a colleague, are even more likely to lodge in memory without any effort on our part (Dolan, 2002).

On the other hand, memories for concepts, such the basic principles of psychology that you are learning about in this book, usually require a deliberate encoding effort, called *elaboration*, in order to establish a usable memory. During this elaboration, you connect a new concept with existing information in memory. One way to do this is to link it with concrete examples, as when you associated the term "negative reinforcement" to the removal of pain when you take an aspirin. (As an aid to elaboration, this book provides many such examples that we hope will connect with your experience.) In another form of elaboration, you connect the new idea to old concepts already in memory. This happens, for example, when you realize that "elaboration" is essentially the same process that Piaget called *assimilation*.

Storage, the second essential memory task, involves the retention of encoded material over time. But, as we get deeper into the workings of memory, you will learn that memory consists of three *stages*, each of which stores memories for different lengths of time and in different forms. The "trick" of getting difficult-to-remember material into long-term storage, then, is to recode the information before the time clock runs out. For example, while listening to a lecture, you have just a few seconds to find some pattern or meaning in the sound of your professor's voice before the information is lost.

Retrieval, the third basic memory task, is the payoff for your earlier efforts in encoding and storage. When you have a properly encoded memory, it takes only a split second for a good cue to access the information, bring it to consciousness, or, in some cases, to influence your behavior at an unconscious level. (Let's test the ability of your conscious retrieval machinery to recover the material we just covered: Can you remember which of the three memory tasks comes before *storage*?)

Alas, retrieval doesn't always go well, because the human memory system—marvelous as it is—sometimes makes errors, distorts information, or even fails us completely. In the last section of the chapter, we will take a close

◄ **CONNECTION: CHAPTER 4**

In Piaget's theory, *assimilation* involves absorbing new information into existing schemes.

■ **Encoding** One of the three basic tasks of memory, involving the modification of information to fit the preferred format for the memory system.
■ **Storage** One of the three basic tasks of memory, involving the retention of encoded material over time.
■ **Retrieval** The third basic task of memory, involving the location and recovery of information from memory.

look at these problems, which memory expert Daniel Schacter (1996) calls the "seven sins of memory." The good news is that there are effective techniques that you can use to combat memory's "sins."

PSYCHOLOGY IN YOUR LIFE: WOULD YOU WANT A "PHOTOGRAPHIC" MEMORY?

Suppose that your memory were so vivid and accurate that you could use it to "read" paragraphs of this book out of memory during the next psychology exam. Such was the power of a 23-year-old woman tested by Charles Stromeyer and Joseph Psotka (1970). For example, she could look at the meaningless configuration of dots in the left-hand pattern in the "Do It Yourself!" box on the facing page and combine it mentally with the right-hand image. The combined pattern was the image shown in Figure 7.2. (Did you see the number "63"?) So, wouldn't it be great to have such a "photographic" memory? Not entirely, it turns out.

The technical term for "photographic memory" is **eidetic imagery.** Psychologists prefer this term because eidetic images are, in many important respects, different from images made by a camera (Haber, 1969, 1980). For example, a photographic image renders everything in minute detail, while an eidetic image portrays the most interesting and meaningful parts of the scene most accurately.

Eidetic memories also differ in several respects from the normal memory images that most of us experience. For one thing, *eidetikers* describe their memory images as having the vividness of the original experience (Neisser, 1967). For another, eidetic images are visualized as being "outside the head," rather than inside—in the "mind's eye." (Even though they see the image "outside," eidetikers realize that it is a mental image.) Further, an eidetic image can last for several minutes—even for days, in some cases. For example, the woman tested by Stromeyer and Psotka could pass the dot-combining test even when the two patterns were shown to her 24 hours apart. Remarkable as this is, however, the persistence of eidetic images can be a curse. Eidetikers report that their vivid imagery can clutter their minds and interfere with other things they want to think about (Hunter, 1964).

Eidetic imagery appears most commonly in children but only rarely in adults. One estimate says that up to 5% of children show some eidetic ability—although in most it's not good enough to pass the dot-combining test (Gray & Gummerman, 1975). While no one knows why eidetic imagery tends to disappear in adults, it may follow some sort of developmental sequence—like losing one's baby teeth. Possibly its disappearance is related to the child's development of formal operational thinking, which often begins to develop at about age 11 or 12.

Alternatively, case studies suggest a connection between the decline of eidetic imagery and the development of language skills: Eidetikers report that describing an eidetic image in words makes the image fade from memory, and they learn to exploit this fact to control their intrusive imagery (Haber, 1969, 1970). A cross-cultural study from Nigeria further supports the idea that the loss of eidetic ability may result from a conflict between language skills and visual imagery. In this research, eidetic imagery was found to be common, not only among children, but among adults of the Ibo tribe who were living in rural villages. Although the villagers could correctly draw details of images seen sometime earlier, tests showed that members of the same tribe who had moved to the city and had learned to read evidenced little eidetic ability (Doob, 1964).

◀ **CONNECTION: CHAPTER 4**

In Piaget's theory, the *formal operational stage* marks the appearance of abstract thought.

■ **Eidetic imagery** An especially clear and persistent form of memory that is quite rare; sometimes known as "photographic memory."

Whatever eidetic memory may be, it is clearly rare—so rare, in fact, that some psychologists have questioned its existence (Crowder, 1992). The few studies of "photographic memory" have portrayed it as different from everyday memory, as we have seen. But the fact is that we know relatively little about the phenomenon, and few psychologists are currently studying it.

Eidetic imagery presents not only a practical problem for those rare individuals who possess it but also a theoretical problem for cognitive psychologists. If eidetic imagery exists, what component of memory is responsible? On the other hand, if it proves to be a unique form of memory, it doesn't fit well with the widely accepted three-stage model of memory—which we will discuss next.

DO IT YOURSELF! | A Test of Eidetic Imagery

Look at the dot pattern on the left in the figure for a few moments and try to fix it in your memory. With that image in mind, look at the dot pattern on the right. Try to put the two sets of dots together by recalling the first pattern while looking at the second one. If you are the rare individual who can mentally combine the two patterns, you will see something not apparent in either image alone. Difficult? No problem if you have eidetic imagery—but impossible for the rest of us. If you want to see the combined images, but can't combine them in your memory, look at Figure 7.2.

 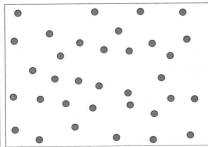

● **A Test of Eidetic Imagery** People with good eidetic imagery can mentally combine these two images to see something that appears in neither one alone.

CHECK YOUR UNDERSTANDING

1. **ANALYSIS:** Which of the following is a major objection to the "video recorder" theory of memory?
   a. Like perception, memory is an interpretation of experience.
   b. Memories are never accurate.
   c. Unlike a video recorder, memory takes in and stores an enormous quantity of information from all the senses, not just vision.
   d. Unlike a tape-recorded video memory, human memory cannot be edited and changed at a later time.

2. **RECALL:** Which of the following are the three essential tasks of memory?
   a. encoding, storage, and retrieval
   b. sensory, working, and long-term
   c. remembering, forgetting, and repressing
   d. recall, recognition, and relearning

3. **ANALYSIS:** When you get a new cat, you will note her unique markings, so that you can remember what she looks like in comparison with other cats in the neighborhood. What would a cognitive psychologist call this process of identifying the distinctive features of your cat?
   a. eidetic imagery
   b. encoding
   c. recollection
   d. retrieval

4. **UNDERSTANDING THE CORE CONCEPT:** Which one of the following memory systems reconstructs material during retrieval?
   a. computer memory
   b. human memory
   c. video recorder memory
   d. information recorded in a book

HOW DO WE FORM MEMORIES?

If the information in your professor's lecture is to become a permanent memory, it must be processed in three sequential stages: first in *sensory memory*, then in *working memory*, and finally in *long-term memory*. The three stages work like an assembly line to convert a flow of incoming stimuli into meaningful patterns that can be stored and later remembered. This model, originally developed by Richard Atkinson and Richard Shiffrin (1968), is now widely accepted—with some elaborations and modifications. Figure 7.3 shows how information flows through these three stages. (Please don't get these *stages* confused with the three basic *tasks* of memory that we covered earlier.)

Sensory memory, the most fleeting of the three stages, typically holds sights, sounds, smells, textures, and other sensory impressions for only a fraction of a second. You have experienced a sensory memory as you watched a moving Fourth of July sparkler leave a fading trail of light or heard the flow of one note into another as you listen to music. One function of these short-lived images is to maintain incoming sensory information long enough to be screened for possible entry into working memory.

Working memory, the second stage of processing, takes information selectively from the sensory registers and connects it with items already in long-term storage. (It is this connection we mean when we say, "That rings a bell!") Working memory is built to hold information for only a few seconds, making it a useful buffer for temporarily holding items, such as a phone number you have just looked up. Originally, psychologists called this stage short-term memory (STM), a term still in use (Beardsley, 1997b; Goldman-Rakic, 1992). The newer term *working memory* emphasizes some elaborations on the short-term stage originally proposed in Atkinson and Shiffrin's model (Baddeley, 2001; Engle, 2002), as we will discuss below.

It is noteworthy that everything entering consciousness passes into working memory. The opposite is also true: We are conscious of everything that enters working memory. Because of this intimate relationship, some psychologists have suggested that working memory is actually the long-sought seat of consciousness that we discussed in Chapter 3 (LeDoux, 1996).

Long-term memory (LTM), the final stage of processing, receives information from working memory and can store it for much longer periods—sometimes for the rest of a person's life. Information in long-term memory constitutes our knowledge about the world and holds material as varied as an image of your mother's face, the lyrics to your favorite song, and the year that Wilhelm Wundt established the first psychology laboratory. (You remember: That was in 18??) Long-term memory holds each person's total knowledge of the world and of the self.

■ **Sensory memory** The first of three memory stages, preserving brief sensory impressions of stimuli.
■ **Working memory** The second of three memory stages, and most limited in capacity. It preserves recently perceived events or experiences for less than a minute without rehearsal.
■ **Long-term memory (LTM)** The third of three memory stages, with the largest capacity and longest duration; LTM stores material organized according to meaning.

| Sensory memory | → | Working memory (includes short-term memory) | → ← | Long-term memory |

● **FIGURE 7.3** The Three Stages of Memory (Simplified)

The "standard model," developed by Atkinson and Shiffrin, says that memory is divided into three stages. Everything that goes into long-term storage must first be processed by sensory memory and working memory.

These, then, are the three stages of memory—which this section of the chapter will explore in detail. As you read, you should attend to the differences in the ways each stage processes and stores information. With these differences in mind, then, you will begin to discover ways of exploiting the quirks of each stage to enhance your own memory abilities. In briefer terms, our Core Concept says:

Each of the three memory stages encodes and stores memories in a different way, but they work together to transform sensory experience into a lasting record that has a pattern or meaning.

In this section you will find out just how the three stages each make unique contributions to the final memory product. (See Table 7.1.) As we consider each stage, we will look at its storage *capacity*, its *duration* (how long it retains information), its *structure and function*, and its *biological basis.*

The First Stage: Sensory Memory

One of the big problems memory must confront is this: Your senses take in far more information than you can possibly use. While reading this book, your senses serve up the words on the page, sounds in the room, the feel of your clothes on your skin, the temperature of the air, the slightly hungry feeling in your stomach . . . And how do you deal with all of this? It's the job of sensory memory to hold the barrage of incoming sensation just long enough (about ¼ second) for your brain to scan it and decide which stream of information needs attention. But just how much information can sensory memory hold? Cognitive psychologist George Sperling answered this question by devising one of psychology's simplest and most clever experiments.

TABLE 7.1	The Three Stages of Memory Compared		
	Sensory memory	Working memory (STM)	Long-term memory (LTM)
Function	Briefly holds information awaiting entry into working memory	Involved in control of attention Attaches meaning to stimulation Makes associations among ideas and events	Storage of information
Encoding	Sensory images: no meaningful encoding	Encodes information (especially by meaning) to make it acceptable for long-term storage	Stores information in meaningful mental categories
Storage capacity	12–16 items	"Magic number 7" ± 2 chunks	Unlimited
Duration	About ¼ second	About 20–30 seconds	Unlimited
Structure	A separate sensory register for each sense	Central executive Phonological loop Sketchpad	Procedural memory and declarative memory (further subdivided into semantic and episodic memory)
Biological Basis	Sensory pathways	Involves the hippocampus and frontal lobes	Cerebral cortex

● The sensory image of a friend's face is quickly taken into working memory. There it is elaborated with associations drawn from long-term storage.

The Capacity and Duration of Sensory Memory

In brief, Sperling found that this first stage of memory holds far more information than ever reaches consciousness. His method involved an array of letters, like the one below, flashed on a screen for a fraction of a second. (You might try glancing at the array briefly and then seeing how many you can recall.)

D J B W
X H G N
C L Y K

In the experiment, Sperling first asked volunteers to report as many of the letters as they could remember from the array (as you just did). As expected, most people could remember only three or four items from such a brief exposure.

But, Sperling conjectured, it might be possible that far more information than these three or four items enters a temporary memory buffer and then vanishes before it can be reported. To test this possibility, he modified the task in the following way. Immediately after the array of letters appeared, an auditory cue signaled which row of letters the subject was to report: A high-pitched tone indicated the top row, a medium tone the middle row, and a low tone meant the bottom row. Thus, immediately after seeing a flash of letters and hearing a beep, respondents were to report items *from only one row,* rather than items from the whole array.

Under this *partial report* condition, most people achieved almost perfect accuracy—no matter which row was signaled. That is, Sperling's subjects could accurately report *any* single row, but not *all* rows. This result suggested that the actual storage capacity of sensory memory can be 12 or more items—even though all but three or four items usually disappear from sensory memory before they can enter consciousness (Sperling, 1960, 1963).

Would it be better if our sensory memories lasted longer, so we would have more time to scan them? Probably not. New information is constantly coming in, and it must also be monitored. Sensory memories last just long enough to dissolve into one another and give us a sense of flow and continuity in our experience. But they usually do not last long enough to interfere with new incoming sensory impressions (Loftus et al., 1992).

The Structure and Function of Sensory Memory

You might think of sensory memory as having something like a movie screen, where images are "projected" fleetingly and then disappear. In fact, it is this blending of images in sensory memory that allows us to have the impression of motion in a "motion picture"—which is really just a rapid series of still images.

But, not all sensory memory consists of visual images. There is a separate *sensory register* for each sense, with each register holding a different kind of sensory information, as you can see in Figure 7.4. The register for vision, called *iconic memory,* stores the encoded light patterns that we see as visual images. Similarly, the sensory memory for hearing, known as *echoic memory,* holds encoded auditory stimuli. Experiments have shown that echoic memory, like iconic memory, holds more information than can pass on into working memory (Darwin et al., 1972).

We should also emphasize that the sensory images have no meaning attached to them, just as an image on photographic film has no meaning to a camera. The job of sensory memory is simply to store the images briefly. As we will see, it's the job of the next stage, working memory, to add meaning to sensation.

The Biological Basis of Sensory Memory   The biology of sensory memory appears to be relatively simple. Psychologists now believe that, in this initial stage, memory images take the form of nerve impulses in the sense organs and their pathways to the brain. In this view, sensory memory merely consists of the rapidly fading trace of stimulation in our sensory systems (Bower, 2000b; Glanz, 1998). Working memory, then somehow "reads" these fading traces, as it decides which information to admit into the spotlight of attention and which to ignore and allow to disappear. It is this transition step—the handoff between sensory and working memory—that we only vaguely understand.

The Second Stage: Working Memory

The second stage, working memory, is where you process conscious experience (LeDoux, 1996). It is the buffer in which you put the new name you have just heard. It is the temporary storage site for the words at the first part of this sentence as you read toward the end. Thus, working memory is the mechanism that selects information from sensory memory.

Working memory also provides a mental "work space" where we sort and encode information before adding it to long-term memory (Shiffrin, 1993). In doing so, it accesses and retrieves information from long-term storage. So, it is also the register into which a long-term memory of yesterday's psychology class can be retrieved as you review for tomorrow's test.

You might think of working memory, then, as the "central processing chip" for the entire memory system. In this role, it typically holds information for about 20 seconds—far longer than does sensory memory. If you make a special effort to rehearse the material, it can keep information active even longer, as when you repeat a phone number to yourself before dialing. It is also the mental work space in which we consciously mull over ideas and images pulled from long-term storage, in the process that we call "thinking." In all of these roles, then, working memory acts much like the central processing chip in a computer—as not only the center of mental action but as a go-between for the other components of memory.

The Capacity and Duration of Working Memory   This stage of memory is associated with the "magic number" seven (Miller, 1956). That is, working memory holds about seven items (give or take two)—a fact that caused lots of

Look at the following list of numbers and scan the four-digit number, the first number on the list. Don't try to memorize it. Just read it quickly; then look away from the page and try to recall the number. If you remember it correctly, go on to the next longer number, continuing down the list until you begin to make mistakes. How many digits are in the longest number that you can squeeze into your STM?

```
7  4  8  5
3  6  2  1  8
4  7  9  1  0  3
2  3  8  4  9  7  1
3  6  8  9  1  7  5  6
7  4  7  2  1  0  3  2  4
8  2  3  0  1  3  8  4  7  6
```

The result is your digit span, or your working (short-term) memory capacity for digits. Studies show that, under ideal testing conditions, most people can remember five to seven digits. If you remembered more, you may have been using special "chunking" techniques.

complaints when phone companies began requiring callers to add an area code to the old 7-digit phone number. Working memory's storage capacity does vary slightly from person to person, so you may want to assess how much yours can hold by trying the test in the "Do It Yourself!" box. Although there is some variation in STM capacity for different kinds of material, that variation is not large. Whatever your capacity is, it will be roughly the same, whether you are dealing with letters, numbers, words, shapes, or sounds. Seven items of nearly any sort will fill up short-term memory for most people.

When we try to overload working memory, earlier items are usually lost to accommodate more recent ones. On the other hand, when working memory is filled with information that demands attention, we may not notice new information that we might otherwise think was important. This limited capacity of working memory, in the opinion of some experts, makes it unsafe to talk on your cell phone while driving (Wickelgren, 2001).

It's important to note that working memory's meager storage capacity is significantly smaller than that of sensory memory. In fact, working memory has the smallest capacity of the three memory stages. This limitation, combined with a tendency to discard information after about 20 seconds, makes this part of memory the information "bottleneck" of the memory system. (See Figure 7.5.) As you might have suspected, the twin problems of limited capacity and short duration are obstacles for students, who must process and remember large amounts of information when they hear a lecture or read a book. Fortunately, there are ways to work around these difficulties, as we will see below.

● **FIGURE 7.5** The STM Bottleneck

Caught in the middle, with a much smaller capacity than sensory and long-term memories, working memory (short-term memory) becomes an information bottleneck in the memory system. As a result, much incoming information from sensory memory is lost.

The Structure and Function of Working Memory

Three important parts of working memory are shown in Figure 7.6. A *central executive* directs attention to material retrieved from long-term memory or to important input from sensory memory, such as someone calling a name. A second component consists of a *phonological loop*, which temporarily stores sounds—helping you to remember the mental "echo" of a name or to follow a melody. The third part of working memory is known as the *sketchpad*, used to store and manipulate visual images, as when you are imagining the route between your home and class.

Even with these tools, however, working memory still must face the twin limitations of limited capacity and short duration. For this purpose, it has two options, known as *chunking* and *rehearsal*. Successful students know how to use both strategies.

FIGURE 7.6 A Model of Working Memory

Atkinson and Shiffrin's original model divided memory into three stages. Events must first be processed by *sensory memory* and *short-term memory* (now called *working memory*) before they finally go into *long-term memory* storage–from which they can later be retrieved back into working memory. Baddeley's (2001) updated version of working memory, shown here, includes a *central executive* that directs attention, a *sketchpad* for visual and spatial information, and a *phonological loop* for sounds. (*Source:* Adapted from "Episodic Buffer: A New Component of Working Memory?" by A. Baddeley, *Trends in Cognitive Sciences* (2002), 4, pp. 417–423, American Psychological Association.)

Chunks and Chunking In memory, a *chunk* is any pattern or meaningful unit of information. A chunk can be a single letter or number, a name, or even a concept. For example, the sequence 1–4–5–9 consists of four digits that could constitute four chunks. However, if you recognize this sequence as the last four digits of your social security number—which is already available in your long-term memory—the four numbers need occupy only one chunk in STM. By **chunking** you can get more material into the seven slots of working memory.

The phone company figured this out years ago—which is why they put hyphens in phone numbers. So, when they group the seven digits of a phone number (e.g., 6735201) into two shorter strings of numbers (673-5201), they have helped us arrange seven separate items into two chunks—which leaves room for the area code.

The Role of Rehearsal Speaking of phone numbers, suppose that you have just looked up the number mentioned in the preceding paragraph. To keep it alive in working memory, you probably repeat the digits to yourself over and over. This technique is called **maintenance rehearsal,** and it serves well for maintaining information temporarily in working memory. Maintenance rehearsal not only keeps information fresh in working memory, but it prevents competing inputs from crowding it out. However, it is not an efficient way to transfer information to long-term memory—although it is a strategy commonly used for this purpose by people who don't know how memory operates. So, the student who "crams" for a test using simple repetition (maintenance rehearsal) probably won't remember much of the material.

A better strategy for getting information into long-term memory involves **elaborative rehearsal.** With this method, information is not merely repeated but is actively connected to knowledge already stored. So, suppose that you are an ophthalmologist, and you want your patients to remember your phone number. Because numbers are notoriously difficult to remember, you can help your customers with their elaborative rehearsal by using a "number" that makes use of the letters on the phone buttons, such as 1-800-EYE-EXAM. The

■ **Chunking** Organizing pieces of information into a smaller number of meaningful units (or chunks)—a process that frees up space in working memory.

■ **Maintenance rehearsal**
A working-memory process in which information is merely repeated or reviewed to keep it from fading while in working memory. Maintenance rehearsal involves no active elaboration.

■ **Elaborative rehearsal** A working-memory process in which information is actively reviewed and related to information already in LTM.

■ **Acoustic encoding** The conversion of information, especially semantic information, to sound patterns in working memory.

■ **Levels-of-processing theory** The explanation for the fact that information that is more thoroughly connected to meaningful items in long-term memory (more "deeply" processed) will be remembered better.

same principle can be used with more complex material, such as you are learning in psychology. For example, when you read about *echoic* memory, you may have elaborated it with a connection to "echo," also an auditory sensation.

Acoustic Encoding: The Phonological Loop   While reading words like "whirr," "pop," "cuckoo," and "splash," you can hear in your mind the sounds they describe. Much the same thing happens, less obviously, even with words that don't have imitative sounds because working memory converts them into the sounds of spoken language in its phonological loop. There, verbal patterns in working memory acquire an acoustic (sound) form, whether they come through our eyes or our ears (Baddeley, 2001). And this can cause some interesting memory errors. When people are asked to recall lists of letters they have just seen, the mistakes they make tend to involve confusions of letters that have a similar sound—such as D and T—rather than letters that have a similar look—such as E and F (Conrad, 1964). Mistakes aside, however, this **acoustic encoding** has its advantages. Specifically, it seems to have a role in learning and using language (Baddeley et al., 1998; Schacter, 1999).

Visual and Spatial Encoding: The Sketchpad   Serving much the same role for visual and spatial information, the sketchpad in working memory encodes visual images and mental representations of objects in space (Baddeley, 2001). For example, it holds the visual images you mentally rummage through when you're trying to imagine where you left your car keys. Neurological evidence suggests that the sketchpad involves the coordination of several brain systems, including the frontal and occipital lobes, while the phonological loop uses the temporal lobes.

Levels of Processing in Working Memory   The more connections you can make with new information while it is in working memory, the more likely you are to remember it later (Craik, 1979). Obviously this requires an interaction between working memory and long-term memory. According to the **levels-of-processing theory** proposed by Fergus Craik and Robert Lockhart (1972), "deeper" processing—establishing more connections with long-term memories—makes new information more meaningful and more memorable. An experiment will illustrate this point.

Craik and his colleague Endel Tulving (1975) had volunteer subjects examine a list of 60 common words presented on a screen one at a time. As each word appeared, the experimenters asked questions designed to control how deeply subjects processed each word. For example, when BEAR appeared on the screen, the experimenters would ask one of three questions: "Is it in capital letters?" "Does it rhyme with 'chair'?" "Is it an animal?" Craik and Tulving theorized that merely scanning the word for capital letters would not require processing the word as deeply as would comparing its sound with that of another word. But the deepest level of processing, they believed, would occur when some aspect of the word's *meaning* was analyzed, as when they asked whether BEAR was an animal. Thus, Craik and Tulving predicted that items processed more deeply would leave more robust traces in memory. And their prediction was correct. When the subjects were later asked to pick the original 60 words out of a larger list of 180, they remembered the deeply processed words much better than words processed more superficially, as the graph in Figure 7.7 shows.

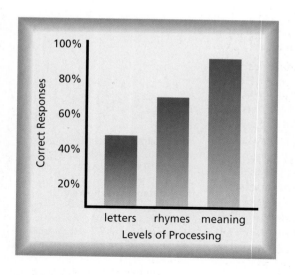

■ **FIGURE 7.7**   Results of Levels-of-Processing Experiment

Words that were processed more deeply (for meaning) were remembered better than words examined for rhymes or for target letters.

The Biological Basis of Working Memory   Although the exact biological mechanism is not clear, working memory probably holds information in actively firing nerve circuits. Brain-imaging studies suggest a likely location for these short-term circuits is in the frontal cortex, regions that are active across a variety of working memory tasks (Beardsley, 1997b; Smith, 2000). And, as we might expect, the working memory circuits have connections with all the sensory parts of the brain and to areas known to be involved in long-term storage.

The research also suggests that the frontal regions house some "executive processes" that are involved in focusing attention and thinking about the information in short-term storage. These mental processes involve attention, priorities, planning, updating the contents of working memory, and monitoring the time sequence of events. Brain imaging studies indicate that the executive processes of working memory are anatomically distinct from the sites of short-term storage (Smith & Jonides, 1999).

The Third Stage: Long-Term Memory

Can you remember who discovered classical conditioning? What is the name of a play by Shakespeare? How many birthdays have you had? Such information, along with everything else you know, is stored in your long-term memory (LTM), the last of the three memory stages.

Given the vast amount of data stored in LTM, it is a marvel that so much of it is so easily accessible. The method behind the marvel involves a special feature of long-term memory: Words and concepts are encoded by their meanings, which interconnects them with other items that have similar meanings. Accordingly, you might picture LTM as a huge web of interconnected associations. The result is that good retrieval cues (stimuli that prompt the activation of a long- term memory) can help you quickly locate the item you want amid all the data stored there. Computer scientists would very much like to understand this feature of LTM and use it to increase the search and retrieval speed of their machines.

The Capacity and Duration of Long-Term Memory   How much information can long-term memory hold? As far as we know, it has unlimited storage capacity. (No one has yet maxed it out, so you don't have to conserve memory by cutting back on your studying.) LTM uses its capacity to store all the experiences, events, information, emotions, skills, words, categories, rules, and judgments that have been transferred to it from working memory. Thus, your LTM contains your total knowledge of the world and of yourself. And, unless it falls victim to injury or dementia, long-term memory is potentially capable of storing information for a lifetime—which makes long-term memory clearly the champion in both duration and storage capacity among the three stages of memory. How does LTM manage to have unlimited capacity? That's still an unsolved mystery of memory, but we do know that the metaphor of LTM being like a computer's hard drive is somewhat misleading. Instead, we suggest that you conceive of LTM as a sort of mental scaffold, so the more associations you make, the more information it can hold.

The Structure and Function of Long-Term Memory   With a broad overview of LTM in mind, let's look at some of the details. First, let's examine the two main parts of LTM, each distinguished by the sort of information it holds. One, a register for the things we know how to *do*, is called *procedural memory*. The other, which acts as storage for the information that we can *describe*—the facts we know and the experiences we remember—is called *declarative memory*.

Procedural Memory   Mental directions, or "procedures," for how things are done are stored in **procedural memory**. (See Figure 7.8.) We use it to remember the

■ **Procedural memory**   A division of LTM that stores memories for how things are done.

● **FIGURE 7.8** Components of Long-Term Memory

Declarative memory involves knowing specific information—knowing "what." It stores facts, personal experiences, language, concepts—things about which we might say, "I remember!" *Procedural memory* involve knowing "how"—particularly motor skills and behavioral learning.

● Procedural memory allows experts like pitcher Pedro Martinez to perform complex tasks automatically, without conscious recall of the details.

■ **Declarative memory**   A division of LTM that stores explicit information; also known as fact memory. Declarative memory has two subdivisions: episodic memory and semantic memory.

■ **Episodic memory**   A subdivision of declarative memory that stores memory for personal events, or "episodes."

■ **Semantic memory**   A subdivision of declarative memory that stores general knowledge, including the meanings of words and concepts.

■ **Engram**   The physical changes in the brain associated with a memory. It is also known as the *memory trace*.

"how to" skills we have learned, such as riding a bicycle, tying shoelaces, or playing a musical instrument (Anderson, 1982; Tulving, 1983). Most often, we are conscious of the details of our performance only during the early phases of acquisition, when we must think about every move we make. Later, after the skill is thoroughly learned, it occurs mainly at or beyond the fringes of awareness, as when a concert pianist performs a piece without consciously recalling the details.

Declarative Memory   The other major division of LTM, **declarative memory,** stores specific information, such as facts and events. Recalling the directions for driving to a specific location requires declarative memory (although knowing how to drive a car depends on procedural memory). In contrast with procedural memory, declarative memory more often requires some conscious mental effort. You may be able to see evidence of this when people roll their eyes or make facial gestures while searching their memories. As they do so, they are looking in one of declarative memory's two subdivisions: *episodic memory* and *semantic memory.*

Episodic memory is the portion of declarative memory that stores personal experiences: your memory for events, or "episodes" in your life. It also stores *temporal coding* (or time tags) to identify *when* the event occurred and *context coding* that indicates *where* it took place. For example, memories of your recent vacation or of an unhappy love affair are stored in episodic memory, along with codes for where and when these episodes occurred. Thus, episodic memory acts as your internal diary or *autobiographical memory.* You consult it when someone says, "Where were you on New Year's Eve?" or "What did you do in class last Tuesday?"

Semantic memory is the other division of declarative memory. (Again, refer to Figure 7.8, if this is becoming confusing.) It stores the basic meanings of words and concepts. Usually, semantic memory retains no information about the time and place in which its contents were acquired. Thus, you keep the meaning of "cat" in semantic memory—but probably not a recollection of the occasion on which you first learned the meaning of "cat." In this respect, semantic memory more closely resembles an encyclopedia or a database than an autobiography. It stores a vast quantity of facts about names, faces, grammar, history, music, manners, scientific principles, and religious beliefs. All the facts and concepts you know are stored there, and you consult its registry when someone asks you, "Who was the third president?" or "What are the two divisions of declarative memory?"

The Biological Basis of Long-Term Memory   The search for the **engram,** the biological basis of long-term memory has taken two approaches. One has

1. **APPLICATION:** Remembering names is usually harder than remembering faces because names require _____, while faces require _____.

    a. short-term memory/long-term memory
    b. declarative memory/procedural memory
    c. encoding/retrieval
    d. recall/recognition

2. **APPLICATION:** At a high-school class reunion you are likely to experience a flood of memories that would be unlikely to come to mind under other circumstances. What memory process explains this?

    a. implicit memory
    b. anterograde amnesia
    c. encoding specificity
    d. the TOT phenomenon

3. **RECALL:** A person experiencing the TOT phenomenon is unable to _____ a specific word.

    a. recognize
    b. recall
    c. encode
    d. learn

4. **UNDERSTANDING THE CORE CONCEPT:** An implicit memory may be activated by priming, and an explicit memory may be activated by a recognizable stimulus. In either case, a psychologist would say that these memories are being

    a. cued.
    b. recalled.
    c. stored.
    d. chunked.

ANSWERS: 1.d 2.c 3.b 4.a

WHY DOES MEMORY SOMETIMES FAIL US?

We forget appointments and anniversaries. During today's test we can't remember the terms we studied the night before. Or a familiar name seems just out of our mental reach. Yet, ironically, we sometimes cannot rid memory of an unhappy event. Why does memory play these tricks on us—making us remember what we would rather forget and forget what we want to remember?

According to memory expert Daniel Schacter, the blame falls on what he terms the "seven sins" of memory: *transience, absent-mindedness, blocking, misattribution, suggestibility, bias,* and unwanted *persistence* (Schacter, 1999, 2001). Further, he claims that these seven problems are really the consequences of some very useful features of human memory. They are features that stood our ancestors in good stead and so are passed down and preserved in our own memory system. Our Core Concept puts this notion more succinctly:

Most of our memory problems arise from memory's "seven sins"—which are really by-products of otherwise adaptive features of human memory.

As we look into the "seven sins," we will also have the opportunity to consider such practical problems as the reliability of eyewitness testimony and ways that memory contributes to certain mental disorders, such as depression. In this section we will also revisit the "memory wars," involving disputes about recovered memories of trauma and sexual abuse—the problem that we encountered in Donna Smith's case at the beginning of the chapter. Finally, we will look at some strategies for improving our memories by overcoming some of Schacter's "seven sins." We begin, however, with the frustration of fading memories.

Transience: Fading Memories Cause Forgetting

Memories seem to weaken with time. (How would you do on a rigorous test of the course work you took a year ago?) Although no one has directly observed

60
50
40
30
20
10

Percent savings

0 12345   10   15   20   25   30
Days

● **FIGURE 7.10** Ebbinghaus's Forgetting Curve

Ebbinghaus's forgetting curve shows that the savings demonstrated by relearning drops rapidly and reaches a plateau, below which little more is forgotten. The greatest amount of forgetting occurs during the first day after learning. (*Source:* From PSYCHOLOGY AND LIFE 15th ed. by P. G. Zimbardo and R. J. Gerrig. Copyright © 1999 by Pearson Education. Reprinted by permission of Allyn & Bacon, Boston, MA.)

◀ **CONNECTION: CHAPTER 2**

PET and *fMRI* are brain scanning techniques that form images of especially active regions in the brain.

● Misplacing your car keys results from a shift in attention. Which of the seven "sins" does this represent?

a human memory trace fade and disappear, much circumstantial evidence points to the **transience,** or impermanence, of long-term memory—the first of Schacter's "sins."

In a classic study of transience, pioneering psychologist Hermann Ebbinghaus (1908/1973) learned lists of *nonsense syllables* (such as POV, KEB, and RUZ) and tried to recall them over varying time intervals. This worked well to assess his retention over short periods up to a few days. But to measure memory after long delays of weeks or months, when recall had failed completely, Ebbinghaus had to invent another method that measured the number of trials required to *relearn* the original list. If it took fewer trials to relearn the list than were required to learn it originally, the difference indicated a "savings" that could serve as a measure of memory. (If the original learning required 10 trials and relearning required 7 trials, the savings was 30%.) By using the *savings method,* Ebbinghaus could trace what happened to memory over long periods of time. The curve obtained from his data is shown in Figure 7.10. There you can see how the graph initially plunges steeply and then flattens out over longer intervals. This represents one of Ebbinghaus's most important discoveries: *For relatively meaningless material, there is a rapid initial loss of memory, followed by a declining rate of loss.* Subsequent research shows that this **forgetting curve** captures the pattern of transience by which we forget much of the verbal material we learn.

Modern psychologists have built on Ebbinghaus's work, but they are now more interested in how we remember *meaningful* material, such as information you read in this book. Meaningful memories seem to fade, too—just not as rapidly as did Ebbinghaus's nonsense syllables. Much of this modern work uses brain scanning techniques, such as fMRI and PET, to visualize diminishing brain activity during forgetting (Schacter, 1996, 1999).

Some memories, however, do not follow the classic forgetting curve as closely. Motor skills, for example, are often retained substantially intact in procedural memory for many years, even without practice—"just like riding a bicycle." The same goes for certain especially memorable emotional experiences, such as "flashbulb" incidents or certain childhood events (although they may become distorted, as we have seen). Obviously, the transiency hypothesis—that memories fade over time—doesn't describe the fate of all our memories. As we will see next, even some memories that seem to be forgotten haven't faded away completely. Instead, they may only be temporarily lost.

Absent-Mindedness: Lapses of Attention Cause Forgetting

When you misplace your car keys or forget an anniversary, you have had an episode of **absent-mindedness.** It's not that the memory has disappeared from your brain circuits. Rather, you have suffered a retrieval failure caused by shifting your attention elsewhere. In the case of a forgotten anniversary, the attention problem occurred on the retrieval end—when you were concentrating on something that took your attention away from the upcoming anniversary. And as for the car keys, your attentive shift probably occurred during the original encoding—when you should have been paying attention to where you laid the keys. In college students, this form of absent-mindedness commonly comes from listening to music or watching TV while studying.

For a demonstration of this sort of encoding error, please see our magic trick in Figure 7.11. The same process was at work in the "depth of processing" experiments, in which people who encoded information shallowly (retrieval cue: Does the word contain an *e*?) were less able to recall the target word (Craik & Lockhart, 1972). Another example can be found in demonstrations of *change blindness:* In one study, participants viewed a movie clip in which one actor who was asking directions was replaced by another actor while they were briefly hidden by two men carrying a door in front of them. Amazingly, fewer than half of the viewers noticed the change (Simons & Levin, 1998).

Blocking: Interference Causes Forgetting

You are most likely to notice this next memory "sin" when you have a "tip-of-the-tongue" experience. It also occurs when you attempt to learn two conflicting things in succession, such as would happen if you had a French class followed by a Spanish class. In general, **blocking** occurs when information has encountered *interference*—that is, when one item acts as an obstacle to accessing and retrieving another memory. And what is likely to cause interference? Three main factors top the list:

1. The greater the similarity between two sets of material to be learned, the greater the interference between them is likely to be. So, French and Spanish classes are more likely to interfere with each other than are psychology and accounting.

2. Meaningless material is more vulnerable to interference than meaningful material. Because LTM is organized by meaning, you will have more trouble remembering your locker combination than you will a news bulletin.

3. Emotional material is a powerful cause of interference. So, if you broke up with your true love last night, you will probably forget what your literature professor says in class today.

A common source of interference comes from an old habit getting in the way of a new one. This can happen, for example, when people switch from one word-processing program to another. Interference also accounts for the legendary problem old dogs have in learning new tricks. Everyday life offers many more examples, but interference theory groups them in two main categories: *proactive interference* and *retroactive interference.*

Proactive Interference When an old memory disrupts the learning and remembering of new information, **proactive interference** is the culprit. An example of proactive interference occurs when, after moving to a new home, you still look for items in the old places where you used to store them, although no such locations exist in your new environment. *Pro-* means "forward," so in *pro*active interference, old memories act forward in time to block your attempts at new learning.

Retroactive Interference When the opposite happens—when newly learned information prevents the retrieval of previously learned material—we can blame forgetting on **retroactive interference.** *Retro-* means "backward"; the newer material reaches back into your memory to block access to old material. Retroactive interference describes what happens when you drive a car with an automatic transmission and then forget to use the clutch when you return to one with a "stick shift." That is, recent experience retroactively interferes with your ability to retrieve an older memory. (See Figure 7.12.)

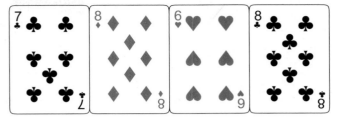

● **FIGURE 7.11** The "Magic" of Memory

Pick one of the cards. Stare at it intently for at least 15 seconds, being careful not to shift your gaze to the other cards. Then turn the page.

■ **Transience** The impermanence of a long-term memory. Transience is based on the idea that long-term memories gradually fade in strength over time.

■ **Forgetting curve** A graph plotting the amount of retention and forgetting over time for a certain batch of material, such as a list of nonsense syllables. The typical forgetting curve is steep at first, becoming flatter as time goes on.

■ **Absent-mindedness** Forgetting caused by lapses in attention.

■ **Blocking** Forgetting that occurs when an item in memory cannot be accessed or retrieved. Blocking is caused by *interference.*

■ **Proactive interference** A cause of forgetting by which previously stored information prevents learning and remembering new information.

■ **Retroactive interference** A cause of forgetting by which newly learned information prevents retrieval of previously stored material.

FIGURE 7.11 The "Magic" of Memory (*continued*)

Your card is gone! How did we do it? We didn't read your mind; it was your own *reconstructive memory* and the "sin" of *absent-mindedness* playing card tricks on you. If you don't immediately see how the trick works, try it again with a different card.

The Serial Position Effect In yet another example of blocking, you may have noticed that the first and last parts of a poem or a vocabulary list are easier to learn and remember than the middle portion—which receives interference from both ends. In general, the *primacy effect* refers to the relative ease of remembering the first items in a series, while the *recency effect* refers to the robustness of memory for the most recent items. Together, with diminished memory for the middle portion, we term this the **serial position effect.** You can see it at work when you meet a series of people: You are more likely to remember the names of those you met first and last than you are those you met in between (other factors being equal, such as the commonness of their names, distinctiveness of their appearance, and their personalities).

■ **Serial position effect** A form of interference related to the sequence in which information is presented. Generally, items in the middle of the sequence are less well remembered than items presented first or last.

How does interference theory explain the serial position effect? Unlike the material at the ends of the poem or list, the part in the middle is exposed to a double dose of interference—both retroactively and proactively. That is, the middle part receives interference from both directions, while material at either end gets interference from only one side. (This suggests that you might find it helpful to pay special attention to the material in the middle of this chapter.)

FIGURE 7.12 Two Types of Interference

In proactive interference, earlier learning (Spanish) interferes with memory for later information (French). In retroactive interference, new information (French) interferes with memory for information learned earlier (Spanish).

Misattribution: Memories in the Wrong Context

All three "sins" discussed so far make memories inaccessible. Sometimes, however, memories are retrievable, but they are associated with the wrong time, place, or person. Schacter (1999) calls this **misattribution.** This is caused by the reconstructive nature of long-term memory. In the penny demonstration at the beginning of the chapter, you learned that memories are typically retrieved as fragments that we reassemble in such a way as to make them meaningful to us. This opens the way to connecting information with the wrong, but oh-so-sensible, context.

Here's an example: Psychologist Donald Thompson was accused of rape, based on a victim's detailed, but mistaken, description of her assailant (Thompson, 1988). Fortunately for Thompson, his alibi was indisputable. At the time of the crime he was being interviewed live on television—about memory distortions. The victim, it turned out, had been watching the interview just before she was raped and had misattributed the assault to Thompson.

Misattribution also can cause people to believe mistakenly that other people's ideas are their own. This sort of misattribution occurs when a person hears an idea and keeps it in memory, while forgetting its source. Unintentional plagiarism comes from this form of misattribution, as we saw earlier in the case of Beatle George Harrison.

Yet another type of misattribution can cause people to remember something they did not experience at all. Such was the case with volunteers who were asked to remember a set of words associated with a particular theme: *door, glass, pane, shade, ledge, sill, house, open, curtain, frame, view, breeze, sash, screen,* and *shutter.* Under these conditions, many participants later remembered *window,* even though that word was not on the list (Roediger & McDermott, 1995, 2000). This result again shows the power of context cues in determining the content of memory. It also demonstrates how people tend to create and retrieve memories based on meaning.

Suggestibility: External Cues Distort or Create Memories

Memories can also be distorted or created by suggestion, a possibility of particular importance to the law. Witnesses may be interviewed by attorneys or by the police, who may make suggestions about the facts of a case—either deliberately or unintentionally—which might alter a witness's testimony. Such concerns about **suggestibility** prompted Elizabeth Loftus and John Palmer to investigate the circumstances under which eyewitness memories can be distorted.

Memory Distortion   Participants in the classic Loftus and Palmer study first watched a film of two cars colliding. Then, the experimenters asked them to estimate how fast the cars had been moving. The witnesses' responses depended heavily on how the questions were worded (Loftus, 1979, 1984; Loftus & Palmer, 1973). Half were asked, "How fast were the cars going when they *smashed* into each other?" Their estimates, it turned out, were about 25% higher than those given by respondents who were asked, "How fast were the cars going when they *hit* each other?" This distortion of memory caused by misinformation is known, appropriately enough, as the **misinformation effect.**

Clearly, the Loftus and Palmer study shows that memories can be distorted and embellished by cues and suggestions given at the time of recall. Memories can even be created by similar methods—all without the individual's awareness that memory has been altered. We'll show you how.

■ **Misattribution**   A memory fault that occurs when memories are retrieved but are associated with the wrong time, place, or person.

■ **Suggestibility**   The process of memory distortion as the result of deliberate or inadvertent suggestion.

■ **Misinformation effect**
The distortion of memory by suggestion or misinformation.

● Our criminal justice system relies heavily on eyewitness identifications and descriptions. How well does this system work? You can judge for yourself in the case of a Catholic priest, Father Pagano (right), who was arrested and accused of a series of robberies. The police and the prosecutor were certain that they had the right man, because seven witnesses had identified him as the culprit. Father Pagano was finally exonerated during his trial, when the real robber (left)—hardly a look-alike—confessed.

Fabricated Memories   To create entirely false memories, Elizabeth Loftus and her colleagues contacted the parents of college students and obtained lists of childhood events, which the students were asked to recall. Added to those lists were plausible events that never happened, such as being lost in a shopping mall, spilling the punch bowl at a wedding, meeting Bugs Bunny at Disneyland (impossible because Bugs is not a Disney character), or experiencing a visit by a clown at a birthday party (Braun et al., 2002; Hyman et al., 1995; Loftus, 1997a, 1997b; Loftus & Ketcham, 1994). After repeated recall attempts over a period of several days, many of the students claimed to remember the bogus events. All that was required were some credible suggestions.

Factors Affecting the Accuracy of Eyewitnesses   In the wake of studies such as these, much attention has focused on the accuracy of eyewitness recall. You can verify this by typing "eyewitness" into the PsychInfo database or looking up the following sources: Bruck and Ceci, 1997; Lindsay, 1990, 1993; Loftus, 1992, 1993, 2003b; Loftus and Ketcham, 1991, 1994; and Weingardt and colleagues, 1995. Here are the most important factors this research has identified:

▌ People's recollections are less influenced by leading questions if they are forewarned that interrogations can create memory bias.

▌ When the passage of time allows the original memory to fade, people are more likely to misremember information.

▌ Each time a memory is retrieved, it is reconstructed and then restored (much like a word-processing document that is retrieved, modified, and saved), increasing the chances of error.

▌ The age of the witness matters: Younger children and adults over 65 may be especially susceptible to influence by misinformation in their efforts to recall.

▌ Confidence in a memory is not a sign of an accurate memory. In fact, misinformed individuals can actually come to believe the misinformation in which they feel confidence.

The Recovered Memory Controversy   At the beginning of the chapter, the Smith family's ordeal began with Donna Smith's claim that she had been sexually abused by her father. Subsequently, Donna came to believe her own claims, although she later stated that they were all fabrications. And now we see that research on eyewitness memory confirms the notion that suggestion can lead people not only to report false memories but to believe them (Hyman et al., 1995; Loftus, 1997a, 1997b).

So, are all recovered memories suspect? The truth is that we frequently recover memories—accurate memories—of long-forgotten events. A chance remark, a peculiar odor, or an old tune can cue vivid recollections that haven't surfaced in years. The ones to be especially suspicious of, however, are memories cued by suggestion or leading questions—as were Donna Smith's recollections.

One notorious source of suggestion that pops up in many recovered memory cases is a book: *The Courage to Heal.* This book suggests repeatedly that forgotten memories of incest and abuse may lie behind people's feelings of powerlessness, inadequacy, vulnerability, and a long list of other unpleasant thoughts and emotions (Bass & Davis, 1988). The authors state, "If you . . . have a feeling that something abusive happened to you, it probably did" (pp. 21–22).

The belief that buried memories of traumatic experiences can cause mental and physical symptoms was originally proposed by Sigmund Freud. In his theory of *repression,* Freud taught that threatening or traumatic memories can be stored in the unconscious mind, where they indirectly influence our thoughts and behavior. He also taught that the only way to be free of these repressed memories is to root them out during therapy—bringing them into the daylight of consciousness, where they could be dealt with rationally. Freud, however, never offered more than anecdotes and testimonials to support his repression theory.

CONNECTION: CHAPTER 11

Psychoanalyst *Sigmund Freud* taught that most of the mind is not accessible to consciousness.

In fact, modern cognitive research suggests just the opposite. Emotionally arousing events, including threatening ones, are usually remembered vividly (McNally, 2003; Shobe & Kihlstrom, 1997). Most people, however, are unaware of this fact, retaining a strong, but unfounded, belief in repression and in the Freudian unconscious. Likewise, many people also hold a strong belief that memory makes an accurate record of events, even though psychological science has abundant evidence showing that memory is prone to error (Neimark, 2004).

We are not suggesting that all therapists use suggestive techniques to recover repressed memories, although some still do (Poole et al., 1995). Patients should be especially wary of therapists who go "fishing" for unconscious causes of mental problem, using such techniques as hypnosis, dream analysis, and repeated leading questions about early sexual experiences. There is no evidence to support the validity of these methods for the recovery of accurate memories.

We should also note that the issue of recovered memories is both complex and charged with emotion. It is also one that strikes many people close to home. Thus, it remains controversial, even among psychologists, where it has caused bitter dispute between therapists and experimental psychologists. Yet, despite the controversy, most experts agree on the following points.

▌ Sexual abuse of children *does* occur, and it is more prevalent than most professionals had suspected just a generation ago (McAnulty & Burnette, 2004).

▌ Memories cued by suggestion are particularly vulnerable to distortion and fabrication (Loftus, 2003a).

▌ Early memories, especially those of incidents that may have happened in infancy, are likely to be fantasies or misattributions. Episodic memories of events before age 3 are extremely rare (Schacter, 1996).

▌ There is no infallible way to be sure about memories of sexual abuse (or any other memories) without independent supporting evidence (Ceci & Bruck, 1993).

- Although traumatic events can be forgotten, they are much more likely to form persistent and intrusive memories that people would rather forget. Moreover, such events can permanently alter the structure of the hippocampus (Teicher, 2002).

- There is no solid evidence for repression, in the Freudian sense of an unconscious memory that can cause physical and mental symptoms (Schacter, 1996).

Bias: Beliefs, Attitudes, and Opinions Distort Memories

The sixth memory "sin," which Schacter calls bias, refers to the influence of personal beliefs, attitudes, and experiences on memory. Lots of domestic arguments of the "Did not! Did, too!" variety owe their spirited exchanges to bias. Naturally, it's easier to see in another person than in ourselves. Here are two other, more subtle forms that memory bias can take.

Expectancy Bias   Suppose that you are among a group of volunteers for an experiment in which you read a story about Bob and Margie, a couple who plan to get married. Part of the story reveals that Bob doesn't want to have children, and he is worried how Margie is going to take this disclosure. When he does tell her, Margie is shocked, because she desperately wants children. Then, after reading the story you are informed that Bob and Margie did get married. Another group of volunteers is told that the couple ended their relationship. Will those in the two groups remember the Bob and Margie story differently?

Those who heard the unexpected ending (the condition in which Bob and Margie decided to get married) gave the most erroneous reports. Their errors made sense, however because what they recalled made the outcome fit their expectations (Sohcter, 1999; Spiro, 1980). One person, for example, "remembered" that Bob and Margie had separated but decided their love could overcome their differences. Another related that the couple had decided on adoption, as a compromise. This **expectancy bias** stems from an unconscious tendency to remember events as being congruent with our expectations.

Self-Consistency Bias   People abhor the thought of being inconsistent, even though research suggests that they are kidding themselves. This Schacter calls the **self-consistency bias.** It showed itself, for example, in one study that found people are less consistent than they remembered themselves being in their support for political candidates (Levine, 1997). Another study showed that people believe themselves to be more consistent than they actually are on their stands concerning equality of women, aid to minority groups, and the legalization of marijuana (Marcus, 1986).

The self-consistency bias appears in emotional memories, as well as in memories for attitudes and beliefs (Levine & Safer, 2002). Earlier in the chapter we saw that our moods could affect which memories we retrieve. Here, however, we are more interested in how our emotions can distort our memories. For example, a study of dating couples who were interviewed twice, two months apart, found that memories could be biased by how well the relationship had progressed over the interval. Those who had grown to like each other more remembered their initial evaluations of their partners as more positive than they actually were, while those whose relationships had become more negative had the opposite response (Scharfe & Bartholomew, 1998). In each

■ **Expectancy bias**   In memory, a tendency to distort recalled events to make them fit one's expectations.

■ **Self-consistency bias**   The commonly held idea that we are more consistent in our attitudes, opinions, and beliefs than we actually are.

of these studies, whether they involve attitudes, beliefs, opinions, or emotions, we see that our biases act as a sort of distorted mirror in which our memories are reflected.

Persistence: When We Can't Forget

The seventh "sin" of memory, **persistence,** reminds us that memory sometimes works all too well, especially when intense negative emotions are involved. In fact, intrusive recollections of unpleasant events lie at the heart of certain psychological disorders. Depressed people can't stop ruminating about unhappy events in their lives. Similarly, patients with *phobias* may become obsessed by fearful memories about snakes, dogs, crowds, spiders, or lightning. All of this again points to the powerful role that emotion plays in memory. Neuroscientists believe that it does so by strengthening the physical changes in the synapses that hold our memories (LeDoux, 1996).

CONNECTION: CHAPTER 12

People with *phobias* have extreme and unreasonable fears of specific objects or situations.

The Advantages of the "Seven Sins" of Memory

Despite the grief they cause us, the "seven sins" are actually by-products of adaptive features of memory, argues Daniel Schacter (1999). Thus, transience— maddening as it is to the student taking a test—is actually a way the memory system prevents itself from being overwhelmed by information that is no longer needed. Similarly, blocking may be viewed as a process that usually allows only the most relevant information (the information most strongly associated with the present cues) to come to mind. Again, this is a process that prevents us from a flood of unwanted and distracting memories.

In contrast, absent-mindedness is the by-product of the useful ability to shift our attention. Similarly, misattributions, biases, and suggestibility result from a memory system built to deal with *meaning* and discard details. (The alternative would be a computer-like memory filled with information at the expense of understanding.) And, finally, we can see that the "sin" of persistence is really a feature of a memory system that is especially responsive to emotional experiences, particularly those involving fear. In general, then, the picture that emerges of memory's "failures" is also one of a system that is well adapted to the conditions people have faced for thousands of years.

PSYCHOLOGY IN YOUR LIFE: IMPROVING YOUR MEMORY WITH MNEMONICS

To improve your memory, try using some mental strategies called *mnemonics* (pronounced *ni-MON-ix,* from the Greek word meaning "remember"). **Mnemonics** are methods memory experts use for encoding information to be remembered by associating it with information already in long-term memory. To illustrate, we will take a detailed look at two mnemonic strategies: the *method of loci* and *natural language mediators.*

The Method of Loci Dating back to the ancient Greeks, the **method of loci** (pronounced *LOW-sye,* from the Latin *locus,* "place"), is literally one of the oldest tricks in this book. It was originally devised to help orators remember the major points of their speeches. You will also find it a practical means of learning and remembering lists.

To illustrate, imagine a familiar sequence of places, such as the bed, desk, and chairs in your room. Then, using the method of loci, mentally move from

■ **Persistence** A memory problem in which unwanted memories cannot be put out of mind.
■ **Mnemonics** Techniques for improving memory, especially by making connections between new material and information already in long-term memory.
■ **Method of loci** A mnemonic technique that involves associating items on a list with a sequence of familiar physical locations.

● Mnemonic strategies help us remember things by making them meaningful. Here an elementary school teacher helps students remember the letter *K* by showing that "*K* does karate."

place to place in your room, and as you go imagine putting one item from your list in each place. To retrieve the series, you merely take another mental tour, examining the places you used earlier. There you will "see" the item you have put in each locus. To remember a grocery list, for example, you might mentally picture a can of *tuna* on your bed, *shampoo* spilled on your desktop, and a box of *eggs* open on a chair. Bizarre or unconventional image combinations are usually easier to remember; a can of tuna in your bedroom will make a more memorable image than tuna in your kitchen (Bower, 1972).

The mental images used in this technique work especially well because they employ both verbal and visual memories (Paivio, 1986). It's worth noting, by the way, that visual imagery is one of the most effective forms of encoding: You can easily remember things by associating them with vivid, distinctive mental pictures. In fact, you could remember your grocery list by using visual imagery alone. Simply combine the mental images of tuna, shampoo, and eggs in a bizarre but memorable way. So, you might picture a tuna floating on an enormous fried egg in a sea of foamy shampoo. Or you might imagine a politician you dislike eating tuna from the can, her hair covered with shampoo suds, while you throw eggs at her.

Natural Language Mediators   Memory aids called **natural language mediators** associate meaningful word patterns with new information to be remembered. For instance, you can make up a story to help you remember a grocery list (the same one, consisting of tuna, shampoo, and eggs). The story might link the items this way: "The cat discovers I'm out of *tuna* so she interrupts me while I'm using the *shampoo* and meows to *egg* me on." Similarly, advertisers know that rhyming slogans and rhythmic musical jingles can make it easier for customers to remember their products and brand names ("Oscar Mayer has a way with . . ."). The chances are that a teacher in your past used a simple rhyme to help you remember a spelling rule ("*I* before *E* except after *C*") or the number of days in each month ("Thirty days has September . . ."). In a physics class you may have used a natural language mediator in the form of an *acronym*—a word made up of initials—to learn the colors of the visible spectrum in their correct order: "Roy G. Biv" stands for red, orange, yellow, green, blue, indigo, violet.

Remembering Names   The inability to remember people's names is one of the most common complaints about memory. So, how could you use the power of association to remember names? In the first place, you must realize that remembering names doesn't happen automatically. People who do this well must work at it by making associations between a name and some characteristic of the person—the more unusual the association, the better.

Suppose, for example, you have just met a man whose name is Bob. You might visualize his face framed in a big "O," taken from the middle of his name. To remember his friend Ann, think of her as "Queen Ann," sitting on a throne. And, as for their companion Phil, you might visualize putting a hose in Phil's mouth and "fill"-ing him with water. (It is usually best not to tell people about the mnemonic strategy you are using to remember their names.)

In general, the use of mnemonics teaches us that memory is flexible, personal, and creative. It also teaches us that *memory ultimately works by meaningful associations.* With this knowledge and a little experimentation, you can devise techniques for encoding and retrieval that work well for you based on your own personal associations and, perhaps, on your own sense of humor.

■ **Natural language mediators**
Words associated with new information to be remembered.

1. **RECALL:** Which one of the following statements best describes forgetting, as characterized by Ebbinghaus's forgetting curve?
   a. We forget at a constant rate.
   b. We forget slowly at first and then more rapidly as time goes on.
   c. We forget rapidly at first and then more slowly as time goes on.
   d. Ebbinghaus's method of relearning showed that we never really forget.

2. **APPLICATION:** Which kind of forgetting is involved when the sociology I studied yesterday makes it more difficult to learn and remember the psychology I am studying today?
   a. proactive interference
   b. retroactive interference
   c. decay
   d. retrieval failure

3. **RECALL:** What is the term for the controversial notion that memories can be blocked off in the unconscious, where they may cause physical and mental problems?

   a. interference
   b. repression
   c. persistence
   d. absent-mindedness

4. **RECALL:** Which one of the seven "sins" of memory is disputed by those who believe that memories of childhood abuse can, in many cases, be recovered during adulthood?
   a. transience
   b. persistence
   c. absent-mindedness
   d. suggestibility

5. **UNDERSTANDING THE CORE CONCEPT:** Which one of the "sins" of memory probably helps us avoid dangerous situations we have encountered before?
   a. suggestibility
   b. bias
   c. persistence
   d. misattribution

ANSWERS: 1.c 2.a 3.b 4.d 5.c

MEMORY: THE STATE OF THE ART

The three-stage model, with the modifications we have discussed, gives a good snapshot of memory taken from the information-processing perspective. It is widely accepted by cognitive psychologists, yet relatively unknown by the general public. What surprises and frightens the public most, however, are the distortions and errors that our memories are heir to. In fact, these "sins" of memory are among the hottest topics for research at the moment.

Two other topics can also be found at the cutting edge of current memory research. One involves the apparently vast and poorly explored domain of implicit memory. What, cognitive psychologists wonder, does memory do while it is "off line"? The other hot topic centers on the biological basis of memory, especially the changes that take place as our synapses lay down long-term memories. And, once the biology of memory becomes clearer, the ultimate goal of memory researchers will come into view: making a connection between the biology and all the quirks of memory we have studied in this chapter.

USING PSYCHOLOGY TO LEARN PSYCHOLOGY

How to Avoid Memory Failure on Exams

Mnemonic strategies designed for memorizing lists of unrelated items won't help much with the material you need to learn in your psychology class. There the important material consists of concepts—often abstract concepts, such as "operant conditioning" or "retroactive interference." Such material calls for different mnemonic strategies geared both to concept learning and to avoiding the two memory "sins" feared most by college students: *transience* and *blocking*. So, let's see what advice cognitive psychologists would give to students for avoiding these two quirks of memory.

Studying to Avoid Transience

▪ *Make the material meaningful to you.* Many studies have shown that memories will remain stronger if the information is approached in a way that makes it meaningful, rather than just a collection of facts and definitions (Baddeley, 1998; Haberlandt, 1999; Terry, 2000). One strategy for doing this involves using the **whole method,** a technique often used by actors who must learn a whole script in a short time. With this approach, the learner begins by getting an overview of all the material to be learned—the "big picture" into which the details can be assimilated. Suppose, for example, that you have a test on this chapter coming up next week. Using the whole method, you would look over the chapter outline and summary, along with all the Key Questions and Core Concepts on the chapter-opening page, before beginning to read the details of the chapter. This approach erects a mental framework on which you can hang the details of encoding, interference, retrieval, and other memory topics.

▪ *Spread your learning out over time.* A second way to build strong memories that are resistant to transience involves **distributed learning** (Baddeley, 1998; Terry, 2000). In less technical terms, the research suggests that you should study your psychology frequently (distributed, or spaced, learning), rather than trying to learn it all at once in a single "cram" session ("massed" learning). This approach not only avoids the lowered efficiency of learning brought about by fatigue but it seems to strengthen memories that are in the process of consolidation. One study found that students could double the amount of information they learned in a given amount of time and also increase their understanding of the material by studying in two separate sessions, rather than in one session (Bahrick et al., 1993). Studies have also shown that distributed learning results in the material being retained longer (Schmidt & Bjork, 1992).

Studying to Avoid Blocking on the Test

The strategies mentioned above will help you get to the test with a strong memory for the material you need to know. But you also will want to avoid block-ing, the inability to find and retrieve what you have in memory. To help you achieve this, we suggest some techniques that apply four ideas you have learned in this chapter: *interference theory, repetition, elaborative rehearsal,* and *encoding specificity:*

▪ *Take active steps to minimize interference.* You can't avoid interference altogether, but you can avoid studying for another class after your review session for tomorrow's psychology test. And you can make sure that you understand all the material and that you have cleared up any potentially conflicting points well before you go to the test. If, for example, you are not sure of the difference between *declarative memory* and *semantic memory,* you should discuss this with your instructor.

▪ *Rehearse and relearn what you have already learned.* Students often think that, just because they have read and understood the material, they will remember it. With complex concepts and ideas, you will probably need to use *repetition* in a form called **overlearning.** With this method, you continue to review the material, even after you think you understand it. Overlearning not only boosts the strength of a memory, but it gives you repeated opportunities to link it with other ideas in LTM (which is our next point).

▪ *Elaborate on the material by thinking of examples and other associations.* One of the best ways of doing *elaborative rehearsal* when studying for a test is to create your own examples of the concepts. So, as you study about proactive interference, think of an example from your own experience. And don't forget to think of examples involving the Core Concepts, too. This approach will help to prevent blocking because adding associations to the material you are learning adds more ways that the material can be accessed when you need it.

▪ *Test yourself with retrieval cues you expect to see on the examination.* Finally, by using the principle of *encoding specificity,* you can learn the material in a form that is most likely to be cued by the questions your psychology professor puts on the test. To do this it is helpful to work with a friend who is also studying for the same test. We also recommend that you get together for this purpose a day or two before the test, after both of you have studied the material thoroughly enough to feel you understand it. Your purpose, at this point, will not be to learn new material but to anticipate the most likely test items. Does your professor prefer essay questions? Short-answer questions? Multiple choice? Try to think up and answer as many questions as you can of the type most likely to appear on the test. Don't overlook the Key Questions throughout the chapter.

▪ **Whole method**   The mnemonic strategy of first approaching the material to be learned "as a whole," forming an impression of the overall meaning of the material. The details are later associated with this overall impression.
▪ **Distributed learning**   A technique whereby the learner spaces learning sessions over time, rather than trying to learn the material all in one study period.
▪ **Overlearning**   A strategy whereby the learner continues to study and rehearse the material after it has been initially brought to mastery.

And please don't overlook the other mnemonic features we have included throughout this book to guide you in your study. These include the "Check Your Understanding" quizzes and "Chapter Review" tests, as well as the "Do It Yourself!" demonstrations. All these mnemonic devices are based on well-established principles of learning and memory. Studying this way may sound like a lot of work—and it is. But the results will be worth the mental effort.

CHAPTER SUMMARY

WHAT IS MEMORY?

Any memory system involves three important processes: encoding, storage, and retrieval. Although many people believe that memory makes a complete and accurate record, cognitive psychologists see human memory from an information processing perspective, as a cognitive system that interprets, distorts, and reconstructs information. Eidetic imagery, however, is a rare and poorly understood form of memory that produces especially vivid and persistent memories that may interfere with thought. It is not clear how eidetic memory fits with the widely accepted three-stage model of memory.

● **Human memory is an information processing system that works constructively to encode, store, and retrieve information.**

HOW DO WE FORM MEMORIES?

The memory system is composed of three distinct stages: sensory memory, working memory, and long-term memory. The three stages work together sequentially to convert incoming sensory information into useful patterns or concepts that can be stored and retrieved when needed later.

Sensory memory holds 12 to 16 visual items for about ¼ second, making use of the sensory pathways. A separate sensory register for each sense holds material just long enough for important information to be selected for further processing.

Working memory, which has the smallest storage capacity of the three stages and a duration of a few seconds, draws information from sensory memory and long-term memory and processes it consciously. It has at least three components: a central executive, a phonological loop, and a sketch pad. We can cope with its limited duration and capacity by chunking, rehearsal, and acoustic encoding. The biological basis of working memory is not clear, but it is believed to involve actively firing nerve circuits, probably in the frontal cortex.

Long-term memory has apparently unlimited storage capacity and duration. It has two main partitions: declarative memory (for facts and events) and procedural memory (for perceptual and motor skills). Declarative memory can be further divided into episodic memory and semantic memory. Semantic information is encoded, stored, and retrieved according to the meaning and context of the material. The case of H. M. showed that the hippocampus is involved in transferring information to long-term memory. Other research has found long-term memories associated with relatively permanent changes at the synaptic level.

Flashbulb memories are common for highly emotional experiences. While most people have a great deal of confidence in such vivid memories, studies have shown that these memories can become distorted over time, especially the material that was not the focus of attention.

● **Each of the three memory stages encodes and stores memories in a different way, but they work together to transform sensory experience into a lasting record that has a pattern or meaning.**

HOW DO WE RETRIEVE MEMORIES?

H. M.'s case also demonstrated that information can be stored as explicit or implicit memories. Implicit memories can be cued by priming. Explicit memories can be cued by recall or recognition tasks. The accuracy of memory retrieval depends on several factors, including encoding specificity and mood. When there is a poor match between retrieval cues and the encoding, we may experience the TOT phenomenon.

● **Whether memories are implicit or explicit, successful retrieval depends on how they were encoded and how they are cued.**

WHY DOES MEMORY SOMETIMES FAIL US?

Memory failures involve the "seven sins" of memory. These include forgetting, resulting from weakening memory traces (transience), lapses of attention (absent-mindedness), and inability to retrieve a memory (blocking). Much forgetting can also be attributed to a form of blocking called interference. Memory can fail when recollections are altered through misattribution, suggestibility, and bias. An important example involves eyewitness memories, which are subject to distortion. Suggestibility can also produce false memories that seem believable to the rememberer. This may be the case with some recovered memories. The final "sin" occurs when unwanted memories persist in memory, even though we would like to forget them.

The "seven sins" of memory, however, are by-products of a memory system that is well suited to solving problems of day-to-day living. Some of these problems can be overcome by mnemonic strategies, such as the method of loci, natural language mediators, and other associative methods.

● **Most of our memory problems arise from memory's "seven sins"—which are really by-products of otherwise adaptive features of human memory.**

For each of the following items, choose the single correct or best answer. The correct answers appear at the end.

1. Unlike a video recorder, human memory is
   a. accurate.
   b. reconstructive.
   c. temporary.
   d. fast.

2. Which of the following is *not* one of the three essential tasks of memory?
   a. encoding
   b. storage
   c. retrieval
   d. consistency

3. There is no meaning attached to information when it is in:
   a. sensory memory.
   b. working memory.
   c. long-term memory.
   d. declarative memory.

4. Your knowledge of how to use a can opener, boot up your computer, address an envelope, and program a VCR are all examples of _____ memory.
   a. sensory
   b. semantic
   c. procedural
   d. constructive

5. Which part of memory would contain your knowledge of the material you studied in the first chapter of this book?
   a. episodic memory
   b. semantic memory
   c. procedural memory
   d. working memory

6. H. M.'s _____ memory was more profoundly affected by the surgery than was his _____ memory.
   a. episodic/procedural
   b. eidetic/sensory
   c. implicit/explicit
   d. recognition/recall

7. Which one of the following best illustrates the reconstructive nature of retrieval from long-term memory?
   a. the Loftus and Palmer study of eyewitnesses
   b. H. M.'s difficulties with episodic memories
   c. priming of implicit memories
   d. the TOT phenomenon

8. If you wanted to remember the major divisions of long-term memory, which method would be the most effective?
   a. repetition: repeating them over and over to yourself
   b. elaborative rehearsal: thinking of examples of each division
   c. acoustic encoding: trying to remember the sounds associated with each term
   d. temporal coding: identifying when you heard of each division

9. Elise used to live in a house with a large kitchen, where all the silverware was stored in a drawer to the right of the sink. Since she moved to her new apartment, she finds that she habitually looks for the silverware in a drawer to the right of the sink, although no such drawer exists. Her behavior reflects forgetting due to
   a. absence of retrieval cues.
   b. retroactive interference.
   c. proactive interference.
   d. repression.

10. Studies of eyewitness testimony and recovery of "repressed" memories show that
   a. our unconscious minds remember events as they actually happened.
   b. distorted memories are a sign of mental disorder.
   c. memories can be severely distorted, even when we have confidence in them.
   d. the more confident we are of a memory, the more likely it is to be true.

ANSWERS: 1.b 2.d 3.a 4.c 5.b 6.a 7.a 8.b 9.c 10.c

OUR RECOMMENDED BOOKS AND VIDEOS

BOOKS

Gross, D. (2000). *On remembering and forgetting in late modern culture.* Amherst: University of Massachusetts Press. Early humans and earlier societies depended on memory for personal survival and cultural traditions. But, in modern times, remembering equals worrying, and we are urged to "forget your troubles" or generally just "forget about it." David Gross examines the social meaning of remembering and forgetting for the self and society.

Hilts, P. J. (1995). *Memory's ghost: The strange tale of Mr. M. and the nature of memory.* New York: Simon & Schuster. The author describes meeting the famous subject of memory research, whose unusual brain injury left him unable to form new memories.

Rupp, R. (1998). *Committed to memory: How we remember and why we forget.* New York: Crown Publishing. A biochemist well-versed in world literature explains what science knows about memory: how it begins, what goes in, what stays or leaves, why some things cannot be retrieved, and what we can do to improve our memory for the things that matter to us.

Schacter, D. L. (1997). *Searching for memory: The brain, the mind, and the past.* New York: HarperCollins. This book includes brain scans, word games, and how the brain's memory processing makes you the individual you are.

VIDEOS

Eternal Sunshine of the Spotless Mind. (2004, color, 108 min.). Directed by Michael Gondry; starring Jim Carrey, Kate Winslet. After a painful breakup, both ex-partners go through an experimental procedure in which the painful memories are selectively removed—but it doesn't work as planned, and as later unpleasant memories go, earlier feelings of passion re-emerge, and seem worth keeping and "hiding" from the memory-removal process. But all one's memories are interconnected, so removing or protecting will have serious consequences.

Memento. (2001, color/b&w, 113 min.). Directed by Christopher Nolan; starring Guy Pearce, Joe Pantoliano, Carrie-Ann Moss. Suffering short-term memory loss that causes him to wake every morning with no recall of his life or purpose, a man struggles to create reliable connections and avenge his wife's murder. The story unfolds in reverse, so the audience begins with what ends up happening but has yet to learn why.

Johnny Mnemonic. (1995, color, 98 min.). Directed by Robert Longo; starring Keanu Reeves, Dolph Lundgren, Takeshi, Ice-T, Dina Meyer. This is an ugly futuristic tale of an "information" courier, who travels the globe with messages stored in his head and must elude an evil corporation after his latest cargo of "memories."

Random Harvest. (1942, black-&-white, 126 min.). Directed by Mervyn LeRoy; starring Ronald Colman, Greer Garson, Philip Dorn. A shell-shocked World War I veteran escapes from a mental hospital and starts a new life—only to be jarred by a mild injury into remembering his old identity. An essential for film buffs, this classic set the stage for decades of portrayals of memory loss in drama and soap opera.

Total Recall. (1990, color, 109 min.). Directed by Paul Verhoeven; starring Arnold Schwarzenegger, Rachel Ticotin, Sharon Stone, Ronny Cox. This futuristic suspense is about a man who realizes that his memory—of who he is as well as of events—is a fake record implanted by his enemies. Oscar-winning special effects highlight the film, based on sci-fi writer Philip K. Dick's "We Can Remember It for You Wholesale."

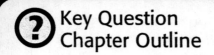

Key Question
Chapter Outline

CORE CONCEPTS

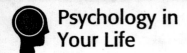

Psychology in
Your Life

How and Why Do We Experience Stress?

Stressors, Ancient and Modern
Traumatic Stressors
Chronic Stressors

How Does Stress Affect Us Physically?

The Physical Stress Response
The General Adaptation Syndrome
Stress and the Immune System

How Do We Respond Psychologically to Stress?

Personality Factors in Stress
How Personal Qualities Can
      Reduce Stress

What Strategies Can Promote Health Rather than Stress?

Psychological Coping Strategies
Physical Coping Strategies
Using Drugs for Stress Relief:
      A Costly Defense

Stress, Health, and Well-Being: The State of the Art

The human stress response to perceived threat activates thoughts, feelings, behaviors, and physiological arousal that normally promote adaptation and survival.

The physical stress response begins with arousal, which stimulates the body's adaptive responses—which can turn harmful after prolonged stress.

Our psychological responses to stressors—both healthy and harmful—depend on perception, personality, and learned patterns of response.

▼

To a large extent, stress, health, and well-being are influenced by lifestyle choices.

Change can be hazardous to your health

Some life changes count more than others—but they all count.

Student stress

College students face stress from both pressure and freedom.

Developing resilience

Individuals can learn to "bounce back" from adversity.

Happiness and well-being

Happiness depends on how you feel—not what you have.

USING PSYCHOLOGY TO LEARN PSYCHOLOGY:

Stress, Health, and Well-Being

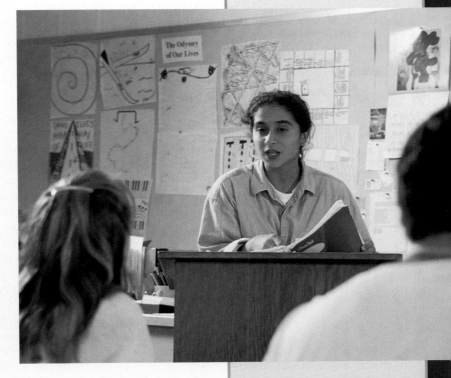

ON SEPTEMBER 11, 2001, at 8:46 A.M., retired firefighter Dennis Smith sat outside a New York clinic, waiting for his annual physical, when a nurse hurried in, announcing that a plane had just crashed into the north tower of the World Trade Center in lower Manhattan (Smith, 2003). The engine and ladder companies of New York's fire department (FDNY) were already responding to the alarms, trucks racing to the scene, men running *into* the same buildings that hordes of people desperately sought to escape. Smith asked himself what "conditions" the men were facing: the heat of the fire; the best access to the buildings; the stairwells' integrity. How many were already trapped inside and facing death?

One firefighter later described the chaos: "It looked like a movie scene, where the monster was coming . . . [W]e got showered with debris . . . Things were hitting—*bing, bang, boom*—over your head" (Smith, 2003, pp. 70–71). He had climbed high into the North Tower when the South Tower was hit, and "suddenly, there was this loud, loud noise overhead." He recalled huddling inside a stairwell, inventorying his resources, just as Smith had imagined: "I was thinking of my situation—what should I do, what can I do? What do I have that is positive? What tools do I have? . . . The main thing I had was my helmet. I remember thinking how important it was to have had that helmet. That was the biggie: the helmet, and holding on to my helmet . . ." (Smith, p. 75).

● Firefighters and other emergency workers responding to the September 11 terrorist attacks needed to quickly determine the conditions they faced and the resources they had to meet those demands.

But the critical need for the helmet was forgotten in one moment by Kross's fellow firefighter, Father Mychael Judge. The FDNY chaplain, among the first to arrive and help people out of the building, heard that firefighters were trapped inside and rushed back into the smoke. While performing last rites, he removed his helmet out of respectful habit—just as a shower of debris fell, killing him instantly (Downey, 2004).

In the weeks and months after the terrorist attacks, firefighters continued to search for bodies, to bury, memorialize, and mourn their brothers. Few bodies of the 343 lost were ever recovered. Those who had made it—while their buddies died just a few feet away—endured *survivor's guilt,* ambivalent and uncertain why they deserved to live, asking themselves, "Why me?" One survivor noted there was no simple answer: "The flip side of 'Why me?' is 'Why *not* me?' That is probably the healthier way to look at it" (Smith, 2003, pp. 82–83).

But surviving firefighters continued to grieve. They rejected phony reverence or gloom in remembering their friends, preferring instead to laugh and joke about the dead men's quirks and screw-ups. Still, everyone wonders what really happened to those who were never found. Manhattan's Engine 40/Ladder 35 lost 12 comrades, more than any other firehouse. Then, five months after 9/11, the men of 40/35 got hold of a newsman's tape that appeared to show their 12 lost comrades entering the tower minutes before it collapsed on them. The video had been shot at a distance, but the moving figures gradually became recognizable. Staring intently at the screen, the surviving firefighters gazed once more on friends who did not return. They played the video over and over again (Halberstam, 2002).

Of the many heroes recognized in the aftermath of the terrorist attacks of September 11, 2001, few were as glamorized as the engine and ladder companies of the FDNY, the Fire Department of New York. Even on a "normal" day, the work of firefighters and other emergency responders involves daunting levels of *stress,* the emotional arousal created by change and threat. But as we explore the psychology of stress, illness, health, and well-being, we hope you will remember that stress doesn't necessarily mean major trauma, tragedy, and disaster. Sources of stress can also include jobs, relationships, school, traffic, and illness—the problems and irritations of everyday life. Amazingly, we deal with stress effectively most of the time, managing to be not only healthy but even happy.

But, as you will see, there can be serious consequences when we don't deal effectively with stress—no matter what its source. On the positive side, we should emphasize that the emotional arousal we call stress usually works to our advantage. It brings threatening events into focus and readies us to respond. On the negative side, extreme or prolonged emotional arousal carries a threat to our health. Too much arousal can turn our defenses against us in a destructive form of the stress response—often called *distress.* The results can include high blood pressure, a stroke, a heart attack, or other life-threatening physical conditions. We see these consequences, for example, not only emergency response workers but also employees in high-pressure corporate environments and air traffic control towers. And we also see among such workers the psychological consequences when stress leads to mental confusion, chronic anxiety, or depression.

Why do some people seem to "bounce back," even after severely traumatic experiences, such as the death of a loved one, while others are derailed by seemingly minor hassles? We can see a snapshot of the individual differences

CONNECTION: CHAPTER 9

Emotions are normally adaptive responses that help us focus our energies on important events.

in response to stress in the way people handle being caught in a traffic jam. Some drivers calmly daydream or listen to their radios, while others frantically hit their horns or "rubberneck" impatiently, straining to see what the obstruction is. To a large extent, the stressful effects of an unpleasant event are a personal matter. How much stress we experience is determined not only by the quality and intensity of the stressful situation but by how we interpret the stressor, the resources we have available to deal with it, and the consequent difficulty of meeting the demands placed on us.

Whether stress comes from the 9/11 disaster, a long illness, or a traffic jam, how we respond depends on an interaction of the same basic elements that you see in Figure 10.1: the stressor, our personal characteristics, the resources we have available. Many of the individual differences seen in responses stem from how we consciously and unconsciously evaluate the stressor and assess our resources for coping with it. Together these two sets of perceptions—identifying the threat and determining how one will cope—comprise the process of *cognitive appraisal.*

And, yes—it's the same cognitive appraisal that we found at work in emotion in the previous chapter. You see, the stress response has the same components as the emotional response. This means that it has four major components, shown in Figure 10.1. In addition to cognitive appraisal, the stress response includes a physiological response (such as a "knot" in the stomach), subjective feelings (such as fear), and behavior (such as aggression). But stress is not just another emotion. In its most worrisome form, it is an emotional

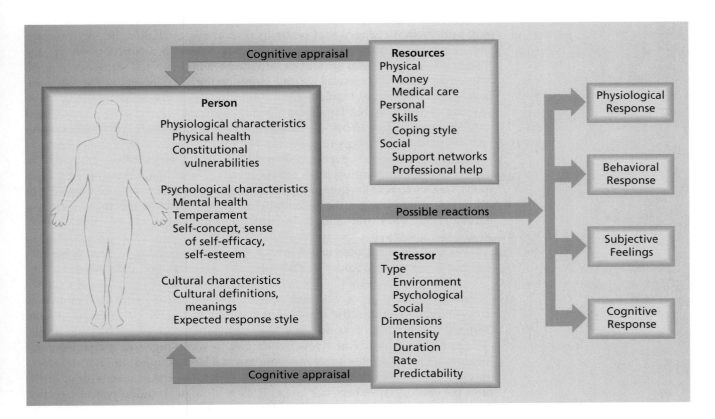

● **FIGURE 10.1**   A Model of Stress

Cognitive appraisal of the stress situation interacts with the stressor and the physical, social, and personal resources available for dealing with the stressor. Individuals respond to threats on various levels—physical, behavioral, emotional, and cognitive. Some responses are adaptive, and others are maladaptive or even lethal.

response that people can experience for long periods—which makes the physiological arousal potentially so dangerous. You cannot remain in a state of arousal for months or years without some dire consequences. As we will see, however, cognitive appraisal can be turned to our advantage, as one of the most effective tools for coping with stress.

HOW AND WHY DO WE EXPERIENCE STRESS?

What images come to mind when you hear the word *stress*? Most people think of the pressures in their lives: difficult jobs, unhappy relationships, financial woes, health problems, and final exams. You may have some visceral associations with stress, too: a churning stomach, perspiration, headache, or high blood pressure. And, as we have noted, stress is also linked with physical illness. In fact, stress is associated with many aspects of modern society, and it is also associated with our internal reactions. This is what makes stress a slippery concept.

We use the word *stress* loosely in everyday conversation, referring to a *situation* that confronts us (Lazarus et al., 1985). For example, if your employer or professor has been giving you a difficult time, you may say that you are "under stress," as though you were being squashed by a heavy object. In this conversational sense, stress means an external threat or pressure, an unpleasant event.

However, psychologists use the term in a more specific way: For them, stress is not a situation but a *response*. They see **stress** as referring to the physical and mental changes that occur in response to a challenging or threatening situation (Krantz et al., 1985). It is useful to make a distinction, on the one hand, between stressful stimuli or situations, which we call **stressors** and, on the other hand, the arousal we call stress or the *stress response*. Thus a stressor is the large, angry man climbing out of the car you just bashed into; stress is your response to that large, angry man: your racing heart, shaky hands, and sudden perspiration. Your demanding boss is the stressor; your upset stomach is part of your stress response.

This section of the chapter begins with a review of the stressors that have drawn the most attention from psychologists. These include everything from petty hassles to relationship problems to terrorist attacks. The Core Concept for this section emphasizes the essentially adaptive nature of the stress response stressors that vary dramatically in nature and intensity:

The human stress response to perceived threat activates thoughts, feelings, behaviors, and physiological arousal that normally promote adaptation and survival.

Whatever one perceives as a stressor, the sense of being challenged or threatened precipitates the same effort to adapt and survive. It's easy to blame "stress" for our problems and symptoms, but the problem is not that simple. The normal experience of stress is essential to surviving, and it enables us to deal with life's challenges and meet our goals. The problem is not normal stress but *excessive* or *prolonged* stress and our ineffective efforts to deal with it. Stress is a psychological experience as well as a biological and physical process, because in order to experience stress, you must first perceive and interpret an event or condition as stressful—psychological processes involving attention, memory, and emotion. For example, the victims of the 9/11 terrorist attacks indisputably experienced stress, recognizing the dangers in which they were immersed. But much later, any American citizen might also feel some stress

■ **Stress** A physical and mental response to a challenging or threatening situation.
■ **Stressor** A stressful stimulus, a condition demanding adaptation.

when the Homeland Security Advisory System announces an increase from Yellow to Orange Alert. These color-coded warnings cannot in themselves harm anyone, but each color symbolizes a level of threat deemed reasonable by the government. If you know and accept the psychological meaning of the color alerts, you experience stress—although it may not be clear how you should behave or what to do differently under Orange as opposed to Yellow conditions (Zimbardo, 2004b). The key role of interpretation, and its dependence on the context of the world we live in, suggests how both severe trauma and vague threats can evoke the same human stress response.

Stressors, Ancient and Modern

Early humans survived mortal dangers by responding quickly and decisively to potentially lethal attacks by predators or hostile tribes, and some of the ways we respond to stressors in modern times are the result of our ancestors' evolutionary legacy. Modern life, of course, adds some new dangers: demanding jobs, financial worries, and computer crashes. Most recently we have faced the stressors of international terrorism. Yet while we are exposed to new stressors, our stress response reflects the body's millennia-old ability to become quickly aroused to meet emergencies. So, when the power company threatens to cut off your power or your boss criticizes your work, an ancient response pattern occurs, as your muscles tighten, your hormones surge, and you feel an urge to flee or fight. Unfortunately, these old remedies don't always work as well with the new problems.

● Traffic can be a hassle—and a significant source of stress for some people.

Some of the serious stressors confronting our ancestors, such as catastrophe or combat, do continue to face us today. Thus we begin our review with a look at primitive threats to survival and the responses that evolved to meet them. Next we contrast sudden, traumatic stressors with more gradual chronic stressors. Finally we consider stress of adapting to normal life-changing events.

Primitive Stressors   Human beings have adapted to an enormous variety of living environments and environmental conditions worldwide, confronting climate extremes, scarce reources, and hostile neighbors. Those who responded most quickly and effectively to danger survived and passed those responsive genes to their offspring; slower or less clever individuals were less likely to survive in the course of human evolution. In all the variety of challenges humans faced, three mortal threats continually demanded quick action: the danger of *starvation, exposure* to the elements, and mortal *attack*. Wherever we have lived, whatever we have done, we always must find a way to feed ourselves, to obtain shelter and protection, and to defend ourselves. While these goals are unmet, there is no time to waste; we must be quick to appraise the problem and solve it. The quicker we are to feel fear or anger and take appropriate action, the better our chances of success and survival.

Responding to Threat   Thus we are the descendants of ancestors who were best suited to *fight or flee* when faced with threats to survival. This evolutionary script is retained in our body's automatic responses to frightening or enraging conditions. If someone insults you, your face feels hot and your fists seem to clench by themselves, readying you for a physical contest. Facing a very different sort of "threat": Suppose you are unprepared for class discussion, but the instructor calls on *you*. Your heart races, your knees feel wobbly, and you feel the urge to run away. These examples illustrate the two poles of the fight-or-flight response, a sequence of internal processes triggered when a threat is perceived, preparing the organism for either struggle or escape.

An individual's fight-or-flight pattern depends on an innate "program" built into the brain. However, responses to different stressors are also affected by how an individual has *learned* to deal with threat. The built-in impulse to either fight or flee from a stressor can cause you to overreact to a mild problem, one that cannot be solved with either action. So, you may feel intimidated by an unwanted phone call, but running away won't make the caller stop pursuing you. Or an obnoxious television talk show might upset you, but yelling or throwing the remote control at the set won't change the host's politics. Thus you find what works and what doesn't work and refine your responses to various stressors accordingly.

Since prehistoric times, humans have been individually challenged by loss and catastrophe. As people collected into communities, societal issues and group conflict has also led us to "worry ourselves sick" by anticipating what might go wrong, from minor irritants to major traumas (Sapolsky, 1994). Both traumatic events and chronic stressors continue to challenge us today.

Traumatic Stressors

Catastrophic events such as natural disaster and major terrorist attacks both qualify as types of **traumatic stressors,** situations that threaten your own or others' physical safety, arousing feelings of fear, horror, or helplessness. On a more personal level, the loss of a loved one constitutes a trauma, despite the fact that death and separation are likely to affect everyone at some time. We examine traumatic stress by considering first natural and human-made catastrophes, then the power of personal loss, and finally the complexity of post-traumatic stress.

Catastrophe Stress and loss in the extreme accompanies *catastrophic events—* sudden, violent calamities, including both natural disasters, such as the 2004 tsunami in Southeast Asia, and human-made tragedies such as terrorist attacks and warfare. Anyone caught up in such a catastrophic event can lose loved ones or possessions; less obvious is the fact that one's *response* to a catastrophe can have devastating effects on physical and mental health. As we saw in the chapter's opening story, firefighters and emergency workers find themselves reliving the events in nightmares and in daytime flashbacks.

Studies of catastrophe survivors have taught psychologists how individuals who have undergone such traumas and losses respond to these ordeals (Asarnow et al., 1999; Baum, 1990; Sprang, 1999). Such research is difficult: Ethics prevent psychologists from creating disastrous events in order to study their effects on volunteer subjects. The only way to study these events is to be on the scene after the catastrophe, getting the story from the survivors while it is fresh in their minds.

One opportunity to understand disaster response presented itself in San Francisco in the early fall of 1989, just as the baseball World Series was about to begin at Candlestick Park. Spectators were still settling into their seats when the entire stadium began to shake violently, the lights went out, and the scoreboard turned black. Sixty thousand fans fell silent. They had just experienced a major earthquake. Elsewhere in the city, fires erupted, a bridge collapsed, highways were crushed—and people were dying.

One week after the quake, a team of research psychologists conducted follow-up surveys by telephone with about 800 regional residents. Survey responses revealed a pattern: The lives of respondents who had been through the earthquake continued to revolve around the disaster for about a month. After this period, they ceased obsessing about the quake, but at the same time reported an increase in other stress-related symptoms, including sleep disruption and relationship problems. Survivors relived the trauma in frequent nightmares about earthquakes (Wood et al., 1992). Most symptoms diminished over the next two months, although one year later, as many as 20% of

■ **Traumatic stressor** A situation that threatens one's physical safety, arousing feelings of fear, horror, or helplessness.

San Francisco area residents remained distressed about the quake (Pennebaker & Harber, 1991).

Natural disasters are violent, destroying life and property in the affected area. But human-made catastrophes such as massive crime and terrorism have an added dimension of threat, because they are produced intentionally by other people. *Terrorism* has been defined as a type of disaster caused by "human malevolence" with a goal of disrupting society by creating fear and danger (Hall et al., 2002).

Psychological responses to extreme natural and human-caused disasters have been theorized to occur in stages, as victims experience shock, feel intense emotion, and struggle to reorganize their lives (Beigel & Berren, 1985; Horowitz, 1997). Cohen and Ahearn (1980) identified five stages that we pass through:

1. Immediately after the event, victims experience *psychic numbness*, including shock and confusion, and for moments to days cannot comprehend what has happened.

2. During a phase of *automatic action*, victims have little awareness of their own experiences and later show poor recall for what occurred. This phase is worsened by a lack of preparedness, delaying rescue and costing lives.

3. In a third stage of *communal effort*, people pool resources and collaborate, proud of their accomplishments but also weary and aware they are using up precious energy reserves. Without better planning, many survivors lose hope and initiative for rebuilding their lives.

4. In the fourth phase, survivors may experience a *letdown* as, depleted of energy, they comprehend and feel the tragedy's impact. Public interest and media attention fade, and survivors feel abandoned although the state of emergency continues.

5. An extended final period of *recovery* follows as survivors adapt to the changes created by the disaster. The fabric of the community will change as the natural and business environment are altered. On the national scale after 9/11, survivors demanded to know how the attacks could have happened in the first place—reflecting a basic need to know "why?" and to find meaning in loss.

Stage theories of stress response are useful because they help us to anticipate what survivors will go through and what kinds of assistance they need. To learn from and make sense of catastrophic loss, we formulate *accounts,* narratives that explain what happened and why. These stories help us to explain ourselves to each other; sharing them may even reflect a more general human need to tell our stories and be understood by those close to us (Harvey, 1996; Harvey et al., 1990). When an event is surprising or unpleasant, we are especially likely to formulate explanations (Holtzworth-Munroe & Jacobson, 1985). By confiding our stories to others, we begin to work through the pain of loss (Harvey, 2000; Weber & Harvey, 1994b).

People who undergo any sort of trauma generally become more susceptible to physical illness. The power of stories holds even here, however: Survivors who discuss their experiences in detail with others suffer fewer health problems (Niederhoffer & Pennebaker, 2002; Pennebaker, 1990; Pennebaker & Harber, 1991; Pennebaker et al., 1988, 1989).

Newsworthy events such as natural disasters merit news coverage, broadcasting the sounds and images of others' pain. Viewers are not immune to such programs, however, and may experience a sort of "second-hand" traumatization.

Trauma in the Media Media news coverage expands the experience of catastrophe, so all viewers can experience it, over and over. How many times have you watched television replay the tsunami hitting the coast of Thailand or the towers collapsing on 9/11? Recall that, in our opening story, members of the Manhattan firefighters' crew who survived 9/11 repeatedly viewed a videotape showing their now-dead comrades as they rushed into the World Trade Center just before the building collapsed. At last they knew for certain the fate of their friends, but was repeated viewing really therapeutic for them? Identifying the figures on the tape as being their friends might give them some *closure,* a sense of completion, and their friends' heroism could help them find meaning in tragedy.

But there is a dark side to the "instant replay" of catastrophe. While New York firefighters were responding to the terrorist attacks, a research team in Washington state had already been conducting a longitudinal (long-term) study of firefighters in their region. Though safely distant from the dangers in the East, firefighters in the study could still experience the events of the eastern United States via the media, especially repeated television coverage of the Twin Towers' collapse. Counselors and therapists had already found that secondhand experiences of catastrophe could create severe stress for emergency rescue and medical workers who heard or watched others' trauma (McCann & Pearlman, 1990; Pearlman & Mac Ian, 1995). The Washington researchers found that, one week after 9/11, firefighters in their study were significantly stressed by constant news of the terrorist attacks. Specifically, they felt greater personal risk and threat from their jobs than they had before. They questioned their own competence in handling mass casualties, and they felt dissatisfied with the level of social support available on the job (Murphy et al., 2004). Just being exposed to media coverage of such intense, relevant news had brought the catastrophe to these firefighters 3000 miles away from Ground Zero.

Vicarious traumatization Revisiting and reliving catastrophe causes its own stress, an experience stress researchers call **vicarious traumatization,** severe stress caused when one is exposed to others' accounts of trauma in which the observer becomes engaged with the stressful material (McCann & Pearlman, 1990). (The term *trauma* refers to a wound or injury; *traumatization* describes the process of creating or experiencing that trauma). To be vicariously traumatized, you need not identify with the victims of tragedy. All media viewers

■ **Vicarious traumatization** Severe stress caused by exposure to traumatic images or stories causing the observer to become engaged with the stressful material.

is correlated with longer life. How can we reconcile this apparent contradiction? It appears that getting married can be a stressful experience, but once the stress of a wedding has dissipated, being married can provide a buffer against stress. In fact, any stable, long-term relationship seems to offer some protection against stress (Friedman et al., 1995). We will see, below, that other forms of social support also are associated with longevity.

Finally, critics point out that the correlations between life changes and health changes are moderate. A high score does not mean that illness is certain, nor does a low score guarantee health. Then too, certain groups, such as students, who are at change points in their lives, tend to get high scores, although it is not clear that they are more at risk for illness. Their youth may offer some protection. In general, people's chances of incurring an illness may be more related to their interpretations and responses to life changes than to the changes themselves (Lazarus et al., 1985). People differ in their abilities to deal with change, presumably because of genetic differences, general physical condition, lifestyles, and coping skills. The SRRS takes none of these factors into account, but it remains the most widely used measure of stress-related risk for illness.

CHECK YOUR UNDERSTANDING

1. **RECALL:** Which of the following is an example of chronic stress?
   a. burnout
   b. terrorism
   c. loss of a loved one
   d. catastrophe

2. **RECALL:** Victims of a natural disaster go through a stage of feeling depletion of energy and abandoned by public and media attention. This is the ____ stage.
   a. psychic numbness
   b. automatic action
   c. communal effort
   d. letdown

3. **APPLICATION:** You have taken the Holmes and Rahe SRRS and have a high score—say 400 points. What does this score mean?

   a. Your risk of developing stress-related illness is extremely low.
   b. The typical stressors in your life are minor problems worth few life-change units.
   c. No matter what your score is, making more friends will reduce your risk by half.
   d. You have a much higher than average risk of developing a major health problem within the next year.

4. **UNDERSTANDING THE CORE CONCEPT:** The human stress response to perceived threat activates psychological reactions that usually
   a. threaten health and survival.
   b. promote adaptation and survival.
   c. slow and reduce one's ability to respond.
   d. produce increasing pain.

Answers: 1.a 2.d 3.d 4.b

HOW DOES STRESS AFFECT US PHYSICALLY?

There is no scientific evidence that mental power alone can alter external physical events, such as the roll of the dice or dealing of cards. The mind can control matter outside our bodies only by controlling our behavior. Mental influence on internal events, however, is another story: Evidence for this internal mind-over-matter effect abounds in psychology and medicine. How this works during stress—to our advantage and disadvantage—is the subject of this section of the chapter, where we look at the physical components of stress. According to our Core Concept,

The physical stress response begins with arousal, which stimulates the body's adaptive responses—which can turn harmful after prolonged stress.

We have seen that stress has many sources, and it can have serious health consequences. Now we will learn how it works on us both biologically and psychologically.

The Physical Stress Response

Firefighters usually report that they love their work, and for some the job is a family tradition. But these individuals' camaraderie and commitment cannot lessen the threat, the risk of injury and death—the stress they experience—when they must answer the alarm, race into harm's way, grieve, and adapt. Even for an experienced firefighter, how does the body respond to the perception of that stressor?

The physical response to nearly any stressor follows the same sequence:

1. An initial arousal
2. A protective behavioral reaction, often taking the form of the fight-or-flight response
3. Internal responses of the autonomic nervous system (ANS) and endocrine system
4. A decrease in the effectiveness of the immune system

As we examine each physical response, note that these are the same processes we reviewed in the experience of emotion in the last chapter. As we have stated, the stress response is a form of emotional response.

Arousal   When a stressful situation begins suddenly—as when a professional firefighter first hears the alarm—the stress response is likely to begin with abrupt and intense physiological arousal, including accelerated heart rate, quickened breathing, increased blood pressure, and profuse perspiration. This response involves the same unconscious brain circuits involved in emotional arousal (recall Figure 9.2). This scenario illustrates a case of **acute stress,** a temporary pattern of stressor-activated arousal with a distinct onset and limited duration.

Sometimes, however, arousal may merely fester, or it may grow slowly, as when jealousy first tugs at you, then distracts you, and finally disrupts your life with fear or outrage. This sort of long-term arousal is an example of **chronic stress.** It involves a continuous state of stressful arousal persisting over time, a state in which the demands may be greater than one's resources for dealing with them.

Arousal does us no good if it creates panic and confusion that keep us from responding to a threat. Fortunately, the human brain evolved to coordinate several simultaneous reactions involving the nervous system, the endocrine system, and the muscles. As a result, we are biologically equipped to make efficient and effective responses to changing environmental demands. So, when one perceives an external threat, these bodily mechanisms are set in motion. Many are automatic or reflexive because instant action and extra strength may be required if the organism is to survive. As introduced earlier, this basic pattern of internal activity constitutes the *fight-or-flight response.*

Fight or Flight   Imagine you are attending a meeting with your coworkers. Suddenly the department head criticizes you and claims that you have failed to attend to tasks that were really someone else's responsibility. As everyone's eyes quickly turn your way, you feel your face getting hot, your jaw tightening,

CONNECTION: CHAPTER 9

One of the brain's two *emotion circuits* relies on lower brain structures that operate outside of consciousness.

■ **Acute stress**   A temporary pattern of stressor-activated arousal with a distinct onset and limited duration.
■ **Chronic stress**   Continuous stressful arousal persisting over time.

and your fists clenching. You would not dream of shouting or hitting anyone—but you feel like it.

Now imagine another stressful scenario: You walk into class a few moments late, only to find everyone putting their books and notes away, apparently clearing their desks for a test you did not realize was scheduled for today. Your heart seems to stop, your mouth is dry, and your knees feel weak. Momentarily you consider hurrying back out the door. Why does this feel like a threat? Your life is not really in danger, and running away won't solve your problem. So why do you feel a physical urge to escape?

These two scenarios illustrate the two poles of the **fight-or-flight response,** a sequence of internal processes that prepares the aroused organism for struggle or escape. It occurs when a situation is *interpreted* as threatening. When a fight-or-flight reaction does occur, its pattern depends on how the organism has learned to deal with threat, as well as on an innate fight-or-flight "program" built into the brain. Thus you have an *internal* urge to flee from an unexpected test, but you have *learned* from experience that sooner or later, you'll have to face the music, and make up the missed work—so fleeing does no good and could even worsen your problem.

While the fight-or-flight response can be acquired or influenced by learning, it is essentially an innate reaction operating largely outside consciousness. This autonomic response was first recognized early in the 20th century by physiologist Walter Cannon, whose research revealed that a threat stimulates a sequence of activities in the organism's nerves and glands (Cannon, 1914; 1936). We now know that the amygdala and the hypothalamus control this response by initiating a cascade of events in the autonomic nervous system (ANS), endocrine system, and immune system (Jansen et al., 1995; LeDoux, 1996).

As you recall, the autonomic nervous system (ANS) regulates the activities of our internal organs. When an individual perceives a situation as threatening, the hypothalamus sends an emergency message to the ANS, which sets in motion several bodily reactions to stress. See Figure 10.2 for a detailed list of how the body is prepared for an emergency response by the ANS and endocrine system (system of internal glands). The response can be helpful when you need to escape a mudslide, confront a hostile rival, or protect your children from a tsunami. And it served our ancestors well—but it has a cost. Staying physiologically "on guard" against a threat eventually wears down the body's natural defenses. In this way, suffering from frequent stress—or frequently interpreting experiences as stressful—can create a serious health risk: An essentially healthy stress response can become distress.

In sudden emergencies, these automatic responses can be helpful, producing effective action without requiring the time and effort of complex thinking and planning. But, as we have seen, modern living has produced a different class of stressors—*psychosocial stressors*—that act over far longer periods and threaten not our immediate survival but our status, lifestyles, health, or self-respect. In the face of chronic psychological stressors, our emergency response may offer little help—or may even backfire. The automatic response that evolved for quick action and to ensure survival can, when prolonged, exhaust bodily resources and actually *impede* survival. Stress researcher Robert Sapolsky notes that our powerful stress-response system works effectively for short-term emergencies, "but we turn it on for months on end, worrying about mortgages, relationships, and promotions" (1998, p. 7).

While fight-or-flight behaviors—efforts to counterattack or flee—are visible in our behavior, the accompanying autonomic and endocrine responses occur invisibly inside us. Like fight-or-flight, these internal responses are adaptive for dealing with acute, life-threatening stressors. But, if a stressor is chronic and long-term, or not a definable external threat, then our internal stress

● In cases of acute stress, such as this woman faces as a fire races through her house, the stressful situation arises suddenly, and the stress response begins with abrupt and intense physiological arousal.

◀ **CONNECTION: CHAPTER 2**

The *autonomic nervous system* operates outside of consciousness and sends messages to the internal organs.

■ **Fight-or-flight** Sequence of internal processes preparing an organism for struggle or escape.

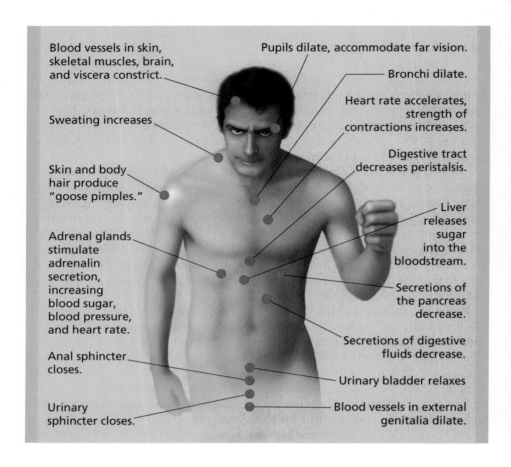

Blood vessels in skin, skeletal muscles, brain, and viscera constrict.

Pupils dilate, accommodate far vision.

Bronchi dilate.

Heart rate accelerates, strength of contractions increases.

Sweating increases

Digestive tract decreases peristalsis.

Skin and body hair produce "goose pimples."

Liver releases sugar into the bloodstream.

Adrenal glands stimulate adrenalin secretion, increasing blood sugar, blood pressure, and heart rate.

Secretions of the pancreas decrease.

Secretions of digestive fluids decrease.

Anal sphincter closes.

Urinary bladder relaxes

Urinary sphincter closes.

Blood vessels in external genitalia dilate.

response can become prolonged, producing physical weakness and illness—even death.

The General Adaptation Syndrome

How do victims of stress and persistent negative emotions become candidates for disease? Our understanding of how stress causes illness began in the early 20th century with the work of Canadian endocrinologist Hans Selye (pronounced *SELL-yeh*). In brief, he discovered that different stressors trigger essentially the same systemic reaction, or general physical response, which mobilizes the body's resources to deal with the threat. Moreover, he found, all stressors provoke some attempt at adaptation, or adjustment of the body to the stressor. Because the bodily response was a general rather than a specific adaptation effort, Selye dubbed it the **general adaptation syndrome (GAS).** (See Figure 10.3.) Normally, these responses are helpful, but under chronically stressful conditions, they can lead to heart disease, asthma, headache, gastric ulcers, arthritis, and a variety of other disorders (Carlson, 2004; Friedman & Booth-Kewley, 1988; Salovey et al., 2000).

Selye's model of the GAS describes a three-stage response to any threat, consisting of an *alarm reaction,* a *stage of resistance,* and a *stage of exhaustion* (Hughes et al., 1984; Johnson, 1991; Selye, 1956, 1991).

The Alarm Reaction. In the first stage of stress, the body's warning system activates and begins to mobilize its resources against the stressor. In this **alarm reaction,** the hypothalamus sets off an emergency response in the hormone system, especially in the adrenal glands, through the pathway shown in Figure 10.4. The result is a flood of steroid hormones into the bloodstream—

■ **General adaptation syndrome (GAS)** Pattern of general physical responses that take essentially the same form in responding to any serious chronic stressor.

■ **Alarm reaction** First stage of the GAS, during which the body mobilizes its resources to cope with a stressor.

itself (Segerstrom & Miller, 2004). Thus, a person who faces, for example, the long-term stress of caring for a parent with Alzheimer's disease runs the risk of dangerous immunosuppression—which increases vulnerability to physical disease. Ironically, immune function can also be accompanied by less serious problems that we *interpret* as stressors. So, when next you feel upset over seemingly uncontrollable events or possible future problems, such as grades, career choices, or relationships, consider the signals you are sending to your brain and immune system. You may literally be worrying yourself sick. (Which, of course, can be just one more thing to worry about, if you are a chronic worrier!)

How do mental processes affect the immune system? The central nervous system and immune systems maintain a communication "loop" in response to stress, injury, or infection—a cold virus, for example (Maier & Watkins, 1999). In response to a stressor, the brain sends messages to the autonomic nervous system and endocrine system, which have links to organs that produce the immune response. (Components of the immune system include the blood, bone marrow, the liver, and the thymus gland.) The brain then receives feedback from the immune system via neural and endocrine pathways (Maier & Watkins, 2000). Among the chemical messengers shuttling between the brain and the immune system are proteins known as **cytokines.** After these hormonelike chemicals alert the brain to distress in the body, the brain releases its own cytokines to reduce energy output, causing symptoms like fever and listlessness—responses that usually help fight disease but can sometimes get out of control (DeAngelis, 2002a). In addition to tiredness, cytokines may produce feelings of depression, involving a spiral of negative emotion and thought. Such a response can prolong stress and illness (National Public Radio, 2004a).

One of the main factors that determine whether immune reaction will harm rather than support health is the nature of the stressor (Pert, 1997). Many physical stressors, such as strenuous exercise or an attack by an aggressive animal, begin and end abruptly. These *acute* stressors trigger *natural immunity* responses, which help reduce the risk of injury. In contrast, *chronic* psychological stressors—a difficult marriage, a bad supervisor, an unfair professor—emerge gradually, last a long time, and are not readily solved with fight or flight or with an immune response. There is no physical enemy to battle, no safe haven to seek—no quick fix. Bodily responses become maladaptive, the body becomes more vulnerable to infection and injury, and eventually immune disorders can develop. This immunosuppression, a diminished effectiveness of immune response, entails serious health risks.

In fact, many chronic stressors are conditions that challenge our emotional well-being or social status. We have seen that such conditions can cause physical disease just as surely as can viruses, bacteria, and physical trauma. Not surprisingly, then, it has been psychology rather than medicine that has had the most to say about the ways people cope with stress, both successfully and unsuccessfully. We will look at these *coping strategies* right after we focus on some common sources of stress in the lives of students.

■ **Cytokines** Hormonelike chemicals facilitating communication between brain and immune system.

PSYCHOLOGY IN YOUR LIFE:
STUDENT STRESS

It's timely for you to be studying stress and well-being right now, because merely being a college student qualifies as a stressor. College freshmen in particular have been found to undergo major challenges in making the transition. One study found that freshman stress unfolds in three phases. First, new students experience the *shock and excitement* of new roles, environments, and social relationships. Next comes a protracted period of *disillusionment and struggle* as students face both the serious work and mundane chores of academic life. Finally, as roles gel and mastery is developed in at least some efforts, a sense of *improved well-being and possibilities* emerges (Rambo-Chroniak, 1999). But stress isn't limited to first-year students. Whatever their year in college, students experience a specific pattern of stress during the school year, with stress peaks at the beginning, middle, and end of each semester (Bolger, 1997). Two points in time are particularly difficult: the "midwinter crash" and the final exam period, when studying competes with regular sleep and healthy eating, and when flu and cold viruses afflict those with low resistance.

Some causes of student stress are obvious. Academic pressure comes at the top of the list (Bolger, 1997). With more and new social interactions, it's not surprising that interpersonal relationships also cause problems, including negative social exchanges, such as having friends lose their temper, being taken advantage of, or having one's privacy invaded (Edwards et al., 2001). Romantic love can also be a source of not only joy but stress and illness, especially among college women (Riessman et al., 1991). Students also complain of stress caused by their families, particularly interactions involving difficult emotions, control, and manipulation (Anderson, 1987). Perhaps the essential source of stress for college students is *freedom*—specifically, the lack of structure or monitoring students experience in a college environment as contrasted with the structure of home and high school curriculum (*USA Today*, 1996).

Finally, college students are certainly not insulated from external crises and world events. After the 9/11 terrorist attacks, students not directly affected by the violence still experienced anxiety, although this impact lessened over time for most students. Anxiety was prolonged for individuals who focused on their own emotions and vented their feelings rather than channeling them into constructive activity (Liverant et al., 2004).

Solutions for student stress, fortunately, may be within arm's reach—the distance needed to reach for the phone and call a friend for support or the college health or counseling center for professional advice. Most students express a reluctance to seek help (Rambo-Chroniak, 1999), so simply overcoming this ambivalence—especially as an enlightened student of the many uses of psychology—can be a step toward feeling better. Young-adult freshmen in particular also do better if they have positive attitudes about becoming independent individuals on a course of normal separation from their parents (Smith, 1995).

In terms of self-help, students also report better results with *problem-focused coping*, taking action to fix whatever is wrong, as opposed to *emotion-focused strategies* that make a person "feel" better but don't help (and might worsen) the stressful situation (Smith, 1995). Cultivating more hopeful attitudes and better self-esteem—for example, by setting and meeting realistic goals—leads to lower stress and better adjustment. Students also appear to be more adaptive if they report better social support and a greater sense of control in their lives (Rambo-Chroniak, 1999). Involvement in student organizations can offer both structure and social contact, but beware of the stress of excessive commitment (Bolger, 1997). Two qualities in particular characterize students who are especially effective in preventing and coping with stress: *resilience*, based in part in self-acceptance, effective communication, and coping skills; and *cognitive hardiness*, an ability to interpret potential stressors as challenging rather than threatening (Nowack, 1983; Yeaman, 1995).

1. **RECALL:** Stress-management behavior that identifies, reduces, and eliminates the stressor is called ____-focused coping.
   a. problem
   b. defense
   c. emotion
   d. control

2. **RECALL:** "Life inflicts the same setbacks and tragedies" on most people, claims psychologist Martin Seligman, "but the ____ weathers them better."
   a. debriefed individual
   b. emotion-focused person
   c. Type A
   d. optimist

3. **APPLICATION:** Suppose that, after reading the section on subjective well-being, you decide you want to help yourself to feel happier. Which of the following is one of the things you might do to achieve your goal?

   a. Spend more time on your own and less involved with other people.
   b. Evaluate the world around you more realistically even if it is less positive.
   c. Develop a more involved spiritual dimension in your life.
   d. Earn a much higher income.

4. **UNDERSTANDING THE CORE CONCEPT:** Which has been shown to be the most effective strategy for coping with stress?
   a. exercise
   b. psychological debriefing
   c. antidepressant medication
   d. setting high goals and working very hard to achieve them

Answers: 1.a 2.d 3.c 4.a

STRESS, HEALTH, AND WELL-BEING: THE STATE OF THE ART

The idea that stress and stress-induced illness are "all in your mind" is now known to be dead wrong. The biological pathways that link stress with disease are well charted. We also know much about healthy methods of coping with stress. So what remains?

The big problems are now motivational. We know that people under stress will benefit, for example, from exercise and good nutrition. We just don't know how to get people to do what's good for them. If you go into health psychology or behavioral medicine and find the solution to the problem of motivating people to maintain healthy lifestyles, your name will appear in introductory psychology books, alongside along with Selye, Maslach, Holmes, Rahe, Taylor, and the others who have made a mark in the psychology of stress, health, and well-being.

USING PSYCHOLOGY TO LEARN PSYCHOLOGY

Writing To Heal

You've just suffered a loss: a friend picked a fight and insulted you, violating your sense of trust; the one you love doesn't return your feelings and has rejected you; or your family pet has died, leaving you grief-stricken though friends insist you should "get over it." Perhaps it's not loss but fear that has you losing sleep, anxiety about your performance in school or a health problem you keep secret from others. Whatever the stress, you are suffering but aren't sure where to go or whom to talk to. You can feel the need to express it, to work it out. What can you do? Here's a place to start: Write it out. In the process, you'll learn more about your own psychology.

Why write? Why not just rant and rave and get it out of your system? For one thing, *venting* emotions is not enough to relieve stress or support your health; it may even have aggravating or harmful effects (Gross & Psaki, 2004; Smythe, 1998). When you write out your thoughts and feelings, you talk only to and for yourself. With no audience to perform for, and no patient listener to please, you can use frank language, tell all, and rest assured you don't have to "explain" anything. Writing about your fears and losses has therapeutic emotional effects (Pennebaker, 1990, 1997; Zimmerman, 2002). Writing about feelings and worries has been found to support the health of patients with immune disorders (Pennebaker, 1997). You need not start or keep a regular journal. You are under no restrictions to stick to a certain format or schedule. All you need is a place, a time, the materials you need, and commitment to maintain the habit. There are ways to make the practice easier and more effective:

■ Write in any medium that is efficient or comforting to you—it's OK to type at your keyboard, but it may not always be convenient to access your computer. Handwriting is more personally expressive, and you don't have to make it legible—it's for your eyes only. By using a pen and paper, you can not only write but draw or doodle, expressing yourself nonverbally. And a small notebook is inexpensive and easy to keep handy.

■ Choose a topic or theme to get your started. If a loss or fear has prompted your writing exercise, start with that. If not, choose an "assignment" that prompts emotions and ideas about important challenges in your life. One professor asks students in a class on psychology of loss to develop a journal of loss, referring either to personal losses or to memorable events such as a terrorist attack or the death of a celebrity, and what that has meant to the writer (Harvey & Hofmann, 2001).

■ Write out your thoughts, not only your feelings. Focus on finding the meaning in difficult expe-

riences. You may not know the answers ("Why didn't our relationship last?") but you can reason and fantasize ("Maybe this is a good time for me to be on my own anyway"). An important purpose in therapeutic writing or talking is to achieve insight, growth, and change. It helps to write out memories as if telling a story: with a beginning, middle, and end; descriptions of characters and events; and your own conclusions about the "moral of the story" and lessons you have learned (Harvey et al., 1990; Murray, 2002).

■ Write in spare moments, setting a goal like a few pages every week. Write as if you were a reporter, including every detail to get past the trauma and achieve resolution (DeSalvo, 2000). Experiment with various forms, such as writing love or hate letters. Identify blessings-in-disguise or categorize various things you do (e.g., things you do for others versus things you do for yourself) (Zimmerman, 2002).

■ Stick with it. Make writing a habit, not just a release for the bad times. One researcher found that writing only about trauma intensified the pain and left subjects less able to open up or work it through. So even at times when you don't "need" to write, because you feel fine—in fact, *especially* at such times—write a few lines, so you can later remember that you have felt good—and remind yourself how you got that way!

Your goal in using writing is not to become a great writer (though it's possible!) but to work through your stress and heal. You set the goals, you make the rules. And because you issue these writing "assignments" to yourself, you can relax knowing there is no deadline pressure and no grade to worry about.

CHAPTER SUMMARY

● HOW AND WHY DO WE EXPERIENCE STRESS?

At the root of most stress is change and the need to adapt to environmental, physical, psychological, and social demands. Primitive stressors included mortal threats such as the struggle to survive, catastrophe, and loss. Modern stressors include vicarious trauma and posttraumatic stress, chronic burnout, societal problems, and daily hassles. The Holmes–Rahe SRRS, a measure of event-related stress, has correlated life changes with impaired health.

● The human stress response to perceived threat activates thoughts, feelings, behaviors, and physiological arousal that normally promote adaptation and survival.

● HOW DOES STRESS AFFECT US PHYSICALLY?

Stress begins with arousal triggered by interpreting an event or condition as a stressor. The autonomic nervous system produces bodily responses to adapt to such experiences. Both acute threats and chronic conditions can trigger a fight-or-flight response, expressing aggression or fear. Hans Selye identified three stages in the general adaptation syndrome: alarm, resistance, and exhaustion. Other theories propose a passive withdrawal or entrapment response, and a tend-and-befriend pattern more characteristic of women. Stress can either excite or suppress the body's immune response. College students may find their health compromised by the stress of adjusting to both increased personal freedom and greater academic pressure.

● **The physical stress response begins with arousal, which stimulates the body's adaptive responses—which can turn harmful after prolonged stress.**

● HOW DO WE RESPOND PSYCHOLOGICALLY TO STRESS?

Individuals' psychological reactions to stress vary according to what those stressors mean. Those with Type A personality traits risk adverse stress reactions, while Type Bs are more relaxed. As a result of experiencing failure, learned helplessness produces passive resignation in the face of threat. Personal qualities can also reduce stress. People who have learned a pattern of cognitive hardiness are more resistant to stress. From an early age, some individuals demonstrate resilience, a capacity to "bounce back" from and overcome adversity. A more resilient mindset can be developed by increasing your sense of control, effectiveness, confidence, and realism.

● Our psychological responses to stressors—both healthy and harmful—depend on perception, personality, and learned patterns of response.

● WHAT STRATEGIES CAN PROMOTE HEALTH RATHER THAN DISTRESS?

Defending strategies reduce stress symptoms; coping actions reduce or eliminate the stressor. Coping techniques include both psychological and physical techniques, which may focus on either the emotions produced by stress or the problems that produce stress. Social support can be provided through survivors' groups and psychological counseling, although the effectiveness of psychological debriefing has been questioned. Cognitive strategies for coping include developing an optimistic thinking style and reappraising stressors in a technique known as cognitive restructuring. Physical coping techniques include regular exercise, a healthy diet, and avoiding the use and abuse of drugs such as tobacco. The relatively new fields of health psychology and behavioral medicine focus on coping with stress and developing healthy lifestyles. Happy people, those with high subjective well-being, tend to have more positive and fewer negative emotions and high life satisfaction. Spirituality may enhance subjective well-being, but happiness is not an outcome of one's particular age, gender, race, or wealth.

● **To a large extent, stress, health, and well-being are influenced by lifestyle choices.**

REVIEW TEST

For each of the following items, choose the single correct answer:

1. According to psychologists, which of the following experiences would be considered an example of *stress*?
   a. an earthquake that destroys your home and possessions
   b. an angry neighbor who demands that you turn down your stereo
   c. a pop quiz your instructor announces just as you take your seat
   d. your arousal and behaviors when you are threatened by a stranger

2. An example of a chronic societal stressor would be
   a. burnout.
   b. vicarious trauma.
   c. being stuck in traffic.
   d. widespread unemployment.

3. Which of the following statements about daily hassles is true?
   a. Some of the most common hassles involve threats to survival.
   b. As daily hassles diminish, people's sense of well-being increases.
   c. More frequent and intense hassles are associated with better health.
   d. The effects of hassles do not accumulate: Several hassles are no worse than only a few.

4. Like the experience of emotion, the physical response to stress almost always begins with
   a. a protective behavior.
   b. a state of arousal.
   c. a reduction in immune effectiveness.
   d. fear.

5. In the ___ stage of Selye's GAS, the organism's defenses are fully engaged and the organism shows signs of recovery from the initial stress.
   a. alarm
   b. withdrawal
   c. resistance
   d. exhaustion

6. Which of the following stressors is the type that would most likely cause the immune system to malfunction and even cause harm?
   a. accidentally slipping and falling on an icy surface
   b. caring for a dying family member for a prolonged period
   c. being rejected by someone you are romantically interested in
   d. receiving a bad grade on a test in an important college course

7. What is the most difficult task facing health psychology?
   a. identifying sources of stress
   b. winning turf battles with behavioral medicine
   c. finding a way to measure SWB
   d. motivating people to adopt healthy lifestyles

8. Amanda possesses many Type A personality traits; this means Amanda has a higher probability of suffering from ___ than non–Type A individuals.
   a. heart disease
   b. colds and flu
   c. accidents
   d. cancer

9. The "three Cs"—challenge, commitment, and control—are the distinctive attitudes that make up
   a. the stage of resistance.
   b. cognitive hardiness.
   c. cognitive restructuring.
   d. an optimistic style of thinking.

10. A program of regular exercise for fitness has been found to
   a. improve one's self-concept.
   b. reduce the symptoms of depression.
   c. improve relaxation and social interaction.
   d. all of the above.

Answers: 1.d 2.d 3.b 4.b 5.c 6.b 7.d 8.a 9.b 10.d

KEY TERMS

Stress (p. 396)

Stressor (p. 396)

Traumatic stressor (p. 398)

Vicarious traumatization (p. 400)

Posttraumatic stress disorder (PTSD) (p. 403)

Burnout (p. 404)

Hassles (p. 406)

Cognitive appraisal (p. 406)

Social Readjustment Rating Scale (SRRS) (p. 407)

Acute stress (p. 410)

Chronic stress (p. 410)

Fight-or-flight (p. 411)

General adaptation syndrome (GAS) (p. 412)

Alarm reaction (p. 412)

Stage of resistance (p. 414)

Stage of exhaustion (p. 415)

Immune system (p. 416)

Tend-and-befriend model (p. 416)

Psychoneuroimmunology (p. 416)

Cytokines (p. 417)

Type A (p. 420)

Type B (p. 420)

Learned helplessness (p. 421)

Cognitive hardiness (p. 422)

Resilience (p. 423)

Coping (p. 426)

Emotion-focused coping (p. 426)

Problem-focused coping (p. 427)

Social support (p. 427)

Psychological debriefing (p. 428)

Optimistic style of thinking (p. 429)

Cognitive restructuring (p. 429)

Behavioral medicine (p. 433)

Health psychology (p. 433)

Subjective well-being (SWB) (p. 434)

OUR RECOMMENDED BOOKS AND VIDEOS

BOOKS

Adams, P. (with an introduction by Robin Williams). (1998). *House calls: How we can all heal the world one visit at a time.* San Francisco: Robert D. Reed. This primer on wellness includes suggestions to visit loved ones, how to make healthy choices, how to be a good doctor, and how to be a successful hospital patient. The key, says Adams, is having a meaningful connection between doctor and patient—a healing bond for both of them.

Berglas, S. (2001). *Reclaiming the fire: How successful people overcome burnout.* New York: Random House. Arguing that many successful professionals' midcareer crises result from self-handicapping, a self-defeating behavior pattern caused by fear of failure, a psychologist offers advice for coping with the distress of believing there is nowhere to go but down.

Groopman, J. (2003). *The anatomy of hope: How people prevail in the face of illness.* New York: Random House. Surveying cancer patients and lab researchers, the author, a medical doctor, uses stories and personalities to explore the origins of hope and its impact on healing, doctors' impact on their patients' optimism, and why some severely or terminally ill persons are able to hang onto hope—while others let go and give up.

McEwen, B. S., & Lasley, E. N. (2004). *The end of stress as we know it.* Washington, DC: The Dana Press. Not another pop-psych book for consumers of quick techniques, this book offers updated research and applied neuroscience for understanding how the brain and immune system interact, with the ironic result that stress *protects* you from temporary stressors but can *harm* you in responding to chronic stressors.

Pyszczynski, T., Solomon, S., & Greenberg, J. (2003). *In the wake of 9/11: The psychology of terror.* Washington, DC: American Psychological Association. Relying on terror management theory, the authors show how the threat of death triggers the thoughts and emotions produced by terrorist attack.

Reivich, K., & Shatté, A. (2002). *The resilience factor.* New York: Broadway. Two psychologists argue that resilience, the ability to "bounce back" from adversity, is built from habits of mind and cognitive style, and offer "seven essential skills for overcoming life's inevitable obstacles," including turning off negative thoughts and restoring perspective.

Sapolsky, R. M. (1998). *Why zebras don't get ulcers: An updated guide to stress-related diseases, and coping.* New York: W. H. Freeman. Cutting-edge research-based advice laced with humor and insight, this work examines the utterly human dilemma of life-threatening stress and how it can be understood, modified, and controlled.

Schlosser, E. (2002). *Fast food nation: The dark side of the all-American meal.* New York: Perennial. This book reveals some grim, fascinating, and unappetizing facts about the origins and realities of fast-food, including industry history, working conditions, factory farming, animals' treatment, slaughterhouses and meatpacking, and unexpected additives in your burgers and fries. It explains why fast food can be a slow killer—and offers alternatives to addictive, high-calorie/low-benefit foods.

Siegel, B. S. (1986). *Love, medicine, and miracles.* New York: Harper & Row. These stories of people who made remarkable recoveries show their new perspectives on life and the characteristics that may have helped them to become survivors.

Taylor, S. E. (2003). *The tending instinct: Women, men, and the biology of relationships.* New York: Owl Books. Psychologist Shelley Taylor, disagreeing with theories that all survival depends on a self-preservation instinct, argues that human survival thrives on social motivations, including cooperation, caregiving, and altruism—especially for women.

VIDEOS

Born on the Fourth of July. (1989, color, 144 min.). Directed by Oliver Stone; starring Tom Cruise, Willem Dafoe, Raymond J. Barry, Carolyn Kava, Kyra Sedgwick. This is the powerful true story of Ron Kovic, who joined the Marines as an eager volunteer during the Vietnam War and returned a paraplegic to face a hostile society, a family in denial, a torturous rehabilitation, and a complete political change of heart. The film shows one of the best depictions of posttraumatic stress disorder (PTSD).

The Doctor. (1991, color, 123 min.). Directed by Randa Haines; starring William Hurt, Christine Lahti, Elizabeth Perkins, Mandy Patinkin. Based on *A Taste of My Own Medicine* by Ed Rosenbaum, M.D., this is the story of a cold though brilliant physician whose feeling about his life and work are changed forever when he is diagnosed with cancer and views the world from the patient's perspective.

The Fisher King. (1991, color, 137 min.). Directed by Terry Gilliam; starring Robin Williams, Jeff Bridges, Amanda Plummer, Mercedes Ruehl, Michael Jeter. When a talk-radio announcer's flip remark to an unstable caller has tragic consequences, he seeks to make amends by helping one of the victims. The film includes powerful imagery of fantastic visions, paranoid delusions, and posttraumatic stress—with poignant and comic moments, too.

Patch Adams. (1998, color, 103 min.). Directed by Tom Shadyac; starring Robin Williams, Monica Potter, Daniel London, Bob Gunton, Peter Coyote. The film is based on the true story of Hunter "Patch" Adams, M.D., who became a physician despite his irreverence regarding the power and money of modern medicine and his desire to make medical care reassuring and even fun for patients. (See the recommendation for Adams's book, above).

Shine. (1999, color, 105 min.). Directed by Scott Hicks; starring Geoffrey Rush, Sonia Todd, Armin Mueller-Stahl. Based on the true story of concert pianist David Helfgott, this film shows his recuperation from a crushing breakdown by reviewing the stress and abuse of his early life and choosing to prevail and work toward an acclaimed comeback.

Super Size Me. (2004, color, 96 min.). Directed by, written by, and starring Morgan Spurlock. Documentary creator Morgan Spurlock forced himself for 30 days to eat only McDonald's food, three meals per day, trying every menu item at least once and accepting any time he was offered the "super size" of a meal. The resulting story reveals funny and scary changes in both physical and mental health, as well as insights into the dangers of Americans' fast-food lifestyle.

Unbreakable. (2000, color, 106 min.). Directed by M. Night Shyamalan; starring Bruce Willis, Samuel L. Jackson, Robin Wright Penn. Urged by an eccentric stranger with a rare chronic illness, a diffident man slowly recognizes that he is uniquely talented—and apparently invulnerable to all sickness and harm.

CORE CONCEPTS

▼

According to the psychodynamic, humanistic, and cognitive theories, personality is a continuously changing process, shaped by our internal needs and cognitions and by external pressures from the social environment.

▼

Another approach describes personality in terms of stable patterns known as temperaments, traits, and types.

▼

People everywhere develop implicit assumptions ("folk theories") about personality, but these assumptions vary in important ways across cultures.

Psychology in Your Life

Explaining Unusual People and Unusual Behavior

You don't need a theory of personality to explain why people do the expected.

Finding Your Type

When it comes to classifying personality according to types, a little caution may be in order.

Developing Your Own Theory of Personality

You'll probably want to be eclectic.

USING PSYCHOLOGY TO LEARN PSYCHOLOGY:
Your Academic Locus of Control

Personality

WHAT DROVE MARGARET SANGER? A psychologist trying to understand this powerful and charismatic figure might conclude that the balance in her life shifted on a sweltering day in July of 1912. She had responded to a call from the slums in New York City's Lower East Side, where Jake Sachs had found his wife, Sadie, unconscious and bleeding on the kitchen floor. The cause: Sadie had attempted to give herself an abortion. It was Sanger's job as an emergency-response nurse to save Sadie's life.

In those days, unwanted pregnancy—and botched abortions—were often the result of ignorance. Giving medical advice on sex was illegal, and birth control devices, such as condoms and diaphragms, were nearly impossible to obtain. As a result, some 100,000 illegal abortions were performed in the state every year—many of them by dangerous quack practitioners. People like Sadie, the poor and uneducated—those least able to bear the costliness of many children—had nowhere to turn for competent help with reproduction and family planning (Asbell, 1995).

Thanks to swift action by Margaret Sanger, Sadie Sachs survived. Nevertheless, Sanger was angry that she could do nothing to help prevent unwanted pregnancies. She was limited by the law to providing after-the-fact treatment for the victims of incompetent abortionists. It only added fuel to her inner fire when she later heard Sachs ask the doctor, "What can I do to stop having babies?" and heard his sarcastic reply, "Better tell Jake to sleep on the roof" (Sanger, 1971).

Sanger saw Sadie Sachs only one more time: Three months later, pregnant once again, Sadie died of another abortion attempt. This needless death spurred Sanger to seek an answer to her patients' pleas for safe contraception, "no matter what it might cost" (Sanger, 1938, in Conway, 1992, p. 567).

The cost was high. Sanger left the nursing profession and put her own family in the background as she began to research and promote contraception full time. In 1914 the threat of a prison term for "indecency" forced her to flee for England, where she spent a year waiting for the charges to be dropped. But she couldn't avoid jail altogether: In 1916, when she opened a public birth-control clinic, Sanger had to serve several jail sentences for illegally distributing information about contraception.

For 40 years, Sanger persistently challenged laws making contraception a criminal act and insisted that women take control of—and responsibility for—their bodies, sexuality, and childbearing (Kennedy, 1970; Sanger, 1971). But her single-minded focus on the birth-control cause eventually cost her a marriage to a man who had adored her and supported her work. Finally, in 1952, Sanger, then in her 70s, joined forces with philanthropist Katharine McCormick to commission the development of an oral contraceptive. The result: The first birth-control pills for women were approved for prescription eight years later.

■ Personality The psychological qualities that bring continuity to an individual's behavior in different situations and at different times.

CONNECTION: CHAPTER 12

Multiple personality and *split personality* are older terms for *dissociative identity disorder.*

The pattern of dogged determination seen in Sanger across these 40 years of struggle illustrates the central idea of this chapter: **Personality** consists of the psychological qualities that bring continuity to an individual in different situations and at different times. So, the *theories* of personality we will discuss in this chapter are "big picture" explanations that attempt to tie together all the important influences on an individual's thoughts and behavior. Thus, we might think of personality as the thread of consistency that runs through our lives (Cervone & Shoda, 1999). And when the "thread" of personality breaks, we see certain mental disorders involving extreme inconsistencies in personality: bipolar disorder, schizophrenia, and so-called "multiple personality" disorder.

What processes were at work to produce the pattern and consistency that we see in the life of Margaret Sanger? Was her personality shaped primarily by the people and events in her life? Those events were often so chaotic that we are forced to consider another possibility—that her strength and determi-

● Personality is the thread of continuity in an individual in different situations.

nation arose from internal traits—from her basic makeup. You may recognize these alternatives as another instance of the nature–nurture question. The answer, of course, lies with *both*: Experience *and* innate factors shaped Margaret Sanger's personality, just as they shape our own.

In this chapter we will examine a number of theoretical explanations for personality. As we do so, you will find that some place more emphasis on nature and others on nurture. You will also find that particular theories are suited to dealing with particular kinds of issues:

■ If your goal is to understand a depressed friend, a troublesome child—any individual—as a developing, changing being, you will probably find one of the *psychodynamic, humanistic,* or *cognitive theories* of personality most helpful. These theories are described in the first part of the chapter.

■ If what you need is a snapshot of a person's current personality characteristics—as you might want if you were screening job applicants for your company—a theory of *temperaments, traits,* or *types* may be your best bet. You will find these in the second section of the chapter.

■ If you are most interested in how people understand each other—as you might be if you were doing marriage counseling or conflict management—you will want to know the assumptions people make about each other. That is, you will want to know their *implicit theories of personality.* These will be discussed in the final section of the chapter.

■ And, if you are wondering whether people understand each other in the same ways the world around, you will want to know about the *cross-cultural* work in personality. Such issues are also discussed in the final section of the chapter.

WHAT FORCES SHAPE OUR PERSONALITIES?

If you have ever attended a family or high school reunion, you know that people change and grow relentlessly. They develop new interests and new friends, they move to new places, and they have new experiences. In this section we will consider three ways of accounting for the paths their personalities take: the *psychodynamic,* the *humanistic,* and the *cognitive theories.* Each describes personality from a different perspective, but all portray it as a dynamic, developing process. And all emphasize the interplay of internal mental processes and external social interactions—as our Core Concept says:

According to the psychodynamic, humanistic, and cognitive theories, personality is a continuously changing process, shaped by our internal needs and cognitions and by external pressures from the social environment.

Although the three viewpoints we will consider in this section of the chapter—the psychodynamic, humanistic, and cognitive theories—share some common ground, each emphasizes a different combination of factors. Most *psychodynamic theories* of personality call attention to motivation, especially unconscious motives, and the influence of past experiences on our mental health. *Humanistic theories* emphasize our present, subjective reality: What we believe is important now and how we think of ourselves in relation to others. Because the humanistic and psychodynamic theories were influenced so much by clinical practice—psychologists working with people who seek counseling and therapy—we grouped them together as the *clinical perspective* in Chapter 1.

The *social-cognitive theories* come out of the research experimental in psychology, rather than clinical practice. They are based on the idea that personality is influenced by learning, perception, and social interaction. In some respects, however, the social-cognitive theories complement rather than contradict the clinical perspective: All agree that our lives include past, present, and future; that our minds have both conscious and unconscious levels; and that our behaviors are sometimes emotional and impulsive and at other times cooler and more calculated. (As you are coming to see, it is impossible to place these theories in neat and tidy categories.) Which theory you choose will depend, to some extent, on what aspect of personality and behavior you want to explain. So, let us look more closely at each perspective.

Psychodynamic Theories

The psychodynamic approach originated in the late 1800s with a medical puzzle called *hysteria,* now known as *conversion disorder.* In this condition, the physician finds physical symptoms, such as a muscle weakness, loss of sensation in a part of the body, or even paralysis—but no apparent physical cause, such as nerve damage. The psychological nature of hysteria finally became apparent when the French physician Jean Charcot demonstrated that he could make hysterical symptoms disappear by suggestion. He did this while his patients were in a hypnotic trance.

Sigmund Freud (1856–1939), a young and curious doctor, heard of Charcot's work and traveled to Paris to watch his renowned hypnotic demonstrations. Inspired, Freud returned to Vienna, resolving to try the hypnotic cure on his own patients. But to his dismay, Dr. Freud found that many could not be hypnotized deeply enough to affect their symptoms. Moreover, even the ones who lost their symptoms under hypnosis regained them after the trance was lifted. Finally, a frustrated Freud resolved to find another way to understand and treat the mysterious illness. The new approach he created became known as **psychoanalysis** or **psychoanalytic theory.** Technically, *psychoanalytic theory* is the term for Freud's explanation of personality and mental disorder, while *psychoanalysis* refers to his system of treatment for mental disorder. In practice, however, it has always been difficult to separate Freud's theory from his therapeutic procedures. Thus the term *psychoanalysis* is often used to refer to both (Carver & Scheier, 2000).

Freud's Psychoanalytic Theory   At center stage in the personality, Freud placed the concept of the **unconscious.** He saw this hidden part of the mind as the source of powerful impulses, instincts, motives, and conflicts that energize the personality. We are normally unaware of this psychic domain, said Freud, because its contents are too threatening and anxiety provoking. Only by using the special techniques of psychoanalysis would we find that a person who had, for example, been sexually molested in childhood still holds these memories in the unconscious. But these memories attempt to escape from the unconscious and reemerge in disguised form—perhaps as a dream or a symptom of a mental disorder, such as depression or a phobia. Even in the healthiest of us, said Freud, behavior originates in unconscious drives that we don't want to acknowledge. Consequently, we go about our daily business without knowing the real motives behind our behavior. Today, many psychologists consider this concept of the unconscious to be Freud's most important contribution to psychology. (See Figure 11.1.)

Drives and Instincts   The actions of the unconscious mind are powered by psychological energy—that is by motives, drives, and desires. In one of his graphic analogies, Freud described the personality as the mental equivalent of steam in a boiler. Psychoanalysis focuses on how the mind's energy is exchanged,

● Sigmund Freud was the founder of psychoanalysis and the psychodynamic perspective. He is seen here walking with his daughter Anna Freud, who later became a psychoanalyst in her own right.

■ **Psychoanalysis**   Freud's system of treatment for mental disorders. The term is often used to refer to psychoanalytic theory, as well.

■ **Psychoanalytic theory**   Freud's theory of personality.

■ **Unconscious**   In Freudian theory, this is the psychic domain of which the individual is not aware but that is the storehouse of repressed impulses, drives, and conflicts unavailable to consciousness.

transformed, and expressed. For example, the "mental steam" of the sex drive could be expressed directly through sexual activity or indirectly through joking or creative pursuits. Freud named this drive *Eros*, for the Greek god of passionate love. And the energy behind this drive he called **libido**, from the Latin word for "lust." It is libidinal energy that fuels not only our sexual behavior but our work and our leisure activities: drawing, dancing, reading, body building—nearly everything we do.

But Eros did not explain everything that fascinated Freud. Specifically, it did not explain acts of human aggression and destruction. It also did not explain the symptoms of the war veterans he saw who continued to relive their wartime traumas in nightmares and hallucinations. Such misery could only be explained with another drive, which he called *Thanatos* (from the Greek word for "death"). Freud conceived of Thanatos as the "death instinct" that drives the aggressive and destructive acts that humans commit against each other and themselves.

Was Freud right about Eros and Thanatos? You might gauge his theory against your own experience. Have you observed any human behavior that could not, broadly speaking, be assigned to one of these two categories: life and death—or, if you prefer, creation and destruction?

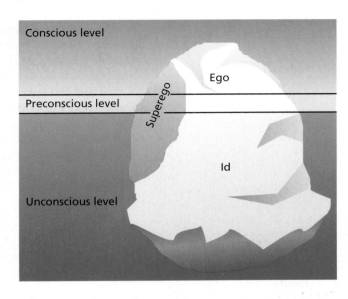

● **FIGURE 11.1** Freud's Model of the Mind

In another famous metaphor, Freud likened the mind to an iceberg, because only a small portion appears "above the surface"—in consciousness. Meanwhile, the vast unconscious mind lurks "beneath the surface" of our awareness.

Personality Structure   Freud pictured a continuing battle between two antagonistic parts of the personality, the *id* and the *superego*. This conflict is moderated by yet another part of the mind, the *ego*. (See Figure 11.1.)

He conceived of the **id** as the primitive, unconscious reservoir that houses the basic motives, drives, and instinctive desires that determine our personalities. Like a child, the id always acts on impulse and pushes for immediate gratification—especially sexual, physical, and emotional pleasures—to be experienced here and now without concern for consequences. It is the *only* part of the personality present at birth.

By contrast, the superego serves as the mind's "police force" in charge of values and morals learned from parents and from society. The **superego** corresponds roughly to our common notion of conscience. It develops as the child forms an internal set of rules based on the external rules imposed by parents and other adults. It is the inner voice of "shoulds" and "should nots." The superego also includes the *ego ideal,* an individual's view of the kind of person he or she should strive to become. Understandably, the superego frequently conflicts with the id's desires because the id wants to do what feels good, while the superego insists on doing what is right and moral.

Resolving the conflicts between id and superego is the job of the third major part of the personality's trinity, the **ego**—the conscious, rational portion of the mind. The ego must choose actions that will gratify the id's impulses but without violating one's moral principles or incurring undesirable consequences. For example, if you found that you had been given too much change at the grocery store, the superego would insist that you give it back, while the id might urge you to spend it on ice cream. The ego, then, would try to find a compromise, which might include returning the money and buying ice cream with your own money. That is, when the id and superego conflict, the ego tries to satisfy both. However, as pressures from the id, superego, and environment intensify, it becomes more difficult for the ego to find workable compromises. The result may be the conflicted or disturbed thoughts and behaviors that signify mental disorder.

■ **Libido** The Freudian concept of psychic energy that drives individuals to experience sensual pleasure.

■ **Id** The primitive, unconscious portion of the personality that houses the most basic drives and stores repressed memories.

■ **Superego** The mind's storehouse of values, including moral attitudes learned from parents and from society; roughly the same as the common notion of the conscience.

■ **Ego** The conscious, rational part of the personality, charged with keeping peace between the superego and the id.

Personality Development and Early Experiences As Freud talked with his patients about their past, he began to understand that personality follows predictable patterns of development throughout childhood and adolescence. He concluded, however, that "forgotten" experiences in infancy and early childhood have the strongest impact on personality formation and later behavior. These early experiences continue to influence the unconscious mind as the child progresses through a series of **psychosexual stages.** These stages consist of successive periods in which the developing child associates pleasure with stimulation of specific bodily areas.

In the *oral stage,* pleasure is associated with the mouth: suckling, crying, spewing. In the *anal stage,* pleasure comes from stimulating parts of the body associated with elimination. Next, in the *phallic stage,* pleasure comes from "immature" sexual expression, such as masturbation. (This also explains the humor popular with the prepubescent set.) Finally, after a quiet period of *latency*, the adult *genital stage* brings (to some) mature sexual relationships. These stages are detailed in Table 11.1.

Why such a seemingly bizarre theory of psychosexual development? Among the issues that Freud was trying to understand with his theory of psychosexual development were those of gender identity and gender roles. Why is it that boys usually develop a masculine identity, even though most boys are raised

■ **Psychosexual stages** Successive, instinctive patterns of associating pleasure with stimulation of specific bodily areas at different times of life.

TABLE 11.1	Freud's Stages of Psychosexual Development	
Psychosexual Stage	**Later Signs of Problems Beginning at This Stage**	
Oral Stage (1st year)	Smoking	Obesity
Desires: Oral stimulation by sucking, eating, crying, babbling	Nail-biting	Talkativeness
Challenge: Overcoming dependency	Chewing	Dependency
	Gluttony	Gullibility
Anal Stage (approximately 1–3 years)	Messiness	Excessive cleanliness
Desires: Anal stimulation by bladder and bowel function	Temper tantrums	Stinginess
Challenge: Toilet training	Destructiveness	Coldness, distance, aloofness
Self-control	Cruelty	
Phallic Stage (approximately 3–6 years)	Masturbation (not considered abnormal by modern psychology and psychiatry; see Chapter 9)	
Desires: Stimulation of genitals	Jealousy	
Challenge: Resolving Oedipus complex, involving erotic attraction to parent of opposite sex and hostility to parent of same sex	Egocentric sex	
	Sexual conquests	
	Problems with parents	
Latency (approximately 6 years to puberty)	Excessive modesty	
Desires: Repression of sexual and aggressive desires, including those involved in the Oedipus complex	Preference for company of same sex	
Challenge: Consciously: learning modesty and shame	Homosexuality (considered by Freud to be a disorder, but not by modern psychology and psychiatry; see Chapter 9)	
Unconsciously: dealing with repressed Oedipal conflict		
Genital Stage (puberty and adulthood)	(none)	
Desires: Mature sexual relationships		
Challenge: Displacing energy into healthy activities		
Establishing new relationship with parents		

primarily by their mothers? Why do girls, as they become adults, most often develop a sexual attraction to males—and boys to females? And why do some not follow this pattern?

Freud's answers to these questions were convoluted and, many psychologists would say, contrived. His inside-the-mind perspective ignored the influence of vastly different forms of socialization for boys and girls. It also ignored the possibility of differences in genetic programming, about which little was known in Freud's day. Instead, he invoked the notion of the **Oedipus complex,** whereby boys feel an erotic attraction toward their mothers. Successful resolution of the Oedipal conflict requires boys to *displace* (shift) their attraction to females of their own age and, at the same time, develop an **identification** with their fathers. Girls, he proposed, develop **penis envy** (because they don't have one!) and are usually attracted to males (who do). Most psychologists today reject these Freudian notions of psychosexual development because they lack scientific support. It is important, however, to remember two things: First, these Freudian concepts—strange as they may seem—continue to have a wide impact outside psychology, particularly in the humanities. Second, while Freud may have been wrong about the details of psychosexual development, he may have been right about other aspects of human personality (Bower, 1998b).

Freud might have been right, for example, in his assertion that certain difficulties early in life lead to **fixation:** arrested psychological development. An *oral stage* fixation, caused by a failure to throw off the dependency of the first year of life, may lead to dependency on others in later childhood and adulthood. We also see an oral fixation in certain behaviors involving the mouth, such as overeating, alcoholism, and tendencies toward sarcasm. Among these diverse problems we find a common theme: using the mouth as the way to connect with what one needs. Fixation in the *anal* stage is presumed to come from problems associated with the second year of life when toilet training is a big issue. Anal fixations can result in a stubborn, compulsive, stingy, or excessively neat pattern of behavior—all related to common themes of "holding on" and not losing control of one's body or life. In Table 11.1 you will find examples of fixation at other developmental stages.

Ego Defenses The ego has an arsenal of **ego defense mechanisms** for dealing with conflict between the id's impulses and the superego's demand to deny them. All operate, said Freud, at the *preconscious level*—just beneath the surface of consciousness. Under mild pressure from the id we may, for example, rely on simple ego defenses, such as *fantasy* or *rationalization*. But if unconscious desires become too insistent, the ego may solve the problem by "putting a lid on the id." To do so, the ego must push extreme desires and threatening memories out of conscious awareness and into the recesses of the unconscious mind.

Repression is the name for the ego defense mechanism that excludes unacceptable thoughts and feelings from awareness. So, for example, repression may explain the behavior of a student who suspects she failed an important test and "forgets" to attend class the day the graded tests are returned. This memory lapse protects her from feeling upset or anxious—at least temporarily. In fact, that is the problem with repression and most of the other ego defense mechanisms, said Freud: They solve the problem only for the moment, leaving the underlying conflict unresolved.

Freud also taught that repression can block access to feelings, as well as memories. For example, if a child has strong feelings of anger toward her

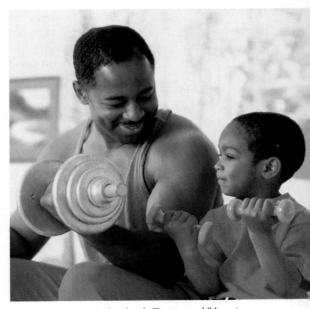

● During the phallic stage, a child must resolve feelings of conflict and anxiety by identifying more closely with the same-sex parent—said Freud.

■ **Oedipus complex** According to Freud, a largely unconscious process whereby boys displace an erotic attraction toward their mother to females of their own age and, at the same time, identify with their fathers.

■ **Identification** The mental process by which an individual tries to become like another person, especially the same-sex parent.

■ **Penis envy** According to Freud, the female desire to have a penis—a condition that usually results in their attraction to males.

■ **Fixation** Occurs when psychosexual development is arrested at an immature stage.

■ **Ego defense mechanisms** Largely unconscious mental strategies employed to reduce the experience of conflict or anxiety.

■ **Repression** An unconscious process that excludes unacceptable thoughts and feelings from awareness and memory.

"All right, deep down it's a cry for psychiatric help—but at one level it's a stick-up."

© Punch/Rothco

father—which, if acted out, would risk severe punishment—repression may take over. The repressed hostile impulse can no longer operate consciously. But, although the impulse is not consciously felt, it is not gone, said Freud. At an unconscious level it continues to influence behavior, but in less direct ways, perhaps disguised as dreams, fantasies, or symptoms of mental disorder.

Freud—always the keen observer of human behavior—proposed many other ego defense mechanisms in addition to fantasy, rationalization, and repression. Here are some of the most important:

- *Denial:* "I don't have a problem." This defense avoids a difficult situation by simply denying that it exists. Denial is a defense frequently seen, for example, in alcoholics, child abusers, people who have problems managing anger, and people who engage in risky behavior, such as casual, unprotected sex.

- *Rationalization:* People using this defense mechanism give socially acceptable reasons for actions that are really based on motives that they believe to be unacceptable. So, a student who feels stressed by academic pressures may decide to cheat on a test, rationalizing it by saying that "everyone does it."

- *Reaction formation:* This ego defense mechanism occurs when people act in exact opposition to their true feelings. Accordingly, those troubled by their own sexual desires may initiate a crusade against "dirty books" in the city library. Or a child with low self-esteem may become a bully.

- *Displacement:* When your boss makes you angry, you may later displace your anger by yelling at your mate or kicking the dog. This ego defense mechanism involves shifting your reaction from the real source of your distress to a safer individual or object.

- *Regression:* Under stress, some people hide; others cry, throw things, or even wet their pants. That is, they adopt immature, juvenile behaviors that were effective ways of dealing with stress when they were younger.

- *Sublimation:* Gratifying sexual or aggressive desires in ways that are acceptable in one's culture, as in acting or sports.

- *Projection:* When we are upset or aroused, we may use the defense of projection to attribute our own unconscious desires to other people or objects. An example frequently seen in small children involves each accusing the other of starting a conflict.

This latter concept—projection—led to the development of *projective tests,* which have been used extensively in clinical psychology for evaluating personality and mental disorders. We take a brief detour at this point to introduce you to these projective techniques.

Projective Tests   What do you see in Figure 11.2? Ambiguous images such as these are the basis for **projective tests.** Freudian clinicians often employ such instruments to probe their patients' innermost feelings, motives, conflicts and desires. The assumption is that people will *project* their hidden motives and conflicts onto the images. In fact, you may have noticed that, when gazing at the clouds, different people see different images, and the images people report seem to reflect their own personalities.

In the most famous of projective techniques, the **Rorschach inkblot technique** (pronounced *ROAR-shock*), the ambiguous stimuli are symmetrical inkblots (Rorschach, 1942). The technique calls for showing the blots one at a time and asking the respondent, "What do you see? What does this seem to be?" The examiner usually interprets responses in light of psychoanalytic theory by noting how they might reflect unconscious sexual and aggressive impulses (Erdberg, 1990).

■ **Projective tests** Personality assessment instruments, such as the Rorschach and TAT, which are based on Freud's ego defense mechanism of projection.
■ **Rorschach inkblot technique** A projective test requiring subjects to describe what they see in a series of ten inkblots.

The Rorschach's value as a testing instrument has been questioned because objective studies of its accuracy have been disappointing (Anastasi, 1988; Lilienfeld et al., 2000a, b; Wood et al., 1996). Moreover, critics claim that the test is based on theoretical concepts (such as unconscious motives) that are impossible to demonstrate objectively. Despite these criticisms, many clinicians have continued to champion the Rorschach, arguing that it can provide unique insights as part of a broader personality assessment (Exner, 1974, 1978; Exner & Weiner, 1982; Hibbard, 2003).

By comparison, the **Thematic Apperception Test (TAT),** developed by Henry Murray, is a projective test that stands on somewhat firmer scientific ground. This test consists of ambiguous pictures, for which respondents are instructed to generate a story (see Figure 11.3). The story should describe what the characters in the scenes are doing and thinking, what led up to each event, and how each situation will end. According to the theory behind the TAT, the respondent perceives the elements in the actual picture and further *apperceives* (fills in) personal interpretations and explanations, based on his or her own thoughts, feelings, and needs. The examiner then interprets the responses by looking for psychological themes, such as aggression, sexual needs, and relationships among people mentioned in the stories. Unlike the Rorschach, the TAT has proved its mettle, especially for assessing achievement motivation, as we saw in Chapter 9 (McClelland, 1987b).

Psychic Determinism To the Freudian analyst, everything a person does has meaning. In particular, mental symptoms such as fears and phobias are interpreted as signs of unconscious

■ **Thematic Apperception Test (TAT)** A projective test requiring subjects to make up stories that explain ambiguous pictures.

● **FIGURE 11.3** Sample Card from the TAT

difficulties. Similarly, a so-called *Freudian slip* occurs when "accidental" speech or behavior belies an unconscious conflict or desire. You might commit such a slip, as you leave a boring social function, by telling your host, "I really had a terrible—I mean *terrific*—time." Likewise, being consistently late for a date with a particular person is no accident, Freud would have said. Rather, your behavior expresses the way you feel unconsciously. This idea supposes that nothing we do is accidental. Rather, according to his principle of **psychic determinism,** all our acts are determined by unconscious processes involving traumas, desires, or conflicts.

In his work with hysterical patients, Freud observed that physical symptoms often seemed connected to a traumatic event that had been "forgotten" (repressed). For instance, a patient who was hysterically "blind" might, during therapy, suddenly recall seeing her parents having intercourse when she was a small child. How had this produced blindness? As she becomes an adult, she may have anticipated her first sexual encounter, which aroused powerful feelings associated with that upsetting memory. Thus, the young woman's blindness could represent an unconscious attempt to undo her vision of the original event—and to deny her own sexual feelings. Blindness would also bring her attention, comfort, and sympathy from others. In this way, her inner psychic motives both determine and maintain her condition.

Evaluating Freud's Work   Whatever your feelings about Freud, you must give him credit for developing the first comprehensive theory of personality, mental disorder, and psychotherapy. His writing was compelling and his observations astute—so perceptive, in fact, that he has had a greater impact than any other theorist on the way all of us think about personality and mental abnormality (Fisher & Greenberg, 1985).

Nevertheless, psychologists today give Freud mixed reviews (Azar, 1997b; McCullough, 2001). One problem is that many Freudian concepts, such as "libido," "anal stage," or "repression," are vague. Because they lack clear operational definitions, much of the theory is impossible to evaluate scientifically.[1] In an earlier chapter we saw the results of this lack of objectivity in the controversy over recovery of repressed memories—a notion that arises directly from Freud's ideas but that has no solid empirical support. Elizabeth Loftus warns that, by blithely accepting vague Freudian notions of repression and "recovery" of memories, society risks dangerous levels of paranoia, persecution of the innocent, and self-inflicted misery (Loftus & Ketcham, 1991, 1994). It should be noted, however, that valiant efforts are being made to put Freud's concepts on a scientific footing (Cramer, 2000).

A second criticism says that Freudian "theory" is a seductive explanation for the past but a poor predictor of future responses. That is, its focus is on retrospective explanation. By overemphasizing historical origins of behavior, psychoanalysis directs attention away from current events that may be responsible for maintaining the behavior.

A third criticism says that Freud gave short shrift to women. For example, we have seen that he portrayed women as suffering from "penis envy." In fact, Freud's theory may simply describe the attitudes that permeated the male-dominated world of his time.

A final criticism claims that the unconscious mind is not as smart or purposeful as Freud believed (Loftus & Klinger, 1992). In this newer view, the unconscious acts reflexively, sometimes based on innate response patterns and

CONNECTION: CHAPTER 1

Operational definitions are stated in objective, observable, and measurable terms.

■ **Psychic determinism**   Freud's assumption that all our mental and behavioral responses are caused by unconscious traumas, desires, or conflicts.

---

[1]Because many of Freud's ideas are not testable, his psychoanalytic theory is not a *scientific* theory, as we defined the term in Chapter 1. Here we follow common usage, which calls it a theory.

sometimes based on conditioned responses. Research in the neuroscience of emotion has, as we saw in Chapter 3, supported this new view of an unconscious emotional processing system in the brain—much less malign and deliberate than anything that Freud imagined (LeDoux, 1996).

Despite these shortcomings, Freud's ideas have found a receptive audience with the public at large (Gray, 1993, p. 47). Much of his appeal may be explained by his accessibility to nonpsychologists and by his emphasis on sexuality, a topic that grabs everyone's interest. As a result, Freudian images and symbols abound in the art and literature of the 20th century. His ideas have had an enormous influence on marketing as well. For example, advertisers often promote new products by associating them with a sexy model and hinting that the product will bring sexual satisfaction to its owner. Alternatively, some advertisers capitalize on Freud's destructive instinct. In this vein, television commercials for everything from antibacterial soap and other "personal products" to life insurance remind us of threats to our happiness (social rejection, irregularity, untimely death) and then offer products and services to reduce our anxiety and restore hope.

Let us end our discussion of Freud by seeing whether his explanation of personality can give us a useful perspective on Margaret Sanger. A psychoanalyst interpreting her drive and sense of mission would scrutinize her childhood, looking for conflicts with parents and anxiety about sexual feelings. The analyst might also focus on her mother's death, which occurred when Sanger was 19, and on her later claim that she blamed her father for exhausting her mother with so many births. Unresolved anger toward her mother (a vestige of the phallic stage of psychosexual development) would be transformed into guilt over her mother's death. By projecting blame onto her father, she removed her conscious sense of guilt. Perhaps Sanger took up the banner of birth control in order to deal with the presence of her now-unconscious guilt and anxiety about unhappy family experiences. Or perhaps she identified with her mother's sacrifice and sought to punish her father and other would-be fathers by depriving them of their control over women's reproductive fate. As is usual with psychoanalysis, these guesses are guided by hindsight—and cannot be either proved or disproved.

The Neo-Freudians Freud was always a controversial figure—an image which he liked to promote (Sulloway, 1992). As such, he attracted many followers. But he brooked no criticism of the basic principles in his theories. As a result, several of Freud's equally strong-willed disciples broke away from the psychoanalytic fold to establish their own systems of personality, mental disorder, and treatment. Whatever these **neo-Freudians** (literally, "new Freudians") changed in Freud's theory, they always retained a *psychodynamic* emphasis. That is, they kept Freud's idea of personality as a process driven by motivational energy—although they often disagreed about the specific motives that energize personality: Are our motives primarily sexual or social? Conscious or unconscious? The next few pages will give you a sense for the divergent paths followed by these neo-Freudians.

Carl Jung: Extending the Unconscious Freud attracted many disciples, but none more famous than Carl Jung (pronounced *YOONG*), a member of the inner circle of colleagues who helped Freud develop and refine psychoanalytic theory during the first decade of the 1900s. For a time, Freud viewed the somewhat younger Jung as his "crown prince" and probable successor. But Freud's paternal attitude increasingly vexed Jung, who was developing theoretical ideas of his own (Carver & Scheier, 1992). Eventually this personality conflict—which Freud interpreted as Jung's unconscious wish to usurp his fatherly authority—caused a split in their relationship.

■ **Neo-Freudians** Literally "new Freudians"; refers to theorists who broke with Freud but whose theories retain a psychodynamic aspect, especially a focus on motivation as the source of energy for the personality.

● Jungian archetypes abound in art, literature, and film. This photo, from *The Lord of the Rings,* shows Gandalf, who embodies the archetype of magician or trickster. The same archetype is evoked by the coyote in Native American legends and by Merlin in the King Arthur legends.

■ **Personal unconscious** Jung's term for that portion of the unconscious corresponding roughly to the Freudian id.

■ **Collective unconscious** Jung's addition to the unconscious, involving a reservoir for instinctive "memories," including the archetypes, which exist in all people.

■ **Archetypes** The ancient memory images in the collective unconscious. Archetypes appear and reappear in art, literature, and folktales around the world.

■ **Introversion** The Jungian dimension that focuses on inner experience—one's own thoughts and feelings–making the introvert less outgoing and sociable than the extravert.

■ **Extraversion** The Jungian personality dimension involving turning one's attention outward, toward others.

TABLE 11.2	Jung's Opposing Tendencies in Personality

conscious–unconscious
extravert–introvert
rational–irrational
thinking–feeling
intuition–sensation
good–bad
masculine–feminine

For Jung, the break with Freud centered on two issues. First, Jung thought that his mentor had overemphasized sexuality at the expense of other unconscious needs and desires that Jung saw at the heart of personality. He believed spirituality, for example, to be a fundamental human motive, coequal with sexuality. Moreover, he disputed the very structure of the unconscious. This new vision of the unconscious, Jung's most famous invention, warrants closer examination.

The Collective Unconscious In place of the Freudian id, Jung installed a two-part unconscious, consisting of both a *personal unconscious* and a *collective unconscious.* While the Jungian **personal unconscious** spanned essentially the same territory as the Freudian id, its collective twin was another matter—and wholly a Jungian creation. He saw in the **collective unconscious** a reservoir for instinctive "memories" held by people everywhere—in much the same way that humans all share a common genetic code. These collective memories tie together countless generations of human history and give us the ancient images, called **archetypes,** that appear and reappear in art, literature, and folktales around the world (Jung, 1959).

Among these archetypal memories, Jung identified the *animus* and the *anima,* which represent the masculine and feminine sides of our personality. Other archetypes give us the universal concepts of mother, father, birth, death, the hero, the trickster, God, and the self. On the darker side of the self lurks the *shadow* archetype, representing the destructive and aggressive tendencies that we don't want to acknowledge in our personalities. You can recognize your shadow at work the next time you take an instantaneous dislike to someone: This occurs when the other person reminds you of your shadow characteristics.

For Jung, the causes of mental disorder include not only repressed traumas and conflicts in the personal unconscious but failure to acknowledge the archetypes we find unacceptable in our collective unconscious. Applying Jungian theory to the case of Margaret Sanger, a therapist might suspect that Sanger's determination originated in conflicts between the masculine and feminine sides of her nature: the animus and anima. Another Jungian possibility would be that her mother's early death made her deny her own maternal archetype, resulting in her obsession with birth control.

Personality Types Jung's *principle of opposites* portrays each personality as a balance between opposing pairs of tendencies or dispositions, which you see in Table 11.2. Jung taught that most people tend to favor one or the other in each pair. The overall pattern of such tendencies, then, was termed a *personality type,* which Jung believed to be a stable and enduring aspect of the individual's personality.

The most famous of these pairs is **introversion** and **extraversion.** Extraverts turn attention outward, on external experience. As a result, extraverts are more in tune with people and things in the world around them than they are with their inner needs. They tend to be outgoing and unaffected by self-consciousness. Introverts, by contrast, focus on inner experience—their own thoughts and feelings—which makes them seem more shy and less sociable. Few people have all pairs of forces in perfect balance. Instead, one or another dominates, giving rise to personality types (Fadiman & Frager, 2001).

Evaluating Jung's Work   Like Freud, Jung's influence is strongest outside of psychology, especially in literature and the popular press. Psychology has not found Jung so attractive, mainly because his ideas, like Freud's, do not lend themselves to objective observation and testing. In two respects, however, Jung has had a big impact on psychological thinking. First, he challenged Freud and thereby opened the door to a spate of alternative personality theories. Second, his notion of *personality types* makes Jung not only a psychodynamic theorist but a pillar of the temperament/trait/type approach that we will review in the middle segment of this chapter. There you will see that Jung's type theory is the basis for the most widely used psychological test in the world, the *Myers–Briggs Type Indicator.*

Karen Horney: A Feminist Voice in Psychodynamic Psychology   Karen Horney (*HORN-eye*) and Anna Freud, Sigmund Freud's daughter, represent virtually the only feminine voices within the early psychoanalytic movement. In this role Horney disputed the elder Freud's notion of the Oedipus complex and his assertion that women must suffer from penis envy (Horney, 1939). Instead, said Horney, women want the same opportunities and rights that men enjoy and that many personality differences between males and females result from social roles, not from unconscious urges. She also disputed Freud's contention that personality is determined mainly by early childhood experiences. For Horney, normal growth involves the full development of social relationships and of one's potential. This development, however, may be blocked by a sense of uncertainty and isolation that she called **basic anxiety.** It is this basic anxiety that leads to adjustment problems and mental disorder. In Horney's view, the neurotic person—the individual who is unhappy and anxious—suffers from "unconscious strivings developed in order to cope with life despite fears, help-lessness, and isolation" (1942, p. 40).

Neurotic Needs   When people feel anxious and unsafe, healthy psychological development is thwarted, and they become *neurotic.* In Horney's theory, the signs of unhealthy development and neurosis involve ten **neurotic needs,** which are normal desires taken to extremes. You can see these neurotic needs listed in Table 11.3.

Horney also identified three patterns of attitudes and behavior that people use to deal with basic anxiety, either in a healthy or neurotic way: moving *toward others, against others,* or *away from others.* Those who move toward others in a neurotic fashion have a pathological need for constant reminders of love and approval. Such persons may need someone to help, to take care of, or for whom to "sacrifice" themselves. Alternatively, they may seek someone on whom they can become dependent. They may end up behaving passively and feeling victimized. In contrast, those who move against others earn power and respect by competing or attacking successfully, but they risk being feared and ending up "lonely at the top." Those who take the third route, moving away from others to protect them-selves from imagined hurt and rejection, are likely to close themselves off from intimacy and support.

What analysis would Horney have made of Margaret Sanger? We suspect that she would have focused on Sanger's achievements, attempting to determine whether they were the result of a healthy drive to fulfill her poten-tial or a neurotic need for power, status, self-respect, achievement, and independence. Undoubtedly, Horney would have reminded us that society often praises these needs in men and punishes them in women. So, from this

■ **Basic anxiety**   An emotion, proposed by Karen Horney, that gives a sense of un-certainty and loneliness in a hostile world and can lead to maladjustment.
■ **Neurotic needs**   Signs of neurosis in Horney's theory, these 10 needs are normal desires carried to a neurotic extreme.

TABLE 11.3	Horney's Ten Neurotic Needs

1. Need for affection and approval
2. Need for a partner and dread of being left alone
3. Need to restrict one's life and remain inconspicuous
4. Need for power and control over others
5. Need to exploit others
6. Need for recognition or prestige
7. Need for personal admiration
8. Need for personal achievement
9. Need for self-sufficiency and independence
10. Need for perfection and unassailability

● How would Karen Horney have interpreted Margaret Sanger's personality? Margaret Sanger had a flair for publicity. Here she has her lips sealed with tape so that she cannot be accused of illegally preaching birth control in Boston. Instead, she will write her message on a blackboard.

point of view, it is likely that Horney may have seen in Sanger a robust and healthy personality.

Evaluating Horney's Work Neglect engulfed Karen Horney's ideas during midcentury (Monte, 1980). Then her 1967 book, *Feminine Psychology,* appeared at just the right time to elevate her among those seeking a feminist perspective within psychology and psychiatry. But, having attracted renewed interest, will Horney eventually slip again into oblivion? Her theory suffers from the same flaw that plagues the other psychodynamic theories: a weak scientific foundation. It awaits someone to translate her concepts into verifiable form so that they can be put to a scientific test.

Other Neo-Freudian Theorists Sigmund Freud's revolutionary ideas attracted many others to the psychoanalytic movement—some of whom, like Erik Erikson and Alfred Adler, also broke from Freud to develop their own ideas. For the most part, the post-Freudian theorists accepted the notions of psychic determinism and unconscious motivation. But they did not always agree with Freud on the details, especially about the sex and death instincts or the indelible nature of early life experiences. In general, the post-Freudians made several significant changes in the course of psychoanalysis:

▌ They put greater emphasis on ego functions, including ego defenses, development of the self, and conscious thought as the major components of the personality—whereas Freud focused primarily on the unconscious.

▌ They viewed social variables (culture, family, and peers) as having an important role in shaping personality—whereas Freud focused mainly on instinctive urges and conflicts.

▌ They extended personality development beyond childhood to include the entire lifespan—whereas Freud focused mainly on early childhood experiences.

In doing so, the post-Freudians broke Freud's monopoly on personality theory and paved the way for new ideas from the humanistic and cognitive theorists.

Humanistic Theories

With its emphasis on internal conflict and mental disorder, the Freudians and neo-Freudians had compelling explanations for mental disorders, but they largely failed to provide a usable theory of the healthy, "normal" personality. And so the humanistic approach grew to fill that need.

The humanistic theories are optimistic about the core of human nature. For humanists, personality is not driven by unconscious conflicts and defenses against anxiety but rather by needs to adapt, learn, grow, and excel. They retained the idea of motivation as one of the central components of personality, but they accentuated the positive rather than negative motives. Mental disorders, when they do occur, are seen as stemming from unhealthy *situations* that cause low self-esteem and unmet needs, rather than from unhealthy *individuals.*

Thus, the humanists emphasized the positive in human nature. Once people are freed from negative situations, such as a abusive relationships, and negative self-evaluations, such as "I'm not smart," the tendency to be healthy should actively guide them to life-enhancing choices. These ideas brought a new focus on the individual's self-concept and subjective interpretation of reality, rather than the external perspective of an observer or therapist.

Abraham Maslow and the Healthy Personality Abraham Maslow referred to the humanistic view as psychology's "third force," to contrast his ideas with the psychoanalytic and behavioristic movements that had dominated psychol-

■ **Abraham Maslow** (1908–1970): The son of Russian-Jewish immigrants to New York, remembered his childhood as unhappy, lonely, isolated, depressing. A good student, his focus moved from music and drama to psychology, in which he became fascinated with behaviorism — which he later rejected. Early in his career as a psychology professor in New York, he came in contact with many of the finest Jewish scholars who had fled Nazi persecution in Europe during World War II. He became interested in ways that psychology could be used to promote world peace.

1930   1940   1950   1960   1970   1980   1990   2000

Attack on Pearl Harbor.

World War II: Hitler's shadow across Europe and extermination of Jews reinforced Freud's idea of *thanatos* and Jung's notion of *the shadow*.

U.S. War in Vietnam: Widespread student protests; "the pill" ushers in the sexual revolution — which encouraged questioning of Freud's theory of sexuality. The peace movement nurtured the humanistic perspective.

The Reagan presidency: emphasis on individual responsibility and national pride.

Kennedy assassination.

The Great Depression: Widespread unemployment led to massive government programs, such as Social Security. Psychologically, the Depression was a blow to many people's self-esteem.

Watergate scandal: Distrust of government and resignation of President Nixon; along with war in Vietnam, this led to diminished national pride.

● **FIGURE 11.4** The Historical Context of Personality Theories

Theories of personality have often been influenced by the historical context in which they were developed.

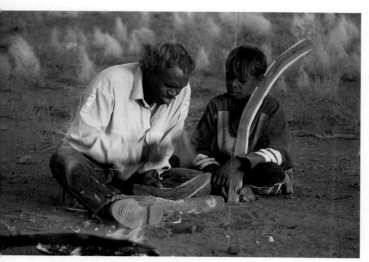

Children develop a clearer sense of identity by observing how men and women behave in their culture.

In Bandura's theory, cognitions are another a major component of our personalities. But cognition doesn't occur in a vacuum: Cognitive processes involve an ongoing relationship between the individual and the environment—an interaction of our behavior, our environment, and our cognitions. Bandura calls this **reciprocal determinism** (Bandura, 1981, 1999). The simple but powerful relationship of these variables is summarized in Figure 11.5.

How does reciprocal determinism work in real life? If, for example, you like psychology, your interest (a cognition) will probably lead you to spend time in the psychology department on campus (an environment) interacting with students and faculty (social behavior) who share your interest. To the extent that you find this stimulating and rewarding, this activity will reciprocally strengthen your interest in psychology and encourage you to spend more time with your friends in the psychology department. This, then, is one instance of the reciprocal determinism among cognition (interest in psychology), environment (the psychology department) and behavior (interacting with others who like psychology).

Locus of Control: Rotter's Theory   Another cognitive psychologist, Julian Rotter (rhymes with *voter*) tells us that the way we act depends on our sense of personal power or **locus of control.** To illustrate, we ask you this question: Do you feel you can control the grade you achieve in your psychology class? If you do, you have an *internal* locus of control, and you probably work hard to get good grades. On the other hand, if you have the feeling that the professor will arbitrarily give you whatever she or he wants you to have—regardless of how much studying you do or the quality of your work—you have an *external* locus of control, and you probably study relatively little.

Scores on Rotter's *Internal–External Locus of Control Scale* correlate with people's emotions and behavior in many situations (Rotter, 1990). For example, those with an internal locus of control are not only more likely to get good grades, but they also are more likely to exercise and watch their diets than are externals (Balch & Ross, 1975; Findley & Cooper, 1983). As you might expect, externals are more likely to be depressed (Benassi et al., 1988).

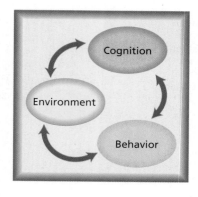

● **FIGURE 11.5**   Reciprocal Determinism

In reciprocal determinism, the individual's cognitions, behavior, and the environment all interact.

■ **Reciprocal determinism**
The process in which cognitions, behavior, and the environment mutually influence each other.
■ **Locus of control**   An individual's sense of where his or her life influences originate.

While we may feel more in control of certain situations than others, many studies suggest that locus of control is an important characteristic of our personalities. That is, people tend to approach different situations with assumptions about their ability to control their fate. Therefore, an internal or external disposition seems to be a reliable personality characteristic—although Rotter resists calling this a *trait* because he believes the term conveys the erroneous idea that internality–externality is fixed and unchangeable. You can evaluate your own locus of control by following the instructions in the "Do It Yourself!" box on the facing page.

Evaluating the Social-Cognitive Approach to Personality   Critics argue that the cognitive theories generally overemphasize rational information processing and overlook both emotion and unconscious processes as important components of personality. So, for those who feel that emotions and motives are central to the functioning of human personality, the cognitive approaches to personality have a blind spot. However, because emotion and associated unconscious processes have assumed a greater role in cognitive psychology recently, we can anticipate a new generation of cognitive theories of personality that do take these aspects of personality into account (Mischel & Shoda, 1995).

Julian Rotter (1966) has developed a test that assesses a person's sense of internal or external control over events. The test items consist of pairs of contrasting statements, and subjects must choose one statement with which they most agree from each pair. This format is called a forced choice test. Unlike many other personality tests, the scoring for each item on Rotter's Internal–External Scale is transparent: The test-taker can easily tell in which direction most items are scored. Here are some items from a preliminary version of the test (Rotter, 1971).

You can see which direction you lean by counting up the number of statements with which you agreed in each column. Agreement with those in the left column suggests an internal locus of control.

1a. Promotions are earned through hard work and persistence.

2a. In my experience I have noticed that there is usually a direct connection between how hard I study and the grades I get.

3a. If one knows how to deal with people they are really quite easily led.

4a. People like me can change the course of world affairs if we make ourselves heard.

5a. I am the master of my fate.

1b. Making a lot of money is largely a matter of getting the right breaks.

2b. Many times the reactions of teachers seem haphazard to me.

3b. I have little influence over the way other people behave.

4b. It is only wishful thinking to believe that one can really influence what happens in society at large.

5b. A great deal that happens to me is probably a matter of chance.

A real strength of the social-cognitive theories is their foundation of solid psychological research—unlike most of the ideas proposed by the Freudians, neo-Freudians, and humanists. You will recall, for example, Bandura's famous Bobo doll experiment, which we discussed in Chapter 6. The price paid for the social-cognitive theories, however, is that they are much less comprehensive than the old and grand theories of personality proposed by Freud and his followers. The payoff, however, has come in the form of both explanations and treatments for a number of mental disorders that often seem to involve observational learning, particularly anxiety-based disorders, such as phobias, and behavior disorders in children.

So, how would a cognitive psychologist explain Margaret Sanger? A cognitive interpretation of Sanger's work and personality would focus on how she interpreted the rewards and punishments she experienced and how these interpretations shaped her behavior. Each time she gave a public lecture about birth-control methods or printed and distributed an illegal pamphlet, Sanger's actions brought punitive consequences—but she was also rewarded with public attention and admiration, press coverage, and ultimately the revocation of unjust laws. Margaret Sanger learned that by enduring hardships, she raised public awareness and changed the social climate. In turn, these successes shaped her, making her less a private citizen and more a public figure.

A cognitive personality theorist would also call attention to the lessons Sanger learned in her social relationships. As she became a celebrity—someone whom others saw as a symbol of a movement rather than a mere individual—she acquired a sense of personal power and an internal locus of control that had eluded her in her early efforts to speak about health education. In her 1938 autobiography, she styled herself as a heroine and martyr, interweaving fanciful stories with accurate information about her life. A cognitive theorist would wonder whether she had come to believe the legendary side of the personality that she had strived to create.

CONNECTION: CHAPTER 12

Other anxiety disorders include *panic disorder* and *obsessive–compulsive disorder*.

Current Trends

Gone are the days when Freud, Jung, Horney, and others were building the grand, sweeping theories of personality that attempted to explain everything we humans do. The humanistic and cognitive theorists arose and pointed out blind spots in the older psychodynamic theories. Now the emphasis has shifted again, as psychologists have brought elements of the psychodynamic, humanistic, and cognitive perspectives together with new knowledge about the impact of culture, gender, and family dynamics. You should be especially aware of three important trends in our thinking about personality.

In *family systems theory*, for example, the basic unit of analysis is not the individual but the family (Gilbert, 1992). This perspective says that personality is shaped by the ways people interacted first in the family and, later, in the peer group. While Freud and others did recognize that parents influence children, the new emphasis is on *interaction*—on the ways that members of the family or the peer group influence each other. This has led to viewing people with psychological problems as individuals embedded in dysfunctional groups, rather than as "sick" persons. This emphasis has also given us a new interpersonal language for personality. We often speak now of *codependence* (instead of *dependent* personalities) and *communication* (instead of mere *talk*). We also have a heightened awareness of relationships and process (the changes that occur as relationships develop).

A second trend comes from psychology's increasing awareness of cultural differences. An increasing number of publications on personality come from psychologists around the world—not just from Europe and America (Quiñones-Vidal et al., 2004). As Stanley Sue (1991) reminds us, our society is becoming ethnically more diverse. No longer can we assume that everyone shares the same cultural experience or the same values. And Harry Triandis (1995) has warned us that people who grow up in *collectivistic* societies may not have the need for individual achievement learned by those who grow up in *individualistic* societies. Triandis also tells us that no culture's approach is superior to the others: They are merely different. We will consider the question of personality differences across cultures in more detail near the end of this chapter.

A third trend comes from an increasing appreciation of gender influences. While we do not know the weights to assign nature and nurture in our attempts to understand gender differences, we do know that males and females often perceive situations differently (Tavris, 1991). For example, males tend to be more physically aggressive than females. Females tend to form close relationships in small, equal-status groups, while males tend to connect in larger groups (teams) organized hierarchically with leaders and followers.

Together these three trends have enlarged our understanding of the forces that shape personality. The new emphasis is on diversity and group processes, rather than on commonalities and individuals. As a result, the picture of personality has become much more complex—but it has undoubtedly become far more accurate.

 ## PSYCHOLOGY IN YOUR LIFE: EXPLAINING UNUSUAL PEOPLE AND UNUSUAL BEHAVIOR

You don't need a theory of personality to explain why people usually get to work on time, sing along at concerts, or spend weekends with their family and friends. That is, you don't need a theory of personality to explain why people do what you would expect them to do. But when they behave in odd and unexpected ways a personality theory becomes handy. A good theory can help you understand interesting and unusual people whom you read about in the newspaper—those who risk their lives to save another, politicians embroiled in scandal, a serial killer, the charismatic leader of a religious cult, and the controversial CEO of a Fortune 500 company.

Which approach to personality offers the best explanations? Unfortunately, none has the whole truth. But each perspective we have covered so far—the psychodynamic, the humanistic, and the cognitive—can help you see personality from a different angle, so you will need to use them all to get the whole picture. To illustrate, let's suppose that you are a counseling psychologist, working at a college counseling center, and a client, a young woman, tells you that she is contemplating suicide. How can your knowledge of personality help you understand her?

The cognitive perspective, with its emphasis on perception and social learning, suggests that her difficulty may lie in her interpretation of some depressing or threatening event. It also alerts you to the possibility that her suicidal thoughts reflect a suicidal role model—perhaps a friend or a family member.

The humanistic view suggests that you explore her unmet needs, such as feeling alone, unloved, or not respected. This view also calls your attention to the possibility of suicidal thoughts arising from low self-esteem.

The psychodynamic perspective suggests that you consider your client's internal motivation. Is she a hostile person who has turned her hostility on herself? Does she have some unfinished emotional business from an earlier developmental stage, such as guilt for angry feelings toward her parents? Does she have an unresolved identity crisis?

No one has a simple answer to the problem of understanding why people do what they do. That is for the counselor and client to work out together. What these theories of personality can do, however, is call your attention to factors you might otherwise overlook.

● A theory of personality is helpful in understanding unusual personalities.

CHECK YOUR UNDERSTANDING

1. **RECALL:** The psychodynamic theories emphasize
   a. motivation.
   b. learning.
   c. consciousness.
   d. the logical basis of behavior.

2. **RECALL:** Freud believed that mental disorders stem from conflicts and drives that are repressed in the
   a. ego.   c. id.
   b. superego.   d. Eros.

3. **APPLICATION:** Which of the following behaviors would a Freudian say is driven by Thanatos?
   a. sexual intercourse
   b. a violent assault
   c. dreaming
   d. flying an airplane

4. **RECALL:** What is the ego defense mechanism on which the Rorschach and TAT are based?
   a. displacement
   b. fantasy
   c. regression
   d. projection

5. **APPLICATION:** If you react strongly to angry outbursts in others, you may be struggling with which Jungian archetype?
   a. the anima
   b. the shadow
   c. introversion
   d. the hero

6. **RECALL:** Karen Horney believed that the main forces behind our behaviors are
   a. social.
   b. sexual.
   c. aggressive and destructive.
   d. the result of the Oedipus complex.

7. **RECALL:** The humanistic theorists were very different from the psychodynamic theorists because of their emphasis on
   a. the cognitive forces behind behavior.
   b. the healthy personality.
   c. mental disorder.
   d. emotional intelligence.

(continues)

8. **RECALL:** Our expectations of reward and punishment play a major role in
   a. the psychodynamic theories.
   b. the humanistic theories.
   c. the cognitive theories.
   d. none of the above theories of personality.

9. **UNDERSTANDING THE CORE CONCEPT:** What do the psychodynamic, humanistic, and cognitive theories of personality have in common?

   a. They all view personality as largely unconscious.
   b. They all acknowledge the internal mental processes underlying our personality characteristics.
   c. They all say that men and women have entirely different motives underlying their behaviors.
   d. They all have a strong basis in psychological research.

ANSWERS: 1.a 2.c 3.b 4.d 5.b 6.a 7.b 8.c 9.b

WHAT PERSISTENT PATTERNS ARE FOUND IN PERSONALITY?

■ **Humors** Four body fluids—blood, phlegm, black bile, and yellow bile—that, according to an ancient theory, control personality by their relative abundance.

Two thousand years before academic psychology appeared, people were classifying each other according to four *temperaments,* based on a theory proposed by the Greek physician Hippocrates (*Hip-POCK-rah-tees*). A person's temperament, he suggested, resulted from the balance of the four **humors,** or fluids, secreted by the body. A *sanguine,* or cheerful, person was characterized by strong, warm blood. A *choleric* temperament, marked by anger, came from yellow bile (called *choler*), believed to flow from the liver. Hippocrates thought that the liver also produced black bile, from which arose a *melancholic,* or depressed, temperament. Finally, if the body's dominant fluid is phlegm, or mucus, the person will have a *phlegmatic* temperament: cool, aloof, slow, and unemotional. Hippocrates' biology may have been a little off the mark, but his notion of temperaments established themselves as "common sense." Even today you will occasionally encounter his terms used to describe people's personalities.

Since the days of Hippocrates, many other personality classification systems have been developed. The most simplistic ones are just streeotypes: If fat, then jolly; if an engineer, then conservative; if female, then sympathetic. Unfortunately, they oversimplify the very complicated problem of understanding the patterns found in personality. In fact, even you may be guilty of such oversimplifications, if you group people strictly according to college class, major, sex, ethnicity, and qualities such as honesty, shyness, or sense of humor.

Still, something in human nature seems to encourage us to group people by categories, according to certain distinguishing features. In modern psychology, some personality theorists describe people in terms of *temperaments:* global dispositions of personality, such as "outgoing" or "shy." Others prefer to look for *traits,* which are more specific characteristics in the personality, such as "cautious." Still others group people according to their personality *types,* which are clusters of traits. As you will see, however, most agree on certain fundamental dimensions of personality. Our Core Concept says:

> Another approach describes personality in terms of stable patterns known as temperaments, traits, and types.

◄ **CONNECTION: CHAPTER 1**

The *trait perspective* is one of the seven major viewpoints in modern psychology.

As you can see, the terms *temperament, trait,* and *type* overlap—which allows us to use the generic term *trait perspective* for this general approach to understanding human personality.

What makes these theories different from mere stereotypes—the conservative engineer, the macho male, or the dismal economics professor? It's all in the science. A good temperament, trait, or type theory has a solid research base. Let's look a few prominent examples.

Personality and Temperament

Psychologists define **temperament** as the inherited personality dispositions that are apparent in early childhood and that establish the tempo and mood of the individual's behaviors (Hogan et al., 1996; Mischel, 1993). When they speak of temperaments, psychologists are usually referring to a single, dominant "theme," such as shyness or moodiness, that characterizes a person's personality. Modern psychology has, of course, abandoned the four humors theory of temperament, but it has retained its most basic concept: *Biological dispositions do affect our basic personalities.* In support of this view, psychologists can point to structures in the brain that are known to regulate fundamental aspects of personality (Canli et al., 2002; Carpenter, 2001a; Craik et al., 1999; Davidson, 2002; LeDoux, 2002; Zuckerman, 1995). You will recall, for example, the case of Phineas Gage, who received an accidental lobotomy and thereby demonstrated the role of the frontal lobes in social interaction and the suppression of impulsive behavior.

Biological psychologists now suspect that some individual differences in disposition also arise from the balance of chemicals in the brain, which may have a genetic basis (Azar, 2002; Sapolsky, 1992). In this sense, the theory of humors still lives, but in a different guise: Modern biological psychology has replaced the humors with neurotransmitters. So, depression—which characterizes most suicidal people—may result from an imbalance of certain transmitters. Likewise, anxiety, anger, and euphoria may each arise from other neurochemical patterns. As developmental psychologist Jerome Kagan says (in Stavish, 1994a), "We all have the same neurotransmitters, but each of us has a slightly different mix" (p. 7). That, says Kagan, is what accounts for many of the temperamental differences among people, especially with regard to negative traits, such as fearfulness, sadness, and shyness.

In fact, Kagan runs a fascinating research program focusing on the inherited basis of shyness (Kagan et al., 1994). This program has clearly demonstrated that on the very first day of life, newborns already differ in the degree to which they are "inhibited" or "uninhibited"—that is, shy versus bold. About 10 to 15% of all children appear to be born shy or introverted, while a similar percentage appear to be born bold or extraverted, as assessed by a variety of measures. These initial differences in temperament persist over time, with the majority of children being classified with the same temperament in measurements taken over an 11-year interval. On the other hand, we know that the percentage of shy college-age students—40% or more—is much higher than the percentage of shy children (Zimbardo, 1990). It is thus reasonable to assume that some shyness is inherited, while even more is learned through negative experiences in one's social life. It is also the case that if a child is withdrawn, startles easily, is unlikely to smile, and is fearful of both strangers and novelty, then that child will create an environment that is not friendly, playful, or supportive. In this way, heredity and environment interact, with initially inherited characteristics becoming amplified—or perhaps muted—over time, because they produce social signals telling others to either approach or stay away.

So does biology determine your destiny? An inherited temperament may set the *range* of your responses to some life situations. However, temperament by itself does not fully determine your life experiences (Kagan & Snidman, 1998). Even among your biological relatives, your unique family position, experiences, and sense of self guarantee that your personality pattern is unlike that of anyone else (Bouchard et al., 1990).

● Some shyness is inherited, and some is learned through experience.

■ **Temperament** The basic and pervasive personality dispositions that are apparent in early childhood and that establish the tempo and mood of the individual's behaviors.

Personality as a Composite of Traits

If you were to describe a friend, you might speak of temperament—a single dominant theme in his or her personality. But you might also describe your friend on several dimensions, using the language of *traits:* moody, cheerful, melancholy, enthusiastic, volatile, friendly, or smart. **Traits** are stable personality characteristics that are presumed to exist within the individual and guide his or her thoughts and actions under various conditions. In this sense, then, traits work to channel the way our motives are expressed in behavior (Winter et al., 1998).

The "Big Five" Traits: The Five-Factor Theory By restricting the definition of personality to motivational and emotional characteristics (excluding such attributes as IQ, skills, and creativity), trait theorists are building a consensus on the major components of personality. Using the mathematical tool of *factor analysis* (which helps an investigator look for relationships, or clusters, among personality test items), many researchers have found five dominant personality factors, sometimes called the *Big Five* (Carver & Scheier, 2000; Digman, 1990; Goldberg, 1981, 1993). As yet, we have no universally accepted names for these factors, although the first term in the list below may be the most widely used. (You will note that each dimension is *bipolar,* describing a range from high to low on that trait. The first term we have listed is a label referring to the "high" pole for each trait.)

- *Openness to experience* (also called inquiring intellect, curiosity, independence, or, at the opposite pole, closed-mindedness)
- *Conscientiousness* (also called dependability, cautiousness, perseverance, superego strength, prudence, or constraint, and, at the opposite pole, impulsiveness, carelessness, or irresponsibility)
- *Extraversion* (also called social adaptability, assertiveness, sociability, boldness, or self-confidence, and, at the opposite pole, introversion)
- *Agreeableness* (also called conformity, likeability, friendly compliance, warmth, or, at the opposite pole, coldness or negativity)
- *Neuroticism* (also called anxiety or emotionality and, at the opposite pole, emotional stability or emotional control)

As an aid to remembering these dimensions, think of the acronym *OCEAN,* standing for *O*penness, *C*onscientiousness, *E*xtraversion, *A*greeableness, and *N*euroticism.

This **five-factor theory** is important because it greatly simplifies a formerly confusing picture. Various theorists, such as Freud, Jung, Adler, Horney, Erikson, and Maslow, had suggested a wide array of "fundamental" personality dimensions. In addition, the dictionary gives us several hundred terms commonly used to describe personality (Allport & Odbert, 1936). While psychologists had attempted to simplify this daunting list of personality characteristics, it wasn't until the last decade or so that agreement has emerged on which traits were fundamental. Although debate still continues about the details, a broad coalition of theorists has now concluded that we can describe people with reasonable accuracy by specifying their position on each of these five dimensions. The five-factor theory also offers the advantage of describing personality in the familiar terms of everyday language.

Significantly, the five-factor model also seems to have validity across cultures. An Israeli sample produced the same five factors as those found in Americans (Birenbaum & Montag, 1986). A study drawing on people from Canada, Germany, Finland, and Poland also supported the five-factor theory (Paunonen et al., 1992), as did still other studies of individuals from Germany, Portugal, Israel, China, Korea, and Japan (McCrae & Costa, 1997), as well as

■ Traits Stable personality characteristics that are presumed to exist within the individual and guide his or her thoughts and actions under various conditions.

■ Five-factor theory A trait perspective suggesting that personality is composed of five fundamental personality dimensions: openness to experience, conscientiousness, extraversion, agreeableness, and neuroticism.

Japanese university students (Bond et al., 1975) and Filipino students (Guthrie & Bennet, 1970). Note that the same five factors stood out in each of these cultures as the basic framework of personality. Digman (1990) notes that these strikingly consistent results, coming in from such diverse cultures, lead to the suspicion "that something quite fundamental is involved here" (p. 433).

Assessing Traits   If you were a clinical or counseling psychologist, you would have your choice of dozens of instruments for measuring personality. We have already met some of these in our discussion of the Rorschach inkblot technique, along with its projective cousin, the TAT, which came to us from the psychodynamic perspective. Now let us examine some of the personality tests spawned in part by the theories of traits, types, and temperaments.

One of the newer trait-based instruments comes from the five-factor theory: the NEO-PI or "Big Five Inventory" (Caprara et al., 1993; Costa & McCrae, 1992a, b). This personality assessment device has been used to study personality stability across the lifespan and the relationship of personality characteristics to physical health and various life events.

One of the most widely used of the personality inventories is the *Minnesota Multiphasic Personality Inventory*, usually called the **MMPI-2**. (The "2" means it is a revised form of the original *MMPI*.) Strictly speaking, it doesn't measure enduring personality traits. Rather, its ten clinical scales were developed to measure serious mental problems, such as depression and schizophrenia (Butcher et al., 1989; Butcher & Williams, 1992; Greene, 1991; Helmes & Reddon, 1993). It consists of 567 statements dealing with attitudes, habits, fears, preferences, physical health, beliefs, and general outlook, such as:

- I am often bothered by thoughts about sex.
- Sometimes I like to stir up some excitement.
- If people had not judged me unfairly, I would have been far more successful.

Respondents are asked to indicate whether each statement describes them, and their answers are scored on the ten clinical dimensions listed in Table 11.4.

Attempting to fake a good or bad score on the *MMPI-2* is not a smart idea. The test has four "lie" scales that will most likely signal that something is amiss. All are sensitive to unusual responses. Here are some items similar to those on the lie scales:

- Sometimes I put off doing things I know I ought to do.
- On occasion I have passed on some gossip.
- Once in a while, I find a dirty joke amusing.

MMPI-2   A widely used personality assessment instrument that gives scores on ten important clinical traits. Also called the *Minnesota Multiphasic Personality Inventory.*

TABLE 11.4	MMPI-2 Clinical Scales

Hypochondriasis (Hs): Abnormal concern with bodily functions

Depression (D): Pessimism; hopelessness; slowing of action and thought

Conversion hysteria (Hy): Unconscious use of mental problems to avoid conflicts or responsibility

Psychopathic deviate (Pd): Disregard for social custom; shallow emotions; inability to profit from experience

Masculinity–femininity (Mf): Differences between men and women

Paranoia (Pa): Suspiciousness; delusions of grandeur or persecution

Psychasthenia (Pt): Obsessions; compulsions; fears; low self-esteem; guilt; indecisiveness

Schizophrenia (Sc): Bizarre, unusual thoughts or behavior; withdrawal; hallucinations; delusions

Hypomania (Ma): Emotional excitement; flight of ideas; overactivity

Social introversion (Si): Shyness; disinterest in others; insecurity

Too many attempts to make yourself look good or bad will boost your lie scale scores into the questionable range.

From a scientific standpoint, the *MMPI-2* is an exemplary instrument, for two reasons. First, it has **reliability.** This means that it provides consistent and stable scores. So, for example, when a person takes the test on two different occasions, the scores are likely to be much the same. Any good test must have reliability, otherwise the scores would be erratic and undependable.

Second, the *MMPI-2* has **validity**—which means that it actually measures what it was designed to measure: indicators of mental disturbance. The instrument does a credible job, for example, of identifying depressed or psychotic persons (Greene, 1991). So, as a diagnostic instrument, the *MMPI-2* has a good record—although it must be used with care in non-Western cultures because some of its items have culture-specific content (Lonner, 1990). Clinicians should also be cautious when giving the *MMPI-2* to members of ethnic minorities in the United States, because minority groups were not well represented in the original sample used in developing the test (Butcher & Williams, 1992; Graham, 1990).

Evaluating Temperament and Trait Theories   Several criticisms have been leveled at the temperament and trait theories and the tests they have spawned. For one, these theories give us a "snapshot" of personality—a picture that portrays personality as fixed and static, rather than as a dynamic and changing process. Another criticism is that they oversimplify our complex natures by describing personality on just a few dimensions. As evolution scholar Stephen Jay Gould remarked, "The world does not come to us in neat little packages" (1996, p. 188). And what would we gain, for example, by judging Margaret Sanger as "passionate" or by finding that she scored high on traits such as outgoingness and dominance but low on agreeableness or conventional thinking? Such judgments would validate others' observations of her and even her own self-descriptions. But brief labels and concise categories also leave out important detail. Although many women may have possessed similar traits, no one else did what Margaret Sanger did. A simple sketch of personality cannot provide the insight of a more complex portrait.

On the positive side, trait theories give us some ability to *predict* behavior in common situations, such as work settings—to select employees who are well trained and to screen out those who might cause problems. But trait theories suffer from the same difficulty as the instinct theories. Both *describe* behavior with a label but do not *explain* it. For example, we can attribute depression to a depressive trait or an outgoing personality to extraversion without really understanding the behavior. In short, trait theories identify common traits, but they do not tell us much about their source or how traits interact (McAdams, 1992; Pervin, 1985). Moreover, because most people display a trait only to a moderate degree, we must ask how useful traits are for understanding all but the extreme cases. In contrast, dynamic theories of personality (which we examined in the first part of this chapter) emphasize changing, developing forces within the individual and the environment.

Finally, with trait theory we again encounter the problem of the *self-fulfilling prophecy.* When given trait labels, people may begin to act as those labels suggest, making it more difficult for them to change. A child labeled "shy," for example, may have to struggle against both the label and the trait.

Traits and the Person–Situation Debate   Cognitive theorist Walter Mischel dropped a scientific bombshell on the trait theorists with evidence suggesting that we behave far less consistently from one situation to another than most had assumed (1968, 1973). A person who is extraverted in one situation can become shy and retiring in another; an emotionally stable person may fall

◀ **CONNECTION: CHAPTER 8**

The original *self-fulfilling prophecy* involved students whose academic performance was altered by teachers' expectations.

apart when the situation changes radically. Therefore, Mischel argued, knowledge of the *situation* is more important in predicting behavior than knowing a person's traits. The ensuing tumult within the field has become known as the **person–situation controversy** (Pervin, 1985).

In fact, Mischel's position challenged the very foundations of most personality theories. After all, if people do act inconsistently in different situations, then what good is a theory of personality? Critics mounted withering attacks on Mischel's thesis, pointing out that his methods underestimated a thread of consistency across situations (Epstein, 1980). Bem and Allen (1974) have also pointed out that some people behave more consistently than others. Moreover, people are most consistent when others are watching (Kenrick & Stringfield, 1980) and when in familiar situations (Funder, 1983a, b; Funder & Ozer, 1983).

Nevertheless, it is true that personality traits as measured by personality tests typically account for less than 10% of all the factors that affect behavior (Digman, 1990)—a small number, indeed! But don't make the mistake of assuming that the situation accounts for the remaining 90%. Correlations between situations and behaviors are relatively weak, too. The lesson to be learned here is that the majority of factors affecting behavior simply cannot be assigned to one category or the other. Behavior seems to result from an *interaction* of trait and situational variables (Kenrick & Funder, 1988). In fact, Mischel has never suggested that we abandon theories of personality. Rather, he sees behavior as a function of the situation, the individual's *interpretation* of the situation, and personality (1990; Mischel & Shoda, 1995).

Mischel has argued that personality variables have their greatest impact on behavior when cues in the situation are *weak* or *ambiguous.* When situations are strong and clear, there will be less individual variation in response. For example, suppose that one day when you are in class, a student collapses, apparently unconscious, onto the floor. After a stunned silence, the instructor asks the class to keep their seats and then points *at you*, demanding loudly, "Use your cell phone to call 911, and get an ambulance here!" What do you do? This is a "strong" situation: Someone is in control, an instructor you already see as an authority figure; that person has told you unambiguously what to do. You are likely to comply—as would most people in that situation. In Mischel's characterization of person–situation interactions, there would be very little variation in how individuals respond to these circumstances.

But now suppose that you are walking leisurely through campus and you see a crowd gathered around a student who has collapsed on the sidewalk. Will you go for help? This is a "weak" situation, and your actions are likely to depend more strongly on your past experience and on such personality variables as independence and extraversion.

THE FAR SIDE® By GARY LARSON

The four basic personality types

● Often the situation is a more powerful predictor of behavior than are personality traits.

PSYCHOLOGY IN YOUR LIFE:
FINDING YOUR TYPE

The notion of **type** refers to especially important dimensions or clusters of traits that are found in essentially the same pattern in many people. As we saw earlier, Carl Jung made the concept of type a feature of his theory of personality. (Thus, we could classify Jung as both a psychodynamic theorist and a trait/type theorist.) Jung's typology scheme, especially his notions of introversion and extraversion, have enjoyed wide influence and, as we have seen, is now recognized as one of the Big Five trait dimensions. Of particular importance is the use of Jung's typology as the foundation for the world's most widely used test of personality: the *Myers–Briggs Type Indicator.*

You are likely to have taken the **Myers–Briggs Type Indicator (MBTI)** because it is given to nearly two million people each year (Druckman & Bjork, 1991). It is used in many college counseling centers, where students may be advised to select a career that fits with their personality type. It is also used in relationship counseling, where couples are taught to accommodate to each other's personality styles. And the *MBTI* is commonly used by consultants in management training sessions to convey the message that people have distinct personality patterns that suit them for different kinds of jobs.

We pause to give the *MBTI* a close look for two reasons. First, as the only objective measure of personality based on Jung's type theory, it presents an opportunity to examine some of his ideas critically. Second, as one of the most widely used of psychological instruments, the *MBTI* deserves critical scrutiny. We suggest that there are some good reasons to be cautious when interpreting the results on an *MBTI* profile.

On the Myers–Briggs test, examinees answer a series of questions about how they make judgments, perceive the world, and relate to others (Myers, 1962, 1976, 1987; Myers & Myers, 1995). Based on these responses, a scoring system assigns an individual to a four-dimensional personality type, derived from the Jungian dimensions of Introversion–Extraversion, Thinking–Feeling, Sensation–Intuition, and Judgment–Perception. You will recall that, according to Jung, personality types are stable patterns over time.

■ **Type** Refers to especially important dimensions or clusters of traits that are not only central to a person's personality but are found with essentially the same pattern in many people.

■ ***Myers–Briggs Type Indicator (MBTI)*** A widely used personality test based on Jungian types.

So, what does the *Myers–Briggs Type Indicator* tell us about the stability or *reliability* of types? Remember that reliable test gives consistent results. But the research suggests that the reliability of the *MBTI* is questionable. One study found that fewer than half of those tested on the *MBTI* had exactly the same type when retested five weeks later (McCarley & Carskadon, 1983). Another study found a change in at least one of the four type categories in about 75% of respondents (see Druckman & Bjork, 1991). Such results certainly raise questions about the fundamental concept of "type."

A second issue concerns the *validity* of the Myers–Briggs test (Pittenger, 1993). We have said that a valid test actually measures what it is being used to measure. And again the research on the *MBTI* gives a mixed picture (Druckman & Bjork, 1991). As you might expect, people who work with people—entertainers, counselors, managers, and sellers—tend to score higher on extraversion. By comparison, librarians, computer specialists, and physicians number many introverts in their ranks. The danger lies, however, in turning averages into stereotypes. In fact, the data show a diversity of types within occupations. Further, we find a conspicuous lack of evidence documenting a relationship between personality type and occupational success. Although proponents of the *MBTI* claim

● Extraversion is thought by some to represent a major personality type.

it to be useful in vocational counseling, a review of the literature by a team from the National Academy of Sciences found no relationship between personality type, as revealed by the *MBTI,* and performance on a particular job (Druckman & Bjork, 1991). This report has, however, been hotly disputed by users of the instrument (Pearman, 1991). Clearly, the *Myers–Briggs Type Indicator* needs more validity work before we can confidently encourage people to make life choices on the basis of its results.

Counselors using the *Myers–Briggs* to assess Jungian personality types often argue that its value lies not in its accuracy but in its ability to suggest new avenues for exploration—previously unknown personality patterns that might suggest career possibilities that might never have come to the individual's attention. Moreover, those who take the test often report that they have gained insight into themselves from the experience. Thus, the instrument may have some value in counseling, especially when counselors resist the temptation to interpret the results rigidly. Unfortunately, no research has been done that documents these benefits over the long term. Says the National Academy of Sciences Report (Druckman & Bjork, 1991), "Lacking such evidence, it is a curiosity why the instrument is used so widely" (p. 99).

CHECK YOUR UNDERSTANDING

1. **RECALL:** Temperament refers to personality characteristics that
   a. cause people to be "nervous" or unpredictable.
   b. are learned, especially from one's parents and peers.
   c. have a substantial biological basis.
   d. cause mental disorders.

2. **APPLICATION:** A friend of yours always seems agitated and anxious, even when nothing in the circumstances would provoke such a response. Which one of the Big Five traits applies to this characteristic of your friend?
   a. introversion
   b. agreeableness
   c. neuroticism
   d. conscientiousness

3. **RECALL:** Walter Mischel argues that _____ is (are) less important than _____.

   a. traits/the situation
   b. traits/temperament
   c. the conscious mind/the unconscious
   d. emotions/reason

4. **UNDERSTANDING THE CORE CONCEPT:** What is found in most psychodynamic, humanistic, and cognitive theories but is not found in most temperament, trait, and type theories?
   a. a description of the components of the personality
   b. labels for common mental disorders
   c. concepts that are useful for individuals involved in personnel selection decisions
   d. a description of the processes of development and change underlying personality

ANSWERS: 1.c 2.c 3.a 4.d

WHAT "THEORIES" DO PEOPLE USE TO UNDERSTAND EACH OTHER?

We have seen how psychologists view personality. But how do people who are *not* psychologists think about people? This is an important matter because we all regularly make assumptions—right or wrong—about other people's personalities. You do so when you meet someone new at a party, when you apply for a job, and when you form your first impression of a professor or classmate. Do people make similar assumptions about each other in other cultures? These questions are significant because the "folk theories," or *implicit personality theories*, that people use to understand each other can support or undermine relationships among individuals—or even among nations. Our Core Concept says:

> People everywhere develop implicit assumptions ("folk theories") about personality, but these assumptions vary in important ways across cultures.

In this section we will examine the assumptions commonly found in implicit theories of personality. Then, at the end, we will help you discover what implicit assumptions you make about others.

Implicit Personality Theories

Think of someone who has been a role model for you. Now think of someone you can't stand to be around. In both cases, what immediately springs to mind are personal attributes—traits—that you have learned to use to describe people: honesty, reliability, sense of humor, generosity, outgoing attitude, aggressiveness, moodiness, or pessimism, for example. Even as a child, you had a rudimentary system for appraising personality. You tried to determine which new acquaintances would be friend or foe; you worked out ways of dealing with your parents or teachers based on how you read their personalities. You have probably also spent a great deal of time trying to get a handle on who you are—on what qualities distinguish you from others, which ones to develop, and which to discard.

In each case, your judgments were personality assessments reflecting your **implicit personality theory,** your personal explanation of how people's qualities and experiences influence their response patterns. Like the implicit memories we studied in Chapter 7, implicit theories of personality operate in the background, largely outside of our awareness. There they simplify the task of understanding other people (Fiske & Neuberg, 1990; Macrae et al., 1994).

Implicit theories often rely on naive assumptions about traits. For example, people tend to assume that certain clusters of traits go together—creativity and emotional sensitivity, for example. Consequently, when they observe one of these traits, they may assume that the person possesses the other (Hochwalder, 1995). People's personal experiences and motives can also influence their judgment of others. So, if you have had your heart broken by someone who was attractive but unwilling to make a commitment, you may quickly judge other attractive persons to be "insincere" or "untrustworthy."

In judging people, Americans and Europeans also tend to make the **fundamental attribution error.** This error in judgment relies on the assumption that another person's behavior, especially clumsy, inappropriate, or otherwise undesirable behavior, is the result of a flaw in the personality, rather than in the situation. For example, if you trip and fall as you enter a psychology class at an American college or university, other students are likely to assume that you are a clumsy person. But, if you were stumbling into a psychology class in China or Japan, the students would be more likely to assume that your bizarre behavior had some external cause, such as someone bumping you or an irregularity in the floor tiles. Cross-cultural research shows that the fundamental attribution error is less common in group-oriented, *collectivistic* cultures, such as are found in China and India (Lillard, 1997; Miller, 1984; Morris & Peng, 1994).

Personality across Cultures

The very concept of personality theory is a Western (Euro-American) invention, said cross-cultural psychologist Juris Draguns (1979). Therefore, it is not surprising that all formal theories of personality have been created by people

■ **Implicit personality theory**
Assumptions about personality that are held by people (especially nonpsychologists) to simplify the task of understanding others.

■ **Fundamental attribution error**
The assumption that another person's behavior, especially clumsy, inappropriate, or otherwise undesirable behavior, is the result of a flaw in the personality, rather than in the situation.

trained in the framework of the Western social sciences, with a built-in bias toward individualism (Guisinger & Blatt, 1994; Segall et al., 1999). Other cultures, however, address many of the same issues in their own ways. Most of these non-Western perspectives have originated in religion (Walsh, 1984). Hindus, for example, see personality as a union of opposing characteristics (Murphy & Murphy, 1968). The Chinese concept of complementary opposite forces, yin and yang, provides a similar perspective (which influenced Carl Jung's *principle of opposites*).

Individualism, Collectivism, and Personality According to Harry Triandis (1989, 1990, 1994; Triandis & Gelfand, 1998), cultures differ most fundamentally on the dimension of *individualism* versus *collectivism*, which we alluded to above. For those raised in the Euro-American tradition, the individual is the basic unit of society, while those raised in many Asian and African cultures emphasize the family or other social groups. In collectivistic cultures people tend to form identities that blend harmoniously with the group, and they expect that others are motivated to do the same. In individualistic cultures, a person tends to form a unique identity and assume that others are similarly motivated to stand out from the crowd (Pedersen, 1979). Thus, for Euro-Americans, the self is a whole, while for many Asians and Africans the self is only a part (Cohen & Gunz, 2002; Gardiner et al., 1998; Markus & Kitayama, 1994). For Euro-Americans, a group is composed of separate individuals; when they work together they become a "team." By contrast, for Asians and Africans the group is the natural unit; the individual is incomplete without the group. Much of the conflict and misunderstanding arising from business dealings and political negotiations across cultures stems from different expectations about personality and the individual's relationship to the group.

● Most Asian cultures have a collectivist tradition that affirms the group, rather than the individual, as the fundamental social unit.

Many aspects of peoples' personalities and behavior are related to their culture's position on the individualism versus collectivism dimension. We have already seen how the fundamental attribution error is more common in individualistic cultures. Two other topics related to individualism versus collectivism and to personality have received special emphasis by cross-cultural psychologists: (1) competition versus cooperation and (2) the need for achievement. In brief, when given the choice of competition or cooperation, individualistic Americans characteristically choose to compete (Aronson, 2004; Gallo & McClintock, 1965). Americans, on the average, also score higher on measures of need for achievement than do people in collectivist cultures.

Other Cultural Differences Cultures differ on other personality-related dimensions that are not so obviously related to individualism–collectivism. These include:

▌ *Status of different age groups and sexes:* The status of the elderly is higher in many Asian cultures than in the United States; women have second-class status in many traditional societies (Segall et al., 1999).

▌ *Romantic love:* The assumption that romantic love should be the basis for marriage is a historically recent European invention and is most often found in individualistic cultures (Rosenblatt, 1966).

▌ *Stoicism:* Asian cultures teach people to suppress the expression of intense feelings (Tsai & Uemura, 1988), while Euro-Americans are much more likely to express strong emotions (although there are pronounced gender differences).

▌ *Locus of control:* Persons in industrialized nations, such as the United States and Canada, more often have an internal locus of control than do those in developing countries, such as Mexico or China (Berry et al., 1992; Draguns, 1979; Shiraev & Levy, 2004).

■ *Thinking versus feeling:* Many cultures (e.g., in Latin America) do not make the strong distinction between thoughts and emotions that Americans do (Fajans, 1985; Lutz, 1988).

Cultures even differ in their views of the ideal personality (Matsumoto, 1996). In the Western psychological tradition, mental health consists of integrating opposite and conflicting parts of the personality. This can be seen especially clearly in Freudian and Jungian theory. By contrast, some Asian psychologies, particularly those associated with Buddhism, seek the opposite: to dissociate consciousness from sensation and from memories of worldly experience (Gardiner et al., 1998; Pedersen, 1979).

Despite these differences, can we say that people are fundamentally the same the world over? On the level of neurons and brain circuits, the answer is certainly "Yes." But personality is also locked in the embrace of culture, so a more comprehensive answer would be "No—but perhaps they can be described on the same Big Five dimensions." In the words of Erika Bourguignon (1979), "It is one of the major intellectual developments of the twentieth century to call into question the concept of a universal human nature."

Even though personality and culture are partners in a perpetual dance, we can make this distinction between them:

> "Culture" refers to those aspects of a society that all its members share, are familiar with, and pass on to the next generation. "Personality" refers to unique combinations of traits (which all people in a culture know about, even though a given trait does not describe a given person) which differentiate individuals within a culture. (Brislin, 1981, pp. 51–52)

But don't forget that culture and personality interact. A culture shapes the personalities of the individuals within it, just as individuals can influence a culture. So, your personality is, to a certain extent, a product of your society's values, attitudes, beliefs, and customs about morality, work, child rearing, aggression, achievement, competition, death, and dozens of other matters important to humans everywhere. And, in a larger sense, a culture is the "personality" of a society (Benedict, 1934).

PSYCHOLOGY IN YOUR LIFE: DEVELOPING YOUR OWN THEORY OF PERSONALITY

Each of the theories we have examined has its limitations and strengths. Consequently, most psychologists become **eclectic.** That is, they either switch theories as the situation requires or construct a theory of personality by borrowing ideas from many perspectives. While an eclectic approach may appear to offer the easiest route, it presents difficulties that arise from certain fundamental conflicts among theories. To give one example: How could we reconcile Freud's concept of our behavior being driven by primitive instincts with humanism's assumption of the innate goodness of our nature?

It may help to think of a personality theory as a map showing the major pathways through a person's psychological landscape. As you formulate your own theory, you must decide how to weight the forces that determine which paths we select—the forces of conditioning, motivation and emotion, heredity and environment, individualism and collectivism, cognition, traits, culture,

■ **Eclectic** Either switching theories to explain different situations or building one's own theory of personality from pieces borrowed from many perspectives.

self-concept, and potential. We propose the following questions, which will help you sort out the assumptions in your implicit theory of personality.

▮ In your opinion, are people more rational and logical (as the cognitive theories contend), or do they more often act on the basis of feelings and emotions (as the psychodynamic theories argue)?

▮ Are people usually conscious of the reasons for their behavior, as many of the post-Freudians claimed? Or, are their actions mainly caused by unconscious needs, desires, and urges (as Freud suggested)?

▮ What do you see as the basic motives behind human behavior: sex, aggression, power, love, spirituality . . . ?

▮ Are human motives essentially egocentric and self-serving? Or are they altruistic, unmotivated by the desire for personal gain (as the humanists suggest)?

▮ When you try to understand another person's actions, which of the following do you consider to be most important: the situation (as Mischel says); the person's inner needs, drives, motives, and emotions (as the psychodynamic theories say); or the person's basic personality characteristics (as the trait and type theories say)?

▮ Is our basic, inner nature essentially healthy and good (as the humanists see it) or composed of primitive and self-serving desires (as Freud saw it)?

No one has yet found the "right" answers, but the answers you give say a great deal about your own personality.

● Do you think these people are conscious of the reasons for their behavior? Some views of personality assert that anger comes from an inner drive that arises in the unconscious mind. Other views emphasize conscious cognitions of environmental stimuli.

C H E C K   Y O U R   U N D E R S T A N D I N G

1. **APPLICATION:** You would expect to find the concept of self emphasized in
   a. the culture of an industrialized society.
   b. a wealthy culture.
   c. an individualistic culture.
   d. a collectivistic culture.

2. **RECALL:** Cross-cultural psychologists say that a basic distinction among cultures is their emphasis on
   a. capitalism or socialism.
   b. external or internal locus of control.
   c. thoughts or feelings.
   d. individualism or collectivism.

3. **APPLICATION:** You are making the *fundamental attribution error* when

   a. you decide to dislike someone who speaks angrily to you.
   b. you see someone who is nice looking and assume that she is self-centered and arrogant.
   c. you go to a foreign country and assume that everyone thinks the same way you do.
   d. you think someone is clumsy when he trips and drops his books.

4. **UNDERSTANDING THE CORE CONCEPT:** Implicit personality theories involve
   a. the assumptions that people make about each other's motives, intentions, and behaviors.
   b. assumptions about themselves that people want to hide from others.
   c. unconscious instincts, memories, and conflicts.
   d. opinions that people privately hold about others but will not say openly.

ANSWERS: 1. c 2. d 3. d 4. a

PERSONALITY: THE STATE OF THE ART

Everyone acknowledges that no single theory explains everything we lump under "personality" as the enduring psychological characteristics that provide continuity to our behavior and distinguish one person from another. Modern theories have a more scientific base than did those of Freud, Jung, Horney, and their contemporaries. Moreover, as Mischel tells us, the situation may be even more influential than the personality in determining what we do.

So where does that leave the cutting edges in the science of personality? Some researchers are looking for genetic connections to temperament and the major personality traits. There have been no "breakthroughs" yet—but stay tuned. Others, as we have noted, are exploring how families, cultures, and gender influence personality. Our guess is that one of the most volatile areas for personality research in the coming decade is going to involve neuroscience. We will gain a deeper understanding of how personality is manifested in the brain, especially in brain chemistry. We hope, however, that an emphasis on the *nature* of personality doesn't make researchers loose sight of its *nurture*—of how experience can alter the very circuits and chemicals that the brain uses to create personality.

USING PSYCHOLOGY TO LEARN PSYCHOLOGY

Your Academic Locus of Control

Although an internal or external locus of control can be a central feature of your personality, your perceived locus of control can also change from situation to situation. When you are speaking in front of a group, for example, you may feel that the situation is beyond your control, but when you are on skis you may feel that your are fully the master of your fate. And what about your education? Do you have a sense of internal or external control with regard to—say—your grade in psychology?

An external locus of control concerning grades poses a danger for the college student because college life is so full of distractions and temptations. If you believe that your grades are largely beyond your control, you can easily be driven by the enticements of the moment and let your studies slide. This attitude can, of course, become a self-fulfilling prophecy that ruins your grades not only in psychology but across the board.

The following questions will help you discover your academic locus of control:

- On a test do you often find that, even if you know the material, anxiety wipes the information from your memory?

- On a test do you often know the material well but find that the test is unfair or covers material that the teacher did not indicate would be on the test?

- Do you feel poorly motivated to cope with college-level work?

- Are you so easily distracted that you can never quite get around to studying?

- Do you believe that some people are born to be good students and some are not?

- Do you feel that you have no control over the grades you receive?

- Do you feel that you are not smart enough to cope with college-level work?

- Do you feel that success in college is largely a matter of luck?

If you answered "yes" to several of these questions, then you probably have an *external* locus of control with respect to your college work—an attitude that can hamper your chances of college success. What can be done? Nothing, if you are completely convinced that your success in college is beyond your control. If, however, you are open to the idea of establishing more control over your college experience, here are several suggestions:

- Get help with test anxiety from your counseling center or learning resources center.

- Find a tutor either among friends or at your learning resources center.

- Talk to your professors individually: Ask them to give you some pointers on what they consider to be especially important (and testable) in their classes.

- Go to your college's learning resources center and get an assessment of your strengths and weaknesses and of your interest patterns. Then make a

plan to correct your weaknesses (e.g., with remedial classes in your weak areas) and build on your strengths. Select a major that capitalizes on your strengths and interests.

We would wish you good luck—but that's only of concern to externalizers!

CHAPTER SUMMARY

● WHAT FORCES SHAPE OUR PERSONALITIES?

The psychodynamic, humanistic, and cognitive theories all seek to explain the influences that mold our personalities. Freud's psychoanalytic theory states that the personality is shaped by unconscious desires and conflicts. None of our thoughts or behaviors happen by accident, according to the principle of psychic determinism. Early childhood experiences also have a strong influence on personality, as the child goes through predictable psychosexual stages in which conflicts are dealt with unconsciously. Freud believed that the personality consisted of three main structures, the id (the reservoir of unconscious desires), the ego (the largely conscious part of the mind), and the superego (which contains the conscience and the ego ideal). Part of the ego, involving the ego defense mechanisms, operates outside of consciousness. One of these defense mechanisms, projection, is the basis for widely used projective tests.

Freud's theory has been extremely influential. Still, critics fault Freud's work for being scientifically unsound, a poor basis for prediction, and unfair to women. Modern psychology also suggests that the unconscious mind is less clever and purposeful than Freud believed.

Other psychodynamic theories, such as those proposed by Jung and Horney, also assume that personality is a dynamic process that involves strong and often-conflicting motives and emotions. Each of these neo-Freudians, however, emphasizes different aspects of personality. Jung proposed a collective unconscious, populated by archetypes. He also proposed that people fall into certain personality types, characterized especially by tendencies to introversion and extraversion. Horney, on the other hand, emphasized conscious processes, basic anxiety, and feminist issues in personality theory. Healthy people, she said, move toward others, while neurotic people move against others.

The humanistic theories, such as those of Maslow and Rogers, argue that people are naturally driven toward self-actualization, but this tendency can be suppressed by unhealthy conditions and perceptions. Maslow emphasized a hierarchy of needs, suggesting that when the deficiency needs are met, a person is more likely to pursue self-actualization. Rogers taught that the fully functioning person has a positive self-concept that is congruent with reality, while mental disorder arises from incongruence. High self-esteem is more likely which a child comes from a family that provides unconditional positive regard. The human-

istic theories have had considerable impact on psychotherapy, but they have been criticized for lacking a strong scientific base.

The social-cognitive theories, by contrast, do have a scientific basis. Bandura's theory suggests that personality is shaped by observational learning. This occurs in an interaction of cognition, behavior, and the environment known as reciprocal determinism. According to Rotter's locus-of-control theory, those with an internal locus are more likely to feel they can control events in their lives than those who have an external locus of control. The social-cognitive theories are much more limited in scope than the psychodynamic or humanistic theories.

Modern theories of personality, unlike those of Freud, Jung, Horney, and the other psychodynamic theorists, have not attempted to provide comprehensive explanations for all aspects of personality. Emphasis has turned to the individual acting in a social environment, such as the family. Other emphases include cultural influences on personality, as well as an awareness of gender differences.

● **According to the psychodynamic, humanistic, and cognitive theories, personality is a continuously changing process, shaped by our internal needs and cognitions and by external pressures from the social environment.**

● WHAT PERSISTENT PATTERNS ARE FOUND IN PERSONALITY?

Temperament, trait, and type theories are descriptive approaches to personality with a long history stretching back to the ancient Greeks. Modern trait/type/temperament theories are frequently used as the basis for diagnosis, personnel selection, and psychological testing. *Temperament* refers to innate personality dispositions, which may be tied to factors in the brain. Traits give personality consistency across situations and may be influenced by both heredity and learning. Many psychologists now agree on the Big Five traits. Trait assessment is the basis for many psychological tests. The person–situation controversy, however, has raised questions about the relative contribution of personality traits and situations to behavior. Type theory is seen especially in the contro-versial and widely used MBTI, based on Jung's personality typology.

● **Another approach describes personality in terms of stable patterns known as temperaments, traits, and types.**

● WHAT "THEORIES" DO PEOPLE USE TO UNDERSTAND EACH OTHER?

People everywhere deal with each other on the basis of their implicit personality theories, which simplify the task of understanding others. Implicit theories may rely on naive assumptions, such as the fundamental attribution error. Moreover, cross-cultural psychologists have found that the assumptions people make about personality and behavior vary widely across cultures—

depending especially on whether the culture emphasizes individualism or collectivism. Most psychologists develop their own eclectic theories of personality by combining ideas from various perspectives.

● People everywhere develop implicit assumptions ("folk theories") about personality, but these assumptions vary in important ways across cultures.

REVIEW TEST

For each of the following items, choose the single best answer. The correct answers appear at the end.

1. Which sort of personality theory would most likely emphasize unconscious motivation?
   a. psychodynamic theory
   b. trait theory
   c. humanistic theory
   d. cognitive theory

2. Which one of the following is an ego defense mechanism that may cause us to forget unpleasant or threatening experiences?
   a. displacement   c. regression
   b. projection   d. repression

3. Critics fault Freud's psychoanalytic theory because it
   a. does not explain the source of mental disorders.
   b. has no theory of psychological development.
   c. has little basis in scientific research.
   d. has had little impact on popular culture.

4. One of the biggest differences between Freud and Jung can be seen in Jung's idea of
   a. the collective unconscious.
   b. locus of control.
   c. implicit personality theories.
   d. shyness.

5. The humanistic theorists were the first to emphasize
   a. unconscious motives.
   b. mental disorder.
   c. the healthy personality.
   d. how people are similar to other animals.

6. According to Rogers, children may grow up with feelings of guilt and anxiety in homes where

   a. parents are not good role models.
   b. one of the parents is absent most of the time.
   c. parental love is conditional on good behavior.
   d. the parents are in conflict with each other.

7. Reciprocal determinism involves the interaction of
   a. the id, ego, and superego.
   b. self-actualization, unconditional positive regard, and the phenomenal field.
   c. the conscious mind, the conscience, and the collective unconscious.
   d. cognitions, behavior, and the environment.

8. Explaining why a new classmate does not seem attractive, your friend remarks, "I don't much like thin people, because they're too nervous!" This assumption reveals that your friend favors a _____ theory of personality.
   a. type
   b. psychodynamic
   c. cognitive
   d. collectivistic

9. Which of the following is not one of the Big Five personality factors?
   a. neuroticism
   b. intelligence
   c. conscientiousness
   d. openness to experience

10. Your implicit theory of personality would help you
   a. know that a friend needs comforting when she loses her job.
   b. laugh at a joke.
   c. shout at a friend when you are angry at your employer.
   d. feel rewarded when you receive your paycheck.

ANSWERS: 1.a 2.d 3.c 4.a 5.c 6.c 7.d 8.a 9.b 10.a

KEY TERMS

Personality (p. 444)

Psychoanalysis (p. 446)

Psychoanalytic theory (p. 446)

Unconscious (p. 446)

Libido (p. 447)

Id (p. 447)

Superego (p. 447)

Ego (p. 447)

Psychosexual stages (p. 448)

Oedipus complex (p. 449)

Identification (p. 449)

Penis envy (p. 449)

OUR RECOMMENDED BOOKS AND VIDEOS

BOOKS

Angier, N. (1999). *Woman: An intimate geography.* Boston: Houghton Mifflin. Pulitzer Prize-winning writer Natalie Angier discusses, with wit and expertise, how the female body distinguishes the development of the "feminine" personality and the experience of becoming and being a woman.

Carducci, B. J., with Golant, S. (1999). *Shyness: A bold new approach.* New York: HarperCollins. Not a workbook for "changing" shy people into extroverts, this book is rather a set of strategies for living a "successfully shy life," including managing shyness when meeting others, working, falling in love, making small talk, and caring for shy children.

Janda, L. H. (1996). *The psychologist's book of self-tests: 25 love, sex, intelligence, career, and personality tests developed by professionals to reveal the real you.* New York: Perigee/Berkley. Just remember that any self-report technique depends on *your* responses—meaning that, to a large extent, you already know or can somewhat control the "outcome." Nonetheless, well constructed, valid, and reliable psychological assessments can cast individual data in a new light according to various theories of development, individual difference, and aptitude.

Kagan, J. (1995). *Galen's prophecy: Temperament in human nature.* Boulder, CO: Westview Press. Since ancient times, healers have believed each human being is born one of a few types: introvert or extrovert; sanguine, choleric, melancholy, or phlegmatic—and dozens of other typologies based on bodily shape or humors. The author, a renowned child psychologist, examines the scientific evidence for two basic types—shy (introverted) or bold—and how these inborn patterns determine one's life experiences in adjustment, work, and love.

VIDEOS

Catch Me If You Can. (2002, color, 141 min.). Directed by Steven Spielberg; starring Leonardo DiCaprio, Tom Hanks, Christopher Walken. Based on the best-selling memoir of con artist Frank Abagnale, Jr. (subtitled *The True Story of a Real Fake*), this is the story of a young man who succeeded in impersonating an airline pilot, pediatrician, hospital supervisor, assistant attorney general, and college professor—but was he motivated by greed or by love for his failed father?

The Cooler. (2003, color, 101 min.). Directed by Wayne Kramer; starring William H. Macy, Alec Baldwin, Maria Bello. In a Las Vegas casino, one employee, merely by his presence, can "cool" the luck of overly successful gamblers—until he finds love and happiness and loses both his deadly touch and his usefulness to his ruthless employer. A different example of internal versus external locus of control!

Identity. (2003, color, 90 min.). Directed by James Mangold; starring John Cusack, Ray Liotta, Amanda Peet, Alfred Molina. Ten strangers, trapped together in a storm-bound motel, deal in dramatically different ways with the threat of a killer amongst them—and all seem to have some mysterious connection with a legal proceeding taking place in a distant location.

The Talented Mr. Ripley. (1999, color, 139 min.). Directed by Anthony Minghella; starring Matt Damon, Gwyneth Paltrow, Jude Law. A poor, amoral young man, sent to retrieve a wayward heir from his European adventures, soon befriends the heir and tragically envies his target's beautiful life. Based on the late Patricia Highsmith's novel, the original U.S. film title listed Ripley's many personality traits and states: "The Mysterious, Yearning, Secretive, Sad, Lonely, Troubled, Confused, Loving, Musical, Gifted, Intelligent, Beautiful, Tender, Sensitive, Haunted, Passionate, Talented Mr. Ripley."

The Truman Show. (1998, color, 102 min.). Directed by Peter Weir; starring Jim Carrey, Laura Linney, Ed Harris. In an eerie tale of a phony life, Truman Burbank, born and raised to be a character living his life in a 24-hour television program, longs to see the world out there—unaware that his world is actually an enormous sound stage, and the "people" in his life merely roles played by actors and extras. The film raises questions not only about the origins of personality and the reality of relationships, but also the price of fame.

Key Question
Chapter Outline

 CORE CONCEPTS

 Psychology in
Your Life

What Is Psychological Disorder?

Changing Concepts of Psychological Disorder

Indicators of Abnormality

▼

The medical model takes a "disease" view, while psychology sees psychological disorder as an interaction of biological, mental, social, and behavioral factors.

A Caution to Readers

If you find that you have some signs of psychological disorder, don't jump to conclusions.

How Are Psychological Disorders Classified?

Overview of the *DSM-IV* Classification System

Mood Disorders

Anxiety Disorders

Somatoform Disorders

Dissociative Disorders

Eating Disorders

Schizophrenia

Personality Disorders

Developmental Disorders

Adjustment Disorders and Other Conditions

▼

The *DSM-IV*, the most widely used system, classifies disorders by their mental and behavioral symptoms.

Shyness

If you have it, it doesn't have to be permanent. (And, by the way, it's not a mental disorder.)

What Are the Consequences of Labeling People?

Diagnostic Labels Can Compound the Problem

The Cultural Context of Psychological Disorder

▼

Ideally, accurate diagnoses lead to proper treatments, but diagnoses may also become labels that depersonalize individuals and ignore the social and cultural contexts in which their problems arise.

The Plea of Insanity

It's not a psychological or psychiatric term, and, contrary to popular opinion, it is a defense that is seldom used.

Psychological Disorders: The State of the Art

USING PSYCHOLOGY TO LEARN PSYCHOLOGY:
Diagnosing Your Friends and Family

Psychological Disorders

THE VOLUNTEERS KNEW they were on their own. If they managed to get into the hospital, the five men and three women could only get out by convincing the staff that they were sane. None had ever been diagnosed with a mental illness, but perhaps they were not so "normal" after all: Would a normal person lie to get into such a place? In fact, all were collaborators in an experiment designed to find out whether normality would be recognized in a mental hospital.

The experimenter, David Rosenhan—himself one of the pseudopatients—suspected that terms such as *sanity, insanity, schizophrenia, mental illness,* and *abnormal* might have fuzzier boundaries than the psychiatric community thought. He also suspected that some strange behaviors seen in mental patients might originate in the abnormal atmosphere of the mental hospital, rather than in the patients themselves. To test these ideas, Rosenhan and his collaborators decided to see how mental hospital personnel would deal with patients who were not mentally ill.

Individually, they applied for admission at different hospitals, complaining that they had recently heard voices that seemed to say "empty," "hollow," and "thud." Aside from this, they claimed no other symptoms of disorder. All used false names, and the four who were mental health professionals gave false occupations—but, apart from these fibs, the subjects answered all questions truthfully. They tried to act normally, although the prospect of entering the alien hospital environment made them feel anxious; they also worried about not being admitted and—worse yet—being exposed as frauds.

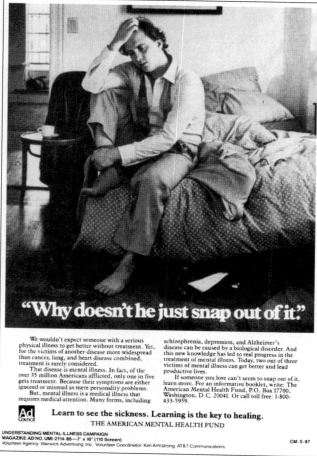

"Why doesn't he just snap out of it."

We wouldn't expect someone with a serious physical illness to get better without treatment. Yet, for the victims of another disease more widespread than cancer, lung, and heart disease combined, treatment is rarely considered.

That disease is mental illness. In fact, of the over 35 million Americans afflicted, only one in five gets treatment. Because their symptoms are either ignored or misread as mere personality problems.

But, mental illness is a medical illness that requires medical attention. Many forms, including

schizophrenia, depression, and Alzheimer's disease can be caused by a biological disorder. And this new knowledge has led to real progress in the treatment of mental illness. Today, two out of three victims of mental illness can get better and lead productive lives.

If someone you love can't seem to snap out of it, learn more. For an informative booklet, write: The American Mental Health Fund, P.O. Box 17700, Washington, D.C. 20041. Or call toll free: 1-800-433-5959.

Learn to see the sickness. Learning is the key to healing.

THE AMERICAN MENTAL HEALTH FUND

UNDERSTANDING MENTAL ILLNESS CAMPAIGN
MAGAZINE AD NO. UMI-2114-86—7" x 10" (110 Screen)
Volunteer Agency: Warwick Advertising, Inc. Volunteer Coordinator: Kim Armstrong. AT&T Communications.   CM-5-87

● Advertisements like the one shown here have gone a long way toward correcting our views of mental illness and creating sympathy for its sufferers.

CONNECTION CHAPTER 14

Social psychology has taught us about the *power of the situation*—that is, the powerful and often unrecognized influence that the social context has on our behavior.

Their concerns about fraud vanished quickly, for all readily gained admittance at 12 different hospitals (some did it twice). All but one were diagnosed with "schizophrenia," a major psychological disorder often accompanied by hearing imaginary voices.

After admission, the pseudopatients made no further claims of hearing voices or any other abnormal symptoms. Indeed, all wanted to be on their best behavior to gain release. Their only apparent "deviance" involved taking notes on the experience—at first privately and later publicly, when they found that the staff paid little attention. The nursing records indicated that, when the staff did notice, they interpreted the note-taking as part of the patient's illness. (One comment: "Patient engages in writing behavior.") But in spite of the absence of abnormal symptoms, it took an average of 19 days for the pseudopatients to convince the hospital staff that they were ready for discharge. One unfortunate individual wasn't released for almost two months.

Two main findings from this classic study jarred the psychiatric community to its core. First, *no professional staff member at any of the hospitals ever realized that any of Rosenhan's pseudopatients was a fraud.* Of course, the staff may have assumed that the patients had been ill at the time of admission and had improved during their hospitalization. But that possibility did not let the professionals off Rosenhan's hook: Despite apparently normal behavior, not one pseudopatient was ever labeled as "normal" or "well" while in the hospital. And, upon discharge, they were still seen as having schizophrenia—but "in remission."

The mistaken diagnosis does not suggest that the hospital staff members were unskilled or unfeeling. The fact that they did not detect the pseudopatients' normal behavior is probably because they spent little time observing and interacting with the patients. Most of the time they kept to themselves in a glassed-in central office that patients called "the cage." As Rosenhan (1973) said:

> It could be a mistake, and a very unfortunate one, to consider that what happened to us derived from malice or stupidity on the part of the staff. Quite the contrary, our overwhelming impression of them was of people who really cared, who were committed and who were uncommonly intelligent. Where they failed, as they sometimes did painfully, it would be more accurate to attribute those failures to the environment in which they, too, found themselves than to personal callousness. Their perceptions and behavior were controlled by the situation . . . (p. 257)

A second finding tells us volumes about the patients and the nature of psychological disorder itself: *To everyone's surprise, the hospital patients readily detected the ruse, even though the professional staff did not.* The pseudopatients reported that the other patients regularly voiced their suspicions: "You're not crazy. You're a journalist or a professor. . . . You're checking up on the hospital." In his report of this experience, entitled

"On Being Sane in Insane Places," Rosenhan (1973) noted dryly: "The fact that the patients often recognized normality when staff did not raises important questions" (p. 252). You will hear the echo of these "important questions" as we critically examine the medical view of mental disorder in this chapter.

Please note that Rosenhan did not deny the existence of psychological disorders. People do suffer the anguish of **psychopathology** (also called *mental disorder or mental illness*). According to a study conducted by the National Institutes of Mental Health, about 15.4% of the population suffers from diagnosable mental health problems. Another study found that, during any given year, the behaviors of over 56 million Americans meet the criteria for a diagnosable psychological disorder (Carson et al., 1996; Regier et al., 1993). Over the lifespan, as many as 32% of Americans will suffer from some psychological disorder (Regier et al., 1988).

Neither did Rosenhan deny that the initial diagnoses given his pseudopatients were justified. After all, they claimed to be hearing voices—a strong indicator of abnormality. Rosenhan's interest in mental hospitals centered on the assumptions made there about people who have been diagnosed with a "mental illness." These conditions, he argued, blinded caregivers to the needs of their patients. As we look at the problem of diagnosing and describing psychological disorder in this chapter, it will be helpful to keep Rosenhan's study in mind. Even though this research was done some 30 years ago, the terms *abnormal, disorder,* and *mental illness* still carry meanings that can prevent us from seeing people with psychological problems as individuals.

WHAT IS PSYCHOLOGICAL DISORDER?

Distinguishing "normal" from "abnormal" is no simple task. Consider, for example, how you would classify such eccentric personalities as Robin Williams or Madonna or Marilyn Manson. And what about a soldier who risks his or her life in combat: Is that "normal"? Or consider a grief-stricken woman who is unable to return to her normal routine three months after her husband died: Does she have a psychological disorder?

More extreme disorders are more easily detected. Clinicians (specialists in the treatment of psychological problems) look for three classic symptoms of severe psychopathology: *hallucinations, delusions,* and extreme *affective disturbances*. **Hallucinations** are false sensory experiences, such as hearing nonexistent voices (as Rosenhan's pseudopatients said they did). **Delusions** are extreme disorders of thinking that involve persistent false beliefs. If you think you are the President of the United States (and you are not), you have a symptom of psychopathology. Or if you think people are out to "get" you, you may also have a delusional disorder. Similarly, those whose **affect** (emotion) is characteristically depressed, anxious, or manic—or those who seem to have no emotional response at all—have other possible signs of severe psychological disorder.

Beyond such extreme signs of distress, the experts do not always agree, however. What is abnormal and what is not become a judgment call, a judgment made more difficult because no sharp boundary separates normal from abnormal thought and behavior. It may be helpful to think of psychological disorder as part of a continuum ranging from the absence of disorder to severe disorder, as shown in Table 12.1. The big idea here is that people with

■ **Psychopathology** Any pattern of emotions, behaviors, or thoughts inappropriate to the situation and leading to personal distress or the inability to achieve important goals. Other terms having essentially the same meaning include *mental illness, mental disorder,* and *psychological disorder.*

■ **Hallucinations** False sensory experiences that may suggest mental disorder. Hallucinations can have other causes, such as drugs or sensory isolation.

■ **Delusions** Extreme disorders of thinking, involving persistent false beliefs. Delusions are the hallmark of paranoid disorders.

■ **Affect** A term referring to emotion or mood.

TABLE 12.1 | The Spectrum of Mental Disorder

Mental disorder occurs on a spectrum that ranges from the absence of signs of pathology to severe disturbances, such as are found in major depression or schizophrenia. The important point is that there is no sharp distinction that divides those with mental disorders from those who are "normal."

No Disorder	Mild Disorder	Moderate Disorder	Severe Disorder
Absence of signs of psychological disorder	Few signs of distress or other indicators of psychological disorder	Indicators of disorder are more pronounced and occur more frequently	Clear signs of psychological disorder, which dominate the person's life
Absence of behavior problems	Few behavior problems; responses usually appropriate to the situation	More distinct behavior problems; behavior is often inappropriate to the situation	Severe and frequent behavior problems; behavior is usually inappropriate to the situation
No problems with interpersonal relationships	Few difficulties with relationships	More frequent difficulties with relationships	Many poor relationships or lack of relationships with others

psychological disorders are not in a class by themselves. Rather, their disorders are an exaggeration of normal responses.

In this section of the chapter, we will focus on two contrasting views of psychological disorder. One, coming to us from medicine, is sometimes called the "medical model." It portrays mental problems much as it does physical disorders: as sickness or disease. The other view, a psychological view, sees psychological disorders as the result of multiple factors that can involve both nature and nurture. As our Core Concept puts it:

> The medical model takes a "disease" view, while psychology sees psychological disorder as an interaction of biological, mental, social, and behavioral factors.

No matter how we conceptualize psychopathology, nearly everyone agrees that psychological disorder is common. It touches the daily lives of millions. It can be insidious, working its way into thoughts and feelings, diminishing its victims' emotional and physical well-being, along with their personal and family relationships. And it can create an enormous financial burden through lost productivity, lost wages, and the high costs of prolonged treatment. Yet the way people think of psychopathology does have a consequence: As we will see, it determines how they attempt to treat it—whether with drugs, charms, rituals, talk, torture, brain surgery, hospitalization, or commitment to an "insane asylum."

In this section of the chapter, we will find that the two main ways of looking at psychopathology, the medical model and the psychological view, are often at odds. Some of this conflict is territorial, resulting from professional infighting. But some of the conflict has historical roots, as we shall see next.

Changing Concepts of Psychological Disorder

Before December 10, 1973, homosexuality was considered an illness. But on that day the American Psychiatric Association voted to drop homosexuality from its list of officially recognized disorders. The membership had decided that this sexual orientation was not associated with mental problems, a decision which has since been shown repeatedly to be accurate—with the understandable exception of problems related to the stress of discrimination (Cochran et al., 2003; Meyer, 2003). This change, however, was only one of the most recent in a continuously evolving concept of mental disorder that stretches back thousands of years.

Historical Roots   In the ancient world, people assumed that supernatural powers were everywhere, accounting for good fortune, disease, and disaster. In this context, psychopathology was believed to be caused by demons and spirits that had taken possession of the person's mind and body (Sprock & Blashfield, 1991). If you had been living in the ancient world, your daily routine would have included rituals aimed at outwitting or placating these supernatural beings.

In about 400 B.C., the Greek physician Hippocrates took humanity's first step toward a scientific view of mental disturbance when he declared that abnormal behavior has physical causes. He taught his disciples to interpret the symptoms of psychopathology as an imbalance among four body fluids called "humors": blood, phlegm (mucus), black bile, and yellow bile. Those with an excess of black bile, for example, were inclined to melancholy or depression, while those who had an abundance of blood were sanguine, or warmhearted. With this revolutionary idea, Hippocrates incorporated mental disorder into medicine, and his view influenced educated people in the Western world until the end of the Roman Empire.

Then, in the Middle Ages, superstition eclipsed the Hippocratic model of mental disorder. Under the influence of the medieval Church, physicians and clergy reverted to the old ways of explaining abnormality in terms of demons and witchcraft. In these harsh times, the Inquisition was driven by the belief that unusual behavior was the work of the Devil. The "cure" involved attempts to drive out the demons who possessed the unfortunate victim's soul. As a

◀ **CONNECTION** CHAPTER 11

Hippocrates' humor theory was a theory of *temperaments*.

Humors	Origin	Temperament
blood	heart	sanguine (cheerful)
choler (yellow bile)	liver	choleric (angry)
melancholer (black bile)	spleen	melancholy (depressed)
phlegm	brain	phlegmatic (sluggish)

● **FIGURE 12.1**   Hippocrates' Humor Theory

In Hippocrates' view, mental disorder was caused by an excess of the body fluids, or "humors."

● A painting of the witchcraft trials held in Salem, Massachusetts, in 1692. Twenty people were executed before the hysteria subsided.

result, thousands of mentally disturbed people were tortured and executed all across the European continent. And, in 1692, the same view of mental disorder led the young colony in Salem, Massachusetts, to convict and execute a group of its residents for witchcraft (Karlsen, 1998). A group of young girls had frightened the community with a rash of convulsions and reports of sensory disturbances that were interpreted as signs of demonic possession. A modern analysis of the Salem witch trials has concluded that the girls were probably suffering from poisoning by a fungus growing on rye grain—the same fungus that produces the hallucinogenic drug LSD (Caporeal, 1976; Matossian, 1982, 1989).

The Medical Model   In the latter part of the 18th century, the "disease" view that originated with Hippocrates re-emerged with the rise of science. The resulting **medical model** held that mental disorders are *diseases* of the mind that, like ordinary physical diseases, have objective causes and require specific treatments. People began to perceive individuals with psychological problems as sick (suffering from illness), rather than as demon-possessed or immoral. And what a difference a new theory made! Treating mental disorders by torture and abuse no longer made sense. The new view of mental illness brought sweeping reforms that were implemented in "asylums" for the "insane." In this supportive atmosphere, many patients actually improved—even thrived—on rest, contemplation, and simple but useful work (Maher & Maher, 1985). Unfortunately, political pressures eventually turned the initially therapeutic asylums into overcrowded warehouses of neglect.

Despite such problems, however, the medical model was unquestionably an improvement over the demon model. Yet modern psychologists think that the medical model has its own weaknesses. They point out that the assumption of "disease" leads to a doctor-knows-best approach in which the therapist takes all the responsibility for diagnosing the illness and prescribing treatment. Under this assumption, the patient may become a passive recipient of medication and advice, rather than an active participant in treatment. Psychologists believe that this attitude wrongly encourages dependency on the doctor, encourages unnecessary drug therapy, and does little to help the patient develop good coping skills.

Not incidentally, a doctor-knows-best approach also takes responsibility away from psychologists and gives it to psychiatrists. Psychologists bristle at the medical model's implication that their treatment of mental "diseases" should be done under the supervision of a physician. In effect, the medical model assigns psychologists to second-class professional status. As you can see, ownership of the whole territory of psychological disorder is hotly contested.

Psychological Models   What does psychology have to offer in place of the medical model? Most clinical psychologists have now turned to a combination of psychological perspectives that derive from *behaviorism, cognitive psychology, social learning,* and *biological psychology.* We will look at these more closely.

The Social–Cognitive–Behavioral Approach   Modern psychologists often combine ideas from perspectives that were once considered incompatible: cognitive psychology and behaviorism. In brief, cognitive psychology looks inward, emphasizing mental processes, while behaviorism looks outward, emphasizing the influence of the environment. As we saw in the chapter on learning,

◀ **CONNECTION: CHAPTER 1**

Psychiatrists, but not psychologists, are trained in medicine.

■ **Medical model**   The view that mental disorders are diseases that, like ordinary physical diseases, have objective physical causes and require specific treatments.

bridges between these perspectives were built by social-learning theorists and others. As a result, a major shift in psychological thinking in recent years now views these traditions as complementary, rather than competitive. Moreover, both sides now acknowledge that cognition and behavior usually occur in a social context, requiring a *social perspective*.

The *behavioral perspective* tells us that abnormal behaviors can be acquired in the same fashion as healthy behaviors—through behavioral learning. This view focuses on our behavior and the environmental conditions, such as rewards, punishments, and social pressures, that maintain it. For example, the behavioral perspective would suggest that a fear of public speaking could result from a humiliating public speaking experience and a subsequent avoidance of any opportunity to develop public speaking skills.

The *cognitive perspective*, by contrast, suggests that we must also consider how people *perceive* or *think about* themselves and their relations with other people. Among the important cognitive variables are these: whether people believe they have control over events in their lives (an internal or external locus of control), how they cope with threat and stress, and whether they attribute behavior to situational or personal factors (Bandura, 1986).

The **social–cognitive–behavioral approach,** then, is a psychological alternative to the medical model, combining three of psychology's major perspectives. Typical of this approach is Albert Bandura's theory of *reciprocal determinism,* which proposes that behavior, cognition, and social/environmental factors all influence each other. From this viewpoint, a fear of public speaking can be understood as a product of behavioral learning, cognitive learning, and social learning.

The Biopsychology of Mental Disorder Although most psychologists have reservations about the medical model, they do not deny the influence of biology on thought and behavior. Modern biopsychology assumes that some mental disturbances involve the brain or nervous system in some way, and this view is taking an increasingly prominent position. An explosion of research in neuroscience during the past decade confirms the role of the brain as a complex organ whose mental functions depend on a delicate balance of chemicals and ever-changing circuits. Subtle alterations in the brain's tissue or in its chemical messengers—the neurotransmitters—can profoundly alter thoughts and behaviors. Genetic factors, brain injury, infection, and learning are a few factors that can tip the balance toward psychopathology.

On the heredity front, the Human Genome Project has specified the complete human genetic package. Many psychologists see this accomplishment as a ripe opportunity for specialists in behavioral genetics who are searching for genes associated with specific psychological disorders (Plomin, 2003). It won't be easy, however. So far, only a few genetic abnormalities have been linked with specific mental problems, despite the fact that some of the most severe pathologies, such as schizophrenia and bipolar disorder, do run in families. Most such disorders are likely to result from multiple genes interacting with forces in the environment (Boomsma et al., 1997). Watch the news for further developments.

Indicators of Abnormality

While clinicians sometimes disagree about the *etiology* (causes) of psychological disorders, they usually agree broadly on the indicators of abnormality (Rosenhan & Seligman, 1995). What are these indicators? Earlier we noted that hallucinations, delusions, and extreme affective changes are signs of severe mental disorder. But many psychological problems don't reveal themselves in

● Phillippe Pinel was one of the first to humanely treat inmates with mental disorders. He is best known for removing the shackles from from mental patients at La Bicêtre hospital in Paris in 1792. To almost everyone's amazement, the patients responded favorably.

■ **Social–cognitive–behavioral approach** A psychological alternative to the medical model that views psychological disorder through a combination of the social, cognitive, and behavioral perspectives.

such stark ways. Accordingly, clinicians also look for the following more subtle signs that may also indicate psychological disturbances, ranging from mild to severe (see Table 12.1):

- *Distress:* Does the individual show unusual or prolonged levels of unease or anxiety? For example, almost anyone will get nervous before an important test, but feeling so overwhelmed with unpleasant emotions that concentration becomes impossible for long periods is a sign of abnormality.

- *Maladaptiveness:* Does the person act in ways that make others fearful or interfere with his or her well-being? We can see this, for example, in someone who drinks so heavily that she or he cannot hold down a job or drive a car without endangering others.

- *Irrationality:* Does the person act or talk in ways that are irrational or incomprehensible to others? A woman who converses with her long-dead sister, whose voice she hears in her head, is behaving irrationally. Likewise, behavior or emotional responses that are inappropriate to the situation, such as laughing at the scene of a tragedy, show irrational loss of contact with one's social environment.

- *Unpredictability:* Does the individual behave erratically and inconsistently at different times or from one situation to another, as if experiencing a loss of control? For example, a child who suddenly smashes a fragile toy with his fist for no apparent reason is behaving unpredictably. Similarly, a manager who treats employees compassionately one day and abusively the next is acting unpredictably.

- *Unconventionality and undesirable behavior:* Does the person behave in ways that are statistically rare and violate social norms of what is legally or morally acceptable or desirable? Being merely "unusual" is not a sign of abnormality—so feel free to dye your hair red and green at Christmastime. But if you decide to act beyond the bounds of social acceptability by strolling naked in the mall, that would be considered abnormal.

Is the presence of just one indicator enough to demonstrate abnormality? It's a judgment call. Clinicians are more confident in labeling behavior as "abnormal" when two or more of the indicators are present. And, the more extreme and prevalent the indicators are, the more confident psychologists can be about identifying an abnormal condition. Moreover, none of these criteria is a condition shared by all forms of disorder that we will describe later in this chapter. Different diagnoses, we shall see, include different combinations from the above list.

While these indicators may suggest a disorder, the clinician still must decide which disorder it is. This can be difficult, because psychopathology takes many forms. Some diagnoses may have a familiar ring: *depression, phobias,* and *panic disorder.* You may be less well acquainted with others, such as *conversion disorder* or *catatonic schizophrenia.* In all, a bewildering 300-plus specific varieties of psychopathology are described in the *Diagnostic and Statistical Manual of Mental Disorders* (4th edition), known by clinicians and researchers as the *DSM-IV* ("DSM-four") and used by mental health professionals of all backgrounds to describe and diagnose psychopathology. So influential is this system that we will devote the entire middle section of this chapter to an explanation of it.

● Behaviors that make other people feel uncomfortable or threatened may be a sign of abnormality.

PSYCHOLOGY IN YOUR LIFE: A CAUTION TO READERS

As you read about the symptoms of psychological disorder, you are likely to wonder about your own mental health. All students studying abnormal psychology face this hazard. To see what we mean, you might answer the following questions, which are based on the indicators of abnormality discussed earlier.

1. Have you had periods of time when you felt "blue" for no apparent reason? (distress)

2. Have you ever gone to a party on a night when you knew you should be studying? (maladaptiveness)

3. Have you had an experience in which you thought you heard or saw something that wasn't really there? (irrationality)

4. Have you had a flash of temper in which you said something that you later regretted? (unpredictability)

5. Have you had unusual thoughts that you told no one about? (unconventionality)

6. Have you made someone fearful or distressed because of something you said or did? (maladaptiveness)

● Sadness or crying is not necessarily a sign of abnormality. Some occasions call for sadness and tears.

The fact is that almost everyone will answer "yes" to at least one—and perhaps all—of these questions. This does not necessarily mean abnormality. Whether you, or anyone else, is normal or abnormal is a matter of degree and frequency—and clinical judgment.

So, as we take a close look at specific psychological disorders in the next section of the chapter, you will most likely find some symptoms that you have experienced. So will your classmates. Even though they may not say so, most other students will find themselves in one or more of the disorders that we will be studying. (A similar problem is common among medical students, who begin to notice that they, too, have symptoms of the physical diseases they learn about.) You should realize that *this is normal.* One reason, of course, that you may see yourself in this chapter arises from the fact that no sharp line separates psychopathology from normalcy. All psychological disorders involve exaggerations of normal tendencies. Moreover, people who are basically healthy may occasionally become depressed, for example— although they do not *stay* depressed or develop the depths of despair that clinically depressed people do. We are not suggesting that concerns about psychological disorder should be taken lightly, however. If, after reading this chapter, you suspect that you may have a problem, you should discuss it with a professional.

CHECK YOUR UNDERSTANDING

1. **RECALL:** In Rosenhan's study, who discovered that the "pseudopatients" were feigning mental illness?
   a. psychiatrists
   b. psychologists
   c. nurses and aides working on the ward
   d. other patients

2. **APPLICATION:** Which of the following symptoms most clearly suggests the presence of abnormality?
   a. hallucinations
   b. worries
   c. unusual behavior
   d. creativity

(continues)

3. **RECALL:** Hippocrates proposed that mental disorder was caused by
   a. possession by demons.
   b. an imbalance in four body fluids.
   c. a fungus growing on rye grain.
   d. traumatic memories in the unconscious.

4. **RECALL:** The behavioral perspective emphasizes the influence of
   _____, while the cognitive perspective emphasizes _____.
   a. the environment/mental processes
   b. conscious processes/unconscious processes
   c. heredity/environment
   d. medical factors/psychological factors

5. **UNDERSTANDING THE CORE CONCEPT:** Which of the
   following would be least likely to be noticed by a clinician using strictly
   the medical model of mental disorder?
   a. delusions
   b. severe disturbances in affect
   c. an unhealthy family environment
   d. a degenerative brain disease

ANSWERS: 1.d 2.a 3.b 4.a 5.c

HOW ARE PSYCHOLOGICAL DISORDERS CLASSIFIED?

Imagine that you have entered a music store looking for a particular CD. Anything you could possibly want is there, but the employees do not bother grouping albums by musical category: They just dump everything randomly into the bins. With so many selections, but no organization, shopping there would be impossible—which is why music stores never operate this way. Instead, they organize selections into categories, such as rock, blues, classical, rap, country, and jazz. In much the same way, the *Diagnostic and Statistical Manual of Mental Disorders* (4th ed.) brings order to the more than 300 recognized mental disorders. Usually called simply the **DSM-IV,** this manual represents the most widely used system for classifying such disorders. We will use it as the scheme for organizing the disorders we have selected for discussion in this chapter.

What is the organizing pattern employed by the *DSM-IV?* It groups nearly all recognized forms of psychopathology into categories, according to mental and behavioral symptoms, such as anxiety, depression, sexual problems, and substance abuse. Our Core Concept states:

> The DSM-IV, the most widely used system, classifies disorders by their mental and behavioral symptoms.

It would be impossible to cover all the recognized psychological disorders in this chapter. Therefore we must focus on those that you are most likely to encounter in daily life and in the study of psychopathology in more advanced courses.

Overview of the *DSM-IV* Classification System

The fourth edition of the *Diagnostic and Statistical Manual of Mental Disorders,* the *DSM-IV,* was published in 1994 by the American Psychiatric Association. Then, in 2000, that volume was given a midedition update, the *DSM-IV-TR* (TR means *Text Revision*). It offers practitioners a common and concise language for the description of psychopathology. It also contains criteria for diagnosing each of the disorders it covers. Even though the manual was developed primarily by psychiatrists, its terminology has been adopted by clinicians of

■ **DSM-IV** The fourth edition of the *Diagnostic and Statistical Manual of Mental Disorders,* published by the American Psychiatric Association; the most widely accepted psychiatric classification system in the United States.

all stripes, including psychiatrists, psychologists, and social workers. In addition, most health insurance companies use *DSM-IV* standards in determining what treatments they will pay for—a fact that gives this manual enormous economic clout.

The fourth edition of the *DSM* has brought with it some big changes. For example, it has banished the term *neurosis* from the official language of psychiatry (although you will frequently hear the term used in more casual conversation). Originally, a **neurosis** or *neurotic disorder* was conceived of as a relatively common pattern of subjective distress or self-defeating behavior that did not show signs of brain abnormalities or grossly irrational thinking. In short, a "neurotic" was someone who might be unhappy or dissatisfied but not considered dangerously ill or out of touch with reality. In the *DSM-IV*, the term *neurosis* has been dropped or replaced by the term *disorder* (Carson et al., 1996; Holmes, 2001). So, for example, "obsessive–compulsive neurosis" is now simply *obsessive–compulsive disorder*.

In contrast, a **psychosis** was previously thought to differ from neurosis in both the quality and severity of symptoms. A condition was frequently designated as *psychotic* if it involved profound disturbances in perception, rational thinking, or affect (emotion)—the three classic signs we discussed earlier. As a result, a clinician using previous editions of the *DSM* would have been more likely to diagnose severe depression, for example, as "psychotic." In the *DSM-IV*, the term *psychotic* is restricted mainly to a loss of contact with reality, as is found in the *schizophrenic disorders*, which we shall discuss below (Carson et al., 1996; Holmes, 2001).

As you may have surmised from its origins in psychiatry, the *DSM-IV* has close ties to the medical model of mental illness. Its language is the language of medicine—symptoms, syndromes, diagnoses, and diseases—and its final form is a curious mixture of science and tradition. (Note: It contains no diagnosis of "norm___.") Yet, in contrast with early versions of the manual, which had a distinc___ ___dian flavor, the *DSM-IV* manages, for the most part, to avo___ ___ theories of cause or treatment. It also differs from earl___ ___ *DSM* by giving extensive and specific descripti___ ___ each disorder. So, while the *DSM-IV* has its ___ ___mon language of psychological disorder___ ___.

L___ ___ disorders described in the *DSM-IV*. ___ ___gin will give you an overview of the sch___ ___sify these disorders. We begin with those ___ ___tremes of emotion: the *mood disorders*.

● Dutch artist Vincent Van Gogh showed signs of bipolar disorder. This problem seems to have a high incidence among very creative people.

> ***Mood Disorders:*** Extremes of Mood, from Mania to Depression
> ● Major depression
> ● Bipolar disorder

Mood Disorde___

Everyone, of course, experiences occasional strong or unpleasant emotional reactions. Emotionality is a normal part of our ability to interpret and adapt to our world. However, when moods career out of control, soaring to extreme elation or plunging to deep depression, the diagnosis will probably be one of the **mood disorders.** The clinician will also suspect an affective disorder when an individual's moods are consistently inappropriate to the situation. Here we will discuss the two best-known of these affective disturbances: *major depression* and *bipolar disorder*.

Major Depression If you fail an important examination, lose a job, or lose a love, it is normal to feel depressed for a while. If a close friend dies, it is also normal to feel depressed. But if you remain depressed for weeks or months, long after the depressing event has passed, then you may have the clinically

■ **Neurosis** Before the *DSM-IV*, this term was used as a label for subjective distress or self-defeating behavior that did not show signs of brain abnormalities or grossly irrational thinking.
■ **Psychosis** A disorder involving profound disturbances in perception, rational thinking, or affect.
■ **Mood disorders** Abnormal disturbances in emotion or mood, including bipolar disorder and unipolar disorder. Mood disorders are also called affective disorders.

■ Major depression A form of depression that does not alternate with mania.

significant condition called **major depression** or *major depressive disorder*, among the commonest of all major mental disturbances.

Novelist William Styron (1990) writes movingly about his own experience with severe depression. The pain he endured convinced him that clinical depression is much more than a bad mood: He characterized it as "a daily presence, blowing over me in cold gusts" and "a veritable howling tempest in the brain" that can begin with a "gray drizzle of horror." Major depression does not give way to manic periods.

Incidence Psychologist Martin Seligman (1973, 1975) has called depression the "common cold" of psychological problems. Nearly everyone has, at some time, suffered either major depression or a milder form that clinicians call *dysthymia*. In the United States, depression accounts for the majority of all mental hospital admissions, but it is still believed to be underdiagnosed and undertreated (Kessler et al, 2003; Robins et al., 1991). *The Wall Street Journal* estimates that depression costs Americans about $43 billion each year, including the costs of hospitalization, therapy, and lost productivity (Miller, 1993). But the human cost cannot be measured in dollars. Countless people in the throes of depression may feel worthless, lack appetite, withdraw from friends and family, have difficulty sleeping, lose their jobs, and become agitated or lethargic. In severe cases, they may also have psychotic distortions of reality. You can give yourself a quick evaluation for signs of depression in the box, "Do It Yourself! A Depression Check," on the facing page.

Most worrisome of all, suicide claims one in 50 depression sufferers (Bostwick & Pankratz, 2000). Significantly, suicide is a greater risk when a depressed person is on the way down in a depressive episode—or on the mend. That is, in the depths of depressive despair, there is usually no energy or will to do *anything,* much less carry out a plan for suicide.

Incidentally, we advise that a suicide threat always be taken seriously, even though you may think it is just a bid for attention—and even if you see no other signs of depression. Other factors may be at work. Abuse of alcohol or other drugs, for example, multiplies the likelihood of suicide, as do chronic physical diseases or brain abnormalities (Ezzell, 2003; Shneidman, 1987). You should direct any person who suggests he or she is thinking about suicide to a competent professional for help.

Cross-cultural studies indicate that depression is the single most prevalent form of disability around the globe (Holden, 2000a), although the incidence of major depression varies widely throughout the world, as Table 12.2 shows. While some of the variation may be the result of differences in reporting and in readiness or reluctance to seek help for depression, other factors seem to be at work, too. In Taiwan and Korea, for example, these factors include low rates of marital separation and divorce—factors known to be associated with high risk of depression in virtually all cultures. On the other hand, the stresses of war have undoubtedly inflated the rate of depression in the Middle East (Horgan, 1996; Weissman et al., 1996).

Causes of Depression Some cases of major depression almost certainly have a genetic predisposition. Severe bouts with depression often run in families (Andreasen et al., 1987; Plomin et al., 1994; Weissman et al., 1986). Further indication of a biological basis for depression comes from the favorable response that many depressed patients have to drugs that affect the brain's neurotransmitters norepinephrine, serotonin, and dopamine (Ezzell, 2004; Hirschfeld & Goodwin, 1988; Nemeroff, 1998). Evidence also indicates that depression is related to lower

TABLE 12.2	Lifetime Risk of a Depressive Episode Lasting a Year or More
Taiwan	1.5%
Korea	2.9%
Puerto Rico	4.3%
United States	5.2%
Germany	9.2%
Canada	9.6%
New Zealand	11.6%
France	16.4%
Lebanon	19%

Most people think that depression is marked by outward signs of sadness, such as weeping. But depression affects other aspects of thought and behavior, as well. For a quick check on your own tendencies to depression, please answer "yes" or "no" to each of the following questions, all adapted from the signs of depression listed in the *DSM-IV:*

1. Do you feel deeply depressed, sad, or hopeless most of the day?
2. Do you feel you have lost interest in most or all activities?
3. Have you experienced any major change in appetite or body weight, though not from dieting?
4. Have you experienced a significant change in your sleeping patterns?

5. Do you feel more restless than usual—or more sluggish than usual?
6. Do you feel more fatigued than you ought to?
7. Do you feel persistently hopeless or inappropriately guilty?
8. Have you been finding it increasingly difficult to think or concentrate?
9. Do you have recurrent thoughts of death or suicide?

Your answers to these items do not constitute any proof that you are, or are not, depressed. While there is no "magic number" of items you must answer "yes" to in order to qualify as depressed, if you answered "yes" to some of them and if you are concerned, you might want to seek a professional opinion. Remember that a diagnosis of depression is

a clinical judgment call, based on the signs listed in the *DSM-IV:* Essentially, it is the pattern and the quality of your life, your feelings, and your behavior that determine whether or not you are depressed. Remember also that self-report is always subject to some bias. If you are concerned after considering the signs of depression in your life, we recommend an examination by a competent mental health professional, who will take into account not only your self-descriptions but also your behavior, your social context, and the rewards and aversive circumstances in your life.

---

brain wave activity in the left frontal lobe (Davidson, 1992a, b, 2000; Robbins, 2000). In a few cases, depression may be caused by viral infection (Bower, 1995b). Such evidence leads some observers to believe that depression is really a collection of disorders having a variety of causes (Kendler & Gardner, 1998).

A special form of depression seems to be related to sunlight deprivation. It appears most frequently during the long, dark winter months among people who live in high latitudes (Wehr & Rosenthal, 1989). (See Figure 12.2.) Aptly named, **seasonal affective disorder,** or **SAD,** is related to levels of the light-sensitive hormone melatonin, which regulates our internal biological clocks (Campbell & Murphy, 1998; Oren & Terman, 1998). Based on this knowledge, researchers have developed an effective therapy that regulates melatonin by exposing SAD sufferers daily to bright artificial light (Lewy et al., 1987).

Biology alone cannot entirely explain depression, however. We must also understand it as a mental, social, and behavioral condition. Initially, a negative event, such as losing a job, can make anyone feel depressed, but low self-esteem and a pessimistic attitude can fuel a cycle of depressive thought patterns (Abramson et al., 1989; Sweeney et al., 1986; Wood et al., 1990a, b). (See Figure 12.3.) Probably because of low self-esteem, depression-prone people are more likely to perpetuate the depression cycle by attributing negative events

◀ **CONNECTION** CHAPTER 3

The "biological clock," located in the hypothalamus, regulates our *circadian rhythms.*

■ **Seasonal affective disorder** or **SAD**   A form of depression believed to be caused by deprivation of sunlight.

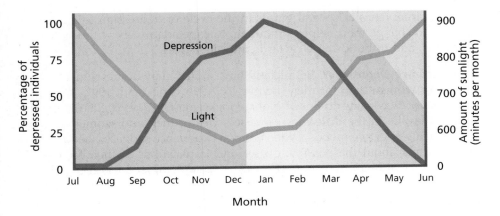

● **FIGURE 12.2**   Seasonal Affective Disorder

People who suffer from seasonal affective disorder are most likely to experience symptoms of depression during months with shortened periods of sunlight. (*Source:* Adaptation of Fig. 1, p. 74 from "Seasonal Affective Disorder: A Description of the Syndrome and Preliminary Findings with Light Therapy" by N. E. Rosenthal et al., *Archives of General Psychiatry, 41* (1984), pp. 72–80. American Medical Association.

● **FIGURE 12.3** The Cognitive–
Behavioral Cycle of Depression

As you follow Fred around the cycle, note how
his depression feeds on itself.

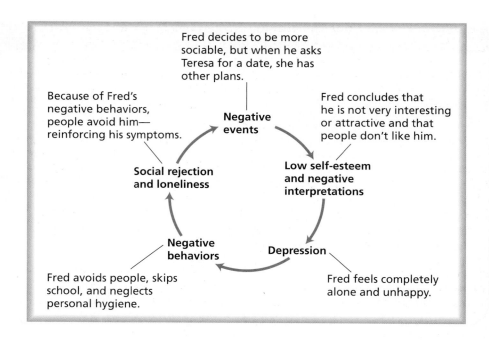

to their own personal flaws or external conditions that they feel helpless to change (Azar, 1994; Robins, 1988; Seligman, 1991; Seligman et al., 1979). Martin Seligman calls this *learned helplessness.* The resulting negative self-evaluation generates a depressed mode, which leads in turn to negative behaviors such as crying. These behaviors encourage others to avoid the depressed individual. Consequently, depressed people feel rejected and lonely, which also feeds the cycle of their despair (Coyne et al., 1991).

If you think this description of depression sounds a lot like the definition of stress that we gave in Chapter 10—you're right! One of the most promising approaches to research on this disorder sees depression as fundamentally a stress disorder (Holden, 2003b). Specifically, stress hormones adversely affect neurons, especially in the hippocampus—a part of the brain known to be a site of action for antidepressant drugs.

The cognitive approach to depression points out that negative thinking styles are learned and modifiable. This implies that, if you work on changing the way you *think,* perhaps blaming yourself less and focusing more on constructive plans for doing better, you can ultimately change your feelings and your performance. Indeed, Peter Lewinsohn and his colleagues (Lewinsohn et al., 1980, 1990; Lewinsohn & Gottlib, 1995) have found that they can treat many cases of depression effectively with cognitive–behavioral techniques. Their approach intervenes at several points in the cycle of depression to teach people how to change their helpless thinking, to cope adaptively with unpleasant situations, and to build more rewards into their lives.

Who Becomes Depressed? Clinicians have noted that depression rates are higher for women than for men (Leutwyler, 1995; Strickland, 1992; Weissman et al., 1996). According to Susan Nolen-Hoeksema (1987, 1990, 2001), the difference may lie in the differing response styles of men and women who are experiencing negative moods. When women experience sadness, she says, they tend to think about the possible causes and implications of their feelings. In contrast, men attempt to distract themselves from depressed feelings, either by shifting their attention to something else or by engaging in a physical activity that will take their minds off their mood. This model suggests that the more *ruminative* response of women—characterized by a tendency to concentrate on problems—increases women's vulnerability to depression (Shea, 1998).

The incidence of depression and the age at which it strikes are changing—at least in the United States. According to Martin Seligman, depression is between 10 and 20 times as common as it was 50 years ago (National Press Club, 1999). In the mid-1900s, most casualties of depression were middle-aged women, but now depression is more often a teenage problem—still more prevalent in females than in males (NIMH, 2000). Seligman, who has studied depression extensively, blames this increase in occurrence and decrease in age to three factors: (1) an out-of-control individualism and self-centeredness that focuses on individual success and failure, rather than group accomplishments; (2) the self-esteem movement, which has taught a generation of schoolchildren that they should feel good about themselves, irrespective of their efforts and achievements; and (3) a culture of *victimology,* which reflexively points the finger of blame at someone or something else.

Bipolar Disorder Another mood disorder also involves periods of depression—but, in addition, alternating periods of extreme elation. Formerly known as *manic–depressive disorder,* the condition is now listed in the *DSM-IV* as **bipolar disorder.** The alternating periods of *mania* (excessive elation or manic excitement) and the profound sadness of depression represent the two "poles."

During the manic phase, the individual becomes euphoric, energetic, hyperactive, talkative, and emotionally wound tight like a spring. It is not unusual for people, swept up in mania, to spend their life savings on extravagant purchases or to engage promiscuously in a number of sexual liaisons or other potentially high-risk actions. When the mania diminishes, they are left to deal with the damage they have created during their frenetic period. Soon, in the depressive phase, a dark wave of melancholy sweeps over the mind, producing symptoms indistinguishable from the "unipolar" form of depression we discussed earlier. Biologically speaking, however, these two forms of depression differ: We know this because the antidepressant drugs that work well on major depression are not usually effective for bipolar disorder.

A genetic component in bipolar disorder is well established, although the exact genes involved have not been pinpointed (Bradbury, 2001; Plomin et al., 1994). While only 1% of the general population has bipolar attacks, having an identical twin afflicted with the problem inflates one's chances to about 70% (Allen, 1976; Tsuang & Faraone, 1990). The fact that bipolar disorder usually responds well to medication also suggests biological factors at work.

Anxiety Disorders

Would you pick up a snake or let a tarantula rest on your shoulder? For some people the mere thought of snakes or spiders is enough to send chills of fear down their spines. Everyone, of course, has experienced anxiety or fear in threatening or dangerous situations. But pathological anxiety is far more severe than the normal anxiety associated with life's challenges. It is also relatively common—even more common than major depression (Barlow, 2000). One estimate says that 15% of the general population has, at some time, experienced the symptoms that are serious enough to qualify as one of the **anxiety disorders** recognized in the *DSM* (Regier et al., 1988).

Here we will review four major disorders that have anxiety as their main feature: (1) generalized anxiety disorder, (2) panic disorder, (3) phobic disorder, and (4) obsessive–compulsive disorder. You will note that the major differences among them have to do with the focus and duration of anxiety: Is anxiety present only occasionally or most of the time? Does the anxiety seem to come from

■ **Bipolar disorder** A mental abnormality involving swings of mood from mania to depression.
■ **Anxiety disorders** Mental problems characterized mainly by anxiety. Anxiety disorders include panic disorder, specific phobias, and obsessive–compulsive disorder.

CONNECTION CHAPTER 9

The brain has two main *emotional pathways;* one operates mainly at an unconscious level.

Anxiety Disorders: Fear, Anxiety, Panic Attacks

- Generalized anxiety disorder
- Panic disorder
- Agoraphobia
- Specific phobias
- Obsessive–compulsive disorder

nowhere—unrelated to the individual's environment or behavior? Does it come from an external object or situation, such as the sight of blood or a snake? Does it involve the victim's own ritualistic behavior, as in a person who compulsively avoids stepping on cracks in the sidewalk? (See the chart in the margin.)

Generalized Anxiety Disorder   Some people spend months or years of their lives coping with anxiety. Charles, a heavy-equipment operator, says he has dizzy spells, headaches, cold sweats, and frequent feelings of anxiety. But he has no clue why he feels anxious. It's "free-floating" anxiety, as clinicians sometimes call it, and they would diagnose his condition as **generalized anxiety disorder.** People with this disorder have a pervasive and persistent sense of anxiety. They are not just worried or fearful about specific situations or objects, such as heights or spiders. Nor does the anxiety come in waves, punctuated by periods of relative calm. Such patterns of anxiety signify different anxiety disorders, to which we turn next.

Panic Disorder   While calmly eating lunch, an unexpected wave of panic sweeps over you, seemingly from nowhere. Your heart races, your body shakes, you feel dizzy, your hands become clammy and sweaty, you are afraid that you might be dying. You are having a *panic attack.*

The distinguishing feature of **panic disorder** is a strong feeling of anxiety that has no connection with present events (Barlow, 2001). As in generalized anxiety disorder, the feeling is one of "free-floating anxiety." Attacks usually last for only a few minutes and then subside (McNally, 1994). Because of the unexpected nature of these "hit-and-run" attacks, *anticipatory anxiety* often develops as an added complication. The dread of the next attack and of being helpless and suddenly out of control can lead a person to avoid public places, yet fear being left alone. Cognitive–behavioral theorists view panic attacks as conditioned responses to physical sensations that may have initially been learned during a period of stress (Antony et al., 1992).

Biologically, we have evidence of a genetic influence in panic disorder (Plomin et al., 1994). However, the brain mechanism responsible for this condition probably lies in the limbic system—especially in the amygdala, which appears abnormal on PET scans of many patients (Barlow, 2000, 2001; Resnick, 1992). Significantly, it is this part of the brain that houses the unconscious emotional-arousal pathway described by Joseph LeDoux (1996). Overstimulation of these circuits can produce lasting physical changes that make the individual more susceptible to anxiety attacks in the future (Rosen & Schulkin, 1998).

To complicate matters, many victims of panic disorder have additional symptoms of **agoraphobia.** This condition involves panic that develops when they find themselves in situations from which they cannot easily escape, such as crowded public places or open spaces (Antony et al., 1992; Magee et al., 1996). The term *agoraphobia* is a literal translation from the ancient Greek for "fear of the marketplace." Victims of agoraphobia often fear that, if they experience an attack in one of these locations, help might not be available or the situation will be embarrassing to them. These fears deprive afflicted persons of their freedom, and some become prisoners in their own homes. If the disorder becomes this extreme, they cannot hold a job or carry on normal daily activities.

You may know someone who has panic disorder or agoraphobia. These problems occur in about 2% of the population (McNally, 1994), and they are much more common in women than in men. Fortunately, the treatment outlook is good. Medical therapy involves antianxiety drugs to relieve the panic attacks. Purely psychological treatment is also effective: Studies have shown that cog-

■ **Generalized anxiety disorder** A psychological problem characterized by persistent and pervasive feelings of anxiety, without any external cause.

■ **Panic disorder**   A disturbance marked by panic attacks that have no obvious connection with events in the person's present experience. Unlike generalized anxiety disorder, the victim is usually free of anxiety between panic attacks.

■ **Agoraphobia**   A fear of public places and open spaces, commonly accompanying panic disorder.

nitive–behavioral therapy may equal or outperform drug therapy in combating panic attacks ("Cognitive–Behavior Therapy," 1991; Craske et al., 1991).

Phobic Disorders In contrast with panic disorder, **phobias** involve a persistent and irrational fear of a specific object, activity, or situation—a response all out of proportion to the circumstances. (These are sometimes called *specific phobias,* as contrasted with the broader fears found in agoraphobia.) Many of us respond fearfully to certain stimuli, such as spiders or snakes—or perhaps to multiple-choice tests! But these emotional responses become full-fledged phobic disorders only when they cause substantial disruption to our lives.

Phobias are relatively common. Studies suggest that 12.5% of Americans suffer from a phobic disorder at some point in their lives (Regier et al., 1988). Some specific phobias are quite rare, as in a fear of a certain type of insect. Others, such as fear of public speaking, are quite common—so common that they seem almost normal (Stein et al., 1996). (See Table 12.3.) Among the most

■ **Phobias** A group of anxiety disorders involving a pathological fear of a specific object or situation.

TABLE 12.3	Phobias	
DSM-IV Category	Object/Situation	Incidence
Agoraphobia	Crowds, open spaces	Common (3.5–7% of adults)
Social phobias	Fear of being observed or doing something humiliating	common (11–15%)
Specific phobias Animals	Varies by category Cats (ailurophobia) Dogs (cynophobia) Insects (insectophobia) Spiders (arachnophobia) Birds (avisophobia) Horses (equinophobia) Snakes (ophidiophobia) Rodents (rodentophobia)	(up to 16% of adults)
Inanimate objects or situations	Closed spaces (claustrophobia) Dirt (mysophobia) Thunder (brontophobia) Lightning (astraphobia) Heights (acrophobia) Darkness (nyctophobia) Fire (pyrophobia)	
Bodily conditions	Illness or injury (nosophobia) Sight of blood (hematophobia) Cancer (cancerophobia) Venereal disease (venerophobia) Death (thanatophobia)	
Other specific phobias	Numbers (numerophobia) The number 13 (triskaidekaphobia) Strangers, foreigners (xenophobia) String (linonophobia) Books (bibliophobia) Work (ergophobia)	rare rare rare

Note: Hundreds of phobias have been described and given scientific names; this table provides only a sample. Some of the rare and strange-sounding phobias may have been observed in a single patient.

common phobic disorders are *social phobias,* irrational fears of normal social situations (Magee et al., 1996). Phobic responses to heights (acrophobia), snakes (ophidiophobia), and closed-in spaces (claustrophobia) are also common.

What causes phobias? Long ago, John Watson and Rosalie Rayner demonstrated that fears can be learned. We also have abundant evidence that fears and phobias can be unlearned through cognitive–behavioral therapy based on conditioning. But learning may not tell the whole story. Martin Seligman (1971) has argued that humans are biologically predisposed to learn some kinds of fears more easily than others. This **preparedness hypothesis** suggests that we carry an innate biological tendency, acquired through natural selection, to respond quickly and automatically to stimuli that posed a survival threat to our ancestors (Öhman & Mineka, 2001). This explains why we develop phobias for snakes and lightning much more easily than we develop fears for automobiles and electrical outlets—objects that have posed a danger only in recent times.

Obsessive–Compulsive Disorder   Seventeen-year-old Jim seemed to be a normal adolescent with many talents and interests. Then, almost overnight, he was transformed into a lonely outsider, excluded from social life by his psychological disabilities. Specifically, he developed an obsession with washing. Haunted by the notion that he was dirty—in spite of what his senses told him—Jim began to spend more and more time cleansing himself. At first his ritual ablutions were confined to weekends and evenings, but soon they consumed all his time, forcing him to drop out of school (Rapoport, 1989).

Jim had developed **obsessive–compulsive disorder,** or *OCD,* a condition characterized by patterns of persistent, unwanted thoughts and behaviors. Obsessive–compulsive disorder affects about 2.5% of Americans at some point during their lives (Regier et al., 1988). Nearly everyone has had some of its symptoms in a mild form.

The *obsession* component of OCD consists of thoughts, images, or impulses that recur or persist despite a person's efforts to suppress them. For example, a person with an obsessive fear of germs may avoid using bathrooms outside his or her home or refuse to shake hands with strangers. And, because sufferers realize that their obsessive thoughts and compulsive rituals are senseless, they often go to great lengths to hide their compulsive behavior from other people. This, of course, places restrictions on their domestic, social, and work lives. Not surprisingly, OCD patients have extremely high divorce rates.

You probably have had some sort of mild obsessional experience, such as petty worries ("Did I remember to lock the door?") or a haunting phrase or melody that kept running through your mind. Such thoughts are normal if they occur only occasionally and have not caused significant disruptions of your life. As we have noted in other disorders, it is a matter of degree.

Compulsions, the other half of obsessive–compulsive disorder, are repetitive, purposeful acts performed according to certain private "rules," in response to an obsession. Victims feel that their compulsive behavior will reduce the tension associated with their obsessions. Typical compulsions include irresistible urges to clean, to check that lights or appliances have been turned off, and to count objects or possessions. When they are calm, people with obsessive–compulsive disorder view the compulsion as senseless, but when their anxiety rises, they can't resist performing the compulsive behavior ritual to relieve tension. Part of the pain experienced by people with this problem is that they are frustrated by the irrationality of their obsessions and their powerlessness to eliminate them.

The tendency for OCD to run in families suggests a genetic link. Another hint comes from the finding that many people with OCD also display *tics,* unwanted involuntary movements, such as exaggerated eye blinks. In these

CONNECTION CHAPTER 6

Watson and Rayner's infamous experiment with Little Albert showed that fears could be learned by *classical conditioning.*

● A common form of social phobia involves an extreme fear of public speaking.

■ **Preparedness hypothesis** The notion that we have an innate tendency, acquired through natural selection, to respond quickly and automatically to stimuli that posed a survival threat to our ancestors.

■ **Obsessive–compulsive disorder** A condition characterized by patterns of persistent, unwanted thoughts and behaviors.

patients, brain imaging often shows oddities in the deep motor control areas, suggesting something amiss in the brain (Resnick, 1992). OCD expert Judith Rapoport tells us to think of compulsions as "fixed software packages" programmed in the brain. Once activated, she theorizes, the patient gets caught in a behavioral "loop" that cannot be switched off (Rapoport, 1989).

Curiously, certain drugs that are commonly prescribed for depression can alleviate both the obsessions and the compulsive rituals (Poling et al., 1991). In further support of a biological basis for OCD, investigators have found that these drugs can reverse compulsive behavior in dogs that display a preoccupation with grooming themselves (Ross, 1992).

Again, however, we must note that biology cannot explain everything. Some victims of OCD have clearly *learned* that their anxiety-provoking thoughts are connected to harmful consequences (Barlow, 2000). Further evidence that learning plays a role can be seen in the results of behavioral therapy, which is effective in reducing compulsive actions. The behavioral strategy for treating compulsive hand-washing, for example, calls for a form of extinction, in which the therapist soils the patient's hands and prevents him or her from washing for progressively longer periods. Indeed, behavioral therapy can produce changes that show up in PET scans of OCD sufferers' brains (Schwartz et al., 1996). Thus, when we change behavior, we inevitably change the wiring of the obsessive–compulsive brain. This disorder shows us, once again, that biology and behavior are inseparable.

● Obsessive–compulsive disorder makes people engage in senseless, ritualistic behaviors, such as repetitive hand washing.

Somatoform Disorders

"Soma" means *body*. Thus, we use the term **somatoform disorders** for psychological problems appearing in the form of bodily symptoms or physical complaints, such as weakness or excessive worry about disease. The somatoform disorders are not especially common, occurring in about 2% of the population (Holmes, 2001). Yet despite their rarity, they have captured the popular imagination under their more common names: "hysteria" and "hypochondria." (See the chart in the margin.)

The *DSM-IV* recognizes several types of somatoform disorders, but we will cover only two: *conversion disorder* and *hypochondriasis.* And, while we're talking about somatoform disorders, please note their potential for confusion with *psychosomatic disorders,* in which mental conditions—especially stress—lead to actual physical disease. The *DSM-IV* places psychosomatic disorders under a separate heading, "Psychological Factors Affecting Medical Condition."

Conversion Disorder Paralysis, weakness, or loss of sensation—with no discernible physical cause—distinguishes **conversion disorder** (formerly called "hysteria"). Patients with this diagnosis may, for example, be blind, deaf, unable to walk, or insensitive to touch in part of their bodies. Yet they have no organic disease that shows up on neurological examinations, laboratory tests, or X rays. In conversion disorder, the problem really is "all in the mind."

"Glove anesthesia" represents a classic form of conversion disorder. As you can see in Figure 12.4, the pattern of insensitivity to touch or pain fits the patient "like a glove." The tip-off that the problem is *psychogenic*, not physical, comes from the pattern of the patient's symptoms: They do not match any possible pattern of nerve impairment. Other cases, however, are not always so clear-cut. Some physicians may rush too quickly to diagnose conversion

> ***Somatoform Disorders:***
> **Physical Symptoms or Overconcern with One's Health**
>
> ● **Conversion disorder**
> ● **Hypochondriasis**

■ **Somatoform disorders**
Psychological problems appearing in the form of bodily symptoms or physical complaints, such as weakness or excessive worry about disease. The somatoform disorders include conversion disorder and hypochondriasis.

■ **Conversion disorder** A type of somatoform disorder, marked by paralysis, weakness, or loss of sensation but with no discernible physical cause.

● **FIGURE 12.4** Glove Anesthesia

The form of conversion disorder known as "glove anesthesia" (A) involves a loss of sensation in the hand, as though the patient were wearing a thick glove. This cannot be a neurological disorder because the pattern of "anesthesia" does not correspond to the actual pattern of nerves in the hand, shown in (B).

disorder when they are confronted with baffling symptoms or especially difficult patients. Concluding that the problem is "all in their heads" conveniently tosses it into somebody else's lap. Women, particularly, have charged that physicians dismiss their physical complaints as "just a hysterical reaction" and refer the patient to a psychiatrist.

We should point out that the term *conversion disorder* carries with it some baggage from our Freudian past. Originally, the term implied an unconscious displacement (or *conversion*) of anxiety into physical symptoms—although many clinicians no longer subscribe to that explanation. Some cases of conversion disorder are now thought to be physical stress responses.

Mysteriously, conversion disorder was much commoner a century ago in Europe and the United States. The problem has declined in industrialized countries, probably due to increased public understanding of physical and mental disorders (American Psychiatric Association, 1994; Nietzel et al., 1998). It is still relatively common in economically undeveloped regions, such as China (Spitzer et al., 1989) and Africa (Binitie, 1975) and among poorly educated persons in the U.S. (Barlow & Durand, 2005).

Hypochondriasis "Hypochondriacs" worry about getting sick. Every ache and pain signals a disease. Because of their exaggerated concern about illness, patients with **hypochondriasis** often bounce from physician to physician until they find one who will listen to their complaints and prescribe some sort of treatment—often minor tranquilizers or placebos. Naturally, these individuals represent easy marks for health fads and scams. They also find their way to the fringes of the medical community, where they may buy extensive treatment packages from disreputable practitioners.

The other side of the problem is a mistaken diagnosis of hypochondriasis (similar to the problem we found with conversion disorder). Clinicians may sometimes be too ready to conclude that the patient's concerns are imaginary. This can have disastrous consequences, such as overlooking the symptoms of very real and very serious physical diseases, such as cancer or a chronic infection.

Dissociative Disorders: Nonpsychotic Fragmentation of the Personality

- Dissociative amnesia
- Dissociative fugue
- Depersonalization disorder
- Dissociative identity disorder

◀ **CONNECTION** CHAPTER 7

Compare with *anterograde amnesia* in the case of H. M.

Dissociative Disorders

The common denominator for all the **dissociative disorders** is "fragmentation" of the personality—a sense that parts of the personality have detached (dissociated) from others. Among the dissociative disorders, we find some of the most fascinating forms of mental pathology, including dissociative fugue, depersonalization disorder, and the controversial dissociative identity disorder (formerly called "multiple personality"), made famous by the fictional Dr. Jekyll and Mr. Hyde. Unfortunately, the underlying causes of dissociative disorders remain unclear. (See the chart in the margin.)

Dissociative Amnesia Sometimes memory loss is too extensive or too specific to be explained by normal forgetting. In some such cases we call it *amnesia*. You may know an amnesia victim who has suffered a memory loss as the result of a severe blow to the head, perhaps in an auto accident. Sometimes, however, people may sustain a purely psychological form of amnesia, known as **dissociative amnesia,** as the result of a traumatic or highly stressful experience. In this disorder, the memory loss involves a specific event or series of events—usually a threatening experience in childhood.

You can see that dissociative amnesia is closely related to *posttraumatic stress disorder*, which we discussed in Chapter 10. In both cases, memory loss is related to a stressful incident or period in the person's life. We should also

● These two paintings by Sybil, a dissociative identity disorder (DID) victim, illustrate the differences among the personalities. The painting on the left was done by Peggy, Sybil's angry, fearful personality. The painting above was done by Mary, a home-loving personality.

note, however, that dissociative amnesia can be a controversial diagnosis when it is associated with recovered memories of childhood abuse. As we discussed in Chapter 7, some psychologists have raised important questions about the accuracy of such recovered memories. And, as the *DSM-IV* states, dissociative amnesia may have "been overdiagnosed in individuals who are highly suggestible" (p. 479).

Dissociative Fugue Now consider the case of "Jane Doe," a woman with *dissociative fugue*. She was found near death in a Florida park, where she was incoherent and suffering the effects of exposure. In contrast with victims of dissociative amnesia, discussed above, Jane Doe had a pervasive memory loss: no memory of her identity nor any ability to read or write. Therapy revealed general information about the kind of past she must have had, but no good clues to her origins. After a nationwide television appeal, Jane Doe and her doctors were flooded with calls from possible relatives, the most promising of which was an Illinois couple, certain she was their daughter. They had not heard from her for over four years, since she had moved from Illinois to Florida. Despite their confidence that they had found her, she was never able to remember her past or what had happened to her (Carson et al., 1996).

Jane Doe had **dissociative fugue,** which is a combination of fugue, or "flight," and *amnesia*. In such persons amnesia takes the form of a lost sense of identity. They also flee their homes, families, and jobs—which is why the disorder is termed *fugue.* Some victims appear disoriented and perplexed. Others may travel to distant locations and take up new lives, appearing unconcerned about the unremembered past. Usually the fugue state lasts only hours or days, followed by complete and rapid recovery. A few cases may continue for months—or, as with Jane Doe, for years.

Heavy alcohol use may predispose a person to dissociative fugue. This suggests that it may involve some brain impairment—although no certain cause has been established. Like dissociative amnesia, fugue occurs more often in those under prolonged high stress, especially in times of war and other calamities. Some psychologists also suspect memory dissociation and repression

■ **Hypochondriasis** A somatoform disorder involving excessive concern about health and disease; also called *hypochondria*.
■ **Dissociative disorders** A group of pathologies involving "fragmentation" of the personality, in which some parts of the personality have become detached, or dissociated, from other parts.
■ **Dissociative amnesia** A psychologically induced loss of memory for personal information, such as one's identity or residence.
■ **Dissociative fugue** Essentially the same as dissociative amnesia, but with the addition of "flight" from one's home, family, and job. Fugue (pronounced *FEWG*) means "flight."

accompany instances of sexual and physical childhood abuse (Spiegel & Cardeña, 1991). As with dissociative amnesia, this conjecture, however, is disputed.

Depersonalization Disorder   Yet another form of dissociation involves a sensation that mind and body have separated. Patients with **depersonalization disorder** commonly report "out-of-body experiences" or feelings of being external observers of their own bodies. Some patients feel as if they are in a dream. (Fleeting, mild forms of this are common, so there is no cause for alarm!) A study of 30 such cases found that obsessive–compulsive disorder and certain personality disorders often accompany this condition (Simeon et al., 1997). The causes are unknown.

People undergoing severe physical trauma, such as a life-threatening injury in an auto accident, may also report symptoms of depersonalization. So do some patients who have had near-death experiences. Usually the sensation passes quickly, although it can recur. In such individuals, investigators have attributed the disorder to hallucinations and to natural changes in the brain that occur during shock (Siegel, 1980).

Dissociative Identity Disorder   Robert Louis Stevenson's famous story of Dr. Jekyll and Mr. Hyde has become a misleading stereotype of **dissociative identity disorder.** In reality, most such cases occur in women, and most display more than two identities (Ross et al., 1989). Unlike the homicidal Mr. Hyde, rarely do they pose a danger to others.

Although it was once thought to be rare, some specialists now believe that dissociative identity disorder has always been common but hidden or misdiagnosed. It usually first appears in childhood (Vincent & Pickering, 1988), and its victims frequently report having been sexually abused (Putnam et al., 1986; Ross et al., 1990). The formation of multiple identities or selves may be a form of defense by the dominant self to protect itself from terrifying events.

Dissociative identity disorder (DID) has now become a familiar diagnosis because of its portrayal in books such as *Sybil* (Schreiber, 1973) and *The Flock* (Casey & Wilson, 1991) and films such as the 1996 production *Primal Fear*. Each emerging personality contrasts in some significant way with the original self. For example, the new personality might be outgoing if the original personality is shy, tough if the original is weak, and sexually assertive if the other is fearful and sexually naive. These alternate personalities, each with its own consciousness, emerge suddenly—usually under stress.

What lies behind this mysterious disturbance? Psychodynamic theories explain it as a fracturing of the ego, as a result of ego defense mechanisms that do not allow energy from conflicts and traumas to escape from the unconscious mind. Cognitive theories see it as a form of role-playing or mood-state dependency, a form of memory bias in which events experienced in a given mood are more easily recalled when the individual is again in that mood state (Eich et al., 1997). Others suggest that at least some cases are frauds (as in the case of a student, charged with plagiarizing a term paper, who claimed that he had multiple personalities and that one of them copied the paper without the knowledge of his dominant personality). Some observers have even suggested that the disorder exists only in the minds of a few therapists (Piper, 1998). In this view, patients may initially be led by the suggestive questioning of their therapists, who seek to uncover what they suspect are repressed memories of trauma and molestation (Loftus, 1993; Loftus & Ketcham, 1994; Ofshe & Watters, 1994).

In an unfortunate choice of terms, dissociative identity disorder is sometimes called "split personality." This causes confusion because schizophrenia (which literally means "split mind") has no relationship to dissociative iden-

■ **Depersonalization disorder**
An abnormality involving the sensation that mind and body have separated, as in an "out-of-body" experience.
■ **Dissociative identity disorder**
A condition in which an individual displays multiple identities, or personalities; formerly called "multiple personality disorder."
■ **Anorexia nervosa**   An eating disorder involving persistent loss of appetite that endangers an individual's health and stemming from emotional or psychological reasons rather than from organic causes.
■ **Bulimia nervosa**   An eating disorder characterized by eating binges followed by "purges," induced by vomiting or laxatives; typically initiated as a weight-control measure.

tity disorder. In schizophrenia, the "split" refers to a psychotic split from reality, not to a fracturing of one personality into many personalities. Dissociative identity disorder, on the other hand, is *not* a psychotic disorder. We suggest that the reader avoid confusion by avoiding the term "split personality."

Eating Disorders

Like a drug addiction, Carla's eating disorder is so powerful that she cannot resume healthy eating patterns without great difficulty. She (it is usually a she) has always felt overweight, and recently she has put herself on a severe diet—a starvation diet. Little does Carla realize that she has become the victim of an eating disorder that will ultimately alter her body in undesirable, and even lethal, ways. After some months, she may become dangerously underweight. Food has become repugnant. She feels "full" after eating only a bite or two. The original motivation may have been the same with Carla's friend Jennifer, but Jennifer has resorted to another extreme method of weight control: She often overeats, but she makes herself vomit after a meal. Eventually, her teeth and the tissues in her mouth and esophagus come under attack by the action of refluxed stomach acid. And she, like Carla, may become dangerously malnourished.

Significantly, such eating disorders are most prevalent in Western cultures in which hunger is not widespread. They are especially likely to develop among middle- and upper-middle-class young women. Here we examine the two best-known eating disorders, exemplified above: *anorexia nervosa* and *bulimia nervosa*. (See the chart in the margin at the bottom of the page.)

Anorexia Nervosa   The condition called *anorexia* (persistent lack of appetite) may develop as a consequence of certain physical diseases or conditions, such as shock, nausea, or allergic reactions. However, when loss of appetite that endangers an individual's health stems from emotional or psychological causes, the syndrome is called **anorexia nervosa** ("nervous anorexia"). A person suffering from anorexia nervosa may act as though she is unconcerned with her condition, although she is emaciated. Commonly, anorexia nervosa is associated with extreme dieting, as in Carla's case. (Most dieters, by contrast, have an increased desire for food.)

What causes anorexia nervosa? A strong hint comes from the finding that most anorectic persons are young white females from middle-class American homes. They typically have backgrounds of good behavior and academic success, but they starve themselves, hoping to become acceptably thin and attractive (Grice et al., 2002; Kaye et al, 2004; Keel & Klump, 2003). While cultural ideals of feminine beauty change over time, in recent decades the mass media—including fashion magazines and MTV—have promoted extremely slim models and celebrities (Andersen & DiDomenico, 1992; Rolls et al., 1991). Especially during adolescence, when people tend to evaluate themselves in terms of physical attractiveness, they judge themselves harshly for failing to live up to cultural ideals (Conger & Petersen, 1984). A victim of anorexia typically holds a distorted body image, believing herself to be unattractively fat, and rejects others' reassurances that she is not overweight (Bruch, 1978; Fallon & Rozin, 1985). In an effort to lose imagined "excess" weight, the anorectic victim rigidly suppresses her appetite, feeling rewarded for such self-control when she does lose pounds and inches—but never feeling quite thin enough. (See Figure 12.5.)

Bulimia   In the "binge-and-purge" syndrome known as **bulimia nervosa,** the sufferer overeats (binges) and then attempts to lose weight (purges) by means of self-induced vomiting, laxative use, or fasting

● Billboards, magazines, TV, the fashion world, and the movies promote images of body shapes that are unrealistic for most people—yet people often judge themselves against these standards.

◀ **CONNECTION** CHAPTER 9

Genetic factors may also be at work in anorexia nervosa and bulimia nervosa.

Eating Disorders
● Anorexia nervosa
● Bulimia nervosa

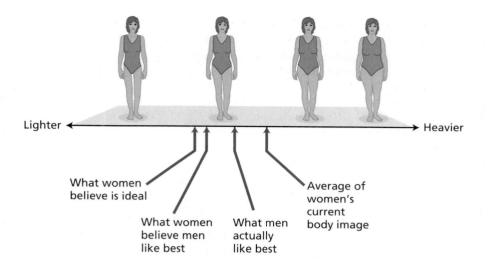

● **FIGURE 12.5** Women's Body Images

April Fallon and Paul Rozin (1985) asked female college students to give their current weight, their ideal weight, and the weight they believed men would consider ideal. The results showed that the average woman felt that her current weight was significantly higher than her ideal weight—and higher than the weight she thought men would like. To make matters worse, women also see their bodies as looking larger than they actually are (Thompson, 1986). When men were asked to rate themselves on a similar questionnaire, Fallon and Rozin found no such discrepancies between ideal and actual weights. But, when asked what they saw as the ideal weight for women, they chose a higher weight than women did. No wonder women go on diets more often than men and are more likely to have a major eating disorder (Mintz & Betz, 1986; Striegel-Moore et al., 1986).

Lighter ← → Heavier

What women believe is ideal

What women believe men like best

What men actually like best

Average of women's current body image

(Rand & Kuldau, 1992). Those who suffer from bulimia usually keep their disorder inconspicuous and may even be supported in their behavior patterns by peers and by competitive norms in their academic, social, and athletic lives (Polivy & Herman, 1993; Rodin et al., 1985; Squire, 1983; Striegel-Moore et al., 1993).

Eating disorders are commonly associated with other forms of psychopathology. For example, bulimia nervosa is a predictor of depression (Walters et al., 1992). It has been observed that anorectic and bulimic individuals apparently take little joy in their thinner profiles, even though their original rationale might have been to lose weight. Further, while hungry normal people look forward to eating and enjoying a good meal, eating-disordered individuals do not associate pleasure with food and may even dread having to eat. Corroborating this observation, bulimic patients in one study took longer to begin eating a scheduled meal, ate more slowly, and reported significantly more negative moods during eating than did control subjects (Hetherington et al., 1993).

Cognitive explanations for eating disorders analyze how the individual sees herself and thinks about food, eating, and weight. Accordingly, many successful treatments of eating disorders employ strategies that alter self-perception and boost feelings of self-efficacy (Baell & Wertheim, 1992).

Schizophrenia

Literally, the word *schizophrenia* means "split or broken mind"—and the "split" is from reality. In psychological terms, **schizophrenia** is a severe form of psychopathology in which personality seems to disintegrate and perception is distorted. Schizophrenia is the disorder that people have in mind when they use the terms "madness," "psychosis," or "insanity."

For the victim of schizophrenia, the mind can be twisted in terrible ways. The world may become bleak and devoid of meaning, or it may become so filled with sensation that everything appears in a confusion of multiple realities layered with hallucinations and delusions. In schizophrenia, emotions often become blunted, thoughts turn bizarre, and language takes strange twists. Memory may also become fragmented (Danion et al., 1999). The disorder breaks the unity of the mind, sending its victims on meaningless mental detours, sometimes riding trains of "clang" associations (associations involving similar-sounding words), and producing confused verbalizations that clinicians call "word salads." (See the chart in the margin on the facing page.) Here is an example of schizophrenic speech:

■ **Schizophrenia** (pronounced *skits-o-FRENNY-a*) A psychotic disorder involving distortions in thoughts, perceptions, and/or emotions.

The lion will have to change from dogs into cats until I can meet my father and mother and we dispart some rats. I live on the front of Whitton's head. You have to work hard if you don't get into bed . . . It's all over for a squab true tray and there ain't no squabs, there ain't no men, there ain't no music, there ain't no nothing besides my mother and my father who stand alone upon the Island of Capri where is no ice. Well it's my suitcase sir. (Rogers, 1982)

In a lifetime, more than one of every 100 Americans—more than 2 million over the age of 18—will become afflicted (Holmes, 2001; McGuire, 2000; NIMH, 2003; Regier et al., 1993). For as yet unknown reasons, the first appearance of schizophrenia typically occurs for men before they are 25 and for women between 25 and 45 years of age.

For years, schizophrenia has consistently been the primary diagnosis for about 40% of all patient admissions to public mental hospitals—far out of proportion to all other categories of mental illness (Manderscheid et al., 1985). Because schizophrenic patients require prolonged or recurrent treatment, they can be expected to occupy about half of all mental hospital beds in the nation (American Psychiatric Association, 2000; Carson et al., 2000). Most sobering, about one-third of all schizophrenic patients will never fully recover, even with the best therapy available.

Major Types of Schizophrenia Many investigators consider schizophrenia a constellation of separate disorders. Here are the five most common:

- *Disorganized type* represents everyone's image of mental illness, featuring incoherent speech, hallucinations, delusions, and bizarre behavior. A patient who talks to imaginary people most likely has this diagnosis.

- *Catatonic type,* involving a spectrum of motor dysfunctions, appears in two forms. Persons with the more common *catatonic stupor* may remain motionless for hours—even days—sometimes holding rigid, statuelike postures. In the other form, called *catatonic excitement,* patients become agitated and hyperactive.

- *Paranoid type* features delusions and hallucinations but no catatonic symptoms and none of the incoherence of disorganized schizophrenia. The paranoid delusions of persecution or of grandiosity (highly exaggerated self-importance) found in this type of schizophrenia are less well organized—more illogical—than those of the patient with a purely delusional disorder.

- *Undifferentiated type* serves as a catchall category for schizophrenic symptoms that do not clearly meet the requirements for any of the other categories above.

- *Residual type* is the diagnosis for individuals who have suffered from a schizophrenic episode in the past but currently have no major symptoms such as hallucinations or delusional thinking. Instead, their thinking is mildly disturbed, or their emotional lives are impoverished. The diagnosis of residual type may indicate that the disease is entering remission, or becoming dormant. (This diagnosis was assumed in most of Rosenhan's pseudopatients, whom we met at the beginning of the chapter.)

Our understanding of schizophrenia suffers from the fact that most schizophrenic patients display such a hodgepodge of symptoms that they drop into the "undifferentiated" category. Trying to make more sense of the problem, many investigators now merely divide the symptoms of schizophrenia into *positive* and *negative* categories (Javitt & Coyle, 2004; Sawa & Snyder, 2002).

Schizophrenia: Psychotic Deterioration of the Personality, Including Disturbances in Affect, Thinking, and Socialization
- Disorganized type
- Catatonic type
- Paranoid type
- Undifferentiated type
- Residual type

Positive symptoms refer to active processes, such as delusions and hallucinations, while negative symptoms refer to passive processes and deficiencies, such as social withdrawal and poverty of thinking. Patient responses to drug therapy support this division: Those with positive schizophrenia usually respond to antipsychotic drugs, while those with negative schizophrenia do not (Andreasen et al., 1995; Heinrichs, 1993). But even this distinction has its problems. Negative schizophrenia often looks like major depression. In addition, both positive and negative symptoms may occur in a single patient. All these difficulties have led some researchers to conclude that schizophrenia is a name for many separate disturbances.

CONNECTION CHAPTER 13

Antipsychotic drugs work by reducing the activity of the neurotransmitter dopamine in the brain.

Possible Causes of Schizophrenia   No longer do most theorists look through the Freudian lens to see schizophrenia as the result of defective parenting or repressed childhood trauma (Johnson, 1989). Studies show that adopted children with *no* family history of the disorder run no increased risk of developing schizophrenia when placed in a home with a schizophrenic parent (Gottesman, 1991). Thus, an emerging consensus among psychiatrists and psychologists views schizophrenia as fundamentally a brain disorder—or a group of disorders (Sawa & Snyder, 2002).

Support for this brain-disorder view comes from many quarters. As we have noted, the antipsychotic drugs (sometimes called *major tranquilizers*)—which interfere with the brain's dopamine receptors—can suppress the symptoms of positive schizophrenia (Carlsson, 1978; Snyder, 1986). On the other hand, drugs that stimulate dopamine production (e.g., the amphetamines) can actually produce schizophrenic symptoms (Dracheva et al., 2001; Lewis et al., 2001; Smith et al., 2001). Recently, attention has turned to deficiencies in the neurotransmitter glutamate (Javitt & Coyle, 2004). Other evidence of a biological basis for schizophrenia comes in the form of brain abnormalities shown by computerized imaging techniques (Mesulam, 1990; Raz & Raz, 1990; Resnick, 1992; Suddath et al., 1990). (See Figure 12.6.)

Yet another line of evidence for the biological basis of schizophrenia comes from family studies (Holden, 2003a; Lencer et al., 2000; Plomin et al., 1994). As we found with the mood disorders, the closer one's relationship to a person with schizophrenia, the greater one's chances of developing it (Gottesman, 1991, 2001; Heston, 1970; Nicol & Gottesman, 1983). This conclusion comes from impressive studies of identical twins reared apart and from adoption studies of children having schizophrenic blood relatives. While only about 1% of us in the general population become schizophrenic, the child of a schizophrenic parent incurs a risk about 14 times higher. The worst case would be to have an identical twin who has developed the condition. In that event, the other twin's chances of becoming schizophrenic jump to nearly 50%.

As with the mood disorders, biology does not tell the whole story of schizophrenia. We can see the effect of the environment, for example, in the fact that 90% of the relatives of schizophrenic patients do not have schizophrenia (Barnes, 1987). Even in identical twins who share *exactly* the same genes, the *concordance rate* (the rate at which the disorder is shared by both) for schizophrenia is only about 50%. That is, in half the cases in which schizophrenia strikes identical

● **FIGURE 12.6**   MRI Scans of a Twin with Schizophrenia and a Twin without Schizophrenia

The normal twin is on the left. Note the enlarged ventricles (fluid-filled spaces) in the brain of the schizophrenic twin on the right.

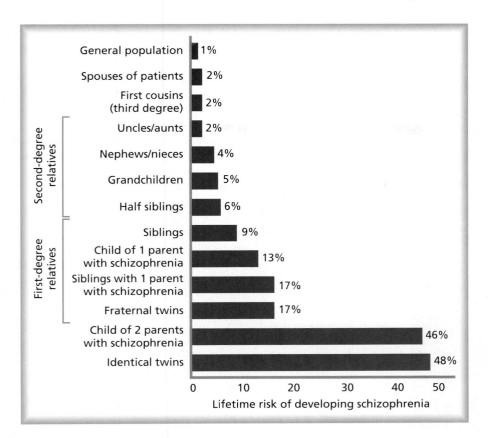

● **FIGURE 12.7** Genetic Risk of Developing Schizophrenia

The graph shows average risks for developing schizophrenia in persons with a schizophrenic relative. Data were compiled from family and twin studies conducted in European populations between 1920 and 1987; the degree of risk correlates highly with the degree of genetic relatedness. (*Source:* Fig. 10, p. 96, "Genetic Risk of Developing Schizophrenia," from SCHIZOPHRENIA GENESIS: The Origins of Madness by Irving Gottesman. Copyright © 1991. Reprinted by permission of W. H. Freeman and Company/Worth Publishers.)

twins, it leaves one twin untouched. A hopeful Finnish study found that being raised in a healthy family environment can actually lower the risk of schizophrenia in adopted children who have a genetic predisposition to the disease (Tienari et al., 1987). Apparently, schizophrenia requires a biological predisposition plus some unknown environmental agent to "turn on" the hereditary tendency (Cromwell, 1993; Iacono & Grove, 1993). This agent could be a chemical toxin, stress, or some factor we have not yet dreamed of. Taken as a whole, this research suggests that genetic factors may not themselves be sufficient for the disorder to develop (Nicol & Gottesman, 1983). (See Figure 12.7.) Despite all the biological evidence, we must remember that psychological disorder is always an interaction of biological, cognitive, and environmental factors, as our first Core Concept of the chapter suggested.

This broader perspective is often called the **diathesis–stress hypothesis.** It says that biological factors may place the individual at risk for schizophrenia (as well as many other disorders), but environmental stressors transform this potential into an actual disorder (Walker & Diforio, 1997). (The word *diathesis* refers to a predisposition or physical condition that makes one susceptible to disease.) Thus, schizophrenia can be seen as a stress response by one who is predisposed to the disorder. In this view, then, susceptible individuals may never develop schizophrenia if they are spared certain damaging conditions or stressors that might push them "over the edge."

Personality Disorders

The **personality disorders** show themselves in a chronic history of poor judgment, disordered thinking, emotional disturbances, disrupted social relationships, or lack of impulse control. The key is that the condition derives from a

■ **Diathesis–stress hypothesis**
In reference to schizophrenia, the proposal that says that genetic factors place the individual at risk while environmental stress factors transform this potential into an actual schizophrenic disorder.

■ **Personality disorders**   Conditions involving a chronic, pervasive, inflexible, and maladaptive pattern of thinking, emotion, social relationships, or impulse control.

● The films *Silence of the Lambs* and *Hannibal* portray an extreme antisocial personality in the character of Hannibal Lecter.

■ **Narcissistic personality disorder**
Characterized by a grandiose sense of self-importance, a preoccupation with fantasies of success or power, and a need for constant attention or admiration.

■ **Antisocial personality disorder**
Characterized by a long-standing pattern of irresponsible behavior indicating a lack of conscience and a diminished sense of responsibility to others.

■ **Borderline personality disorder**
An unstable personality given to impulsive behavior.

■ **Autism** A developmental disorder marked by disabilities in language, social interaction, and the ability to understand another person's state of mind.

personality pattern of long standing. These patterns can seriously impair an individual's ability to function in social or work settings.

Ten types of personality disorder are recognized in the *DSM-IV* (see the chart in the margin). Here we will consider three of the better known: *narcissistic personality disorder, antisocial personality disorder,* and *borderline personality disorder.*

People with a **narcissistic personality disorder** have an exaggerated sense of self-importance, a need for constant attention or admiration, and often a preoccupation with fantasies of success or power. These people often respond inappropriately to criticism or minor defeat, either by acting indifferent or by overreacting. They have problems in interpersonal relationships, feel entitled to favors without obligations, exploit others selfishly, and have difficulty understanding how others feel. For example, an individual with narcissistic personality disorder might express annoyance—but not empathy—when a friend has to cancel a date because of a death in the family.

Another personality disorder, **antisocial personality disorder,** is marked by a long-standing pattern of irresponsible or harmful behavior that indicates a lack of conscience and a diminished sense of responsibility to others. Chronic lying, stealing, and fighting are common signs. People with antisocial personality disorder may not experience anxiety, shame, or any other sort of intense emotion. They can "keep cool" in situations that would arouse and upset normal people. Violations of social norms begin early in their lives—disrupting class, getting into fights, and running away from home. Individuals who show a criminal pattern of antisocial personality disorder, such as committing murders and other serious crimes, are popularly referred to as "psychopaths" or "sociopaths."

Although carriers of the antisocial type of personality disorder can be found among street criminals and con artists, they are also well represented among successful politicians and businesspeople who put career, money, and power above everything and everyone. Two to three percent of the population in the United States may have antisocial personality disorder. Men are four times more likely to be so diagnosed than women (Regier et al., 1988, 1993).

The main signs of **borderline personality disorder** are instability and impulsivity (Carson et al., 2000; Holmes, 2001). People with this diagnosis have unpredictable moods and stormy interpersonal relationships, often becoming upset and abusive in response to perceived slights. They also have little tolerance for frustration. Their impulsivity may be seen in a tendency for substance abuse, gambling, sexual promiscuity, binge eating, reckless driving, self-mutilation, or suicide attempts. As with the other personality disorders, the treatment outlook for borderline personality disorder is guarded. (See Table 12.4.)

Developmental Disorders

Developmental problems can appear at any age, but several common ones are first seen in childhood, including *autism, attention-deficit hyperactivity disorder (ADHD),* and *dyslexia.* Here we will give you a brief description of these disorders, because you have already encountered them in earlier chapters. (See the chart in the margin on the facing page.)

Autism A complex and poorly understood disorder, **autism** involves an impoverished ability to "read" other people, use language, and interact socially.

TABLE 12.4	Types of Personality Disorders
Type clusters*	**Dominant feature**
Odd or eccentric	
Paranoid personality disorder	Unwarranted suspicion and mistrust of people
Schizoid personality disorder	Lack of interest in people or social relationships
Schizotypal personality disorder	Symptoms of schizophrenia, but not severe enough to be considered psychotic
Erratic or Emotional	
Borderline personality disorder	Instability and impulsivity
Histrionic personality disorder	Need for attention; shallow social relationships
Narcissistic personality disorder	Preoccupation with self; exaggerated sense of self-importance
Antisocial personality disorder	Antisocial behavior, without anxiety or guilt
Anxious or Fearful	
Avoidant personality disorder	Hypersensitivity to social rejection
Dependent personality disorder	Excessive reliance on others; reluctance to make independent decisions
Obsessive–compulsive personality disorder	Rigid need for perfection, order, and control; preoccupation with details

*Based on categories in the *DSM-IV,* with cluster names suggested by Holmes (2001).

To illustrate, imagine the following situation: Sally and Anne are playing together, when Sally puts a piece of candy in a box and then leaves the room. While Sally is gone, Anne opens the box, removes the candy, and stashes it in her purse. When Sally comes back, where will she look for the candy? Normal children will say that Sally will look in the box. Autistic children are most likely to say (if they communicate at all) that Sally will look in the purse. Thus, the autistic child lacks a *theory of mind* (Frith, 1993). Severely autistic children cannot imagine themselves in Sally's place, believing something they know is not the case. As a result of this deficit, the autistic child has difficulty in social relationships, usually existing in a world of extreme social isolation.

Besides the theory-of-mind deficiencies and social isolation, most autistic persons also have language difficulties. In fact, many never achieve functional language at all. Perhaps because of all these difficulties, many are classified as mentally retarded (although most mentally retarded persons are *not* autistic). In severe cases, such children may engage in destructive self-stimulation, such as head-banging. Often they will also display repetitive behavior, such as rocking, for extended periods.

Autism occurs in about 1 in 500 children and often is first suspected at about 1½ to 2 years of age, when the child fails to develop language (Kabot, Masi, & Segal, 2003). Most experts believe that autism is fundamentally a brain disorder, with a genetic basis. At present there is no cure, although there are treatment programs that can improve socialization and speech—but they are intensive and relatively expensive.

Dyslexia Reading is a key that opens many doors in a modern, information-driven society. But those doors can remain closed for people who have difficulty in reading—people with **dyslexia.** The disorder affects about 1 of 5 children to some degree, often leading to poor school performance. And, because

Developmental Disorders:
Disorders Usually First Diagnosed in Infancy, Childhood, or Adolescence

- Autism
- Dyslexia
- Attention-Deficit Hyperactivity Disorder (ADHD)

◄ **CONNECTION** CHAPTER 1

Facilitated communication was a discredited attempt to communicate with autistic individuals.

■ **Dyslexia** A reading disability, thought by some experts to involve a brain disorder.

school is so important in our society, it often leads to diminished self-esteem and eventually to lost career opportunities (Shaywitz, 1996).

Contrary to popular presumption, dyslexia is not a visual disorder. It doesn't cause letters and words to "jump around" or reverse themselves. Research over the last 15 years suggests, instead, that the disorder involves the abnormalities in the brain's language processing circuits (Breier et al., 2003). Ironically, another "cause" may be language itself: Speakers of English—with its bizarre spelling menagerie, containing some 1120 ways to spell only 40 different sounds—are much more likely to be dyslexic than are Italian speakers, who must contend with only 33 combinations of letters for 25 sounds (Helmuth, 2001c; Paulesu et al., 2001).

In a sense, dyslexia may not even be a distinct disorder. Researcher Sally Shaywitz and her colleagues have made a case that there is no marker that sets dyslexic individuals entirely apart from others who are merely average readers. She argues that dyslexia is simply the diagnosis we give to an arbitrarily defined group of people occupying the lower end of the reading-abilities spectrum (Shaywitz et al., 1990).

Everyone does agree that dyslexia involves reading difficulties. Everyone also agrees that recent years have seen great strides made in understanding the neurological basis of the disorder, debunking some of the myths surrounding dyslexia (smart people, like Einstein, *can* have dyslexia), and developing treatments. Currently, the most effective treatments are special reading programs that emphasize the matching of sounds to letter combinations.

Attention-Deficit Hyperactivity Disorder (ADHD)   Some children have more trouble than others sitting still and focusing attention on a task, such as solving a math problem or listening to directions from the teacher. Many things can cause these symptoms, including distracting problems at home, abuse from peers, or merely a cultural tradition that places low value on the tasks that demand quiet attention. Besides those, there seems to be a brain-based condition, known as **attention-deficit hyperactivity disorder (ADHD),** that can interfere with even the best of intentions to focus attention and sit quietly (Barkley, 1998). The disorder is estimated to affect some 3 to 5% of school-age children (Brown, 2003b). (Contrary to a belief widely held among the general public, hyperactivity is *not* caused by eating sugar [Wolraich et al., 1995].)

ADHD is a controversial diagnosis, and its treatment is even more controversial (Sax & Kautz, 2003). Critics have claimed that ADHD is overdiagnosed, often being used to describe normal rambunctiousness or to blame children for the mistakes made by unskilled parents and teachers. In addition, drug treatment consisting of stimulant drugs strikes many people as being wrongheaded. On the other hand, many careful studies have demonstrated that properly administered drug therapy, along with behavioral therapy, can improve attention and diminish hyperactivity in a majority (about 70%) of individuals diagnosed with ADHD (Daley, 2004; MTA Cooperative Treatment Group, 2004).

Adjustment Disorders and Other Conditions

Although the large majority of everyday psychological problems involve making choices and dealing with confusion, frustration, and loss, the *DSM-IV* gives these problems short shrift under *adjustment disorders* and under the awkwardly named category, *other conditions that may be a focus of clinical attention.* Together, these categories represent a catch basin for relatively mild problems that do not fit well under other headings. They span a diverse range of con-

■ **Attention-deficit hyperactivity disorder (ADHD)**   A developmental disability involving short attention span, distractibility, and extreme difficulty in remaining inactive for any period.

"Wait! Come back! I was just kidding about wanting to be happy."

ditions that include mild depression, physical complaints, marital problems, academic problems, job problems, parent–child problems, bereavement, and even *malingering* (faking an illness). Consequently, the largest group of people suffering from mental problems may fit these headings—even though the *DSM-IV* devotes disproportionately little space to them. Ironically, because these adjustment difficulties are so prevalent, sufferers who turn to psychologists and psychiatrists account for a large proportion of the patient load seen by professionals in private practice.

PSYCHOLOGY IN YOUR LIFE:
SHYNESS

Being shy is a common problem, but it is not a *DSM-IV* disorder. Rather, *shyness* is a distressing pattern of avoiding or withdrawing from social contact. At the extreme, shy behavior may resemble a social phobia or avoidant personality disorder, as afflicted individuals seek to limit or escape from social interactions. As we have seen many times before, it is a matter of degree. Shy people are not utterly incapacitated by fear, yet they may suffer from loneliness and from lost opportunities to pursue interests and relationships.

What are the origins of this painful problem? For some people it may begin at birth: Shyness is one of three basic temperaments that have been observed among infants and traced through adult life (Kagan et al., 1988, 1994). Jerome Kagan has also recently proposed that shyness may have its origin in an overly excitable amygdala (Kagan, 2001). But shyness and other forms of social anxiety are also *learned* responses, so that even those who are not "born shy" can acquire shy behavior patterns.

On a hopeful note, shyness does not have to be a permanent condition. Many people overcome it on their own. Organizations such as Toastmasters help people build verbal skills and confidence in social situations. And many others have found the help they need in cognitive–behavioral therapy groups. If you suffer from shyness, we recommend Phil Zimbardo's (1990) book *Shyness* as a good place to look for help.

● Shyness may be painful, but it is not a *DSM-IV* disorder.

1. **RECALL:** The *DSM-IV* is based on the
   a. cognitive perspective.
   b. behavioral perspective.
   c. medical model.
   d. psychoanalytic view.

2. **RECALL:** Which disorder involves extreme swings of mood from elation to depression?
   a. panic disorder
   b. bipolar disorder
   c. schizophrenia
   d. unipolar depression

3. **APPLICATION:** According to the preparedness hypothesis, which one of the following phobias would you expect to be most common?
   a. fear of snakes (ophidiophobia)
   b. fear of books (bibliophobia)
   c. fear of horses (equinophobia)
   d. fear of the number 13 (triskaidekaphobia)

4. **RECALL:** Which of the following disorders involves a deficiency in memory?
   a. phobia
   b. antisocial personality
   c. dissociative fugue
   d. obsessive–compulsive disorder

5. **RECALL:** Which of the following is a disorder in which the individual displays more than one distinct personality?
   a. schizophrenia
   b. depersonalization disorder
   c. bipolar disorder
   d. dissociative identity disorder

6. **RECALL:** Which of the following is primarily a disorder of young American women?
   a. bipolar disorder
   b. schizophrenia
   c. anorexia nervosa
   d. antisocial personality disorder

7. **RECALL:** Hallucinations and delusions are symptoms of
   a. schizophrenia.
   b. somatoform disorders.
   c. anxiety disorders.
   d. depersonalization disorder.

8. **RECALL:** Which category of disorder is most common?
   a. schizophrenia
   b. dissociative disorders
   c. eating disorders
   d. the adjustment disorders and "other conditions that may be a focus of clinical attention"

9. **UNDERSTANDING THE CORE CONCEPT:** The *DSM-IV* groups most mental disorders by their
   a. treatments.
   b. causes.
   c. symptoms.
   d. theoretical basis.

ANSWERS: 1.c 2.b 3.a 4.c 5.d 6.c 7.a 8.d 9.c

DO IT YOURSELF! | The Insanity Plea: How Big Is the Problem?

How often is the plea of insanity used? Before you read about the insanity defense in the next part of the chapter, try to guess the approximate percentage of accused criminals in the United States who use a plea of insanity in court: _____%. You will find the correct answer in the "Psychology in Your Life" section on p. 516. (An answer within 10% indicates that you have an exceptionally clear grasp of reality!)

Hint: Research shows that the public has an exaggerated impression of the problem.

WHAT ARE THE CONSEQUENCES OF LABELING PEOPLE?

"Mad." "Maniac." "Mentally ill." "Crazy." "Insane." "Disturbed." "Neurotic." These, along with all the official diagnostic terms that appear in the *DSM-IV*, are labels used by the public, the courts, and mental health professionals to describe people who display mental disturbances. Ideally, an accurate diagnosis leads to an effective treatment program for the afflicted individual. Sometimes, however, labels create confusion and hurt. They can turn people into abnormality, however, should prompt a consult with a mental health professional.

● The medical model takes a "disease" view, while psychology sees psychological disorder as an interaction of biological, mental, social, and behavioral factors.

● HOW ARE PSYCHOLOGICAL DISORDERS CLASSIFIED?

The most widely used system for classifying mental disorders is the *DSM-IV,* which derives from psychiatry and has a bias toward the medical model. The *DSM-IV* recognizes more than 300 specific disorders, categorized by symptom patterns, but it has no category for "normal" functioning.

Among the *DSM-IV* categories are the *mood disorders,* which involve emotional disturbances. *Major depression* is the most common affective disorder, while *bipolar disorder* occurs less commonly. The *anxiety disorders* include *generalized anxiety disorder, panic disorder, phobic disorders,* and *obsessive–compulsive disorder.* The *somatoform disorders* involve the mind–body relationship in various ways. Those with *conversion disorder* have physical symptoms but no organic disease, while those with *hypochondriasis* suffer from exaggerated concern about illness. The *dissociative disorders* include *dissociative amnesia, dissociative fugue, depersonalization disorder,* and *dissociative identity disorder.* All disrupt the integrated functioning of memory, consciousness, or personal identity. Two patterns of *eating disorder* are common: *anorexia nervosa* (self-starvation) and *bulimia nervosa* (binging and purging). Both are related to unrealistic, negative body images and are difficult to treat. *Schizophrenia* is a psychotic disorder, characterized by extreme distortions in perception, thinking, emotion, behavior, and language. Schizophrenia takes five forms: *disorganized, catatonic, paranoid, undifferentiated,* and *residual* types. Evidence for the causes of schizophrenia has been found in a variety of factors including genetics, abnormal brain structure, and biochemistry. *Personality disorders* are patterns of perception, thinking, or behavior that are long-standing and inflexible and that impair an individual's functioning. They include the *narcissistic, antisocial,* and *borderline personality disorders.* The *DSM-IV* also lists a variety of *developmental disorders,* including *autism, dyslexia,* and *attention-deficit hyperactivity disorder.*

The most common forms of disorder are classified in the *DSM-IV* as the *adjustment disorders* and *"other conditions that may be a focus of clinical attention."* These include a wide range of problems in living. *Shyness* is a widespread problem—and a treatable one—but it is not officially a disorder, unless it goes to the extreme of a social phobia or avoidant personality disorder.

● The *DSM-IV,* the most widely used system, classifies disorders by their mental and behavioral symptoms.

● WHAT ARE THE CONSEQUENCES OF LABELING PEOPLE?

Labeling someone as psychologically or mentally disordered is ultimately a matter of human judgment. Yet even professional judgments can be biased by prejudices. Those labeled with psychological disorders may be depersonalized in ways that most physically ill people are not. Culture has an effect on whether a behavior is called normal, abnormal, or merely unusual. Cross-cultural research suggests that people everywhere distinguish between psychotic individuals and those whom they label shamans, prophets, or visionaries.

"Insanity" is a special sort of label that is awarded by the courts. Insanity, however, is not a psychological or psychiatric term. In fact, the insanity defense is not often used, much less used successfully—although a few high-profile cases have captured public attention.

● Ideally, accurate diagnoses lead to proper treatments, but diagnoses may also become labels that depersonalize individuals and ignore the social and cultural contexts in which their problems arise.

REVIEW TEST

For each of the following items, choose the single correct or best answer. The answer key appears at the end.

1. The medical model views mental disorder as
   a. a character defect.
   b. a disease or illness.
   c. an interaction of biological, cognitive, behavioral, social, and cultural factors.
   d. normal behavior in an abnormal context.

2. Which of the following is *not* one of the six indicators of possible abnormality agreed upon by psychologists?
   a. chronic physical illness
   b. observer discomfort
   c. unconventionality
   d. irrationality

3. The *DSM-IV* is
   a. a personality inventory.
   b. the most widely used classification system for mental disorders.
   c. the neurochemical implicated in anxiety disorders.
   d. a class of psychoactive drugs effective in the treatment of schizophrenia.

4. A long-standing pattern of irresponsible behavior that hurts others without causing feelings of guilt or remorse is typical of
   a. an obsessive–compulsive disorder.
   b. an antisocial personality disorder.
   c. a narcissistic personality disorder.
   d. paranoid schizophrenia.

5. A young woman wanders into a hospital, claiming not to know who she is, where she came from, or how she got there. Her symptoms indicate that she might be suffering from a(n) _____ disorder.
   a. anxiety
   b. affective
   c. personality
   d. dissociative

6. Which of the following statements about phobic disorders is true?
   a. Any extreme and irrational fear of a situation or thing, such as of spiders, is considered a "phobia."
   b. The preparedness hypothesis suggests that some people learn their fears from their parents at an early age.
   c. Phobias represent one form of affective disorders.
   d. all of the above

7. _____ has been called the "common cold of psychopathology," because it occurs so frequently and because almost everyone has experienced it, at least briefly, at some time.
   a. Obsessive–compulsive disorder
   b. Bipolar disorder
   c. Depression
   d. Paranoid schizophrenia

8. A person who suffers from _____ cannot eat normally but engages in a ritual of "binging"—periodic binges of overeating—followed by "purging" with induced vomiting or use of laxatives.
   a. anorexia nervosa
   b. bulimia nervosa
   c. inhibition
   d. mania

9. The _____ type of schizophrenia is characterized by delusions.
   a. residual
   b. catatonic
   c. paranoid
   d. undifferentiated

10. Rosenhan believes that his "pseudopatients" were not recognized as normal because
   a. the staff members in the mental hospitals were stupid and foolish.
   b. the staff members in the mental hospitals were just as disturbed as the patients.
   c. mental illness is a myth.
   d. staff members did not expect patients to be normal.

ANSWERS: 1. b 2. a 3. b 4. b 5. d 6. a 7. c 8. b 9. c 10. d

KEY TERMS

Psychopathology (p. 485)

Hallucinations (p. 485)

Delusions (p. 485)

Affect (p. 485)

Medical model (p. 488)

Social–cognitive–behavioral approach (p. 489)

DSM-IV (p. 492)

Neurosis (p. 493)

Psychosis (p. 493)

Mood disorders (p. 493)

Major depression (p. 494)

Seasonal affective disorder or **SAD** (p. 495)

Bipolar disorder (p. 497)

Anxiety disorders (p. 497)

Generalized anxiety disorder (p. 498)

Panic disorder (p. 498)

Agoraphobia (p. 498)

Phobias (p. 499)

Preparedness hypothesis (p. 500)

Obsessive–compulsive disorder (p. 500)

Somatoform disorders (p. 501)

Conversion disorder (p. 501)

Hypochondriasis (p. 502)

Dissociative disorders (p. 502)

Dissociative amnesia (p. 502)

Dissociative fugue (p. 503)

Depersonalization disorder (p. 504)

Dissociative identity disorder (p. 504)

Anorexia nervosa (p. 505)

Bulimia nervosa (p. 505)

Schizophrenia (p. 506)

Diathesis–stress hypothesis (p. 509)

Personality disorders (p. 509)

Narcissistic personality disorder (p. 510)

Antisocial personality disorder (p. 510)

Borderline personality disorder (p. 510)

Autism (p. 510)

Dyslexia (p. 511)

Attention-deficit hyperactivity disorder (ADHD) (p. 512)

Insanity (p. 517)

OUR RECOMMENDED BOOKS AND VIDEOS

BOOKS

Casey, N. (Ed.). (2002). *Unholy ghost: Writers on depression.* New York: Perennial. In this "reader on depression"—including observations and stories by writers including Russell Banks, Susanna Kaysen, William Styron, and Anne Beattie—the selections offer vivid descriptions of how depression feels, the behaviors it causes, its effects on others, and the drama of wide-ranging treatments of depression.

Colas, E. (1998). *Just checking: Scenes from the life of an obsessive-compulsive.* New York: Pocket Books. The author discusses her incessant, obsessive–compulsive tendency to worry about *everything,* and her inability to resist the urge to check and double-check every threat and possible action in everyday life, from electric lights and appliances to the dangers of driving accidents.

Corrigan, P., & Lundin, J. (1997). *Don't call me nuts.* Tinley Park, IL: Recovery Press. Media attention to mental disorders (including books and films such as those we recommend in this text) can both inform and misinform. How can those recovering from mental illness overcome social stigma and rejection and become accepted and respected? The authors—respectively a psychiatrist and a recovering mental patient—address the many forms of rejection and fear confronting those diagnosed with and recovering from mental illness.

Gabbard, G. O., & Gabbard, K. (1999). *Psychiatry and the cinema.* Arlington, VA: American Psychiatric Association. The authors present an examination of the three eras of psychiatric portrayals in the history of film—Experts or Quacks; Healers; and Evil Agents—and an in-depth look at seven films that capture these distinctive types of portrayals.

Gregory, J. (2003). *Sickened: A memoir of a Munchausen by proxy childhood.* New York: Bantam. In search of attention, excitement, or purpose, Julie Gregory's disordered mother made and kept her sick, then dragged her to doctors and hospitals in search of drugs and surgery for nonexistent ailments. Even as an adult, Gregory never recognized she had been abused until she heard a lecture on MBP.

Jamison, K. R. (1996). *Touched with fire: Manic depressive illness and the artistic temperament.* New York: Free Press. Best-selling psychiatrist-author Kay Redfield Jamison, who chronicled her own manic–depressive illness in *An Unquiet Mind* (1995), examines the many cases of lives whose genius in music, art, and the sciences were also afflicted—not coincidentally—with extreme and uncontrollable moods.

Moskovitz, R. (2001). *Lost in the mirror: An inside look at borderline personality disorder* (2nd ed.). Dallas, TX: Taylor Publishing. Most borderline personality disordered individuals have a history of abuse; most are women. Moskovitz reviews several case histories of BPD, and suggests treatments for the variety of symptoms: guilt, self-mutilation, self-hate, and suicide risk, among others. With a preface by Chris Costner Sizemore, the real person behind the multiple-personality subject of the book and movie *The Three Faces of Eve.*

Porter, R. (2003). *Madness: A brief history.* Oxford, U.K.: Oxford University Press. Today the attitude is widespread that most people struggle with some degree of mental illness at some point in life. But for most of history, the mentally ill have been ostracized as unacceptably different, persecuted, imprisoned, "treated" with torture, or at best dismissed as "sick." The author's engaging account recounts how attitudes shifted over centuries of recognizing and responding to mental illness in human societies.

Sheehan, S. (1982). *Is there no place on earth for me?* New York: Vintage. Journalist Susan Sheehan lived with a young schizophrenic woman and her family members off and on for several years in order to compose this chronicle of the life, times, and marginally helpful treatment of a complex, colorful, difficult disorder.

Torrey, E. F., & Miller, J. (2002). *The invisible plague: The rise and fall of mental illness from 1750 to the present.* Rutgers, NJ: Rutgers University Press. Here is a comprehensive and well-presented history of mental illness in the Western world, with no pat answers about causes or treatment, with a lighter and more literary tone than you'd expect in a sad history.

Wahl, O. F. (1999). *Media madness: Public images of mental illness.* Rutgers, NJ: Rutgers University Press. This review of decades of films portraying mental illness reveals that most media images characterize disordered individuals as frightening or dangerous and contribute to general social stigmatization of mental health problems.

VIDEOS

A Beautiful Mind. (2001, color, 135 min.). Directed by Ron Howard; starring Russell Crowe, Jennifer Connelly, Ed Harris. This absorbing, Oscar-winning film is based on the true story of the early career of Nobel Prize–winning mathematician John Forbes Nash, who suffered life-long from paranoid schizophrenia.

As Good as It Gets. (1997, color, 138 min.). Directed by James Brooks; starring Jack Nicholson, Helen Hunt, Greg Kinnear, Cuba Gooding, Jr., Shirley Knight. An obsessive–compulsive writer becomes entangled, much against his will and inclinations, in the lives of a neighbor, a waitress, and their families, in his efforts to keep his world predictable and protected. For all its funny as well as tragic moments, the film makes clear the struggle of those who suffer from anxiety disorders.

K-Pax. (2001, color, 120 min.). Directed by Iain Softley; starring Kevin Spacey, Jeff Bridges. A mental hospital patient, claiming actually to be visitor from another planet, baffles his psychiatrist, whose own life is touched by the "alien's" abilities as he searches for clues to the patient's true past.

Mr. Jones. (1993, color, 114 min.). Directed by Mike Figgis; starring Richard Gere, Lena Olin, Delroy Lindo. A melodramatic romance between a psychiatrist and her bipolar patient allows Richard Gere to portray vividly the scary highs of mania and the desolate lows of depression.

One Flew over the Cuckoo's Nest. (1975, color, 133 min.). Directed by Milos Forman; starring Jack Nicholson, Louise Fletcher, Brad Dourif, Will Sampson. Nicholson won the Oscar for his portrayal of McMurphy, a petty criminal whose "soft sentence" in a psychiatric hospital turns into a war between the patients and the controlling nurse who supervises their ward. Depictions of electroconvulsive therapy and psychosurgery are inaccurate and disturbing but essential for the story's drama and its lessons about the abuses of power.

Sling Blade. (1996, color, 134 min.). Directed by Billy Bob Thornton; starring Billy Bob Thornton, Dwight Yoakam, J. T. Walsh, John Ritter, Lucas Black, Natalie Canerday. This is the fascinating picture of a mentally deficient man, a lifelong victim of abuse, whose devotion to his first friend outside an institution has violent consequences. Superb performances sharpen this film, which won the Oscar for Best Screenplay Adaptation.

The Three Faces of Eve. (1957, black-and-white, 91 min.). Directed by Nunnally Johnson; starring Joanne Woodward, Lee J. Cobb, David Wayne. This classic film is based on the true story of a woman found to have at least three distinct personalities and the efforts she and her therapists made to find the source—and the resolution—of her dissociative disorder. Woodward won the Oscar for her astonishing performance.

Vertigo. (1958, color, 128 min.). Directed by Alfred Hitchcock; starring James Stewart, Kim Novak, Barbara Bel Geddes. A police detective with a fear of heights (acrophobia) is lured first into a mysterious romance and then a crime in this dramatic cinematic portrayal of anxiety and terror.

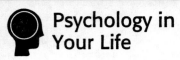

CORE CONCEPTS

▼

We usually adapt our behavior to the demands of the social situation, and in ambiguous situations we take our cues from the behavior of others in that setting.

▼

The judgments we make about others depend not only on their behavior but also on our interpretation of their actions within a social context.

▼

The power of the situation can help us understand violence and terrorism, but a broader understanding requires multiple perspectives that go beyond the boundaries of traditional psychology.

Psychology in Your Life

On Being "Shoe" at Yale

How college students dress may be a matter of their "taste," but it may also be a matter of unconscious social influence to dress like the "in crowd" dresses.

Loving Relationships

The end of a relationship can be difficult for everyone. Social psychologists have begun to study what it takes to keep people caring about each other.

Multiple Perspectives on Terrorism

A field experiment on groups of Boy Scouts holds lessons for dealing with conflict in the Middle East.

USING PSYCHOLOGY TO LEARN PSYCHOLOGY:

Social Psychology

ON A SUMMER SUNDAY in California, a siren shattered the serenity of college student Tommy Whitlow's morning. A police car screeched to a halt in front of his home. Within minutes, Tommy was charged with a felony, informed of his constitutional rights, frisked, and handcuffed. After he was booked and fingerprinted at the city jail, Tommy was blindfolded and transported to the Stanford County Prison, where he was stripped and issued a smock-type uniform with an I.D. number on the front and back. Tommy became "Prisoner 647." Eight other college students were also arrested and assigned numbers during that mass arrest by the local police.

The prison guards were anonymous in their khaki military uniforms, reflector sunglasses, and nameless identity as "Mr. Correctional Officer," but with symbols of power shown off in their big night sticks, whistles, and handcuffs. To them, the powerless prisoners were nothing more than their worthless numbers.

The guards insisted that prisoners obey all of their many arbitrary rules without question or hesitation. Failure to do so led to losses of privileges. At first, privileges included opportunities to read, write, or talk to other inmates. Later, the slightest protest resulted in the loss of "privileges" of eating, sleeping, washing, or having visitors during visiting nights. Failure to obey rules also resulted in a variety of unpleasant tasks

Scenes from the Stanford prison experiment.

such as endless push-ups, jumping jacks, and number count-offs that lasted for hours on end. Each day saw an escalation of the level of hostile abuse by the guards against their prisoners: making them clean toilets with bare hands, do push-ups while a guard stepped on the prisoner's back, spend long hours naked in solitary confinement, and finally engage in degrading forms of sexual humiliation. "Prisoner 647" encountered some guards whose behavior toward him and the other prisoners was sadistic, taking apparent pleasure in cruelty; others were just tough and abusive, but none of the few "good" guards ever challenged the extremely demeaning actions of the "perpetrators of evil."

Less than 36 hours after the mass arrest, "Prisoner 8412," the ringleader of an aborted prisoner rebellion that morning, had to be released because of an extreme stress reaction of screaming, crying, rage, and depression. On successive days, three more prisoners developed similar stress-related symptoms. A fifth prisoner developed a psychosomatic rash all over his body when the parole board rejected his appeal, and he too was released from the Stanford County Jail.

At night, "Prisoner 647" tried to remember what Tommy Whitlow had been like before he became a prisoner. He also tried to imagine his tormentors before they became guards. He reminded himself that he was a college student who had answered a newspaper ad and agreed to be a subject in a two-week psychological experiment on prison life. He had thought it would be fun to do something unusual, and he could always use some extra money.

Everyone in the prison, guard and prisoner alike, had been selected from a large pool of student volunteers. On the basis of extensive psychological tests and interviews, the volunteers had been judged as law-abiding, emotionally stable, physically healthy, and "normal-average" on all psychological measures. In this mock prison experiment, assignment of participants to the independent variable treatment of "guard" or "prisoner" roles had been determined by random assignment. Thus, in the beginning there were no systematic differences between the "ordinary" college males who were in the two different conditions. By the end of the study, there were no similarities between these two alien groups. The prisoners lived in the jail around the clock, and the guards worked standard eight-hour shifts.

As guards, students who had been pacifists and "nice guys" in their usual life settings behaved aggressively—sometimes even sadistically. As prisoners, psychologically stable students soon behaved pathologically, passively resigning themselves to their unexpected fate of learned helplessness. The power of the simulated prison situation had created a new social reality—a functionally real prison—in the minds of both the jailers and their captives. The situation became so powerfully disturbing that the researchers were forced to terminate the two-week study after only six days.

Although Tommy Whitlow said he wouldn't want to go through it again, he valued the personal experience because he learned so much about himself and about human nature. Fortunately, he and the other students were basically healthy, and extensive debriefing showed that they readily bounced back from the prison experience. Follow-ups over many years revealed no lasting negative effects on these students. The participants had all learned an important lesson: Never underestimate the power of a bad situation to overwhelm the personalities and good upbringing of even the best and brightest among us (Haney et al., 1973; Haney & Zimbardo, 1998; Zimbardo, 1973,

1975; Zimbardo et al., 1999; replicated in Australia by Lovibond et al., 1979). For detailed information about this study and its relationship to recent abuses of Iraqi prisoners by American military police guards, see *www.prisonexperiment.org.*

Suppose *you* had been a subject in the Stanford prison experiment. Would you have been a good guard—or a sadist? A model compliant prisoner—or a rebel? Could you have resisted the pressures and stresses of these circumstances? We'd all like to believe we would be good guards and heroic prisoners; we would never step across that line between good and evil. And, of course, we all believe that we would be able to keep things in perspective, knowing that it was "just an experiment," only role-playing and not real. But the best bet is that most of us would react the same way as these participants did. This disturbing study raises many questions about how well we really know ourselves, our inner dispositional qualities, and how much we appreciate the subtle powers of external forces on us, the situational qualities.

● Scene at the Abu Ghraib prison .

Welcome to social psychology, the field that investigates how individuals affect each other. It may be a relief to hear that not all of social psychology brings such bad news about ourselves as does the Stanford prison experiment. This exciting field of psychology also explores the forces that bring people together for friendships and loving relationships. As you study **social psychology** in this chapter, you will learn how people's thoughts, feelings, perceptions, motives, and behavior are influenced by interactions with others. Social psychologists try to understand behavior within its *social context.* Defined broadly, the **social context** includes the real, imagined, or symbolic *presence of other people;* the *activities and interactions* that take place among people; the *settings* in which behavior occurs; and the *expectations* and social *norms* governing behavior in a given setting (Sherif, 1981).

Most of all, the Stanford prison experiment conducted by Philip Zimbardo (one of your authors) underscores the *power of social situations* to control human behavior. This is a major theme to emerge from social psychological research of the past 50 years. In the first part of this chapter, you will see how seemingly minor features of social settings can have a huge impact on what we think and how we feel and act. In these studies you will see how the situation can produce conformity to group standards—even when the group is clearly "wrong." Other studies will demonstrate how situational forces can lead many average people to blindly follow orders—even orders to harm others.

Yet, as powerful as the situation can be, psychologists know that it is not *objective reality* to which we respond. Rather, we respond to our *subjective interpretation* of the situation—to our perception—which can differ significantly from person to person. This, then, is the second great theme in social psychology: the construction of a *subjective social reality.* We must grasp this world of expectations and perceptions in order to understand the attractive forces at work in building friendships and romantic relationships as well as the repulsive forces underlying prejudice and violence.

Our examination of prejudice will set the stage for a third theme that will combine the first two. We will see how social psychologists have experimented with altering the situation to change subjective social reality that, in turn, helps *to promote the human condition.* This, we will discover, has important implications for understanding violence and terrorism and for resolving conflicts among individuals, groups, and even nations. We begin now with the first of these three themes, the power of the situation.

■ **Social psychology**   The branch of psychology that studies the effects of social variables and cognitions on individual behavior and social interactions.
■ **Social context**   The combination of (a) people, (b) the activities and interactions among people, (c) the setting in which behavior occurs, and (d) the expectations and social norms governing behavior in that setting.

HOW DOES THE SOCIAL SITUATION AFFECT OUR BEHAVIOR?

Suppose that you find yourself in an interview, with the possibility of being hired for the job of your dreams. Afterward, the interview suggests that you go to lunch together in the company cafeteria. Will you order a sandwich, a salad, or a full-course meal? Will you leave the plastic tray under your plate as you eat? Will you put the tiny paper napkin in your lap? Will you shift your fork from your left hand to your right hand as you put the food you cut into your mouth? Even in this simple social situation, there are many social and cultural rules governing what is appropriate and acceptable behavior. If you are like most people in an unfamiliar situation such as this, you will take your cues from those around you.

Social psychologists believe that, even when the situation is a familiar one, such as a college classroom, the primary determinant of individual behavior is the social situation in which that behavior occurs. So powerful is the situation that it can sometimes dominate our personalities and override our past history of learning, values, and beliefs. We will see that the pressures of the situation can create powerful psychological effects, such as prejudice, blind obedience, and violence. Social roles, rules, how we are dressed, competition, or the mere presence of others can profoundly influence how we behave. Often, these subtle situational variables affect us in many ways even without our awareness. Our Core Concept emphasizes this point:

CORE CONCEPT

> We usually adapt our behavior to the demands of the social situation, and in ambiguous situations we take our cues from the behavior of others in that setting.

In this section, we will review some research that explores this concept, called **situationism.** Situationism assumes that the environment, or the behavioral context, can have both subtle and forceful effects on people's thoughts, feelings, and behaviors. Situationism is contrasted with *dispositionism,* the tendency to attribute behavior to internal factors, such as genes, traits, and character qualities. Here we will look particularly at the power of the situation to create conformity, obedience, and sometimes even the willingness to inflict harm on others.

Social Standards of Behavior

A job interview, such as the one described above, provides an example of a situational influence on your behavior as you try to do "what is right" in front of your prospective employer. You will also notice the power of the situation when you compare the way students talk to their friends versus their professors. Most people learn to size up their social circumstances and conform their behavior to situational demands. The responses most people make depend heavily on two factors: the social roles they play and social norms of the group. Let us look at both of these closely.

Social Roles   Whether you are at a concert, a department meeting, a pizza parlor, or in a rock concert mosh pit, you will see that people operate by rules that depend on their *social roles.* You can see this more clearly by responding to the question: Who are you? Almost certainly you and other readers of this book are students or professors of psychology—social roles that imply different sets of behaviors. (One, for example, takes exams; the other grades them.)

■ **Situationism**   The view that environmental conditions influence people's behavior as much or more than their personal dispositions do.

It is likely that you take on many other social roles in different parts of your life. Are you a part-time employee? Someone's child? A cyclist? A musician? A friend? A lover? A spammer? A **social role** is one of several socially defined patterns of behavior that are expected of persons in a given setting or group. The roles you assume may result from your interests, abilities, and goals—or they may be imposed on you by the group or by cultural, economic, or biological conditions beyond your control. In any case, social roles prescribe your behavior by making obvious what you should do, how you should do it, and when.

The situations in which you live and function also determine the roles that are available to you and the behaviors others expect of you. Being a college student, for example, is a social role that carries certain implicit assumptions about attending classes, studying, and handing in papers before deadline. In addition, the adoption of this role makes other roles less likely. Thus, your role as college student diminishes the chances that you will assume the role of homeless person, drug pusher, or witch doctor, for example. By the same token, because you have college experience, numerous other roles (such as manager, teacher, attorney, doctor, and politician) are available to you.

The Stanford prison experiment cast guards and prisoners in different social roles. Yet, just a week before, their roles (college students) were very similar. Chance, in the form of random assignment, had decided their new roles as guards or prisoners, and these roles created status and power differences that influenced everyone's behavior in that prison situation.

Remember that no one taught the participants to play their roles. Each student called upon *scripts* about those roles. A **script** involves a person's knowledge about the sequence of events and actions that are expected of a particular social role. So, if an individual understands the role of "guard" as someone who uses coercive rules to limit the freedom of "prisoners," then that person is likely to use a script derived from that schema to become an authoritarian guard under conditions such as the Stanford prison experiment. In fact, many students in the guard role were surprised at how easy it was for them to enjoy controlling and dominating other people, just as did guards whom they read about or saw in films.

In trying to understand what happened in the Stanford prison experiment, we should note that all the prisoners and guards were male. Would it have made any difference if women had been in the roles of prisoner and guard? We will never know because the unanticipated negative impact of the experiment on both the guards and prisoners would make it unethical to do the experiment again. The possibility of gender differences, however, is raised by this fact: The experiment was called off after a graduate student, Christina Maslach, visited the "prison" and was shocked by what she saw. Immediately she conferred with Dr. Zimbardo, whom she implored to end the study. After some intense discussion, he agreed to do so. (Drs. Maslach and Zimbardo were later married and have lived happily ever after.)

Social Norms In addition to specific social roles, groups develop many "unwritten rules" for the ways that members should act. These expectations, called **social norms,** dictate socially appropriate attitudes and behaviors. Social norms can be broad guidelines, such as ideas about which political or religious attitudes are considered acceptable. Social norms can also be quite specific, embodying standards of conduct such as being quiet in the library or shining your shoes for a job interview. Norms can guide conversation, as when they restrict discussion of sensitive or taboo subjects in the presence of certain

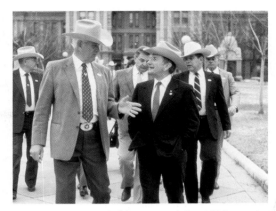

● Social norms can define rigid dress codes for group members.

"GOSH, ACKERMAN, DIDN'T ANYONE IN PERSONNEL TELL YOU ABOUT OUR CORPORATE CULTURE?"

◄ **CONNECTION: CHAPTER 8**

Schemas are cognitive structures that integrate knowledge and expectations about a topic or concept.

■ **Social role** One of several socially defined patterns of behavior that are expected of persons in a given setting or group.
■ **Script** Knowledge about the sequence of events and actions that is expected in a particular setting.
■ **Social norms** A group's expectations regarding what is appropriate and acceptable for its members' attitudes and behaviors.

company. And norms can define dress codes, whether requiring uniforms or business suits or prohibiting shorts and tank tops. In the Stanford prison experiment, the guards quickly developed norms for abusive behavior. That norm was not already present in the situation, it was an *emergent norm*, one that emerged out of the transactions between guards and prisoners in that situation. Some norms exist in unwritten rules that are built into various situations, such as when teachers are lecturing, students are expected to listen and not talk simultaneously. However, what about the norms governing your behavior in elevators? We bet you always face the front of the elevator and either stop talking to a friend or talk lower when others are there as well. Why? Where are those rules written? How did you learn them? What will happen the next time when you enter an elevator filled with other people and *you face the rear?* Try that little experiment and see how others react.

When a person joins a new group, such as a work group or a group of friends, there is always an adjustment period during which the individual tries to discover how best to fit in. Adjustment to a group typically involves discovering its social norms. Individuals experience this adjustment in two ways: by first noticing the *uniformities and regularities* in certain behaviors, and then by observing the *negative consequences* when someone violates a social norm. For example, a new student in your school who carries books and notes in an attaché case will be seen as "out of it" if backpacks are in, and vice versa in other schools.

Social Norms Influence Students' Political Views   Social scientist Theodore Newcomb wanted to know if the political views of faculty can influence those of their students. The college: Vermont's Bennington College. The time: the 1930s. The students: from wealthy, conservative homes with decidedly conservative values. The faculty: young, dynamic, and liberal. Bennington's campus culture had a prevailing norm of political and economic liberalism. Social psychologist Theodore Newcomb wondered: Which forces most shape the attitudes of these students, their family's or their faculty's? His data showed that the norms of the campus won the war of influence against the norms of the family. In most women, their initial attitude of conservatism were transformed as they progressed through their college years, so that by their senior year they had clearly converted to liberal thinking and causes (Newcomb, 1943). But was that shift in attitudes enduring?

Twenty years later, the social influence of the Bennington experience was still evident. Women who had graduated as liberals were still liberals; the minority who had resisted the prevailing liberal norm had remained conservative. This was accomplished in part by marrying their "own kind" politically. Most of the women had married husbands with values similar to their own—either liberal or conservative—and created supportive new home environments that sustained those different ideologies. The liberal Bennington allegiance was evident in the 1960 presidential election when 60% of the class Newcomb had investigated voted for liberal John Kennedy, rather than conservative Richard Nixon—in contrast to less than 30% support for Kennedy among graduates of comparable colleges at that time (Newcomb et al., 1967).

Campus culture is not the only source of norms and group pressure, of course. One's workplace, neighborhood, religious group, and family all communicate standards for behavior—and threaten sanctions (such as firing, social rejection, or excommunication) for violating those norms. But a college or university environment can have a powerful impact on young people. This is especially true if they have had narrow life experiences and not previously encountered attitudes radically different from their own. For example, new college students commonly adopt classmates' political opinions, as in the Bennington study, and also frequently take on religious beliefs of classmates, as

CONNECTION: CHAPTER 6

Bandura demonstrated that we acquire many social behaviors through *observational learning*.

well as attitudes about sex and alcohol (see Prentice & Miller, 1993; Schroeder & Prentice, 1995).

Conformity

How powerful are these social pressures? We can see the effects of social pressure in people's moods, clothing styles, and leisure activities (Totterdell, 2000; Totterdell et al., 1998). This tendency to mimic other people is called the *chameleon effect* (Chartrand & Bargh, 1999). A personal example of the effects of pervasive social pressures in a college environment on the way students dress can be seen in the study outlined in the "Psychology in Your Life" feature at the end of this section.

We have seen how social pressure in political attitudes influenced Bennington College students. But, can social influence be strong enough to make people follow a group norm that is clearly and objectively wrong? Could the power of that situation prove stronger than the evidence of your own eyes?

The Asch Effect   Solomon Asch (1940, 1956) set out to answer just such questions by having a group of his confederates challenge the perception of individual students by making them think that their eyes were deceiving them. In Asch's study, male college students were told they would be participating in a study of visual perception. They were shown cards with three lines of differing lengths and asked to indicate which of the three lines was the same length as a separate, standard line (see Figure 14.1). The problem was simple: The lines were different enough so that mistakes were rare when volunteers responded alone. But when those same individuals were put in a group of other students who had been coached to give wrong answers, then everything changed.

Here's how the experiment worked. On the first three trials, everyone agreed on the correct answer. But the first person to respond on the fourth trial reported an obviously incorrect judgment, reporting as equal two lines that were clearly different. So did the next person and so on, until all members of the group but the remaining one (the only real subject in the experiment) had unanimously agreed on an erroneous judgment. That person then had to decide whether to go along with everyone else's view of the situation and conform or remain independent, standing by the objective evidence of his own eyes. This group pressure was imposed on 12 of the 18 trials.

What did he and other participants in his position finally do? As you might expect, nearly everyone showed signs of disbelief and discomfort when faced with a majority who saw the world so differently from the way they did. But despite their distress the group pressure usually prevailed. Three-quarters of those subjected to group pressure conformed to the false judgment of the group one or more times, while only one-fourth remained completely independent on all trials. In various related studies, between 50 and 80% conformed with the majority's false estimate at least once; a third yielded to the majority's wrong judgments on half or more of the critical trials.

Social psychologists call this the **Asch effect:** the influence of a group majority on the judgments of an individual. The Asch effect has become the classic illustration of **conformity**—the tendency for people to adopt the behavior and opinions presented by other group members. Even though individuals were judging matters of fact, not merely personal opinions, most caved in to conformity pressures.

At the same time, we should recognize that the Asch effect, powerful as it is, still does not make everyone conform. Conformity researchers do regularly find "independents," individuals who are bothered and even dismayed to find themselves in disagreement with the majority, but who nonetheless stand their

◀ **CONNECTION: CHAPTER 5**

Asch made us realize that *perceptual interpretation* involves the social situation.

■ **Asch effect**   A form of conformity in which a group majority influences individual judgments.
■ **Conformity**   The tendency for people to adopt the behaviors, attitudes, and opinions of other members of a group.

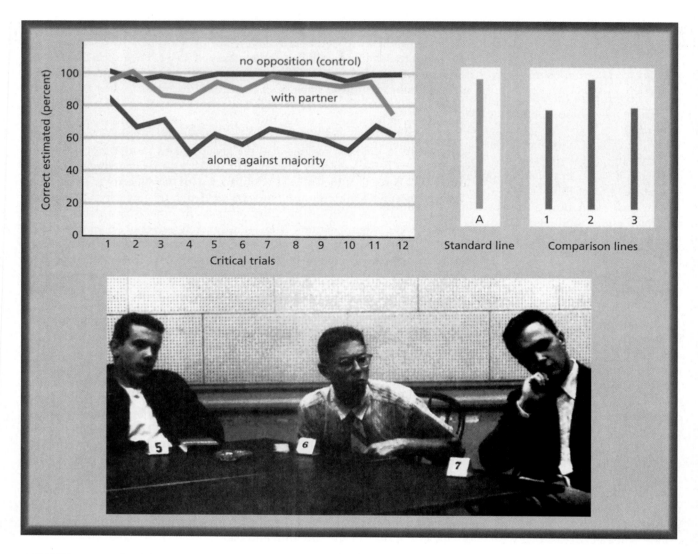

● FIGURE 14.1 Conformity in the Asch Experiments

In this photo from Asch's study, the naive individual, number 6, displays obvious concern about the majority's erroneous judgment. At top right, you see a typical stimulus array. At top left, the graph illustrates conformity across 12 critical trials, when individuals were grouped with a unanimous majority or had the support of a single dissenting partner. (A lower percentage of correct estimates indicates a greater degree of conformity with the group's false judgment.)

ground and "call 'em as they see 'em"—even to the point of deliberately giving a wrong answer when the group gives a correct one (Friend et al., 1990). As we will see in a host of other studies in this chapter, more often than not the majority conforms, complies, and gives up personal standards for group standards. However, this situational power faces one challenge, that of *individual heroic defiance. Heroes* are people who are able to resist situational forces that overwhelm their peers and remain true to their personal values. They are the "whistle blowers" who challenge corrupt or immoral systems by not going along with the company norm. Sherron Watkins (Schwartz & Watkins, 2003), a vice president at Enron Corporation, did that when she exposed the illegal transactions of Enron, and Army Reservist Joe Darby exposed the horrendous abuses of prisoners by his buddies at Iraq's Abu Ghraib Prison. But these "heroes" are often despised by their former colleagues and made to pay a high price for not being a silent "team player." Darby, for example, had to go into hiding under protective custody for many months because of death threats against him by soldiers in his battalion for humiliating them by exposing the photos of sadistic abuse of prisoners.

Group Characteristics That Produce Conformity In further experiments, Asch identified three factors that influence whether a person will yield to group pressure: (1) *the size of the majority,* (2) *the presence of a partner who dissented* from the majority, and (3) *the size of the discrepancy* between the correct answer and the majority's position. He found that individuals tended to conform with a unanimous majority of as few as three people, but not if they faced only one or two. However, even in a large group, giving the person one ally who dissented from the majority opinion sharply reduced conformity (as shown in Figure 14.1). With such a "partner," nearly all subjects resisted the pressures to conform. Remarkably, however, some individuals continued to yield to the group even with a partner present. All who yielded underestimated the influence of the social pressure and the frequency of their conformity; a few even claimed that they really had seen the lines as the majority had claimed so were not conforming, only reporting accurately what they were seeing (Asch, 1955, 1956).

Numerous studies have revealed additional factors that influence conformity. (These experiments have included both females and males.) Specifically, a person is more likely to conform under the following circumstances:

▌ When a judgment task is difficult or ambiguous (Deutsch & Gerard, 1955; Lott & Lott, 1961; Saltzstein & Sandberg, 1979).

▌ When the group members are perceived as especially competent.

▌ When responses are given publicly rather than privately.

▌ When the group majority is unanimous—but once that unanimity is broken, the rate of conformity drops dramatically (Allen & Levine, 1969; Morris & Miller, 1975).

So now imagine you are about to vote openly in a group, as is common in clubs or on boards of directors. You will probably conform to the group majority if: (a) the issue being decided is complex or confusing, (b) others in the group seem to know what they are talking about, (c) you must vote by raising your hand instead of casting an anonymous ballot, (d) the entire group casting their votes before you all vote in a certain way, and especially if (e) the leader votes first.

Groupthink Groups can also be pressured to conform. This important social psychological process that encourages conformity in the thinking and decision making of individuals when they are in groups, like committees, has been termed "groupthink" by psychologist Irving Janis (1972; Janis & Mann, 1977). In *groupthink,* members of the group attempt to conform their opinions to what each believes to be the consensus of the group. This conformity bias leads the group to take actions on which each member might normally consider to be unwise. Seven conditions likely to promote groupthink are:

▌ Isolation of the group

▌ High group cohesiveness

▌ Directive leadership

▌ Lack of norms requiring methodical procedures

▌ Homogeneity of members' social background and ideology

▌ High stress from external threats with low hope of a better solution than that of the group leader

This concept was first developed to help understand bad decisions made by the U.S. government regarding the bombing of Pearl Harbor, the Vietnam War, and the invasion of Cuba's Bay of Pigs. Later, others have cited groupthink as a factor that contributed to the faulty decisions in the space shuttle disasters, the bankruptcy of Enron Corporation, and, more recently, the 2003 decision to wage war against Iraq (see Shwartz & Wald, 2003). The U.S.

● Sharron Watkins, an executive at Enron, realized that illegal activities were taking place and exposed the mess publicly; she is a heroic whistle blower.

CONNECTION: CHAPTER 8

Our judgments are often affected by personal *biases.*

CONNECTION: CHAPTER 11

Most personality theories focus on internal processes, while social psychology now emphasizes the external situation.

Senate Intelligence Committee investigating the justifications for the Iraq War cited groupthink as one of the processes involved in that decision. It is interesting to note the use of this social psychological concept in an official report of that government committee:

> The Intelligence Community (IC) has long struggled with the need for analysts to overcome analytic biases .... This bias that pervaded both the IC's analytic and collection communities represents 'group think,' a term coined by psychologist Irving Janis in the 1970's to describe a process in which a group can make bad or irrational decisions as each member of the group attempts to conform their opinions to what they believe to be the consensus of the group. IC personnel involved in the Iraq WMD issue demonstrated several aspects of groupthink: examining few alternatives, selective gathering of information, pressure to conform within the group or withhold criticism, and collective rationalization. (U.S. Senate, 2004, p. 4)

Obedience to Authority

So far, we have seen how groups influence individuals. But the arrow of influence also points the other way: Certain individuals, such as leaders and authorities, can command the obedience of groups—even large masses of people. The ultimate demonstration of this effect was seen in the World War II era, with the emergence of Adolf Hitler in Germany and Benito Mussolini in Italy. These dictators transformed the rational citizens of whole nations into mindlessly loyal followers of a fascist ideology bent on world conquest.

Modern social psychology had its origins in this wartime crucible of fear and prejudice. It was natural, then, that many of the early social psychologists focused on the personalities of people drawn into fascist groups. Specifically, they looked for an *authoritarian personality* behind the fascist group mentality (Adorno et al., 1950). But that dispositional analysis failed to recognize the social, economic, historical, and political realities operating on those populations at that time. To clarify this point, let us reflect for a moment on some more recent examples of unquestioning obedience to authority.

In 1978, a group of American citizens left California to relocate their Protestant religious order, called "Peoples Temple," in the South American jungle of Guyana. There, following the orders of their charismatic leader, the Reverend Jim Jones, over 900 members of the Peoples Temple willingly administered lethal doses of cyanide to hundreds of their children, then to their parents, and then to themselves. Then, in 1993, 100 members of a religious sect in Waco, Texas, joined their leader, David Koresh, in defying federal agents who had surrounded their compound. After a standoff of several weeks, the Branch Davidians set fire to their quarters rather than surrender. In the resulting conflagration, scores of men, women, and children perished. Four years later, the college-bred members of another group calling itself "Heaven's Gate" followed their leader's command to commit mass suicide in order to achieve a "higher plane" of being. And, on September 11, 2001, followers of Osama bin Laden commandeered commercial airliners and piloted them into the Pentagon and the World Trade Center. In addition to murdering thousands of people on those planes and working at those sites, they knowingly committed suicide. And even more recently, scores of suicide bombers, both men and women, have blown themselves apart as "revolutionary martyrs" in the Palestinian campaign against Israel. Were these people mentally deranged, stupid, and totally strange creatures—unlike us? Are there any conditions under which *you* would blindly obey an order from a person you love and respect (or fear) to do such extreme deeds? Would you, for example, obey an authority figure who told you to electrocute a stranger? Of course, you are saying to yourself, "No way," "Not me," "I am not that kind of person." But think about what each of the people we have described above must have been thinking *before* they were caught up in their obedience trap—the same thing as you, probably.

After reading this chapter, you may be more likely to answer, "I hope not—but I have a better understanding of the social forces that can pressure ordinary people like me to commit horrible acts." And, your authors hope, your study of social psychology will make you more resistant to the forces that produce unquestioning obedience and conformity. We want you to be one of the thoughtful heroes and not one of the mindless majority.

On that note, let us now turn to the most convincing demonstration of situational power ever created in the laboratory. In a dramatic experiment, social psychologist Stanley Milgram (1965, 1974) showed that a willingness of people to follow the orders of an authority, even potentially lethal ones, is not confined to a few extreme personalities or deranged individuals. This finding, along with certain ethical issues that the experiment raises, places Milgram's work at the center of one of the biggest controversies in psychology (Blass, 1996; Miller, 1986; Ross & Nisbett, 1991). Let us begin with a look at the controversial methods Milgram used.

Milgram's Obedience Experiment The experiment was first conducted on Yale College students where Milgram was teaching at the time. After his initial surprising results, he advertised for more paid volunteers among ordinary citizens in several towns in Connecticut and conducted variations of his original paradigm on more than 1000 participants from a variety of backgrounds. The volunteers thought that they were participating in a scientific study of memory and learning. Specifically, they were led to believe that the research aimed to help improve learning and memory by punishing errors as soon as they were made, as well as rewarding correct responding. Cast in the role of "teacher," a volunteer subject was instructed to punish memory errors made by another person (actually a confederate of the experimenter) playing the role of "learner." To administer punishment, the teacher was told to throw a switch that would deliver an electric shock to the learner each time the learner made an error. Moreover, the teacher was told to increase the level of shock by a fixed amount for every new error. Overseeing the whole procedure was a white-coated experimenter. This authority figure presented the rules, arranged for the assignment of roles (by a rigged drawing of lots), and ordered the teachers to do their job whenever they hesitated or dissented.

The real question driving the experiment was this: How far would people go before they defied the authority figure by refusing to obey? The dependent variable was the teacher's response, measured by the highest shock level he was willing to deliver. The level of shock could be clearly seen on a "shock generator" that featured a row of 30 switches that apparently could deliver shocks in 30-volt steps from a weak start of 15 volts all the way up to 450 volts, marked on the generator as "XXX."

To make the situation realistic, Milgram gave each "teacher" a mild sample shock. This convinced them that the apparatus was actually delivering shocks and that they would be causing the "learner" increasing pain and suffering each time they flipped a switch. Except for this demonstration shock, however, no shocks were actually administered: You will remember that the learner was actually a part of the experimental team.

The part of the learner was played by a pleasant, mild-mannered man, about 50 years old. He mentioned having a "heart condition" but said he was willing to go along with the procedure. The experimenter obliged by strapping

● Milgram's obedience experiment. Top, generator; bottom, the "learner" being strapped into his electrified chair. Experts incorrectly predicted the behavior of the "teachers" because they failed to consider the influence of the special situation created in the experiment. Although many of the participants in Milgram's study dissented verbally, the majority obeyed.

him into an "electric chair" in an adjacent room. As the learner, his task was to memorize pairs of words, then choose the correct response for each stimulus word from a multiple-choice listing. Following the experimental script, the learner soon began making mistakes.

At 75 volts, the script called for the learner to moan and grunt; at 150 volts he would demand to be released from the experiment. At 180 volts he would cry out that he could not stand the pain any longer. The plan then called for the learner's protests to increase with increasing shock levels. For any teachers still delivering punishment at the 300-volt level, the learner would shout that he would no longer take part in the experiment and must be freed. As you might imagine, this situation was stressful. If the teacher hesitated or protested about delivering the required shock at any level, the experimenter interrupted, stating that the experiment "must continue," demanding that the teacher "please continue." Most volunteers dissented often; when they asked who would be responsible for the consequences, the authority figure said he would assume full responsibility. But when the shock level rose to 375 volts, the "learner" screamed out, and there was a thud and then silence. Virtually all of the participants stopped shocking but then continued when the authority reminded them that failure to respond was an error that also had to be punished. The experiment ended only when the shock level reached the 450-volt maximum—or when the "teacher" refused to obey.

The Shocking Results Suppose for a moment that you were the "teacher." Ask yourself the following questions:

▌ How far up the shock scale would you go?

▌ At which level would you refuse to continue?

In Milgram's experiment, nearly two-thirds delivered the maximum 450 volts to the learner. Most of those who refused to give the maximum shock obeyed until reaching about 300 volts. And no one who got within five switches of the end refused to go all the way. By then their resistance was broken; they had resolved their own conflicts and just tried to get it over with as quickly as possible. Most verbally dissented but behaviorally obeyed the white-coated authority. These same results were found with Yale College students as with the many ordinary citizens from all walks of life.

These were not sadistic people who obeyed happily. They dissented verbally, even though they continued to deliver shocks. One person complained to the unwavering experimenter, "He can't stand it! I'm not going to kill that man in there! You hear him hollering? He's hollering . . . Who is going to take the responsibility if anything happens to that gentleman?" Clearly upset, this individual added, "You mean I've got to keep going up with that scale? No sir, I'm not going to kill that man!" (Milgram, 1965, p. 67). But, the shocks continued. When the learner simply stopped responding to the questions, some teachers called out to him, urging him to get the answer right so they would not have to continue shocking him. All the while they protested loudly to the experimenter, but the experimenter responded with stern commands: "You have no other choice, you *must* go on." Even when there was only silence from the learner's room, the teacher was ordered to keep shocking him more and more strongly, all the way up to the button that was marked "Danger: Severe Shock XXX (450 volts)." Most people obeyed.

Of course, no shocks were ever delivered to the learner. The "victim" of the "shocks" was an accomplished actor who congenially chatted with his "teacher" after the experiment and assured him he was fine and had never felt any shocks. All of his comments during the study had been tape recorded to standardize the procedure across the many trials and variations of the study. Moreover, the powerful authority figure in the white lab coat was not a "real" authority, not Milgram himself, but a hired actor. And, for all the "teachers" knew, when once the learner fell silent, he may have been unconscious or dead—but in any case his memory could not be improved by further shocks. Nevertheless, hundreds of people, young and old, educated or not, mindlessly obeyed and continued doing as ordered even though it made no sense—had they thought rationally about what they were doing.

● This Chinese man risked his life by defying authority. Would you have done the same?

The controversy about Milgram's research concerns the ethics of deception and the potentially disturbing effects on those in the role of teacher.

Why Do We Obey Authority?   From the many variations Milgram conducted on his original study, we can conclude that people tended to be obedient under the following conditions (Milgram, 1965, 1974; Rosenhan, 1969):

▮ *When a peer modeled obedience* by complying with the authority figure's commands

▮ *When the victim was remote from the "teacher"* and could not be seen or heard

▮ *When the "teacher" was under direct surveillance of the authority figure* so that he was aware of the authority's presence

▮ *When a participant acted as an intermediary bystander,* merely "assisting" the one who was delivering the shock, rather than actually throwing the switches

▮ *When the authority figure had higher relative status,* as when the participant was a student and the experimenter was billed as "professor" or "doctor"

What are the lessons to be learned? If you carefully review these conditions (Figure 14.2), you can see that the obedience effect results from *situational* variables and not *personality* variables. In fact, personality tests administered to the subjects did *not* reveal any traits that differentiated those who obeyed from those who refused, nor did they identify any psychological disturbance or abnormality in the obedient punishers. These findings enable us to rule out personality as a variable in obedient behavior. And what about gender? Milgram later found that women were just as obedient as men (Milgram, 1974).

Like the Stanford prison study, obedience research challenges the myth that evil lurks in the minds of evil people—that the bad "they" differ from the good "us" who would never do such things. The purpose in recounting these findings is not to debase human nature or to excuse evil deeds but to make clear that even normal, well-meaning individuals can give in to strong situational and social influences to behave wrong when they know fully the right way they should behave. In a sense, this reflects one view of "evil" as knowing better but doing worse.

Before moving on to our next major issue, there is an important matter for us to add. Although you should remember the Milgram effect as "two-thirds

● **FIGURE 14.2** Obedience in
Milgram's Experiments

The graph shows a profile of weak or strong
obedience effects across situational variations
of Milgram's study of obedience to authority.
(*Source:* From THE OBEDIENCE EXPERIMENTS:
A Case Study of Controversy in the Social
Sciences by A. G. Miller. Copyright © 1986
by Praeger Publishers, Inc. Reprinted by
permission of Greenwood Publishing Group,
Inc., Westport, CT.)

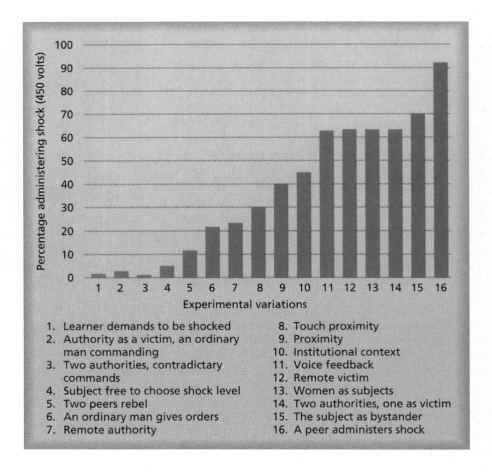

1. Learner demands to be shocked
2. Authority as a victim, an ordinary man commanding
3. Two authorities, contradictory commands
4. Subject free to choose shock level
5. Two peers rebel
6. An ordinary man gives orders
7. Remote authority
8. Touch proximity
9. Proximity
10. Institutional context
11. Voice feedback
12. Remote victim
13. Women as subjects
14. Two authorities, one as victim
15. The subject as bystander
16. A peer administers shock

◀ **CONNECTION: CHAPTER 4**

Moral judgments depend not only on the
situation but on one's stage of *moral
development.*

went all the way," in the many variations he conducted obedience went all the
way up to 90% if the teacher first observed others going all the way, although
it dropped down to only 10% when the teacher saw peers refusing to go all
the way. The other take-home message from these experiments is that social
models can have an enormous impact on how you behave and that you should
be aware that you are a social model for others. And just to make you more
aware when such influence may be at work, in Table 14.1 we have listed some
general tactics of influence that can get good people to do harmful deeds (Zimbardo, 2004).

TABLE 14.1	Ten Steps toward Evil—Getting Good People to Harm Others

- Provide people with an ideology to justify beliefs for actions.
- Make people take a small first step toward a harmful act with a minor, trivial action and then gradually increase those small actions.
- Make those in charge seem like a "just authority."
- Slowly transform a once compassionate leader into a dictatorial figure.
- Provide people with vague and ever-changing rules.
- Relabel the situation's actors and their actions to legitimize the ideology.
- Provide people with social models of compliance.
- Allow verbal dissent but only if people continue to comply behaviorally with orders.
- Encourage dehumanizing the victim.
- Make exiting the situation difficult.

The Bystander Problem: The Evil of Inaction

Harm doesn't always come from a hurtful act. It can also come from *inaction* when someone needs help. We can illustrate this fact with a news event that stunned the nation and then inspired some vital psychological research. In Queens, New York, 38 ordinary citizens watched for more than half an hour, as a man with a knife stalked and killed Kitty Genovese in three separate attacks. Twice the sound of the bystanders' voices and the sudden glow of their bedroom lights interrupted the assailant and frightened him. Each time, however, he returned and stabbed her again. Not a single person telephoned the police during the assault! Only one witness called the police—after the woman was finally raped and murdered (*The New York Times*, March 13, 1964, as cited in Darley & Latané, 1968). The newspaper and TV accounts of this gruesome story played up the angle of bystander "apathy," the callous indifference of New Yorkers, and a bewildered nation.

Why didn't bystanders help? Was it something in the *person* (again the dispositional analysis: New Yorkers being "callous" types), or was it something in the *situation* (something outside of any of the individuals)? Come let us see again how social psychology is done.

Contrived Emergencies   Soon after hearing of the Kitty Genovese murder and the analysis in the press, social psychologists Bibb Latané and John Darley began a series of studies on the bystander intervention problem. These studies all ingeniously created laboratory analogues of the difficulties faced by bystanders in real emergency situations. In one such experiment, a college student, placed alone in a room with an intercom, was led to believe that he was communicating with one or more students in adjacent rooms. During a discussion about personal problems, this individual heard what sounded like another student having a seizure and gasping for help. During the "seizure" the bystander couldn't talk to the other students or find out what, if anything, they were doing about the emergency. The dependent variable was the speed with which he reported the emergency to the experimenter. The independent variable was the number of people he believed were in the discussion group with him.

It turned out that the speed of response by those in this situation depended on the number of bystanders they thought were present. The more other people they believed to be listening in on the situation in other rooms, the *slower* they were to report the seizure, if they did so at all. As you can see in Figure 14.3, all those in a two-person situation intervened within 160 seconds, but only 60% of those who believed they were part of a large group ever informed the experimenter that another student was seriously ill (Latané & Darley, 1968).

Was it the person or the situation? Personality tests showed no significant relationship between particular personality characteristics of the participants and their speed or likelihood of intervening. The best predictor of bystander intervention was the situational variable of *group size* present. By way of explanation, Darley and Latané proposed that the likelihood of intervention *decreases* as the group *increases* in size, because each person assumes that others will help, so he or she does not have to make that commitment. Individuals who perceive themselves as part of a large group of potential interveners experience a **diffusion of responsibility:** a dilution or weakening of each group member's obligation to help, to become personally involved. You may have experienced moments of diffused responsibility if you have driven past a disabled car beside a busy highway because "surely someone else" would stop and help.

Another factor was undoubtedly also at work: conformity. As you will remember from our Core Concept and from Asch's studies of conformity,

● Kitty Genovese was murdered in her neighborhood while 38 of her neighbors watched. Why didn't somebody help? The answer is not what most people think.

◀ **CONNECTION: CHAPTER 1**

The *independent variable* refers to the various stimulus conditions for different groups in an experiment.

■ **Diffusion of responsibility**
Dilution or weakening of each group member's obligation to act when responsibility is perceived to be shared with all group members.

● **FIGURE 14.3** Bystander Intervention in an Emergency

The more people present in a crisis, the less likely it is that any one bystander will intervene. As this summary of research findings shows, bystanders act most quickly in two-person groupings. (*Source:* From "Bystander Intervention in Emergencies: Diffusion of Responsibilities," by S. M. Darley and B. Latané, *Journal of Personality & Social Psychology,* 1968, Vol. 8, No. 4, pp. 377–384. Copyright © 1968 by the American Psychological Association. Reprinted by permission of the American Psychological Association.)

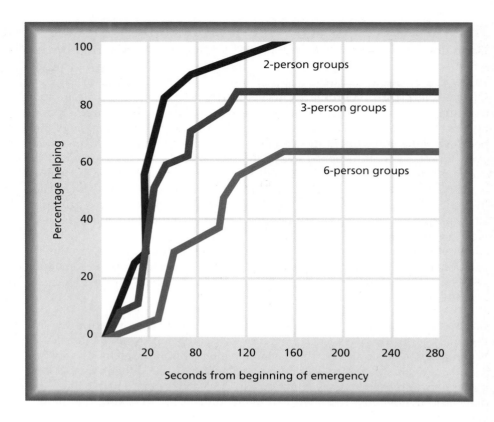

when people don't know what to do, they take their cues from others. The same thing occurred in the bystander studies, where subjects who failed to intervene were observing and conforming to the behavior of other people who were doing nothing.

Does Training Encourage Helping? Two studies suggest that the bystander problem can be countered with appropriate training. Ted Huston and his colleagues (1981) found no personality traits that distinguished people who had helped in actual emergency situations from those who had not. But they did find that helpers more often had had some medical, police, first-aid, or CPR training in dealing with emergency situations. And another study shows that even a psychology class lecture on the bystander problem can help (Beaman et al., 1978). Students had an opportunity to help a "victim" slumped in a doorway while walking by with a nonresponsive confederate of the experimenter. Those who had attended a lecture on bystander intervention were twice as likely to stop and attempt to help as those who had not received the lecture on helping. Education apparently makes some difference.

Need help? Ask for it! To demonstrate the positive effects of situational power, social psychologist Tom Moriarity (1975) arranged two fascinating experiments. In the first study, New Yorkers watched as a thief snatched a woman's suitcase in a restaurant when she left her table. In the second, they watched a thief grab a portable radio from a beach blanket when the owner left it for a few minutes. What did these onlookers do? Some did nothing, letting the thief go on his merry way. But others did intervene. What were the conditions under which some helped and others did not?

In each experiment, the would-be theft victim (the experimenter's accomplice) had first asked the soon-to-be observer of the crime either "Do you have the time?" or "Will you please keep an eye on my bag (radio) while I'm gone?"

Now that you know something about bystander intervention, let's see how good you are at picking the crucial variable out of a bystander situation inspired by the biblical tale of the Good Samaritan (see Luke 10:30–37). In the biblical account, several important people are too busy to help a stranger in distress. He is finally assisted by an outsider, a Samaritan, who takes the time to offer aid. Could the failure of the distressed individual's countrymen to help be due to character flaws or personal dispositions? Or was it determined by the situation?

Social psychologists decided to put students at the Princeton Theological Seminary into a similar situation. It was made all the more ironic because they thought that they were being evaluated on the quality of the sermons they were about to deliver on the parable of the Good Samaritan. Let's see what happened when these seminarians were given an opportunity to help someone in distress.

With sermon in hand, each was directed to a nearby building where the sermon was to be recorded. But as the student walked down an alley between the two buildings, he came upon a man slumped in a doorway, in obvious need of help. The student now had the chance to practice what he was about to preach. What would you guess was the crucial variable that predicted how likely a seminarian—ready to preach about the Good Samaritan—was to help a person in distress? Choose one:

a. How religious the seminarian was (as rated by his classmates)
b. How "neurotic" the seminarian was (as rated on the "Big Five" personality traits)
c. How much of a hurry the seminarian was in
d. How old the seminarian was

All of the dispositional variables (personal characteristics) of the seminarians were controlled by random assignment of subjects to three different conditions. Thus, we know that personality was not the determining factor. Rather, it was a situational variable: time. Before the seminarians left the briefing room to have their sermons recorded in a nearby building, each was told how much time he had to get to the studio. Some were assigned to a late condition, in which they had to hurry to make the next session; others to an on-time condition, in which they would make the next session just on time; and a third group to an early condition, in which they had a few spare minutes before they would be recorded.

What were the results? Of those who were in a hurry, only 10% helped. Ninety percent failed to act as Good Samaritans! If they were on time, 45% helped the stranger. The greatest bystander intervention came from 63% of those who were not in any time bind.

Remarkably, the manipulation of time urgency made those in the "late" condition six times less likely to help than those in the "early" condition. While fulfilling their obligation to hurry, these individuals appeared to have a single-minded purpose that blinded them to other events around them. Again, it was the power of the situation.

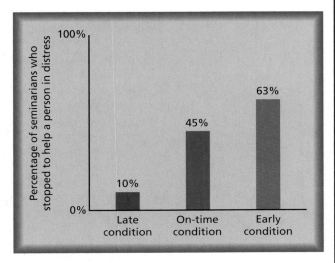

● Results of the "Good Samaritan" Study

Even with a sermon on the Good Samaritan in hand, seminary students who were in a hurry didn't usually stop to help (Darley & Batson, 1973).

The first interaction elicited no personal responsibility, and almost all of the bystanders stood by idly as the theft unfolded. However, of those who had agreed to watch the victim's property, almost every bystander intervened. They called for help, and some even tackled the runaway thief on the beach.

The encouraging message is that we can often convert apathy to action and transform callousness to kindness just by asking for it. The mere act of requesting a favor forges a special human bond that involves other people in ways that materially change the situation. It makes them feel responsible to you, and thereby responsible for what happens in your shared social world. You can use this knowledge to increase your chances of getting aid from would-be helpers in several ways (Schroeder et al., 1995):

▪ *Ask for help.* Let others know you need it rather than assuming they realize your need or know what is required.

▪ *Reduce the ambiguity* of the situation by clearly explaining the problem and what should be done: "She's fainted! Call an ambulance right away," or "Someone broke into my house—call the police and give them this address!"

▪ *Identify specific individuals* so they do not diffuse responsibility with others present: "You, in the red shirt: Call 911!" or "Will the person in the blue Toyota please call for a tow truck right away?"

None of these tactics guarantees the safety of your person or possessions, of course. (Kitty Genovese did call for help.) Nevertheless they probably represent your best hope if you find yourself, alone in a crowd, facing a real emergency.

PSYCHOLOGY IN YOUR LIFE: ON BEING "SHOE" AT YALE[1]

When I (PGZ) arrived at Yale University to start my graduate career in the mid-1950s, I was dressed in all my south Bronx splendor—blue suede shoes, peg pants, big rolled collar (Billy Eckstein model), and other cool clothes. A month or two later, I was wearing chino pants, button-down shirt, and loafer-type shoes. I was not fully aware of the subtle social pressures to change my "taste" in apparel but knew that I felt more "in" in those weird Yalie clothes than I had in my good old Bronx duds. But as a budding psychologist, I used my personal case study to motivate me to find out more about that unwritten dress code, one that everyone around the campus at that time was following as if a Marine drill instructor was ordering our total mindless compliance.

Interviews with seniors revealed that indeed there was a powerful dress code that the "in group" formulated regularly in order to distinguish them from the mass of "out group" pretenders. Every single item of clothing could be identified by those in the know as socially appropriate at that time for real Yale men to wear (it was all male at that time). I was informed that the underlying concept was termed "shoe." (Yale men of that era and earlier could be identified as wearing white buck shoes.) To be "shoe" was to be in, to be cool, to be with it, to be right on, and so forth. Not only was every bit of clothing indexed as to its degree of shoeness, but so was everything else in that universe. Tennis, golf, and crew were shoe, basketball was not. Asking questions in lecture classes was not shoe; tailgating before football games was shoe, but only if done with the right style, or panache. Of equal interest to me was the fact that shoe ratings changed periodically to keep outsiders from being mistaken as really true blue shoe. One year the Yale Senior ring was shoe to wear, the next year it might be un-shoe; or handmade bow ties would become un-shoe and clip-on bow ties would vault from low-shoe to high-shoe rating.

My team of informants helped me to form an index of the shoe strengths of every conceivable item of clothing that a Yale student might wear that year. With the help of my introductory psychology students, we went into the dormitories and found out what students from each college class actually had in their wardrobes. We then multiplied each of those items of clothing by their Shoe Index and averaged those ratings across each class from frosh to senior. Next, we separated out students' shoe scores by whether they had come from prep schools versus public high schools.

Three major significant results were obvious from our graphs of the quantification of Shoeness at Yale:

1. Student wardrobes become ever more shoe as they progress from lowly frosh up to high-powered seniors.

2. Preppy frosh were much more shoe than were their classmates from public high schools.

---

[1]Zimbardo, P. G. (2004). *On being "shoe" at Yale: A study in institutional conformity.* In preparation, Stanford University.

3. Over the four years, the gap between prep schoolers and high schoolers diminished, so that by senior year they were almost equally shoe.

When Yale became co-ed in the next decade, this kind of shoeness became less apparent, went undergound, and now may exist only in very modified forms. But let this be a lesson to you whatever school you are in: Much of what you think is the You in Your Taste, is really the Them in social conformity pressures subtly imposed on you to be like Them and liked by Them.

CONSTRUCTING SOCIAL REALITY: WHAT INFLUENCES OUR JUDGMENTS OF OTHERS?

KEY QUESTION

Powerful as a social situation is, it doesn't account for everything that people do. For example, it does not account for the individual differences we see in people's choices of friends and romantic partners, nor does it account for their prejudices. To explain the patterns we find in social interaction, we must also look at cognitive processes. In the language of social psychology, we need to understand how we construct our **social reality**—our subjective interpretations of other people and of our relationships. Thus, the social reality that we construct determines whom we find attractive, whom we find threatening, whom we seek out, and whom we avoid. This, then, leads us to the second lesson of social psychology, captured in our next Core Concept:

■ **Social reality** An individual's subjective interpretation of other people and of relationships with them.

CORE CONCEPT

The judgments we make about others depend not only on their behavior but also on our interpretation of their actions within a social context.

We will illustrate how these cognitive factors operate by analyzing how they affect our attitudes toward other people. Let's start out on the positive end of the scale by asking a simple question: What makes people like each other? That is, what produces *interpersonal attraction?* Then we will move to the opposite end of the scale with a look at the negative feelings that often underlie *prejudice.*

Interpersonal Attraction

It is no surprise that we are attracted to people who have something to offer us (Brehm et al., 2002; Simpson & Harris, 1994). We tend to like those who give us gifts, agree with us, act friendly toward us, share our interests, entertain us, and help us in times of need—unless, of course, we suspect that their behavior is self-serving. Although we don't necessarily mind giving something back in the form of a social exchange, we shrink from relationships that merely take from us and offer nothing in return. In the best of relationships, as in a friendship, partnership, marriage, or business relationship, both parties receive rewards. You might consider whether this is true in your own relationships as we look at the *reward theory of attraction* next.

Reward Theory: We (Usually) Prefer Rewarding Relationships Most good relationships can be seen as an exchange of benefits (Batson, 1987; Clark et al., 1989). The benefits could be some combination of money and material possessions. Or the exchange might involve something intangible like praise, status, information, sex, or emotional support.

Social psychologist Elliot Aronson (2004) summarizes this in a **reward theory of attraction,** which says that attraction is a form of social learning. By looking at the social costs and benefits, claims Aronson, we can usually understand why people are attracted to each other. In brief, reward theory says that we like best those who give us maximum rewards at minimum cost. After we look at the evidence, we think you will agree that this theory explains (almost) everything about interpersonal attraction.

Social psychologists have found four especially powerful sources of reward that predict interpersonal attraction: *proximity, similarity, self-disclosure,* and *physical attractiveness.* Most of us choose our friends, associates, and lovers because they offer some combination of these factors at a relatively low social cost.

Proximity An old saying advises, "Absence makes the heart grow fonder." Another contradicts with "Out of sight, out of mind." Which one is correct? Studies show that frequent sightings best predict our closest relationships and the people we see most often are the people who live and work nearest us (Simpson & Harris, 1994). In college dormitories, residents more often become close friends with the person who lives in the next room than they do with the person who lives two doors down (Priest & Sawyer, 1967). Residents of apartments make more friendships among people who live on the same floor than among those who live on other floors (Nahemow & Lawton, 1975). Those who live in neighborhoods more often become friends with the occupants of the house next door than with people living two houses away (Festinger et al., 1950). This **principle of proximity** (nearness) also accounts for the fact that many people end up married to the boy or girl next door (Ineichen, 1979). And it correctly predicts that people at work will make more friends among those with whom they have the most contact (Segal, 1974).

Although you don't have to like your neighbors, the proximity rule says that when two individuals are equally attractive, you are more likely to make friends with the nearest one: The rewards are equal, but the cost is less in time and inconvenience (Gilbertson et al., 1998). Apparently, another old saying,

◀ **CONNECTION: CHAPTER 6**

Social learning involves expectations of rewards and punishments learned through social interaction and the observation of others.

■ **Reward theory of attraction**
A social learning view that says we like best those who give us maximum rewards at minimum cost.

■ **Principle of proximity** The notion that people at work will make more friends among those who are nearby—with whom they have the most contact. Proximity means "nearness."

that familiarity breeds contempt, should be revised in light of social psychological research: In fact, familiarity more often breeds friendship. Increased contact, itself, often increases peoples' liking for each other (Bornstein, 1989).

Similarity   People usually find it more rewarding to strike up a friendship with someone who shares their attitudes, interests, values, and experiences than to bother with people who are disagreeable or merely different (Hatfield & Rapson, 1993; Hendrick & Hendrick, 1992; Kelley et al., 1983; Simpson & Harris, 1994). If two people have just discovered that they share tastes in music, politics, and attitudes toward education, they will probably hit it off because they have, in effect, exchanged compliments that reward each other for their tastes and attitudes (Byrne, 1969). The **similarity principle** also explains why teenagers are most likely to make friends among those who share their political and religious views, educational aspirations, and attitudes toward music, alcohol, and drugs (Kandel, 1978). Likewise, similarity accounts for the fact that most people find marriage partners of the same age, race, social status, attitudes, and values (Brehm, 1992; Hendrick & Hendrick, 1992). In general, similarity, like proximity, makes the heart grow fonder.

Self-Disclosure   Good friends and lovers share intimate details about themselves (Sternberg, 1998). This practice not only allows people to know each other more deeply, but it sends signals of trust. It is as if I say, "Here is a piece of information that I want you to know about me, and I trust you not to hurt me with it." Friends and lovers usually find such exchanges highly rewarding. When you observe people exchanging confidences and details about their lives, you can predict that they are becoming more and more attracted to each other. Given that sharing personal disclosures comes after a sense of trust has been created in a relationship, it both takes time to reach this level of intimacy and is an index of that trust which the disclosing person has in the other.

Physical Attractiveness   Yet another old saying tells us that beauty is only skin deep. Nevertheless, people usually find it more rewarding to associate with people they consider physically attractive than with those they consider to be plain or homely (Patzer, 1985). Fair or not, good looks are a real social asset. Potential employers, for example, prefer good-looking job candidates to plainer applicants (Cash & Janda, 1984). Looks also affect people's judgments of children. Attractive children are judged as happier and more competent than their peers (Dion, 1986; Eagly et al., 1991; Hatfield & Sprecher, 1986). Even babies judge people by their appearances. We know this because babies gaze longer at pictures of normal faces than at those of distorted faces (Langlois et al., 1987).

Most people are repelled by the idea that they might make judgments based only on looks. Indeed, when asked what they look for in a dating partner, college students rank physical attractiveness last. But what people *say* does not match what they *do*—at least as far as their first impressions go. Across many studies, involving a variety of characteristics, including intelligence, sincerity, masculinity, femininity, and independence, physical attractiveness overwhelmed everything else as the best predictor of how well a person would be liked after a first meeting (Aronson, 1999; Feingold, 1990; Langlois et al., 1998; Tesser & Brodie, 1971).

Other research shows that the principle of attractiveness applies equally to same-sex and opposite-sex relationships (Maruyama & Miller, 1975). Gender

● The principle of proximity predicts that coworkers are likely to become friends.

◀ **CONNECTION: CHAPTER 5**

The Gestalt principle of *similarity* refers to perceptual grouping of objects that share common features.

■ **Similarity principle**   The notion that people are attracted to those who are most similar to themselves.

differences do exist, however. While both males and females are strongly influenced by physical attractiveness, men seem to be more influenced by looks than are women (Cash & Killcullen, 1985; Feingold, 1990; Folkes, 1982; Hatfield & Sprecher, 1986).

These findings may come as bad news for the majority of us, who consider ourselves rather average-looking at best. But we can take some comfort in a study that suggests that people actually consider a composite of "average" features to be the most attractive. Investigators fed images of many students' faces into a computer program that manipulated the facial features to be more or less of an average combination of all features from the many different student portraits. Surprisingly, they found that people usually liked best the images having features closest to the average size and shape (Langlois & Roggman, 1990; Langlois et al., 1994; Rhodes et al., 1999).

Now some bad news for exceptionally attractive readers: While we usually associate positive qualities with attractive individuals (Calvert, 1988), extreme attractiveness can also be a liability. Although physically attractive people are seen as more poised, interesting, sociable, independent, exciting, sexual, intelligent, well-adjusted, and successful, they are also perceived as more vain and materialistic (Brigham, 1980; Cash & Duncan, 1984; Hassebrauck, 1988; Moore et al., 1987). A "double standard" also comes into play. For example, the public favors good-looking male politicians but disparages their attractive female counterparts (Sigelman et al., 1986). It is also double trouble to be shy and handsome or beautiful because others mistake their reserved demeanor as being cold, indifferent, or feeling superior.

These effects of physical attractiveness hint that reward, as powerful as it is, does not account for everything. We will see this more clearly below, as we explore some important exceptions to the reward theory of attraction.

Exceptions to the Reward Theory of Attraction   While the rules of proximity, similarity, self-disclosure, and physical attractiveness may explain a lot about interpersonal attraction, a casual look around reveals lots of relationships that don't seem especially rewarding. Why, for example, might a woman be attracted to a man who abuses her? Or, why would a person want to join an organization that requires a difficult or degrading initiation ritual? Such relationships pose most interesting puzzles (Aronson, 2004). Could some people actually feel *more* attraction when they find that another person has *less* to offer them? Let's try to uncover the principles of social cog____ n operating behind some interesting exceptions to a reward theory of att___

Expectations and the Influence of Self-Esteem   We_____ rd theory predicts our attraction to smart, good-lookin_____ike-minded, and powerful people. Yet, you have pr_____ o-ple end up with friends and mates whom you _____ eir same level of attractiveness—the so-called r_____ old, 1988; Harvey & Pauwels, 1999). How does thi_____ sso-ciates the result of a sort of bargaining for th_____ per-sonal marketplace?

Yes, says **expectancy-value theory.** Peop_____ pur-sue a relationship by weighing the value the_____ ding such qualities as physical attractiveness, wit_____ ainst their expectation of success in the relatic_____ n be attracted to me?). Most of us don't waste too_____ auses we think are lost. Rather, we initiate relatior_____ peo-ple we think will probably like us in return. _____ e the-ory is not so much a competitor of reward _____ it.

■ **Matching hypothesis**   The prediction that most people will find friends and mates that are perceived to be of about their same level of attractiveness.

■ **Expectancy-value theory**   A theory in social psychology that states how people decide whether or not to pursue a relationship by weighing the potential value of the relationship against their expectation of success in establishing the relationship.

tion to this argument
from low self-esteem.
ainions of themselves
ips with people who
s. people who devalue
th erally feel a stronger
co o when their partner
thi they do when the
par Swann et al., 1992).
ear to be extremely
com the expectancy-
value of us keep such people
at a di aably because we fear that they
will be ck to reject our approaches. But, if you
happen to be one of these stunningly superior
people, do not despair: Social psychologists have
found hope! When highly competent individuals
commit minor blunders—spilling a drink or dropping a sheaf of papers—other
people actually like them better, probably because blunders bring them down
to everyone else's level and "normalize" them (Aronson et al., 1966, 1970).
Don't count on this, however, unless you are so awesomely competent as to
be unapproachable. The latté-in-the-lap trick only makes most of us look like
klutzes whom people like less.

● Cognitive dissonance theory predicts that these recruits will increase their loyalty to the Marine Corps as a result of their basic training ordeal.

Attraction and Self-Justification *Semper fidelis,* says the Marine Corps motto: "Always faithful." Considering the discomforting experiences that people must go through to become Marines (grueling physical conditioning, loss of sleep, lack of privacy, being yelled at, suffering punishment for small infractions of rules), it may seem remarkable that recruits routinely develop so much loyalty to their organization. Obviously, some powerfully attractive and interesting forces are at work.

Cognitive dissonance theory offers a compelling explanation for the mental adjustments that occur in people who voluntarily undergo unpleasant experiences (Festinger, 1957). The theory says that when people voluntarily act in ways that produce discomfort or otherwise clash with their attitudes and values, they develop a highly motivating mental state, called **cognitive dissonance.** A Republican politician who makes a public statement agreeing with a Democratic opponent is likely to feel cognitive dissonance. The same holds true for people who find themselves acting in ways that cause them to experience physical discomfort. Thus, our Marine recruits may feel cognitive dissonance when they find that they have volunteered for an experience that is far more punishing than they had imagined. And what is the psychological result?

According to cognitive dissonance theory, people are motivated to avoid the uncomfortable state of dissonance. If they find themselves experiencing cognitive dissonance, they attempt to reduce it in ways that are predictable, even if not always entirely logical. The two main ways of reducing dissonance are to change either one's behavior or one's cognitions. So, in civilian life, if the boss is abusive, you might avoid dissonance by simply finding another job. But in the case of a Marine recruit, changing jobs is not an option: It is too late to turn back once basic training has started. A recruit experiencing cognitive dissonance therefore is motivated to adjust his or her thinking. Most likely the recruit will resolve the dissonance by rationalizing the experience ("It's tough, but it builds character!") and by developing a stronger loyalty to the organization ("Being a member of such an elite group is worth all the suffering!").

◀ **CONNECTION: CHAPTER 9**

Social psychologists view *cognitive dissonance* as a powerful psychological motive.

■ **Cognitive dissonance** A highly motivating state in which people have conflicting cognitions, especially when their voluntary actions conflict with their attitudes.

In general, cognitive dissonance theory says that *when people's cognitions and actions are in conflict (a state of dissonance) they often reduce the conflict by changing their thinking to fit their behavior.* Why? People don't like to see themselves as being foolish or inconsistent. So, to explain their own behavior to themselves, people are motivated to change their attitudes. Otherwise, it would threaten their self-esteem.

One qualification on this theory has recently come to light. In Japan, and, perhaps, in other parts of Asia, studies show that people have a lesser need to maintain high self-esteem than do North Americans (Bower, 1997a; Heine et al., 1999). As a result, cognitive dissonance was found to have less power to change attitudes among Japanese. Apparently, cognitive dissonance is yet another psychological process that operates differently in collectivist and individualistic cultures.

The Explanatory Power of Dissonance   Despite cultural variations, cognitive dissonance theory explains many things that people do to justify their behavior and thereby avoid dissonance. For example, it explains why smokers so often rationalize their habit. It explains why people who have put their efforts into a project, whether it be volunteering for the Red Cross or writing a letter of recommendation, become more committed to the cause as time goes on—in order to justify their effort. It also explains why, if you have just decided to buy a Chevrolet, you will attend to new information supporting your choice (such as Chevrolet commercials on TV), but you will tend to ignore dissonance-producing information (such as a Chevy broken down alongside the freeway).

Cognitive dissonance theory also helps us understand certain puzzling social relationships, such as a woman who is attracted to a man who abuses her. Her dissonance might be summed up in this thought: "Why am I staying with someone who hurts me?" Her powerful drive for self-justification may make her reduce the dissonance by focusing on his good points and minimizing the abuse. And, if she has low self-esteem, she may also tell herself that she deserved his abuse. To put the matter in more general terms: *Cognitive dissonance theory predicts that people are attracted to those for whom they have agreed to suffer.* A general reward theory, by contrast, would never have predicted that outcome.

To sum up our discussion on interpersonal attraction: You usually will not go far wrong if you use a reward theory to understand why people are attracted to each other. People initiate social relationships because they expect some sort of benefit. It may be an outright reward, such as money or status or sex, or it may be an avoidance of some feared consequence, such as pain. But social psychology also shows that a simple reward theory cannot, by itself, account for all the subtlety of human social interaction. A more sophisticated and useful understanding of attraction must take into account such cognitive factors as expectations, self-esteem, and cognitive dissonance. That is, a complete theory must take into account the ways that we *interpret* our social environment. This notion of interpretation also underlies other judgments that we make about people, as we shall see next in our discussion of *attributions.*

Making Cognitive Attributions

We are always trying to explain to ourselves why people do what they do. Suppose you are riding on a bus when a middle-aged woman with an armload of packages gets on. In the process of finding a seat, she drops everything on the floor as the bus starts up. How do you explain her behavior? Do you think of her as the victim of circumstances, or is she a klutz, or eliciting sympathy so someone will give up a seat to her?

CONNECTION: CHAPTER 4

Collectivist cultures socialize people to put the needs of the group before the desires of the individual.

els to change the minds of people who are already prejudiced. Role models may serve better to prevent prejudice than to cure it.

Equal Status Contact   Slave owners had always had plenty of contact with their slaves, but they always managed to hang onto their prejudices. Obviously, mere contact with people from an out-group is not enough to erase prejudices against them. Evidence, however, from integrated public housing (where the economic threat of lowered property values is not an issue) suggests that when people are placed together under conditions of equal status, where neither wields power over the other, the chances of developing understanding increase (Deutsch & Collins, 1951; Wilner et al., 1955). In an extensive review of all available literature, Tom Pettigrew (1998) found strong support for the power of equal status contact to prevent and reduce prejudice among many different kinds of groups.

Legislation   You can't legislate morality. Right? The evidence of several studies suggests, however, that the old cliché may be wrong. One of the most convincing of these studies was an experiment, done in the late 1940s, comparing the attitudes of white tenants toward black tenants in public housing projects. In one project, white and black occupants were assigned to different buildings, that is, the project was racially segregated. A second project mixed or integrated the two racial groups by assigning housing in the same buildings. Only in the racially integrated project did prejudicial attitudes sharply decrease (Deutsch & Collins, 1951). This result strongly suggests that rules requiring equal status contact can diminish prejudice.

This notion is reinforced by a larger social "experiment" that was done under far less controlled conditions. During the past half century, the United States has adopted laws abolishing racial discrimination. The consequences were sometimes violent, but prejudice and discrimination have gradually diminished. Evidence for this shift comes from polls showing that, in the 1940s, fewer than 30% of white Americans favored desegregation. That percentage has steadily climbed to well above 90% today (Aronson, 2004).

Because these changes in public opinion were not part of a carefully controlled experiment, we cannot say that the data prove that legislation has caused peoples' prejudices to diminish. Nevertheless, we can argue that the increased number of white Americans favoring desegregation is exactly what one might predict from cognitive dissonance theory: When the law requires people to act in a less discriminatory fashion, people have to justify their new behavior by softening their prejudiced attitudes. From this vantage point, it appears that legislation can affect prejudiced attitudes, after all.

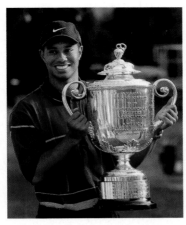

● Golfer Tiger Woods is a role model in a sport that has traditionally had few representatives of minority groups.

PSYCHOLOGY IN YOUR LIFE: LOVING RELATIONSHIPS

We end this section on a more positive note. Although people often do terrible things to one another, the complexity and beauty of the human mind also enable people to be caring and loving. Liking and loving are essential for happiness (Kim & Hatfield, 2004). Further, the pleasure of attraction and love appear to be part of the very circuitry and chemistry of our brains (Bartels & Zeki, 2004).

How do we know when attraction becomes love? To a large extent, our culture tells us how. Each culture has certain common themes defining love—such as sexual arousal, attachment, concern for the other's welfare, and a willingness to make a commitment. But the idea of "love" can vary greatly from culture to culture (Aron & Aron, 1994; Beall & Sternberg, 1995;

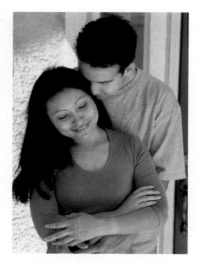

● Is it love? Social psychologists have been exploring the psychology of the human heart, collecting and interpreting data about how people fall in love and strengthen their bonds of intimacy. Most recently the emphasis has shifted to the factors that keep relationships together.

Berscheid, 1988; Fehr, 1988; Hatfield, 1988; Sprecher & McKinney, 1994; Sternberg, 1998).

There are also many kinds of love. The love that a parent has for a child differs from the love that longtime friends have for each other. Both differ from the commitment found, say, in a loving couple who have been married for 40 years. Yet, for many Americans, the term *love* brings to mind yet another form of attraction based on infatuation and sexual desire: **romantic love,** a temporary and highly emotional condition that generally fades after a few months (Hatfield et al., 1995; Hatfield & Rapson, 1993, 1998). But the American assumption that romantic love is the basis for a long-term intimate commitment is not universal. In many other cultures marriage is seen as an economic bond or, perhaps, as a political relationship linking families.

Psychologist Robert Sternberg (1998) has proposed an interesting view in his **triangular theory of love.** He says that love can have three components: passion (erotic attraction), intimacy (sharing feelings and confidences), and commitment (dedication to putting this relationship first in one's life). Various forms of love can be understood in terms of different combinations of these three components. Thus, Sternberg suggests that:

▮ *Romantic love* is high on passion and intimacy but low on commitment.

▮ Liking and friendship are characterized by intimacy but not by passion and commitment.

▮ *Infatuation* has a high level of passion, but it has not developed into intimacy or a committed relationship.

▮ *Complete love* (consummate love) involves all three: passion, intimacy, and commitment.

The need to understand what strengthens and weakens loving relationships in our own culture has acquired some urgency because of the "divorce epidemic" in the United States (Brehm, 1992; Harvey & Pauwels, 1999). If current rates hold, approximately half of all today's first marriages—and up to 60% of second marriages—will end in divorce. Much research stimulated by concern about high divorce rates has focused on the effects of divorce on children (Ahrons, 1994; Edwards, 1995b).

In the past decade or so, however, research emphasis has shifted to the processes by which couples maintain loving relationships and the environments that challenge relationships (Berscheid, 1999; Brehm, 1992; Duck, 1992; Hatfield & Rapson, 1993). We now know, for example, that for a relationship to stay healthy and to thrive both partners must see it as rewarding and equitable. As we saw in our discussion of reward theory, both must, over the long run, feel that they are getting something out of the relationship, not just giving. What they get—the rewards of the relationship—can involve many things, including adventure, status, laughter, mental stimulation, and material goods, as well as nurturance, love, and social support.

In addition, for a relationship to thrive, communication between partners must be open, ongoing, and mutually validating (Gottman et al., 1998; Gottman & Silver, 1994; Harvey & Omarzu, 1997; Monaghan, 1999). Research shows that couples in lasting relationships have five times more positive interactions than negative ones—including exchanges of smiles, loving touches, laughter, and compliments (Gottman, 1994). Yet, because every relationship experiences an occasional communication breakdown, the partners must know how to deal with conflicts effectively. Conflicts must be faced early and resolved fairly and effectively. Ultimately, each partner must take responsibility for his or her own identity, self-esteem, and commitment to the relationship—rather than expect the partner to engage in mind reading or self-sacrifice.

■ **Romantic love** A temporary and highly emotional condition based on infatuation and sexual desire.
■ **Triangular theory of love** A theory that describes various kinds of love in terms of three components: passion (erotic attraction), intimacy (sharing feelings and confidences), and commitment (dedication to putting this relationship first in one's life).

This has been the briefest sampling from the growing social psychology of relationships. Such research has practical applications. Teachers familiar with research findings can now inform their students about the basic principles of healthy relationships. Therapists apply these principles in advising clients on how to communicate with partners, negotiate the terms of their relationships, and resolve inevitable conflicts. More immediately, as you yourself learn about the factors that influence how you perceive and relate to others, you should gain a greater sense of self-control and well-being in your own intimate connections with others (Harvey, 1996; Harvey et al., 1990).

CHECK YOUR UNDERSTANDING

1. **RECALL:** According to Aronson, we can explain almost everything about interpersonal attraction with a theory of
   a. love.
   b. rewards.
   c. genetics.
   d. gender.

2. **RECALL:** Which of the following does the research say is most important in predicting initial attraction?
   a. physical attractiveness
   b. money
   c. personality
   d. nurturing qualities

3. **RECALL:** Which theory of attraction best explains why people who are considered to be extremely competent are often not the people we are most attracted to?
   a. reward theory
   b. expectancy-value theory
   c. cognitive dissonance theory
   d. psychoanalytic theory

4. **APPLICATION:** According to cognitive dissonance theory, which of the following would be the best strategy for getting people to like you?
   a. Give them presents.
   b. Show interest in their interests.
   c. Tell them that you like them.
   d. Persuade them to perform a difficult or unpleasant task for you.

5. **RECALL:** Prejudice is a(n) _____, while discrimination is a(n) _____.
   a. behavior/attitude
   b. instinct/choice
   c. attitude/behavior
   d. stimulus/response

6. **RECALL:** The evidence suggests that one of the most effective techniques for eliminating racial prejudice has been
   a. education.
   b. threat and force.
   c. legislation.
   d. tax incentives.

7. **UNDERSTANDING THE CORE CONCEPT:** Reward theory, expectancy-value theory, cognitive dissonance theory, and attribution theory all tell us that we respond not just to situations but to
   a. our cognitive interpretations.
   b. our social instincts.
   c. the intensity of the stimuli.
   d. our biological needs and drives.

ANSWERS: 1. b 2. a 3. b 4. d 5. c 6. c 7. a

WHAT ARE THE ROOTS OF VIOLENCE AND TERRORISM?

The terrorist attacks of September 11, 2001, raise questions for which there are no easy answers. In this section, however, we will see that social psychology's findings on the *power of the situation* offer a useful starting point for understanding why people commit violent acts. But, your authors will argue, a complete picture of violence and terrorism requires the combined insights of many perspectives—and not just those from psychology. Issues of money, power, resources, and ancient grudges must be considered as well. Our Core Concept says:

> The power of the situation can help us understand violence and terrorism, but a broader understanding requires multiple perspectives that go beyond the boundaries of traditional psychology.

◀ **CONNECTION: CHAPTER 6**

Aggression often results from *punishment* or the threat of punishment.

Before we plunge into these chilling waters, however, let us clarify two basic terms, **violence** and **aggression,** that have overlapping definitions. In the following discussion, we will use these terms interchangeably for any behavior that is intended to cause harm to others (whether or not harm actually results). A key component of this definition is *intent,* but it is also important to note that violence and aggression are social—or, perhaps more aptly, anti-social—phenomena.

The Social Psychology of Aggression and Violence

In this chapter we have seen repeatedly that the pressures of a social situation can make ordinary people commit horrible acts (Zimbardo, 2003). Social influence was at work in Milgram's obedience studies, where subjects obeyed orders to deliver apparently lethal shocks to a stranger. Likewise, the social situation provoked aggression in the Stanford prison study, where ordinary students acting as guards behaved with brutality toward fellow students in the role of prisoners. Still other research has shown that aggressive behavior can be induced by situations that create prejudice, conformity, frustration, threat, or wounded pride (Aronson, 2004; Baumeister et al., 1996). Now, let us take a detailed look at another important study that showed how aggression could arise out of intergroup conflict—again caused by the power of the situation.

The Robbers Cave: An Experiment in Conflict

The setting was a Boy Scout Camp known as the "Robbers Cave." There, the experimenters, Muzafer Sherif and his colleagues (1961) randomly assigned 11- and 12-year-old boys to two groups, dubbed the Eagles and the Rattlers. The experiment called for conditions similar to those at many other summer camps for boys: days filled with competitive games and activities. Competition, the experimenters hoped, would create conflict between the two groups.

Initially, the Eagles and Rattlers were kept apart, allowing within-group activities to build group **cohesiveness** (solidarity, loyalty, and a sense of group membership). Later the experimenters brought the two groups together for competitions, such as tug-of-war and football. Prizes for the winners heightened the competitive atmosphere. The final straw was a "party" at which the experimenters arranged to have the Eagles arrive an hour early. Half the food was mouth watering, and half was deliberately unappealing. As you might expect, when the Rattlers arrived they found that the Eagles had devoured the more desirable food. This led to name calling and scuffling, which culminated in a food fight.

With a rancorous atmosphere well established, Sherif and his colleagues tried various tactics for promoting cooperation between the groups. Their initial attempts were, however, complete failures. In particular, it did not help merely to bring the Eagles and Rattlers together for social events, such as movies or eating in the same dining room. Such occasions just offered opportunities for more hostility.

What *did* help was to contrive situations in which the groups had to cooperate in order to serve their mutual interests. First, however, the experimenters

■ **Violence and aggression** Terms that refer to behavior that is intended to cause harm.

■ **Cohesiveness** Solidarity, loyalty, and a sense of group membership.

called a halt to the competitive games. Then, they assembled the boys to inform them of a "problem" that had developed with the camp's vital water line. Both groups agreed to search the line for the trouble spot, which they did together—harmoniously. On another day, the experimenters arranged for the camp's truck to break down—which meant that it could not go to town for food. To get the truck running, the two groups had to work cooperatively by pulling it with the same rope previously used for the divisive tug-of-war game.

To serve its own needs, each group had to cooperate with the "enemy." And, as dissonance theory would predict, hostility changed to friendliness. The change in behavior led directly to a change in attitude. That is, the attitude change resulted from a need to justify the altered behavior.

It took several such crises to break down the hostile barriers between the two groups and to build a sense of **mutual interdependence,** a working relationship based on shared goals. But, in the end, the groups actively sought opportunities to mingle with each other, and friendships developed between members of the Eagles and Rattlers. One group even used its own money to buy treats for members of the other group. (Do you see a parallel between this study and the ethnic conflicts in the Middle East?)

● Competition can promote aggressive behavior.

Fuel for Terrorism

The flammable combination of poverty, powerlessness, and hopelessness are the tinder that the September 11 attacks were intended to ignite, says Jonathan Lash, president of the World Resources Institute in Washington, D.C. (2001). Much of the world lives in poverty and hunger and sees no way out. Ethnic hatred and wars aggravate their plight. Moreover, the number of people living in these miserable conditions is increasing, as most of the world's population explosion is occurring in poorer countries. And, to make matters more volatile, says Lash, a large proportion of these desperate people depend directly on resources that are rapidly being depleted: fisheries, forests, soils, and water resources. As a result, every day thousands flee their traditional homelands and stream into the largest and poorest cities. Most are young—a result of the high birth rates in the Third World. Mr. Lash warns that urban slums, filled with restless, jobless young men, are "tinderboxes of anger and despair; easy recruiting grounds for bin Laden or those who may come after him" (p. 1789). Consider this warning in light of Milgram's obedience studies: If ordinary, well-fed people can be induced to deliver apparently lethal shocks, how much easier it would be to persuade angry, hopeless young men and women to commit violent acts.

Thus, says Lash, removing the flint that sets off the spark is not sufficient; the Western world must also deal with the tinder. In other words, even if the terrorists' leaders are struck down and their resources captured, the anger and despair of the world's poor and desperate people will continue to pose a threat to the United States and other wealthy nations. As psychologists, we can understand this threat as a political restatement of the pain–aggression relationship that we saw in Chapter 6.

Understanding the tinderbox conditions that arise from poverty and despair and the tension between rich and poor nations, then, requires that we take economic and political perspectives. In addition, we must see that many of the conflicts that breed terrorism have historical roots. We cannot understand, for example, the tensions between Christianity and Islam without knowing about

■ **Mutual interdependence** A shared sense that individuals or groups need each other in order to achieve common goals the 200-year-war that the Western world calls the Crusades (1095–1291) or the fall of the six-centuries-old Ottoman empire (1300–1922) at the end of World War I. Although such events may seem remote, they changed the trajectory of history, and their religious significance continues to fuel conflict in the Middle East today.

What We Can Do about Terrorism Terrorism is really about psychology. It typically involves a relatively small group of people who take dramatic, violent actions against a larger group with the intention of spreading fear among them and inducing anxiety and uncertainty about their government's ability to protect them. Terrorists do not want to conquer other nations' land, as in traditional wars, but to conquer the minds of their enemies by making them feel victimized and fearful. Your authors believe that taking multiple perspectives can provide important insights on the problems of aggression, violence, and terrorism. In this vein, please consider the following suggestions.

As citizens and critical thinkers, we need to call for better information from our politicians, educators, journalists, and others who may try to assign easy answers to complex problems. Meeting aggression with aggression may be necessary, but it is never sufficient. We should encourage our political representatives to consider responses based on multiple perspectives. More specifically, we can support efforts to find common goals—in much the same way that Sherif and his colleagues reduced conflict among the Eagles and Rattlers.

Unfortunately, the easiest and most simplistic response is to demonize those who perpetrate evil deeds—but that is merely name-calling, and we should resist it. This tactic blinds us to the power of the situation to create aggression in ordinary people. More important, it prevents us from dealing with the situations that nurture violence. Labeling others as "evil," or "pathological" usually prevents any attempt to understand the reasons for their actions, instead making them into objects of scorn or disdain.

A related mistake is to think of violence and terrorism as "senseless." On the contrary, destructive deeds always make sense from the perpetrator's frame of reference. As Shakespeare's Hamlet said, there is "method" in madness: We must understand the method in the minds of potential terrorists, if we are to deter them.

Finally, as individuals and as a society, we must refuse to adopt the terrorists' devaluing of human life. If we act on the desire to destroy our enemy at any cost, we have succumbed to the power of the situation. Moreover, we will have played into the hands of the ones we would destroy.

Kelman's Conflict Resolution Approach The hope that the psychology of cooperation and conflict reduction might ease international tensions lies behind a quiet program currently operating in Israel. There, social psychologist Herbert Kelman applies the lessons of the Eagles and Rattlers to the long-standing hostilities and prejudices between the Israelis and the Palestinians (Kelman, 1997, 1999; Rouhana & Kelman, 1994). His approach involves bringing community leaders from both sides together for small-group discussions of mutual problems. Not just anyone could have started such a program: Kelman's credibility with both sides is a product of his stature as a scholar and the prestige of his affiliation with Harvard University.

Kelman's approach was carefully planned to encourage cooperation and minimize the rewards for hostile behaviors. Representatives of both groups are invited to attend a series of meetings. These are not the usual, high-profile public negotiation sessions, however. Kelman has found that the process works best when the participants are midlevel community leaders, who have some power and status but who are in close touch with ordinary, grassroots

■ **Terrorism** The use of violent, unpredictable acts by a small group against a larger group for political, economic, or religious goals.

citizens. Also important is the fact that meetings are held in private to avoid competitive posturing for the press. Removed from the public spotlight, tensions between the two factions have eased, and earnest communication has developed.

Proof that this approach works is difficult to come by, especially in these times of political crisis and upheaval, although Kelman can recite case studies in which old hatreds have been soothed. In fact, several participants in these workshops have later become involved in other peace efforts in their communities. While the method is inspired by solid science, Kelman is performing no laboratory experiment. Rather, he is applying principles of social psychology to the world beyond the laboratory, where most of the variables remain uncontrolled.

 ## PSYCHOLOGY IN YOUR LIFE: MULTIPLE PERSPECTIVES ON TERRORISM

How does the Robbers Cave experiment apply to our understanding of the terrorist attacks of September 11? Admittedly, it is a stretch between experiments in the laboratory and conflicts on the international stage. Nevertheless, please consider the following ideas.

First, understanding terrorism does not mean condoning or accepting it—any more than understanding prejudice means approving of it. There can be no moral justification for the vicious attacks on the United States—or any other terrorist attacks. But—like it or not—many people in the world perceive the United States as the enemy. Understanding this perception—and dealing constructively with it—demands that Americans see the conflict from someone else's point of view: those who consider the United States to be the enemy. Doing so involves a cultural perspective.

Second, the Eagles and Rattlers study suggests that effective conflict resolution can come from identifying goals of mutual benefit and persuading the antagonistic groups to pursue these shared goals. This task requires leadership of exceptional vision and skill. It will take this same level of leadership to resolve the conflict resulting from the terrorist attacks on the United States.

Third, we must realize that terrorism does not always involve international conflict. The shootings at Columbine High School were terrorist acts, as was the bombing of the Federal Building in Oklahoma City, along with thousands of racial/ethnic hate crimes, attacks against gays, and violence directed at abortion providers that have made news in recent years (Doyle, 2001). It would be a mistake to believe that terrorism is always an outside threat from foreigners: Even though some cultures are more violent than others, every culture can breed violent people who terrorize others (Moghaddam et al., 1993; Shiraev & Levy, 2001).

Fourth, as in other areas of psychology, understanding the problem of violence and terrorism requires application of multiple perspectives—perhaps the most profound and far-reaching idea in psychology. In an earlier chapter, for example, we viewed aggression from a biological perspective, noting its association with testosterone and with certain parts of the brain (Davidson et al., 2000; Enserink, 2000; Holden, 2000b). From a behavioral perspective, we saw how aggression often results from pain or punishment (Shiraev & Levy, 2001). From an evolutionary perspective, we can see that aggression involves an impulse built into our genetic makeup and triggered by fear, threat, scarce resources, and sexual rivalry. Experiments in social learning have also shown how role models can stimulate aggression. And, in this chapter, we have seen how other forms of social influence can lead to aggression and violence.

CONNECTION: CHAPTER 6

Through social learning we acquire behaviors observed in our role models.

A complete picture, however, necessitates taking perspectives that extend beyond psychology (Segall et al., 1999). When we expand our view of terrorism, we can see that long-standing hostilities arise from religious, ethnic, and racial prejudices and from poverty, powerlessness, and hopelessness. To arrive at this understanding, however, we must view terrorism from historical, economic, and political perspectives—again, not to excuse violent acts but to understand their origins.

CHECK YOUR UNDERSTANDING

1. **RECALL:** Conflict between the groups in the Robbers Cave experiment was encouraged by
   a. punishing nonaggressive boys.
   b. showing movies featuring hostile role models.
   c. competitive games.
   d. putting a particularly aggressive boy in charge of each group.

2. **RECALL:** In Kelman's work in the Middle East, he removed much of the incentive for competitive responses by
   a. punishing those who responded competitively.
   b. holding the meetings in private.
   c. taking hostages from both sides.
   d. publicly denouncing those who responded competitively.

3. **UNDERSTANDING THE CORE CONCEPT:** In both the Robbers Cave experiment and Kelman's work in the Middle East, helping people to build a sense of mutual interdependence encouraged them to
   a. alter their perceptions of each other.
   b. punish those who had encouraged hostilities.
   c. become more creative.
   d. adopt new personality traits.

ANSWERS: 1.c 2.b 3.a

SOCIAL PSYCHOLOGY: THE STATE OF THE ART

More than anything else, social psychology has demonstrated the *power of the situation* to shape people's behavior. Depending on how it is structured, the situation can make people conform, obey, act aggressively, develop prejudices, and even commit terrorist acts. On the other hand, the power of the situation can induce cooperation, liking, and loving. The most recent research has focused not only on the conditions but the *social processes* that shape these attitudes and behaviors. And, despite the complexity of their subject matter, social psychologists have been exemplars in the use of the experimental method in studying social processes.

In our opinion, the social psychology of the future lies in two domains: (a) work on validating (or invalidating) our knowledge across cultures and (b) the application of basic principles, theories, and methods to political and social problems at home and abroad—to situations as diverse as discrimination, poverty, crime, prisoner abuse, terrorism, ethnic conflict, and war.

Persuasion in the Classroom

You may associate persuasion with advertising and politics, but persuasion does not stop there. It is woven into all human interaction—including the exchanges of ideas that occur in the classroom. There, your professors and fellow students will attempt to persuade you with reasoned arguments, and they will expect you to set out your points of view in the same fashion. But, aside from the open exchange of ideas and opinions, there are other, more subtle persuasive pressures of which you should be aware, says social psychologist Robert Cialdini (2001a, b). If you don't know about these, you run the risk of letting other people make up your mind for you. We will discuss three such subtle forms of influence that you will encounter in your college or university experience.

Social Validation

Although you may see a popular movie because your friends like it, going along with the crowd is a poor basis for judging the theories you encounter in your classes. Many of the world's discarded ideas were once accepted by nearly everyone. In psychology, these include the false notions that we use only 10% of our brain, that personality is determined by the first two years of life, and that IQ tests are a good measure of innate abilities. So, rather than accepting what you hear and read, questioning even the most widely held concepts is a good habit. In fact, most famous scientists have built their careers on challenging ideas that everyone else accepted.

Authority

The lectures you hear and the textbooks you read are full of authority figures. Every parenthetical reference in this book, for example, cites an authority. Most are given, in part, to persuade you that the argument being offered is credible. The problem, of course, is that ideas are not true merely because some authority says so. For example, just a few years ago, every introductory psychology text in print taught that no new neurons were created in the brain after birth. Now we know that the textbooks and the experts they cited were wrong. Real proof of such assertions, however, requires more objective evidence obtained by the scientific method—not just the declaration of an authority.

The Poison Parasite Argument

In advertising, a good way to undermine a competitor, says Cialdini, is with a message that calls into question the opponent's credibility. Then, to get people to remember what you have said, you can infect your opponent with a "parasite"—a mnemonic link that reminds people of your message every time they hear your opponent's pitch (Brookhart, 2001). A classic example involved antismoking ads that looked like Marlboro commercials, except that they featured a coughing, sickly "Marlboro Man." You may encounter the same sort of poison parasite argument in a lecture or a textbook that attempts to hold someone's ideas up to ridicule. That's not necessarily bad: In the academic world, weak ideas should perish. The sneaky, dishonest form of this technique, however, involves a misrepresentation or oversimplification of the opponent's arguments. The antidote is to be alert for ridicule and to check out the other side of the argument yourself.

The social psychology of persuasion, of course, involves much more than we have discussed here. A good place to look for more information is Cialdini's book, *Influence: Science and Practice* (2001a). Perhaps the most important idea is that some knowledge of persuasion can forearm you against the persuasive techniques you will encounter, both in and out of the classroom. When you know how effective persuaders operate, you are less likely to donate money to causes you don't care about, buy a car you don't really like, or accept a theory without examining the evidence critically.

A PERSONAL ENDNOTE

And so we come to the end of our journey together through psychology. If you are a curious people-watcher, perhaps you will continue on to the next phase of the journey into more advanced psychology and social science courses and into the books and films we have suggested at the end of each chapter. If you scan back through the Core Concepts in this book, you will realize that you have learned much already. Yet, because people are so complex, we have scarcely scratched the surface of the excitement and challenges that the field of psychology has to offer you.

One day you may be among those who contribute to this dynamic enterprise as a scientific researcher. (Wouldn't it be great if your name could appear in a future edition of this book? Please send us word of your discoveries!) Or perhaps you will decide to be a practitioner who applies what is known in psychology to the solution of personal and social problems. (Again, we would like to know if your career in psychology began with our journey together.) But, even if you don't become a professional psychologist, your authors hope that this introduction to psychology has sparked a lasting interest in mind and behavior because you cannot help but be an intuitive psychologist—psychology is all around you, and in you.

Playwright Tom Stoppard reminds us that, "Every exit is an entry somewhere else." We would like to believe that the entry into the next phase of your life will be facilitated by what you have learned from *Psychology: Core Concepts*, and from your introductory psychology course. In that next journey, may you infuse new life into the study of human nature, while strengthening the human connections among all people you encounter. Here's to a long, mindful, and wonderful journey through life.

CHAPTER SUMMARY

● HOW DOES THE SOCIAL SITUATION AFFECT OUR BEHAVIOR?

The Stanford prison experiment demonstrated how norms and social roles can be major sources of situational influence. The Asch studies demonstrated the powerful effect of the group to produce conformity, even when the group is clearly wrong. Another shocking demonstration of situational power came from Stanley Milgram's controversial experiments on obedience to authority. Situational influence can also lead to inaction: The bystander studies showed that individuals are inhibited by the number of bystanders, the ambiguity of the situation, and their resultant perception of their social role and responsibility.

● **We usually adapt our behavior to the demands of the social situation, and in ambiguous situations we take our cues from the behavior of others.**

● CONSTRUCTING SOCIAL REALITY: WHAT INFLUENCES OUR JUDGMENTS OF OTHERS

The situation, by itself, does not determine behavior. Rather, it is our interpretation of the situation—our constructed social reality— that regulates behavior, including our social interactions. Usually we are attracted to relationships that we find rewarding, although there are exceptions, predicted by expectancy-value theory and cognitive dissonance theory. Attribution theory predicts that we

will attribute other people's blunders to their traits or character (the fundamental attribution error) and our own to the situation (the self-serving bias), although this tendency depends on one's culture. Prejudice and discrimination also demonstrate how we construct our own social reality through such cognitive processes as the perception of social distance and threats, the influence of media stereotypes, scapegoating, and self-justification. Healthy loving relationships also demonstrate the social construction of reality, because there are many kinds of love and many cultural variations in the understanding of love.

● **The judgments we make about others depend not only on their behavior but also on our interpretation of their actions within a social context.**

● WHAT ARE THE ROOTS OF VIOLENCE AND TERRORISM?

Many studies in social psychology—particularly those dealing with obedience and conformity—show that the power of the situation can pressure ordinary people to commit horrible acts. In the Robbers Cave experiment, conflict between groups arose from an intensely competitive situation. Cooperation, however, replaced conflict when the experimenters contrived situations that fostered mutual interdependence and common goals for the groups.

The Robbers Cave experiment may hold a valuable lesson about dealing with violence and terrorism: the need for leadership that will find common goals for groups in conflict. A fuller understanding of violence and terrorism, however, requires taking multiple perspectives—including those that go beyond the boundaries of psychology to include the historical, economic, and political roots. Unfortunately, the easiest responses involve demonizing those who commit violent acts or labeling such acts as "senseless"—responses that interfere with our understanding them and dealing with them effectively.

A constructive approach, based on understanding conflict

from multiple perspectives, is now underway in the Middle East. There, social psychologist Herbert Kelman has created noncompetitive situations in which Israeli and Palestinian community leaders are seeking solutions that benefit all sides.

● **The power of the situation can help us understand violence and terrorism, but a broader understanding requires multiple perspectives that go beyond the boundaries of psychology.**

REVIEW TEST

For each of the following items, choose the single correct or best answer. The answer key appears at the end.

1. Which of the following is the social psychological principle illustrated by the Stanford prison experiment and its findings about participants' behavior?
   a. Social situations have powerful influences on human behavior.
   b. An experience is only socially real when the group is unanimous about interpreting it.
   c. Because everyone is basically different, no two people will respond to the same circumstances in the same way.
   d. Even in healthy circumstances, disturbed people will behave in unhealthy ways.

2. Theodore Newcomb's study of the attitudes of Bennington College students showed that, 20 years after they were first studied,
   a. all the women had gradually shifted to more conservative attitudes.
   b. all the women had gradually shifted to more liberal attitudes.
   c. the liberals were still liberal, and the conservatives still conservative.
   d. none of the above

3. According to research on the Asch effect, which of the following is not a condition that encourages greater conformity?
   a. The task being judged is difficult or ambiguous.
   b. Each group member responds privately and anonymously.
   c. The group is extremely cohesive.
   d. The group members perceive each other to be highly competent.

4. Which of the following statements about Milgram's obedience experiments is true?
   a. All participants were unable to resist the authority figure's orders, no matter how high the level of shock they believed they were administering.
   b. The majority of subjects delivered increasingly intense shocks until the learner complained of a heart condition, at which point most subjects refused to go on.
   c. Although most subjects verbally dissented and complained, most obeyed.

   d. Despite predictions by human nature experts that no one would comply, subjects enjoyed the experiment and had no trouble obeying the authority figure's commands.

5. Research on the factors that influence helping behavior suggests that the best predictor of bystander intervention is
   a. each individual's measurable level of personal altruism.
   b. the appearance or attractiveness of the victim.
   c. an individual's degree of religiousness or agreement with conventional religious values.
   d. the size of the group of bystanders to the emergency.

6. According to research on interpersonal attraction and close relationships, which of the following is *false*?
   a. The more you interact with someone, the more likely you are to like him or her.
   b. We form friendships on the basis of our similarity of backgrounds and attitudes.
   c. As far as first impressions go, a pleasing personality counts more than good looks.
   d. If you voluntarily undergo a hardship or suffering at someone's request, you will probably like them more than you did before.

7. Which of the following situations would be likely to create a feeling of cognitive dissonance in the mind of the individual described?
   a. A woman who has said she is on a diet declines the offer of dessert.
   b. A young man who says he loves his girlfriend spends a great deal of time choosing just the right valentine card to send her.
   c. When a man finds out the car he wants costs more than he can afford, he decides not to buy it and looks instead for a less expensive vehicle.
   d. A woman with a prejudice against Jews finds herself agreeing to do a favor for a Jewish neighbor.

8. Which of the following illustrates the effects of the fundamental attribution error?
   a. Explaining why he is turning his paper in late, a student tells the professor that he had car trouble on the way to campus.

b. Watching an acquaintance hurry from the overcrowded dining hall, a woman remarks, "Amy's in such a hurry—she must be a pretty impatient person."

c. After waiting an unusually long time to be waited on in a restaurant, a customer thinks there must be something wrong in the kitchen that is interfering with the waitress's ability to work as quickly as usual.

d. All of the above

9. In the Robbers Cave experiment, hostility between the groups was reduced by
a. having the groups engage in social activities with each other.
b. creating crisis situations that the groups had to work on cooperatively.

c. punishing aggressive behavior.
d. allowing the groups to take out their hostilities in competitive sports.

10. In an application of social psychological findings on promoting cooperation between hostile groups, Herbert Kelman has
a. used the power of conformity (the Asch effect) to reduce hostilities.
b. advocated the use of rewards for peaceful actions and punishments for hostile actions.
c. brought community officials on both sides together for private discussions of mutual problems.
d. promoted "friendly" athletic competition as a means of displacing harmful aggressions and "burning off" energy that could explode into violence.

ANSWERS: 1.a 2.c 3.b 4.c 5.d 6.c 7.d 8.b 9.b 10.c

KEY TERMS

Social psychology (p. 567)
Social context (p. 567)
Situationism (p. 568)
Social role (p. 569)
Script (p. 569)
Social norms (p. 569)
Asch effect (p. 571)
Conformity (p. 571)
Diffusion of responsibility (p. 579)

Social reality (p. 583)
Reward theory of attraction (p. 584)
Principle of proximity (p. 584)
Similarity principle (p. 585)
Matching hypothesis (p. 586)
Expectancy-value theory (p. 586)
Cognitive dissonance (p. 587)

Fundamental attribution error (FAE) (p. 589)
Self-serving bias (p. 589)
Prejudice (p. 590)
Discrimination (p. 590)
In-group (p. 590)
Social distance (p. 590)
Out-group (p. 591)
Scapegoating (p. 591)

Romantic love (p. 594)
Triangular theory of love (p. 594
Violence and aggression (p. 596)
Cohesiveness (p. 596)
Mutual independence (p. 597)
Terrorism (p. 598)

OUR RECOMMENDED BOOKS AND VIDEOS

BOOKS

Aronson, E. (2000). *Nobody left to hate: Teaching compassion after Columbine.* New York: W. H. Freeman. Renowned social psychologist Elliot Aronson argues that violent shootings by young students are in part fostered by the pressures and negativity in the schools themselves, including bullying, taunting, and exclusion. To end the tragedy, he offers strategies by which students, teachers, and communities might work to make schools humane, compassionate, and respectful.

Beck, A. T. (1999). *Prisoners of hate: The cognitive basis of anger, hostility, and violence.* New York: HarperCollins. The author, an expert on cognitive therapy and depression, finds parallels between the crimes of terrorists and extremists and the genocides perpetrated by warring nations. The book can be taken as a primer on the cognitive distortions that justify violence and destruction.

Cialdini, R. B. (2001). *Influence: Science and Practice.* Boston: Allyn & Bacon. Noted social psychologist Robert Cialdini summarizes the key principles of social influence, by which you get others to do what you want—or they get you to obey, agree, or buy. Whether you're selling, buying, or trying not to buy, this review arms you with the principles and research explaining how ideas and relationships alter behavior.

Coplin, W. D. (2000). *How you can help: An easy guide to doing good deeds in your everyday life.* New York: Routledge. Since September 11, 2001, many citizens want to "do good" but aren't sure how to start. This guide lists needy groups and worthwhile causes, strategies and principles for efficient helping, and brief, inspiring case histories of people who have made a difference in ways both large and small.

Davis, J. M. (2003). *Martyrs: Innocence, vengeance, and despair in the Middle East.* New York: Macmillan. What are the origins of the hatred and fanaticism that turn people into terrorists? Journalist Joyce Davis interviews people on both sides of the Israeli–Palestinian conflict to uncover the conditions and motives that turn young men, mothers, and children into warriors and suicide bombers.

Gay, P. (1994). *The cultivation of hatred.* New York: W. W. Norton & Co. This is volume 3 of a series exploring the bourgeois experience at the turn of the last century, examining the Victorians' ambivalence about aggression, so that it becomes channeled into sports, duels, wars of "honor," myths of "manliness," and finally old-fashioned warfare, prejudice, racism, sexism, and repression.

Friday, N. (1996). *The power of beauty.* New York: HarperCollins. Bestselling author Nancy Friday takes a careful, critical look at life in the "age of the empty package," when looks take precedence over personal qualities and everyone lusts for beauty.

Kohn, A. (1990). *The brighter side of human nature: Altruism and empathy in everyday life.* New York: Basic Books. Kohn provides an uplifting review of the many ways in which people help and cooperate with each other and the challenge this poses for more cynical views of human nature as "naturally" warlike and selfish.

Pope, H. G., Phillips, K. A., & Olivardia, R. (2000). *The Adonis complex: The secret crisis of male body obsession.* New York: The Free Press. Much has been written about the damage done to girls and women by society's unreal expectations and impossible images of female thinness and beauty. But what about males? This book examines a pressure to be not anorexic but "bigorexic," pumped up and bulging with muscles to achieve the look of strength and power, a pressure the authors relate to women's gains in social power and men's inability to define masculinity in new ways. It includes recommendations for identifying and treating symptoms of dangerously disordered behavior.

Stern, J. (2003). *Terror in the name of God: Why religious militants kill.* New York: Ecco. Jessica Stern, former fellow on terrorism at the Council of Foreign Relations, traveled the world to study the people and issues behind "religious" murders, ranging from Muslim jihadists in Indonesia to Americans who murder abortion providers in the name of Christianity. Religious militancy, she notes, is maintained by religious groups' support and the façade of normality and can be countered only with effective nonviolent strategies.

VIDEOS

Fahrenheit 451. (1966, color, 111 min.). Directed by François Truffaut; starring Oskar Werner, Julie Christie, Cyril Cusack. Based on the Ray Bradbury novel, this is a futuristic tale of a book-burning society (paper burns at 451 degrees Fahrenheit) in which a conforming "fireman" is tempted to explore the illicit, underground world of book-reading nonconformists.

Fahrenheit 9/11. (2004, color, 122 min.). Written, directed by, and starring Michael Moore. This satirical documentary by commentator Moore has itself become the provocative target of documentaries, censorship, and high-level critics unhappy with Moore's attack on President George W. Bush's personal and political motives for declaring war on Iraq. Winner of several awards, *Fahrenheit 9/11* also explores (and represents) the relationships between media and power.

The Fog of War: Eleven Lessons from the Life of Robert S. McNamara. (2004, color, 107 min.). Directed by Errol Morris; starring Robert S. McNamara. As Secretary of Defense in both the Kennedy and Johnson administrations, McNamara has been cited as the architect of U.S. involvement in and escalation of the war in Vietnam. Interviews with a haunted McNamara are here mixed with grim documentary footage and ironic imagery, making this hidden view of U.S. government and history all the more vivid and disquieting.

Ghosts of Mississippi. (1996, color, 130 min.). Directed by Rob Reiner; starring Alec Baldwin, Whoopi Goldberg, James Woods. This is the involving drama of the murder of civil rights leader Medgar Evers, the campaign by his widow to arrest and convict Byron De La Beckwith (the admitted but not confessed killer), and the attorney who finally agreed to prosecute the case at great cost to his own life. It is a portrait of a culture's doomed efforts to protect their prejudices and resist change.

Pay It Forward. (2001, color, 123 min.). Directed by Mimi Leder; starring Kevin Spacey, Helen Hunt, Haley Joel Osment. Challenged by a talented but afflicted new teacher, a young boy initiates a program of helping others in threes, with each recipient obligated to do the same for others in need. The engaging plot about the personalities and relationships of the principal characters also shows how such a plan might work and suggests that altruism might yet prevail.

Ridicule. (1992, color, 102 min. [French w/subtitles]). Directed by Patrice Leconte; starring Charles Berling, Jean Rochefort, Fanny Ardant. In the reign of Louis XVI, an environmentally conscious landowner seeking an audience with the king learns that he must meet social norms for sardonic wit and putdown in order to win influence and attention.

Separate but Equal. (1991, color, 193 min.). Directed by John Stevens, Jr., starring Sidney Poitier, Richard Kiley, Burt Lancaster. Originally a two-part TV movie, this docudrama tells the story of a young Thurgood Marshall's 1954 argument of *Brown v. Board of Education* before the Supreme Court, of which he was later to become the first black justice. Includes depiction of classic research by black psychologists Kenneth and Mamie Clark, who discovered that segregated children's self-concepts had been harmed, even to the point of preferring white dolls to black ones.

Six Degrees of Separation. (1993, color, 111 min.). Directed by Fred Schepisi; starring Stockard Channing, Donald Sutherland, Will Smith. Social psychologist Stanley Milgram once demonstrated that a letter with only an unknown addressee and city, but no address, could be hand delivered via a series of only five or six go-betweens, each of whom knew each other if no one else in the "chain." In this film, based on John Guare's stage play, an affluent urban couple find their lives surprisingly connected to and affected by a young man impersonating a celebrity's son.

Sliding Doors. (1998, color, 108 min.). Directed by Peter Howitt; starring Gwyneth Paltrow, John Hannah, John Lynch, Jeanne Tripplehorn, Zara Turner. This romantic comedy explores how situations and chance events—like catching or not catching a subway home—can set in motion a sequence of life-changing events. Two parallel stories are told of a woman's experiences after she either does or does not get through the sliding doors in time to catch the departing train.

To Kill a Mockingbird. (1962, b&w, 129 min.). Directed by Robert Mulligan; starring Gregory Peck, Mary Badham, Philip Alford, Brock Peters, Robert Duvall. This dramatization of Harper Lee's novel about a small-town Southern lawyer defending a black man falsely accused of rape shows the impact of his unpopular efforts on his young children and his community.

12 Angry Men. (1957, b&w, 95 min.). Directed by Sidney Lumet; starring Henry Fonda, Lee J. Cobb, E. G. Marshall, Ed Begley, Jack Klugman, Jack Warden, Robert Webber. In this absorbing drama of 12 jurors' deliberation over a verdict in a murder trial, their own prejudices, eyewitness memory, and group influence all play a part.

Making Sense of the Data: Descriptive and Inferential Statistics

The famous Bennington College study, discussed in Chapter 14, showed that students' political views can be profoundly influenced by their campus culture—which should make it interesting for you to think about the climate of political opinion on your own campus. Do the students and faculty at your college or university lean toward the liberal or toward the conservative end of the spectrum? And, are the students at your school typical of their counterparts elsewhere in the country? In the following pages we will use these questions as a starting point for an exploration of the statistical methods psychologists use to make sense of the data they gather in their research.

Every fall, the *Chronicle of Higher Education* publishes its "Almanac Issue," which reports the results of a survey of first-year students at colleges and universities across the country. Table A.1 shows how a national sample stood on a number of political issues (*Chronicle of Higher Education*, 2004). We will use this survey as the basis for assessing the political attitudes of your classmates and comparing them with those of other students across the United States.

We will begin by converting the items in the national survey into a scale that measures liberal and conservative attitudes. The second step will be to determine how you might use that scale to assess your psychology class or some other sample of students at your college or university. Next, we will show you how the resulting data might be organized and analyzed so that you could compare your own survey results with the national student survey data. In addition, we will discuss how your data could be linked, or

Agree strongly or somewhat that:	Conservative/ liberal wording	Agree	Majority response	Liberal response[a]
1. There is too much concern in the courts for the rights of criminals.	Conservative	61.1%	Conservative	38.9%
2. Abortion should be legal.	Liberal	54.5%	Liberal	54.5%
3. The death penalty should be abolished.	Liberal	32.6%	Conservative	32.6%
4. Marijuana should be legalized.	Liberal	38.8%	Conservative	38.8%
5. It is important to have laws prohibiting homosexual relationships.	Conservative	26.1%	Liberal	73.9%
6. The federal government should do more to control the sale of handguns.	Liberal	76.5%	Liberal	76.5%
7. Racial discrimination is no longer a problem in America.	Conservative	22.4%	Liberal	77.6%
8. Wealthy people should pay a larger share of taxes than they do now.	Liberal	53.1%	Liberal	53.1%
9. Same-sex couples should have the right to legal marital status.	Liberal	59.4%	Liberal	59.4%
10. Affirmative action in college admissions should be abolished.	Conservative	52.8%	Conservative	52.8%
11. The activities of married women are best confined to the home and family.	Conservative	21.7 %	Liberal	78.3%
12. Federal military spending should be increased.	Conservative	38.4%	Liberal	61.6%

[a]The score in this column has been converted to accord with the LCS scoring system. So, when the question has been worded conservatively, the LCS score is calculated by subtracting the percentage who agree from 100.

correlated, with other measures, such as income, gender, or grade-point average. Then, in the final section of this Appendix, we will point out some of the statistical pitfalls into which the unwary researcher may fall.

DEVELOPING YOUR OWN SURVEY

A look at Table A.1 reveals that the items on the national survey are written in two different ways. Some questions are worded so that agreement is a "conservative" response. (Item #1 is an example of conservative wording: "There is too much concern in the courts for the rights of criminals.") Other items are worded so that agreement is a "liberal" response. (Item #3, for example, is worded in the liberal direction: "The death penalty should be abolished.") Good surveys are constructed in this way to be neutral and to control for the tendency some people have of simply agreeing or disagreeing with each statement.

In Table A.1 we have indicated on each item whether agreement with the statement indicates a liberal or a conservative attitude. While you may disagree with our judgment about the liberalness or conservativeness of a particular item, it is important to note that you can clearly see what we mean by "liberal" and "conservative" by the way we have designated each item. By doing so, we have given *operational definitions* of the terms *liberal* and *conservative*. Together these items comprise what we will call our Liberal–Conservative Scale (LCS). By administering the LCS to your class, not only can you obtain political attitude scores for students in your class, but you can also compare the class's responses with the national survey data.

To score the responses obtained on the LCS, we will give one point for each of the following "liberal" items with which a respondent *agrees:* 2, 3, 4, 6, 8, and 9. Further, we will give another point for each of the following "conservative" items with which a respondent *disagrees:* 1, 5, 7, 10, 11, and 12. Accordingly, high scores will indicate a liberal tendency, and low scores will indicate a conservative tendency. (There is no value judgment here: Neither a high or low score is judged as being better.)

To illustrate how we might use the LCS in a study of students' political attitudes, let's suppose that we have administered the LCS to a class of 50 students. The resulting data (which we have contrived) appear in Table A.2. By merely counting the questions on which the majority gave a liberal response,

◄ CONNECTION: CHAPTER 1

An *operational definition* specifies the researcher's meaning in concrete, observable terms.

TABLE A.2	Distribution of LCS Responses from a Class of 50 College Students			
Agree strongly or somewhat that:	Number of respondents who agree	Agree	Majority response	Liberal response
1. There is too much concern in the courts for the rights of criminals.	36	72%	Conservative	28%
2. Abortion should be legal.	28	56%	Liberal	56%
3. The death penalty should be abolished.	19	38%	Conservative	38%
4. Marijuana should be legalized.	24	48%	Conservative	48%
5. It is important to have laws prohibiting homosexual relationships.	16	32%	Liberal	68%
6. The federal government should do more to control the sale of handguns.	24	48%	Conservative	48%
7. Racial discrimination is no longer a problem in America.	14	28%	Liberal	72%
8. Wealthy people should pay a larger share of taxes than they do now.	24	48%	Conservative	48%
9. Same-sex couples should have the right to legal marital status.	32	64%	Liberal	64%
10. Affirmative action in college admissions should be abolished.	31	62%	Conservative	38%
11. The activities of married women are best confined to the home and family.	13	26%	Liberal	74%
12. Federal military spending should be increased.	19	38%	Liberal	62%

we find that our class was more conservative (with conservative majorities on six items) than was the national sample (which had liberal majorities on eight items).

While this is an interesting result, there is much more that can be learned by organizing the data obtained from our survey. Let's first take a look at the *raw data* in the next section.

ORGANIZING THE DATA

In addition to the data showing how students responded on each question, we obtained the following set of LCS scores for the class:

4	4	8	3
3	3	7	9
6	7	8	9
6	6	1	4
3	6	11	8
7	1	8	5
8	7	5	7
1	1	6	5
4	6	10	7
9	8	5	8
2	4	8	4
5	6	2	3
10	2		

As you can see immediately, a set of raw data in this form is nearly impossible to interpret. Accordingly, our first task is to arrange the LCS scores into a **frequency distribution,** as shown in Table A.3. In the "Frequency" column of the table, you will see, for example, that four students received a score of 1, three scored 2, and so on. Grouping of the data in this way makes much more

■ **Frequency distribution** A summary chart, showing how frequently each of the various scores in a set of data occurs.

TABLE A.3	Frequency Distribution of LCS Scores for a Class	
LCS score	Frequency	LCS score × frequency
1	4	4
2	3	6
3	5	15
4	6	24
5	5	25
6	7	42
7	6	42
8	8	64
9	3	27
10	2	20
11	1	11
12	0	0
	$\Sigma = 50$	$\Sigma = 280$

sense than did the array of raw data above. Going one step further, we can convert the data into a bar graph called a **histogram,** which we have drawn in Figure A.1. In this diagram, you can more readily see that the students' scores are not evenly distributed across the scale. The histogram also makes it obvious that the scores are more clustered near the middle of the distribution than they are at the ends.

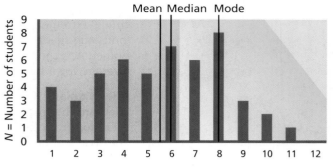

DESCRIBING THE DATA WITH DESCRIPTIVE STATISTICS

We can bring our data into even sharper focus by calculating some simple **descriptive statistics,** which are numbers that describe the main characteristics of the data. In particular, psychologists often find it useful to find a number that represents the middle of a distribution—the central point around which the scores seem to cluster. This is called a *measure of central tendency.* Additionally, researchers usually want a statistic that indicates the spread of the distribution—how closely the scores bunch up around the central point. This is called a *measure of variability.*

Measures of Central Tendency: Finding the Center of the Distribution

You are undoubtedly more familiar with the everyday name for measures of central tendency: *averages.* As their more formal name suggests, measures of central tendency help us locate the center of a set of measurements, such as we have from the responses we obtained on the Liberal–Conservative Scale. Three forms of central tendency are most commonly used: the *mean,* the *median,* and the *mode.* Let's look briefly at each in turn.

The Mean Most people think only of the **mean** when they hear the word *average.* The mean is, no doubt, familiar to you as the statistic used to calculate your grade-point average. And it is the statistic psychologists most often use to describe sets of data. To find the mean, you simply add up all the scores in a distribution and divide by the total number of scores. The calculation is summarized by the following formula:

$$M = \Sigma X \div N$$

Here M is the mean, Σ (the Greek letter *sigma*) is the summation of what immediately follows it, X represents each individual score, and N represents the total number of scores. In our example, to calculate the mean we would first add up all the Liberal–Conservative Scale scores (ΣX). The resulting sum is 280. Then, we would divide that sum by the total number of scores ($N = 50$). Thus, our mean (M) of the LCS scores for the class would be:

$$M = 280 \div 50 = 5.6$$

Usually the mean is a good indicator of the center of the distribution, as you will note in Figure A.1. Unfortunately, it has one potential flaw: Under some circumstances the mean can be unduly influenced by extreme scores. When the distribution is relatively symmetrical, this is not a problem. But when

FIGURE A.1 Distribution of Liberal–Conservative Scale (LCS) Scores for a Hypothetical Class

The height of each bar indicates how many respondents obtained exactly that score on the LCS. Note that the three averages, the *mean,* the *median,* and the *mode* are in different locations with the distribution not perfectly symmetrical. The mean is heavily influenced by extreme outlying scores, such as the four students who scored 1 on the LCS.

■ **Histogram** A bar graph depicting a frequency distribution. The height of the bars indicates the frequency of a group of scores.
■ **Descriptive statistics** Statistical procedures used to describe characteristics and responses of groups of subjects.
■ **Mean** The measure of central tendency most often used to describe a set of data—calculated by adding all the scores and dividing by the number of scores.

the scores bunch up toward one end of a distribution (in a *skewed* distribution), a few extreme scores at the other end can have a disproportionate effect that pulls the mean toward the extreme score. Because of this effect, researchers sometimes choose one of the other measures of central tendency to find an average for a highly skewed distribution.

The Median One of the alternative measures of central tendency is the **median,** the middle score—the score that separates the upper half of the distribution from the lower half. In our example, the median is 6. That is, half of the scores are 6 or higher, and the other half are 6 or lower. (See Figure A.1.) The big advantage of the median is that it is not distorted by extreme scores.

The Mode The third and simplest of the averages, or measures of central tendency, is called the **mode.** It is merely the score that occurs more often than any other. In our data, more students received a score of 8 than any other number, as shown in Figure A.1. The modal responses for this class on our conservative–liberal scale, therefore, is 8. While the mode is the easiest index of central tendency to determine, it is often the least useful, especially when the sample is relatively small.

Take a look again at the distribution of scores in Table A.3 and Figure A.1. Which of the averages seems to best fit the distribution? Is it the mean of 5.6, the median of 6, or the mode of 8?

Using Averages How can we use averages to compare the class we tested with student responses on the national survey? As shown in the last two columns of Table A.1, it is easy to convert the national survey percentages to indicate liberal responses—much as we did for the LCS scores. The mean of these national percentages is 58.2. That figure is higher than the mean of our own data set, which is 53.7. These two scores jibe with our earlier comparison of the two groups and further confirm that our class gave, on the average, more conservative responses than did the national sample.

Measures of Variability: Finding the Spread of the Distribution

In addition to knowing which score best represents the distribution's center, it is often useful to know how well the average represents the distribution as a whole. That is, we may want to know whether most of the scores cluster closely near the average or whether they are spread widely. We use statistics called *measures of variability* to describe the "spread-outness," of scores around some measure of central tendency.

To illustrate why variability is important, suppose that you are a third-grade teacher, and it is the beginning of the school year. Knowing that the average child in your class can read a third-grade-level book will help you to plan your lessons. You could plan more effectively, however, if you knew how similar or how divergent the reading abilities of the 30 children are. Do they all read at about the same level—that is, do they have *low variability?* If so, then you can develop a fairly standard third-grade lesson. But what if the group has *high variability,* with several who can read fourth-grade material and others who can barely read at all? In the latter case, the average reading level is not so representative of the entire class, and you will have to plan a variety of lessons to meet the children's varied needs.

The simplest measure of variability is the **range,** the difference between the highest and the lowest values in a frequency distribution. Returning to the

■ **Median** A measure of central tendency for a distribution, represented by the score that separates the upper half of the scores in a distribution from the lower half.

■ **Mode** A measure of central tendency for a distribution, represented by the score that occurs more often than any other.

■ **Range** The simplest measure of variability, represented by the difference between the highest and the lowest values in a frequency distribution.

Glossary

Absent-mindedness   Forgetting caused by lapses in attention.

Absolute threshold   The amount of stimulation necessary for a stimulus to be detected. In practice, this means that the presence or absence of a stimulus is detected correctly half the time over many trials.

Accommodation   A mental process that restructures existing schemes so that new information is better understood.

Acoustic encoding   The conversion of information, especially semantic information, to sound patterns in working memory.

Acquisition   The initial learning stage in classical conditioning, during which the conditioned response comes to be elicited by the conditioned stimulus.

Action potential   The nerve impulse caused by a change in the electrical charge across the cell membrane of the axon. When the neuron "fires," this charge travels down the axon and causes neurotransmitters to be released by the terminal buttons.

Activation-synthesis theory   The theory that dreams begin with random electrical *activation* coming from the brain stem. Dreams, then, are the brain's attempt to make sense of—to *synthesize*—this random activity.

Active listener   A person who gives the speaker feedback in such forms as nodding, paraphrasing, maintaining an expression that shows interest, and asking questions for clarification.

Acute stress   A temporary pattern of stressor-activated arousal with a distinct onset and limited duration.

Addiction   A condition in which a person continues to use a drug despite its adverse effects—often despite repeated attempts to discontinue using the drug. Addiction may be based on physical or psychological dependence.

Adolescence   In industrial societies, a developmental period beginning at puberty and ending (less clearly) at adulthood.

Affect   A term referring to emotion or mood.

Afterimages   Sensations that linger after the stimulus is removed. Most visual afterimages are *negative afterimages*, which appear in reversed colors.

Agonist   Drug or other chemical that enhances or mimics the effects of neurotransmitters.

Agoraphobia   A fear of public places and open spaces, commonly accompanying panic disorder.

Alarm reaction   First stage of the GAS, during which the body mobilizes its resources to cope with a stressor.

Algorithms   Problem-solving procedures or formulas that guarantee a correct outcome, if correctly applied.

All-or-none principle   Refers to the fact that the action potential in the axon occurs either full-blown or not at all.

Alzheimer's disease   A degenerative brain disease usually noticed first by its debilitating effects on memory.

Ambiguous figures   Images that are capable of more than one interpretation. There is no "right" way to see an ambiguous figure.

Amplitude   The physical strength of a wave. This is usually measured from peak (top) to valley (bottom) on a graph of the wave.

Amygdala   A limbic system structure involved in memory and emotion, particularly fear and aggression. Pronounced *a-MIG-da-la*.

Analysis of transference   The Freudian technique of analyzing and interpreting the patient's relationship with the therapist, based on the assumption that this relationship mirrors unresolved conflicts in the patient's past.

Analytical intelligence   According to Sternberg, the ability measured by most IQ tests; includes the ability to analyze problems and find correct answers.

Anchoring bias   A faulty heuristic caused by basing (anchoring) an estimate on a completely unrelated quantity.

Animistic thinking   A preoperational mode of thought in which inanimate objects are imagined to have life and mental processes.

Anorexia nervosa   An eating disorder involving persistent loss of appetite that endangers an individual's health and stemming from emotional or psychological reasons rather than from organic causes.

Antagonist   Drug or other chemical that inhibits the effects of neurotransmitters.

Anterograde amnesia   The inability to form memories for new information (as opposed to retrograde amnesia, which involves the inability to remember information previously stored in memory).

Antianxiety drugs   A category of drugs that includes the barbiturates and benzodiazepines, drugs that diminish feelings of anxiety.

Antidepressant drugs   Medicines that affect depression, usually by their effect on the serotonin and/or norepinephrine pathways in the brain.

Antipsychotic drugs   Medicines that diminish psychotic symptoms, usually by their effect on the dopamine pathways in the brain.

Antisocial personality disorder   Characterized by a long-standing pattern of irresponsible behavior indicating a lack of conscience and a diminished sense of responsibility to others.

Anxiety disorders   Mental problems characterized mainly by anxiety. Anxiety disorders include panic disorder, specific phobias, and obsessive–compulsive disorder.

Applied psychologists   Psychologists who use the knowledge developed by experimental psychologists to solve human problems.

Aptitudes   Innate potentialities (as contrasted with abilities acquired by learning).

Archetypes   The ancient memory images in the collective unconscious. Archetypes appear and reappear in art, literature, and folktales around the world.

Artificial concepts   Concepts defined by rules, such as word definitions and mathematical formulas.

Asch effect   A form of conformity in which a group majority influences individual judgments.

Assimilation   A mental process that modifies new information to fit into existing schemes.

Association cortex   Cortical regions throughout the brain that combine information from various other parts of the brain.

Attachment   The enduring social-emotional relationship between a child and a parent or other regular caregiver.

Attention-deficit hyperactivity disorder (ADHD)   A developmental disability involving short attention span, distractibility, and extreme difficulty in remaining inactive for any period; a common problem in children who have difficulty controlling their behavior and focusing their attention.

Autism   A developmental disorder marked by disabilities in language, social interaction, and the ability to understand another person's state of mind.

Autonomic nervous system   The portion of the peripheral nervous system that sends communications between the central nervous system and the internal organs and glands.

Availability bias   A faulty heuristic strategy that estimates probabilities based on information that can be recalled (made available) from personal experience.

Aversion therapy   As a classical conditioning procedure, aversive counterconditioning involves presenting individuals with an attractive stimulus paired with unpleasant (aversive) stimulation in order to condition a repulsive reaction.

Axon   In a nerve cell, an extended fiber that conducts information from the *soma* to the *terminal buttons.* Information travels along the axon in the form of an electric charge, called the *action potential.*

Basic anxiety   An emotion, proposed by Karen Horney, that gives a sense of uncertainty and loneliness in a hostile world and can lead to maladjustment.

Basilar membrane   A thin strip of tissue sensitive to vibrations in the cochlea. The basilar membrane contains hair cells connected to neurons. When a sound wave causes the hair cells to vibrate, the associated neurons become excited. As a result, the sound waves are converted (transduced) into nerve activity.

Behavior modification   Another term for behavior therapy.

Behavior therapy   Any form of psychotherapy based on the principles of behavioral learning, especially operant conditioning and classical conditioning.

Behavioral learning   Forms of learning, such as classical conditioning and operant conditioning, that can be described in terms of stimuli and responses.

Behavioral medicine   Medical field specializing in the link between lifestyle and disease.

Behavioral view   A psychological perspective that finds the source of our actions in environmental stimuli, rather than in inner mental processes.

Behaviorism   A historical school (as well as a modern perspective) that has sought to make psychology an objective science that focused only on behavior—to the exclusion of mental processes.

Binding problem   Refers to the process used by the brain to combine (or "bind") the results of many sensory operations into a single percept. This occurs, for example, when sensations of color, shape, boundary, and texture are combined to produce the percept of a person's face. No one knows exactly how the brain does this. Thus, the binding problem is one of the major unsolved mysteries in psychology.

Binocular cues   Information taken in by both eyes that aids in depth perception, including binocular convergence and retinal disparity.

Biological view   The psychological perspective that searches for the causes of behavior in the functioning of genes, the brain and nervous system, and the endocrine (hormone) system.

Biomedical therapies   Treatments that focus on altering the brain, especially with drugs, psychosurgery, or electroconvulsive therapy.

Biopsychology   The specialty in psychology that studies the interaction of biology, behavior, and mental processes.

Bipolar disorder   A mental abnormality involving swings of mood from mania to depression.

Blind spot   The point where the optic nerve exits the eye and where there are no photoreceptors. Any stimulus that falls on this area cannot be seen.

Blocking   Forgetting that occurs when an item in memory cannot be accessed or retrieved. Blocking is caused by *interference.*

Borderline personality disorder   An unstable personality given to impulsive behavior.

Bottom-up processing   Perceptual analysis that emphasizes characteristics of the stimulus, rather than our concepts and expectations. "Bottom" refers to the stimulus, which occurs at step one of perceptual processing.

Brain stem   The most primitive of the brain's three major layers. It includes the medulla, pons, and the reticular formation.

Brightness   A psychological sensation caused by the intensity of light waves.

Bulimia nervosa   An eating disorder characterized by eating binges followed by "purges," induced by vomiting or laxatives; typically initiated as a weight-control measure.

Burnout   Syndrome of emotional exhaustion, depersonalization, and reduced personal accomplishment, often related to work.

Cannon–Bard theory   The counterproposal that an emotional feeling and an internal physiological response occur at the same time: One is not the cause of the other. Both were believed to be the result of cognitive appraisal of the situation.

Case study   Research involving a single individual (or, at most, a few individuals).

Central nervous system   The brain and the spinal cord.

Centration   A preoperational thought pattern involving the inability to take into account more than one factor at a time.

Cerebellum   The "little brain" attached to the brain stem. The cerebellum is responsible for coordinated movements.

Cerebral cortex   The thin gray-matter covering of the cerebral hemispheres, consisting of a ¼-inch layer dense with cell bodies of neurons. The cerebral cortex carries on the major portion of our "higher" mental processing, including thinking and perceiving.

Cerebral dominance   The tendency of each brain hemisphere to exert control over different functions, such as language or perception of spatial relationships.

Chromosome   Tightly coiled threadlike structure along which the genes are organized, like beads on a necklace. Chromosomes consist primarily of DNA.

Chronic stress   Continuous stressful arousal persisting over time.

Chronological age (CA)   The number of years since the individual's birth.

Chunking   Organizing pieces of information into a smaller number of meaningful units (or chunks)—a process that frees up space in working memory.

Circadian rhythms   Physiological patterns that repeat approximately every 24 hours—such as the sleep–wakefulness cycle.

Classical conditioning   A form of behavioral learning in which a previously neutral stimulus acquires the power to elicit the same innate reflex produced by another stimulus.

Client-centered therapy   A humanistic approach to treatment developed by Carl Rogers, emphasizing an individual's tendency for healthy psychological growth through self-actualization.

Clinical view   The psychological perspective emphasizing mental health and mental illness. Psychodynamic and humanistic psychology are variations on the clinical view.

Closure   The Gestalt principle that identifies the tendency to fill in gaps in figures and to see incomplete figures as complete.

Cochlea   The primary organ of hearing; a coiled tube in the inner ear, where sound waves are transduced into nerve messages.

Cognitions Mental processes, such as thinking, memory, sensation, and perception.

Cognitive appraisal Assessment of a stressor and one's resources for dealing with it.

Cognitive–behavioral therapy A newer form of psychotherapy that combines the techniques of cognitive therapy with those of behavior therapy.

Cognitive dissonance A highly motivating state in which people have conflicting cognitions, especially when their voluntary actions conflict with their attitudes.

Cognitive hardiness Mental quality of resistance to stress, based on a sense of challenge (welcoming change), commitment (purposeful activity), and control (maintaining an internal guide for action).

Cognitive map A mental representation of physical space.

Cognitive neuroscience An interdisciplinary field emphasizing brain activity as information processing; involves cognitive psychology, neurology, biology, computer science, linguistics, and specialists from other fields who are interested in the connection between mental processes and the brain.

Cognitive restructuring Psychotherapeutic technique based on client's learning to reappraise stressors as less uncertain and more within one's control.

Cognitive therapy Emphasizes rational thinking (as opposed to subjective emotion, motivation, or repressed conflicts) as the key to treating mental disorder.

Cognitive view The psychological perspective emphasizing mental processes, such as learning, memory, perception, and thinking, as forms of information processing.

Cohesiveness Solidarity, loyalty, and a sense of group membership.

Collective unconscious Jung's addition to the unconscious, involving a reservoir for instinctive "memories," including the archetypes, which exist in all people.

Collectivism The view, common in Asia, Africa, Latin America, and the Middle East, that values group loyalty and pride over individual distinction.

Color Also called *hue*. Color is *not* a property of things in the external world. Rather, it is a *psychological sensation* created in the brain from information obtained by the eyes from the wavelengths of visible light.

Color blindness Typically a genetic disorder (although sometimes the result of trauma, as in the case of Jonathan) that prevents an individual from discriminating certain colors. The most common form is red–green color blindness.

Community mental health movement An effort to deinstitutionalize mental patients and to provide therapy from outpatient clinics. Proponents of community mental health envisioned that recovering patients could live with their families, in foster homes, or in group homes.

Computer metaphor The idea that the brain is an information-processing organ that operates, in some ways, like a computer.

Concept hierarchies Levels of concepts, from most general to most specific, in which a more general level includes more specific concepts—as the concept of "animal" includes "dog," "giraffe," and "butterfly."

Concepts Mental representations of categories of items or ideas, based on experience.

Concrete operational stage The third of Piaget's stages, when a child understands conservation but still is incapable of abstract thought.

Conditioned reinforcers or secondary reinforcers Stimuli, such as money or tokens, that acquire their reinforcing power by a learned association with primary reinforcers.

Conditioned response (CR) In classical conditioning, a response elicited by a previously neutral stimulus that has become associated with the unconditioned stimulus.

Conditioned stimulus (CS) In classical conditioning, a previously neutral stimulus that comes to elicit the conditioned response. Customarily, in a conditioning experiment, the neutral stimulus is called a conditioned stimulus when it is first paired with an unconditioned stimulus (UCS).

Cones Photoreceptors in the retina that are especially sensitive to colors but not to dim light. You may have guessed that the cones are cone-shaped.

Confirmation bias The tendency to attend to evidence that complements and confirms our beliefs or expectations, while ignoring evidence that does not.

Conformity The tendency for people to adopt the behaviors, attitudes, and opinions of other members of a group.

Conscious motivation Having the desire to engage in an activity and being aware of the desire.

Consciousness The process by which the brain creates a model of internal and external experience.

Conservation The understanding that the physical properties of an object or substance do not change when appearances change but nothing is added or taken away.

Consolidation The process by which short-term memories are changed to long-term memories over a period of time.

Contact comfort Stimulation and reassurance derived from the physical touch of a caregiver.

Contingency management An operant conditioning approach to changing behavior by altering the consequences, especially rewards and punishments, of behavior.

Continuity view The perspective that development is gradual and continuous—as opposed to the discontinuity (stage) view.

Continuous reinforcement A type of reinforcement schedule by which all correct responses are reinforced.

Control group Participants who are used as a comparison for the experimental group. The control group is not given the special treatment of interest.

Conversion disorder A type of somatoform disorder, marked by paralysis, weakness, or loss of sensation but with no discernible physical cause.

Coping Dealing with stress by reducing or eliminating stressful conditions and their effects.

Corpus callosum The band of nerve cells that connects the two cerebral hemispheres.

Correlation A relationship between variables, in which changes in one variable are reflected in changes in the other variable—as in the correlation between a child's age and height.

Correlation coefficient A number between –1 and +1, expressing the degree of relationship between two variables.

Correlational study A form of research in which the relationship between variables is studied, but without the experimental manipulation of an independent variable. Correlational studies cannot determine cause-and-effect relationships.

Creative intelligence According to Sternberg, the form of intelligence that helps people see new relationships among concepts; involves insight and creativity.

Creativity A mental process that produces novel responses that contribute to the solutions of problems.

Crystallized intelligence The knowledge a person has acquired, plus the ability to access that knowledge.

CT scanning or **computerized tomography** A computerized imaging technique that uses X rays passed through the brain at various angles and then combined into an image.

Culture A complex blend of language, beliefs, customs, values, and traditions developed by a group of people and shared with others in the same environment.

Cytokines Hormonelike chemicals facilitating communication between brain and immune system.

Data Pieces of information, especially information gathered by a researcher to be used in testing a hypothesis. (Singular: *datum*.)

Daydreaming A common (and quite normal) variation of consciousness in which attention shifts to memories, expectations, desires, or fantasies and away from the immediate situation.

Declarative memory A division of LTM that stores explicit information; also known as fact memory. Declarative memory has two subdivisions: episodic memory and semantic memory.

Deinstitutionalization The policy of removing patients, whenever possible, from mental hospitals.

Delusions Extreme disorders of thinking, involving persistent false beliefs. Delusions are the hallmark of paranoid disorders.

Dendrite A branched fiber that extends outward from the main cell body and carries information into the neuron.

Dependent variable The measured outcome of a study; the responses of the subjects in a study.

Depersonalization disorder An abnormality involving the sensation that mind and body have separated, as in an "out-of-body" experience.

Depressants Drugs that slow down mental and physical activity by inhibiting transmission of nerve impulses in the central nervous system.

Descriptive statistics Statistical procedures used to describe characteristics and responses of groups of subjects.

Developmental psychology The psychological specialty that studies how organisms change over time as the result of biological and environmental influences.

Developmental stages Periods of life initiated by significant transitions or changes in physical or psychological functioning.

Developmental view The psychological perspective emphasizing changes that occur across the lifespan.

Diathesis–stress hypothesis In reference to schizophrenia, the proposal that says that genetic factors place the individual at risk while environmental stress factors transform this potential into an actual schizophrenic disorder.

Difference threshold The smallest amount by which a stimulus can be changed and the difference be detected half the time.

Diffusion of responsibility Dilution or weakening of each group member's obligation to act when responsibility is perceived to be shared with all group members.

Discontinuity view The perspective that development proceeds in an uneven (discontinuous) fashion—as opposed to the continuity view.

Discrimination A negative action taken against an individual as a result of his or her group membership.

Display rules The permissible ways of displaying emotions in a particular society.

Dissociative amnesia A psychologically induced loss of memory for personal information, such as one's identity or residence.

Dissociative disorders A group of pathologies involving "fragmentation" of the personality, in which some parts of the personality have become detached, or dissociated, from other parts.

Dissociative fugue Essentially the same as dissociative amnesia, but with the addition of "flight" from one's home, family, and job. Fugue (pronounced *FEWG*) means "flight."

Dissociative identity disorder A condition in which an individual displays multiple identities, or personalities; formerly called "multiple personality disorder."

Distributed learning A technique whereby the learner spaces learning sessions over time, rather than trying to learn the material all in one study period.

DNA A long, complex molecule that encodes genetic characteristics. DNA is an abbreviation for deoxyribonucleic acid.

Double-blind study An experimental procedure in which both researchers and participants are uninformed about the nature of the independent variable being administered.

Drive Biologically instigated motivation.

DSM-IV The fourth edition of the *Diagnostic and Statistical Manual of Mental Disorders*, published by the American Psychiatric Association; the most widely accepted psychiatric classification system in the United States.

Dyslexia A reading disability, thought by some experts to involve a brain disorder.

Eclectic Either switching theories to explain different situations or building one's own theory of personality from pieces borrowed from many perspectives.

Ego The conscious, rational part of the personality, charged with keeping peace between the superego and the id.

Ego defense mechanisms Largely unconscious mental strategies employed to reduce the experience of conflict or anxiety.

Egocentrism In Piaget's theory, the self-centered inability to realize that there are other viewpoints beside one's own.

Eidetic imagery An especially clear and persistent form of memory that is quite rare; sometimes known as "photographic memory."

Elaborative rehearsal A working-memory process in which information is actively reviewed and related to information already in LTM.

Electroconvulsive therapy (ECT) A treatment used primarily for depression and involving the application of an electric current to the head, producing a generalized seizure. Sometimes called "shock treatment."

Electroencephalograph or **EEG** A device for recording brain waves, typically by electrodes placed on the scalp. The record produced is known as an electroencephalogram (also called an EEG).

Electromagnetic spectrum The entire range of electromagnetic energy, including radio waves, X rays, microwaves, and visible light.

Embryo In humans, the name for the developing organism during the first eight weeks after conception.

Emotion A four-part process that involves physiological arousal, subjective feelings, cognitive interpretation, and behavioral expression—all of which *interact,* rather than occurring in a linear sequence. Emotions help organisms deal with important events.

Emotion-focused coping Responding to stress by controlling one's emotional responses.

Emotional intelligence The ability to understand and control emotional responses.

Empirical investigation An approach to research that relies on sensory experience and observation as research data.

Encoding One of the three basic tasks of memory, involving the modification of information to fit the preferred format for the memory system.

Encoding specificity principle The doctrine that memory is encoded and stored with specific cues related to the context in which it was formed. The more closely the retrieval cues match the form in which the information was encoded, the better it will be remembered.

Endocrine system The hormone system—the body's chemical messenger system, including the endocrine glands: pituitary, thyroid, parathyroid, adrenals, pancreas, ovaries, and testes.

Engram The physical changes in the brain associated with a memory. It is also known as the *memory trace.*

Episodic memory A subdivision of declarative memory that stores memory for personal events, or "episodes."

Eugenics A philosophy and a political movement that encouraged biologically superior people to interbreed and sought to discourage biologically inferior people from having offspring.

Event-related potentials Brain waves shown on the EEG in response to stimulation.

Evolution The gradual process of biological change that occurs in a species as it adapts to its environment.

Evolutionary psychology A relatively new specialty in psychology that sees behavior and mental processes in terms of their genetic adaptations for survival and reproduction.

Expectancy bias The researcher allowing his or her expectations to affect the outcome of a study; or, in memory, a tendency to distort recalled events to make them fit one's expectations.

Expectancy-value theory A theory in social psychology that states how people decide whether or not to pursue a relationship by weighing the potential value of the relationship against their expectation of success in establishing the relationship.

Experiment A kind of research in which the researcher controls all the conditions and directly manipulates the conditions, including the independent variable.

Experimental group Participants in an experiment who are exposed to the treatment of interest.

Experimental neurosis A pattern of erratic behavior resulting from a demanding discrimination learning task, typically one that involves aversive stimuli.

Experimental psychologists Psychologists who do research on basic psychological processes—as contrasted with applied psychologists; also called *research psychologists.*

Experts Individuals who possess well-organized funds of knowledge, including the effective problem-solving strategies, in a field.

Explicit memory Memory that has been processed with attention and can be consciously recalled.

Exposure therapy A form of desensitization therapy in which the patient directly confronts the anxiety-provoking stimulus (as opposed to imagining the stimulus).

Extinction (in classical conditioning) The weakening of a conditioned response in the absence of an unconditioned stimulus.

Extinction (in operant conditioning) A process by which a response that has been learned is weakened by the absence or removal of reinforcement. (Compare with *extinction in classical conditioning.*)

Extraversion The Jungian personality dimension involving turning one's attention outward, toward others.

Extrinsic motivation The desire to engage in an activity to achieve an external consequence, such as a reward.

Feature detectors Cells in the cortex that specialize in extracting certain features of a stimulus.

Fetus In humans, the term for the developing organism between the embryonic stage and birth.

Fight-or-flight Sequence of internal processes preparing an organism for struggle or escape.

Figure The part of a pattern that commands attention. The figure stands out against the ground.

Five-factor theory A trait perspective suggesting that personality is composed of five fundamental personality dimensions: openness to experience, conscientiousness, extraversion, agreeableness, and neuroticism.

Fixation Occurs when psychosexual development is arrested at an immature stage.

Fixed-action patterns Genetically based behaviors, seen across a species, that can be set off by a specific stimulus. The concept of fixed-action patterns has replaced the older notion of instinct.

Fixed interval (FI) schedules Programs by which reinforcement is contingent upon a certain, fixed time period.

Fixed ratio (FR) schedules Programs by which reinforcement is contingent upon a certain, unvarying number of responses.

Flashbulb memory A clear and vivid long-term memory of an especially meaningful and emotional event.

Flow In Csikszentmihalyi's theory, an intense focus on an activity, accompanied by increased creativity and near-ecstatic feelings. Flow involves intrinsic motivation.

Fluid intelligence The ability to see complex relationships and solve problems.

Forgetting curve A graph plotting the amount of retention and forgetting over time for a certain batch of material, such as a list of nonsense syllables. The typical forgetting curve is steep at first, becoming flatter as time goes on.

Formal operational stage The last of Piaget's stages, during which abstract thought appears.

Fovea The tiny area of sharpest vision in the retina.

Fraternal twins A pair who started life as two separate fertilized eggs that happened to share the same womb. Fraternal twins, on the average, have about 50% of their genetic material in common.

Frequency The number of cycles completed by a wave in a given amount of time, usually a second.

Frequency distribution A summary chart, showing how frequently each of the scores in a set of data occurs.

Frontal lobes Cortical regions at the front of the brain that are especially involved in movement and in thinking.

Fully functioning person Carl Rogers's term for a healthy, self-actualizing individual, who has a self-concept that is both positive and congruent with reality.

Functional fixedness The inability to perceive a new use for an object associated with a different purpose; a form of mental set.

Functionalism A historical school of psychology that believed mental processes could best be understood in terms of their adaptive purpose and function.

Fundamental attribution error (FAE) The assumption that another person's behavior, especially clumsy, inappropriate, or otherwise undesirable behavior, is the result of a flaw in the personality, rather than in the situation; the tendency to emphasize internal causes and ignore external pressures. The FAE is more common in individualistic cultures than in collectivistic cultures.

g factor A general ability, proposed by Spearman as the main factor underlying all intelligent mental activity.

Gate-control theory An explanation for pain control that proposes we have a neural "gate" that can, under some circumstances, block incoming pain signals.

Gene Segment of a chromosome that encodes the directions for the inherited physical and mental characteristics of an organism. Genes are the functional units of a chromosome.

General adaptation syndrome (GAS) Pattern of general physical responses that take essentially the same form in responding to any serious chronic stressor.

Generalized anxiety disorder A psychological problem characterized by persistent and pervasive feelings of anxiety, without any external cause.

Generativity In Erikson's theory, a process of making a commitment beyond oneself to family, work, society, or future generations.

Genotype An organism's genetic makeup.

Gestalt psychology A historical school of psychology that sought to understand how the brain works by studying perception and perceptual learning. Gestalt psychologists believed that percepts consist of meaningful wholes (in German, *Gestalts*).

Gestalt psychology From a German word (pronounced *gush-TAWLT*) that means "whole" or "form" or "configuration." (A Gestalt is also a *percept*.) The Gestalt psychologists believed that much of perception is shaped by innate factors built into the brain.

Giftedness Often conceived as representing the upper 2% of the IQ range, commencing about 30 points above average (at about 130 IQ points).

Glial cells Cells that bind the neurons together. Glial cells also provide an insulating covering (the myelin sheath) of the axon for some neurons, which facilitates the electrical impulse.

Grammar The rules of a language, specifying how to use words, morphemes, and syntax to produce understandable sentences.

Ground The part of a pattern that does not command attention; the background.

Group therapy Any form of psychotherapy done with more than one client/patient at a time. Group therapy is often done from a humanistic perspective.

Gustation The sense of taste—from the same word root as "gusto"—also called the *gustatory sense*.

Habituation Learning not to respond to the repeated presentation of a stimulus.

Hallucinations False sensory experiences that may suggest mental disorder. Hallucinations can have other causes, such as drugs or sensory isolation.

Hallucinogens Drugs that create hallucinations or alter perceptions of the external environment and inner awareness.

Hassles Situations that cause minor irritation or frustration.

Health psychology Psychological specialty devoted to understanding how people stay healthy, why they become ill, and how they respond when ill.

Heritability The amount of trait variation within a group, raised under the same conditions, that can be attributed to genetic differences. Heritability tells us nothing about between-group differences.

Heuristics Cognitive strategies or "rules of thumb" used as shortcuts to solve complex mental tasks. Unlike algorithms, heuristics do not guarantee a correct solution.

Hierarchy of needs In Maslow's theory, the notion that needs occur in priority order, with the biological needs as the most basic.

Hindsight bias The tendency, after learning about an event, to "second guess" or believe that one could have predicted the event in advance.

Hippocampus A component of the limbic system, involved in establishing long-term memories.

Histogram A bar graph depicting a frequency distribution. The height of the bars indicates the frequency of a group of scores.

Homeostasis The body's tendency to maintain a biologically balanced condition, especially with regard to nutrients, water, and temperature.

Hormone A chemical messenger used by the endocrine system. Many hormones also serve as neurotransmitters.

Humanistic psychology A clinical viewpoint emphasizing human ability, growth, potential, and free will.

Humanistic therapies Treatment techniques based on the assumption that people have a tendency for positive growth and self-actualization, which may be blocked by an unhealthy environment that can include negative self-evaluation and criticism from others.

Humors Four body fluids—blood, phlegm, black bile, and yellow bile—that, according to an ancient theory, control personality by their relative abundance.

Hypnosis An induced state of awareness, usually characterized by heightened suggestibility, deep relaxation, and highly focused attention.

Hypochondriasis A somatoform disorder involving excessive concern about health and disease; also called *hypochondria.*

Hypothalamus A limbic structure that serves as the brain's blood-testing laboratory, constantly monitoring the blood to determine the condition of the body.

Hypothesis A statement predicting the outcome of a scientific study; a statement describing the relationship among variables in a study.

Id The primitive, unconscious portion of the personality that houses the most basic drives and stores repressed memories.

Identical twins A pair who started life as a single fertilized egg, which later split into two distinct individuals. Identical twins have exactly the same genes.

Identification The mental process by which an individual tries to become like another person, especially the same-sex parent.

Illusion You have experienced an illusion when you have a demonstrably incorrect perception of a stimulus pattern, especially one which also fools others who are observing the same stimulus. (If no one else sees it the way you do, you could be having a *delusion* or a *hallucination.* We'll take those terms up in a later chapter on mental disorder.)

Immune system Bodily organs and responses that protect the body from foreign substances and threats.

Implicit memory A memory that was not deliberately learned or of which you have no conscious awareness.

Implicit personality theory Assumptions about personality that are held by people (especially nonpsychologists) to simplify the task of understanding others.

Imprinting A primitive form of learning in which some young animals follow and form an attachment to the first moving object they see and hear.

In-group The group with which an individual identifies.

Independent variable A stimulus condition so named because the experimenter changes it independently of all the other carefully controlled experimental conditions.

Individualism The view, common in the Euro-American world, that places a high value on individual achievement and distinction.

Infancy In humans, infancy spans the time between the end of the neonatal period and the establishment of language—usually at about 18 months to 2 years.

Inferential statistics Statistical techniques (based on probability theory) used to assess whether the results of a study are reliable or whether they might be simply the result of chance. Inferential statistics are often used to determine whether two or more groups are essentially the same or different.

Information-processing model A cognitive understanding of memory, emphasizing how information is changed when it is encoded, stored, and retrieved.

Insanity A legal term, not a psychological or psychiatric one, referring to a person who is unable, because of a mental disorder or defect, to conform his or her behavior to the law.

Insight learning A form of cognitive learning, originally described by the Gestalt psychologists, in which problem solving occurs by means of a sudden reorganization of perceptions.

Insight therapies Psychotherapies in which the therapist helps patients/clients understand (gain insight into) their problems.

Insomnia The most common of sleep disorders—involving insufficient sleep, the inability to fall asleep quickly, frequent arousals, or early awakenings.

Instinct theory The now-outmoded view that certain behaviors are completely determined by innate factors. The instinct theory was flawed because it overlooked the effects of learning and because it employed instincts merely as labels, rather than as explanations for behavior.

Intelligence The mental capacity to acquire knowledge, reason, and solve problems effectively.

Intelligence quotient (IQ) A numerical score on an intelligence test, originally computed by dividing the person's mental age by chronological age and multiplying by 100.

Interaction A process by which forces work together or influence each other—as in the interaction between the forces of heredity and environment.

Intermittent reinforcement A type of reinforcement schedule by which some, but not all, correct responses are reinforced; also called *partial reinforcement.*

Interneuron A nerve cell that relays messages between nerve cells, especially in the brain and spinal cord.

Interval schedule A program by which reinforcement depends on the time interval elapsed since the last reinforcement.

Intrinsic motivation The desire to engage in an activity for its own sake, rather than for some external consequence, such as a reward.

Introspection The process of reporting on one's own conscious mental experiences.

Introversion The Jungian dimension that focuses on inner experience—one's own thoughts and feelings—making the introvert less outgoing and sociable than the extravert.

Inverted U function Describes the relationship between arousal and performance. Both low and high levels of arousal produce lower performance than does a moderate level of arousal.

Irreversibility The inability, in the preoperational child, to think through a series of events or mental operations and then mentally reverse the steps.

James–Lange theory The proposal that an emotion-provoking stimulus produces a physical response that, in turn, produces an emotion.

Just noticeable difference (JND) Same as the difference threshold.

Kinesthetic sense The sense of body position and movement of body parts relative to each other (also called *kinesthesis*).

Language acquisition device or LAD A biologically organized mental structure in the brain that facilitates the learning of language because (according to Chomsky) it is innately programmed with some of the fundamental rules of grammar.

Latent content The symbolic meaning of objects and events in a dream. Latent content is usually an interpretation based on Freud's psychoanalytic theory or one of its variants. The latent content of a dream involving clocks might involve fear of the menstrual cycle and, hence, of one's sexuality.

Lateralization of emotion Different influences of the two brain hemispheres on various emotions. The left hemisphere apparently influences positive emotions (for example, happiness), and the right hemisphere influences negative emotions (anger, for example).

Law of common fate The Gestalt principle that we tend to group similar objects together that share a common motion or destination.

Law of continuity The Gestalt principle that we prefer perceptions of connected and continuous figures to disconnected and disjointed ones.

Law of effect The idea that responses that produced desirable results would be learned, or "stamped" into the organism.

Law of Prägnanz The most general Gestalt principle, which states that the simplest organization, requiring the least cognitive effort, will emerge as the figure. *Prägnanz* shares a common root with *pregnant,* and so it carries the idea of a "fully developed figure." That is, our perceptual system prefers to see a fully developed Gestalt, such as a complete circle—as opposed to a broken circle.

Law of proximity The Gestalt principle that we tend to group objects together when they are near each other. *Proximity* means *nearness.*

Law of similarity The Gestalt principle that we tend to group similar objects together in our perceptions.

Laws of perceptual grouping The Gestalt principles of similarity, proximity, continuity, and common fate. These "laws" suggest how our brains prefer to group stimulus elements together to form a percept (Gestalt).

Learned helplessness Pattern of failure to respond to noxious stimuli after an organism learns its responses are ineffective.

Learning A lasting change in behavior or mental processes that results from experience.

Learning-based inference The view that perception is primarily shaped by learning (or experience), rather than by innate factors.

Levels-of-processing theory The explanation for the fact that information that is more thoroughly connected to meaningful items in long-term memory (more "deeply" processed) will be remembered better.

Libido The Freudian concept of psychic energy that drives individuals to experience sensual pleasure.

Limbic system The middle layer of the brain, involved in emotion and memory. The limbic system includes the hippocampus, amygdala, hypothalamus, and other structures.

Lithium carbonate A simple chemical compound that is highly effective in dampening the extreme mood swings of bipolar disorder.

Locus of control An individual's sense of where his or her life influences originate—internally or externally.

Long-term memory (LTM) The third of three memory stages, with the largest capacity and longest duration; LTM stores material organized according to meaning.

Long-term potentiation A biological process, involving physical changes that strengthen the synapses in groups of nerve cells, which is believed to be the neural basis of learning.

Loudness A sensory characteristic of sound produced by the *amplitude* (intensity) of the sound wave.

Maintenance rehearsal A working-memory process in which information is merely repeated or reviewed to keep it from fading while in working memory. Maintenance rehearsal involves no active elaboration.

Major depression A form of depression that does not alternate with mania.

Manifest content The story line of a dream, taken at face value without interpretation.

Matching hypothesis The prediction that most people will find friends and mates that are perceived to be of about their same level of attractiveness.

Maturation The process by which the genetic program manifests itself over time.

Mean The measure of central tendency most often used to describe a set of data—calculated by adding all the scores and dividing by the number of scores.

Median A measure of central tendency for a distribution, represented by the score that separates the upper half of the scores in a distribution from the lower half.

Medical model The view that mental disorders are diseases that, like ordinary physical diseases, have objective physical causes and require specific treatments.

Meditation A state of consciousness often induced by focusing on a repetitive behavior, assuming certain body positions, and minimizing external stimulation. Meditation may be intended to enhance self-knowledge, well-being, and spirituality.

Medulla A brain-stem structure that controls breathing and heart rate. The sensory and motor pathways connecting the brain to the body cross in the medulla.

Memory Any system—human, animal, or machine—that encodes, stores, and retrieves information.

Mental age (MA) The average age at which normal (average) individuals achieve a particular score.

Mental operations Solving problems by manipulating images in one's mind.

Mental representation The ability to form internal images of objects and events.

Mental retardation Often conceived as representing the lower 2% of the IQ range, commencing about 30 points below average (below about 70 points). More sophisticated definitions also take into account an individual's level of social functioning and other abilities.

Mental set The tendency to respond to a new problem in the manner used for a previous problem.

Mere exposure effect A learned preference for stimuli to which we have been previously exposed.

Method of loci A mnemonic technique that involves associating items on a list with a sequence of familiar physical locations.

Misattribution A memory fault that occurs when memories are retrieved but are associated with the wrong time, place, or person.

Misinformation effect The distortion of memory by suggestion or misinformation.

MMPI-2 A widely used personality assessment instrument that gives scores on ten important clinical traits. Also called the Minnesota Multiphasic Personality Inventory.

Mnemonics Techniques for improving memory, especially by making connections between new material and information already in long-term memory.

Mode A measure of central tendency for a distribution, represented by the score that separates the upper half of the scores in a distribution from the lower half.

Monocular cues Information about depth that relies on the input of just one eye—includes relative size, light and shadow, interposition, relative motion, and atmospheric perspective.

Mood-congruent memory A memory process that selectively retrieves memories that match (are congruent with) one's mood.

Mood disorders Abnormal disturbances in emotion or mood, including bipolar disorder and unipolar disorder. Mood disorders are also called *affective disorders.*

Morphemes The meaningful units of language that make up words. Some whole words are morphemes (example: "word"); other morphemes include grammatical components that alter a word's meaning (examples: "-ed," "-ing," and "un-").

Motivation Refers to all the processes involved in starting, directing, and maintaining physical and psychological activities.

Motive An internal mechanism that selects and directs behavior. The term *motive* is often used in the narrower sense of a motivational process that is learned, rather than biologically based (as are drives).

Motor cortex A narrow vertical strip of cortex in the frontal lobes, lying just in front of the central fissure; controls voluntary movement.

Motor neuron Nerve cell that carries messages away from the central nervous system toward the muscles and glands. Also called an *efferent neuron.*

MRI or **magnetic resonance imaging** An imaging technique that relies on cells' responses in a high-intensity magnetic field.

Multiple intelligences A term used to refer to Gardner's theory, which proposes that there are seven (or more) forms of intelligence.

Mutual interdependence A shared sense that individuals or groups need each other in order to achieve common goals

Myers–Briggs Type Indicator (MBTI) A widely used personality test based on Jungian types.

Narcissistic personality disorder Characterized by a grandiose sense of self-importance, a preoccupation with fantasies of success or power, and a need for constant attention or admiration.

Narcolepsy A disorder of REM sleep, involving sleep-onset REM periods and sudden daytime REM-sleep attacks usually accompanied by cataplexy.

Natural concepts Mental representations of objects and events drawn from our direct experience.

Natural language mediators Words associated with new information to be remembered.

Natural selection The driving force behind evolution, by which the environment "selects" the fittest organisms.

Naturalistic observation A form of descriptive research involving behavioral assessment of people or animals in their home surroundings.

Nature–nurture issue The long-standing discussion over the relative importance of nature (heredity) and nurture (environment) in their influence on behavior and mental processes.

Need for achievement (*n Ach*) In Murray and McClelland's theory, a mental state that produces a psychological motive to excel or to reach some goal.

Need In drive theory, a need is a biological imbalance (such as dehydration) that threatens survival, if the need is left unmet. Biological needs are believed to produce drives.

Negative correlation A correlation coefficient indicating that the variables change simultaneously in opposite directions: as one becomes larger, the other gets smaller.

Negative punishment The removal of an attractive stimulus after a response.

Negative reinforcement The removal of an unpleasant or aversive stimulus, contingent upon a particular behavior. Compare with *punishment.*

Neo-Freudian psychodynamic therapies Therapies for mental disorder that were developed by psychodynamic theorists who embraced some of Freud's ideas but disagreed with others.

Neo-Freudians Literally "new Freudians"; refers to theorists who broke with Freud but whose theories retain a psychodynamic aspect, especially a focus on motivation as the source of energy for the personality.

Neonatal period In humans, the neonatal (newborn) period extends through the first month after birth.

Nervous system The entire network of neurons in the body, including the central nervous system, the peripheral nervous system, and their subdivisions.

Neural pathway Bundle of nerve cells that follow generally the same route and employ the same neurotransmitter.

Neuron Cell specialized to receive and transmit information to other cells in the body—also called a *nerve cell*. Bundles of many neurons are called *nerves*.

Neuroscience A relatively new interdisciplinary field devoted to understanding how the brain creates thoughts, feelings, motives, consciousness, memories, and other mental processes.

Neurosis Before the *DSM-IV*, this term was used as a label for subjective distress or self-defeating behavior that did not show signs of brain abnormalities or grossly irrational thinking.

Neurotic needs Signs of neurosis in Horney's theory, these 10 needs are normal desires carried to a neurotic extreme.

Neurotransmitters Chemical messengers that relay neural messages across the synapse. Many neurotransmitters are also hormones.

Neutral stimulus Any stimulus that produces no conditioned response prior to learning. When it is brought into a conditioning experiment, the researcher will call it a conditioned stimulus (CS). The assumption is that some conditioning occurs after even one pairing of the CS and UCS.

Night terrors Deep sleep episodes that seem to produce terror, although any terrifying mental experience (such as a dream) is usually forgotten upon awakening. Night terrors occur mainly in children.

Nonconscious processes Any brain process that does not involve conscious processing, including both preconscious memories and unconscious processes.

Non-REM (NREM) sleep The recurring periods, mainly associated with the deeper stages of sleep, when a sleeper is not showing rapid eye movements.

Normal distribution or normal curve A bell-shaped curve, describing the spread of a characteristic throughout a population.

Normal range Scores falling near the middle of a normal distribution.

Object permanence The knowledge that objects exist independently of one's own actions or awareness.

Observational learning A form of cognitive learning in which new responses are acquired after watching others' behavior and the consequences of their behavior.

Obsessive–compulsive disorder A condition characterized by patterns of persistent, unwanted thoughts and behaviors.

Occipital lobes The cortical regions at the back of the brain, housing the visual cortex.

Oedipus complex According to Freud, a largely unconscious process whereby boys displace an erotic attraction toward their mother to females of their own age and, at the same time, identify with their fathers.

Olfaction The sense of smell.

Operant An observable, voluntary behavior that an organism emits to "operate" on, or have an effect on, the environment.

Operant chamber A boxlike apparatus that can be programmed to deliver reinforcers and punishers contingent on an animal's behavior. The operant chamber is often called a "Skinner box."

Operant conditioning A form of behavioral learning in which the probability of a response is changed by its consequences—that is, by the stimuli that follow the response.

Operational definitions Specific descriptions of concepts involving the conditions of a scientific study. Operational definitions are stated in terms of how the concepts are to be measured or what operations are being employed to produce them.

Opiates Highly addictive drugs, derived from opium, that can produce a profound sense of well-being and have strong pain-relieving properties.

Opponent-process theory The idea that cells in the visual system process colors in complementary pairs, such as red or green or as yellow or blue. The opponent-process theory explains color sensation from the bipolar cells onward in the visual system.

Optic nerve The bundle of neurons that carries visual information from the retina to the brain.

Optimistic style of thinking Pattern of thinking that interprets stressors as external in origin, temporary, and specific in their effects.

Out-group Those outside the group with which an individual identifies.

Overjustification The process by which extrinsic (external) rewards can sometimes displace internal motivation, as when a child receives money for playing video games.

Overlearning A strategy whereby the learner continues to study and rehearse the material after it has been initially brought to mastery.

Overregularization Applying a grammatical rule too widely and creating incorrect forms.

Panic disorder A disturbance marked by panic attacks that have no obvious connection with events in the person's present experience. Unlike generalized anxiety disorder, the victim is usually free of anxiety between panic attacks.

Parasympathetic division The part of the autonomic nervous system that monitors the routine operations of the internal organs and returns the body to calmer functioning after arousal by the sympathetic division.

Parietal lobes Cortical areas lying toward the back and top of the brain; involved in touch sensation and in perceiving spatial relationships (the relationships of objects in space).

Participant modeling A social learning technique in which a therapist demonstrates and encourages a client to imitate a desired behavior.

Penis envy According to Freud, the female desire to have a penis—a condition that usually results in their attraction to males.

Percept The meaningful product of perception—often an image that has been associated with concepts, memories of events, emotions, and motives.

Perception A process that makes sensory patterns meaningful. It is perception that makes these words meaningful, rather than just a string of visual patterns. To make this happen, perception draws heavily on memory, motivation, emotion, and other psychological processes.

Perceptual constancy The ability to recognize the same object as remaining "constant" under different conditions, such as changes in illumination, distance, or location.

Perceptual set Readiness to detect a particular stimulus in a given context—as when a person who is afraid interprets an unfamiliar sound in the night as a threat.

Peripheral nervous system All parts of the nervous system lying outside the central nervous system. The peripheral nervous system includes the autonomic and somatic nervous systems.

Persistence A memory problem in which unwanted memories cannot be put out of mind.

Personal bias The researcher allowing personal beliefs to affect the outcome of a study.

Personal unconscious Jung's term for that portion of the unconscious corresponding roughly to the Freudian id.

Personality disorders Conditions involving a chronic, pervasive, inflexible, and maladaptive pattern of thinking, emotion, social relationships, or impulse control.

Personality The psychological qualities that bring continuity to an individual's behavior in different situations and at different times.

Person–situation controversy A theoretical dispute concerning the relative contribution of personality factors and situational factors in controlling behavior.

PET scanning or **positron emission tomography** An imaging technique that relies on the detection of radioactive sugar consumed by active brain cells.

Phenomenal field Our psychological reality, composed of one's perceptions and feelings.

Phenotype An organism's observable physical characteristics.

Pheromones Chemical signals released by organisms to communicate with other members of their species. Pheromones are often used by animals as sexual attractants. It is unclear whether or not humans employ pheromones.

Phobias A group of anxiety disorders involving a pathological fear of a specific object or situation.

References

ABC News. (1995). "My Family, Forgive Me." *20/20*, Transcript #1526, June 30, pp. 6–10. New York: American Broadcasting Companies, Inc.

Abelson, P., & Kennedy, D. (2004, June 4). Editorial: The obesity epidemic. *Science, 304,* 1413.

Abelson, R. P. (1981). Psychological status of the script concept. *American Psychologist, 36,* 715–729.

Abrams, A. R. (1992). *Electroconvulsive therapy.* New York: Oxford University Press.

Abramson, L. Y., Metalsky, G. I., & Alloy, L. B. (1989). Hopelessness depression: A theory-based subtype. *Psychological Review, 96,* 358–372.

Ackerman, S. J., Benjamin, L. S., Beutler, L. E., Gelso, C. J., Goldfried, M. R., Hill, C., Lambert, M. J., Norcross, J. C., Orlinsky, D. E., & Rainer, J. (2001). Empirically supported therapy relationships: Conclusions and recommendations of the Division 29 task force. *Psychotherapy, 38,* 495–497.

Adams, J. (1979). Mutual-help groups: Enhancing the coping ability of oncology clients. *Cancer Nursing, 2,* 95–98.

Adelson, R. (2003, December). Conquering fear: Kick-starting extinction through massed exposure helps mice overcome conditioned fear faster. *Monitor on Psychology,* 20–21.

Ader, R., & Cohen, N. (1993). Psychoneuroimmunology: Conditioning and stress. *Annual Review of Psychology, 44,* 53–85.

Adolphs, R., Jansari, A., & Tranel, D. (2001). Hemispheric perception of emotional valence from facial expressions. *Neuropsychology, 15,* 516–524.

Adorno, T. W., Frenkel-Brunswick, E., Levinson, D. J., & Sanford, R. N. (1950). *The authoritarian personality.* New York: Harper.

Aftergood, S. (2000, November 3). Polygraph testing and the DOE National Laboratories. *Science, 290,* 939–940.

Agras, W. S., Brandt, H. A., Bulik, C. M., Dolan-Sewell, R., Fairburn, C. G., Halmi, K. A., Herzog, D. B., Jimerson, D. C., Kaplan, A. S., Kaye, W. H., le Grange, D., Lock, J., Mitchell, J., Rudorfer, M. V., Street, L. L., Striegel-Moore, R., Vitousek, K. M., Walsh, B. T., & Wilfley, D. E. (2004). Report of the National Institutes of Health workshop on overcoming barriers to treatment research in anorexia nervosa. *International Journal of Eating Disorders, 35,* 509–521.

Ahern, G. L., & Schwartz, G. E. (1985). Differential lateralization for positive and negative emotion in the human brain: EEG spectral analysis. *Neuropsychologia, 23,* 744–755.

Ahrons, C. R. (1994). *The good divorce: Keeping your family together when your marriage comes apart.* New York: HarperCollins.

Ainsworth, M. D. S. (1973). The development of infant–mother attachment. In B. M. Caldwell & H. N. Ricciuti (Eds.), *Review of child development research* (Vol. 3). Chicago: University of Chicago Press.

Ainsworth, M. D. S. (1989). Attachments beyond infancy. *American Psychologist, 44,* 709–716.

Ainsworth, M. D. S., Blehar, M., Water, E., & Wall, S. (1978). *Patterns of attachment.* Hillsdale, NJ: Erlbaum.

Ainsworth, M. D. S., & Wittig, B. A. (1969). Attachment and exploratory behavior of one-year-olds in a strange situation. In B. M. Foss (Ed.), *Determinants of infant behavior* (Vol. 4). London, U.K.: Methuen.

Alford, G. S., & Bishop, A. C. (1991). Psychopharmacology. In M. Hersen, A. E. Kazdin, & A. S. Bellack (Eds.), *The clinical psychology handbook* (2nd ed., pp. 667–694). New York: Pergamon Press.

Allen, M. G. (1976). Twin studies of affective illness. *Archives of General Psychiatry, 33,* 1476–1478.

Allen, V. S., & Levine, J. M. (1969). Consensus and conformity. *Journal of Experimental Social Psychology, 5,* 389–399.

Allport, G. W. (1954). *The nature of prejudice.* Cambridge, MA: Addison-Wesley.

Allport, G. W., & Odbert, H. S. (1936). Trait-names, a psycho-lexical study. *Psychological Monographs, 47*(1, Whole No. 211).

Alper, J. (1985, March). The roots of morality. *Science 85,* 70–76.

Alper, J. (1993). Echo-planar MRI: Learning to read minds. *Science, 261,* 556.

Amabile, T. M. (1983). *The social psychology of creativity.* New York: Springer-Verlag.

Amabile, T. M. (1987). The motivation to be creative. In S. Isaksen (Ed.), *Frontiers in creativity: Beyond the basics.* Buffalo, NY: Bearly Limited.

Amabile, T. M. (2001). Beyond talent: John Irving and the passionate craft of creativity. *American Psychologist, 56,* 333–336.

Amabile, T. M., Hadley, C. N., & Kramer, S. J. (2002, August). Creativity under the gun, *Harvard Business Review, 80*(8), 52–60.

American Academy of Pediatrics, Subcommittee on Attention Deficit Hyperactivity Disorder, Committee on Quality Improvement. (2001). Clinical practice guideline: Treatment of the school-aged child with attention-deficit/hyperactivity disorder. *Pediatrics, 108,* 1033–1044.

American Psychiatric Association. (1994). *Diagnostic and statistical manual of mental disorders* (4th ed.). Washington, DC: American Psychiatric Association.

American Psychiatric Association. (2000). *Diagnostic and statistical manual of mental disorders, 4th edition, text revision.* Washington, DC: American Psychiatric Association.

American Psychological Association. (2002). Ethical principles of psychologists and code of conduct. *American Psychologist, 57,* 1060–1073.

American Psychological Association. (2003a). Careers in psychology for the twenty-first century. Retrieved on October 14, 2004, from http://www.apa.org/students/brochure/brochurenew.pdf

American Psychological Association. (2003b). Council policy manual. Retrieved on October 14, 2004, from http://www.apa.org/about/division/cpmscientific.html

American Psychological Association. (2003c). Degree Fields of Psychology PhDs Awarded in 1981–2001. Retrieved on October 14, 2004, from http://research.apa.org/doctoraled05.html

American Psychological Association. (2004). *About APA.* Retrieved on October 14, 2004, from http://www.apa.org/about/

Anand, K. J. S., & Scalzo, F. M. (2000). Can adverse neonatal experiences alter brain development and subsequent behavior? *Biology of the Neonate, 77,* 69–82.

Anastasi, A. (1988). *Psychological testing* (6th ed.). New York: Macmillan.

Anch, A. M., Browman, C. P., Mitler, M. M., & Walsh, J. K. (1988). *Sleep: A scientific perspective.* Englewood Cliffs, NJ: Prentice Hall.

Anderson, A. E., & DiDomenico, L. (1992). Diet vs. shape content of popular male and female magazines: A dose-response relationship to the incidence of eating disorders? *International Journal of Eating Disorders, 11,* 283–287.

Anderson, C. A., & Bushman, B. J. (2002). Media violence and the American public revisited. *American Psychologist, 57,* 448–450.

Anderson, J. R. (1982). Acquisition of cognitive skill. *Psychological Review, 89,* 369–406.

Anderson, W. (1987). Parents as a source of stress for college students. *College Student Journal, 21,* 317–323.

Andreasen, N. C., Arndt, S., Alliger, R., Miller, D., et al. (1995). Symptoms of schizophrenia: Methods, meanings, and mechanisms. *Archives of General Psychiatry, 52,* 341–351.

Andreasen, N. C., Rice, J., Endicott, J., Coryell, W., Grove, W. W., & Reich, T. (1987). Familial rates of affective disorder. *Archives of General Psychiatry, 44,* 461–472.

Andrews, F. M., & Withey, S. B. (1976). *Social indicators of well-being: Americans' perceptions of life quality.* New York: Plenum.

Andrews, J. D. W. (1967). The achievement motive and advancement in two types of organization. *Journal of Personality and Social Psychology, 6,* 163–168.

Angerer, J. M. (2003). Job burnout. *Journal of Employment Counseling, 40,* 98–107.

Anglin, J. M. (1993). Vocabulary development: A morphological analysis. *Monographs of the Society for Research in Child Development, 58*(Serial No. 238).

Anglin, J. M. (1995, March). *Word learning and the growth of potentially knowable vocabulary.* Paper presented at the biennial meetings of the Society for Research in Child Development, Indianapolis, IN.

Angold, A., Erkanli, A., Egger, H. L., & Costello, E. J. (2000). Stimulant treatment for children: a community perspective. *Journal of the American Academy of Child and Adolescent Psychiatry, 39,* 975–984.

Anthony, E. J. (Ed.). (1987). *The invulnerable child.* New York: Guilford Press.

Antonova, I., Arancio, O., Trillat, A-C., Hong-Gang W., Zablow, L., Udo, H., Kandel, E. R., & Hawkins, R. D. (2001, November 16). Rapid increase in clusters of presynaptic proteins at onset of long-lasting potentiation, *Science, 294,* 1547–1550.

Antonuccio, D. (1995). Psychotherapy for depression: No stronger medicine. *American Psychologist, 50,* 450–452.

Antony, M. M., Brown, T. A., & Barlow, D. H. (1992). Current perspectives on panic and panic disorder. *Current Directions in Psychological Science, 1,* 79–82.

APA Online. (2004). *Empirical studies on lesbian and gay parenting.* Retrieved on November 8, 2004, from http://www.apa.org/pi/l&gbib.html

Archer, J. (1996). Sex differences in social behavior: Are the social role and evolutionary explanations compatible? *American Psychologist, 51,* 909–917.

Armstrong, L. (2001). *It's not about the bike: My journey back to life.* Madison, WI: Turtleback Books.

Arnett, J. J. (1999). Adolescent storm and stress, reconsidered. *American Psychologist, 54,* 317–326.

Arnhoff, F. N. (1975). Social consequences of policy toward mental illness. *Science, 188,* 1277–1281.

Arnsten, A. F. T. (1998, June 12). The biology of being frazzled. *Science, 280,* 1711–1712.

Aron, A., & Aron, E. (1994). Love. In A. L. Weber & J. H. Harvey (Eds.), *Perspectives on close relationships* (Chapter 7, pp. 131–152). Boston: Allyn & Bacon.

Aronson, E. (2004). *The social animal* (9th ed.). New York: Worth.

Aronson, E. (2000). *Nobody left to hate: Teaching compassion after Columbine.* New York: W. H. Freeman & Company.

Aronson, E., Helmreich, R., & LeFan, J. (1970). To err is humanizing—sometimes: Effects of self-esteem, competence, and a pratfall on interpersonal attraction. *Journal of Personality and Social Psychology, 16,* 259–264.

Aronson, E., Willerman, B., & Floyd, J. (1966). The effect of a pratfall on increasing interpersonal attractiveness. *Psychonomic Science, 4,* 227–228.

Asarnow, J., Glynn, S., Pynoos, R. S., Nahum, J., Guthrie, D., Cantwell, D. P., & Franklin, B. (1999). When the earth stops shaking: Earthquake sequelae among children diagnosed for pre-earthquake psy-

chopathology. *Journal of the American Academy of Child and Adolescent Psychiatry, 38,* 1016–1025.

Asbell, B. (1995). *The Pill: A biography of the drug that changed the world.* New York: Random House.

Asch, S. E. (1940). Studies in the principles of judgments and attitudes: 11. Determination of judgments by group and by ego standards. *Journal of Social Psychology, 12,* 433–465.

Asch, S. E. (1955). Opinions and social pressure. *Scientific American, 193*(5), 31–35.

Asch, S. E. (1956). Studies of independence and conformity: A minority of one against a unanimous majority. *Psychological Monographs, 70*(9, Whole No. 416).

Aserinsky, E., & Kleitman, N. (1953). Regularly occurring periods of eye mobility and concomitant phenomena during sleep. *Science, 118,* 273–274.

Ashby, F. G., & Waldron, E. M. (2000). The neuropsychological bases of category learning. *Current Directions in Psychological Science, 9,* 10–14.

Atkinson, R. C., & Schiffrin, R. M. (1968). Human memory: A control system and its control processes. In K. Spence (Ed.), *The psychology of learning and motivation* (Vol. 2). New York: Academic Press.

Attig, T. (1996). *How we grieve: Relearning the world.* New York: Oxford University Press.

Austin, J. H. (1998). *Zen and the brain: Toward an understanding of meditation and consciousness.* Cambridge, MA: MIT Press.

Averill, J. A. (1980). A constructivist view of emotion. In R. Plutchik & H. Kellerman (Eds.), *Emotion: Theory, research, and experience: Vol. 1. Theories of emotion.* New York: Academic Press.

Axel, R. (1995, October). The molecular logic of smell. *Scientific American, 273,* 154–159.

Ayllon, T., & Azrin, N. H. (1965). The measurement and reinforcement of behavior of psychotics. *Journal of Experimental Analysis of Behavior, 8,* 357–383.

Ayllon, T., & Azrin, N. H. (1968). *The token economy: A motivational system for therapy and rehabilitation.* New York: Appleton-Century-Crofts.

Azar, B. (1994, October). Seligman recommends a depression "vaccine." *APA Monitor, 4.*

Azar, B. (1995, June). New cognitive research makes waves. *APA Monitor, 16.*

Azar, B. (1996, November). Some forms of memory improve as people age. *APA Monitor, 27.*

Azar, B. (1997, October). Was Freud right? Maybe, maybe not. *American Psychological Association Monitor, 28,* 30.

Azar, B. (1998a, January). Certain smells evoke stronger memories. *APA Monitor, 10.*

Azar, B. (1998b, January). Communicating through pheromones. *APA Monitor, 1,* 12.

Azar, B. (2002, September). Searching for genes that explain our personalities. *Monitor on Psychology, 33*(8), 44–45.

Babyak, M., Blumenthall, J. A., Herman, S., Khatri, P., Doraiswamy, M., Moore, K., Craighead, W. E., Baldewicz, T. T., & Krishnan, K. R. (2000). Exercise treatment for major depression: Maintenance of therapeutic benefit at 10 months. *Psychosomatic Medicine, 62,* 633–638.

Baddeley, A. (1998). *Human memory: Theory and practice.* Boston: Allyn & Bacon.

Baddeley, A., Gathercole, S., & Papagno, C. (1998). The phonological loop as a language learning device. *Psychological Review, 105,* 158–173.

Baddeley, A. D. (2001). Is working memory still working? *American Psychologist, 56,* 851–864.

Baell, W. K., & Wertheim, E. H. (1992). Predictors of outcome in the treatment of bulimia nervosa. *British Journal of Clinical Psychology, 31*(3), 330–332.

Bahrick, H. P., Bahrick, L. E., Bahrick, A. S., & Bahrick, P. E. (1993). Maintenance of foreign language vocabulary and the spacing effect. *Psychology Science, 4,* 316–321.

Bailey, J. M., Bobrow, D., Wolfe, M, & Mikach, S. (1995). Sexual orientation of adult sons of gay fathers. *Developmental Psychology, 31,* 124–129.

Balch, P., & Ross, A. W. (1975). Predicting success in weight reduction as a function of locus of control: A uni-dimensional and multi-dimensional approach. *Journal of Consulting and Clinical Psychology, 43,* 119.

Baldwin, D. A. (2000). Interpersonal understanding fuels knowledge acquisition. *Current Directions in Psychological Science, 9,* 40–45.

Baldwin, M. W. (1992). Relational schemas and the processing of social information. *Psychological Bulleting, 112,* 461–484.

Balter, M. (2000, October 20). Celebrating the synapse. *Science, 290,* 424.

Baltes, M. M. (1995). Dependency in old age: Gains and losses. *Current Directions in Psychological Science, 4,* 14–19.

Baltes, P. B. (1987). Theoretical propositions on life-span developmental psychology: On the dynamics between growth and decline. *Developmental Psychology, 23,* 611–626.

Baltes, P. B. (1990, November). *Toward a psychology of wisdom.* Invited address presented at the annual convention of the Gerontological Society of America, Boston, MA.

Baltes, P. B. (1993). The aging mind: Potential and limits. *The Gerontologist, 33,* 580–594.

Baltes, P. B., & Kliegl, R. (1992). Further testing of limits of cognitive plasticity: Negative age differences in a mnemonic skill are robust. *Developmental Psychology, 28,* 121–125.

Bamshad, M. J., & Olson, S. E. (2003, December). Does race exist? *Scientific American, 289*(6), 78–85.

Bandura, A. (1970). Modeling therapy. In W. S. Sahakian (Ed.), *Psychopathology today: Experimentation, theory and research.* Itasca, IL: Peacock.

Bandura, A. (1981). In search of pure unidirectional determinants. *Behavior Therapy, 12,* 30–40.

Bandura, A. (1986). *Social foundations of thought and action: A social cognitive theory.* Englewood Cliffs, NJ: Prentice-Hall.

Bandura, A. (1992). Exercise of personal agency through the self-efficacy mechanism. In R. Schwarzer (Ed.), *Self-efficacy: Thought control of action* (pp. 3–38). Washington, DC: Hemisphere.

Bandura, A. (1999). Social cognitive theory of personality. In L. A. Pervin & O. P. John (Eds.), *Handbook of personality: Theory and research* (2nd ed., pp. 154–196). New York: Guilford Press.

Bandura, A., Ross, D., & Ross, S. A. (1963). Imitation of film-mediated aggressive models. *Journal of Abnormal and Social Psychology, 66,* 3–11.

Banich, M. T. (1998). Integration of information between the cerebral hemispheres. *Current Directions in Psychological Science, 7,* 32–37.

Banks, M. S., & Bennet, P. J. (1988). Optical and photoreceptor immaturities limit the spatial and chromatic vision of human neonates. *Journal of the Optical Society of America, 5,* 2059–2079.

Barab, S. A., & Plucker, J. A. (2002). Smart people or smart contexts? Cognition, ability, and talent development in an age of situated approaches to knowing and learning. *Educational Psychologist, 37,* 165–182.

Baranowsky, A. B. (2002). The silencing response in clinical practice: On the road to dialogue. In C. R. Figley (Ed.), *Treating compassion fatigue* (pp. 155–170). New York: Brunner-Routledge.

Barber, T. X. (1976). *Hypnosis: A scientific approach.* New York: Psychological Dimensions.

Barber, T. X. (1979). Suggested ("hypnotic") behavior: The trance paradigm versus an alternative paradigm. In E. Fromm & R. E. Shor (Eds.), *Hypnosis: Developments in research and new perspectives.* New York: Aldine.

Barber, T. X. (1986). Realities of stage hypnosis. In B. Zilbergeld, M. G. Edelstein, & D. L. Araoz (Eds.), *Hypnosis: Questions and answers.* New York: Norton.

Barinaga, M. (1994, July 29). To sleep, perchance to . . . learn? New studies say yes. *Science, 265,* 603–604.

Barinaga, M. (1995, December 1). Brain researchers speak a common language. *Science, 270,* 1437–1438.

Barinaga, M. (1996, January 19). Social status sculpts activity of crayfish neurons. *Science, 271,* 290–291.

Barinaga, M. (1997a, July 25). How jet-lag hormone does double duty in the brain. *Science, 277,* 480.

Barinaga, M. (1997b, June 27). New imaging methods provide a better view into the brain. *Science, 276,* 1974–1976.

Barinaga, M. (1998, April 17). Listening in on the brain. *Science, 280,* 376–377.

Barinaga, M. (1999, July 9). The mapmaking mind. *Science, 285,* 189, 191–192.

Barinaga, M. (2000, October 27). Synapses call the shots. *Science, 290,* 736–738.

Barinaga, M. (2002, February 8). How the brain's clock gets daily enlightenment. *Science, 295,* 955–957.

Barinaga, M. (2003a, January 3). Newborn neurons search for meaning. *Science, 299,* 32–34.

Barinaga, M. (2003b, October 3). Studying the well-trained mind. *Science, 302,* 44–46.

Barker, L. M., Best, M. R., & Domjan, M. (Eds.). (1978). *Learning mechanisms in food selection.* Houston: Baylor University Press.

Barkley, R. A. (1998, September). Attention-deficit hyperactivity disorder. *Scientific American, 279*(9), 66–71.

Barlow, D. H. (1996). Health care policy, psychotherapy research, and the future of psychotherapy. *American Psychologist, 51,* 1050–1058.

Barlow, D. H. (2000). Unraveling the mysteries of anxiety and its disorders from the perspective of emotion theory. *American Psychologist, 55,* 1247–1263.

Barlow, D. H. (2001). A modern learning theory perspective on the etiology of panic disorder. *Psychological Review, 108,* 4–32.

Barlow, D. H., & Durand, V. M. (2005). *Abnormal psychology: An integrative approach.* Belmont, CA: Wadsworth.

Barnes, D. M. (1987). Biological issues in schizophrenia. *Science, 235,* 430–433.

Barnett, R. C., & Hyde, J. S. (2001). Women, men, work, and family: An expansionist theory. *American Psychologist, 56,* 781–796.

Barnier, A. J., & McConkey, K. M. (1998). Posthypnotic responding away from the hypnotic setting. *Psychological Science, 9,* 256–262.

Barnouw, V. (1963). *Culture and personality.* Homewood, IL: Dorsey Press.

Baron, L., & Straus, M. A. (1985). *Four theories of rape in American society: A state-level analysis.* New Haven, CT: Yale University Press.

Barron, F., & Harrington, D. M. (1981). Creativity, intelligence and personality. *Annual Review of Psychology, 32,* 439–476.

Bartels, A., & Zeki, S. (2004). The neural correlates of maternal and romantic love. *NeuroImage, 22,* 419–433.

Bartoshuk, L. M. (1990, August–September). Psychophysiological insights on taste. *Science Agenda,* 12–13.

Bartoshuk, L. M. (1993). The biological basis of food perception and acceptance. *Food Quality and Preference, 4,* 21–32.

Bartoshuk, L. M., Duffy, V. B., & Miller, I. J. (1994). PCT/PROP tasting: Anatomy, psychophysics and sex effects. *Physiology and Behavior, 56,* 1165–1171.

Basbaum, A. I., Clanton, C. H., & Fields, H. L. (1976). Opiate and stimulus-produced analgesia: Functional anatomy of a medullospinal pathway. *Proceedings of the National Academy of Sciences, 73,* 4685–4688.

Basbaum, A. I., & Fields, H. L. (1984). Endogenous pain control systems: Brainstem spinal pathways and endorphin circuitry. *Annual Review of Neuroscience, 7,* 309–338.

Basic Behavioral Science Task Force of the National Advisory Mental Health Council. (1996). Basic behavioral science research for mental health: Family processes and social networks. *American Psychologist, 51,* 622–630.

Bass, E., & Davis, L. (1988). *The courage to heal.* New York: Harper-Collins.

Batista, A. P., Buneo, C. A., Snyder, L. H., & Andersen, R. A. (1999, July 9). Reach plans in eye-centered coordinates. *Science, 285,* 257–260.

Batson, C. D. (1987). Prosocial motivation: Is it ever truly altruistic? In L. Berkowitz (Ed.), *Advances in experimental social psychology* (Vol. 20). Orlando, FL: Academic Press.

Bauer, P. J. (2002). Long-term recall memory: Behavioral and neuro-developmental changes in the first 2 years of life. *Current Directions in Psychological Science, 11,* 137–141.

Baum, A. (1990). Stress, intrusive imagery, and chronic distress. *Health Psychology, 9,* 653–675.

Baum, D. (2004, July 12, 19). The price of valor. *The New Yorker, 80,* 44–52.

Baum, W. M. (1994). *Understanding behaviorism: Science, behavior, and culture.* New York: HarperCollins.

Baumeister, A. A. (1987). Mental retardation: Some conceptions and dilemmas. *American Psychologist, 42,* 796–800.

Baumeister, R. F. (Ed.). (1993). *Self-esteem: The puzzle of low self-regard.* New York: Plenum.

Baumeister, R. F., Campbell, J. D., Krueger, J. I., & Vohs, K. D. (2003). Does high self-esteem cause better performance, interpersonal success, happiness, or healthier lifestyles? *Psychological Science in the Public Interest, 4,* 1–44.

Baumeister, R. F., & Leary, M. R. (1995). The need to belong: Desire for interpersonal attachments as a fundamental human motivation. *Psychological Bulletin, 117,* 427–529.

Baumeister, R. F., Smart, L., & Boden, J. M. (1996). Relation of threatened egotism to violence and aggression: The dark side of high self-esteem. *Psychological Review, 103,* 5–33.

Baumeister, R. F., Stillwell, A. M., & Wotman, S. R. (1990). Victim and perpetrator accounts of interpersonal conflict: Autobiographical narratives about anger. *Journal of Personality and Social Psychology, 59,* 994–1005.

Baumrind, D. (1967). Child care practices anteceding three patterns of preschool behavior. *Genetic Psychology Monographs, 75,* 43–88.

Baumrind, D. (1971). Current patterns of parental authority. *Developmental Psychology Monograph, 4*(1, Part 2).

Baumrind, D. (1985). Research using intentional deception: Ethical issues revisited. *American Psychologist, 40,* 165–174.

Baynes, K., Eliassen, J. C., Lutsep, H. L., & Gazzaniga, M. S. (1998). Modular organization of cognitive systems masked by interhemispheric integration. *Science, 280,* 902–905.

Beall, A. E., & Sternberg, R. J. (1995). The social construction of love. *Journal of Social and Personal Relationships, 12*(3), 417–438.

Beaman, A. L., Barnes, P. J., Klentz, B., & McQuirk, B. (1978). Increasing helping rates through information dissemination: Teaching pays. *Personality and Social Psychology Bulletin, 4,* 406–411.

Beardsley, T. (1996, July). Waking up. *Scientific American, 14,* 18.

Beardsley, T. (1997a, August). The machinery of thought. *Scientific American, 277,* 78–83.

Beardsley, T. (1997b, March). Memories are made of . . . *Scientific American,* 32–33.

Beasley, M., Thompson, T., & Davidson, J. (2003). Resilience in response to life stress: The effects of coping style and cognitive hardiness. *Personality and Individual Differences, 34,* 77–95.

Bechara, A., Damasio, H., Tranel, D., & Damasio, A. R. (1997, February 28). Deciding advantageously before knowing the advantageous strategy. *Science, 275,* 1293–1295.

Bechara, A., Tranel, D., Damasio, H., Adolphs, R., Rockland, C., & Damasio, A. R. (1995, August 25). Double dissociation of conditioning and declarative knowledge relative to the amygdala and hippocampus in humans. *Science, 269,* 1115–1118.

Beck, A., Kline, S., & Greenfeld, L. (1988). *Survey of youth in custody, 1987.* Washington, DC: Bureau of Justice Statistics.

Beck, A. T. (1976). *Cognitive therapy and emotional disorders.* New York: International Universities Press.

Beck, A. T., Rush, A. J., Shaw, B. F., & Emery, G. (1979). *Cognitive therapy of depression.* New York: Guilford Press.

Bédard, J., & Chi, M. T. H. (1992). Expertise. *Current Directions in Psychological Science, 1,* 135–139.

Bee, H. (1994). *Lifespan development.* New York: HarperCollins.

Beeman, M. J., & Chiarello, C. (1998). Complementary right- and left-hemisphere language comprehension. *Current Directions in Psychological Science, 7,* 2–8.

Begley, S. (1995, November 20). Lights of madness. *Newsweek,* 76–77.

Behrmann, M. (2000). The mind's eye mapped onto the brain's matter. *Current Directions in Psychological Science, 9,* 50–54.

Beigel, A., & Berren, M. R. (1985). Human-induced disasters. *Psychiatric Annals, 15,* 143–150.

Beilin, H. (1992). Piaget's enduring contribution to developmental psychology. *Developmental Psychology, 28,* 191–204.

Bell, A. P., Weinberg, M. S., & Hammersmith, S. K. (1981). *Sexual preference.* Bloomington: Indiana University Press.

Bem, D. J. (1996). Exotic becomes erotic: A developmental theory of sexual orientation. *Psychological Review, 103,* 320–335.

Bem, D. J. (2001). *Interplay of theory and politics in explaining the enigma of sexual orientation.* Address given at the annual convention of the American Psychological Association in San Francisco, CA.

Bem, D. J., & Allen, A. (1974). On predicting some of the people some of the time: The search for cross-situational consistencies in behavior. *Psychological Review, 81*(6), 506–520.

Benassi, V. A., Sweeney, P. D., & Dufour, C. L. (1988). Is there a relation between locus of control orientation and depression? *Journal of Abnormal Psychology, 97,* 357–367.

Benedict, R. (1934). *Patterns of culture.* Boston: Houghton Mifflin.

Benjamin, L. T., Jr., & Nielsen-Gammon, E. (1999). B. F. Skinner and psychotechnology: The case of the heir conditioner. *Review of General Psychology, 3,* 155–167.

Bennett, K. K., & Elliott, M. (2002). Explanatory style and health: Mechanisms linking pessimism to illness. *Journal of Applied Social Psychology, 32,* 1508–1526.

Benson, H. (1975). *The relaxation response.* New York: Morrow.

Berglas, S. (2001). *Reclaiming the fire: How successful people overcome burnout.* New York: Random House.

Berk, L. E. (2004). *Development through the lifespan.* Boston: Allyn & Bacon.

Berkman, L. F., & Syme, S. L. (1979). Social networks, host resistance, and mortality: A nine-year follow-up study of Alameda County residents. *American Journal of Epidemiology, 109,* 186–204.

Berlyne, D. E. (1960). *Conflict, arousal, and curiosity.* New York: McGraw-Hill.

Berman, J. S., & Norton, N. C. (1985). Does professional training make a therapist more effective? *Psychological Bulletin, 98,* 401–407.

Berndt, T. J. (1992). Friendship and friends' influence in adolescence. *Current Directions in Psychological Science, 1,* 156–159.

Bernstein, I. L. (1988). *What does learning have to do with weight loss and cancer?* Proceedings of the Science and Public Policy Seminar of the Federation of Behavioral, Psychological and Cognitive Sciences. Washington, DC.

Bernstein, I. L. (1990). Salt preference and development. *Developmental Psychology, 26,* 552–554.

Bernstein, I. L. (1991). Aversion conditioning in response to cancer and cancer treatment. *Clinical Psychology Review, 11,* 185–191.

Berry, J. (1992). Cree conceptions of cognitive competence. *International Journal of Psychology, 27,* 73–88.

Berry, J. W., Poortinga, Y. H., Segall, M. H., & Dasen, P. R. (1992). *Cross-cultural psychology: Research and applications.* New York: Cambridge University Press.

Berscheid, E. (1988). Some comments on love's anatomy: or, Whatever happened to old-fashioned lust? In R. J. Sternberg & M. L. Barnes (Eds.), *The psychology of love.* New Haven, CT: Yale University Press.

Berscheid, E. (1999). The greening of relationship science. *American Psychologist, 54,* 260–266.

Beutler, L. E., Brown, M. T., Crothers, L., Booker, K., & Seabrook, M. K. (1996). The dilemma of factitious demographic distinctions in psychological research. *Journal of Consulting and Clinical Psychology, 64,* 892–902.

Beutler, L. E., & Machado, P. P. (1992). Research on psychotherapy. In M. R. Rosenzweig (Ed.), *International psychological science: Progress, problems, and prospects* (pp. 227–252). Washington, DC: American Psychological Association.

Bevins, R. A. (2001). Novelty seeking and reward: Implications for the study of high-risk behaviors. *Current Directions in Psychological Science, 10,* 189–193.

Bicklen, D. (1990). Communication unbound: Autism and praxis. *Harvard Educational Review, 60*(3), 291–314.

Biederman, I. (1989). Higher-level vision. In D. N. Osherson, H. Sasnik, S. Kosslyn, K. Hollerbach, E. Smith, & N. Block (Eds.), *An invitation to cognitive science.* Cambridge, MA: MIT Press.

Biehl, M., Matsumoto, D., Ekman, P., Hearn, V., Heider, K., Kudoh, T., & Ton, V. (1997). Matsumoto and Ekman's Japanese and Caucasian facial expressions of emotion (JACFEE): Reliability data and cross-national differences. *Journal of Nonverbal Behavior, 21,* 3–21.

Billings, A. G., & Moos, R. H. (1985). Life stressors and social resources affect post-treatment outcomes among depressed patients. *Journal of Abnormal Psychology, 94,* 140–153.

Binet, A. (1911). *Les idées modernes sur les enfants.* Paris: Flammarion.

Binitie, A. (1975). A factor-analytical study of depression across cultures (African and European). *British Journal of Psychiatry, 127,* 559–563.

Bink, M. L., & Marsh, R. L. (2000). Cognitive regularities in creative activity. *Review of General Psychology, 4,* 59–78.

Birenbaum, M., & Montag, I. (1986). On the location of the sensation seeking construct in the personality domain. *Multivariate Behavioral Research, 21,* 357–373.

Bjork, R. (1991, November). How do you improve human performance? *APS Observer,* 13–15.

Bjork, R. A. (2000). *Creating desirable difficulties for the learner. Implications for theory and practice.* Address given at the American Psychological Society's annual convention, Miami Beach, FL.

Bjork, R. A., & Richardson-Klarehn, A. (1989). On the puzzling relationship between environmental context and human memory. In C. Izawa (Ed.), *Current issues in cognitive processes: The Tulane-Floweree symposium on cognition.* Hillsdale, NJ: Erlbaum.

Bjorklund, D. F., & Shackelford, T. K. (1999). Differences in parental investment contribute to important differences between men and women. *Current Directions in Psychological Science, 8,* 86–89.

Blass, E. M. (1990). Suckling: Determinants, changes, mechanisms, and lasting impressions. *Developmental Psychology, 26,* 520–533.

Blass, T. (1996). Experimental invention and controversy: The life and work of Stanley Milgram. *The General Psychologist, 32,* 47–55.

Blass, T. (2004). *The man who shocked the world: The life and legacy of Stanley Milgram.* New York: Basic Books.

Blatt, S. J., Sanislow III, C. A., & Pilkonis, P. A. (1996). Characteristics of effective therapists: Further analyses of data from the National Institute of Mental Health treatment of depression collaborative research program. *Journal of Consulting and Clinical Psychology, 64,* 1276–1284.

Bloom, R. W. (2002). On media violence: Whose facts? Whose misinformation? *American Psychologist, 57,* 447–448.

Blum, D. (2002). *Love at Goon Park: Harry Harlow and the science of affection.* New York: Perseus Publishing.

Bodmer, W. F., & Cavalli-Sforza, L. L. (1970, October). Intelligence and race. *Scientific American,* 19–29.

Bolger, M. A. (1997). An exploration of college student stress. *Dissertation Abstracts International, 58,* 5-A, 1597.

Bolger, N., DeLongis, A., Kessler, R. C., & Schilling, E. A. (1989). Effects of daily stress on negative mood. *Journal of Personality and Social Psychology, 57,* 808–818.

Bond, M. H., Nakazato, H. S., & Shiraishi, D. (1975). Universality and distinctiveness in dimensions of Japanese person perception. *Journal of Cross-Cultural Psychology, 6,* 346–355.

Boomsma, D., Anokhin, A., & de Geus, E. (1997, August). Genetics of electrophysiology: Linking genes, brain, and behavior. *Current Directions in Psychological Science, 6,* 106–110.

Booth, A., Johnson, D. R., Granger, D. A., Crouter, A. C., & McHale, S. (2003). Testosterone and child and adolescent adjustment: The moderating role of parent–child relationships. *Developmental Psychology, 39,* 85–98.

Bornstein, R. F. (1989). Exposure and affect: Overview and meta-analysis of research, 1968–1987. *Psychological Bulletin, 106,* 265–289.

Borod, C., Koff, E., Lorch, M. P., Nicholas, M., & Welkowitz, J. (1988). Emotional and non-emotional facial behavior in patients with unilateral brain damage. *Journal of Neurological and Neurosurgical Psychiatry, 5,* 826–832.

Bostwick, J. M., & Pankratz, V. S. (2000). Affective disorders and suicide risk: A reexamination. *American Journal of Psychiatry, 157,* 1925–1932.

Bouchard, T. J., Jr. (1994, June 17). Genes, environment, and personality. *Science, 264,* 1700–1701.

Bouchard, T. J., Lykken, D. T., McGue, M., Segal, N. L., & Tellegen, A. (1990). Sources of human psychological differences: The Minnesota study of twins reared apart. *Science, 250,* 223–228.

Bourguignon, E. (1979). *Psychological anthropology: An introduction to human nature and cultural differences.* New York: Holt, Rinehart and Winston.

Bowden, C. L., Calabrese, J. R., McElroy, S. L., Gyulai, L. Wassef, A., Petty, F., Pope, H. G. Jr., Chou, J. C., Keck, P. E. Jr., Rhodes, L. J., Swann, A. C., Hirschfeld, R. M., & Wozniak, P. J. (2000). A randomized, placebo-controlled 12-month trial of divalproex and lithium in treatment of outpatients with bipolar I disorder. Divalproex Maintenance Study Group. *Archives of General Psychiatry, 57,* 481–489.

Bower, B. (1992, August 22). Genetic clues to female homosexuality. *Science News, 142,* 117.

Bower, B. (1995a, December 23 & 30). "Trauma disorder high, new survey finds." *Science News, 148,* 422.

Bower, B. (1995b, March 4). Virus may trigger some mood disorders. *Science News, 147,* 132.

Bower, B. (1996, April 27). Mom–child relations withstand day care. *Science News, 149,* 261.

Bower, B. (1997a, October 18). My culture, my self: Western notions of the mind may not translate to other cultures. *Science news, 152,* 248–249.

Bower, B. (1997b). Preschoolers get grip on hidden emotions. *Science News, 152,* 70.

Bower, B. (1997c, August 9). The ties that bond: Adult romantic and sexual styles may grow out of parent–child affiliations. *Science News, 152,* 94–95.

Bower, B. (1998a, February 21). All fired up: Perception may dance to the beat of collective neuronal rhythms. *Science News, 153,* 120–121.

Bower, B. (1998b). Dr. Freud goes to Washington. *Science News, 154,* 347–349.

Bower, B. (1998c, April 25). The name game: Young kids grasp new words with intriguing dexterity. *Science News, 153,* 268–269.

Bower, B. (1998d, June 20). Psychology's tangled web. *Science News, 153,* 394–395.

Bower, B. (2000a, January 22). Cultures of reason: Thinking styles may take Eastern and Western routes. *Science News, 157,* 56–58.

Bower, B. (2000b, September, 30). Memory echoes in brain's sensory terrain. *Science News, 158,* 213.

Bower, B. (2004, July 24). Suicide watch: Antidepressants get large-scale inspection. *Science News, 166,* 51.

Bower, G. H. (1972). A selective review of organizational factors in memory. In E. Tulving & W. Donaldson (Eds.), *Organization of memory.* New York: Academic Press.

Bower, G. H. (1981). Mood and memory. *American Psychologist, 36,* 129–148.

Bower, J. M., & Parsons, L. M. (2003, August). Rethinking the "lesser brain." *Scientific American,* 50–57.

Bower, T. G. R. (1971, October). The object in the world of the infant. *Scientific American, 225*(4), 30–39.

Bowers, K. S. (1983). *Hypnosis for the seriously curious* (2nd ed.) New York: Norton.

Bowlby, J. (1969). *Attachment and loss: Vol. 1. Attachment.* New York: Basic Books.

Bowlby, J. (1973). *Attachment and loss: Vol. 2. Separation, anxiety and anger.* London: Hogarth.

Bradbury, J. (2001, May 19). Teasing out the genetics of bipolar disorder. *Lancet, 357,* 1596.

Bradley, G. W. (1978). Self-serving biases in the attribution process: A re-examination of the fact or fiction question. *Journal of Personality and Social Psychology, 35,* 56–71.

Bradshaw, G. (1992). The airplane and the logic of invention. In R. N. Giere (Ed.). *Minnesota studies in the philosophy of science* (pp. 2239–2250). Minneapolis: University of Minnesota Press.

Braine, M. D. S. (1976). Children's first word

combinations. *Monographs of the Society for Research in Child Development, 41* (Serial No. 164).

Bransford, J., Sherwood, R., Vye, N., & Rieser, J. (1986). Teaching thinking and problem solving: Research foundations. *American Psychologist, 41,* 1078–1089.

Bransford, J. D., & Franks, J. J. (1971). The abstraction of linguistic ideas. *Cognitive Psychology, 2,* 331–350.

Braun, K. A., Ellis, R., & Loftus, E. F. (2002). Make our memory: How advertising can change our memories of the past. *Psychology and Marketing, 19,* 1–23.

Breggin, P. R. (1979). *Electroshock: Its brain disabling effects.* New York: Springer.

Breggin, P. R. (1991). *Toxic psychiatry.* New York: St. Martin's Press.

Breggin, P. R., & Breggin, G. R. (1994). *Talking back to Prozac.* New York: St. Martin's Press.

Brehm, S. S. (1992). *Intimate relationships* (2nd ed.). Boston: McGraw-Hill.

Brehm, S. S., Miller, R., Perlman, D., & Campbell, S. M. (2002). *Intimate relationships* (3rd ed). New York: McGraw-Hill.

Breier, J. I., Simos, P. G., Fletcher, J. M., Castillo, E. M., Zhang, W., & Papanicolaou, A. C. (2003). Abnormal activation of temporoparietal language areas during phonetic analysis in children with dyslexia. *Neuropsychology, 17,* 610–621.

Brett, A. S., Phillips, M., & Beary, J. F., III. (1986, March 8). Predictive power of the polygraph: Can the "lie detector" really detect liars? *Lancet, 1*(8480), 544–547.

Brewer, C. L. (1991). Perspectives on John B. Watson. In G. A. Kimble, M. Wertheimer, & C. L. White (Eds.), *Portraits of pioneers in psychology* (pp. 170–186). Washington, DC: American Psychological Association.

Brewer, M. B., Dull, V., and Lui, L. (1981). Perceptions of the elderly: Stereotypes and prototypes. *Journal of Personality and Social Psychology, 41,* 656–670.

Brigham, J. C. (1980). Limiting conditions of the "physical attractiveness stereotype": Attributions about divorce. *Journal of Research in Personality, 14,* 365–375.

Brislin, R. (1974). The Ponzo illusion: Additional cues, age, orientation, and culture. *Journal of Cross-Cultural Psychology, 5,* 139–161.

Brislin, R. (1993). *Understanding culture's influence on behavior.* Fort Worth, TX: Harcourt Brace Jovanovich.

Brislin, R. W. (1981). *Cross-cultural encounters: Face-to-face interaction.* Boston: Allyn & Bacon.

Broman, S. H., Nichols, P. I., & Kennedy, W. A. (1975). *Preschool IQ: Prenatal and early developmental correlates.* Hillsdale, NJ: Erlbaum.

Bronfenbrenner, U., & Ceci, S. J. (1994). Nature–nurture reconceptualized in developmental perspective: A bioecological model. *Psychological Review, 101,* 568–586.

Bronheim, S. (2000, January/February). The impact of the Human Genome Project on the science and practice of psychology. *Psychological Science Agenda, 13*(1), 12.

Brookhart, S. (2001). Persuasion and the "poison parasite." *APS Observer, 14*(8), 7.

Brooks, R., & Goldstein, S. (2004). *The power of resilience: Achieving balance, confidence, and personal strength in your life.* New York: Contemporary Books.

Brown, A. M. (1990). *Human universals.* Unpublished manuscript, University of California, Santa Barbara.

Brown, B. (1999). Optimizing expression of the common human genome for child development. *Current Directions in Psychological Science, 8,* 37–41.

Brown, C. (2003, October). The stubborn scientist who unraveled a mystery of the night. *Smithsonian,* 92–99.

Brown, J. D. (1991). Accuracy and bias in self-knowledge. In C. R. Snyder & D. F. Forsyth (Eds.), *Handbook of social and clinical psychology: The health perspective.* New York: Pergamon.

Brown, J. L., & Pollitt, E. (1996, February). Malnutrition, poverty and intellectual development. *Scientific American, 274*(2), 38–43.

Brown, K. (2003a, March 14). The medication merry-go-round. *Science, 299,* 1646–1649.

Brown, K. (2003b, July 11). New attention to ADHD genes. *Science, 301,* 160–161.

Brown, R., & Kulik, J. (1977). Flashbulb memories. *Cognition, 5,* 73–99.

Brown, R., & McNeill, D. (1966). The "tip of the tongue" phenomenon. *Journal of Verbal Learning and Verbal Behavior, 5,* 325–337.

Brown, S. L., Nesse, R. M., Vinokur, A. D., & Smith, D. M. (2003). Providing social support may be more beneficial than receiving it: Results from a prospective study of mortality. *Psychological Science, 14,* 320–327.

Brown, W. A. (1998, January). The placebo effect. *Scientific American,* 90–95.

Bruce, D. (1991). Integrations of Lashley. In G. A. Kimble, M. Wertheimer, & C. L. White (Eds.), *Portraits of pioneers in psychology* (pp. 306–323). Washington, DC: American Psychological Association.

Bruch, H. (1978). *The golden cage: The enigma of anorexia nervosa.* Cambridge, MA: Harvard University Press.

Bruck, M., & Ceci, S. (1997). The suggestibility of young children. *Current Directions in Psychological Science, 6,* 75–79.

Bruner, J. (1992). Another look at new look 1. *American Psychologist, 47,* 780–783.

Bruner, J. S., Olver, R. R., & Greenfield, P. M. (1966). *Studies in cognitive growth.* New York: Wiley.

Brunner, H. G., Nelen, M., Breakefield, X. O., Ropers, H. H., & van Oost, B. A. (1993). Abnormal behavior associated with a point mutation in the structural gene for monoamine oxidase A. *Science, 262,* 578.

Buck, L., & Axel, R. (1991). A novel multigene family may encode odorant receptors: A molecular basis for odor recognition. *Cell, 65,* 175–187.

Buhrmester, D. (1996). Need fulfillment, interpersonal competence, and the developmental contexts of early adolescent friendship. In W. M. Bukowski, A. F. Newcomb, & W. W. Hartup (Eds.), *The company they keep: Friendship during childhood and adolescence* (pp. 158–185). New York: Cambridge University Press.

Buie, J. (1988, July). "Control" studies bode better health in aging. *APA Monitor,* 20.

Bushman, B. J., & Anderson, C. A. (2001). Media violence and the American public: Scientific facts versus media misinformation. *American Psychologist, 56,* 477–489.

Buss, D. M. (2000). The evolution of happiness. *American Psychologist, 55,* 15–23.

Buss, D. M. (2001). *Human mating strategies and human nature.* Address given at the annual convention of the American Psychological Association, San Francisco, CA.

Buss, D. M. (2004). *Evolutionary psychology: The new science of the mind* (2nd ed.). Boston: Allyn & Bacon.

Buss, D. M., Haselton, M. G., Shackelford, T. K., Bleske, A. L., & Wakefield, J. C. (1998). Adaptations, exaptations, and spandrels. *American Psychologist, 53,* 533–548.

Buss, D. M., & Schmitt, D. P. (1993). Sexual strategies theory: An evolutionary perspective on human mating. *Psychological Review, 100,* 204–232.

Bussey, K., & Bandura, A. (1999). Social cognitive theory of gender development and differentiation. *Psychological Review, 106,* 676–713.

Butcher, J. N., Graham, J. R., Williams, C. L., & Ben-Porath, Y. (1989). *Development and use of the MMPI-2 content scales.* Minneapolis: University of Minnesota Press.

Butcher, J. N., & Williams, C. L. (1992). *Essentials of MMPI-2 and MMPI-A interpretation.* Minneapolis: University of Minnesota Press.

Byne, W. (1995). The biological evidence challenged. *Scientific American, 270*(5), 50–55.

Byrne, D. (1969). Attitudes and attraction. In L. Berkowitz (Ed.), *Advances in experimental social psychology* (Vol. 4). New York: Academic Press.

Cabay, M. (1994). A controlled evaluation of facilitated communication using open-ended and fill-in questions. *Journal of Autism and Developmental Disorders, 24*(4), 517–527.

Cabeza, R. (2002). Hemispheric asymmetry reduction in older adults: The HAROLD model. *Psychology & Aging, 17*(1), 85–100.

Cahill, L., Prins, B., Weber, M., & McGaugh, J. L. (1994). b-Adrenergic activation and memory for emotional events. *Nature, 371,* 702–704.

Cain, C. K., Blouin, A. M., & Barad, M. (2003). Temporally massed CS presentations generate more fear extinction than spaced presentations. *Journal of Experimental Psychology: Animal Behavior Processes, 29,* 323–333.

Caldwell, M. (1995, June). Kernel of fear. *Discover, 16,* 96–102.

Calev, A., Nigal, D., Shapira, B., Tubi, N., Chazan, S., Ben-Yehuda, Y., Kugelmass, S., & Lerer, B. (1991). Early and long-term effects of electroconvulsive therapy and depression on memory and other cognitive functions. *Journal of Nervous and Mental Disorders, 179,* 526–533.

Callahan, J. (1997, May/June). Hypnosis: Trick or treatment? *Health, 11*(1), 52–55.

Callaway, C. W. (1987). Obesity. *Public Health Reports Supplement, 102,* 26–29.

Calvert, J. D. (1988). Physical attractiveness: A review and reevaluation of its role in social skill research. *Behavioral Assessment, 10,* 29–42.

Camara, W. J., & Schneider, D. L. (1994). Integrity tests: Facts and unresolved issues. *American Psychologist, 49,* 112–119.

Campbell, S. S., & Murphy, P. J. (1998, January 16). Extraocular circadian phototransduction in humans. *Science, 279,* 396–399.

Campfield, L. A., Smith, F. J., & Burn, P. (1998, May 29). Strategies and potential molecular targets for obesity treatment. *Science, 280,* 1383–1387.

Campos, J. J., Barrett, K. C., Lamb, M. E., Goldsmith, H. H., & Stenberg, C. (1983). *Socioemotional development* (Vol. 2). New York: Wiley.

Canli, T., Sivers, H., Whitfield, S. L., Gotlib, I. H., & Gabreli, J. D. E. (2002, June 21). Amygdala response to happy faces as a function of extraversion. *Science, 296,* 2191.

Cann, A., Calhoun, L. G., Selby, J. W., & Kin, H. E. (Eds.). (1981). Rape. *Journal of Social Issues, 37* (Whole No. 4).

Cannon, W. B. (1914). The interrelations of emotions as suggested by recent physiological researchers. *American Journal of Psychology, 25,* 256.

Cannon, W. (1936). The interrelations of emotions as suggested by recent physiological researches. *American Journal of Psychology, 25,* 256.

Caplow, T. (1982). *Middletown families: Fifty years of change and continuity.* Minneapolis: University of Minnesota Press.

Caporeal, L. R. (1976). Ergotism: The Satan loosed in Salem? *Science, 192,* 21–26.

Caprara, G. V., Barbaranelli, C., Borgoni, L., & Perugini, M. (1993). The Big Five Questionnaire: A new questionnaire for the measurement of the five-factor model. *Personality and Individual Differences, 15,* 281–288.

Carey, S. (1978). The child as word learner. In M. Halle, J. Bresnan, & G. A. Miller (Eds.), *Linguistic theory and psychological reality* (pp. 265–293). Cambridge, MA: MIT Press.

Carlson, N. R. (2004). *Physiology of behavior* (8th ed.). Boston: Allyn & Bacon.

Carlsson, A. (1978). Antipsychotic drugs, neurotransmitters, and schizophrenia. *American Journal of Psychiatry, 135,* 164–173.

Carmichael, L. (1970). The onset and early development of behavior. In P. H. Mussen (Ed.), *Carmichael's manual of child psychology* (3rd ed., Vol. 1). New York: Wiley.

Carpenter, G. C. (1973). Differential response to mother and stranger within the first month of life. *Bulletin of the British Psychological Society, 16,* 138.

Carpenter, S. (1999, August 14). A new look at recognizing what people see. *Science News, 156,* 102.

Carpenter, S. (2000, September). Stoicism reconsidered. *Monitor on Psychology, 31*(8), 58–61.

Carpenter, S. (2001a, February). Different dispositions, different brains. *Monitor on Psychology, 32*(2), 66–68.

Carpenter, S. (2001b, January). When at last you don't succeed . . . *Monitor on Psychology, 32*(1), 70–71.

Carson, R. C., Butcher, J. N., & Mineka, S. (2000). *Abnormal psychology and modern life* (11th ed.). Boston: Allyn & Bacon.

Carstensen, L. L. (1987). Age-related changes in social activity. In L. L. Carstensen & B. A. Edelstein (Eds.), *Handbook of clinical gerontology* (pp. 222–237). New York: Pergamon Press.

Carstensen, L. L. (1991). Selectivity theory: Social activity in life-span context. In K. W. Schaie (Ed.), *Annual Review of Geriatrics and Gerontology* (Vol. 11). New York: Springer.

Carstensen, L. L., and Freund, A. M. (1994). Commentary: The resilience of the aging self. *Developmental Review, 14,* 81–92.

Cartwright, R. D. (1977). *Night life: Explorations in dreaming.* Englewood Cliffs, NJ: Prentice Hall.

Cartwright, R. D. (1978). *A primer on sleep and dreaming.* Reading, MA: Addison-Wesley.

Cartwright, R. D. (1984). Broken dreams: A study of the effects of divorce and depression on dream content. *Psychiatry, 47,* 251–259.

Carver, C. S., & Scheier, M. F. (2000). *Perspectives on personality* (4th ed.). Boston: Allyn & Bacon.

Casey, J. F., & Wilson, L. (1991). *The flock.* New York: Fawcett Columbine.

Cash, T. F., & Duncan, N. C. (1984). Physical attractiveness stereotyping among black American college students. *Journal of Social Psychology, 122,* 71–77.

Cash, T. F., & Janda, L. H. (1984, December). The eye of the beholder. *Psychology Today, 18,* 46–52.

Cash, T. F., & Kilcullen, R. N. (1985). The aye of the beholder: Susceptibility to sexism and beautyism in the evaluation of managerial applicants. *Journal of Applied Social Psychology, 15,* 591–605.

Caspi, A., McClay, J., Moffitt, T. E., Mill, J., Martin, J., Craig, I. W., Taylor, A., & Poulton, R. (2002, August 2). Role of genotype in the cycle of violence in maltreated children. *Science, 297,* 851–852.

Cattaneo, E., Rigamonti, D., & Zuccato, C. (2002, December). The enigma of Huntington's disease. *Scientific American,* 92–97.

Cattell, R. B. (1963). Theory of fluid and crystallized intelligence: A critical experiment. *Journal of Educational Psychology, 54,* 1–22.

Ceci, S. J., & Bruck, M. (1993). Suggestibility of the child witness: A historical review and synthesis. *Psychological Bulletin, 113,* 403–439.

Ceci, S. J., & Liker, J. K. (1986). A day at the races: A study of IQ, expertise, and cognitive complexity. *Journal of Experimental Psychology: General, 115,* 255–266.

Ceci, S. J., & Williams, W. M. (1997). Schooling, intelligence, and income. *American Psychologist, 52,* 1051–1058.

Centers for Disease Control and Prevention. (2000). *Health, United States, 2000: Adolescent Health Chartbook.* Retrieved on November 8, 2004, from http://www.cdc.gov/nchs/hus.htm

Cervone, D. (2004). The architecture of personality. *Psychological Review, 111,* 183–204.

Cervone, D., & Shoda, Y. (1999). Beyond traits in the study of personality coherence. Current *Directions in Psychological Science, 8,* 27–32.

Chalmers, D. J. (1995, December). The puzzle of conscious experience. *Scientific American, 273*(6), 80–86.

Chamberlain, K., & Zika, S. (1990). The minor events approach to stress: Support for the use of daily hassles. *British Journal of Psychology, 81,* 469–481.

Chambless, D. L., Sanderson, W. C., Shoham, V., Johnson, S. B., Pope, K. S., Crits-Christoph, P., Baker, M., Johnson, B., Woody, S. R., Sue, S., Beutler, L., Williams, D. A., & McCurry, S. (1996). An update on empirically validated therapies. *The Clinical Psychologist, 49,* 5–18.

Chapman, P. D. (1988). *Schools as sorters: Lewis M. Terman, applied psychology, and the intelligence testing movement, 1890–1930.* New York: New York University Press.

Chartrand, T. L., & Bargh, J. A. (1999). The chameleon effect: The perception–behavior link and social interaction. *Journal of Personality & Social Psychology, 76,* 893–910.

Chase, W. G., & Simon, H. A. (1973). The mind's eye in chess. In W. G. Chase (Ed.), *Visual information processing* (pp. 215–281). New York: Academic Press.

Chaudhari, N., Landin, A. M., & Roper, S. D. (2000). A metabotropic glutamate receptor variant functions as a taste receptor. *Nature Neuroscience, 3,* 113–119.

Chi, M., Glaser, R., & Rees, E. (1982). Expertise in problem solving. In R. Sternberg (Ed.)., *Advances in the psychology of human intelligence* (Vol. 1). Hillsdale, NJ: Erlbaum.

Chilman, C. S. (1983). *Adolescent sexuality in a changing American society* (2nd ed.). New York: Wiley.

Chomsky, N. (1965). *Aspects of a theory of syntax.* Cambridge, MA: MIT Press.

Chomsky, N. (1975). *Reflections on language.* New York: Pantheon Books.

Chorney, M. J., Chorney, N. S., Owen, M. J., Daniels, J., McGuffin, P., Thompson, L. A., Detterman, D. K., Benbow, C., Lubinski, D., Eley, T., & Plomin, R. (1998). A quantitative trait locus associated with cognitive ability in children. *Psychological Science, 9,* 159–166.

Christensen, A., & Jacobson, N. S. (1994). Who (or what) can do psychotherapy: The status and challenge of nonprofessional therapies. *Psychological Science, 5,* 8–14.

The Chronicle of Higher Education. (2004, August 27). *2001–2002 Almanac, 51*(1), 19.

Church, R. M. (2001). A turning test for computational and associative theories of learning. *Current Directions in Psychological Science, 10,* 132–136.

Churchland, P. M. (1995). *The engine of reason, the seat of the soul: A philosophical journey into the brain.* Cambridge, MA: MIT Press.

Cialdini, R. B. (2001a). *Influence: Science and practice* (4th ed.). Boston: Allyn & Bacon.

Cialdini, R. B. (2001b, February). The science of persuasion. *Scientific American, 284,* 76–81.

Clark, H. H., & Clark, E. V. (1977). *Psychology and language: An introduction to psycholinguistics.* New York: Harcourt Brace Jovanovich.

Clark, M. S., Mills, J. R., & Corcoran, D. M. (1989). Keeping track of needs and inputs of friends and strangers. *Personality and Social Psychology Bulletin, 15,* 533–542.

Clark, R. E., & Squire, L. R. (1998, April 3). Classical conditioning and brain systems: The role of awareness. *Science, 280,* 77–81.

Clarke-Stewart, K. A. (1989). Infant day care: Maligned or malignant? *American Psychologist, 44,* 266–273.

Clay, R. (2003a, April). An empty nest can promote freedom, improved relationships. *Monitor on Psychology,* 40–41.

Clay, R. (2003b, April). Researchers replace midlife myths with facts. *Monitor on Psychology,* 38–39.

Clay, R. A. (1998, November). Preparing for the future: Practitioners seek training for prescribing medication. *APA Monitor,* 22–23.

Clay, R. A. (2000, January). Psychotherapy is cost-effective. *Monitor on Psychology, 31*(1) 40–41.

Clay, R. A. (2001, January). Research to the heart of the matter. *Monitor on Psychology, 32*(1), 42–49.

Cleek, M. B., & Pearson, T. A. (1985). Perceived causes of divorce: An analysis of interrelationships. *Journal of Marriage and the Family, 47,* 179–191.

Cobb, S. (1976). Social support as a moderator of stress. *Psychosomatic Medicine, 35,* 375–389.

Cochran, S. D., Sullivan, J. G., & Mays, V. M. (2003). Prevalence of mental disorders, psychological distress, and mental health services use among lesbian, gay, and bisexual adults in the United States. *Journal of Consulting and Clinical Psychology, 71,* 53–61.

Coghill, R. C., McHaffie, J. G., & Yen, Y. (2003, July 8). Neural correlates of interindividual differences in the subjective experience of pain. *Proceedings of the National Academy of Sciences, 14,* 8538–8542.

Cognitive–behavior therapy effective for panic disorder. (1991, November). APS Observer, 8.

Cohen, D., & Gunz, A. (2002). As seen by the other . . . : Perspectives on the self in the memories and emotional perceptions of Easterners and Westerners. *Psychological Science,* 55–59.

Cohen, J. (2002, February 8). The confusing mix of hype and hope. *Science, 295,* 1026.

Cohen, J. D., & Tong, F. (2001, 28 September). The face of controversy. *Science, 293,* 2405–2407.

Cohen, M. N. (1998). *Culture of intolerance: Chauvinism, class, and racism in the United States.* New Haven, CT: Yale University Press.

Cohen, R. E., & Ahearn, F. L., Jr. (1980). *Handbook for mental health care of disaster victims.* Baltimore: Johns Hopkins University Press.

Cohen, S. (1988). Psychosocial models of the role of social support in the etiology of physical disease. *Health Psychology, 7,* 269–297.

Cohen, S., & Girgus, J. S. (1973). Visual spatial illusions: Many explanations. *Science, 179,* 503–504.

Cohen, S., & McKay, G. (1983). Social support, stress, and the buffering hypotheses: A theoretical analysis. In A. Baum, S. E. Taylor, & J. Singer (Eds.), *Handbook of psychology and health* (Vol. 4). Hillsdale, NJ: Erlbaum.

Cohen, S., & Syme, S. L. (Eds.). (1985). *Social support and health.* Orlando, FL: Academic Press.

Colby, A., Kohlberg, L., Gibbs, J, & Lieberman, M. (1983). A longitudinal study of moral judgment. *Monographs of the Society for Research in Child Development, 481*(1–2, Serial No. 200).

Colcombe, S. J., Kramer, A. F., Erickson, K. I., Scalf, P., McAuley, E., Cohen, N. J., Webb, A., Jerome, G. J., Marquez, D. X., & Elavsky, S. (2004). Cardiovascular fitness, cortical plasticity, and aging. *Proceedings of the National Academy of Sciences, 101,* 3316–3321.

Collins, A. W., Maccoby, E. E., Steinberg, L., Hetherington, E. M., & Bornstein, M. H. (2000). Contemporary research on parenting: The case for nature *and* nurture. *American Psychologist, 55,* 218–232.

Collins, G. P. (2001, October). Magnetic revelations: Functional MRI highlights neurons receiving signals. *Scientific American,* 21.

Collins, N. L., & Read, S. J. (1990). Adult attachment, working models, and relationship quality in dating couples. *Journal of Personality and Social Psychology, 58,* 644–663.

Collins, S., & Long, A. (2003). Too tired to care? The psychological effects of working with trauma. *Journal of Psychiatric and Mental Health Nursing, 10,* 17–27.

Committee on Substance Abuse and Committee on Children with Disabilities (2000). Fetal alcohol syndrome and alcohol-related neurodevelopmental disorders. *Pediatrics, 106,* 358–361.

Comuzzie, A. G., & Allison, D. B. (1998, May 29). The search for human obesity genes. *Science, 280,* 1374–1377.

Conger, J. J., & Peterson, A. C. (1984). *Adolescence and youth* (3rd ed.) New York: Harper & Row.

Conrad, R. (1964). Acoustic confusions in immediate memory. *British Journal of Psychology, 55,* 75–84.

Consumer Reports. (1995, November). Mental health: Does therapy help? 734–739.

Contrada, R. J., Ashmore, R. D., Gary, M. L., Coups, E., Egeth, J. D., Sewell, A., Ewell, K., Goyal, T. M., & Chasse, V. (2000). Ethnicity-related sources of stress and their effects on well-being. *Current Directions in Psychological Science, 9,* 136–139.

Conway, J. K. (1992). *Written by herself: Autobiographies of American women: An anthology.* New York: Vintage.

Cook, M., Mineka, S., Wolkenstein, B. & Laitsch, K. (1985). Observational conditioning of snake fear in unrelated rhesus monkeys. *Journal of Abnormal Psychology, 94,* 591–610.

Coon, D. J. (1992). Testing the limits of sense and science: American experimental psychologists combat spiritualism, 1880–1920. *American Psychologist, 47,* 143–151.

Cooper, W. H. (1983). An achievement motivation normological network. *Journal of Personality and Social Psychology, 44,* 841–861.

Costa, P. T., Jr., & McCrae, R. R. (1992a). Four ways five factors are basic. *Personality and Individual Differences, 13,* 653–665.

Costa, P. T., Jr., & McCrae, R. R. (1992b). *Revised NEO Personality Inventory (NEO-PI-R) and NEO Five-Factor Inventory (NEO-FFI) professional manual.* Odessa, FL: Psychological Assessment Resources.

Coughlin, E. K. (1994, October 26). Class, IQ, and heredity. *The Chronicle of Higher Education,* A12, A20.

Covington, M. V. (2000). Intrinsic versus extrinsic motivation in schools: A reconciliation. *Current Direction in Psychology Science, 9,* 22–25.

Cowan, P., & Cowan, P. A. (1988). Changes in marriage during the transition to parenthood. In G. Y. Michaels & W. A. Goldberg (Eds.), *The transition to parenthood: Current theory and research.* Cambridge, U.K.: Cambridge University Press.

Coyne, J. C., Burchill, S. A. L., & Stiles, W. B. (1991). An interactional perspective on depression. In C. R. Snyder & D. O. Forsyth (Eds.), *Handbook of social and clinical psychology: The health perspective* (pp. 327–349). New York: Pergamon Press.

Coyne, K. J. C. (2001, February). Depression in primary care: Depressing news, exciting research opportunities. *APS Observer, 14*(2), 1, 18.

Craig, A. D., & Reiman, E. M. (1996, November 21). Functional imaging of an illusion of pain. *Nature, 384,* 258–260.

Craik, F. I. M. (1979). Human memory. *Annual Review of Psychology, 30,* 63–102.

Craik, F. I. M., & Lockhart, R. S. (1972). Levels of processing: A framework for memory research. *Journal of Verbal Learning and Verbal Behavior, 11,* 671–684.

Craik, F. I. M., Moroz, T. M., Moscovitch, M., Stuss, D. T., Winocur, G., Tulving, E., & Shitij, K. (1999). In search of the self: A positron emission tomography study. *Psychological Science, 10,* 26–34.

Craik, F. I. M., & Tulving, E. (1975). Depth of processing and the retention of words in episodic memory. *Journal of Experimental Psychology: General, 104,* 268–294.

Cramer, P. (2000). Defense mechanisms in psychology today. *American Psychologist, 55,* 637–646.

Craske, M. G., Brown, T. A., & Barlow, D. H. (1991). Behavioral treatment of panic disorder: A two year follow-up. *Behavior Therapy, 19,* 577–592.

Cree, G. S., & McRae, K. (2003). Analyzing the factors underlying the structure and computation of the meaning of chipmunk, cherry, cheese, and cello (and many other such concrete nouns). *Journal of Experimental Psychology: General, 132,* 163–201.

Crick, F. (1994). *The astonishing hypothesis: The scientific search for the soul.* New York: Charles Scribner's Sons.

Crick, F., & Mitchison, G. (1983). The function of dream sleep. *Nature, 304,* 111–114.

Crocker, J., & Major, B. (1989). Social stigma and self-esteem: The self-protective properties of stigma. *Psychological Review, 96,* 608–630.

Crohan, S. E., Antonucci, T. C., Adelmann, P. K., & Coleman, L. M. (1989). Job characteristics and well-being at mid-life. *Psychology of Women Quarterly, 13,* 223–235.

Cromwell, R. L. (1993). Searching for the origins of schizophrenia. *Psychological Science, 4,* 276–279.

Crowder, R. G. (1992). Eidetic images. In L. R. Squire (Ed.), *The encyclopedia of learning and memory* (pp. 154–156). New York: MacMillan.

Crowell, T. A. (2002). Neuropsychological findings in combat-related posttraumatic stress disorder. *Clinical Neuropsychologist, 16,* 310–321.

Crowley, B. J., Hayslip, B., Jr., & Hobdy, J. (2003). Psychological hardiness and adjustment to life events in adulthood. *Journal of Adult Development, 10,* 237–248.

Csikszentmihalyi, M. (1990). *Flow: The psychology of optimal experience.* New York: Harper & Row.

Csikszentmihalyi, M. (1996, July/August). The creative personality. *Psychology Today, 29*(4), 34–40.

Csikszentmihalyi, M. (1998). *Finding flow.* New York: Basic Books.

Csikszentmihalyi, M., Larson, R., & Prescott, S. (1977). The ecology of adolescent activity and experience. *Journal of Youth and Adolescence, 6,* 281–294.

Csikszentmihalyi, M., Rathunde, K. R., Whalen, S., & Wong, M. (1993). *Talented teenagers: The roots of success and failure.* New York: Cambridge University Press.

Cushman, P. (1990). Why the self is empty: Toward a historically situated psychology. *American Psychologist, 45,* 599–611.

Dabbs, J. M. (2000). *Heroes, rogues, and lovers: Testosterone and behavior.* New York: McGraw-Hill.

Dackman, L. (1986). Everyday illusions. *Exploratorium Quarterly, 10,* 5–7.

Daily, D. K., Ardinger, H. H., & Holmes, G. E. (2000). Identification and evaluation of mental retardation. *American Family Physician, 61,* 1059–1067.

Daley, K. C. (2004). Update on attention-deficit/hyperactivity disorder. *Current Opinion in Pediatrics, 16,* 217–226.

Daly, R. C., Su, T.-P., Schmidt, P. J., Pagliaro, M., Pickar, D., & Rubinow, D. R. (2003). Neuroendocrine and behavioral effects of high-dose anabolic steroid administration in male normal volunteers. *Psychoneuroendocrinology, 28,* 317–331.

Damasio, A. (2003). *Looking for Spinoza: Joy, sorrow, and the feeling brain.* Orlando, FL: Harcourt.

Damasio, A. B. (1994). *Descartes' error: Emotion, reason, and the human brain.* New York: Avon Books.

Damasio, A. R. (1999, December). How the brain creates the mind. *Scientific American,* 112–117.

Damasio, A. R. (2000). *The feeling of what happens: Body and emotion in the making of consciousness.* New York: Harcourt Brace.

Danion, J., Rizzo, L., & Bruant, A. (1999). Functional mechanisms underlying impaired recognition memory and conscious awareness in patients with schizophrenia. *Archives of General Psychiatry, 56,* 639–644.

Dannefer, D., & Perlmutter, M. (1990). Developmental as a multidimensional process: Individual and social constituents. *Human Development, 33,* 108–137.

Darley, J. M., & Batson, C. D. (1973). From Jerusalem to Jericho: A study of situational and dispositional variables in helping behavior. *Journal of Personality and Social Psychology, 27,* 100–108.

Darley, J. M., & Latané, B. (1968) Bystander intervention in emergencies: Diffusion of responsibility. *Journal of Personality and Social Psychology, 8,* 377–383.

Darling, N., & Steinberg, L. (1993). Parenting style as context: An integrative model. *Psychological Bulletin, 113,* 487–496.

Darwin, C. (1963). *On the origin of species.* London: Oxford University Press. (Original work published in 1859.)

Darwin, C. (1998). *The expression of the emotions in man and animals* (3rd ed., with Introduction, Afterword, and Commentaries by P. Ekman). New York: Oxford University Press. (Original work published in 1862.)

Darwin, C. J., Turvey, M. T., & Crowder, R. G. (1972). The auditory analogue of the Sperling partial report procedure: Evidence for brief auditory stage. *Cognitive Psychology, 3,* 255–267.

Dattilio, F. M., & Padesky, C. A. (1990). *Cognitive therapy with couples.* Sarasota, FL: Professional Resource Exchange.

Davidson, R. J. (1992a). Anterior cerebral asymmetry and the nature of emotion. *Brain and Cognition, 20,* 125–151.

Davidson, R. J. (1992b). Emotion and affective style: Hemispheric substrates. *Psychological Science, 3,* 39–43.

Davidson, R. J. (2000a). *Affective neuroscience.* Address given at the American Psychological Association's annual convention, Washington, DC.

Davidson, R. J. (2000b). Affective style, psychopathology, and resilience: Brain mechanisms and plasticity. *American Psychologist, 55,* 1196–1214.

Davidson, R. J. (2002, April). Synaptic substrates of the implicit and explicit self. *Science, 296,* 268.

Davidson, R. J., Kabat-Zinn, J., Schumacher, J., Rosenkranz, M., Muller, D., Santorelli, S. F., Urbanowski, F., Harrington, A., Bonus, K., & Sheridan, J. F. (2003). Alternations in brain and immune function produced by mindfulness meditation. *Psychosomatic Medicine, 65,* 564–570.

Davidson, R. J., Putnam, K. M., & Larson, C. L. (2000, July 28). Dysfunction in the neural circuitry of emotion regulation—a possible prelude to violence. *Science, 289,* 591–594.

Davis, C. G., & Nolen-Hoeksema, S. (2001). Loss and meaning: How do people make sense of loss? *American Behavioral Scientist, 44,* 726–743.

Davis, C. G., Nolen-Hoeksema, S., & Larson, J. (1998). Making sense of loss and benefiting from the experience: Two construals of meaning. *Journal of Personality and Social Psychology, 75,* 561–574.

Davison, K. P., Pennebaker, J. W., & Dickerson, S. S. (2000). Who talks? The social psychology of illness support groups. *American Psychologist, 55,* 205–217.

Daw, J. (2001, June). The Ritalin debate. *Monitor on Psychology, 32*(6), 64–65.

Daw, J. (2002, November). Why and how normal people go mad. *Monitor on Psychology,* 20–21.

Dawkins, K., Lieberman, J. A., Lebowitz, B. D., & Hsiao, J. K. (1999). Antipsychotics: Past and future. *Schizophrenia Bulletin, 25,* 395–405.

Deadwyler, S. A., & Hampson, R. E. (1995, November 24). Ensemble activity and behavior: What's the code? *Science, 270,* 1316–1318.

DeAngelis, T. (1997, January). Chromosomes contain clues on schizophrenia. *APA Monitor,* 26.

DeAngelis, T. (2002a, June). A bright future for PNI. *Monitor on Psychology,* 46–50.

DeAngelis, T. (2002b, July–August). If you do just on thing, make it exercise. *Monitor on Psychology,* 4–51.

DeAngelis, T. (2003, March). When anger's a plus. *Monitor on Psychology, 34,* 44–45.

DeCasper, A. J., & Fifer, W. P. (1980). Of human bonding: Newborns prefer their mothers' voices. *Science, 208,* 1174–1176.

DeCasper, A. J., & Spence, M. J. (1986). Prenatal maternal speech influences newborns' perception of speech sounds. *Infant Behavior and Development, 9,* 133–150.

Deckers, L. (2001). *Motivation: Biological, psychological, and environmental.* Boston: Allyn & Bacon.

de Gelder, B. (2000, August 18). More to seeing than meets the eye. *Science, 289,* 1148–1149.

DeGrandpre, R. J. (2000). A science of meaning: Can behaviorism bring meaning to psychological science? *American Psychologist, 55,* 721–739.

de Groot, A. D. (1965). *Thought and choice in chess.* The Hague: Mouton.

Delgado, J. M. R. (1969). *Physical control of the mind: Toward a psychocivilized society.* New York: Harper & Row.

Dembroski, T. M., & Costa, P. T., Jr. (1987). Coronary prone behavior: Components of the Type A pattern and hostility. *Journal of Personality, 55,* 211–235.

Dembroski, T. M., Weiss, S. M., Shields, J. L., et al. (1978). *Coronary-prone behavior.* New York: Springer-Verlag.

Dement, W. C. (1980). *Some watch while some must sleep.* San Francisco: San Francisco Book Company.

Dement, W. C. (2000, September 25). *Sleep debt.* Retrieved March 9, 2004, from SleepQuest website: http://www.sleepquest.com/d_column_archive6.html

Dement, W. C., & Kleitman, N. (1957). Cyclic variations in EEG during sleep and their relations to eye movement, body mobility and dreaming. *Electroencephalography and Clinical Neurophysiology, 9,* 673–690.

Dement, W. C., & Vaughan, C. (1999). *The promise of sleep.* New York: Delacorte Press.

Dennis, W. (1960). Causes of retardation among institutionalized children: Iran. *Journal of Genetic Psychology, 96,* 47–59.

Dennis, W., & Dennis, M. G. (1940). The effect of cradling practices upon the onset of walking in Hopi children. *Journal of Genetic Psychology, 56,* 77–86.

DePaulo, B. M., Lindsay, J. J., Malone, B. E., Muhlenbruck, L., Charlton, K, & Cooper, H. (2003). Cues to deception. *Psychological Bulletin, 129,* 74–118.

Deregowski, J. B. (1980). *Illusions, patterns and pictures: A cross-cultural perspective* (pp. 966–977). London, U.K.: Academic Press.

DeSalvo, L. (2000). *Writing as a way of healing: How telling our stories transforms our lives.* Boston: Beacon Press.

Detterman, D. K. (1999). The psychology of mental retardation. *International Review of Psychiatry, 11,* 26–33.

Deutsch, M., & Collins, M. E. (1951). *Interracial housing: A psychological evaluation of a social experiment.* Minneapolis: University of Minnesota Press.

Deutsch, M., & Gerard, H. B. (1955). A study of normative and informational social influence upon individual judgment. *Journal of Abnormal and Social Psychology, 51,* 629–636.

Devereux, G. (1981). *Mohave ethnopsychiatry and suicide: The psychiatric knowledge and psychic disturbances of an Indian tribe. Bureau of American Ethology Bulletin 175.* Washington, DC: Smithsonian Institution.

Devine, P. G., & Zuwerink, J. R. (1994). Prejudice and guilt: The internal struggle to overcome prejudice. In W. J. Lonner & R. Malpass (Eds.), *Psychology and culture* (pp. 203–207). Boston: Allyn & Bacon.

de Waal, F. B. M. (1999, December). The end of nature versus nurture. *Scientific American,* 94–99.

Dewsbury, D. A. (1990). Early interactions between animal psychologists and animal activists and the founding of the APA Committee on Precautions in Animal Experimentation. *American Psychologist, 45,* 315–327.

Dewsbury, D. A. (1997). In celebration of the centennial of Ivan P. Pavlov's (1897/1902) *The work of the digestive glands. American Psychologist, 52,* 933–935.

Dickens, W. T., & Flynn, J. R. (2001). Heritability estimates versus large environmental effects: The IQ paradox resolved. *Psychological Review, 108,* 346–369.

Dickinson, A. (2001). Causal learning: Association versus computation. *Current Directions in Psychological Science, 10,* 127–132.

Diener, E. (1984). Subjective well-being. *Psychological Bulletin, 95,* 542–575.

Diener, E. (2000). Subjective well-being: The science of happiness and a proposal for a national index. *American Psychologist, 55,* 34–43.

Diener, E., & Diener, C. (1996). Most people are happy. *Psychological Science, 7,* 181–189.

Diener, E., Sandvik, E., Seidlitz, L., & Diener, M. (1993). The relationship between income and subjective well-being: Relative or absolute? *Social Indicators Research, 28,* 195–223.

Diener, E., & Seligman, M. E. P. (2002). Very happy people. *Psychological Science, 13,* 81–84.

Digman, J. M. (1990). Personality structure: Emergence of the five-factor model. *Annual Review of Psychology, 41,* 417–440.

Dillbeck, M. C., & Orme-Johnson, D. W. (1987). Physiological differences between transcendental meditation and rest. *American Psychologist, 42*(9), 879–881.

Dion, K. K. (1986). Stereotyping based on physical attractiveness: Issues and conceptual perspectives. In C. P. Herman, M. P. Zanna, & E. T. Higgins (Eds.), *Physical appearance, stigma, and social behavior: The Ontario symposium on personality and social psychology* (Vol. 3). Hillsdale, NJ: Erlbaum.

Dittmann, M. (2003). Psychology's first prescribers. *Monitor on Psychology, 34*(2), 36.

Dittmann, M. (2004). Prescriptive authority. *Monitor on Psychology, 35*(5), 34–35.

Dixon, R. A., Kramer, D. A., & Baltes, P. B. (1985). Intelligence: A life-span developmental perspective. In B. B. Wolman (Ed.), *Handbook of intelligence* (pp. 301–352). New York: Wiley.

Dobbins, A. C., Jeo, R. M., Fiser, J., & Allman, J. M. (1998, July 24). Distance modulation of neural activity in the visual cortex. *Science, 281,* 552–555.

Dobelle, W. (1977). Current status of research on providing sight to the blind by electrical stimulation of the brain. *Journal of Visual Impairment and Blindness, 71,* 290–297.

Doetsch, F. (2002). Genetics of childhood disorders: XXXVIII. Stem cell research, part 2: Reconstructing the brain. *Journal of the American Academy of Child & Adolescent Psychiatry, 41,* 622–624.

Dohrenwend, B. P., & Shrout, P. E. (1985). "Hassles" in the conceptualization and measurement of life stress variables. *American Psychologist, 40,* 780–785.

Dohrenwend, B. S., & Dohrenwend, B. P. (1974). *Stressful life events: Their nature and effects.* New York: Wiley.

Doka, K. J. (1989). *Disenfranchised grief: Recognizing hidden sorrows.* Lexington, MA: Lexington Books.

Doka, K. J. (1995). Friends, teachers, movie stars: The disenfranchised grief of children: Friends, teachers, movie stars. In E. A. Grollman (Ed.), *Bereaved children and teens: A support guide for parents and professionals* (pp. 37–45). Boston: Beacon Press.

Dolan, R. J. (2002). Emotion, cognition, and behavior. *Science, 298,* 1191–1194.

Domhoff, G. W. (1996). *Finding meaning in dreams: A quantitative approach.* New York: Plenum Press.

Doob, L. W. (1964). Eidetic images among the Ibo. *Ethnology, 3,* 357–363.

Dowling, J. E. (1992). *Neurons and networks: An introduction to neuroscience.* Cambridge, MA: Harvard University Press.

Downey, T. (2004). *The last men out: Life on the edge at Rescue 2 Firehouse.* New York: Henry Holt and Co.

Downing, P. E., Jiang, Y., Shuman, M., & Kanwisher, N. (2001, 28 September). A cortical area selective for visual processing of the human body. *Science, 293,* 2470–2473.

Doyle, R. (2001, June). The American terrorist. *Scientific American, 285*(6), 28.

Doyle, R. (2002a). Deinstitutionalization: Why a much maligned program still has life. *Scientific American, 287,* 38.

Doyle, R. (2002b, January). Going solo: Unwed motherhood in industrial nations rises. *Scientific American,* 24.

Dracheva, S., Marras, S. A. E., Elhakem, S. L., Kramer, F. R., Davis, K. L., & Haroutunian, V. (2001). N-methyl-d-aspartic acid receptor expression in the dorsolateral prefrontal cortex of elderly patients with schizophrenia. *American Journal of Psychiatry, 158,* 1400–1410.

Draguns, J. (1980). Psychological disorders of clinical severity. In H. Triandis & J. Draguns (Eds.), *Handbook of cross-cultural psychology, Vol. 6: Psychopathology* (pp. 99–174). Boston: Allyn & Bacon.

Draguns, J. G. (1979). Culture and personality. In A. J. Marsella, R. G. Tharp, & T. J. Ciborowski (Eds.), *Perspectives on cross-cultural psychology* (pp. 179–207). New York: Academic Press.

Drake, R. E., Osher, F. C., & Wallach, M. A. (1991). Homelessness and dual diagnosis. *American Psychologist, 46,* 1149–1158.

Druckman, D., & Bjork, R. A. (1991). *In the mind's eye: Enhancing human performance.* Washington, DC: National Academy Press.

Duck, S. (1992). *Human relationships* (2nd ed.). Newbury Park, CA: Sage.

Duncan, J., Seitz, R. J., Kolodny, J., Bor, D., Herzog, H., Ahmed, A., Newell, F. N., & Emslie, H. (2000, July 21). A neural basis for general intelligence. *Science, 289,* 457–460.

Dutton, D. G., & Aron, A. P. (1974). Some evidence for heightened sexual attraction under conditions of high anxiety. *Journal of Personality and Social Psychology, 30,* 510–517.

Dykema, J., Bergbower, K., & Peterson, C. (1995). Pessimistic explanatory style, stress, and illness. *Journal of Social and Clinical Psychology, 14,* 357–371.

Eaddy, S. L. (2001). An exploration of the relationship between hardiness and resilience for people impacted by HIV. *Dissertation Abstracts International, Section A: Humanities and Social Sciences, 61,* 4301.

Eagly, A. H., Ashmore, R. D., Makhijani, M. G., & Kennedy, L. C. (1991). What is beautiful is good, but. . . : A meta-analytic review of the social psychological literature. *Psychological Bulletin, 100,* 283–308.

Eagly, A. H., & Wood, W. (1999). The origins of sex differences in human behavior: Evolved dispositions versus social roles. *American Psychologist, 54,* 408–423.

Eccles, J. S., Midgley, C., Wigfield, A., Buchanan, C. M., Reuman, D., Flanagan, C., & Mac Iver, D. (1993). Development during adolescence: The impact of stage-environment fit on young adolescents' experiences in schools and in families. *American Psychologist, 48,* 90–101.

Eckensberger, L. H. (1994). Moral development and its measurement across cultures. In W. J. Lonner & R. Malpass (Eds.), *Psychology and culture* (pp. 71–78). Boston, MA: Allyn & Bacon.

Edwards, A. E., & Acker, L. E. (1962). A demonstration of the long-term retention of a conditioned galvanic skin response. *Psychosomatic Medicine, 24,* 459–463.

Edwards, K. J., Hershberger, P. J., Russell, R. K., & Markert, R. J. (2001). Stress, negative social exchange, and health symptoms in university students. *Journal of American College Health, 50,* 75–86.

Ehrlich, P. R. (2000a). *Genes, cultures and the human prospect.* Washington, DC: Island Press.

Ehrlich, P. R. (2000b, September 22). The tangled skeins of nature and nurture in human evolution. *The Chronicle of Higher Education,* B7–B11.

Eich, E., Macaulay, D., Loewenstein, R. J., & Dihle, P. H. (1997). Memory, amnesia, and dissociative identity disorder. *Psychological Science, 8,* 417–422.

Eichenbaum, H. (1997, July 18). How does the brain organize memories? *Science, 277,* 330–332.

Eichorn, D. H., & VandenBos, G. R. (1985). Dissemination of scientific and professional knowledge: Journal publication within the APA. *American Psychologist, 40,* 1309–1316.

Eisenberger, R., & Cameron, J. (1996). Detrimental effects of reward: Reality or myth? *American Psychologist, 51,* 1153–1166.

Eisler, R., & Levine, D. S. (2002). Nurture, nature, and caring: We are not prisoners of our genes. *Brain and Mind, 3,* 9–52.

Ekman, P. (1984). Expression and the nature of emotion. In K. R. Scherer & P. Ekman (Eds.), *Approaches to emotion.* Hillsdale, NJ: Erlbaum.

Ekman, P. (1992). Facial expressions of emotion: New findings, new questions. *Psychological Science, 3,* 34–38.

Ekman, P. (1993). Facial expression and emotion. *American Psychologist, 48,* 384–392.

Ekman, P. (1994). Strong evidence for universals in facial expressions: A reply to Russell's mistaken critique. *Psychological Bulletin, 115,* 268–287.

Ekman, P. (2003). *Emotions revealed: Recognizing faces and feelings to improve communication and emotional life.* New York: Times Books, Henry Holt and Company.

Ekman, P., & Friesen, W. V. (1971). Constants across cultures in the face and emotion. *Journal of Personality and Social Psychology, 17,* 124–129.

Ekman, P., & Friesen, W. V. (1986). A new pan-cultural facial expression of emotion. *Motivation and Emotion, 10,* 159–168.

Ekman, P., Friesen, W. V., O'Sullivan, M., Chan, A., Diacoyanni-Tarlatzis, I., Heider, K., Krause, R., LeCompte, W. A., Pitcairn, T., Ricci-Bitti, P. E., Scherer, K., Tomita, M., & Tzavaras, A. (1987). Universal and cultural differences in the judgments of facial expressions of emotion. *Journal of Personality and Social Psychology, 53,* 712–717.

Ekman, P., & Rosenberg, E. (1997). *What the face reveals.* New York: Oxford University Press.

Ekman, P., Sorenson, E. R., & Friesen, W. V. (1969). Pan-cultural elements in facial displays in emotion. *Science, 764,* 86–88.

Elbert, T., Pantev, C., Wienbruch, C., Rockstroh, B., & Taub, E. (1995, October 13). Increased cortical representation of the fingers of the left hand in string players. *Science, 270,* 305–307.

Eley, T. C. (1997). General genes: A new theme in developmental psychopathology. *Current Directions in Psychological Science, 6,* 90–95.

El-Hai, J. (1999). Uniquely twins. *Minnesota Medicine.* Retrieved on November 8, 2004, from http://www.mnmed.org/Protected/99MNMED/9903/El-Hai.html

Elliott, G. R., & Eisdorfer, C. (Eds.). (1982). *Stress and human health: Analysis and implications of research (A study by the Institute of Medicine/National Academy of Sciences).* New York: Springer.

Ellis, A. (1987). *The practice of rational emotive therapy (RET).* New York: Springer.

Ellis A. (1990). *The essential Albert Ellis: Seminal writings on psychotherapy.* New York: Springer.

Ellis, A. (1996). *Better, deeper, and more enduring brief therapy: The rational emotive behavior therapy approach.* New York: Brunner/Mazel Publishers.

Ellison, J. (1984, June). The seven frames of mind. *Psychology Today, 18,* 21–24, 26.

Ellsworth, P. C. (1994). William James and emotion: Is a century of fame worth a century of misunderstanding? *Psychological Review, 101,* 222–229.

Engle, R. W. (2002). Working memory capacity as executive attention. *Current Directions in Psychological Science, 11,* 19–23.

Ennis, M., Kelly, K. S., & Lambert, P. L. (2001). Sex differences in cortisol excretion during anticipation of a psychological stressor: Possible support for the tend-and-befriend hypothesis. *Stress and Health, 17,* 253–261.

Enserink, M. (2000, July 28). Searching for the mark of Cain. *Science, 289,* 575–579.

Epstein, S. (1980). The stability of confusion: A reply to Mischel and Peake. *Psychological Review, 90,* 179–184.

Epstein, S., & Feist, G. J. (1988). Relation between self- and other-acceptance and its moderation by identification. *Journal of Personality and Social Psychology, 54,* 309–315.

Erdberg, P. (1990). Rorschach assessment. In G. Goldstein & M. Hersen (Eds.), *Psychological assessment* (2nd ed.). New York: Pergamon.

Erdelyi, M. H. (1992). Psychodymanics and the unconscious. *American Psychologist, 47,* 784–787.

Ericsson, K. A., & Charness, N. (1994). Expert performance: Its structure and acquisition. *American Psychologist, 49,* 725–747.

Ericsson, K. A., Krampe, R. T., & Tesch-Römer, C. (1993). The role of deliberate practice in the acquisition of expert performance. *Psychological Review, 100,* 363–406.

Erikson, E. H. (1963). *Childhood and society* (2nd ed.). New York: Norton.

Exner, J. E., Jr. (1974). *The Rorschach: A comprehensive system: Vol. 1.* New York: Wiley.

Exner, J. E., Jr. (1978). *The Rorschach: A comprehensive system: Vol. 2: Current research and interpretation.* New York: Wiley.

Exner, J. E., Jr., & Weiner, I. B. (1982). *The Rorschach: A comprehensive system: Vol. 3: Assessment of children and adolescents.* New York: Wiley.

Eysenck, H. J. (1952). The effects of psychotherapy: An evaluation. *Journal of Consulting Psychology, 16,* 319–324.

Ezzell, C. (2003, February). Why??? The neuroscience of suicide. *Scientific American, 288,* 45–51.

Fackelmann, K. (1998, November 28). It's a girl! Is sex selection the first step to designer children? *Science News, 154,* 350–351.

Fadiman, J., & Frager, R. (2001). *Personality and personal growth.* Upper Saddle River, NJ: Prentice-Hall.

Fajans, J. (1985). The person in social context: The social character of Baining "psychology." In G. M. White & J. Kirkpatrick (Eds.), *Person, self, and experience* (pp. 367–400). Berkeley: University of California Press.

Fallon, A., & Rozin, P. (1985). Sex differences in perceptions of desirable body states. *Journal of Abnormal Psychology, 94,* 102–105.

Fancher, R. E. (1979). *Pioneers of psychology.* New York: W. W. Norton.

Fantz, R. L. (1963). Pattern vision in newborn infants. *Science, 140,* 296–297.

Farina, A., Fischer, E. H., Boudreau, L. A., & Belt, W. E. (1996). Mode of target presentation in measuring the stigma of mental disorder. *Journal of Applied Social Psychology, 26,* 2147–2156.

Farquhar, J. W., Maccoby, N., & Solomon, D. S. (1984). Community applications of behavioral medicine. In W. D. Gentry (Ed.), *Handbook of behavioral medicine* (pp. 437–478). New York: Guilford Press.

Faulkner, M. (2001). The onset and alleviation of learned helplessness in older hospitalized people. *Aging and Mental Health, 5* (379–386).

Fehr, B. (1988). How do I love thee? Let me consult my prototype. *Journal of Personality and Social Psychology, 55*(4), 557–579.

Fein, M. L. (1993). *I.A.M.: A common sense guide to coping with anger.* Westport, CT: Praeger/Greenwood.

Feingold, A. (1988). Matching for attractiveness in romantic partners and same-sex friends: A meta-analysis and theoretical critique. *Psychological Bulletin, 104,* 226–235.

Feingold, A. (1990). Gender differences in effects of physical attractiveness on romantic attraction: A comparison across five research paradigms. *Journal of Personality and Social Psychology, 59,* 981–993.

Ferguson, C. J. (2002). Media violence: Miscast causality. *American Psychologist, 57,* 446–447.

Fernandez, A., & Glenberg, A. M. (1985). Changing environmental context does not reliably affect memory. *Memory and Cognition, 13,* 333–345.

Ferster. D., & Spruston, N. (1995, November 3). Cracking the neuronal code. *Science, 270,* 756–757.

Festinger, L. (1957). *A theory of cognitive dissonance.* Stanford, CA: Stanford University Press.

Festinger, L., Schachter, S., & Back, K. (1950). *Social pressures in informal groups: A study of a housing community.* New York: Harper & Row.

Field, T. F., & Schanberg, S. M. (1990). Massage alters growth and catecholamine production in preterm newborns. In N. Gunzenhauser (Ed.), *Advances in touch* (pp. 96–104). Skillman, NJ: Johnson & Johnson Co.

Fields, H. L. (1978, November). Secrets of the placebo. *Psychology Today, 172.*

Fields, H. L., & Levine, J. D. (1984). Placebo analgesia: A role for endorphins. *Trends in Neuroscience, 7,* 271–273.

Fields, R. D. (2004, April). The other half of the brain. *Scientific American, 290*(4), 54–61.

Figley, C. R. (2002). *Treating compassion fatigue.* New York: Brunner-Routledge.

Filsinger, E. E., & Fabes, R. A. (1985). Odor communication, pheromones, and human families. *Journal of Marriage and the Family, 47,* 349–359.

Finamore, D. C. (2000). *The relationship of learned helplessness, hardiness, and depression in married, abused women.* Doctoral dissertation, University of Sarasota.

Findley, M. J., & Cooper, H. M. (1983). Locus of control and academic achievement: A literature review. *Journal of Personality and Social Psychology, 44,* 419–427.

Finer, B. (1980). Hypnosis and anaesthesia. In G. D. Burrows & L. Donnerstein (Eds.), *Handbook of hypnosis and psychosomatic medicine.* Amsterdam: Elsevier/North Holland Biomedical Press.

Fiorillo, C. D., Tobler, P. N., & Schultz, W. (2003, March 21). Discrete coding of reward probability and uncertainty by dopamine neurons. *Science, 299,* 1898–1902.

Fiorito, G., & Scotto, P. (1992). Observational learning in Octopus vulgaris. *Science, 256,* 545–547.

Fischer, A. H. (1993). Sex differences in emotionality: Fact or stereotype? *Feminism & Psychology, 3,* 303–318.

Fischer, A. H., Rodriguez Mosquera, P. M., van Vianen, A. E. M., & Manstead, A. S. R. (2004). Gender and culture differences in emotion. *Emotion, 4,* 87–94.

Fischer, P. C., Smith, R. J., Leonard, E., Fuqua, D. R., Campbell, J. L., & Masters, M. A. (1993). Sex differences on affective dimensions: Continuing examination. *Journal of Counseling and Development, 71,* 440–443.

Fischer, P. J., & Breakey, W. R. (1991). The epidemiology of alcohol, drug, and mental disorders among homeless persons. *American Psychologist, 46,* 1115–1128.

Fischhoff, B. (1975). Hindsight ≠ foresight: The effect of outcome knowledge on judgment under uncertainty. *Journal of Experimental Psychology: Human Perception and Performance, 1,* 288–299.

Fisher, H. E. (1992). *Anatomy of love: The natural history of monogamy, adultery, and divorce.* New York: W. W. Norton and Company.

Fisher, S., & Greenberg, R. P. (1985). *The scientific credibility of Freud's theories and therapy.* New York: Columbia University Press.

Fishman, H. C. (1993). *Intensive structural therapy: Treating families in their social context.* New York: Basic Books.

Fiske, D. W., & Fogg, L. (1990). But the reviewers are making different criticisms of my paper! Diversity and uniqueness in reviewer comments. *American Psychologist, 45,* 591–598.

Fiske, S. T., & Neuberg, S. L. (1990). A continuum of impression formation, from category-based to individuating processes: Influences of information and motivation on attention and interpretation. In M. P. Zanna (Ed.), *Advances in experimental social psychology* (Vol. 23). San Diego, CA: Academic Press.

Flavell, J. H. (1985). *Cognitive development* (2nd ed.). Englewood Cliffs, NJ: Prentice-Hall.

Flavell, J. H. (1996). Piaget's legacy. *Psychological Science, 7,* 200–203.

Fleischman, J. (2002). *Phineas Gage: A gruesome but true story about brain science.* Boston: Houghton Mifflin.

Fletcher, A., Lamond, N., van den Heuvel, C. J., & Dawson, D. (2003). Prediction of performance during sleep deprivation and alcohol intoxication using a quantitative model of work-related fatigue. *SleepResearch Online, 5,* 67–75. Retrieved on November 6, 2004, from http://www.sro.org/2003/Fletcher/67/

Fletcher, G. J. O., & Ward, C. (1988). Attribution theory and processes: A cross-cultural perspective. In M. H. Bond (Ed.), *The cross-cultural challenge to social psychology* (pp. 230–244). Newbury Park, CA: Sage.

Fogel, A. (1991). Movement and communication in human infancy: The social dynamics of development. *Human Movement Science, 11,* 387–423.

Foley, V. D. (1979). Family therapy. In R. J. Corsini (Ed.), *Current psychotherapies* (2nd ed., pp. 460–469). Itasca, IL: Peacock.

Folkes, V. S. (1982). Forming relationships and the matching hypothesis. *Journal of Personality and Social Psychology, 8,* 631–636.

Folkins, C. H., & Sime, W. (1981). Physical fitness training and mental health. *American Psychologist, 36,* 373–389.

Ford, C. S., & Beach, F. A. (1951). *Patterns of sexual behavior.* New York: Harper & Row.

Forgatch, M. S., Patterson, G. R., & Ray, J. A. (1994). Divorce and boys' adjustment problems: Two paths with a single model. In E. M. Hetherington, D. Reiss, & R. Plomin (Eds.), *Stress, coping, and resiliency in children and the family* (pp. 96–110). Hillsdale, NJ: Erlbaum.

Fowers, B. J., & Richardson, F. C. (1996). Why is multiculturalism good? *American Psychologist, 31,* 609–621.

Fowler, H. (1965). *Curiosity and exploratory behavior.* New York: Macmillan.

Fraser, S. (Ed.). (1995). *The bell curve wars: Race, intelligence, and the future of America.* New York: Basic Books.

Freedman, D. J., Riesenhuber, M., Poggio, T., & Miller, E. K. (2001, January 12). Categorical representation of visual stimuli in the primate prefrontal cortex. *Science, 291,* 312–316.

Freedman, J. L. (1984) Effect of television violence on aggression. *Psychological Bulletin, 96,* 227–246.

Freedman, J. L. (1996, May). Violence in the mass media and violence in society: The link is unproven. *Harvard Mental Health Letter, 12*(11), 4–6.

French, E. G. & Thomas, F. H. (1958). The relation of achievement motivation to problem-solving effectiveness. *Journal of Abnormal and Social Psychology, 56,* 46–48.

Freud, S. (1915a). *The collected papers.* New York: Collier.

Freud, S. (1925). The unconscious. In S. Freud, *The collected papers* (Vol. 4). London: Hogarth.

Freud, S. (1953). *The interpretation of dreams.* New York: Basic Books. (Original edition published in 1900).

Fridlund, A. J. (1990). Evolution and facial action in reflex, social motive, and paralanguage. In P. K. Ackles, J. R. Jennings, & M. G. H. Coles (Eds.), *Advances in psychophysiology.* Greenwich, CT: JAI Press.

Friedman, H. S., & Booth-Kewley, S. (1988). Validity of the Type A construct: A reprise. *Psychological Bulletin, 104,* 381–384.

Friedman, H. S., Hawley, P. H., & Tucker, J. S. (1994). Personality, health, and longevity. *Current Directions in Psychological Science, 3,* 37–41.

Friedman, H. S., Tucker, J. S., Schwartz, J. E., Tomlinson-Keasey, C., Martin, L. R., Wingard, D. L., & Criqui, M. H. (1995). Psychosocial and behavioral predictors of longevity: The aging and death of the "termites." *American Psychologist, 50,* 69–78.

Friedman, J. M. (2003, February 7). A war on obesity, not the obese. *Science, 299,* 856–858.

Friedman, M., & Rosenman, R. F. (1974). *Type A behavior and your heart.* New York: Knopf.

Friedman, M., & Ulmer, D. (1984). *Treating Type A behavior—and your heart.* New York: Knopf.

Friedman, M. J. (2004). Acknowledging the psychiatric cost of war. *New England Journal of Medicine, 351,* 75–77.

Friend, R., Rafferty, Y., & Bramel, D. (1990). A puzzling misinterpretation of the Asch "conformity" study. *European Journal of Social Psychology, 20,* 29–44.

Frincke, J. L., & Pate, W. E., II (2004). Yesterday, today, and tomorrow. Careers in psychology: 2004. What students need to know. Retrieved on October 14, 2004, from http://research.apa.org

Frith, C. D., & Frith, U. (1999, November 26). Interacting minds—A biological basis. *Science, 286,* 1692–1695.

Frith, U. (1993, June). Autism. *Scientific American, 268,* 108–114.

Zajecka, J. (2000, May 18). A comparison of nefazodone, the cognitive behavioral-analysis system of psychotherapy, and their combination for the treatment of chronic depression. *New England Journal of Medicine, 342,* 1462–1461.

Kelley, H. H., Berscheid, E., Christensen, A., Harvey, J., Huston, T., Levinger, G., McClintock, E., Peplau, A., & Peterson, D. (1983). *Close relationships.* San Francisco, CA: Freeman.

Kelley, J. E., Lumley, M. A., & Leisen, J. C. C. (1997). Health effects of emotional disclosure in rheumatoid arthritis patients. *Health Psychology, 16,* 331–340.

Kelman, H. C. (1997). Group processes in the resolution of international conflicts: Experiences from the Israeli–Palestinian case. *American Psychologist, 52,* 212–220.

Kelman, H. C. (1999). Interactive problem solving as a metaphor for international conflict resolution: Lessons for the policy process. *Peace & Conflict: Journal of Peace Psychology, 5,* 201–218.

Kempermann, G., & Gage, F. H. (1999, May). New nerve cells for the adult brain. *Scientific American, 280,* 48–53.

Kendler, K. S., & Gardner, C. O., Jr. (1998). Boundaries of major depression: An evaluation of DSM-IV criteria. *American Journal of Psychiatry, 155,* 172–177.

Kendler, K. S., Hettema, J. M., Butera, F., Gardner, C. O., & Prescott, C. A. (2003). Life event dimensions of loss, humiliation, entrapment, and danger in the prediction of onsets of major depression and generalized anxiety. *Archives of General Psychiatry, 60,* 789–796.

Kennedy, D. M. (1970). *Birth control in America: The career of Margaret Sanger.* New Haven, CT: Yale University Press.

Kennedy, M. B. (2000, October 27). Signal-processing machines at the postsynaptic density. *Science, 290,* 750–754.

Kenrick, D. T., & Funder, D. C. (1988). Profiting from controversy: Lessons from the person–situation debate. *American Psychologist, 43,* 23–34.

Kenrick, D. T., & Stringfield, D. O. (1980). Personality traits and the eye of the beholder: Crossing some traditional philosophical boundaries in the search for consistency in all of the people. *Psychological Review, 87,* 88–104.

Kerlinger, F. N. (1985). *Foundations of behavioral research* (3rd ed.). New York: Holt, Rinehart & Winston.

Kershner, J. R., & Ledger, G. (1985). Effect of sex, intelligence, and style of thinking on creativity: A comparison of gifted and average IQ children. *Journal of Personality and Social Psychology, 48,* 1033–1040.

Kesner, R., & Olton, D. S. (1990). *The neurobiology of comparative cognition.* Hillsdale, NJ: Erlbaum.

Kessler, R. C., Berglund, P., Demler, O., Jin, R., Koretz, D., Merikangas, K. R., Rush, A. J., Walters, E. E., & Wang, P. S. (2003, June). The epidemiology of major depressive disorder: Results from the National Comorbidity Survey Replication (NCS-R). *Journal of the American Medical Association, 289,* 3095–3105.

Keynes, R. (2002). *Darwin, his daughter, and human evolution.* New York: Penguin Putnam.

Kiecolt-Glaser, J. K., & Glaser, R. (1987). Psychosocial moderators of immune function. *Annals of Behavioral Medicine, 9,* 16–20.

Kiecolt-Glaser, J. K., & Glaser, R. (2001). Stress and immunity: Age enhances the risks. *Current Directions in Psychological Science, 10,* 18–21.

Kiesler, C. A. (1982a). Mental hospitals and alternative care: Noninstitutionalization as potential public policy for mental patients. *American Psychologist, 37,* 349–360.

Kiesler, C. A. (1993). Mental health policy and mental hospitalization. *Current Directions in Psychological Science, 2,* 93–95.

Kiester, E. (1980, May/June). Images of the night. *Science, 80,* 36–42.

Kihlstrom, J. F. (1985). Hypnosis. *Annual Review of Psychology, 36,* 385–418.

Kihlstrom, J. F. (1987). The cognitive unconscious. *Science, 237,* 1445–1452.

Kihlstrom, J. F. (1990). The psychological unconscious. In L. Pervin (Ed.), *Handbook of personality: Theory and research* (pp. 445–464). New York: Guilford Press.

Kihlstrom, J. F. (1998). Dissociations and dissociation theory in hypnosis: Comment on Kirsch and Lynn (1998). *Psychological Bulletin, 123,* 186–191.

Kihlstrom, J. F., Barnhardt, T. M., & Tartaryn, D. J. (1992). The psychological unconscious: Found, lost, and regained. *American Psychologist, 47,* 788–791.

Kim, J. E., & Moen, P. (2001). Is retirement good or bad for subjective well-being? *Current Directions in Psychological Science, 10,* 83–86.

Kimble, G. A. (1991). The spirit of Ivan Petrovich Pavlov. In G. A. Kimble, M. Wertheimer, & C. L. White (Eds.), *Portraits of pioneers in psychology* (pp. 26–40). Washington, DC: American Psychological Association.

Kimmel, A. J. (1991). Predictable biases in the ethical decision making of American psychologists. *American Psychologist, 46,* 786–788.

Kinoshita, J. (1992, July). Dreams of a rat. *Discover, 13,* 34–41.

Kinsey, A. C., Pomeroy, W. B., & Martin, C. E. (1948). *Sexual behavior in the human male.* Philadelphia: Saunders.

Kinsey, A. C., Pomeroy, W. B., Martin, C. E., & Gebhard, P. H. (1953). *Sexual behavior in the human female.* Philadelphia: Saunders.

Kintsch, W. (1981). Semantic memory: A tutorial. In R. S. Nickerson (Ed.), *Attention and performance* (Vol. 8). Hillsdale, NJ: Erlbaum.

Kirkpatrick, L. A., & Shaver, P. R. (1992). An attachment-theoretical approach to romantic love and religious belief. *Personality and Social Psychology Bulletin, 18,* 266–275.

Kirsch, I., & Braffman, W. (2001). Imaginative suggestibility and hypnotizability. *Current Directions in Psychological Science, 10,* 57–61.

Kirsch, I., & Lynn, S. J. (1995). Altered state of hypnosis: Changes in the theoretical landscape. *American Psychologist, 50,* 846–858.

Kirsch, I., & Lynn, S. J. (1998). Dissociation theories of hypnosis. *Psychological Bulletin, 123,* 100–115.

Kitayama, S., Duffy, S., Kawamura, T., & Larsen, J. T. (2003). Perceiving an object and its context in different cultures: A cultural look at new look. *Psychological Science, 14,* 201–206.

Klag, M. J., Whelton, P. K., Grim, C. E., & Kuller, L. H. (1991). The association of skin color with blood pressure in U.S. blacks with low socioeconomic status. *Journal of the American Medical Association, 265,* 599– 02.

Klagsbrun, F. (1985). *Married people: Staying together in the age of divorce.* New York: Bantam Books.

Klahr, D., & Simon, H. A. (2001). What have psychologists (and others) discovered about the process of scientific discovery? *Current Directions in Psychological Science, 10,* 75–79.

Klass, D., Silverman, P. R., & Nickman, S. L. (1996). *Continuing bonds: New understandings of grief.* Philadelphia: Taylor and Francis.

Kleinfeld, J. (1994). Learning styles and culture. In W. J. Lonner & R. Malpass, *Psychology and culture* (pp. 151–156). Boston: Allyn & Bacon.

Kleinke, C. (1975). *First impressions: The psychology of encountering others.* Englewood Cliffs, NJ: Prentice Hall.

Kleinman, A., & Cohen, A. (1997). Psychiatry's global challenge. *Scientific American, 276*(3), 86–89.

Kleinmuntz, B., & Szucko, J. J. (1984). Lie detection in ancient and modern times: A call for contemporary scientific study. *American Psychologist, 39,* 766–776.

Klinger, E. (1987, May). The power of daydreams. *Psychology Today,* 37–44.

Klüver, H., & Bucy, P. C. (1939). Preliminary analysis of temporal lobes in monkeys. *Archives of Neurology and Psychiatry, 42,* 979–1000.

Knapp, S., & VandeCreek, L. (2003). An overview of the major changes in the 2002 APA Ethics Code. *American Psychologist, 34,* 301–308.

Knecht, S., Flöel, A., Dräger, B., Breitenstein, C., Sommer, J. Henningsen, H., Ringelstein, E. B., & Pascual-Leone, A. (2002, July 1). Degree of language lateralization determines susceptibility to unilateral brain lesions *Nature Neuroscience, 5,* 695–699.

Kobasa, S. O. (1984). How much stress can you survive? *American Health, 3,* 64–77.

Kobasa, S. O., Hilker, R. R., & Maddi, S. R. (1979). Who stays healthy under stress? *Journal of Occupational Medicine, 21,* 595–598.

Koechlin, E., Ody, C., & Kouneiher, F. (2003, November 14). The architecture of cognitive control in the human prefrontal cortex. *Science, 302,* 1181–1185.

Kohlberg, L. (1964). Development of moral character and moral ideology. In M. L. Hoffman & L. W. Hoffman (Eds.), *Review of child development research* (Vol. 1). New York: Russell Sage Foundation.

Kohlberg, L. (1968, April). The child as a moral philosopher. *Psychology Today, 2*(4), 25–30.

Kohlberg, L. (1981). *The philosophy of moral development.* New York: Harper & Row.

Köhler, W. (1925). *The mentality of apes.* New York: Harcourt Brace Jovanovich.

Kohn, P. M., Barnes, G. E., & Hoffman, F. M. (1979). Drug-use history and experience seeking among adult male correctional inmates. *Journal of Consulting and Clinical Psychology, 47,* 708–715.

Kohout, J. (2000, January). A look at recent baccalaureates in psychology. *Monitor on Psychology,* p. 13.

Kohout, J. (2001, February). Facts and figures: Who's earning those psychology degrees? *Monitor on Psychology, 32*(2). Retrieved on October 14, 2004, from http://www.apa.org/monitor/feb01/facts.html

Kohout, J., & Wicherski, M. (2000, December). Where are the new psychologists working? *Monitor on Psychology,* p. 13.

Kolb, B. (1989). Development, plasticity, and behavior. *American Psychologist, 44,* 1203–1212.

Koob, G. F., & Le Moal, M. (1997, October 3). Drug abuse: Hedonic homeostatic dysregulation. *Science, 278,* 52–58.

Kopta, S. M., Lueger, R. J., Saunders, S. M., & Howard, K. I. (1999). Individual psychotherapy outcome and process research: Challenges leading to greater turmoil or a positive transition? *Annual Review of Psychology, 30,* 441–469.

Kosko, B., & Isaka, S. (1993, July). Fuzzy logic. *Scientific American, 269,* 76–81.

Kosslyn, S., Thompson, W., Kim, I., & Alpert, N. (1995). Topographical representations of mental images in primary visual cortex. *Nature, 378,* 496–498.

Kosslyn, S. M. (1976). Can imagery be distinguished from other forms of internal representation? Evidence from studies of information retrieval times. *Memory and Cognition, 4,* 291–297.

Kosslyn, S. M. (1983). *Ghosts in the mind's machine: Creating and using images in the brain.* New York: Norton.

Kosslyn, S. M., Cacioppo, J. T., Davidson, R. J., Hugdahl, K., Lovallo, W. R., Speigel, D., & Rose, R. (2002). Bridging psychology and biology: The analysis of individuals in groups. *American Psychologist, 57,* 341–351.

Kotchoubey, B. (2002). Do event-related brain potentials reflect mental (cognitive) operations? *Journal of Psychophysiology, 16,* 129–149.

Kramer, A. F., & Willis, S. L. (2002). Enhancing the cognitive vitality of older adults. *Current Directions in Psychological Science, 11,* 173–177.

Kramer, P. D. (1993). *Listening to Prozac: A psychiatrist explores antidepressant drugs and the remaking of the self.* New York: Viking.

Krampe, R. T., & Ericsson, K. A. (1996). Maintaining excellence: Deliberate practice and elite performance in young and older pianists. *Journal of Experimental Psychology: General, 125,* 331–359.

Krantz, D. S., Grunberg, N. E., & Baum, A. (1985). Health psychology. *Annual Review of Psychology, 36,* 349–383.

Kristol, I. (1994, November 3). Children need their fathers. *The New York Times,* A15.

Kukla, A. (1989). Nonempirical issues in psychology. *American Psychologist, 44,* 785–794.

Lachman, R., Lachman, J. L., & Butterfield, E. C. (1979). *Cognitive psychology and information processing: An introduction.* Hillsdale, NJ: Erlbaum.

Lai, C. S. L., Fisher, S. E., Hurst, J. A., Vargha-Khadem, F., & Monaco, A. P. (2001, October 4). A forkhead-domain gene is mutated in a severe speech and language disorder. *Nature, 413,* 519–523.

Lakoff, R. T. (1990). *Talking power.* New York: Basic Books.

Lamb, H. R. (1998). Deinstitutionalization at the beginning of the new millennium. *Harvard Review of Psychiatry, 6,* 1–10.

Lamb, M. E. (1999, May/June). Mary D. Salter Ainsworth 1913–1999 attachment theorist. *APS Observer, 32,* 34–35.

Lambo, T. A. (1978). Psychotherapy in Africa. *Human Nature, 1*(3), 32–39.

Lampl, M., Veldhuis, J. D., & Johnson, M. L. (1992). Saltation and stasis: A model of human growth. *Science, 258,* 801–803.

Landesman, S., & Butterfield, E. C. (1987). Normalization and deinstitutionalization of mentally retarded individuals: Controversy and facts. *American Psychologist, 42,* 809–816.

Landry, D. W. (1997, February). Immunotherapy for cocaine addiction. *Scientific American,* 42–45.

Lang, F. R., & Carstensen, L. L. (1994). Close emotional relationships in late life: Further support for proactive aging in the social domain. *Psychology and Aging, 9,* 315–324.

Lang, P. J., & Lazovik, D. A. (1963). The experimental desensitization of a phobia. *Journal of Abnormal and Social Psychology, 66,* 519–525.

Langleben, D. D., Schroeder, L., Maldjian, J. A., Gur, R. C., McDonald, S., Ragland, J. D., O'Brien, C. P., & Childress, A. R. (2002). Brain activity during simulated deception: An event-related functional magnetic resonance study. *NeuroImage, 15,* 727–732.

Langlois, J. H., Kalakanis, L., Rubenstein, A. J., Larson, A., Hallam, M., & Smoot, M. (2000). Maxims or myths? A meta-analytic and theoretical review. *Psychological Bulletin, 126,* 390–423.

Langlois, J. H., & Roggman, L. A. (1990). Attractive faces are only average. *Psychological Science, 1,* 115–121.

Langlois, J. H., Roggman, L. A., Casey, R. J., Ritter, J. M., Rieser-Danner, L. A., & Jenkins, V. Y. (1987). Infant preferences for attractive faces: Rudiments of a stereotype. *Developmental Psychology, 23,* 363–369.

Langlois, J. H., Roggman, L. A., & Musselman, L. (1994). What is average and what is not average about attractive faces? *Psychological Science, 5,* 214–220.

Larson, R. (1989). Is feeling "in control" related to happiness in daily life? *Psychological Reports, 64,* 775–784.

Larson, R. W. (2000). Toward a psychology of positive youth development. *American Psychologist, 55,* 170–183.

Larson, R. W. (2001). How U.S. children and adolescents spend time: What it does (and doesn't) tell us about their development. *Current Directions in Psychological Science, 10,* 160–164.

Lash, J. (2001). Dealing with the tinder as well as the flint. *Science, 294,* 1789.

Lashley, K. S. (1950). In search of the engram. In *Physiological mechanisms in animal behavior: Symposium of the Society for Experimental Biology* (Vol. 4). New York: Academic Press.

Latané, B., & Darley, J. M. (1968). Group inhibition of bystander intervention in emergencies. *Journal of Personality and Social Psychology, 10,* 215–221.

Laumann, E. O., Gagnon, J. H., Michael, R. T., & Michaels, S. (1994). *The social organization of sexuality: Sexual practices in the United States.* Chicago: University of Chicago Press.

Lawton, M. P. (2001). Emotion in later life. *Current Directions in Psychological Science, 10,* 120–123.

Lazar, I., & Darlington, R. (1982). Lasting effects of early education: A report from the Consortium for Longitudinal Studies. *Monographs of the Society for Research in Child Development, 47*(2–3, Serial No. 195).

Lazarus, R. S. (1981, July). Little hassles can be hazardous to your health. *Psychology Today,* 58–62.

Lazarus, R. S. (1984). On the primacy of cognition. *American Psychologist, 39,* 124–129.

Lazarus, R. S. (1991a). Cognition and motivation in emotion. *American Psychologist, 46,* 352–367.

Lazarus, R. S. (1991b). Progress on a cognitive-motivational-relational theory of emotion. *American Psychologist, 46,* 819–834.

Lazarus, R. S. (1999). *Stress and emotion: A new synthesis.* London, U.K.: Free Association Press.

Lazarus, R. S., DeLongis, A., Folkman, S., & Gruen, R. (1985). Stress and adaptational outcomes: The problem of confounded measures. *American Psychologist, 40,* 770–779.

LeDoux, J. (2002). *Synaptic self: How our brains become who we are.* New York: Viking.

LeDoux, J. E. (1994). Emotion, memory and the brain. *Scientific American, 270*(6), 50–57.

LeDoux, J. E. (1996). *The emotional brain: The mysterious underpinnings of emotional life.* New York: Simon & Schuster.

LeDoux, J. E. (2000). Emotion circuits in the brain. *Annual Review of Neuroscience, 23,* 155–184.

Lee, V. E., Brooks-Gunn, J., & Schnur, E. (1988). Does Head Start work? A 1-year follow-up of disadvantaged children attending Head Start, no preschool. *Developmental Psychology, 24,* 210–222.

Leeper, R. W., & Madison, P. (1959). *Toward understanding human personalities.* New York: Appleton-Century-Crofts.

Leerhsen, C. (1990, February 5). Unite and conquer: America's crazy for support groups. *Newsweek,* 50–55.

Leiter, M. P., & Maslach, C. (2000). *Preventing burnout and building engagement: A complete program for organizational renewal.* San Francisco, CA: Jossey-Bass.

Lencer, R., Malchow, C. P., Trillenberg-Krecker, K., Schwinger, E., & Arolt, V. (2000). Eye-tracking dysfunction (ETD) in families with sporadic and familial schizophrenia. *Biological Psychiatry, 47,* 391–401.

Lensing, V. (2001). Grief support: The role of funeral service. *Journal of Loss and Trauma, 6,* 45–63.

Leonard, J. (1998, May–June). Dream-catchers: Understanding the biological basis of things that go bump in the night. *Harvard Magazine, 100,* 58–68.

Lepper, M. R., Greene, D., & Nisbett, R. E. (1973). Undermining children's intrinsic interest with extrinsic reward: A test of the over-justification hypothesis. *Journal of Personality and Social Psychology, 28*(1), 129–137.

Lerner, R. M., Orlos, J. R., & Knapp, J. (1976). Physical attractiveness, physical effectiveness and self-concept in adolescents. *Adolescence, 11,* 313–326.

Leshner, A. I. (1997, October 3). Addiction is a brain disease, and it matters. *Science, 278,* 45–47.

Leslie, A. M. (2001). Learning: Association or computation? Introduction to a special section. *Current Directions in Psychological Science, 10,* 124–127.

Leslie, M. (2000, July/August). The vexing legacy of Lewis Terman. *Stanford, 28*(4), 44–51.

Lesperance, F., & Frasure-Smith, N. (1996, February 17). Negative emotions and coronary heart disease: Getting to the heart of the matter. *Lancet, 347,* 414–415.

Lettvin, J. Y., Maturana, H. R., McCulloch, W. S., & Pitts, W. H. (1959). What the frog's eye tells the frog's brain. *Proceedings of the Institute of Radio Engineers, 47,* 1940–1951.

Leutgeb, S., Leutgeb, J. K., Treves, A., Moser, M-B., & Moser, E. I. (2004, August 27). Distinct ensemble codes in hippocampal areas ca3 and ca1. *Science, 305,* 1295–1298.

Leutwyler, K. (1994, March). Prosthetic vision: Workers resume the quest for a seeing-eye device. *Scientific American, 270,* 108.

Leutwyler, K. (1995, June). Depression's double standard. *Scientific American, 272,* 23–24.

LeVay, S. (1991). A difference in hypothalamic structure between heterosexual and homosexual men. *Science, 253,* 1034–1037.

LeVay, S., & Hamer, D. (1995). Evidence for a biological influence in male homosexuality. *Scientific American, 270*(5), 44–49.

Levenson, R. W. (1992). Autonomic nervous system differences among emotions. *Psychological Science, 3,* 23–27.

Leventhal, H., & Tomarken, A. J. (1986). Emotion: Today's problems. *Annual Review of Psychology, 37,* 565–610.

Levine, J. A., Eberhardt, N. L., & Jensen, M. D. (1999, January 8). Role of nonexercise activity thermogenesis in resistance to fat gain in humans. *Science, 283,* 212–214.

Levine, K., Shane, H. C., & Wharton, R. H. (1994). What if . . . : A plea to professionals to consider the risk–benefit ratio of facilitated communication. *Mental Retardation, 32*(4), 300–304.

Levine, L. J. (1997). Reconstructing memory for emotions. *Journal of Experimental Psychology: General, 126,* 165–177.

Levine, L. J., & Safer, M. A. (2002). Sources of bias in memory for emotions. *Current Directions in Psychological Science, 11,* 169–173.

Levine, M., & Perkins, D. V. (1987). *Principles of community psychology: Perspectives and applications.* New York: Oxford University Press.

Lewinsohn, P. M., Clarke, G. N., Hops, H., & Andrews, J. A. (1990). Cognitive-behavioral treatment for depressed adolescents. *Behavior Therapy, 21,* 385–401.

Lewinsohn, P. M., & Gotlib, I. H. (1995). Behavioral theory and treatment of depression. In E. E. Beckham, & W. R. Leber (Eds.), *Handbook of depression* (2nd ed., pp. 352–375). New York: Guilford Press.

Lewinsohn, P. M., & Rosenbaum, M. (1987). Recall of parental behavior by acute depressives, remitted depressives, and nondepressives. *Journal of Personality and Social Psychology, 52,* 611–619.

Lewinsohn, P. M., Sullivan, J. M., & Grosscup, S. J. (1980). Changing reinforcing events: An approach to the treatment of depression. *Psychotherapy: Theory, Research and Practice, 17,* 322–334.

Lewis, D. A., Cruz, D. A., Melchitzky, D. S., & Pierri, J. N. (2001). Lamina-specific deficits in parvalbumin-immunoreactive varicosities in the prefrontal cortex of subjects with schizophrenia: Evidence for fewer projections from the thalamus. *American Journal of Psychiatry, 158,* 1411–1422.

Lewis-Fernández, R., & Kleinman, A. (1994). Culture, personality, and psychopathology. *Journal of Abnormal Psychology, 103,* 67–71.

Lewy, A. J., Sack, R. L., Miller, S., & Hoban, T. M. (1987). Antidepressant and circadian phase-shifting effect of light. *Science, 235,* 352–354.

Liegeois, F., Baldeweg, T., Connelly, A., Gadian, D. G., Mishkin, M., & Vargha-Khadem, F. (2001). Language fMRI abnormalities associated with FOXP2 gene mutation. *Nature Neuroscience 11,* 1230–1237.

Liem, R., & Rayman, P. (1982). Health and social costs of unemployment: Research and policy considerations. *American Psychologist, 37,* 1116–1123.

Lilienfeld, S. O., Wood, J. M., & Garb, H. N. (2000a). The scientific status of projective techniques. *Psychological Science in the Public Interest, 1,* 27–66.

Lilienfeld, S. O., Wood, J. M., & Garb, H. N. (2000b). What's wrong with this picture? *Scientific American, 284*(5), 80–87.

Lillard, A. (1999). Developing a cultural theory of mind: The CIAO approach. *Current Directions in Psychological Science, 8,* 57–61.

Lillard, A. S. (1997). Other folks' theories of mind and behavior. *Psychological Science, 8,* 268–274.

Lindsay, D. S. (1990). Misleading suggestions can impair eyewitnesses' ability to remember event details. *Journal of Experimental Psychology: Learning, Memory, and Cognition, 16*(6), 1077–1083.

Lindsay, D. S. (1993). Eyewitness suggestibility. *Current Directions in Psychological Science, 2,* 86–89.

Linsheid, T. R., Iwata, B. A., Ricketts, R. W., Williams, D. E., & Griffin, J. C. (1990). Clinical evaluation of the self-injurious behavior inhibiting system (SIBIS). *Journal of Applied Behavior Analysis, 23,* 53–78.

Lipsey, M. W., & Wilson, D. B. (1993). The efficacy of psychological, educational, and behavioral treatment: Confirmation from meta-analysis. *American Psychologist, 48,* 1181–1209.

Lipsitt, L. P., Reilly, B., Butcher, M. G., & Greenwood, M. M. (1976). The stability and interrelationships of newborn sucking and heart rate. *Developmental Psychobiology, 9,* 305–310.

Liu, W., Vichienchom, K., Clements, M., DeMarco, S.C., Hughes, C., McGucken, E., Humayun, M.S., De Juan, E., Weiland, J.D., & Greenberg, R. (2000, October). A neuro-stimulus chip with telemetry unit for retinal prosthetic device. *IEEE Journal of Solid-State Circuits, 35,* 1487–1497.

Liverant, G. I., Hofmann, S. G., & Litz, B. T. (2004). Coping and anxiety in college students after the September 11th terrorist attacks. *Stress & Coping, 17,* 127–139.

Loftus, E. F. (1979). *Eyewitness testimony.* Cambridge, MA: Harvard University Press.

Loftus, E. F. (1984). The eyewitness on trial. In B. D. Sales & A. Alwork (Eds.), *With liberty and justice for all.* Englewood Cliffs, NJ: Prentice Hall.

Loftus, E. F. (1992). When a lie becomes memory's truth: Memory distortion after exposure to misinformation. *Current Directions in Psychological Science, 1,* 121–123.

Loftus, E. F. (1993). The reality of repressed memories. *American Psychologist, 48,* 518–537.

Loftus, E. F. (1997a, September). Creating false memories. *Scientific American, 227,* 70–75.

Loftus, E. F. (1997b). Memory for a past that never was. *Current Directions in Psychological Science, 6,* 60–65.

Loftus, E. F. (2003a). Make-believe memories. *American Psychologist, 58,* 867–873.

Loftus, E. F. (2003b). Our changeable memories: Legal and practical implications. *Nature Reviews: Neuroscience, 4,* 231–234.

Loftus, E. F., & Ketcham, K. (1991). *Witness for the defense: The accused, the eyewitness, and the expert who puts memory on trial.* New York: St. Martin's Press.

Loftus, E. F., & Ketcham, K. (1994). *The myth of repressed memory: False memories and allegations of sexual abuse.* New York: St. Martin's Griffin.

Loftus, E. F., & Klinger, M. R. (1992). Is the unconscious smart or dumb? *American Psychologist, 47,* 761–765.

Loftus, E. F., & Palmer, J. C. (1973). Reconstruction of automobile destruction: An example of the interaction between language and memory. *Journal of Verbal Learning and Verbal Behavior, 13,* 585–589.

Loftus, G. R., Duncan, J., & Gehrig, P. (1992). On the time course of perceptual information that results from a brief visual presentation. *Journal of Experimental Psychology: Human Perception and Performance, 18*(2), 530–549.

London, K. A., Mosher, W. D., Pratt, W. F., & Williams, L. B. (1989, March). *Preliminary findings from the National Survey of Family Growth, Cycle IV.* Paper presented at the annual meeting of the Population Association of America, Baltimore, MD.

Lonner, W. J., & Malpass, R. (1994). *Psychology and culture.* Boston: Allyn & Bacon.

Lonner, W. J. (1990). An overview of cross-cultural testing and assessment. In R. W. Brislin (Ed.), *Applied cross-cultural psychology.* Newbury Park, CA: Sage.

Lott, A. J., & Lott, B. E. (1961). Group cohesiveness, communication level, and conformity. *Journal of Abnormal and Social Psychology, 62,* 408–412.

Lourenço, O., & Machado, A. (1996). In defense of Piaget's theory: A reply to 10 common criticisms. *Psychological Review, 103,* 143–164.

Lovaas, O. I. (1977). *The autistic child: Language development through behavior modification.* New York: Halstead Press.

Lovaas, O. I. (1993). The development of a treatment-research project for developmentally disabled and autistic children. *Journal of Applied Behavior Analysis, 26,* 617–630.

Lovaas, O. I., Schreibman, L., & Koegel, R. L. (1974). A behavior modification approach to the treatment of autistic children. *Journal of Autism and Childhood Schizophrenia, 4,* 111–129.

Lovibond, S. H., Adams, M., & Adams, W. G. (1979). The effects of three experimental prison environments on the behavior of nonconflict volunteer subjects. *Australian Psychologist, 14,* 273–285.

Luborsky, L., Singer, B., & Luborsky, L. (1975). Comparative studies of psychotherapies: Is it true that everyone has won and all must have prizes? *Archives of General Psychiatry, 32,* 995–1008.

Lutz, C. (1988). *Unnatural emotions.* Chicago: University of Chicago Press.

Lykken, D., & Tellegen, A. (1996). Happiness is a stochastic phenomenon. *Psychological Science, 7,* 186–189.

Lykken, D. T. (2001). Parental licensure. *American Psychologist, 56,* 885–894.

Lykken, D. T., McGue, M., Tellegen, A., & Bouchard, T. J. (1992). Emergenesis: Genetic traits that may not run in families. *American Psychologist, 47,* 1565–1577.

Lynch, G., & Staubli, U. (1991). Possible contributions of long-term potentiation to the encoding and organization of memory. *Brain Research Reviews, 16,* 204–206.

Maas, J. B. (1999). *Power sleep: The revolutionary program that prepares your mind for peak performance.* New York: HarperPerennial.

Maccoby, E. (1998). *The two sexes: Growing up apart, coming together.* Cambridge, MA: Belknap Press.

Maccoby, E. (2000). *Gender differentiation in childhood: Broad patterns and their implications.* Address given at the American Psychological Association annual convention, Washington, DC.

Maccoby, E. E., & Martin, J. A. (1983). Socialization in the context of the family: Parent–child interaction. In E. M. Hetherington (Ed.), *Handbook of child psychology: Vol. 4, Socialization, personality, and social development* (4th ed., pp. 1–101). New York: Wiley.

Maccoby, N., Farquhar, J. W., Wood, P. D., & Alexander, J. K. (1977). Reducing the risk of cardiovascular disease: Effects of a community-based campaign on knowledge and behavior. *Journal of Community Health, 3,* 100–114.

MacCoun, R. J. (1998). Toward a psychology of harm reduction. *American Psychologist, 53,* 1199–1208.

MacLeod, C., & Campbell, L. (1992). Memory accessibility and probability judgments: An experimental evaluation of the availability heuristic. *Journal of Personality and Social Psychology, 63,* 890–902.

Macmillan, J. C. (2000). *An odd kind of fame: Stories of Phineas Gage.* Cambridge, MA: MIT Press.

MacNair, R. M. (1999). *Symptom pattern differences for perpetration-induced traumatic stress in veterans: Probing the National Vietnam Veterans Readjustment Study.* Doctoral dissertation, University of Kansas City, Missouri.

MacNair, R. M. (2002). *Perpetration-induced traumatic stress: The psychological consequences of killing.* Westport, CT: Praeger.

Macrae, C. N., Milne, A. B., & Bodenhausen, G. V. (1994). Stereotypes as energy-saving devices: A peek inside the cognitive toolbox. *Journal of Personality and Social Psychology, 66,* 37–47.

Magee, W. J., Eaton, W. W., Wittchen, H.-U., McGonagle, K. A., & Kessler, R. C. (1996). Agoraphobia, simple phobia, and social phobia in the national comorbidity survey. *Archives of General Psychiatry, 53,* 159–168.

Maher, B. A., & Maher, W. B. (1985). Psychopathology: II. From the eighteenth century to modern times. In G. A. Kimble & K. Schlesinger (Eds.), *Topics in the history of psychology* (Vol. 2, pp. 295–329). Hillsdale, NJ: Erlbaum.

Maher, B. A., & Ross, J. S. (1984). Delusions. In H. E. Adams & P. B. Sutker (Eds.), *Comprehensive handbook of psychopathology* (pp. 383–987). New York: Plenum.

Maier, S. F., & Watkins, L. R. (1999). Bidirectional communication between the brain and the immune system: Implications for behaviour. *Animal Behaviour, 57,* 741–751.

Maier, S. F., & Watkins, L. R. (2000). The immune system as a sensory system: Implications for psychology. *Current Directions in Psychological Science, 9,* 98–102.

Maier, S. F., Watkins, L. R., & Fleshner, M. (1994). Psychoneuroimmunology: The interface between behavior, brain, and immunity. *American Psychologist, 49,* 1004–1017.

Maisto, S. A., Galizio, M., & Connors, G. J. (1995). *Drug use and abuse* (2nd ed). Fort Worth, TX: Harcourt Brace.

Majewska, M. D., Harrison, N. L., Schwartz, R. D., Barker, J. L., & Paul, S. M. (1986). Steroid hormone metabolites are barbiturate-like modulators of the GABA receptor. *Science, 232,* 1004–1007.

Malatesta, V. J., Sutker, P. B., & Treiber, F. A. (1981). Sensation seeking and chronic public drunkenness. *Journal of Consulting and Clinical Psychology, 49,* 282–294.

Malinowski, B. (1927). *Sex and repression in savage society.* London, U.K.: Humanities Press.

Malitz, S., & Sackheim, H. A. (1984). Low dosage ECT: Electrode placement and acute physiological and cognitive effects. *American Journal of Social Psychiatry, 4,* 47–53.

Manderscheid, R. W., Witkin, M. J., Rosenstein, M. J., Milazzo-Sayre, L. J., Bethel, H. E., & MacAskill, R. L. (1985). In C. A. Taube & S. A. Barrett (Eds.), *Mental Health, United States, 1985.* Washington, DC: National Institute of Mental Health.

Manfredi, M., Bini, G., Cruccu, G., Accornero, N., Beradelli, A., & Medolago, L. (1981). Congenital absence of pain. *Archives of Neurology, 38,* 507–511.

Mann, C. C. (1994, June 17). Behavioral genetics in transition. *Science, 264,* 1686–1689.

Manschreck, T. C. (1989). Delusional (paranoid) disorders. In H. I. Kaplan & B. J. Sadock (Eds.), *Comprehensive textbook of psychiatry* (pp. 816–829). Baltimore: Williams & Wilkins.

Manson, S. M. (1994). Culture and depression: Discovering variations in the experience of illness. In W. J. Lonner & R. Malpass (Eds.), *Psychology and culture* (pp. 285–290). Boston: Allyn & Bacon.

Maquet, P. (2001, November 2). The role of sleep in learning and memory. *Science, 294,* 1048–1052.

Marcus, G. B. (1986). Stability and change in political attitudes: Observe, recall, and "explain." *Political Behavior, 8,* 21–44.

Marcus, G. F. (1996). Why do children say "breaked"? *Current Directions in Psychological Science, 3,* 81–85.

Markman, H. J., & Notarius, C. I. (1993). *We can work it out.* Berkeley, CA: Berkeley Publishing Group.

Markus, H. R., & Kitayama, S. (1994). The cultural construction of self and emotion: Implications for social behavior. In H. R. Markus & S. Kitayama (Eds.), *Emotion and culture: Empirical studies of mutual influence* (pp. 89–130). Washington, DC: American Psychological Association.

Marsh, P. (1988). Detecting insincerity. In P. Marsh (Ed.), *Eye to eye: How people interact.* (Ch. 14, pp. 116–119). Oxford, U.K.: Oxford Andromeda.

Marshall, E. (2000, August 4). Duke study faults overuse of stimulants for children. *Science, 289,* 721.

Martin, A., Haxby, J. V., Lalonde, F. M., Wiggs, C. L., & Ungerleider, L. G. (1995). Discrete cortical regions associated with knowledge of color and knowledge of action. *Science, 270,* 102–105.

and distressed mood in everyday life. *Journal of Personality and Social Psychology, 58,* 1027–1036.

Woods, S. C., Seeley, R. J., Porte, Jr., D., Schwartz, M. W. (1998, May 29). Signals that regulate food intake and energy homeostasis. *Science, 280,* 1378–1383.

Woodworth, R. S. (1918). *Dynamic psychology.* New York: Columbia University Press.

Woody, E., & Sadler, P. (1998). On reintegrating dissociated theories: Comment on Kirsch and Lynn (1998). *Psychological Bulletin, 123*(2), 192–197.

World Health Organization. (1973). *Report of the International Pilot Study of Schizophrenia* (Vol. 1). Geneva, Switzerland: Author.

World Health Organization. (1979). *Schizophrenia: An international follow-up study.* New York: Wiley.

Wright, E. R., Gronfein, W. P., & Owens, T. J. (2000). Deinstitutionalization, social rejection, and self-esteem of former mental patients. *Journal of Health and Social Behavior, 41,* 68–90.

Wright, K., & Mahurin, M. (1997, October). Babies, bonds, and brains. *Discover,* 74–78.

Wright, L. (1988). The Type A behavior pattern and coronary artery disease: Quest for the active ingredients and the elusive mechanism. *American Psychologist, 43,* 2–14.

Wu, C. (1998, April 4). Ritalin may work better as a purer compound. *Science News, 153,* 213.

Wurtman, R. J. (1982, April). Nutrients that modify brain functions. *Scientific American, 242,* 50–59.

Wynn, K. (1992). Addition and subtraction by human infants. *Nature, 358,* 749–759.

Wynn, K. (1995). Infants possess a system of numerical knowledge. *Current Directions in Psychological Science, 4,* 172–177.

Yacoubian, G. S. Jr., Deutsch, J. K., & Schumacher, E. J. (2004). Estimating the prevalence of ecstasy use among club rave attendees. *Contemporary Drug Problems, 31,* 163–177.

Yalom, I. D., & Greaves, C. (1977). Group therapy with the terminally ill. *American Journal of Psychiatry, 134,* 396–400.

Yeaman, J. (1995). Who is resilient? Who is vulnerable? *Dissertation Abstracts International, Section A: Humanities and Social Sciences, 55,* 3110.

Yee, A. H., Fairchild, H. H., Weizmann, F., & Wyatt, G. E. (1993). Addressing psychology's problems with race. *American Psychologist, 48,* 1132–1140.

Yee, P. L., Pierce, G. R., Ptacek, J. R., & Modzelesky, K. L. (2003). Learned helplessness, attributional style, and examination performance: Enhancement effects are not necessarily moderated by prior failure. *Anxiety, Stress & Coping, 16,* 359–373.

Yerkes, R. M. (1921). Psychological examining in the United States Army. In R. M. Yerkes (Ed.), *Memoirs of the National Academy of Sciences: Vol. 15.* Washington, DC: U.S. Government Printing Office.

Young, J. R. (2003, February 14). Prozac campus. *The chronicle of Higher Education,* A-37–A-38.

Zajonc, R. B. (1968). Attitudinal effects of mere exposure. *Journal of Personality and Social Psychology. Monograph Supplement, 9*(2, Part 2), 1–27.

Zajonc, R. B. (1980). Feeling and thinking: Preferences need no inferences. *American Psychologist, 35,* 151–175.

Zajonc, R. B. (1984). On the primacy of affect. *American Psychologist, 39,* 117–123.

Zajonc, R. B. (2001). *Mere exposure effects explained . . . finally!* Address given to the Western Psychological Association annual convention in Lahaina (Maui), Hawaii.

Zaman, R. M. (1992). Psychotherapy in the third world: Some impressions from Pakistan. In U. P. Gielen, L. L. Adler, & N. A. Milgram (Eds.), *Psychology in international perspective* (pp. 314–321). Amsterdam: Swets & Zeitlinger.

Zarit, S. H., & Pearlin, L. I. (Eds.). (2003). *Personal control in social and life course contexts: Societal impact on aging* (pp. 127–164). New York: Springer Publishing.

Zatorre, R. J., & Krumhansl, C. L. (2002, December 13). Mental models and musical minds. *Science, 298,* 2138–2139.

Zeki, S. (1992, September). The visual image in mind and brain. *Scientific American, 267,* 68–76.

Zeman, N. (1990, Summer/Fall). The new rules of courtship (Special Edition). *Newsweek,* 24–27.

Zigler, E., & Muenchow, S. (1992). *Head Start: The inside story of America's most successful educational experiment.* New York: Basic Books.

Zigler, E., & Styfco, S. J. (1994). Head Start: Criticisms in a constructive context. *American Psychologist, 49,* 127–132.

Zilbergeld, B. (1986, June). Psychabuse. *Science 86, 7,* 48.

Zimbardo, P. G. (1973). On the ethics of investigation in human psychological research: With special reference to the Stanford Prison Experiment. *Cognition, 2,* 243–256.

Zimbardo, P. G. (1975). On transforming experimental research into advocacy for social change. In M. Deutsch & H. Hornstein (Eds.), *Applying social psychology: Implications for research, practice, and training* (pp. 33–66). Hillsdale, NJ: Erlbaum.

Zimbardo, P. G. (1990). *Shyness: What it is, what to do about it* (Rev. ed.). Reading, MA: Perseus Books. (Original work published 1977).

Zimbardo, P. G. (2002, August). *Why and how normal people go mad.* Address presented at the convention of the American Psychological Association, Chicago.

Zimbardo, P. G. (2004a). *On being shoe at Yale: A study in institutional conformity.* In preparation, Stanford University.

Zimbardo, P. G. (2004b, July). *The politics of fear.* Address given at the annual convention of the American Psychological Association, Honolulu, HI.

Zimbardo, P. G. (2004c, May 9). Power turns good soldiers into "bad apples." *Boston Globe,* D11.

Zimbardo, P. G. (2004d). A situationist perspective on the psychology of evil: Understanding how good people are transformed into perpetrators. In A. G. Miller (Ed.), *The Social Psychology of Good and Evil* (pp. 21–50). New York: Guilford Press.

Zimbardo, P. G., Andersen, S. M., & Kabat, L. (1981). Induced hearing deficit generates experimental paranoia. *Science, 212,* 1529–1531.

Zimbardo, P. G., & Leippe, M. (1991). *The psychology of attitude change and social influence.* New York: McGraw-Hill.

Zimbardo, P. G., Maslach, C., & Haney, C. (1999). Reflections on the Stanford prison Experiment: Genesis, transformations, consequences. In T. Blass (Ed.), *Obedience to authority: Current perspectives on the Milgram paradigm* (pp. 193–237). Mahwah, NJ: Erlbaum.

Zimbardo, P. G., & Montgomery, K. D. (1957). The relative strengths of consummatory responses in hunger, thirst, and exploratory drive. *Journal of Comparative and Physiological Psychology, 50,* 504–508.

Zimmerman, S. (2002). *Writing to heal the soul: Transforming grief and loss through writing.* New York: Three Rivers Press/ Crown Publishing.

Zucker, G. S., & Weiner, B. (1993). Conservatism and perceptions of poverty: An attributional analysis. *Journal of Applied Social Psychology, 23,* 925–943.

Zuckerman, M. (1974). The sensation-seeking motive. In B. Maher (Ed.), *Progress in experimental personality research* (Vol. 7). New York: Academic Press.

Zuckerman, M. (1978, February). The search for high sensation. *Psychology Today, 12,* 38–46.

Zuckerman, M. (1990). Some dubious premises in research and theory on racial differences: Scientific, social, and ethical issues. *American Psychologist, 45,* 1297–1303.

Zuckerman, M. (1995). Good and bad humors: Biochemical bases of personality and its disorders. *Psychological Science, 6,* 325–332.

Zuckerman, M. (2004). The shaping of personality: Genes, environments, and chance encounters. *Journal of Personality Assessment, 82,* 11–22.

Zuckerman, M., Buchsbaum, M. S., & Murphy, D. L. (1980). Sensation seeking and its biological correlates. *Psychological Bulletin, 88,* 187–214.

Zuckerman, M., Depaulo, B. M., & Rosenthal, R. (1981). Verbal and nonverbal communication of deception. *Advances in Experimental Social Psychology, 14,* 1–59.

Zuckerman, M., Eysenck, S., & Eysenck, H. J. (1978). Sensation seeking in England and America: Cross-cultural, age and sex comparisons. *Journal of Consulting and Clinical Psychology, 46,* 139–149.

Zuckerman, M., Kuhlman, D. M., Joireman, J., Teta, P., & Kraft, M. (1993). A comparison of three structural models for personality: The Big Three, the Big Five, and the Alternative Five. *Journal of Personality and Social Psychology, 65,* 575–768.

Subject Index

Authoritarian personality, 574
Authoritative parents, 153, 154t
Authority
    obedience to, 574–578, 578f
    proof of, 601
Autism, 5, 510–511
Autobiographical memory, 276
Automatic action phase, in natural disasters, 399
Autonomic nervous system (ANS)
    anatomy of, 59–60, 60f
    classical conditioning and, 233
    emotions and, 358–359, 359t
    physical stress response and, 410, 411
Autonomy, vs. self-doubt, 156–157, 157t
Availability bias, 318
Average (mean), 611–612
Aversion therapy, 541, 541f
Aversive conditioning, 227
Aversive stimulus, 241
Axon, 54, 54f

Babbling, 145
Baby boomers, 169
"Baby tender" crib, 237–238
"Back links," 301
BackRub, 301
"Backwards knowledge," 334
Bandura, Albert, 251–252, 459, 462
Barbiturates, 115t, 117, 553
Basic anxiety, 455
Basilar membrane, 195, 196f, 197
Bedlam, 529
Behavior
    brain damage and, 81–82
    conformity of, 571–574, 572f
    discrimination as, 590
    genetics, heredity and, 49
    learning and, 227
    negative consequences of, 570
    observable, connecting to internal states, 371
    social standards of, 568–571
    uniformities/regularities of, 570
    unusual, 464–465
    variability, motivation and, 371
Behavioral learning
    in cognitive terms, 252–253
    definition of, 228
    vs. cognitive learning, 253, 253t
Behavioral medicine, 432–434
Behavioral modification therapies, for mentally retarded individuals, 328
Behavioral perspective, 489
Behavioral reactions, of emotion, 359t
Behavioral view, 17, 19t
Behaviorism, 12, 17
Behaviorists, 12
Behavior modification, 231, 539
Behaviors, 2
Behavior self-modification, 542
Behavior therapies, 385, 539, 546f
Beliefs, examination of, 545
The Bell Curve: Intelligence and Class Structure in
    American Life (Hernstein; Murray), 342
Benzodiazepines, 115t, 117, 553
Bias
    anchoring, 317
    availability, 318
    confirmation, 316–317
    definition of, 292
    hindsight, 317
    in intelligence tests, 341
    representativeness, 317–318
    self-serving, 589–590
Bible, consciousness and, 90
"Big Five" personality traits, 17, 133
Binding problem, 205, 213
Binet, Alfred, 322, 330

Binet-Simon approach, for intelligence
    measurement, 322–323, 323f
"Binge-and-purge" syndrome, 505–506
Binocular convergence, 215
Binocular cues, 214–215
Biological clock, 99
Biological differences, in emotions, 354, 355
Biological factors, personality and, 467
Biological needs, 375
Biological origins, of sexual orientation, 387
Biological view, 14–15, 19t
Biology, behavior and, 371
Biomedical approach, for psychological
    disorders, 550–559
Biomedical therapies, 528, 529, 546f
Biopsychology, 43, 83, 489
Bipolar, 468
Bipolar cells, 189f, 190
Bipolar disorder, 497
Blind spot, 190, 191
Blocking
    avoiding, 295, 296–297
    description of, 287–288, 287f, 288f
BoBo doll experiment, childhood
    aggression and, 251–252
Bodily-kinesthetic intelligence, 332
Body images
    adolescent, 160
    of women, 505, 506f
Bonding, 138–139
Borderline personality disorder, 510
Bottom-up processing, 205–206
Brain
    adolescent, 160
    age-related changes in, 171
    auditory cortex, 196
    cells of, 42–43
    changes, from cognitive-behavior therapy,
        545
    changes, on psychoactive drugs, 118
    chemistry, biomedical therapies and, 550
    computer metaphor, 302
    development of, 137
    division of labor in, 76–77
    dreams and, 106
    emotional circuits in, 410
    endocrine and, 51–52
    imaging, 65–67
    injury/damage, 42, 81–82
    knowledge of, 83–84
    language structures of, 144–145
    layers of, 67–73, 68f, 69f, 71f
    localization of function, 73
    long-term memory and, 278
    mapping, with electric probes, 66
    mechanisms, learning and, 253–254
    mind-behavior connection and, 64–65
    nervous system and, 51–52
    neural impulses and, 181–182
    neural plasticity and, 56–57
    pathways, for emotions, 356, 357f
    prenatal development, 136
    in schizophrenia, 508, 508f
    sensation and, 188
    as sexual organ, 385
    size of, 42
    thought and, 308–309
    visual sensation processing in, 191
Brain scans
    computerized, 66–67, 67f
    for detecting deception, 368
Brain stem, 67–69, 68f, 69f
Brain-stimulation therapies, 555–556
Brain surgery, 42
Brain tumor, 41, 42f, 349–350
Brain waves, sensing with EEG, 66
Brightness, 191, 192t
Broca's area, 77

Bulimia nervosa, 382, 504, 505–506
Burnout, 404–405
Bystander problem, 579–582, 580f

CA (chronological age), 322–323, 324, 326
Caffeine, 115t, 119
Cannabis, 114–115, 114–116, 115t
Cannon-Bard theory, 360
Case studies, 29–30
Catastrophe, 398–400
Catatonic schizophrenia, 507, 507t
Catharsis, 428
Cattell, Raymond, 331, 333t
Causation, vs. correlation, 28
Cause and effect, 26, 27
Cell body (soma), 53–54, 54f
Central executive, 272
Central nervous system (CNS), 58f, 59, 553
Centration, 150, 151
Cerebellum, 68f, 69–70, 69f
Cerebral achromatopsia, 179–180
Cerebral cortex
    anatomy of, 68f, 72–73, 74f
    emotions and, 358
    lobes of, 73, 74f, 75–76
Cerebral dominance, 77–79
Cerebral hemispheres, 72, 78, 78f
Cerebrum, 67
Challenge, cognitive hardiness and, 422
Change, gradual vs. abrupt, 132–132
Change blindness, 287
Chemotherapy, taste aversions and, 235
Chess experts, 344
Chicagocentric view of world, 306, 307f
Childhood
    developmental tasks of, 144–158
    influences on personality, 156–158, 157t
    transition to adulthood (See Adolescence)
Chlorpromazine (Thorazine), 551
Choleric temperament, 466
Chromosome, 47
Chronic stress, 410
Chronological age (CA), 322–323, 324, 326
Chunking, 272, 273
Circadian clock, vs. sleep debt, 103
Circadian rhythms, 99
"Circular culture," 210
Classical conditioning
    applications of, 232–235
    conditioned stimulus and, 540
    definition of, 228, 229
    elements of, 229–232, 230f, 231f
    emotional responses and, 356
    learning and, 138, 228–229
    vs. operant conditioning, 245–247, 245t, 246f
Classical conditioning therapies, 539–540
Clever Hans, 1–2
Client-centered therapy, 535
Clinical method, 29–30
Clinical psychologists, 7, 527, 528t
Clinical social worker, 527, 528t
Clinical view, 16, 19t
Cloning, 50
Closure, 212, 400
Clozapine (Clozaril), 551
CNS (central nervous system), 58f, 59
Cocaine, 115t, 118
Cochlea, 195, 196f
Codeine, 115t
Codependence, 464
Cognitions
    definition of, 16
    dreams and, 106
    emotions and, 360–362, 361f
Cognitive appraisal, 395, 406
Cognitive attributions, 588–590
Cognitive-behavioral cycle of depression,
    495–496, 496f

DID (dissociative identity disorder), 504–505
Diet, stress reduction and, 430–431, 431t
Difference threshold, 184
Differentiation, 135
Diffusion of responsibility, 579
Disasters, natural, 399
Discontinuity view, 132, 132f
Discontinuous stage model of development, 148
Discrimination, 590–593
Discrimination learning, 232
Disease, 486
Disenfranchised grief, 402–403
Displacement, 450
Display rules, 352, 355
Dispositionism, 568
Dissimilarity, prejudice and, 590–591
Dissociative amnesia, 502–503
Dissociative disorders, 502–505, 502t
Dissociative fugue, 503–504
Dissociative identity disorder (DID), 504–505
Distortion, perceptual ambiguity and, 207–208, 207f–210f, 210
Distress, psychological disturbances and, 490
Distributed learning, 296
Divorce, 168, 594
DNA, 47
Dopamine, 57t
Dopamine agonists, 253
Double-blind study, 30
The Double Helix, 248
Down syndrome, 49, 327
"Dream explorer," 107
Dreaming, 89–90
Dream interpretation, 532
Dreams
    age and, 105–106
    cognition and, 106
    creative insight and, 107
    culture, 105–106
    Freud's theory of, 105
    gender and, 105–106
    interpretation of, 104
    as meaningful events, 104
    as random brain activity, 106
    recent experience and, 106
Dress codes, 582–583
Drive reduction, 372
Drives, 371, 446–447
Drive theory, 372–373, 374t
Drug therapy
    evaluation of, 554
    for psychological disorders, 550–554
DSM-IV (Diagnostic and Statistical Manual of Mental Disorder 4th edition), 490, 492–493, 516, 518
Duality of consciousness, 81
Dyslexia, 511–512
Dysthymia, 494

Ear, anatomy of, 195, 196f
Eating
    culture and, 381
    emotions and, 381
Eating disorders, 382, 505–506
Ebbinghaus's forgetting curve, 286, 286f
Echoic memory, 270
Echolocation, 180
Economic competition, prejudice and, 591
Education
    in psychology, 20
    vs. therapy, 560
EEG. *See* Electroencephalograph
Efferent neurons (motor), 52, 53f
Efferent system, 59
Ego, 447, 447f, 532
Egocentrism, 149

Ego defense mechanisms, 449
Ego ideal, 447
Ego-integrity, *vs.* despair, 169–170
Eidetic imagery, 266–268
Elaboration, 265
Elaborative rehearsal, 273–274
Elavil, 552
Electroconvulsive therapy (ECT), 555–556
Electroencephalograph (EEG)
    definition of, 66
    event-related potentials, 308
    sleep patterns, 100, 101f
Electromagnetic energy, 193
Electromagnetic spectrum, 193, 193f
Embryo, 135
Embryonic stem cells, 135
Emergency situations
    bystander intervention in, 579–582, 580f
    response to, 359
    training for, 581
Emotional development
    adolescent issues and, 161–162
    day care and, 154–155
    leisure activities and, 155
    school and, 155
Emotional intelligence
    definition of, 332
    development of, 364–365
    nature and nurture of, 365
    predictive power of, 364–365
Emotion-focused coping, 426, 427
Emotion-focused strategies, 418
Emotions
    age-related changes in, 172
    basic, 352
    brain pathways for, 356, 357f
    cerebral cortex and, 358
    cognition and, 360–362, 361f
    control over, 363–369
    counting, 352–353, 353f
    evolution of, 351
    expression of, cultural universals of, 352
    facial expressions of, 352, 353f
    "feeling" component of, 350
    functions of, 351–355
    gender differences in, 354–355
    genetic variations in, 351
    hormones and, 359
    lack of, 349–350
    lateralization of, 358
    limbic system and, 357–358
    memory and, 283–284
    motivation and, 350, 388
    neuroscience of, 356–359
    physical responses and, 360
    psychological theories of, 359–363, 361f, 362f
    reticular formation and, 358
    subjective well-being and, 435
    theories of, 361f
    venting, 437–438
Emotion Wheel, 353f
Empathy, 536, 549
Empirical investigation, 21–22
Encoding, 265
Encoding specificity principle, 283
Endocrine system
    anatomy of, 51, 52, 61–63, 61f
    hormonal functions of, 61–62, 62t
Endorphins, 57t
Engineering psychologists, 7
Engram, 276–277
Environment
    developmental view and, 15
    heredity and, 15, 133–134
    intelligence and, 336, 338
Epilepsy, 66
Epinephrine (adrenalin), 62
Episode, 308

Episodic memory, 276, 278
Equal status contact, in combating prejudice, 593
Erikson's theory
    of psychosocial development, 156–158, 157t
    of young adulthood, 167–168
Eros, 373–374, 447
Escape, from punishment, 243–244
Esteem needs, 375
Estrogen, 160
Ethical issues, in research, 31–32
Ethnicity, intelligence and, 323
Ethnic minority psychologists, 18–19
Eurocentric maps, 306
Event-related potentials, 308
Evolution
    definition of, 44
    natural selection and, 44–46
Evolutionary psychology, 15
Excitatory messages, to neuron, 54
Excitement phase, of sexual response cycle, 384, 385f
Exercise, for stress reduction, 430
Existential crises, 535
Existential intelligence, 332
Expectancy bias, 30, 129, 292
Expectancy-value theory, 586–587
Expectations
    confirmation bias and, 6
    influence on performance, 335
    negative, effects of, 335
    perception and, 216–217, 216f
    reinforcement and, 253
    schemas and, 309
Experimental group, 27, 28f
Experimental neurosis, conditioning as, 232
Experimental psychologists, 6
Experiments, 26–27
Experts, 344–345
Explicit memory, 281–282
Exposure therapy, 541
External locus of control, 373
Extinction
    in classical conditioning, 231, 231f
    in modifying operant behavior, 247–248
    in operant conditioning, 238–239
Extraversion, 454, 468
Extrinsic motivation, 371
Eyes
    anatomy of, 188, 189f
    real *vs.* fake smiles and, 367
Eyewitnesses, accuracy of, factors affecting, 290
Eysenck, Hans, 546–547

Fabricated memories, 290
Facial expressions, 352, 353f
Facilitated communication, 5, 511
Facilitator, 5
Fading memories, forgetting and, 285–286
FAE (fundamental attribution error), 371, 474, 589
Failure to thrive, 141
Family systems theory, 464
Family therapy, 539
Fantasy, 449
Fast fibers, 202
Fear, 133
Fear-of-flying program, 225–226
Feature detectors, 205
Feeling, *vs.* thinking, 476
Feminine Psychology (Horney), 456
Feminist consciousness-raising movement, 538
Fetal alcohol syndrome, 135, 327
Fetus, 135
FI (fixed interval schedules), 240
Fight-or-flight response
    description of, 410–412
    emotion and, 350

Maslow, Abraham, 374–376, 374t, 456–457, 461f
"Master gland," 62
Masturbation, 162–163
Matching hypothesis, 586
Maturation, 141, 142f, 143
MDMA (ecstasy), 115t, 117, 118
Mean, 611–612
Meaningful associations, memory and, 294
Meaningful organization, 282
Median, 612
Media stereotypes, prejudice and, 592
Media violence, 252, 400
Medical model, 488, 526
Meditation, 113
Medulla, 69
Melancholic temperament, 466
Memory/memories
  age-related changes in, 171
  basic tasks of, 265–266
  for concepts, 310
  consciousness and, 122
  definition of, 263
  erroneously recovered, 261–262
  failures on exams, avoiding, 295–297
  formation of, 268–279
  improvement of, 293–294
  during infancy, 138
  metaphors for, 263–265
  mood and, 283–284
  neurons/synapses and, 278–279
  "photographic" or eidetic, 266–268
  problems, 285–295
  retrieval of, 280–284
  "seven sins" of, 293
  stages of, 268–269, 269f, 269t
  working (See Working memory)
  in wrong context, 289
Memory distortion, 289
Memory retrieval, TOT phenomenon, 284
Memory trace, 277
Mental age (MA), 322, 324, 326
Mental health professionals, types of, 527, 528t
Mental illness. See Psychological disorders
Mental images
  learning and, 250–251
  zooming in on, 93–94
Mental operations, 151
Mental processes, 2, 227
Mental representation, 149
Mental retardation, 326–328
Mental rotation, 92–93, 93f
Mental set, 314, 314f
Mere exposure effect, 227
Mescaline, 115t
Methadone, 115t, 116
Methamphetamines, 115t, 118
Method of loci, 293–294
Midlife, challenge of, 168
Midlife crisis, 168
Milgram's obedience experiment, 575–577, 578f
Mindset, resilient, 424
Minimum principle of perception, 214
Minor tranquilizers, 117
Misattribution, 289
Misinformation effect, 289
Mistrust, vs. trust, 156, 157t
MMPI-2 (Minnesota Multiphasic Personality Inventory), 469, 469t
M'Naughten, Daniel, 516–517
Mnemonics, 293
Mode, 612
Money, happiness and, 436
Monitor on Psychology, 34
Monoamine oxidase inhibitors (MAO), 552
Monocular cues, for depth perception, 215
Moñz, Egas, 555
Mood, memory and, 283–284
Mood-congruent memory, 284

Mood disorders, 493–497
Mood stabilizers, 551, 552–553
Moral development, 578
Moral dilemmas, 164
Morality
  culture and, 165
  gender and, 166
Moral thinking, development of, 163–166, 164t
Morphemes, 146–147
Morphine, 115t
Motivation, 370–377
  emotion and, 350, 388
  flow and, 389
  psychologist use of, 370–371
  rewards and, 376–377
  theories of, 372–376, 374t
  types of, 371–372
Motive, 371
Motor control, maturational timetable for, 141, 142f
Motor cortex, 73, 74f
Motor neurons, 52, 53f
Movement, position and, 199
MRI. See Magnetic resonance imaging
MS (multiple sclerosis), 57
Müller-Lyer illusion, 208, 209f, 210
Multiple intelligences, 332–333, 333t
Multiple personality, 444
Multiple sclerosis (MS), 57
Multiple-systems approach, 380–381, 381f
Musical intelligence, 332
Mutual interdependence, 597
Myelin sheath, 57
Myers-Briggs Type Indicator (MBTI), 455, 472–473

Naltrexone, 204
Names, remembering, 294
Naming explosion, 146
Narcissistic personality disorder, 510
Narcolepsy, 109
National Health and Social Life Survey (NHSLS), 383–384, 384t
Native Americans, concept of intelligence and, 334
Natural concepts, 304
Natural immunity, 417
Naturalistic intelligence, 332
Naturalistic observations, 29
Natural language mediators, 294
Natural selection
  definition of, 45
  evolution and, 15, 44–46
Nature-nurture controversy, 46
Nature-nurture issue, 130–132
Nature vs. nurture, 167
Necker, Louis, 13
Necker cube, 12, 13, 13f, 208, 208f
Need, 372
Need for achievement (n Ach), 378–379
Needs, basic, 167
Negative correlation, 29, 614, 614f
Negative punishment, 241–242
Negative reinforcement
  definition of, 237, 247
  vs. punishment, 242, 242f
Neo-Freudian psychodynamic therapies, 534–535
Neo-Freudian theorists, 453, 456
Neonatal period, 136–137
NEO-PI, 469
Nervous system, 51, 52
  divisions of, 58–61, 58f, 60f
  psychoactive drugs and, 63–64, 63f
Network therapy, 530
Neural impulses
  brain and, 181–182
  transduction of, in hearing, 195–196

Neural messages
  excitatory, 54
  inhibitory, 54
  reaction time and, 55
Neural pathways
  definition of, 64
  from eyes to visual cortex, 79–81, 80f, 81f
Neural tube, 136
Neurons
  definition of, 52
  memories and, 278–279
  plasticity of, 56–57
  structure of, 53, 54f
  types of, 52–53, 54f
Neuroscience
  definition of, 15, 43
  of emotions, 356–359
Neurosis, 493
Neuroticism, 468
Neurotic needs, 455–456, 455t
Neurotransmitters, 54f, 56, 57t
Neutral stimulus, 229
Newborns, innate abilities of, 134
NHSLS (National Health and Social Life Survey), 383–384, 384t
Nicotine, 115t, 119, 432
Night terrors, 108–109
Nine-dot problem, 315, 315f, 316f
Nonconscious mind, levels of, 95–97
Nonconscious processes, 92
Nonjudgmental attitude, 549
Non-REM sleep (NREM), 100, 102f
Nontasters, 201
Norepinephrine, 57t
Normal curve, 326, 326f
Normal distribution, 326, 326f, 327f
Normal range, 326, 326f
Norms, social, 569–571
NREM sleep, 100, 102f
Nucleotides, 47
Nurture, of perception, 216
Nutrition, stress reduction and, 430–431, 431t

Obedience, to authority, 574–578, 578f
Objective data, gathering, 24
Object permanence, 149
Observation, 251
Observational learning
  definition of, 251–252
  participant modeling and, 543, 543f, 544f
  personality and, 459, 462
Obsessional neurosis, 532
Obsessive-compulsive disorder (OCD), 133, 493, 500–501, 532
Occipital lobe, 75, 76t
Oedipus complex, 449, 532
Olfaction, 199–200, 199t, 200f
Olfactory bulbs, 200
One-word stage, 146
On the Origin of Species (Darwin), 10, 44
Openness to experience, 468
Operant, 236
Operant behavior, modifying, 247–248
Operant chamber, 237
Operant conditioning
  definition of, 236
  law of effect and, 236
  punishment and, 241–245, 242f, 243t
  reinforcement and, 236–241, 237f, 240f
  studying and, 257
  vs. classical conditioning, 245–247, 245t, 246f
Operant conditioning therapies, 541–543
Operational definitions, 23, 184, 452, 609
Opiates, 115t, 116
Opponent-process theory, 194
Opponent-process theory of color vision, 190
Optic chiasma, 192f
Optic nerve, 190

Optimism, resilience and, 423
Optimistic style of thinking, 429
Oral stage, 448, 448f
Orbicularis occuli muscles, 367
Organization, of data, 610–611
Organized knowledge, expertise as, 344–345
Orgasm phase, of sexual response cycle, 384, 385f
Out-group, 591
Outliers, 128
"Out-of-body experiences," 504
Overjustification, 376
Overlearning, 296
Overregularization, 147

PAG (periaqueductal gray), 203
Pain
    dealing with, 203–204
    features of, 199t
    management, hypnosis for, 112–113
    phantom limb, 202
    tolerance, 204
Panic disorder, 133, 498–499
Papillae, 201
Paranoid schizophrenia, 507, 507t
Paraprofessionals, 530
Parasympathetic division, 60, 60f
Parental love, conditional, 458
Parenting styles, 153–154, 154t, 387
Parietal lobe, 75, 76t
Partial reinforcement, 238
Participant modeling, 543, 543f, 544f
Passive fear response, 415
Pastoral counselor, 527, 528t
Patterns, perception of, 211–212
Pavlov, Ivan, 228–229
PCP (phencyclidine), 114, 115t
Peer marriages, 168
Peers, influence of, 161
Penis envy, 449
Penny Test, 264, 264f
"Peoples Temple," 574
Peptide YY3-36, 380
Percept, 205
Perception
    cultural influences on, 217–219, 218f
    definition of, 181
    meaning from, 13
    sensation and, 219, 220
    social psychology and, 567
    theoretical explanations, 211–219, 213f, 214f, 216f
Perceptual constancy, 206
Perceptual grouping, 212–213, 213f
Perceptual interpretation, 571
Perceptual organization, Gestalt theory and, 211–214
Perceptual processing, 205–206, 205f, 206f
Perceptual psychology, 181
Perceptual set, 216, 217
Performance
    arousal level, task difficulty and, 362–363, 362f
    inverted U function and, 362–363, 362f
Periaqueductal gray (PAG), 203
Periodic table, 10
Peripheral nervous system (PNS), 58f, 59–60, 60f
Permissive parents, 153, 154t
Perpetration-induced traumatic stress (PITS), 403
Perseverance, 371
Persistence, 293
Personal bias, 30
Personal control, sense of, 421–422
Personality
    cognitive theory of, 445
    cross-cultural view of, 474–476
    definition of, 444

development, early experiences and, 448–449, 448t
"folk theories" of, 473–474
fragmentation of, 502–505
healthy, 456–457
humanistic theory of, 445
observational learning and, 459, 462
psychodynamic theories of, 446–456
psychodynamic theory of, 445
self-centered view of, 458
social-cognitive theories of, 446
social-cognitive theory of, 459, 462–463
temperament and, 467
temperaments and, 466
theories of, 445
traits and, 468–471
Personality disorders, 509–510, 510t, 511t
Personality structure, 447, 447f
Personality theories
    comparison of, 477t
    current, 463–464
    eclectic, 476–478
    implicit, 474
    internal processes and, 573
    timeline of, 460f–461f
Personality traits, of creative people, 320
Personality types
    description of, 454–455, 454t, 466
    determining, 472–473
    stress and, 419–421
Personal unconscious, 454
Personal wellness, steps for, 431t
Person-situation controversy, 470–471
Persuasion, in classroom, 601
PET scans. See Positron emission tomography
Phallic stage, 448, 448f
Phantom limb pain, 202
Phencyclidine (PCP), 114, 115t
Phenomenal field, 457–458
Phenotype, 46
Pheromones, 200
Phlegmatic temperament, 466
Phobias, 45, 293, 499–500, 499t
Phonological loop, 272, 274
Phosphenes, 183
"Photographic" memory, 266–268
Photoreceptors, 188
Phrenology, 73
Physical abilities, maturation and, 141, 142f, 143
Physical attractiveness, interpersonal attraction and, 585–586
Physical dependence, 119–120
Physical maturation, in adolescence, 159–160
Piaget, Jean, cognitive development theory of, 147–151
Pitch, 196–197, 197f
PITS (perpetration-induced traumatic stress), 403
Pituitary gland, 62
PKU, 327–328
Placebo effect, 27, 203–204
Placenta, 135
Place theory, 197
Plasticity, 56–57, 82
Plateau phase, of sexual response cycle, 384, 385f
"Pleasure centers," 71, 72
PNS. See Peripheral nervous system
Poison parasite argument, 601
"Poker face," 366
Political issues, national student survey on, 607–608, 608t, 609t
Polygraphers, techniques of, 366–367
Polygraphs, 4, 366
    accuracy of, 367–368
    false positive, 367
Pons, 69
Ponzo illusion, 218, 218f

Population, demographic shift in, 169
Position, movement and, 199
Positive correlation, 29, 614, 614f
Positive psychology, 459
Positive punishment, 241–242
Positive reinforcement, 237, 247
Positron emission tomography (PET)
    of brain, 67, 67f, 92, 92f
    of cognitive-behavior therapy brain changes, 545
    in schizophrenia, 358
    of thought patterns, 308
Posthypnotic amnesia, 112
Posttraumatic stress disorder (PTSD), 278, 403–404, 502–503
Postural reflex, 137
Poverty
    IQ and, 340
    terrorism and, 597–598
Powerlessness, terrorism and, 597–598
Power of social situations, 567
Power of the situation, 484, 595–596
Practical intelligence, 331
Preconscious level of personality, 447f, 449
Preconscious memories, 95–96
Prefrontal lobotomy, 555
Prejudice
    causes of, 590–592
    combating, 592–593
Premack principle, 240–241
Prenatal period
    brain development and, 136
    development in, 135
    toxins and, 135
Preoperational stage, 149–150
Preoperational thought, 151
Preparedness hypothesis, 500
Prevention, of heart disease, 435–436, 436f
Primacy effect, 288
Primary reinforcers, 240
Primary sex characteristics, 159
Priming, implicit memory retrieval and, 281–282
Principle of opposites, 475
Principle of proximity, 584–585
Prison, mock experience, 565–567
Proactive interference, 287, 288f
Problem-focused coping, 418, 426–427
Problems
    identifying, 312
    intense interest in, 320
    mental, help for, 548–549
    nonpsychotic, recovery from, 546–547
    restructuring, willingness for, 320
    situational vs. dispositional aspects of, 539
    solving, selecting a strategy for, 312
Problem-solving, 311–316
    age-related changes in, 171
    obstacles to, 314–316, 314f–316f
    skills for, 311
Procedural memory, 275–276, 278, 280
Procedures, as concepts, 303
Processing styles, 78
Professional organizations, in psychology, 33
Projection, 450
Projective tests, 450–451
Prototype, 304
Proximity, principle of, 584–585
Prozac (fluoxetine), 63–64, 552
Pseudomemories, 261–262
Pseudopsychology, 3, 4–5
Psilocybin, 115t
Psychiatric nurse practitioner, 527, 528t
Psychiatric social worker, 527, 528t
Psychiatrist, 8, 527, 528t
Psychiatry, 8
Psychic determinism, 451–452
Psychic numbness, 399

Psychoactive drugs
 nervous system and, 63–64, 63f
 types of, 113–119, 115t
Psychoanalysis, 12–13, 16, 446
Psychoanalyst, 16, 527, 528t
Psychoanalytic method, 12–13
Psychoanalytic theory, 446, 452–453
Psychobabble, 3
Psychodynamic psychology, 16
Psychodynamic theories
 of motivation, 373–374, 374t
 of personality, 445, 446–456, 477t
Psychodynamic therapies
 neo-Freudian, 534–535
 vs. other therapies, 546f
Psychogenic problems, 501
Psychological addiction, 120
Psychological debriefing, 428–429
Psychological disorders. See also specific
  psychological disorders
 classification of, 492–493
 clinical judgment and, 491
 cultural aspects of, 529–530
 cultural context of, 515–516
 diagnosis of, 518
 diagnostic labeling and, 514–517
 drug therapy for, 550–554
 DSM-IV and, 518
 historical perspective of, 486–489, 487f
 hospitalization for, 556–557
 medical model of, 488
 mistaken diagnosis of, 483–485
 spectrum of, 486t
 therapy for (See Therapy)
 treatment of (See Therapy)
Psychological models, 488–489
Psychological processes, genetics and, 48–49
Psychological research. See Research
Psychological responses, to stress, 419–425
Psychological Science, 34
Psychological sensation, 192
Psychological therapies
 definition of, 528, 529
 evaluating, 545–548
Psychologists
 applied, 7
 counseling vs. clinical, 527, 528t
 ethnic minority, 18–19
 functions of, 6–7
 professional role of, 33–34
 scientific method and, 21–22
 vs. psychiatrists, 8
 vs. psychoanalysts, 16
 work settings for, 6, 6f
Psychology
 biology of, 83
 branches/categories of, 6–7
 changing face of, 18–19
 critical thinking and, 3, 4–6
 definition of, 2–3
 developing expertise in, 344–345
 early contributions of women, 19, 20t
 education in, 20
 electronic resources, 34
 historical roots of, 9–10
 perspectives, 14–18, 19t
 professional organizations, 33
 science of, 2–3
Psychometric theories, of intelligence, 330–331
Psychometric tradition, 330
Psychoneuroimmunology, 416–417
Psychopathology, 485
Psychophysics, 184
Psychosexual stages of development, 448–449,
  448t
Psychosis, 493
Psychosocial development, Erikson's theory of,
  156–158, 157t

Psychosocial dwarfism, 141
Psychosocial stages, 156
Psychosocial stressors, 411
Psychosurgery, 554–555
Psychotherapies, comparison of, 546f
Psychotherapy. See Therapy
Psychotic, 493
PTSD (posttraumatic stress disorder), 278,
  403–404, 502–503
Puberty, 159, 161
Publishing, of research results, 25–26
Punishment, 236, 247
 efficacy of, 244–245
 negative, 241–242
 positive, 241–242
 unequal, 244
 uses/abuses of, 243–244
 vs. negative reinforcement, 242, 242f

Quantification, 24

Race
 intelligence and, 323
 IQ and, 340–341
Radical behaviorism, 236
Rainman, 330
Random assignment, 27
Random presentation, 24
Random sample, 615
Range, 612–613
Rational-emotive behavior therapy (REBT),
  544–545
Rationalization, 449, 450
Ratio schedule, 239
Rave culture, 118
Reaction formation, 450
REBT (rational-emotive behavior therapy),
  544–545
Recall, 282
Recency effect, 288
Receptors
 neurotransmitters and, 56
 for smell, 200f
 taste, 201, 201f
 transduction and, 182
Reciprocal determinism, 462, 462f
Recognition, 282–283
Reconstructive memory, 286–287, 287f, 288f
Recovered memory controversy, 290–291
Recovery phase, of natural disasters, 399
Reflection of feelings, 535–536
Reflexes, 59, 229
Regression, 450
Rehabilitation psychologists, 7
Rehearsal, 272, 273–274
Reinforcement
 across cultures, 241
 power of, 236–237
Reinforcement contingencies, 238
Reinforcement schedules, 239, 240f
Reinforcers
 definition of, 236–237
 preferred activities as, 240–241
 removal of, 241
Relationship concepts, 303
Relative size, as monocular cue, 215
Reliability, 470
REM rebound, 101
REM sleep, 100, 101f, 102, 102f, 106, 109
Replicate, 26
Replication, 547
Representativeness bias, 317–318
Representative sample, 615
Repression
 definition of, 449–450
 of memories, 291
 psychoanalysis and, 532, 533
 of sexual desires, 96

Reputake, 56
Research
 ethical issues in, 31–32
 hypothesis (See Hypothesis)
 results, replication of, 26
 scientific method for (See Scientific method)
 sources of bias in, 30–31
 types of, 26–30
 unanswered questions, 32, 33t
Residual type schizophrenia, 507, 507t
Resilience, 418, 422–424
Resolution phase
 of grieving process, 402
 of sexual response cycle, 384, 385f
Response, 12
Resting potential, 55
Reticular formation, 69, 358
Retina, 188, 189f
Retinal disparity, 215
Retrieval
 definition of, 265
 of explicit memories, 282
 of implicit memory, priming and, 281–282
 influencing factors, 283–284
Retrieval cues, 281
Retroactive interference, 287, 288f
Retrograde amnesia, 277, 279
Reuptake, 54f, 552
Revolutionary martyrs, 574–575
Rewards, 236, 376–377
Reward theory of attraction, 584, 586
Right-brained individuals, 78, 78f, 255
Rites of passage, 159
Robbers Cave, 596–597
Rods, 188
Rogers, Carl, 457–458, 460f, 535
Rohypnol (date-rape drug), 115t, 117
Role models, new, in combating prejudice,
  592–593
Romantic love, 475, 594
Rorschach inkblot technique, 450–451
Rotter, Julian, 462
"Rules of thumb," 312
Rumination, depression and, 496–497

Sachs, Sadie, 443–444
SAD (seasonal affective disorder), 495–496, 495f
Safety needs, 375
Saltation, 143
Samaritans, 581
Same-gender couples, 169
Same-sex orientation, in adolescence, 163
Sampling, 615
Sanger, Margaret, 443–445, 453, 458, 463, 470
Sanguine temperament, 466
Satisfaction, with present life, 435
Savant syndrome, 320, 330
Saving method, 286
Scapegoating, 591
"Scapegoat stimulus," 235
Scarr and Weinberg Adoption Study, 339–340
Schedules of reinforcement, 239
Schemas
 in cognitive development, 148, 309
 event, scripts as, 310
 expectations and, 309
 restructuring/modifying, 148
Schizophrenia
 causes of, 508–509, 508f
 definition of, 506
 diagnostic labeling, 483–484, 515
 genetic risk of, 509, 509f
 hallucinations and, 358
 positive vs. negative, 507–508
 types of, 507–508, 507t
Schizophrenic disorders, 493
School, social/emotional development and, 155
School psychologists, 7

Vestibular sense, 199, 199*t*
VI (variable interval schedules), 240
Vicarious traumatization, 400–401
Victimology, depression and, 497
"Video recorder" metaphor, for memory, 263
Violence, 595–596
    conflict resolution approach for, 598–599
    multiple perspectives on, 599–600
    social psychology of, 596
"Virtual reality" images, 214
Visible light, 193
Visible spectrum, 193
Vision. *See* Visual sensation
Visual cliff, 214
Visual cortex, 75, 191
Visual encoding, 274
Visual sensation (vision)
    aging and, 170
    anatomy of, 188, 189*f*, 190–191
    brightness and, 191, 192*t*
    characteristic features of, 199*t*
    in neonatal period, 136–137
    processing, in brain, 191
    from visual stimulation, 191, 912*f*
    vs. auditory sensation, 198

Visual thinking, 306
Vocabulary, acquisition of, 145–147, 146*f*
Von Helmholtz, Hermann, 216, 218, 219
VR (variable ratio schedules), 239

WAIS (Wechsler Adult Intelligence Scale), 324
Weber's law, 185
Wechsler Adult Intelligence Scale (WAIS), 324
Wechsler Intelligence Scale for Children
    (WISC), 324
Wechsler Preschool and Primary Scale of
    Intelligence (WPPSI), 324
Weeping Woman (Picasso), 212
Weight control, 382–383
Wertheimer, Max, 12
"White bear" experiment, 98
Whole method, 296
Will power, weight control and, 382
WISC (Wechsler Intelligence Scale for
    Children), 324
Witchcraft trials, 488
Withdrawal
    definition of, 120
    in general adaptation syndrome, 413*f*, 415
    symptoms of, 119–120

Women
    dreams and, 105
    early contributions to psychology, 19, 20*t*
    new perspectives on, 168–169
Word scrambles, 314, 314*f*
Work, 167
Working backward heuristic, 313, 313*f*
Working memory
    biological basis of, 274–275
    capacity/duration of, 271–272, 272*f*
    characteristics of, 269*t*
    definition of, 268
    levels of processing in, 274, 274*f*
    model of, 272, 273*f*
    structure/function of, 272–274, 273*f*
WPPSI (Wechsler Preschool and Primary Scale
    of Intelligence), 324
Writing, healing and, 437–438
Wundt, Wilhelm, 10–11

Zero correlation, 29
Zooming in on mental images, 93–94
Zygote, 135